# Classics of
# Organization Theory

# Classics of
# Organization Theory
## Eighth Edition

Jay M. Shafritz
*University of Pittsburgh*

J. Steven Ott
*University of Utah*

Yong Suk Jang
*Yonsei University*

Australia • Brazil • Mexico • Singapore • United Kingdom • United States

# CENGAGE
## Learning®

**Classics of Organization Theory, Eighth Edition**
Jay M. Shafritz, J. Steven Ott, Yong Suk Jang

Product Director: Suzanne Jeans

Product Manager: Carolyn Merrill

Content Developer: Michael B. Kopf

Associate Content Developer: Amy Bither

Media Developer: Laura Hildebrand

Marketing Manager: Valerie Hartman

Content Project Manager: Dan Saabye

Art Director: Linda May

Manufacturing Planner: Fola Orekoya

IP Analyst: Alex Ricciardi

IP Project Manager: Sarah Shainwald

Production Service: Integra

Compositor: Integra

Cover Designer: Jenny Willingham

Cover Image: Dimitri Otis/ Photographer's Choice/Getty Images.

Library of Congress Control Number: 2014948230

ISBN: 978-1-285-87027-4

Cengage Learning
20 Channel Center Street
Boston, MA 02210
USA

Cengage Learning is a leading provider of customized learning solutions with office locations around the globe, including Singapore, the United Kingdom, Australia, Mexico, Brazil, and Japan. Locate your local office at **www.cengage.com/global.**

Cengage Learning products are represented in Canada by Nelson Education, Ltd.

To learn more about Cengage Learning Solutions, visit **www.cengage.com.**

Purchase any of our products at your local college store or at our preferred online store **www.cengagebrain.com.**

Printed in the United States of America
Print Number: 02   Print Year: 2015

# Contents

## Chapter 6
## Power and Politics Organization Theory 245

## Chapter 7
## Theories of Organizational Culture and Change 292

## Chapter 8
## Theories of Organizations and Environments 340

**Chapter 9**
Theories of Organizations and Society   412

# Foreword

Modern societies are filled with organizing. New areas of social life, such as the semi-conductor industry or marriage counseling or international consulting, are carried out by organizations. And, older social patterns, in the school, hospital, firm, or government, are formalized and managed as organizations. Organizations, once restricted to a few institutional areas in political and economic systems, are now to be found in every sector of social life. Further, any given organization, in recent periods, is likely to be more elaborately organized, with more differentiated roles and more activity arenas formalized. A university, for instance, will now have departments and offices that did not exist a few decades ago.

The modern expansion in organizing is by no means a matter of evolutionary drift. Organizations are self-consciously constructed and managed as bounded and purposive entities. This is a matter of definition, because organizations are distinct from other sorts of social collectives precisely in that they are articulated and formalized.

Organizations, thus, are theorized. And they are interdependent with the theories that create them, but that also arise from them. It is a two-way street. The academic theory of organizations develops in good part out of the intellectual examination of life in real-world organizations. But it importantly derives from cultural and ideological notions quite independent from ongoing realities: organization and organizational theory are visions as well as practices. In any case, organizational theory drives the kinds of organizations that people build in the real world, and greatly affects the ways existing organizations change. Theorists and researchers analyze organizations and organizational ideologies, and their analyses, carried into reality by a variety of consultants and trained practitioners, change the organizations that exist.

In this book, Shafritz, Ott, and Jang provide an extraordinary overview of the development of modern organization theory by collecting and integrating discussions in the field that have become classics.

- In part, this overview describes the historical development, to greater maturity and sophistication, of an intellectual enterprise. There is more and better empirical research, and there is a greater variety of theoretical ideas and schemes with which to work.

- But in part, it depicts the development toward more complexity of modern organizations themselves. Organizations arise and expand in more and more settings, carrying out more and more tasks. They thus change. And the theoretical developments displayed in this book change with them.

- And further, social ideas about what activities and domains ought to be brought under formal organizational control expand greatly in the modern system. We want our natural environment to be measured and protected, our expanded human rights as workers or consumers taken carefully into account, and our technical and administrative procedures rendered rational and efficient. So expansions and change in organizational theory reflect not only evolving realities and sophistication in analyzing these realities, but also expanded modern ideologies about what needs to be brought under the systematic control of formal organizational structures.

Thus, the theoretical developments displayed in this book's sweeping portrait of the development of organizational theory show (a) increased theoretical sophistication, but also changes over time both (b) in the actual landscapes of organizational life and (c) in modern ideals or fantasies about the social control of uncertainties.

In all three of these respects, of course, similar developments occur in the world of organizations in practice. Simple structures become more complex and contingent. More and more interdependencies are discovered, created, or desired, and are brought under attempted organizational control. And this occurs on more and more fronts, as organizations are seen at once as managing work, people, and relations with multiple wider environments. In an important sense, rational organizations become less simplistically rational.

In fact, these last sentences capture the evolving complexity of organizational theory. Organization, and its theoretical counterpart, is after all an attempt to simultaneously rationally bring under control activity, people, and linkages to wider environments. This is difficult because each of these dimensions of control poses different and expanding demands with overall cultural change. It all requires much structuring and becomes even more difficult as each of the elements to be linked acquires more and more complexity. Obviously, the work and activity to be controlled is much more complex than in the past. But so are the perceived and legitimated dimensions of the people to be controlled, who now are seen as having many more rights, capacities and agency. And the social and physical environments, too, are filled with more and more perceived complexity.

The history thus starts with the Enlightenment dream, displayed in Chapter 1, of pulling some activities and people out of the messy societal environment and structuring them in rationalized and standardized form under the will of a unitary sovereign. The emphasis may vary from the structuring of economic work with a division of labor to the bureaucratic control of people for political purposes.

It turns out, in social history and in the history of the field, that there are inconsistencies between the requisite elements of the actualities and ideologies of organization. Structuring work effectively is often inconsistent with the sovereign control over people, and both are inconsistent with effective relations with multiple environments. Thus, there is skepticism about the simple rational dream. It is prominently displayed in Chapter 2 of this book, in which theorists raise questions (more than give answers) about the validity of the original dream. The subsequent history of the field takes off from the materials in this chapter.

## 1. COMING TO TERMS WITH THE HUMAN PARTICIPANTS

One early development was to concentrate on the human dimension of organizing. Organizations in practice have to (or anyway do, or should) take into account that the people in them are participants, not just objects of control. And over time, the human rights and recognized (and schooled) capacities of these people have grown rapidly: modern organizational participants, often professionalized, carry much legitimated agency.

Various sacrifices in the rational exercises of sovereign control, or the rational management of work, are necessary in coming to terms with the cultural reality of expanded human complexity. Chapter 3 of this book presents the core theoretical materials that permanently changed the field in this area.

The people who participate in organizations are not the psychologically simple entities of the original formulations. They bring, from wider society, a whole host of cultural meanings and interpretations. On the one side, organizations must come to terms with the expanded rights and capacities involved. More importantly, organizations can (or must) give up some aspects of their rational structuring to use these cultural elements, or build them, or manipulate them. Organizational culture, thus, constrains, but also may facilitate functioning. The line of reasoning involved is displayed in Chapter 7.

## 2. COMING TO TERMS WITH VARIABLE ACTIVITY

Classical theory had tended to treat the work activities going on in organizations as having a rather simple character, and tended to imagine that fairly simple rules could cover them. But organizational activities vary sharply in their character and technologies. And the variance increases over time as more and more human activities are brought under the control of formalized organizations. Uncertainties prevail in many of the domains subjected to newly expanded organizing: religious, educational, medical, and charitable structures are now commonly organizations, and pose problems for rationalized standardization. Chapters 4 and 5 of this book pull together the major lines of theorizing that tried to come to terms with these issues. The agenda here is not about the problematics of people, but about the variable difficulties in controlling activity. The effort is to suggest variations in structure that can come to terms with these difficulties. It is understood in these chapters that sacrifices in simple rationalistic models are made necessary by the complexities involved in muddy arenas of work activity and expanded technical interdependencies.

## 3. COMING TO TERMS WITH VARIABLE SOVEREIGNS AND EXPANDING ENVIRONMENTS

Classical organizational theory tended to imagine rational structuring around singular goals—say, efficient production of work or effective control and standardization of people—under the authority of a single sovereign. Reality is more disordered than that, and in complex modern society becomes more disorderly over time. Chapters 6, 8, and 9 of this book show the lines of contemporary theorizing that result. One dimension of this effort emphasizes the loose power that accumulates within and around organizations, and the constraints (and opportunities) that result. The sovereign is never entirely in command, and must sacrifice rational controls (and unitary goals) to accede to a variety of internal and external pressures.

A second dimension is cultural in character—organizations depend on legitimacy to function. They must use environmentally legitimated forms and meet socially legitimate goals, whether these are most rational or effective or not. And in the contemporary "knowledge" society, the range of rationalized environments (both natural and social) to which an organization must respond has greatly expanded.

A third dimension is competitive. Any given organization is likely to be highly dependent on the competitive, as well as legitimating, environment. The best and most rational way to do things, in principle, may not be feasible in practice, depending on what competitive and supportive elements the environment supplies.

On all these dimensions, the modern societal environment involves a greatly expanded level of cultural rationalization. People inside and outside organizations have more agency, social and natural environments are more rationalized, and thus organization itself becomes more complex. The matter is given special attention in Chapter 9.

All in all, the modern discussions of organizational theory keep an interesting distance from the simple rationalistic dreams of the early classical texts. There is more complexity and more skepticism. Sometimes this takes a pessimistic form, as writers emphasize the failures and pretenses of rationalism. Often it is more optimistic, as theorists see gains in overall effectiveness to be produced by sacrificing simple rationality to incorporate environmental supports, the commitment of human participants, or the complex and variable characteristics of the tasks at hand. Thus, there is an enormous expansion of, and faith in, the possibilities of managerialism and organizational "decision making." The failures of simpler forms of sovereignty have evolved into the striking modern faith in "management" and the MBA degree. This permits the continuing expansion of organization that is central in contemporary society.

In any case, the rational organization is seen as a good deal less rational than it once was imagined. Partly, the field has gotten more sophisticated; partly, organizations themselves have changed; and partly, the original mechanistic and naïve Enlightenment ideals have matured or eroded. The entire history is under display in this extraordinary collection. Shafritz, Ott, and Jang have done students, and the field, a considerable service in creating and updating this work, so that it reflects the continuing growth in both theory and practice.

John W. Meyer
Department of Sociology
Stanford University

# Preface

*C*lassics of Organization Theory is a collection of the most important works in organization theory written by the most influential authors in the field. *Classics* does not simply tell the reader what the "masters" said—it presents their works in their own words. These are theories that have withstood the test of time—the critically acclaimed masterworks in the field. Although this book contains a liberal sprinkling of important newer works, its focus is the enduring classics. *Classics of Organization Theory* thus tells the history of organization theory through the words of the great theorists.

This book is designed to help people who are new to the field of organization theory "get into," understand, and appreciate its important themes, perspectives, and theories. We describe and explain what organization theory is, how it has developed, and how its development coincides with developments in other fields, as well as the contexts in which these great works were written.

Each chapter presents one major perspective or "school" of organization theory. Readers thus can immerse themselves in one perspective at a time, before moving to the next. The major perspectives of organization theory—and the chapters—are as follows:

- Classical Organization Theory
- Neoclassical Organization Theory
- Human Resource Theory, or the Organizational Behavior Perspective
- "Modern" Structural Organization Theory
- Organizational Economics Theory
- Power and Politics Organization Theory
- Theories of Organizational Culture and Change
- Theories of Organizations and Environments
- Theories of Organizations and Society

Several other features that help make *Classics* "reader friendly" include:

- The revised *Foreword* by John W. Meyer explains the book in the context of the field of organization theory.
- The *Introduction* explains why there is no single perspective of organization theory. Instead there are competing perspectives or frames for grouping theories of organization, and we explain why we chose this framework.
- The *Introduction* also explains how theories of organization reflect what was going on in the world at the time (for example, World War II, the "flower child"/antiestablishment/self-development era of the 1960s, the recognition in the 1980s that U.S. industry had lost its global competitiveness, and the blurring of boundaries among the private, government, and nonprofit sectors since the turn of the century); defines the criteria used for including and excluding works (for example, "Should the serious student of organization theory be

expected to identify this author and his or her basic themes?"); and presents the organizing framework for the book.

- The *Introduction* contains a *Chronology* of important events and contributions to the field of organizational theory from 1491 BC up to the present. The chronology allows the reader to see the intellectual development of the myriad themes and perspectives of organization theory and to comprehend the impact of time and context on the development of perspectives across the field.

- The opening pages of each chapter identify the central themes and issues of the perspective, contrast the perspective with others, and briefly summarize the key contributions each article makes to the field.

- Most of the articles have been shortened to make them more readable. The editing helps readers focus on the central ideas that make an article a classic.

- Each chapter contains a bibliography of important books and articles from the perspective— whether or not the works are reproduced in this edition of *Classics*.

## CHANGES FROM THE SEVENTH EDITION TO THE EIGHTH EDITION

In our never-ending attempt to walk a fine line between holding this book true to its purpose and thus including only "true classics" and adding important newer areas of theory, we have held the first four chapters relatively intact from the seventh edition while increasing the emphasis in the later chapters on the interactions and relations of organizations with the social, economic, and political dimensions of their environment—in other words, beyond earlier notions of organizations as open systems.

It is always difficult to choose new inclusions from among the rich variety of alternatives. We have tried to identify a few readings that present important new bodies of theory within perspectives—theories that we believe will become classics in time. For example, we have added a new reading in Chapter 7 (Theories of Organizational Culture and Change) on the effects of differences among national cultures on organizational cultures; in Chapter 8 (Theories of Organizations and Environments) on network organizations; and in Chapter 9 (Theories of Organizations and Society) on cultural competency and on hybrid organizations as a response to the blurring lines between public and private organizations.

As in previous editions, we have inserted replacement readings that communicate theories more clearly or more compellingly, emphasize aspects of theories we believe are more central to the perspective, and reflect how organizations adapt to fundamental shifts in their environment.

We broke with our long-standing tradition of including only original works by "the masters" in one instance. We replaced Chester Barnard's classic "The Economy of Incentives" with William G. Scott's insightful "Chester I. Barnard and the Guardians of the Managerial State: The Moral Obligations of the Elite." Scott positions Barnard's writing about the moral obligation of organization leaders in the context of Barnard's personal ethical code—an important insight into the source of Barnard's views that does not emerge from reading his original chapter.

We also have streamlined the eighth edition to help hold down the cost of the book. We are well aware of the rapid rise in the price of books and the burden this places on students. Therefore, we reluctantly deleted several old favorites.

The following selections have been added and deleted. We hope you agree the changes improve this edition.

### Chapter 2: Neoclassical Organization Theory
*Deletions from the Seventh Edition*

Chester Barnard, "The Economy of Incentives" (1938)

Robert K. Merton, "Bureaucratic Structure and Personality" (1957)

Richard M. Cyert & James G. March, "A Behavioral Theory of Organizational Objectives" (1959)

*Addition to the Eighth Edition*

William G. Scott, "Chester I. Barnard and the Guardians of the Managerial State: The Moral Obligations of the Elite" (1992)

### Chapter 3: Human Resource Theory, or the Organizational Behavior Perspective
*Deletion from the Seventh Edition*

Mary Parker Follett, "The Giving of Orders" (1926)

Fritz J. Roethlisberger, "The Hawthorne Experiments" (1941)

*Addition to the Eighth Edition*

Elton Mayo, "The Hawthorne Experiment. Western Electric Co." (1933)

### Chapter 4: "Modern" Structural Organization Theory
*Deletions from the Seventh Edition*

Tom Burns & G. M. Stalker, "Mechanistic and Organic Systems" (1961)

Henry Mintzberg, "The Five Basic Parts of the Organization" (1979)

Richard M. Burton & Børge Obel, "Technology as a Contingency Factor" (1998)

*Addition to the Eighth Edition*

Henry Mintzberg, "Structure in 5's: A Synthesis of the Research on Organization Design" (1980)

### Chapter 5: Organizational Economics Theory
*Deletions from the Seventh Edition*

Michael C. Jensen & William H. Meckling, "Theory of the Firm: Managerial Behavior, Agency Costs and Ownership Structure" (1976)

Paul H. Rubin, "Managing Business Transactions" (1990)

*Addition to the Eighth Edition*

Elinor Ostrom, "An Institutional Approach to the Study of Self-Organization and Self-Governance (1990)

### Chapter 6: Power and Politics Organization Theory
*Deletions from the Seventh Edition*

Jeffrey Pfeffer, "Understanding the Role of Power in Decision Making" (1981)

Robert Michels, "Democracy and the Iron Law of Oligarchy" (1915/1962)

### Chapter 7: Theories of Organizational Culture and Change
*Deletions from the Seventh Edition*

Joanne Martin, "Organizational Culture: Pieces of the Puzzle" (2002)

William G. Ouchi, "The Z Organization" (1981)

*Addition to the Eighth Edition*

Geert Hofstede, Gert Jan Hofstede, & Michael Minkov, "Cultures and Organizations: Pyramids, Machines, and Families: Organizing Across Nations" (2010)

### Chapter 8: *Theories of Organizations and Environments*

*Deletion from the Seventh Edition*

    Glenn R. Carroll & Michael T. Harmon, "Demography of Corporations and Industries" (2000)

*Addition to the Eighth Edition*

    Wayne Baker, "The Network Organization in Theory and Practice" (1992)

### Chapter 9: *Theories of Organizations and Society*

*Deletions from the Seventh Edition*

    Taylor Cox, "Creating the Multicultural Organization: The Challenge of Managing Diversity" (2001)

    Abigail McWilliams & Donald Siegel, "Corporate Social Responsibility: A Theory of the Firm Perspective" (2001)

    Johanna Mair, Jeffrey Robinson & Kai Hockerts, "Social Entrepreneurship" (2006)

    Helen Haugh, "Social Enterprise: Beyond Economic Outcomes and Individual Returns" (2006)

*Additions to the Eighth Edition*

    Mitchell F. Rice & Audrey L. Mathews, "A New Kind of Public Service Professional" (2012)

    Paul Light, "The Search of Social Entrepreneurship" (2008)

    David Billis, "Towards a Theory of Hybrid Organizations" (2010)

## ACKNOWLEDGMENTS

This eighth edition of *Classics of Organization Theory* has benefited immeasurably from advice we have received from an array of friendly critics of the seventh edition. We wish to thank those who provided ideas, encouragement and criticisms, including Patricia Bromley, Richard Green, Thad Hall, Chris Simon, and Lina Svedin, University of Utah; Al Hyde, San Francisco State University; Hugh Miller, Florida Atlantic University; Joungyoon Hwang, Yonsei University; and Lisa Dicke, University of North Texas. The reviewers selected by Cengage–Wadsworth provided several useful suggestions for deletions and new additions that we acted upon.

    We thank the authors and publishers of these classics for their permission to reproduce their work. As with the previous editions, we sincerely solicit comments, ideas, and suggestions from the scholarly and practitioner communities. Given sufficient encouragement from readers and support from our publisher—and long enough lives—we will continue to revise *Classics of Organization Theory* as new theories and perspectives gain in importance and others fizzle.

Jay M. Shafritz
*University of Pittsburgh*

J. Steven Ott
*University of Utah*

Yong Suk Jang
*Yonsei University*

# Introduction to Organization Theory

O rganization theory is one of the most interesting, useful, and dynamic sub-fields in the applied fields of administration, including business, public, education, health-care, art, and social work administration. But, *there is no such thing as the theory of organizations* Rather, there are many theories that attempt to explain and predict how organizations and the people in them will behave in varying organizational structures, cultures, and circumstances. Therefore, "frameworks," "perspectives," "traditions," "schools," or occasionally "eras" of organization theory are useful for grouping compatible theories that tend to use the same language or jargon.

## A FRAMEWORK: THE "PERSPECTIVES" OF ORGANIZATION THEORY

Some theories of organization are compatible with and build upon others—in what they explain or predict, the aspects of organizations they consider to be important, their assumptions about organizations and the world at large from which they are created, and the suitable methods for studying organizations. Organization theorists from the same schools will quote and cite each other's works regularly. However, they usually ignore theorists and theories from other schools—or acknowledge them only negatively.

In 1961, Harold Koontz described management theory as a "semantics jungle." In 1963, Arthur Kuriloff found that "each [school of organization theory] is at odds with others, each defends its own position, each claims that the others have major deficiencies." But that was 1963, and we have come a long way since then. Or have we? In 1983, Graham Astley and Andrew Van de Ven observed: "The problem is that different schools of [organizational] thought tend to focus only on single sides of issues and use such different logics and vocabularies that they do not speak to each other directly." And, as recently as 2013, Lee Bolman and Terrence Deal observed: "Within the social sciences, major schools of thought have evolved, each with its own view of organizations, its own well-defined concepts and assumptions, and its own ideas about how managers can best bring social collectives under control."

It is reasonable to conclude that not only is there no consensus on what constitutes knowledge in organization theory, but there is not likely to be any such consensus in the foreseeable future. Anyone who studies this subject is free to join the school of organization theory of his or her choice and to accept the philosophic boundaries of one group of serious thinkers over another. But before casting your lot with one school and excluding others, consider the options. Examine each school's strengths and weaknesses. See if its philosophy is in harmony with your already-established beliefs, assumptions, and predispositions.

You may find that no single perspective deserves your loyalty, that each contains important information and insights that are useful in differing circumstances. Remember, these are schools with no tuition, no classes, and no grades. They exist only as intellectual constructs and as mutual support networks of organization theorists. They have one primary purpose: to organize and extend knowledge about organizations and how to study them.

Just as there is disagreement among the various frames about what makes organizations tick, there are also different views about the best way to group organization theories into schools. Each of the major frames of organization theory is associated with a period in time. For example, the classical school was at its prime in the 1920s and 1930s, and the human resources school peaked in the 1960s and early 1970s. Each school had its beginnings while another was dominant, gradually gained acceptance, and eventually replaced its predecessor as the dominant perspective. Some years later, another school came along to challenge and eventually take its position. However, once-dominant frames of organization theory may lose the center stage, but they do not die. Their thinking influences subsequent frames—even those that reject their basic assumptions and tenets. Important works from these earlier perspectives become the timeless classics.

This cycling of schools through struggling ascendancy, dominance, challenge by other schools, and reluctant decline is not unique to organization theory. Thomas Kuhn (1970) postulated that this dialectic process is common in all sciences, including physics, mathematics, and psychiatry. It is quite common for frames that are chronologically close to each other to have widely divergent basic assumptions about the object of their theories.

Despite their differences, most of the better-known approaches to grouping organization theories into schools have commonalities. First, they group theories by their perspectives on organizations—in other words, by basic assumptions about humans and organizations and by those aspects of organizations that they see as most important for understanding organizational processes and structures. Second, they usually group the theories by the period of time during which the most important contributions were written. Other organization theorists use different approaches for labeling the theories. On the other hand, Herbert Simon, among others, has put forward a solid argument that the use of frames (or schools or perspectives) confuses more than it enlightens (1997, pp. 26–27).

In 1983, Graham Astley and Andrew Van de Ven proposed a useful logic for classifying schools of organization "thought" into four fundamental views based on two analytical dimensions: the level of organizational analysis (micro or macro) and the emphasis placed on deterministic versus voluntaristic assumptions about human nature. Thus, Astley and Van de Ven concluded that organization theories could be grouped into the cells of a two-by-two matrix (see Figure 1). Their voluntaristic-to-deterministic dimension (the horizontal continuum in Figure 1) classifies theories by their assumptions about individual organization members' autonomy and self-direction versus the assumption that behavior in organizations is determined by structural constraints. The macro-to-micro continuum (the vertical continuum in Figure 1) groups organization theories by their focus on communities of organizations or single organizations.

W. Richard Scott and Gerald F. Davis (2007) have offered an alternative organizing schema that includes three perspectives of formal organizations: *organizations as rational, natural, and open systems*. The first of these perspectives, *organizations as rational systems*, views organizations as highly formalized rational collectivities pursuing specific goals. The early studies of organizations reflected this rational system perspective. For example, Max

## FIGURE 1 • ASTLEY AND VAN DE VEN'S FOUR VIEWS OF ORGANIZATION

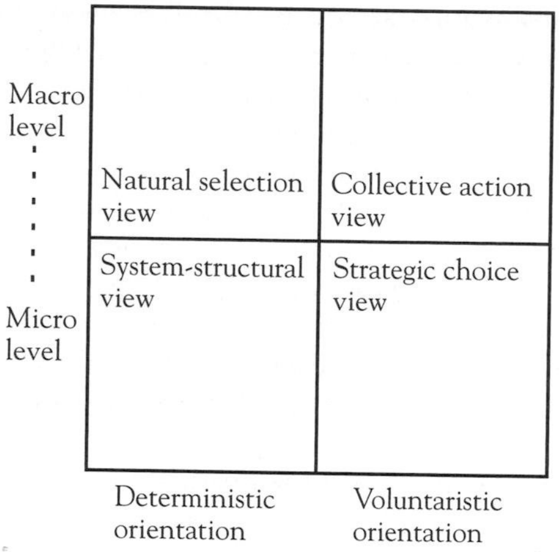

| | Deterministic orientation | Voluntaristic orientation |
|---|---|---|
| Macro level | Natural selection view | Collective action view |
| Micro level | System-structural view | Strategic choice view |

**Examples of some representative organization theorists for each of the four views:**

*System-Structural View:* Blau and Scott (1962), Fayol (1949), Gulick and Urwick (1937), Lawrence and Lorsch (1967), Merton (1940), James D. Thompson (1967)

*Strategic Choice View:* Bittner (1965), Blau (1964), Feldman and March (1981), Strauss et al. (1963), Weick (1969)

*Natural Selection View:* Aldrich (1979), Hannan and Freeman (1977), Pfeffer and Salancik (1978), Porter (1981)

*Collective Action View:* Emery and Trist (1973), Hawley (1950, 1968), Schön (1971)

Adapted from W. G. Astley & A. H. Van de Ven (1983), Central perspectives and debates in organization theory, *Administrative Science Quarterly, 28.*

Weber (1946) and Robert Michels (1949) studied the rise of bureaucracy and the expansion of formalized rules and official hierarchies within organizations at the turn of the twentieth century. Frederick Winslow Taylor (1911) and his associates developed the ideas of scientific management as important mechanisms to restructure and rationalize the activities of business organizations. Henri Fayol (1949) and his colleagues articulated a universal set of principles of administration to guide the specialization and coordination of work activities. These early works viewed formal organizations as rationally designed instruments for achieving goals and maximizing machine-like efficiency.

The second perspective, *organizations as natural systems*, views organizations as social systems with multiple interests, informal relations, and participants with subgoals. Organizational theorists and researchers with this perspective argue there is no one best formal way to maximize organizational efficiency. Rather, they emphasize informal structures that include roles and relationships that emerge among individuals and groups of organizations and shape organizational goals and activities. Exemplary work from this natural system perspective include Elton Mayo's human relations notions (1945) and Chester Barnard's conception of cooperative systems (1938).

Finally, the *organizations as open systems* perspective views organizations as systems of interdependent activities embedded in and dependent on wider environments. Whereas the rational and natural system perspectives view organizations and their environments as separate and closed entities with clear boundaries, this separation is not apparent in the open system perspective. Organizations not only acquire material, financial, and human resources from their environment, they also gain social support and legitimacy. The main focus of theory and research from this perspective is the interactions and interdependencies between organizations and environments. Exemplary works include Hannan and Freeman's organizational ecology model (1977), Pfeffer and Salancik's resource dependence model (1978), and Meyer and Rowan's institutional theory (1977).

Theoretical models of organizations underwent a major change around 1960 when the open system perspective gained support and essentially displaced the closed system models (Scott & Davis, 2007). Although these three perspectives developed historically as distinct research paradigms, recent organizational research tends to combine elements of rational, natural, and open system perspectives and stresses the interactions between organizations and environments.

As the primary focus of organizational research has shifted from the internal characteristics of organizations to the external dynamics of competition, interaction, and interdependency, we have observed an important change in organizational research from a static/structure-centered perspective to a dynamic/process-based perspective. From a static perspective, organizations are depicted as fixed structures that enhance production efficiency and decrease the costs of transactions and controls. Organizations are viewed as tools designed to achieve preset goals, and these approaches tend to pay less attention to organizations' connections to their wider environment. Some of these approaches were developed from a social-psychological perspective—for example, Taylor's scientific management approach—while others focused on structure—for instance, Weber's model of bureaucracy and Fayol's administrative theory.

From the 1930s through to the 1950s, a new set of approaches developed that employed natural system assumptions. Although this line of theory acknowledges that organizational structure becomes more complex and flexible as conflicting goals and the multiple interests of participants are recognized, most of the work from this tradition remains interested in how to build a stable organization structure in order to coordinate conflicts and interests effectively. Once again, some of these approaches were developed primarily from a social-psychological perspective—such as the socio-psychological studies on human relations within small groups—while others focus on structure—for example, Barnard's theory of cooperative systems and Mayo's version of human relations. This line of theory stresses goal complexity and the emergence of informal structures such as interpersonal systems of power, status, communication, and friendship and their impacts on formal organization systems.

In contrast with the natural systems assumptions, the dynamic perspective sees organizations as involved in continually changing and transforming processes of "structuration" while interacting with technical and institutional environments. Not only the internal operations of an organization but also the organization itself persists and evolves as a system (Aldrich & Reuf, 2006). From this perspective, an organization is not a fixed entity but a dynamic system.

This emerging dynamic approach provides a clear example of how recent organization theory has shifted its attention from structure (organization) toward process (organizing). Karl Weick defines "organizing" as "the resolving of equivocality in an enacted environment by means of interlocked behaviors embedded in conditionally related process" (1969: 91). Organizing is directed toward information processing in general and toward removing information ambiguity in particular. Organizing attempts to narrow the range of possibilities and alternatives and to establish a workable level of certainty.

Organizations create or "enact" their environments deliberately, rather than passively awaiting the judgment of the environment to select them into or out of it. When encountering environmental uncertainty, organization leaders try to "make sense" of their environments (Weick, 1995). They construct, rearrange, single out, and edit many features of their surroundings as they define and create their own constraints through an "enactment-selection-retention" process. Enactment is the process by which individuals arrive at an understanding about the opportunities and constraints and construct an ordered picture of their environments. Besides these perceptual processes, organizational members also influence their environments through their own actions, including information gathering, processing, and decision making. Thus, enactment emphasizes that organizational participants interact with and actually constitute their environments. The organization does more than observe and interpret. It modifies the environment while it continually transforms and changes itself.

While organizational participants perceive and evaluate the environment, they also arrive at agreed-upon responses in order to make collective sense of what is going on. This is the *selection process*. That is, some responses are selected from among many alternatives. Some responses that are selected are more useful than others. They are retained and institutionalized as organizational rules and routines. In this way, the dynamic process of sense-making gives rise to a repertoire of repeated routines and patterns of interaction and thereby reduces uncertainty.

Successful organizations need to decrease the degree to which their systems are formalized and structured. They must develop new kinds of flexibilities, including more reliance on contingent workers; more loosely coupled and flexible connections among work units and divisions—some of which operate outside the formal boundaries of the organization; and more reliance on project teams, whose goals, composition, and division of labor shift over time (Scott, 2004). Success today depends on how promptly organizations respond to rapidly changing environments, including, for example, fluctuating market demands, shifting customer needs, and legislated changes. Competitors move quickly in and out of products, markets, and sometimes even entire business. In such an environment, the essence of strategy is not the efficient *structure* of an organization, but the *dynamic process* of organizational interactions in and with turbulent environments.

Because an understanding of organizations from different perspectives is essential for the practice of administrators, we believe that no student in any field of administration should complete their degree without at least one course in organization theory. Unfortunately, however, too many undergraduate and graduate students think organization theory is a stuffy old field that died or at least went dormant in the second half of the twentieth century with giants such as Herbert Simon (1946), J. D. Thompson (1967), and Douglas McGregor (1957)—or perhaps all the way back in the times of Frederick Winslow Taylor (1911), Max Weber (1922), and Luther Gulick (1937). How can theories as old as these be of more than historic interest in today's world of fluid, rapidly changing, and electronically connected organizations?

It may surprise some readers that many older organization theories remain vital and useful in today's world because theorists such as Weber, Taylor, Gulick, Simon, Thompson, and McGregor provided a clear picture of organizations as stable institutions, and thereby continue to serve as bed-rock models in theory and practice. Some early theories provide a basis of comparison for more recent fluid alternative models of organizations that fit better with the realities of current environments. Because of this, many of these legendary theories serve as points of departure for today's exciting, newly emerging organizational forms and functions.

On the other hand, it is important to emphasize that the existence of the long-standing theories should not be used as reasons for not trying and experimenting with creative new organizational forms. Organizations are means, not ends. They are merely legal entities established for the purpose of coordinating activities that lead to desired ends, whether the end is profit, effective and efficient delivery of services, or enabling individuals to collectively challenge the status quo. Organizations should serve people, purposes and societies, not longings for bygone years or myths about a past that never existed.

Older theories need to be adapted to fit with the needs of the times. Henri Fayol (1916) and Luther Gulick (1937) (both reprinted in Chapter 1) never considered government agencies that deliver their services through contracted nonprofit and for-profit organizations. Chester Barnard may have written about chief executives holding their organizations together by creating a culture of cooperation and collaboration among employees (see Reading 9 in Chapter 2 by William G. Scott), but consider how different this challenge is for a firm that contracts with individuals or employs mostly part-time temporary employees who are spread around the globe. These individuals may never meet in person; they work together only briefly, and exclusively through electronic communications. How does a CEO develop loyalty to the organization or collaboration among its personnel? Barnard may have provided the foundational ideas, but alternative theories are needed today.

Accordingly, newer theories are needed for organizations to deal with the world of today. More recent theories tend to address types of circumstances and rates of change that the early giants of organization theory could not have foreseen. They are keeping organization theory interesting, useful, dynamic, and relevant—which is why we believe all students in all fields of administration should take at least one course in organizations theory. Whereas J. D. Thompson (1967) is widely credited with introducing the notion of organizations as "open systems" (reprinted in Chapter 8), theorists today are wrestling with the realities of organizations without boundaries—organizations that are integral components of their environments (Chapter 8) and their communities (Chapter 9). Corporate citizenship or corporate social responsibility is becoming an essential element of an organization's mission, purpose, and business model, not a public relations ploy (Carroll & Buchholtz, 1989, reprinted in Chapter 9). Likewise, many nonprofit organizations use organizational models from business, but utilize them for completely different purposes. Instead of seeking profits, they seek business-like ways to raise funds to help finance their public good ends. This explains why organizational models have evolved over the past several decades to blend profitability from entrepreneurial ventures with social consciousness (Light, 2008, reprinted in Chapter 9).

## THE ORGANIZATION OF THIS BOOK

We believe strongly that a historical approach offers clear advantages for students, and the use of perspectives, schools, or frames as the basis for organizing chapters lends itself quite well to such an approach. Organization theory tends to be somewhat cumulative: Theorists and schools of theorists learn from and build upon each other's works. Sometimes the cumulative building of organization theory has been accomplished through the adoption of prior theorists' assumptions, logic, and empirical research methods and findings. In other instances, the building process has advanced by *rejecting* prior assumptions and theories (Kuhn, 1970). Thus, our rather traditional, historical approach allows readers to follow the ebb and flow among and within the perspectives. Most chapters move from the oldest theories (Chapter 1, Classical Organization Theory) to the most recent (Chapter 9, Theories of Organizations and Society). Within chapters, readings usually are presented in chronological sequence so readers can gain a sense of the evolution of thought in the field. Do not expect all chapters and readings to be in chronological order, however. The evolution of organization theory has never been a straight line.

Keep in mind that many theories include some concepts from multiple perspectives no matter how tightly or loosely the boundaries are defined and drawn. Also, the schools—and therefore the chapters—reflect general periods in time as well as perspectives of organizations. The reader can gain an overview of the historical development of organization theory by referring to the "Chronology of Organization Theory" that follows this Introduction.

Our perspectives, or schools, and the corresponding book chapters are as follows:

Chapter 1    Classical Organization Theory
Chapter 2    Neoclassical Organization Theory
Chapter 3    Human Resource Theory, or the Organizational Behavior Perspective
Chapter 4    "Modern" Structural Organization Theory
Chapter 5    Organizational Economics Theory
Chapter 6    Power and Politics Organization Theory
Chapter 7    Theories of Organizational Culture and Change
Chapter 8    Theories of Organizations and Environments
Chapter 9    Theories of Organizations and Society

Each perspective is described and discussed in the introductory essays in the respective chapters.

## CRITERIA FOR SELECTING READINGS

The editors are neither so vain nor so foolish as to assert that these are *the* classics of organization theory. The academic study of organization theory rests on a foundation of primary and secondary sciences and draws significantly from such diverse disciplines as sociology, psychology, social psychology, cultural anthropology, political science, economics, business administration, public administration, and education leadership and policy. It draws less, but still importantly, from mathematics, statistics, systems theory, industrial engineering, philosophy and ethics, history, and computer sciences. We readily admit that some important contributors and contributions to the field have been omitted from this collection. Some omissions were particularly painful—especially the readings that we deleted from the seventh edition. Considerations of space and balance necessarily had to prevail.

We have continued to use the same criteria for selecting the readings to include in this edition. First, we asked ourselves, "Should the serious student of organization theory be expected to identify these authors and their basic themes?" When the answer was yes, it was because the contribution has long been, or is increasingly being recognized as, representative of an important theme by a significant writer. Whereas we expect to be criticized for excluding other articles and writers, it will be more difficult to honestly criticize us for our inclusions. The writers and readings chosen are among the most widely quoted and reprinted theorists and theories in the field of organization theory. The exceptions are the articles chosen to represent the newer perspectives of organization theory. Obviously, new articles have not been quoted as extensively as those written ten, twenty, or thirty years earlier. Thus, we had to be more subjective when making our editorial decisions about inclusions and exclusions in these chapters. In our judgment, these readings have a reasonable chance to fare well against the test of time.

Although this is a book of classics, we continue to receive requests to include some current and near-current theories. Other readers and reviewers, however, urge us to stay true to the book's purpose. "Stay with the time-tested classics. Don't try to be everything for everybody. Let other anthologies keep readers up to date with the current fads." We hope to appease both points of view by including some recent contributions, particularly in Chapters 7 and 9. Purists can simply pretend these chapters are not included.

The second criterion is related to the first: Each reading had to make a basic statement that has been echoed or attacked consistently. In other words, the selection had to be important—significant in the sense that it must have been (or will be) an integral part of the foundation for the subsequent building of the field of organization theory.

The third criterion was that articles should be readable. Those of you who have already had reason to peruse the literature of organization theory will appreciate the importance of this criterion.

The inclusion of readings from the more recent perspectives raises important questions about our choices of chapters for grouping theories and selections. For example, why are some readings included in Chapter 7, "Theories of Organizational Culture and Change," instead of in Chapter 9, "Theories of Organizations and Society"? The answers to questions such as these reflect our own conceptual and historical construction of organization theory, tempered by the need to limit the size of this volume. It is crucially important, then, to understand where we, the authors/editors, are "coming from." Thus we have written essays to introduce each chapter. Each introductory essay presents a school or perspective of organization theory, but because there is no universally accepted set of schools or perspectives, these words of explanation were needed here.

## BIBLIOGRAPHY

Aldrich, H. (1979). *Organizations and environments*. Englewood Cliffs, NJ: Prentice-Hall.

Aldrich. H., & M. Ruef (2006). *Organizations evolving*. 2nd ed. Thousand Oaks, CA: Sage.

Astley, W. G., & A. H. Van de Ven (1983). Central perspectives and debates in organization theory. *Administrative Science Quarterly, 28,* 245–270.

Barnard, C. I. (1938). *The functions of the executive*. Cambridge, MA: Harvard University Press.

Bittner, E. (1965). The concept of organization. *Social Research, 32*(3), 239–255.

Blau, P. M. (1964). *Exchange and power in social life*. New York: Wiley.

Blau, P. M., & R. G. Scott (1962). *Formal organizations*. San Francisco: Chandler.

Bolman, L. G., & T. E. Deal (1984). *Modern approaches to understanding and managing organizations*. San Francisco: Jossey-Bass.

Bolman, L. G., & T. E. Deal (2013). *Reframing organizations: Artistry, choice, and leadership*. 5th ed. San Francisco: Jossey-Bass/Wiley.

Burton, R. M., & B. Obel (1998). *Strategic organizational diagnosis and design: Developing theory for application*. 2nd ed. Boston: Kluwer Academic.

Christensen, T., P. Lægreid, P. G. Roness & K. A. Røvik (2008). *Organization theory and the public sector: Instrument, culture and myth*. London: Routledge.

Daft., R. L. (2012). *Organization theory and design*. 9th ed. Boston: Cengage Learning.

Davis, G. F., D. McAdam, W. R. Scott, and M. N. Zald (2005). *Social movements and organization theory*. New York: Cambridge University Press.

DeSanctis, G., & J. Fulk, eds. (1999). *Shaping organizational form: Communication, connection, and community*. Thousand Oaks, CA: Sage.

Drori, G. S., J. W. Meyer, & H. Hwang (2006). *Globalization and organization: World society and organizational change*. Oxford: Oxford University Press.

Drucker, P. F. (1954). *The practice of management*. New York: Harper & Row.

Emery, F. E., & Trist, E. L. (1973). *Towards a social ecology: Contextual appreciations of the future in the present*. New York: Plenum.

Fayol, H. (1949). *General and industrial management*. London: Pitman. (Originally published in 1916.)

George, C. S., Jr. (1972). *The history of management thought*. Englewood Cliffs, NJ: Prentice Hall.

Gulick, L., & L. Urwick, eds. (1937). *Papers on the science of administration*. New York: Institute of Public Administration.

Hannan, M., & J. Freeman (1977). The population ecology of organizations. *American Journal of Sociology, 82*, 929–964.

Hannan, M. T., L. Polos, & G. R. Carroll (2007). *Logics of organization theory: audiences, codes, and ecologies*. Princeton: Princeton University Press.

Hatch, M. J. (2011). *Organizations: A very short introduction*. Oxford, UK: Oxford University Press.

Hatch, M. J., and A. L. Cunliffe (2013). *Organization theory: Modern symbolic and postmodern perspectives*. 3rd ed. Oxford, UK: Oxford University Press.

Hawley, A. (1968). Human ecology. In D. L. Sills, ed., *The international encyclopedia of the social sciences*, vol. 4 (pp. 328–337). New York: Crowell-Collier & Macmillan.

Hutchinson, J. O. (1967). *Organizations: Theory and classical concepts*. New York: Holt, Rinehart & Winston.

Ibn Khaldun (1969). *The Muqaddimah: An introduction to history*. Trans. F. Rosenthal. Ed and abridged N. J. Dawood. Princeton, NJ: Bollingen Series/Princeton University Press.

Kendall, K. E., ed. (1999). *Emerging information technologies: Improving decisions, cooperation and infrastructure*. Thousand Oaks, CA: Sage.

Kilduff, M. & W. Tsai (2003). *Social networks and organizations*. Thousand Oaks, CA: Sage.

Koontz, H. (1961). The management theory jungle. *Academy of Management Journal, 4*, 174–188.

Koontz, H. (1980). The management theory jungle revisited. *Academy of Management Review, 5*, 175–187.

Kuhn, T. S. (1970). *The structure of scientific revolutions*. 2nd ed. Chicago: University of Chicago Press.

Kuriloff, Arthur. (1963). An experiment in management: Putting Theory Y to the test. *Personnel, 40*(6), 8–17.

Lawrence, P. R., & J. W. Lorsch (1967). *Organization and environment*. Cambridge, MA: Harvard University Press.

Marrow, A. J. (1969). *The practical theorist: The life and works of Kurt Lewin*. New York: Basic Books.

Mayo, E. (1945). *The social problems of an industrial civilization*. Boston: Graduate School of Business Administration, Harvard University.

Meyer, J. W., & B. Rowan (1977). Institutionalized organizations: Formal structures as myth and ceremony. *American Journal of Sociology, 83,* 340–363.

Michels, R. (1949 trans.). *Political parties*. E. Paul and C. Paul. Glencoe, IL: Free Press (originally published in 1915).

Miles, J. A. (2012). *Management and organization theory: A Jossey-Bass reader*. San Francisco: Jossey-Bass/Wiley.

Nadler, D. A., M. S. Gerstein, & R. B. Shaw, eds. (1992). *Organizational architecture: Designs for changing organizations*. San Francisco: Jossey-Bass.

Osborne, D., & T. Gaebler (1992). *Reinventing government*. Reading, MA: Addison-Wesley.

Ott, J. S., S. J. Parkes, & R. B. Simpson, eds. (2008). *Classic readings in organizational behavior*. 4th ed. Belmont, CA: Thomson-Wadsworth.

Perrow, C. (1973, Summer). The short and glorious history of organizational theory. *Organizational Dynamics, 2*(1), 2–15.

Pershing, S. P., & E. A. Austin (2014). *Organization theory and governance for the 21st century*. Thousand Oaks, CA: CQ Press.

Peters, B. G. (1996). *The future of governing: Four emerging models*. Lawrence, KS: University Press of Kansas.

Pfeffer, J. (1981). *Power in organizations*. Marshfield, MA: Pitman.

Pfeffer, J., & G. R. Salancik (1978). *The external control of organizations: A resource dependence perspective*. New York: Harper & Row.

Schön, D. A. (1971). *Beyond the stable state*. New York: Basic Books.

Scott, W. G. (1961, April). Organization theory: An overview and an appraisal. *Academy of Management Journal, 4*(1), 7–26.

Scott, W. G. *Institutions and organizations: Ideas, interests, and identities*. 4th ed. Thousand Oaks, CA: Sage.

Scott, W. G., & T. R. Mitchell (1972). *Organization theory*. Rev. ed. Chicago: Dorsey Press.

Scott, W. R., & G. F. Davis (2007). *Organizations and organizing: Rational, natural, and open systems*. Upper Saddle River, NJ: Prentice Hall.

Scott, W. R. (2004). Reflections on a half-century of organizational sociology. *Annual Review of Sociology, 30:* 1–21.

Senge, P. M. (1990). *The fifth discipline: The art & practice of the learning organization*. New York: Doubleday Currency.

Simon, H. A. (1997). *Administrative behavior: A study of decision-making processes in administrative organizations*. 4th ed. New York: Free Press.

Taylor, F. W. (1911). *The principles of scientific management*. New York: Harper.

Thompson, J. D. (1967). *Organizations in action*. New York: McGraw-Hill.

Tosi, H. L. (2009). *Theories of organization*. Thousand Oaks, CA: Sage.

Tsoukas, H. (2005). *The Oxford handbook of organization theory: Meta-theoretical perspectives*. New York: Oxford University Press.

Weber, M. (1946 trans.). *From Max Weber: Essays in sociology*, ed. Hans H. Gerth and C. Wright Mills. New York: Oxford University Press (first published in 1906–1924).

Weick, K. E. (1969). *The social psychology of organizing*. Reading, MA: Addison-Wesley.

Weick, K. E. (1995). *Sensemaking in organizations*. Thousand Oaks, CA: Sage.

Williamson, O. E. (1981). The economics of organization: The transaction cost approach. *American Journal of Sociology, 87:* 548–577.

Wren, D. A. (1972). *The evolution of management thought*. New York: Ronald Press.

## A CHRONOLOGY OF ORGANIZATION THEORY

**1491 BC**   During the exodus from Egypt, Jethro, the father-in-law of Moses, urges Moses to delegate authority over the tribes of Israel along hierarchical lines.

**500 BC**   Sun Tzu's *The Art of War* recognizes the need for hierarchical organization, interorganizational communications, and staff planning.

**400 BC**   Socrates argues for the universality of management as an art unto itself.

**370 BC**   Xenophon records the first known description of the advantages of the division of labor when he describes an ancient Greek shoe factory.

**360 BC**   Aristotle, in *The Politics*, asserts that the specific nature of executive powers and functions cannot be the same for all states (organizations) but must reflect their cultural environment.

**c. AD 770**   Abu Yusuf, an important pioneering Muslim scholar, explores the administration of essential Islamic government functions, including public financial policy, taxation, and criminal justice, in *Kitab al-Kharaj* (*The Book of Land Taxes*).

**1058**   *Al-Ahkam As-Sultaniyyah* (*The Governmental Rules*), by al-Mawardi, examines Islamic constitutional law, theoretical and practical aspects of Muslim political thought and behavior, and the behavior of politicians and administrators in Islamic states.

**c. 1093**   Al-Ghazali emphasizes the role of Islamic creed and teachings for the improvement of administrative and bureaucratic organization in Muslim states, particularly the qualifications and duties of rulers, ministers, and secretaries, in *Ihya Ulum ad-Din* (*The Revival of the Religious Sciences*) and *Nasihat al-Muluk* (*Counsel for Kings*).

**c. 1300**   In *As-Siyasah ash-Shariyyah* (*The Principles of Religious Government*), ibn Taymiyyah, "the father of Islamic administration," uses the scientific method to outline the principles of administration within the framework of Islam, including "the right man for the right job," patronage, and the spoils system.

**1377**   *The Muqaddimah: An Introduction to History*, by Muslim scholar ibn Khaldun, argues that methods for organizational improvement can be developed through the study of the science of culture. He specifically introduces conceptions of formal and informal organization, organizations as natural organisms with limits beyond which they cannot grow, and esprit de corps.

**1513**   Machiavelli urges the principle of unity of command in *The Discourses*: "It is better to confide any expedition to a single man of ordinary ability, rather than to two, even though they are men of the highest merit, and both having equal ability."

**1532**   Machiavelli's book of advice to all would-be leaders, *The Prince*, is published five years after its author's death. It became the progenitor of all "how to succeed" books that advocate practical rather than moral actions.

1776    Adam Smith's *The Wealth of Nations* discusses the optimal organization of a pin factory. It becomes the most famous and influential statement of the economic rationale for the factory system and the division of labor.

1813    Robert Owen, in his "Address to the Superintendents of Manufactories," puts forth the then-revolutionary idea that managers should pay as much attention to their "vital machines" (employees) as to their "inanimate machines."

1832    Charles Babbage's *On the Economy of Machinery and Manufactures* anticipates many of the notions of the scientific management movement, including such "basic principles of management" as the division of labor.

1856    Daniel McCallum states his six basic principles of administration in his annual report as superintendent of the New York and Erie Railroad Company.

1885    Captain Henry Metcalfe, the manager of an army arsenal, publishes *The Cost of Manufactures and the Administration of Workshops, Public and Private,* in which he asserts that there is a "science of administration" that is based upon principles discoverable by diligent observation.

1886    Henry Towne's paper "The Engineer as Economist," read at a meeting of the American Society of Mechanical Engineers, encourages the scientific management movement.

1902    Vilfredo Pareto becomes the "father" of the concept of "social systems." His societal notions would later be applied by Elton Mayo and the human relationists in organizational contexts.

1903    Frederick W. Taylor publishes *Shop Management.*

1904    Frank B. and Lillian Gilbreth marry. They proceed to produce many pioneering works on time and motion study, scientific management, and applied psychology.

1910    Louis Brandeis, an associate of Frederick W. Taylor (and later Supreme Court Justice), coins and popularizes the term *scientific management* in his Eastern Rate Case testimony before the Interstate Commerce Commission by arguing that railroad rate increases should be denied because the railroads could save "a million dollars a day" by applying scientific management methods.

1911    Frederick W. Taylor publishes *The Principles of Scientific Management.*

1912    Harrington Emerson publishes *The Twelve Principles of Efficiency,* which describes an interdependent but coordinated management system.

1913    Hugo Munsterberg's *Psychology and Industrial Efficiency* calls for the application of psychology to industry.

1914    Robert Michels formulates his iron law of oligarchy: "Who says organization, says oligarchy," in his analysis of the workings of political parties and labor unions, *Political Parties.*

1916    In France, Henri Fayol publishes his *General and Industrial Management,* the first complete theory of management.

Frederick Winslow Taylor's principles of scientific management are published in the *Bulletin of the Taylor Society* as an abstract of an address given by Taylor before the Cleveland Advertising Club in 1915.

**1922**    Max Weber's structural definition of bureaucracy is published posthumously. It uses an "ideal-type" approach to extrapolate from the real world the central core features that characterize the most fully developed form of bureaucratic organization.

**1924**    The Hawthorne studies begin at the Hawthorne Works of the Western Electric Company in Chicago. They last until 1932 and lead to new thinking about the relationships among work environment, human motivation, and productivity.

**1926**    Mary Parker Follett anticipates the movement toward more participatory management styles in a book chapter, "On the Giving of Orders." Follett calls for "power with" as opposed to "power over."

**1933**    Elton Mayo's *The Human Problems of an Industrial Civilization* is the first major report on the Hawthorne studies and the first significant call for a human relations movement.

**1937**    Luther Gulick's "Notes on the Theory of Organization" draws attention to the functional elements of the work of an executive with his mnemonic device POSDCORB.

**1938**    Chester Barnard's *The Functions of the Executive*, a sociological analysis of organizations, encourages and foreshadows the post-war revolution in thinking about organizational behavior.

**1939**    Roethlisberger and Dickson publish *Management and the Worker*, the definitive account of the Hawthorne studies.

**1940**    Robert K. Merton's article "Bureaucratic Structure and Personality" proclaims that Max Weber's "ideal-type" bureaucracy has inhibiting dysfunctions that lead to inefficiency and worse.

**1943**    Abraham Maslow's "needs hierarchy" first appears in his *Psychological Review* article "A Theory of Human Motivation."

**1946**    Herbert Simon's *Public Administration Review* article "The Proverbs of Administration" attacks the principles approach to management for being inconsistent and often inapplicable.

**1947**    The National Training Laboratories for Group Development (later renamed the NTL Institute for Applied Behavioral Science) is established to conduct research on group dynamics and, later, sensitivity training.

Herbert Simon's *Administrative Behavior* urges the use of a truly scientific method in the study of administrative phenomena. The perspective of logical positivism should be used with questions of policy making, and it should be acknowledged that decision making is the true heart of administration.

**1948**     Dwight Waldo publishes *The Administrative State*, which attacks the "gospel of efficiency" that dominated administrative thinking before World War II.

In their *Human Relations* article "Overcoming Resistance to Change," Lester Coch and John French, Jr., note that employees are less inclined to resist change when the need is effectively communicated to them and when the workers are involved in planning the changes.

Norbert Wiener coins the term *cybernetics* in his book of the same title, which becomes a foundational concept for systems theories of organization.

**1949**     Philip Selznick, in *TVA and the Grass Roots*, discovers "cooptation" when he examines how the Tennessee Valley Authority subsumed new external elements into its policy-making process in order to prevent those elements from becoming threats to the organization.

In a *Public Administration Review* article, "Power and Administration," Norton Long finds that power is the lifeblood of administration. Managers must do more than apply the scientific method to problems—they have to attain, maintain, and increase their power or risk failing in their mission.

Rufus Miles, Jr., of the U.S. Bureau of the Budget, states Miles's Law: "Where you stand depends on where you sit."

Air Force Captain Edsel Murphy articulates Murphy's Law: "If anything can go wrong, it will."

**1950**     George Homans publishes *The Human Group*, the first major application of "systems" to organizational analysis.

**1951**     Kurt Lewin proposes a general model of change consisting of three phases, "unfreezing, change, [and] refreezing," in his *Field Theory in Social Science*. His model becomes a conceptual frame for organization development.

Ludwig von Bertalanffy's article "General Systems Theory: A New Approach to the Unity of Science" is published in *Human Biology*. His concepts become *the* intellectual basis for the systems approach to organizational theory.

**1954**     Peter Drucker's book *The Practice of Management* popularizes the concept of management by objectives.

Alvin Gouldner's *Patterns of Industrial Bureaucracy* describes three possible responses to a formal bureaucratic structure: "mock," where the formal rules are ignored by both management and labor; "punishment-centered," where management seeks to enforce rules that workers resist; and "representative," where rules are both enforced and obeyed.

**1956**     William Whyte, Jr., profiles *The Organization Man*, an individual within an organization who accepts its values and finds harmony in conforming to its policies.

In an issue of *Administrative Science Quarterly*, Talcott Parsons's article "Suggestions for a Sociological Approach to the Theory of Organizations" defines an organization as a social system that focuses on the attainment of specific subgoals and, in turn, contributes to the accomplishment of goals of the larger organization or society itself.

Kenneth Boulding's *Management Science* article "General Systems Theory—The Skeleton of Science" merges Wiener's concept of cybernetics with von Bertalanffy's general systems theory. This article becomes the most-quoted introduction to the systems approach to organization theory.

**1957** C. Northcote Parkinson discovers his law that "work expands so as to fill the time available for its completion."

Chris Argyris asserts in his first major book, *Personality and Organization*, that there is an inherent conflict between the personality of a mature adult and the needs of modern organizations.

Douglas McGregor's article "The Human Side of Enterprise" distills the contending traditional authoritarian and humanistic managerial philosophies into Theory X and Theory Y and applies the concept of "self-fulfilling prophecies" to organizational behavior.

Philip Selznick, in *Leadership in Administration*, anticipates many 1980s notions of "transformational leadership." He asserts that the function of an institutional leader is to help shape the environment in which the institution operates and to define new institutional directions through recruitment, training, and bargaining.

Alvin Gouldner, in "Cosmopolitans and Locals," identifies two latent social roles in organizations: "cosmopolitans," who have little loyalty to the employing organization, high commitment to specialized skills, and an outer-reference group orientation; and "locals," who have high loyalty to the employing organization, a low commitment to specialized skills, and an inner-reference group orientation.

**1958** James March and Herbert Simon attempt to inventory and classify all that is worth knowing about the behavioral revolution in organization theory in *Organizations*.

Leon Festinger, the father of cognitive dissonance theory, writes "The Motivating Effect of Cognitive Dissonance," which becomes the theoretical foundation for inequity theories of motivation.

Robert Tannenbaum and Warren Schmidt's *Harvard Business Review* article "How to Choose a Leadership Pattern" describes "democratic management" and devises a leadership continuum ranging from authoritarian to democratic.

**1959** Charles Lindblom's "The Science of 'Muddling Through'" rejects the rational model of decision making in favor of incrementalism.

Herzberg, Mausner, and Snyderman's *The Motivation to Work* puts forth the motivation–hygiene theory of worker motivation.

Richard Cyert and James March postulate that power and politics influence the formation of organizational goals. Their essay "A Behavioral Theory of Organizational Objectives" is a precursor of the power and politics school of organization theory.

John French, Jr., and Bertram Raven identify five bases of power—expert, referent, reward, legitimate, and coercive—in "The Bases of Social Power." They argue that coercive and expert power bases are least effective.

**1960**      Richard Neustadt's *Presidential Power* asserts that a president's—or any executive's—essential power is that of persuasion.

Herbert Kaufman's *The Forest Ranger* examines how organizational and professional socialization can develop the will and capacity of employees to conform.

**1961**      Victor Thompson's *Modern Organization* finds "an imbalance between ability and authority" that causes bureaucratic dysfunctions.

Harold Koontz's "The Management Theory Jungle" describes the state of management and organization theory as a "semantics jungle."

Burns and Stalker's *The Management of Innovation* articulates the need for different types of management systems—organic or mechanistic—under differing circumstances.

Rensis Likert's *New Patterns of Management* offers an empirically based defense of participatory management and organization development.

William Scott's *Academy of Management Journal* article "Organization Theory: An Overview and an Appraisal" explains the relationship between systems theory and organization theory and the distinction between micro and macro perspectives in theory development.

Amitai Etzioni, in *A Comparative Analysis of Complex Organizations*, argues that organizational effectiveness is affected by the match between an organization's goal structure and its compliance structure.

**1962**      Robert Presthus's *The Organizational Society* introduces his classification of how individuals accommodate to organizations: "upwardmobiles" identify and accept the values of the organization; "indifferents" reject such values and find personal satisfaction off the job; and "ambivalents" want the rewards of organizational life but can't cope with the demands.

Peter Blau and W. Richard Scott, in *Formal Organizations: A Comparative Approach*, assert that all organizations include both a formal and an informal element, and it is impossible to know and understand the true structure of a formal organization without understanding its parallel informal organization.

David Mechanic anticipates the power and politics perspective of organization theory in an *Administrative Science Quarterly* article, "Sources of Power of Lower Participants in Complex Organizations."

**1963**      Strauss, Schatzman, Bucher, Erlich, and Sabshin describe the maintenance of order in a hospital as a dynamic process operating within a framework of negotiated "contracts" among people and groups with different expectations and interests in "The Hospital and Its Negotiated Order."

Cyert and March demonstrate that corporations tend to "satisfice" rather than engage in economically rational profit-maximizing behavior in *A Behavioral Theory of the Firm*.

| | |
|---|---|
| **1964** | Blake and Mouton's *The Managerial Grid* uses a graphic gridiron to explain management styles and their potential impacts on an organization development program. |
| | Michel Crozier, in *The Bureaucratic Phenomenon*, defines a bureaucracy as "an organization which cannot correct its behavior by learning from its errors." |
| | Bertram M. Gross publishes his two-volume *The Managing of Organizations*, a historical analysis of thinking about organizations from ancient times to the present. |
| **1965** | Don Price publishes *The Scientific Estate*, in which he posits that decision authority flows inexorably from the executive suite to the technical office. |
| | Robert Kahn's *Organizational Stress* is the first major study of the mental health consequences of organizational role conflict and ambiguity. |
| | James March edits the huge *Handbook of Organizations*, which sought to summarize all existing knowledge on organization theory and behavior. |
| **1966** | Katz and Kahn seek to unify the findings of behavioral science on organizational behavior through open systems theory in *The Social Psychology of Organizations*. |
| | *Think Magazine* publishes David McClelland's article "That Urge to Achieve," in which he identifies two groups of people: the majority who are not concerned about achieving and the minority who are challenged by the opportunity to achieve. |
| | In *Changing Organizations*, Warren Bennis sounds a death knell for bureaucratic institutions, asserting they are inadequate for a future that will demand rapid organizational change, participatory management, and the growth of a more professionalized work force. |
| | In "The Power of Power" (a chapter in *Varieties of Political Theory*, edited by David Easton), James March explores alternative definitions, concepts, and approaches for empirically studying social power in organizations and communities. |
| **1967** | James D. Thompson's *Organizations in Action* seeks to close the gap between open and closed systems theory by suggesting that organizations deal with environmental uncertainty by creating specific elements to cope with the outside world, which allows other elements to focus on the rational nature of technical operations. |
| | Anthony Downs's *Inside Bureaucracy* seeks to develop laws and propositions to help predict the behavior of bureaus and bureaucrats. |
| | John Kenneth Galbraith's *The New Industrial State* asserts that control of modern corporations has passed to technostructures, and technostructures are more concerned with stability than profits. |
| | Antony Jay applies political principles from Machiavelli's *The Prince* to modern organizational management in *Management and Machiavelli*. |

**1968**        Harold Wilensky's *Organizational Intelligence* presents the pioneering study of the flow and perception of information in organizations.

In *Group Dynamics*, Dorwin Cartwright and Alvin Zander propose that the systematic study of group dynamics would advance knowledge of the nature of groups, how they are organized, and relationships among individuals, other groups, and larger institutions.

Walker and Lorsch grapple with the perennial structural issue of whether to design organizations by product or function in their *Harvard Business Review* article "Organizational Choice: Product vs. Function."

Frederick Herzberg's *Harvard Business Review* article "One More Time, How Do You Motivate Employees?" catapults *motivators* or *satisfiers* and *hygiene factors* into the forefront of organizational motivation theory.

**1969**        Laurence Peter promulgates his principle that "in a hierarchy every employee tends to rise to his level of incompetence."

Lawrence and Lorsch call for a contingency theory that can deal with the appropriateness of different theories under differing circumstances, in *Organization and Environment*. Organizations must solve the problem of simultaneous differentiation and integration.

Paul Hersey and Kenneth Blanchard's "Life Cycle Theory of Leadership" asserts that the appropriate leadership style for a particular situation depends on employees' education, experience level, achievement motivation, and willingness to accept responsibility.

**1970**        In "Expectancy Theory," John Campbell, Marvin Dunnette, Edward Lawler III, and Karl Weick, Jr., theorize that people are motivated by calculating how much they want something, how much of it they think they will get, how likely it is their actions will cause them to get it, and how much others in similar circumstances have received.

Chris Argyris writes *Intervention Theory and Methods*, an enduring work about consulting for organizational change from the organizational behavior/ organization development perspective.

**1971**        Graham Allison's *Essence of Decision* demonstrates the inadequacies of the view that decisions of a government are made by a "single calculating decision maker" who has control over the organizations and officials within the government.

Irving Janis's "Groupthink," first published in *Psychology Today*, proposes that group cohesion can lead to the deterioration of effective group decision making.

**1972**        Harlan Cleveland asserts that decision making in the future will call for "continuous improvisation on a general sense of direction," in *The Future Executive*.

Charles Perrow's *Complex Organizations* is a major defense of bureaucratic forms of organization and an attack on writers who believe that bureaucracy can be easily, fairly, or inexpensively replaced.

Kast and Rosenzweig, in an *Academy of Management Journal* article, "General Systems Theory: Applications for Organization and Management," assesses the success of applications of general systems theory and advocates contingency theory as a less abstract and more applicable theoretical approach.

**1973**      Jay Galbraith articulates the systems/contingency view that the amount of information an organization needs is a function of the levels of its uncertainty, interdependence of units and functions, and adaptation mechanisms in *Designing Complex Organizations*.

**1974**      In a report for the Carnegie Commission on Higher Education, Cohen and March introduce the phrase *organized anarchies* to communicate why colleges and universities are distinctive organizational forms with uniquely difficult leadership needs and problems. The report was published as the book *Leadership and Ambiguity: The American College President*.

Victor Vroom's *Organizational Dynamics* article "A New Look at Managerial Decision-Making" develops a model whereby leaders can diagnose situations to determine which leadership style is most appropriate.

**1975**      Oliver Williamson uses economic market models to analyze organizational decisions about producing products and services internally or purchasing them, and assesses the implications of such decisions on, for example, organizational authority, in *Markets and Hierarchies: Analysis and Antitrust Implications*.

*Behavior in Organizations*, by Porter, Lawler, and Hackman, examines how individual-organizational relationships emerge and grow, including how groups can exert influence on individuals in organizations and how such social influences relate to work effectiveness.

**1976**      Michael Maccoby psychoanalytically interviews 250 corporate managers and discovers "The Gamesman," a manager whose main interest lies in "competitive activity where he can prove himself a winner."

Michael Jensen and William Meckling describe an organization as simply an extension of and a means for satisfying the interests of the myriad individuals and groups that affect and are affected by it, in their *Journal of Fianancial Economics* article "Agency Costs and the Theory of the Firm."

In "A Concept of Organizational Ecology," an article in the *Australian Journal of Management*, Eric Trist proposes a field concept of organizational population ecology. The field is created by the organizations whose interrelations constitute a system; thus, the system is the field, not its component organizations.

Herbert Kaufman concludes in *Are Government Organizations Immortal?* that governmental agencies experience a death rate of less than half the annual rate of business organizational demise.

**1977**      Hannan and Freeman's *American Journal of Sociology* article "The Population Ecology of Organizations" proposes "populations of organizations" as the appropriate unit of analysis for understanding organizations.

John Meyer and Brian Rowan stress that the modern world contains socially constructed practices and norms that provide a framework for the creation and elaboration of formal organizations in an *American Sociological Review* article,

"Institutionalized Organizations: Formal Structure as Myth and Ceremony." Organizations as open systems gain legitimacy and support to the extent that they accept these norms as appropriate ways to organize.

Gerald Salancik and Jeffrey Pfeffer's article in *Organizational Dynamics*, "Who Gets Power—and How They Hold On to It," explains how power and politics help organizations adapt to their environment by reallocating critical resources to subunits that are performing tasks most vital to organizational survival.

In *Matrix*, Davis and Lawrence caution against using a matrix form of organization unless specific organizational conditions exist that are conducive to its success.

In *Men and Women of the Corporation*, Rosabeth Moss Kanter examines the unique problems women encounter with power and politics in organizations.

**1978**      Pfeffer and Salancik explain that the structure and behavior of an organization cannot be understood without also understanding its context in *External Control of Organizations: A Resource Dependence Perspective*. Organizations must acquire resources from their environment, and how important and how scarce these resources are determines the extent of organizational dependency.

Thomas Peters's *Organizational Dynamics* article "Symbols, Patterns, and Settings: An Optimistic Case for Getting Things Done" is the first major analysis of symbolic management to gain significant attention in the mainstream literature of organization theory.

James MacGregor Burns's *Leadership* introduces the concept of transformational leadership, a leader who "looks for potential motives in followers, seeks to satisfy higher needs, and engages the full person of the follower."

**1979**      Rosabeth Moss Kanter's *Harvard Business Review* article "Power Failure in Management Circuits" identifies organizational positions that tend to have power problems and argues that powerlessness is often more of a problem than power for organizations.

*Structuring Organizations* is published, the first book in Henry Mintzberg's integrative series, "The Theory of Management Policy."

**1980**      In "Structure in 5's: A Synthesis of the Research on Organization Design," Mintzberg asserts that elements of organizational structure "show a curious tendency to appear in five's—suggesting a typology of five basic configurations: Simple Structure, Machine Bureaucracy, Professional Bureaucracy, Divisionalized Form, and Adhocracy."

Connolly, Conlon, and Deutsch argue that assessments of organizational effectiveness should employ multiple criteria in order to reflect the diverse interests of the various constituencies involved with organizations in "Organizational Effectiveness: A Multiple Constituency Approach," in the *Academy of Management Review*.

Meryl Reis Louis's *Administrative Science Quarterly* article "Surprise and Sense Making: What Newcomers Experience in Entering Unfamiliar Organizational Settings" proposes that sense making by newcomers usually must rely on inadequate sources of information, which can lead them astray.

1981     W. Richard Scott offers three definitions of formal organizations in *Organizations: Rational, Natural and Open Systems*. The first sees organizations as highly formalized, rational collectives pursuing specific goals. The second views organizations as social systems with multiple interests, informal relations, and subgoals of participants. And the third views organizations as systems of interdependent activities embedded in and dependent on wider environments.

Oliver Williamson's article "The Economics of Organization: The Transaction Cost Approach," in the *American Journal of Sociology*, explains that transaction cost economizing is essential for understanding the emergence and development of hierarchies and organizations. He identifies three types of governance structures: market, hybrid, and hierarchy. His approach helps determine boundaries between firms and markets and can be applied to the organization of internal transactions.

Jeffrey Pfeffer's *Power in Organizations* integrates the tenets and applications of the power and politics school of organization theory.

Thomas Ouchi's *Theory Z* and Pascale and Athos's *The Art of Japanese Management* popularize the Japanese management movement.

1982     Organizational culture becomes "hot" in the general business literature with such books as Peters and Waterman's *In Search of Excellence*, Deal and Kennedy's *Corporate Culture*, and *Business Week*'s cover story "Corporate Culture."

1983     Henry Mintzberg's *Power In and Around Organizations* explains the power and politics school of organizational theory as a coherent theory of management policy.

In *The Change Masters*, Rosabeth Moss Kanter defines change masters as architects of organizational change. They are the right people in the right places at the right time.

Meryl Louis's article "Organizations as Cultural-Bearing Milieux" becomes an early integrative statement of the organizational cultural perspective's assumptions and positions.

"Values in Organizational Theory and Management Education," by Michael Keeley and published in the *Academy of Management Review*, proposes that organizations exist by virtue of agreement on joint activities to achieve separate purposes of important constituencies, not to achieve organizational goals or purposes.

Ian Mitroff's *Stakeholders of the Organizational Mind* describes how the perceptions of internal and external stakeholders influence organizational behavior—particularly decision making about complex problems of organizational policy and design.

Pondy, Frost, Morgan, and Dandridge edit the first definitive volume on symbolic management, *Organizational Symbolism*.

Linda Smircich's "Organizations as Shared Meanings," a chapter in Pondy, Frost, Morgan, and Dandridge's *Organizational Symbolism*, examines how systems of commonly shared meanings develop and are sustained in organizations through symbolic communications processes and how shared meanings provide members of an organizational culture with a sense of commonality and a distinctive character.

**1984**    Sergiovanni and Corbally edit the first notable collection of papers on the organizational culture perspective, *Leadership and Organizational Culture*.

Siehl and Martin report the findings of a quantitative and qualitative empirical study of organizational culture in "The Role of Symbolic Management: How Can Managers Effectively Transmit Organizational Culture?"—a chapter in Hunt, Hosking, Schriesheim, and Stewart's *Leaders and Managers: International Perspectives on Managerial Behavior and Leadership*.

**1985**    Edgar Schein writes the first edition of his highly regarded statement on organizational culture, *Organizational Culture and Leadership*.

In *The Irrational Organization*, Nils Brunsson postulates that rationality may lead to good decisions, but it decreases the probability of organizational action and change.

Kathy Ferguson's *The Feminist Case Against Bureaucracy* becomes the first widely accepted presentation of the feminist perspective on organizations.

*Administrative Development*, by Muhammad A. Al-Buraey, combines western methodology and techniques with Islamic substance, values, and ethics to demonstrate how the Islamic perspective—as a system and a way of life—is a moving force in the process and realization of administrative development worldwide.

**1986**    Michael Harmon and Richard Mayer write a comprehensive text on public sector organization theory, *Organization Theory for Public Administration*.

Gareth Morgan's *Images of Organization* develops the art of reading and understanding organizations starting from the premise that theories of organization are based on metaphors—distinctive but partial mental images.

Jay Barney and William Ouchi provide an overview of themes, such as agency theory and price theory, which have contributed to organizational theory, in *Learning from Organizational Economics*.

**1988**    Michael Keeley combines concepts of multiple constituencies, organizational purposes, systems of justice, values, and organizational worth in the first comprehensive statement of *A Social-Contract Theory of Organizations*.

The *American Journal of Sociology* publishes a heated debate between the leading proponents and detractors of population ecology approaches to organization theory.

**1989**      Rosabeth Moss Kanter's *When Giants Learn to Dance* explores how organizations can gain the advantages of smallness (flexibility) and size (staying power) at the same time.

In a *Business and Society* article, "Corporate Citizenship: Social Responsibility, Responsiveness, and Performance," Archie Carroll and Ann Buchholtz assert that it is partially business's fault that many of today's social problems arose in the first place, and therefore, business should assume a role in remedying these problems.

**1990**      In *Governing the Commons: The Evolution of Institutions for Collective Action*, Elinor Ostrom introduces the concept of a "common pool resource" (CPR) and highlights the role of self-governing, cooperative institutions as a way to manage CPRs effectively. Ostrom puts forth cooperative self-governing institutions as an alternative solution to markets and governments for solving "the tragedy of commons."

Sally Helgesen uses diary studies to explore how women leaders make decisions and gather and disperse information in organizations. In *The Female Advantage*, Helgesen suggests that "women may be the new Japanese" of management.

"In Praise of Hierarchy" by Elliott Jaques, a *Harvard Business Review* article, argues that critics of hierarchy are misguided. Instead of needing new organizational forms, we need to learn how to manage hierarchies better.

Paul Goodman and Lee Sproull describe how organizational behavior is affected by new technologies. They argue in *Technology and Organizations* that technology's impacts are so profound that organizations must find new ways of conducting enterprise in order to survive.

Peter Senge's highly influential management book *The Fifth Discipline* describes organizations with "learning disabilities" and how "learning organizations" defy the odds to overcome them.

David Ulrich and Dale Lake's *Organizational Capability: Competing from the Inside Out* explains what "capability" is and how to develop competitiveness based on management action.

Lex Donaldson's *Academy of Management Review* article "The Ethereal Hand: Organizational Economics and Management Theory" explains the potentialities and pitfalls of organizational economics.

Karl Weick's chapter in Goodman and Sproull's *Technology and Organizations*, "Technology as Equivoque: Sensemaking in New Technologies," examines cognitive processes that people use to adapt to work in environments where important events are unpredictable and often chaotic.

Publication of Roosevelt Thomas Jr.'s *Harvard Business Review* article "From Affirmative Action to Affirming Diversity" introduces cultural diversity as an organizational concept and a definable goal.

Paul Rubin explains the costs of principal-agent relationships, how to minimize costs, and the effects of transaction costs on management decisions in *Managing Business Transactions*.

**1991**     Robert Lord and Karen Maher frame leadership in terms of how organizational "commandants" process information—rational, limited-capacity, expert, and cybernetic—and relate this to how other participants in the environment process information about commandants in *Information Processing: Linking Perceptions and Performance*.

Manfred Kets de Vries demonstrates how individuals' rational and irrational behavior patterns influence organizations in *Organizations on the Couch*.

**1992**     Thierry Pauchant and Ian Mitroff explore crisis-prone organizations and the psychological and emotional factors that enable managers to ignore the possibility of pending crises in *Transforming the Crisis-Prone Organization*.

Jeffrey Pfeffer's *Managing With Power* describes how to consolidate and use power for constructive organizational goals, urging managers to realize that if they do not use power, someone else will.

Barbara Czarniawska-Joerges explains sense making in organizational life—even when organizational behavior does not appear to make sense. *Exploring Complex Organizations: A Cultural Perspective* constitutes a cross-cultural and cross-contextual analysis of sense making in large organizations.

*Organizational Architecture*, by David Nadler, Marc Gerstein, and Robert Shaw, uses architecture as a metaphor to identify evolving forms and features of effective organizations, including autonomous work teams, high-performance work systems, spinouts, networks, self-designed organizations, and fuzzy boundaries.

William G. Scott's *Chester I. Barnard and the Guardians of the Managerial State* provides a penetrating look into the beliefs and philosophies that laid the foundation for Chester Barnard's highly influential 1938 classic *The Functions of the Executive*.

Joan Acker's "Gendering Organization Theory," a chapter in Mills and Tancred's *Gendering Organization Theory*, argues that ordinary activities in organizations are not gender neutral. They perpetuate the "gendered substructure within the organization itself and within the wider society"—as well as in organization theory.

David Osborne and Ted Gaebler's best-selling book *Reinventing Government: How the Entrepreneurial Spirit Is Transforming the Public Sector* claims that public agencies are designed to protect against politicians and bureaucrats gaining too much power or misusing public money. Instead, we need "entrepreneurial government."

Ralph Stacey's *Managing the Unknowable: Strategic Boundaries Between Order and Chaos* challenges the view that organizational success stems from stability, harmony, predictability, and stable equilibrium. Managers should embrace "unbounded instability" because disorder, chance, and irregularity can be beneficial.

Richard Beckhard and Wendy Pritchard's *Changing the Essence* discusses leadership behaviors that are necessary for initiating and managing fundamental organizational change.

In "The Network Organization in Theory and Practice," a chapter in Nohria and Eccles' *Networks and Organizations*, Wayne Baker explores features of network organizations. Baker quantifies their structural properties using the principles of integration and differentiation. Using a real estate service firm as an example, he concludes that a network organization is integrated across formal boundaries while interpersonal ties of different types are formed without respect to vertical, horizontal or spatial differentiation.

**1993**   William Bergquist's *The Postmodern Organization* looks at premodern, modern, and postmodern views on five dimensions of organizational life: size and complexity, mission and boundaries, leadership, communication, and capital and worker values.

*Cultural Diversity in Organizations*, by Taylor Cox, Jr., examines benefits and difficulties that may accrue to an organization from cultural diversity.

Ian Mitroff and Harold Linstone examine four ways of knowing, or "inquiry systems," for assisting decision making in *The Unbounded Mind: Breaking the Chains of Traditional Business Thinking*.

*Reengineering the Corporation*, by Michael Hammer and James Champy, prescribes how to radically redesign a company's processes, organization, and culture to achieve quantum advances in performance.

In *The Corporate Closet*, James Woods and Jay Lucas explore what it is like to be gay in the corporate world and how to manage sexual identity in the workplace. They encourage openness in corporate practices, such as listing sexual preference along with gender and ethnicity in training, recruiting, and retention programs.

Harrison Trice and Janice Beyer write a comprehensive treatise on organizational culture, *The Cultures of Work Organizations*.

Donald Kettl's *Sharing Power* adds to the growing debate about privatization of government goods and services, arguing that government must become a "smart buyer" when it contracts with the private sector.

Camilla Stivers's *Gender Images in Public Administration* examines the role that traditional public administrators—that is, professional experts, visionary leaders, guardians, and citizens—play in creating gender bias.

Michael Diamond's *The Unconscious Life of Organizations* provides a psychodynamic view of modern organizational complexities. Interactions from unconscious hierarchical dynamics and work relationships produce organizational values, rituals, emotions, and identities.

Christopher Pollitt's *Managerialism and the Public Services* applies managerialism to public administration.

Scott Cook and Dvora Yanow's *Culture and Organizational Learning* offers an explanation of organizational culture and organizational learning by suggesting that "the capacity of an organization to learn how to do what it does, where what it learns is possessed not by individual members of the organization but by the aggregate itself."

*The Gore Report on Reinventing Government*, Al Gore's "reinventing government" initiative, is published as the *National Performance Review*.

1994    *Managing Chaos and Complexity in Government*, by Douglas Kiel, applies chaos theory to self-organization in public management. Kiel shows how the deep structures and processes of agency dynamics can foster learning and ability to cope with risk and uncertainty.

Bart Victor and Carroll Stephens sound a warning to those who advocate virtual offices, virtual occupations, and temporary working relationships without acknowledging the importance of "loyalty, dedication, and belonging" in their *Organization Science* article "The Dark Side of the New Organizational Forms."

1995    Thierry Pauchant introduces the concept of "organizational existentialism" and urges the use of the existential tradition when examining managerial and organizational issues in *In Search of Meaning*.

Attribution theory—how people explain causes of their own and other's behavior—is explored through an organizational lens by Mark J. Martinko in *Attribution Theory: An Organizational Perspective*.

1996    *Organizational Communication: Theory and Behavior*'s editor, Peggy Yuhas Byers, presents a collection of essays on human communication in modern organizations.

Espejo, Schuhmann, Schwaninger, and Bilello address issues of organizational complexity and how organizational and managerial cybernetics can be useful in *Organizational Transformation and Learning: A Cybernetic Approach to Management*.

1997    In their book, *In Virtual Organizations and Beyond: Discover Imaginary Systems*, Hedberg, Dahlgren, Hansson, and Olve introduce "the imaginary organization," a new perspective on organizations where information technologies, alliances, and other networks inside and outside the organization are used to describe the entire system.

1998    "Technology as a Contingency Factor," a chapter by Richard Burton and Børge Obel in their book *Strategic Organizational Diagnosis and Design*, assesses technology's impacts on six dimensions of organization design: formalization, centralization, complexity, configuration, coordination and control, and incentives.

1999    David Thomas and John Gabarro compare experiences of successful minority and white executives and conclude that the paths to corporate success are distinctly different for people of color in *Breaking Through: The Making of Minority Executives in Corporate America.*

*Shakespeare on Management: Wise Business Counsel from the Bard*, by Jay Shafritz, offers a compelling twist to Shakespeare's literary contributions by exploring his thoughts on business and management.

In *Organizations Evolving*, Howard Aldrich utilizes an evolutionary approach to explain the development of organizations and institutional change over time. Aldrich is concerned with interorganizational diversity and with the use of interdisciplinary perspectives for understanding why organizations persist and to identify factors that affect whether developing organizations accept or reject existing institutional forms.

Janet Fulk and Gerardine DeSanctis's "Articulation of Communication Technology and Organizational Form" explores the connections between communication technology and organizational form in *Shaping Organization Form: Communication, Connection, and Community.*

2000    Glenn Carroll and Michael Hannan explore the theory, models, methods, and data used in demographic approaches to organizational studies in *Demography of Corporations and Industries*. They demonstrate how corporate populations change over time by exploring the processes of organizational founding, growth, decline, transformation, and mortality.

Scott Snook uses the 1994 shooting down of U.S. Blackhawk helicopters in Iraq as an example of organizational failure at the individual, group, and institutional levels in *Friendly Fire*. Snook offers insights as to how multiple factors cause system failures, not simply organizational shortcomings.

2001    Taylor Cox, Jr., acknowledges the importance of organizational diversity, but asserts that "counting heads for the government" has failed to achieve and maintain multiculturalism in *Creating the Multicultural Organization: A Strategy for Capturing the Power of Diversity*. Cox introduces a proactive model that includes strategies for creating a diverse and multicultural environment through leadership, research, and education.

Abagail McWilliams and Donald Siegel outline a supply and demand model of corporate social responsibility in "Corporate Social Responsibility: A Theory of the Firm Perspective," an article in the *Academy of Management Review*. They conclude that managers can establish an "ideal" level of corporate social responsibility using cost-benefit analysis and that a relationship can be predicted between corporate social responsibility and financial performance.

Neil Fligstein's *The Architecture of Markets: An Economic Sociology of Twenty-First Century Capitalist Societies* uses a sociological and political-culture approach to explain the construction of American markets. His theory of "market institutionalism" offers insights into economic sociology that account for developments in globalization, American capitalism, and the role of government.

David Knoke employs a sociological perspective to assess intra- and interorganizational networks in *Changing Organizations: Business Networks in the*

*New Political Economy*. Knoke considers ecology, institutionalism, power and resource dependence, transaction cost economics, organizational learning, and evolutionary theory as ways to understand a variety of contemporary corporate issues.

**2002**     In *Organizing America: Wealth, Power, and the Origins of Corporate Capitalism*, Charles Perrow asserts that the development of large bureaucratic organizations in America was both intentional and inevitable. Entrepreneurs have been able to take advantage of abundant resources and flourishing markets because many regulatory barriers that impede organizational development in other nations have been eliminated by elected officials or legal decisions.

Although many students of organizational culture seek an integrated, shared set of cultural values, and the unity of cultural beliefs within an organization, Joanne Martin addresses the extent of diversity and the realities of differentiation in organizational culture—a fragmented culture—in *Organizational Culture: Mapping the Terrain*.

Management ideas are shaped and transferred by knowledge carriers, such as business schools and consultants. Kerstin Sahlin-Andersson and Lars Engwall provide a summary of empirical studies on the development, refinement, and diffusion of managerial ideas and explanation about the global explosion of management knowledge in *The Expansion of Management Knowledge: Carriers, Flows, and Sources*.

**2003**     *Social Networks and Organizations*, by Martin Kilduff and Wenpin Tsai, explains social network approaches to organizational research.

**2004**     In "The Concept of Organizational Culture: Why Bother?" Edgar H. Schein articulates a formal definition of organizational culture that consists of a model with three levels of culture, which is particularly useful for sorting through myriad methodological and substantive problems associated with identifying an organizational culture.

Edwin Locke and Gary Latham's *Academy of Management* article "What Should We Do about Motivation Theory? Six Recommendations for the Twenty-First Century" presents recommendations for building theories of work motivation that are valid, complete, broad in scope, and useful to practitioners.

**2005**     *Appreciative Inquiry* by David Cooperrider and Diana Whitney offers a positive, strengths-based approach to organization development and change management. Their approach to organizational development and change engages organizational members in a process for appreciating and valuing what might be rather than analyzing existing problems or their causes.

Barbara Crosby and John Bryson argue that because powerful groups influence what is held to be "rational," altering power distributions and relationships undermines the legitimacy of perceived rationalities about the world as it is, in *Leadership for the Common Good*.

Gerald Davis, Doug McAdam, W. Richard Scott, and Mayer Zald blend organization theory and social movement theory in *Social Movements and Organization Theory*. They provide rich evidence of how the fields of social movement—like organizations and strategically organized movements—inform each other and can be bridged.

2006   Helen Haugh identifies a variety of direct and indirect economic, social, and environmental outcomes from social entrepreneurial initiatives that are benefiting six communities in rural Scotland, in "Social Enterprise: Beyond Economic Outcomes and Individual Returns," a chapter in Robinson and Kocherts' *Social Entrepreneurship*.

In "Abu Ghraib, Administrative Evil, and Moral Inversion," Guy Adams, Danny Balfour, and George Reed analyze why U.S. military personnel could casually engage in torture "and perhaps even believe that it was part of their job to do so." This *Public Administration Review* article concludes that "group and organizational roles and social structures play a far more powerful part in everyday human behavior than most of us would consider.

Johanna Mair, Jeffrey Robinson, and Kai Hockerts explain that social entrepreneurship encompasses "a wide range of activities: enterprising individuals devoted to making a difference; social purpose business ventures dedicated to adding for-profit motivations to the nonprofit sector; new types of philanthropists supporting venture capital-like 'investment' portfolios" in *Social Entrepreneurship*.

Leigh Buchanan and Andrew O'Connell trace the history of intellectual contributions to decision-making models and ideas from Chester Barnard into the twenty-first century, in their *Harvard Business Review* article "A Brief History of Decision Making."

Gili Drori, John Meyer, and Hokyu Hwang explore dimensions of the global trends of expansion, formalization, and standardization of organizing, in *Globalization and Organization: World Society and Organizational Change*. The authors argue that these processes can be attributed to globalization and its tendencies toward universalism, rationalization, and the rise of "social actors" as a concept.

Gary Johns argues that the impact of context is not sufficiently recognized and incorporated into models and theories of organization. He proposes two levels of analysis for theories relating to context in his *Academy of Management Review* article "The Essential Impact of Context on Organizational Behavior."

Christopher Worley and Edward Lawler III explain that many change efforts fail to meet expectations as a result of poor organizational design, cultural barriers, and/or poor management in "Designing Organizations that are Built to Change," an article in *Leadership and Organizational Studies*.

2007   Jagdeep Chhokar, Robert House, and Felix Brodbeck's *Culture and Leadership Across the World* documents a large-scale study of leadership approaches in more than 1,000 organizations in 62 countries. They identify new ideas and conceptual frameworks for leadership models from around the globe.

In *Logics of Organization Theory: Audiences, Codes, and Ecologies*, Michael Hannan, Laszlo Polos, and Glenn Carroll adapt the language and concepts of non-monotonic logic and "fuzzy set theory" to theory building for organizational ecology. They also use insights from cognitive psychology and anthropology to develop an audience-based theory of organizational categories as an approach to analyzing organizations.

2008    In *the Red Queen among Organizations: How Competitiveness Evolves*, William Barnett questions why some organizations are more competitive than others and what makes competitive advantages of these organizations ephemeral. Competing organizations strengthen rivals through the endless cycle of competition, but learning does not guarantee sustained benefits and may lead to the loss of advantages.

The *Sage Handbook of Organizational Institutionalism*, by Royston Greenwood, Christine Oliver, Roy Suddaby, and Kerstin Sahlin-Andersson, explores how institutionalist research applied to organizational behavior has emerged and evolved over time.

*Gender and Communication at Work*, by Mary Barrett and Marilyn Davison, offers a broad contemporary assessment of the ways in which gender affects communications, decisions, opportunities, and individual development in the workplace.

Paul Light's *The Search of Social Entrepreneurship* presents findings from a study on the differences between highly, moderately, and not very socially entrepreneurially oriented organizations using interviews of senior executives in high-performing social benefit organizations.

2009    Frank Dobbin's *Inventing Equal Opportunities* reveals that corporate personnel experts eventually determine what "discrimination in practice" means by changing the methods of hiring, promoting, and firing. By studying the important historical changes in the actions of U.S. corporate personnel, he explains how corporate personnel experts have influenced corporate executives to adopt a wide variety of equal opportunity policies and work-family balance practices.

*Managed by the Markets: How Finance Re-Shaped America*, by Gerald Davis, explains how the focus of the American economy has been shifting from manufacturing industries to the financial markets for the past three decades. Davis insists that the "great recession" of 2008 has proven the danger of overdependence on financial markets.

2010    Geert Hofstede, Gert Jan Hofstede, and Michael Minkov explain how organizational culture is influenced by and partially reflects dimensions of national cultures and how nationality affects organizational rationality, in *Cultures and Organizations: Software of the Mind*.

*The Entrepreneurial Group: Social Identities, Relations, and Collective Action* by Ruef Martin introduces a group-based approach to entrepreneurship. Entrepreneurial groups act together, thereby revealing how the social structure of entrepreneurship influences the emergence of new organizations. Martin includes extensive sociological analyses on the entrepreneurial groups.

David Billis' chapter "Towards a Theory of Hybrid Organizations," a chapter in his book *Hybrid Organizations and the Third Sector*, develops a foundation for theories about organizations that are partly in one sector and partly in another. Billis identifies underlying principles of "ideal type sectors and accountabilities," and "hybrid zones," and the most difficult challenges facing hybrid organization theory builders.

**2012**

In *A Theory of Fields*, Doug McAdam and Neil Fligstein undertake an extensive review of social theories. They assume fields are a sum of every environment in life including the world, and show how these fields affect one another, thereby stimulating social changes. For applications, the book analyzes the Civil Rights Movement and shifts in the U.S. mortgage markets in the 1960s.

"A New Kind of Public Service Professional," by Mitchell Rice and Audrey Mathews, a chapter in Norman-Major and Gooden's *Cultural Competency for Public Administrators*, asserts that organizations and public agencies that develop cultural competency among their personnel can manage diversity well and also tend to be creative problem solvers, innovative, and able to adapt to other inevitable forces of change. Cultural competency requires cultural awareness, cultural knowledge, and cultural skills.

Patricia Thornton, William Ocasio, and Michael Lounsbury's *The Institutional Logics Perspective: A New Approach to Culture, Structure, and Process* charts changes in perspectives on institutional logics and their influence on the transformation of institutional theory. The authors show how these changes have occurred and have developed micro aspects of institutional logics and institutional entrepreneurship.

In *The Emergence of Organizations and Markets*, John Frederick Padgett and Walter Powell elaborate a theory of newly formed organizations and markets that emphasizes interactions of social networks. Actors initially develop relations, and eventually these relations influence the actors.

# CHAPTER 1

# *Classical Organization Theory*

No single date can be pinpointed as the beginning of serious thinking about how organizations work and how they should be structured and managed. Writings about management and organizations can be traced as far back as the known origins of commerce. A lot can be learned from the early organizations of the Muslims, Hebrews, Greeks, and Romans. We could make the case that much of what we know about organization theory has its origins in ancient and medieval times. After all, it was Aristotle who first wrote of the importance of culture to management systems, ibn Taymiyyah who used the scientific method to outline the principles of administration within the framework of Islam, and Machiavelli who gave the world the definitive analysis of the use of power.

Further evidence of organization theory's deep roots in earlier eras are shown in the following two examples of ancient wisdom. In the Book of Exodus, Chapter 18 (see the next page), Jethro, Moses' father-in-law, chastises Moses for failing to establish an organization through which he could delegate his responsibility for the administration of justice. In Verse 25, Moses accepts Jethro's advice. He "chose able men out of all Israel, and made them heads over the people, rulers of thousands, rulers of hundreds, rulers of fifties, and rulers of tens." Moses continued to judge the "hard cases," but his rulers judged "every small matter" themselves. Frederick Winslow Taylor would later develop this concept of "management by exception" for modern audiences.

In the second ancient example (the full text is in the first selection in this chapter, "Socrates Discovers Generic Management"), Socrates anticipates the arguments for "generic management" and "principles of management" when he explains to Nicomachides that a leader who "knows what he needs, and is able to provide it, [can] be a good president, whether he have the direction of a chorus, a family, a city, or an army" (Xenophon, 1869). Socrates lists and discusses the duties of all good presidents of public and private institutions and emphasizes the similarities. This is the first known statement that organizations as entities are basically alike—and that a manager who could cope well with one would be equally adept at coping with others—even though their purposes and functions might differ.

Although it is interesting to connect the wisdom of the ancients to modern times, most scholars consider the beginnings of the factory system in Great Britain in the eighteenth century as the "birthplace" of complex economic organizations and, consequently, of the field of organization theory. Classical organization theory, as its name implies, was the first theory of its kind, is considered traditional, and continues to be the base on which other schools of organization theory have been built and against which they are compared. Thus, an understanding of classical organization theory is essential, not only because of its historical interest, but more importantly, because subsequent analyses and theories presume knowledge of it.

**Exodus Chapter 18**

13  And it came to pass on the morrow, that Moses sat to judge the people: and the people stood by Moses from the morning unto the evening.

14  And when Moses' father-in-law saw all that he did to the people, he said, "What is this thing that thou doest to the people? why sittest thou thyself alone, and all the people stand by thee from morning unto even?"

15  And Moses said unto his father-in-law, "Because the people come unto me to inquire of God:

16  When they have a matter, they come unto me; and I judge between one and another, and I do make *them* know the statutes of God, and his laws."

17  And Moses' father-in-law said unto him, "The thing that thou doest is not good.

18  Thou wilt surely wear away, both thou, and this people that is with thee: for this thing is too heavy for thee: thou art not able to perform it thyself alone.

19  Hearken now unto my voice, I will give thee counsel, and God shall be with thee: Be thou for the people to God-ward, that thou mayest bring the causes unto God:

20  And thou shalt teach them ordinances and laws, and shalt shew them the way wherein they must walk, and the work that they must do.

21  Moreover thou shalt provide out of all the people able men, such as fear God, men of truth, hating covetousness; and place *such* over them, *to be* rulers of thousands, *and* rulers of hundreds, rulers of fifties, and rulers of tens:

22  And let them judge the people at all seasons and it shall be, *that* every great matter they shall bring unto thee, but every small matter they shall judge: so shall it be easier for thyself, and they shall bear *the burden* with thee.

23  If thou shalt do this thing, and God command thee so, then thou shalt be able to endure, and all this people shall also go to their place in peace."

24  So Moses hearkened to the voice of his father-in-law, and did all that he had said.

25  And Moses chose able men out of all Israel, and made them heads over the people, rulers of thousands, rulers of hundreds, rulers of fifties, and rulers of tens.

26  And they judged the people at all seasons: the hard cases they brought unto Moses, but every small matter they judged themselves.

27  And Moses let his father-in-law depart; and he went his way into his own land.

The classical school dominated organization theory into the 1930s and remains highly influential today. Over the years, classical organization theory has expanded and matured. Its basic tenets and assumptions, however, which were rooted in the industrial revolution of the 1700s and the professions of mechanical engineering, industrial engineering, and economics, have never been abandoned. They have been expanded, refined, adapted, and made more sophisticated. These fundamental tenets are as follows:

1. Organizations exist to accomplish production-related and economic goals.
2. There is one best way to organize for production, and that way can be found through systematic, scientific inquiry.
3. Production is maximized through specialization and division of labor.
4. People and organizations act in accordance with rational economic principles.

The evolution of any theory must be viewed in context. The beliefs of early management theorists about how organizations worked or should work were a direct reflection of the societal values of their times—and the times were harsh. It was well into the twentieth century before the industrial workers of the United States and Europe began to enjoy even limited "rights" as organizational citizens. Workers were viewed not as individuals but as interchangeable parts in an industrial machine in which parts were made of flesh only when it was impractical to make them of steel.

The advent of power-driven machinery and hence of the modern factory system spawned our current concepts of economic organizations and organization for production. Power-driven equipment was expensive. Production workers could not purchase and use their own equipment as they had their own tools. Remember, one phrase for being fired, "get the sack," comes from the earliest days of the industrial revolution when a dismissed worker was literally given a sack in which to gather up his tools. But workers without their own tools and often without any special skills had to gather for work where the equipment was—in factories. Expensive equipment had to produce enough output to justify its acquisition and maintenance costs.

The factory system presented managers of organizations with an unprecedented array of new problems. Managers had to arrange for heavy infusions of capital, plan and organize for reliable large-scale production, coordinate and control activities of large numbers of people and functions, contain costs (this was hardly a concern in "cottage industry" production), and maintain a trained and motivated workforce.

Under the factory system, success resulted from well-organized production systems that kept machines busy and costs under control. Industrial and mechanical engineers and their machines were the keys to production. Organizational structures and production systems had to be designed to take best advantage of the machines. Organizations, it was thought, should work like machines, using people, capital, and machines as their parts. Just as industrial engineers sought to design the "best" machines to keep factories productive, industrial and mechanical engineering–type thinking dominated theories about the "best way" to organize for production. Thus, the first theories of organizations were concerned primarily with the anatomy, or structure, of formal organizations. This was the environment and the mode of thinking that shaped and influenced the tenets of classical organization theory.

Centralization of equipment and labor in factories, division of specialized labor, management of specialization, and economic paybacks on factory equipment all were concerns of the Scottish economist Adam Smith, which he described in his *An Inquiry into the Nature and Causes of the Wealth of Nations* (1776). Historian Arnold Toynbee (1956) identified Adam Smith (1723–1790) and James Watt (1736–1819) as the two individuals who were most responsible for pushing the world into industrialization. Watt, of course, invented the steam engine.

Smith, who is considered the father of the academic discipline of economics, provided the intellectual foundation for laissez-faire capitalism. *The Wealth of Nations* devotes its first chapter, "Of the Division of Labour," to a discussion of the optimum organization of a pin factory. Why? Because specialization of labor was a pillar of Smith's "invisible hand" market mechanism in which the greatest rewards would go to those who were most efficient in the competitive marketplace. Traditional pin makers could produce only a few dozen pins a day. When organized in a factory with each worker performing a limited operation, they could produce tens of thousands a day. Smith's "Of the Division of Labour" is reprinted here because, coming as it did at the dawn of the industrial revolution, it is the most famous and influential statement on the economic rationale for the factory system. Smith revolutionized thinking about economics and organizations. As a result, 1776, the year in which *Wealth of Nations* was published, is our choice as the beginning point of organization theory as an applied science and as an academic discipline. Besides, 1776 was a good year for other events as well.

In 1856, Daniel C. McCallum (1815–1878), the visionary general superintendent of the New York and Erie Railroad, elucidated general principles of organization that "may be regarded as settled and necessary." His principles included division of responsibilities, power commensurate with responsibilities, and a reporting system that allowed managers to know promptly if responsibilities were "faithfully executed" and to identify errors and "delinquent" subordinates. McCallum, who is also credited with creating the first modern organization chart, had an enormous influence on the managerial development of the American railroad industry.

In systematizing America's first big business before the Civil War, McCallum provided the model principles and procedures of management for the big businesses that would follow after the war. He became so much *the* authority on running railroads that, as a major general during the Civil War, he was chosen to run the Union's military rail system. However, although McCallum was highly influential as a practitioner, he was no scholar. The only coherent statement of his general principles comes from an annual report he wrote for the New York and Erie Railroad. Excerpts from his "Superintendent's Report" of March 25, 1856, are reprinted in this chapter.

During the 1800s, two practicing managers in the United States independently discovered that generally applicable principles of administration could be determined through systematic, scientific investigation—about 30 years before Frederick Winslow Taylor's *Principles of Scientific Management* or Henri Fayol's *General and Industrial Management*. The first to urge managers to record production events and experiences systematically so they could use the information to improve production processes was Captain Henry Metcalfe (1847–1917) of the United States Army's Frankford Arsenal in Philadelphia. Metcalfe published his propositions in *The Cost of Manufactures and the Administration of Workshops, Public and Private* (1885). He also pioneered in the application of "pre-scientific management" methods to the problems of managerial control and asserted that there is a "science of administration" based upon principles discoverable by diligent observation. Although Metcalfe's work is important historically, it is so similar to that of Taylor and others that it is not included here as a selection.

The second pre-scientific management advocate of the 1880s was Henry R. Towne (1844–1924), cofounder and president of the Yale & Towne Manufacturing Company. In 1886, Towne proposed that shop management was of equal importance to engineering management, and thus, the American Society of Mechanical Engineers (ASME) should take a leadership role in establishing a multi-company, engineering/management "database" on shop practices or, in Towne's words, on "the management of works." The information could then be shared among enterprises. Several years later, ASME adopted his proposal. The paper he presented to the society, "The Engineer as Economist," was published in *Transactions of the American Society of Mechanical Engineers* in 1886 and is reprinted here. Historians have often considered it the first call for scientific management.

Interestingly, Towne was associated with Frederick Winslow Taylor in several ways. The two were fellow draftsmen at the Midvale Steel works in the Nicetown area of Philadelphia during the 1880s. Later, Towne gave Taylor one of his first true opportunities to succeed at applying scientific management principles at Yale & Towne in 1904. Towne also nominated Taylor for the presidency of ASME in 1906, thereby provided him with an international forum for advocating scientific management. Upon election, Taylor promptly reorganized the ASME using scientific management principles.

While the ideas of Adam Smith, Frederick Winslow Taylor, and others are still major influences on the design and management of organizations, it was Henri Fayol (1841–1925), a French executive engineer, who articulated the first comprehensive theory of management. While Taylor was tinkering with the technology employed by the individual worker, Fayol was theorizing about all the elements necessary to organize and manage a major corporation. Fayol's major work, *Administration Industrielle et Générale* (published in France in 1916), was almost entirely ignored in the United States until Constance Storr's English translation, *General and Industrial Management,* was published in 1949. Since that time, Fayol's theoretical contributions have been widely recognized, and his work is considered as significant as that of Taylor.

Fayol believed that his concept of management was universally applicable to every type of organization. He delineated six principles—technical (production of goods), commercial (buying, selling, and exchange activities), financial (raising and using capital), security (protection of property and people), accounting, and managerial (coordination, control, organization, planning, and command of people). Fayol's primary interest and emphasis, however, was on his managerial principle. It addressed such variables as division of work, authority and responsibility, discipline, unity of command, unity of direction, subordination of individual interest to general interest, remuneration of personnel, centralization, scalar chains, order, equity, stability of personnel tenure, initiative, and esprit de corps. Fayol's "General Principles of Management," a chapter from his *General and Industrial Management,* is reprinted here.

About 100 years after Adam Smith declared the factory to be the most appropriate means of mass production, Frederick Winslow Taylor and a group of his followers were "spreading the gospel" that factory workers could be much more productive if their work were designed scientifically. Taylor, the acknowledged father of the scientific management movement, developed time and motion studies, originally under the name "Taylorism," or the "Taylor system." Taylorism, or its successor, "scientific management," was not a single invention but rather a series of methods and organizational arrangements designed by Taylor and his associates to increase the efficiency and speed of machine-shop production. Premised on the notion that there was "one best way" for accomplishing any given task, Taylor's scientific management sought to increase output by using scientific methods to discover the fastest, most efficient, and least fatiguing production methods.

The job of the scientific manager, once the "one best way" was found, was to implement this procedure at his or her organization. Classical organization theory derives from a corollary of this proposition. If there was one best way to accomplish any given production task, then correspondingly, there must also be one best way to accomplish any task of social organization—including organizing firms. Such principles of social organization were assumed to exist and to be waiting to be discovered through diligent scientific observation and analysis.

Scientific management, as espoused by Taylor, also contained a powerful puritanical social message. Taylor (1911) offered scientific management as the way for firms to increase profits, get rid of unions, "increase the thrift and virtue of the working classes," and raise productivity so the broader society could enter a new era of harmony based on higher consumption of mass-produced goods by members of the laboring classes.

Scientific management emerged as a national movement during a series of events in 1910. The railroad companies in the eastern United States filed for increased freight rates with the Interstate Commerce Commission (ICC). The railroads had been receiving poor press—they were being blamed for (among many other things) a cost-price squeeze that was bankrupting farmers—and the rate hearings received extensive media coverage. Louis D. Brandeis, a self-styled populist lawyer who would later be a distinguished Supreme Court justice, took the case against the railroads without pay. Brandeis called in Harrington Emerson, a consultant who had "systematized" the Santa Fe Railroad, to testify that the railroads did not need increased rates: They could "save a million dollars a day" by using what Brandeis initially called "scientific management" methods (Urwick, 1956). At first, Taylor was reluctant to use the phrase because it sounded too academic. But with the ICC hearings, the national scientific management boom was underway, and Taylor was its leader.

Taylor had a profound—almost revolutionary—effect on the fields of business and public administration. He gained credibility for the notion that organizational operations could be planned and controlled systematically by experts using scientific principles. Many of Taylor's concepts and precepts are still in use today, and the legacy of scientific management is substantial. Taylor's is best-known for his 1911 *The Principles of Scientific Management*, but he also wrote numerous other works on the subject. Reprinted here is an article, also entitled "The Principles of Scientific Management," which was the summary of an address Taylor gave on March 3, 1915, two weeks before his death.

Several of Taylor's associates subsequently built reputations for innovations that utilized principles of scientific management, including Frank Gilbreth (1868–1924) and Lillian Gilbreth (1878–1972), leaders in developing the tools and techniques of "time and motion study," including the "therblig" (Spriegel & Myers, 1953); Henry Laurence Gantt (1861–1919), who invented the Gantt chart for planning work output (Alford, 1932); and Carl O. Barth (1860–1939) who, among other accomplishments, in 1908 convinced the dean of the new Harvard Business School to adopt *Taylorism* as the "foundation concept" of modern management (Urwick, 1956). Frank and Lillian Gilbreth also achieved wide public recognition for the book (1948) and movie, *Cheaper by the Dozen*, which described the couple's efforts to raise their 12 children using scientific management principles and practices.

In contrast to the fervent advocates of scientific management, Max Weber (1864–1920) was a brilliant analytical sociologist who happened to study bureaucratic organizations. It is hardly worth mentioning that bureaucracy has emerged as a dominant feature of the contemporary world. Virtually everywhere one looks in both developed and developing nations, economic, social, and political life is influenced extensively by bureaucratic organizations. *Bureaucracy* refers to a specific set of structural arrangements. It also refers to specific patterns of behavior—patterns that are not restricted to formal bureaucracies. It is widely assumed that the structural characteristics of organizations properly defined as bureaucratic influence the behavior of individuals, whether clients or bureaucrats, who interact with them. Contemporary thinking along these lines began with the work of Max Weber. His analysis of bureaucracy, first published in 1922, remains the single most influential statement and the point of departure for all further analyses on the subject (including those of the "modern" structuralists described in Chapter 4).

Drawing on studies of ancient bureaucracies in Egypt, Rome, China, and the Byzantine Empire, as well as on more modern ones emerging in Europe during the nineteenth and early part of the twentieth centuries, Weber used an "ideal-type" approach to extrapolate from the real world the central core of features characteristic of the most fully developed bureaucratic form of organization. Weber's "Bureaucracy," which is included here, is neither a description of reality nor a statement of normative preference. In fact, Weber feared the potential implications of bureaucracies. Rather, his ideal-type bureaucracy is merely an identification of the major variables or features that characterize this type of social institution.

Luther Gulick's "Notes on the Theory of Organization," which was influenced heavily by the work of Henri Fayol, is one of the best-known statements of the "principles" approach to managing the functions of organizations. It appeared in *Papers on the Science of Administration*, a collection that Gulick and Lyndall Urwick edited in 1937. Here, Gulick introduced his famous mnemonic, POSDCORB, which stood for the seven major functions of executive management—planning, organizing, staffing, directing, coordinating, reporting, and budgeting. Gulick's principles of administration also included unity of command and span of control. Overall, *Papers on the Science of Administration* was a statement of the "state of the art" of organization theory. The study of organizations through analysis of management functions continues in the field of organization theory.

Daniel A. Wren and Arthur Bedeian (2009) observed that "the development of a body of knowledge about how to manage has ... evolved within a framework of the economic, social, and political facets of various cultures. Management thought is both a process in and a product of its cultural environment." The selections we have chosen to represent the classical school of organization theory demonstrate Wren's thesis. Looking through today's lenses, it is tempting to denigrate the contributions of the classicalists—to view them as narrow and simplistic. In the context of their times, however, they were brilliant pioneers. Their thinking provided invaluable foundations for the field of organization theory, and their influence continues today.

## BIBLIOGRAPHY

Aitken, H. G. J. (1986). *Scientific management in action: Taylorism at Watertown Arsenal, 1908–1915*. Princeton, NJ: Princeton University Press.

Al-Buraey, M. A. (1985). *Administrative development: An Islamic perspective*. London: Kegan Paul International.

Alford, L. P. (1932). *Henry Laurence Gantt: Leader in industry*. New York: Harper & Row.

Babbage, C. (1832). *On the economy of machinery and manufactures*. Philadelphia, PA: Carey & Lea.

Copley, F. B. (2013). *Frederick W. Taylor, father of scientific management*, Vol. 1. Charleston, SC: Nabu Press.

Durkheim, E., (1893). *The division of labor in society*. Republished in English in 1997 by The Free Press and in 2012 by Martino Fine Books.

Fayol, H. (1949). *General and industrial management*. Trans. C. Storrs. London: Pitman. (Originally published in 1916.)

Fournier, M. (2013). *Emile Durkheim: a biography*. Cambridge, UK: Polity.

Gay, P. du. (2000). *In praise of bureaucracy: Weber—Organization—Ethics*. Thousand Oaks, CA: Sage.

George, C. S., Jr. (1972). *The history of management thought.* 2nd ed. Englewood Cliffs, NJ: Prentice Hall.

Gilbreth, F. B., Jr., & E. G. Carey (1948). *Cheaper by the dozen.* New York: Grosset & Dunlap.

Gulick, L. (1937). Notes on the theory of organization. In L. Gulick & L. Urwick, eds., *Papers on the science of administration* (pp. 3–34). New York: Institute of Public Administration.

Kanigel, R. (2005). *The one best way: Frederick Winslow Taylor and the enigma of efficiency.* Cambridge, MA: MIT Press.

McCallum, D. C. (1856). Superintendent's report, March 25, 1856. In *Annual report of the New York and Erie Railroad Company for 1855.* In A. D. Chandler Jr., ed., *The railroads* (pp. 101–108). New York: Harcourt Brace Jovanovich.

Merkle, J. A. (1980). *Management and ideology: The legacy of the international scientific management movement.* Berkeley, CA: University of California Press.

Metcalfe, H. (1885). *The cost of manufactures and the administration of workshops, public and private.* New York: Wiley.

Schachter, H. L. (1990). *Frederick Taylor and the public administration community: A reevaluation.* Albany, NY: State University of New York Press.

Scott, W. R., & Davis, G. F. (2007). *Organizations and organizing: Rational, natural and open system perspectives.* Hoboken, NJ: Pearson Prentice Hall.

Smith, A. (1776). Of the division of labour. In *An inquiry into the nature and causes of the wealth of nations* (chap. 1, pp. 5–15). Printed for W. Strahan and T. Cadell in the Strand, London, 1776.

Spriegel, W. R., & C. E. Myers, eds. (1953). *The writings of the Gilbreths.* Homewood, IL: Irwin.

Taylor, F. W. (1911). *The principles of scientific management.* New York: Norton. Republished in 2007 by NuVision Publications.

Taylor, F. W. (1911). *Shop management.* New York: American Society of Mechanical Engineers. Republished in 2008 by Enna.

Taylor, F. W. (1916, December). The principles of scientific management: Bulletin of the Taylor Society. An abstract of an address given by Dr. Taylor to the Cleveland Advertising Club, March 3, 1915.

Towne, H. R. (1886, May). The engineer as an economist. *Transactions of the American Society of Mechanical Engineers, 7,* 428–432. Paper presented at a meeting of the Society, Chicago, IL.

Toynbee, A. (1956). *The industrial revolution.* Boston, MA: Beacon Press. Originally published in 1884.

Urwick, L. (1956). *The golden book of management.* London: Newman, Neame.

Weber, M. (1905). *The Protestant ethic and the spirit of capitalism.* Republished in 2013 by CreateSpace Independent Publishing Platform.

Weber, M. (1922). Bureaucracy. In H. Gerth & C. W. Mills, eds., *Max Weber: Essays in sociology.* Oxford, UK: Oxford University Press.

Wood, J. C. (2002). *Henri Fayol: Critical evaluations in business and management.* London, UK: Routledge.

Wrege, C. D., & R. G. Greenwood. (1991). *Frederick W. Taylor: The father of scientific management: Myth and reality.* Homewood, IL: Business One Irwin.

Wren, D. A., & A. G. Bedeian. (2009). *The evolution of management thought.* 6th ed. Hoboken, NJ: Wiley.

Xenophon (1869). *The memorabilia of Socrates.* Trans. Rev. J. S. Watson. New York: Harper & Row.

# 1

# Socrates Discovers Generic Management

*Xenophon*

Seeing Nicomachides, one day, coming from the assembly for the election of magistrates, he asked him, "Who have been chosen generals, Nicomachides?"

"Are not the Athenians the same as ever, Socrates?" he replied; "for they have not chosen me, who am worn out with serving on the list, both as captain and centurion, and with having received so many wounds from the enemy (he then drew aside his robe, and showed the scars of the wounds), but have elected Antisthenes, who has never served in the heavy-armed infantry, nor done anything remarkable in the cavalry, and who indeed knows nothing, but how to get money."

"Is it not good, however, to know this," said Socrates, "since he will then be able to get necessaries for the troops?"

"But merchants," replied Nicomachides, "are able to collect money; and yet would not on that account, be capable of leading an army."

"Antisthenes, however," continued Socrates, "is given to emulation, a quality necessary in a general. Do you not know that whenever he has been chorus-manager he has gained the superiority in all his choruses?"

"But, by Jupiter," rejoined Nicomachides, "there is nothing similar in managing a chorus and an army."

"Yet Antisthenes," said Socrates, "though neither skilled in music nor in teaching a chorus, was able to find out the best masters in these departments."

"In the army, accordingly," exclaimed Nicomachides, "he will find others to range his troops for him, and others to fight for him!"

"Well, then," rejoined Socrates, "if he finds out and selects the best men in military affairs, as he has done in the conduct of his choruses, he will probably attain superiority in this respect also; and it is likely that he will be more willing to spend money for a victory in war on behalf of the whole state, than for a victory with a chorus in behalf of his single tribe."

"Do you say, then, Socrates," said he, "that it is in the power of the same man to manage a chorus well, and to manage an army well?"

"I say," said Socrates, "that over whatever a man may preside, he will, if he knows what he needs, and is able to provide it, to be a good president, whether he have the direction of a chorus, a family, a city, or an army."

"By Jupiter, Socrates," cried Nicomachides, "I should never have expected to hear from you that good managers of a family would also be good generals."

"Come, then," proceeded Socrates, "let us consider what are the duties of each of them, that we may understand whether they are the same, or are in any respect different."

"By all means."

"Is it not, then, the duty of both," asked Socrates, "to render those under their command obedient and submissive to them?"

"Unquestionably."

"Is it not also the duty of both to intrust various employments to such as are fitted to execute them?"

"That is also unquestionable."

"To punish the bad, and to honor the good, too, belongs, I think, to each of them."

*Source:* Xenophon, *The Anabasis or Expedition of Cyrus and the Memorabilia of Socrates*, trans. J. S. Watson. New York: Harper & Row, 1869, 430–433.

"Undoubtedly."

"And is it not honorable in both to render those under them well-disposed toward them?"

"That also is certain."

"And do you think it for the interest of both to gain for themselves allies and auxiliaries or not?"

"It assuredly is for their interest."

"Is it not proper for both also to be careful of their resources?"

"Assuredly."

"And is it not proper for both, therefore, to be attentive and industrious in their respective duties?"

"All these particulars," said Nicomachides, "are common alike to both; but it is not common to both to fight."

"Yet both have doubtless enemies," rejoined Socrates.

"That is probably the case," said the other. "Is it not for the interest of both to gain the superiority over those enemies?"

"Certainly; but to say something on that point, what, I ask, will skill in managing a household avail, if it be necessary to fight?"

"It will doubtless in that case, be of the greatest avail," said Socrates; "for a good manager of a house, knowing that nothing is so advantageous or profitable as to get the better of your enemies when you contend with them, nothing so unprofitable and prejudicial as to be defeated, will zealously seek and provide everything that may conduce to victory, will carefully watch and guard against whatever tends to defeat, will vigorously engage if he sees that his force is likely to conquer, and, what is not the least important point, will cautiously avoid engaging if he finds himself insufficiently prepared. Do not, therefore, Nicomachides," he added, "despise men skillful in managing a household; for the conduct of private affairs differs from that of public concerns only in magnitude; in other respects they are similar; but what is most to be observed, is, that neither of them are managed without men, and that private matters are not managed by one species of men, and public matters by another; for those who conduct public business make use of men not at all differing in nature from those whom the managers of private affairs employ; and those who know how to employ them conduct either public or private affairs judiciously, while those who do not know will err in the management of both."

# 2

# Of the Division of Labour

*Adam Smith*

The greatest improvement in the productive powers of labour, and the greater part of the skill, dexterity, and judgment with which it is any where directed, or applied, seem to have been the effects of the division of labour.

The effects of the division of labour, in the general business of society, will be more easily understood, by considering in what manner it operates in some particular manufactures. It is commonly supposed to be carried furthest in some very trifling ones; not perhaps that it really is carried further in them than in others of more importance: but in those trifling manufactures which are destined to supply the small wants of but a small number of people, the whole number of workmen must necessarily be small; and those employed in every different branch of the work can often be collected into the same workhouse, and placed at once under the view of the spectator. In those great manufactures, on the contrary, which are destined to supply the great wants of the great body of the people, every different branch of the work employs so great a number of workmen, that it is impossible to collect them all into the same workhouse. We can seldom see more, at one time, than those employed in one single branch. Though in such manufactures, therefore, the work may really be divided into a much greater number of parts, than in those of a more trifling nature, the division is not near so obvious, and has accordingly been much less observed.

To take an example, therefore, from a very trifling manufacture; but one in which the division of labour has been very often taken notice of, the trade of the pin-maker; a workman not educated to this business (which the division of labour has rendered a distinct trade), nor acquainted with the use of the machinery employed in it (to the invention of which the same division of labour has probably given occasion), could scarce, perhaps, with his utmost industry, make one pin in a day, and certainly could not make twenty. But in the way in which this business is now carried on, not only the whole work is a peculiar trade, but it is divided into a number of branches, of which the greater part are likewise peculiar trades. One man draws out the wire, another straights it, a third cuts it, a fourth points it, a fifth grinds it at the top for receiving the head; to make the head requires two or three distinct operations; to put it on, is a peculiar business, to whiten the pins is another; it is even a trade by itself to put them into the paper; and the important business of making a pin is, in this manner, divided into about eighteen distinct operations, which, in some manufactories, are all performed by distinct hands, though in others the same man will sometimes perform two or three of them. I have seen a small manufactory of this kind where ten men only were employed, and where some of them consequently performed two or three distinct operations. But though they were very poor, and therefore but indifferently accommodated with the necessary machine, they could, when they exerted themselves, make among them about twelve pounds of pins in a day. There are in a pound upwards of four thousand pins of a middling size. Those ten persons,

*Source:* Adam Smith, *An inquiry into the nature and causes of the wealth of nations* (1776), chap. 1 (footnotes have been omitted).

therefore, could make among them upwards of forty-eight thousand pins in a day. Each person, therefore, making a tenth part of forty-eight thousand pins, might be considered as making four thousand eight hundred pins in a day. But if they had all wrought separately and independently, and without any of them having been educated to this peculiar business, they certainly could not each of them have made twenty, perhaps not one pin in a day; that is, certainly, not the two hundred and fortieth, perhaps not the four thousand eight hundredth part of what they are at present capable of performing, in consequence of a proper division and combination of their different operations.

In every other art and manufacture, the effects of the division of labour are similar to what they are in this very trifling one; though, in many of them, the labour can neither be so much subdivided, nor reduced to so great a simplicity of operation. The division of labour, however, so far as it can be introduced, occasions, in every art, a proportionable increase of the productive powers of labour. The separation of different trades and employments from one another, seems to have taken place, in consequence of this advantage. This separation too is generally carried furthest in those countries which enjoy the highest degree of industry and improvement; what is the work of one man in a rude state of society, being generally that of several in an improved one. In every improved society, the farmer is generally nothing but a farmer; the manufacturer, nothing but a manufacturer. The labour too which is necessary to produce any one complete manufacture, is almost always divided among a great number of hands. How many different trades are employed in each branch of the linen and woollen manufactures, from the growers of the flax and the wool, to the bleachers and smoothers of the linen, or to the dyers and dressers of the cloth! The nature of agriculture, indeed, does not admit of so many subdivisions of labour, nor of so complete a separation of one business from another, as manufactures. It is impossible to separate

so entirely, the business of the grazier from that of the corn-farmer, as the trade of the carpenter is commonly separated from that of the smith. The spinner is almost always a distinct person from the weaver; but the ploughman, the harrower, the sower of the seed, and the reaper of the corn, are often the same. The occasions for those different sorts of labour returning with the different seasons of the year, it is impossible that one man should be constantly employed in any one of them. This impossibility of making so complete and entire a separation of all the different branches of labour employed in agriculture, is perhaps the reason why the improvement of the productive powers of labour in this art, does not always keep pace with their improvement in manufactures. The most opulent nations, indeed, generally excel all their neighbours in agriculture as well as in manufactures; but they are commonly more distinguished by their superiority in the latter than in the former. Their lands are in general better cultivated, and having more labour and expence bestowed upon them, produce more in proportion to the extent and natural fertility of the ground. But this superiority of produce is seldom much more than in proportion to the superiority of labour and expence. In agriculture, the labour of the rich country is not always much more productive than that of the poor; or, at least, it is never so much more productive, as it commonly is in manufactures. The corn of the rich country, therefore, will not always, in the same degree of goodness, come cheaper to market than that of the poor. The corn of Poland, in the same degree of goodness is as cheap as that of France, notwithstanding the superior opulence and improvement of the latter country. The corn of France is, in the corn provinces, fully as good, and most years nearly about the same price with the corn of England, though, in opulence and improvement, France is perhaps inferior to England. The corn lands of England, however, are better cultivated than those of France, and the corn lands of France are said to be much better cultivated than those of Poland. But though the poor country, notwithstanding the inferiority of its cultivation, can, in some measure, rival the rich in the cheapness and goodness of its corn, it can pretend to no such competition in its manufactures; at least if those manufactures suit the soil, climate, and situation of the rich country. The silks of France are better and cheaper than those of England, because the silk manufacture, at least under the present high duties upon the importation of raw silk, does not so well suit the climate of England as that of France. But the hardware and the coarse woollens of England are beyond all comparison superior to those of France, and much cheaper too in the same degree of goodness. In Poland there are said to be scarce any manufactures of any kind, a few of those coarser household manufactures excepted, without which no country can well subsist.

This great increase of the quantity of work, which, in consequence of the division of labour, the same number of people are capable of performing, is owing to three different circumstances; first, to the increase of dexterity in every particular workman; secondly, to the saving of the time which is commonly lost in passing from one species of work to another; and lastly, to the invention of a great number of machines which facilitate and abridge labour, and enable one man to do the work of many.

First, the improvement of the dexterity of the workman necessarily increases the quantity of the work he can perform; and the division of labour, by reducing every man's business to some one simple operation, and by making this operation the sole employment of his life, necessarily increases very much the dexterity of the workman. A common smith, who, though accustomed to handle the hammer, has never been used to make nails, if upon some particular occasion he is obliged to attempt it, will scarce, I am assured, be able to make above two or three hundred nails in a day, and those too very bad ones. A smith who has been accustomed to make nails, but whose sole or principal business

has not been that of a nailer, can seldom with his utmost diligence make more than eight hundred or a thousand nails in a day. I have seen several boys under twenty years of age who had never exercised any other trade but that of making nails, and who, when they exerted themselves, could make, each of them, upwards of two thousand three hundred nails in a day. The making of a nail, however, is by no means one of the simplest operations. The same person blows the bellows, stirs or mends the fire as there is occasion, heats the iron, and forges every part of the nail: In forging the head too he is obliged to change his tools. The different operations into which the making of a pin, or of a metal button, is subdivided, are all of them much more simple, and the dexterity of the person, of whose life it has been the sole business to perform them, is usually much greater. The rapidity with which some of the operations of those manufactures are performed, exceeds what the human hand could, by those who had never seen them, be supposed capable of acquiring.

Secondly, the advantage which is gained by saving the time commonly lost in passing from one sort of work to another, is much greater than we should at first view be apt to imagine it. It is impossible to pass very quickly from one kind of work to another, that is carried on in a different place, and with quite different tools. A country weaver, who cultivates a small farm, must lose a good deal of time in passing from his loom to his field, and from the field to his loom. When the two trades can be carried on in the same workhouse, the loss of time is no doubt much less. It is even in this case, however, very considerable. A man commonly saunters a little in turning his hand from one sort of employment to another. When he first begins the new work he is seldom very keen and hearty; his mind, as they say, does not go to it, and for some time he rather trifles than applies to good purpose. The habit of sauntering and of indolent careless application, which is naturally, or rather necessarily acquired by every country workman who is obliged to change his work and his tools every half hour, and to apply his hand in twenty different ways almost every day of his life, renders him almost always slothful and lazy, and incapable of any vigorous application even on the most pressing occasions. Independent, therefore, of his deficiency in point of dexterity, this cause alone must always reduce considerably the quantity of work which he is capable of performing.

Thirdly, and lastly, every body must be sensible how much labour is facilitated and abridged by the application of proper machinery. It is unnecessary to give any example. I shall only observe, therefore, that the invention of all those machines by which labour is so much facilitated and abridged, seems to have been originally owing to the division of labour. Men are much more likely to discover easier and readier methods of attaining any object, when the whole attention of their minds is directed towards that single object, than when it is dissipated among a great variety of things. But in consequence of the division of labour, the whole of every man's attention comes naturally to be directed towards some one very simple object. It is naturally to be expected, therefore, that some one or other of those who are employed in each particular branch of labour should soon find out easier and readier methods of performing their own particular work, wherever the nature of it admits of such improvement. A great part of the machines made use of in those manufactures in which labour is most subdivided, were originally the inventions of common workmen, who, being each of them employed in some very simple operation, naturally turned their thoughts toward finding out easier and readier methods of performing it. Whoever has been much accustomed to visit such manufactures, must frequently have been shewn very pretty machines, which were the inventions of such workmen, in order to facilitate and quicken their own particular part of the work. In the first fire-engines, a boy was constantly employed to open and shut alternately the communication between the boiler and the cylinder, according as the piston either ascended or descended. One of those boys, who loved to play with his companions, observed that, by tying a string from the handle of the valve which opened this communication to another part of the machine, the valve would open and shut without his assistance, and leave him at liberty to divert himself with his playfellows. One of the greatest improvements that has been made upon this machine, since it was first invented, was in this manner the discovery of a boy who wanted to save his own labour.

All the improvements in machinery, however, have by no means been the inventions of those who had occasion to use the machines. Many improvements have been made by the ingenuity of the makers of the machines, when to make them become the business of a peculiar trade; and some by that of those who are called philosophers or men of speculation, whose trade it is not to do anything, but to observe everything; and who, upon that account, are often capable of combining together the powers of the most distant and dissimilar objects. In the progress of society, philosophy or speculation becomes, like every other employment, the principal or sole trade and occupation of a particular class of citizens. Like every other employment too, it is subdivided into a great number of different branches, each of which affords occupation to a peculiar tribe or class of philosophers; and this subdivision of employment in philosophy, as well as in every other business, improves dexterity, and saves time. Each individual becomes more expert in his own peculiar branch, more work is done upon the whole, and the quantity of science is considerably increased by it.

It is the great multiplication of the productions of all the different arts, in consequence of the division of labour, which occasions, in a well-governed society, that universal opulence which extends itself to the lowest ranks of the people. Every workman has a great quantity of his own work to dispose of beyond what he himself has occasion for; and every other workman being exactly in the same situation, he is enabled to exchange a great quantity of his own goods for a great quantity, or, what comes to the same thing, for the price of a great quantity of theirs. He supplies them abundantly with what they have occasion for, and they accommodate him as amply with what he has occasion for, and a general plenty diffuses itself through all the different ranks of the society.

Observe the accommodation of the most common artificer or day-labourer in a civilized and thriving country, and you will perceive that the number of people of whose industry a part, though but a small part, has been employed in procuring him his accommodation, exceeds all computation. The woollen coat, for example, which covers the day-labourer, as coarse and rough as it may appear, is the produce of the joint labour of a great multitude of workmen. The shepherd, the sorter of the wool, the woolcomber or carder, the dyer, the scribbler, the spinner, the weaver, the fuller, the dresser, with many others, must all join their different arts in order to complete even this homely production. How many merchants and carriers, besides, must have been employed in transporting the materials from some of those workmen to others who often live in a very distant part of the country! How much commerce and navigation in particular, how many ship-builders, sailors, sail-makers, rope-makers, must have been employed in order to bring together the different drugs made use of by the dyer, which often come from the remotest corners of the world! What a variety of labour too is necessary in order to produce the tools of the meanest of those workmen! To say nothing of such complicated machines as the ship of the sailor, the mill of the fuller, or even the loom of the weaver, let us consider only what a variety of labour is requisite in order to form that very simple machine, the shears with which the shepherd clips the wool. The miner, the builder of the furnace for smelting the ore, the feller of the timber, the burner of the charcoal to be made use of in the smelting-house, the brick-maker, the brick-layer, the work-men who attend the furnace, the millwright, the forger, the smith, must all of them join their different arts in order to produce them. Were we to examine, in the same manner, all the different parts of his dress and household furniture, the coarse linen shirt which he wears next his skin, the shoes which cover his feet, the bed which he lies on, and all the different parts which compose it, the kitchen grate at which he prepares his victuals, the coals which he makes use of for that purpose, dug from the bowels of the earth, and brought to him perhaps by a long sea and a long land carriage, all the other utensils of his kitchen, all the furniture of his table, the knives and forks, the earthen or pewter plates upon which he serves up and divides his victuals, the different hands employed in preparing his bread and his beer, the glass window which lets in the heat and the light, and keeps out the wind and the rain, with all the knowledge and art requisite for preparing that beautiful and happy invention, without which these northern parts of the world could scarce have afforded a very comfortable habitation, together with the tools of all the different workmen employed in producing those different conveniences; if we examine, I say, all these things, and consider what a variety of labour is employed about each of them, we shall be sensible that without the assistance and cooperation of many thousands, the very meanest person in a civilized country could not be provided, even according to, what we very falsely imagine, the easy and simple manner in which he is commonly accommodated. Compared, indeed, with the more extravagant luxury of the great, his accommodation must no doubt appear extremely simple and easy; and yet it may be true, perhaps, that the accommodation of an European prince does not always so much exceed that of an industrious and frugal peasant, as the accommodation of the latter exceeds that of many an African king....

## 3

# Superintendent's Report

*Daniel C. McCallum*

Office General Sup't N.Y. &
Erie R. R.
New York, March 25, 1856

Homer Ramsdell, Esq.
President of the New York and
Erie Railroad Company:

Sir:
The magnitude of the business of this road, its numerous and important connections, and the large number of employés engaged in operating it, have led many, whose opinions are entitled to respect, to the conclusion, that a proper regard to details, which enter so largely into the elements of success in the management of all railroads, cannot possibly be attained by any plan that contemplates its organization as a whole; and in proof of this position, the experience of shorter roads is referred to, the business operations of which have been conducted much more economically.

*Theoretically,* other things being equal, a long road should be operated for a less cost per mile than a short one. This position is so clearly evident and so generally admitted, that its truth may be assumed without offering any arguments in support of it; and, notwithstanding the reverse, so far as *practical* results are considered, has generally been the case, we must look to other causes than the mere difference in length of roads for a solution of the difficulty.

A Superintendent of a road fifty miles in length can give its business his personal attention, and may be almost constantly upon the line engaged in the direction of its details; each employé is familiarly known to

him, and all questions in relation to its business are at once presented and acted upon; and any system, however imperfect, may under such circumstances prove comparatively successful.

In the government of a road five hundred miles in length a very different state of things exists. Any system which might be applicable to the business and extent of a short road, would be found entirely inadequate to the wants of a long one; and I am fully convinced, that in the want of a system perfect in its details, properly adapted and vigilantly enforced, lies the true secret of their failure; and that this disparity of cost per mile in operating long and short roads, is not produced by *a difference in length,* but is in proportion to the perfection of the system adopted.

Entertaining these views, I had the honor, more than a year since, to submit for your consideration and approval a plan for the more effective organization of this department. The system then proposed has to some extent been introduced, and experience, so far, affords the strongest assurances that when fully carried out, the most satisfactory results will be obtained.

In my opinion a system of operations, to be efficient and successful, should be such as to give to the principal and responsible head of the running department a complete daily history of details in all their minutiae. Without such supervision, the procurement of a satisfactory annual statement must be regarded as extremely problematical. The fact that dividends are earned without such control does not disprove the position, as in many cases the extraordinarily

*Source:* Daniel C. McCallum, "Superintendent's Report," March 25, 1856, in *Annual Report of the New York and Erie Railroad Company for 1855* (New York, 1856).

remunerative nature of an enterprise may ensure satisfactory returns under the most loose and inefficient management.

It may be proper here to remark that in consequence of that want of adaptation before alluded to, we cannot avail ourselves to any great extent of the plan of organization of shorter lines in framing one for this, nor have we any precedent or experience upon which we can fully rely in doing so. Under these circumstances, it will scarcely be expected that we can at once adopt any plan of operations which will not require amendment and a reasonable time to prove its worth. A few general principles, however, may be regarded as settled and necessary in its formation, amongst which are:

1. A proper division of responsibilities.
2. Sufficient power conferred to enable the same to be fully carried out, that such responsibilities may be real in their character.
3. The means of knowing whether such responsibilities are faithfully executed.
4. Great promptness in the report of all derelictions of duty, that evils may be at once corrected.
5. Such information, to be obtained through a system of daily reports and checks that will not embarrass principal officers, nor lessen their influence with their subordinates.
6. The adoption of a system, as a whole, which will not only enable the General Superintendent to detect errors immediately, but will also point out the delinquent.

# 4

# The Engineer as Economist

*Henry R. Towne*

The monogram of our national initials, which is the symbol of our monetary unit, the dollar, is almost as frequently conjoined to the figures of an engineer's calculations as are the symbols indicating feet, minutes, pounds, or gallons. The final issue of his work, in probably a majority of cases, resolves itself into a question of dollars and cents, of relative or absolute values. This statement, while true in regard to the work of all engineers, applies particularly to that of the mechanical engineer, for the reason that his functions, more frequently than in the case of others, include the executive duties of organizing and superintending the operations of industrial establishments, and of directing the labor of the artisans whose organized efforts yield the fruition of his work.

To insure the best results, the organization of productive labor must be directed and controlled by persons having not only good executive ability, and possessing the practical familiarity of a mechanic or engineer with the goods produced and the processes employed, but having also, and equally, a practical knowledge of how to observe, record, analyze, and compare essential facts in relation to wages, supplies, expense accounts, and all else that enters into or affects the economy of production and the cost of the product. There are many good mechanical engineers;—there are also many good "business men";—but the two are rarely combined in one person. But this combination of qualities, together with at least some skill as an accountant, either in one person or more, is essential to the successful management of industrial works, and

has its highest effectiveness if united in one person, who is thus qualified to supervise, either personally or through assistants, the operations of all departments of a business, and to subordinate each to the harmonious development of the whole.

Engineering has long been conceded a place as one of the modern arts, and has become a well-defined science, with a large and growing literature of its own, and of late years has subdivided itself into numerous and distinct divisions, one of which is that of mechanical engineering. It will probably not be disputed that the matter of shop management is of equal importance with that of engineering, as affecting the successful conduct of most, if not all, of our great industrial establishments, and that the *management of works* has become a matter of such great and far-reaching importance as perhaps to justify its classification also as one of the modern arts. The one is a well-defined science, with a distinct literature, with numerous journals and with many associations for the interchange of experience; the other is unorganized, is almost without literature, has no organ or medium for the interchange of experience, and is without association or organization of any kind. A vast amount of accumulated experience in the art of workshop management already exists, but there is no record of it available to the world in general, and each old enterprise is managed more or less in its own way, receiving little benefit from the parallel experience of other similar enterprises, and imparting as little of its own to them; while each new enterprise, starting *de novo* and with much labor, and usually at

Source: *Transactions of the American Society of Mechanical Engineers,* vol. 7 (paper presented at the May, 1886, meeting of the society, Chicago), 428–432.

much cost for experience, gradually develops a more or less perfect system of its own, according to the ability of its managers, receiving little benefit or aid from all that may have been done previously by others in precisely the same field of work.

Surely this condition of things is wrong and should be remedied. But the remedy must not be looked for from those who are "business men" or clerks and accountants only; it should come from those whose training and experience has given them an understanding of both sides (viz.: the mechanical and the clerical) of the important questions involved. It should originate, therefore, from those who are also engineers, and, for the reasons above indicated, particularly from mechanical engineers. Granting this, why should it not originate from, and be promoted by The American Society of Mechanical Engineers?

To consider this proposition more definitely, let us state the work which requires to be done. The questions to be considered, and which need recording and publication as conducing to discussion and the dissemination of useful knowledge in this specialty, group themselves under two principal heads, namely: Shop Management and Shop Accounting. A third head may be named which is subordinate to, and partly included in each of these, namely: Shop Forms and Blanks. Under the head of Shop Management fall the questions of organization, responsibility, reports, systems of contract and piece work, and all that relates to the executive management of works, mills and factories. Under the head of Shop Accounting fall the questions of time and wages systems, determination of costs, whether by piece or day-work, the distribution of the various expense accounts, the ascertainment of profits, methods of bookkeeping, and all that enters into the system of accounts which relates to the manufacturing departments of a business, and to the determination and record of its results.

There already exists an enormous fund of information relating to such matters, based upon actual and most extensive experience. What is now needed is a medium for the interchange of this experience among those whom it interests and concerns. Probably no better way for this exists than that obtaining in other instances, namely, by the publication of papers and reports, and by meetings for the discussion of papers and interchange of opinions.

The subject thus outlined, however distinct and apart from the primary functions of this society, is, nevertheless, germane to the interests of most, if not all, of its members. Conceding this, why should not the function of the society be so enlarged as to embrace this new field of usefulness? This work, if undertaken, may be kept separate and distinct from the present work of the society by organizing a new "section" (which might be designated the "Economic Section"), the scope of which would embrace all papers and discussions relating to the topics herein referred to. The meetings of this section could be held either separately from, or immediately following the regular meetings of the society, and its papers could appear as a supplement to the regular transactions. In this way all interference would be avoided with the primary and chief business of the society, and the attendance at the meetings of the new section would naturally resolve itself into such portion of the membership as is interested in the objects for which it would be organized.

As a single illustration of the class of subjects to be covered by the discussions and papers of the proposed new section, and of the benefit to be derived therefrom, there may be cited the case of a manufacturing establishment in which there are now in use, in connection with the manufacturing accounts and exclusive of the ordinary commercial accounts, some twenty various forms of special record and account books, and more than one hundred printed forms and blanks. The primary object to which all of these contribute is the systematic recording of the operations of the different departments of the works, and the computation therefrom of such statistical information

## FIGURE 4.1 • THE ENGINEER AS ECONOMIST

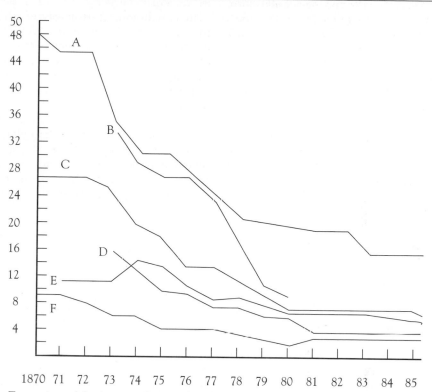

*Source*: Transactions of the American Society of Mechanical Engineers, vol. 7 (paper presented at May 1886 meeting of the society, Chicago), 428–432.

as is essential to the efficient management of the business, and especially to increased economy of production. All of these special books and forms have been the outgrowth of experience extending over many years, and represent a large amount of thoughtful planning and intelligent effort at constant development and improvement. The methods thus arrived at would undoubtedly be of great value to others engaged in similar operations, and particularly to persons engaged in organizing and starting new enterprises. It is probable that much, if not all, of the information and experience referred to would be willingly made public through such a channel as is herein suggested, particularly if such action on the part of one firm or corporation would be responded to in like manner by others, so

that each member could reasonably expect to receive some equivalent for his contributions by the benefit which he would derive from the experience of others.

In the case of the establishment above referred to, a special system of contract and piece-work has been in operation for some fifteen years, the results from which, in reducing the labor cost on certain products without encroaching upon the earnings of the men engaged, have been quite striking. A few of these results selected at random, are indicated by the accompanying diagram (Figure 4.1), the diagonal lines on which represent the fluctuations in the labor cost of certain special products during the time covered by the table, the vertical scale representing values.

Undoubtedly a portion of the reductions thus indicated resulted from improved appliances, larger product, and increased experience, but after making due allowance for all of these, there remains a large portion of the reduction which, to the writer's knowledge, is fairly attributable to the operation of the peculiar piece-work system adopted. The details and operations of this system would probably be placed before the society, in due time, through the channel of the proposed new section, should the latter take definite form. Other, and probably much more valuable, information and experience relating to systems of contract and piece-work would doubtless be contributed by other members, and in the aggregate a great amount of information of a most valuable character would thus be made available to the whole membership of the society.

In conclusion, it is suggested that if the plan herein proposed commends itself favorably to the members present at the meeting at which it is presented, the subject had best be referred to a special committee, by whom it can be carefully considered, and by whom, if it seems expedient to proceed further, the whole matter can be matured and formulated in an orderly manner, and thus be so presented at a future meeting as to enable the society then intelligently to act upon the question, and to decide whether or not to adopt the recommendations made by such committee.

## 5
# General Principles of Management
*Henri Fayol*

The managerial function finds its only outlet through the members of the organization (body corporate). Whilst the other functions bring into play material and machines the managerial function operates only on the personnel. The soundness and good working order of the body corporate depend on a certain number of conditions termed indiscriminately principles, laws, rules. For preference I shall adopt the term principles whilst dissociating it from any suggestion of rigidity, for there is nothing rigid or absolute in management affairs, it is all a question of proportion. Seldom do we have to apply the same principle twice in identical conditions; allowance must be made for different changing circumstances, for men just as different and changing and for many other variable elements.

Therefore principles are flexible and capable of adaptation to every need; it is a matter of knowing how to make use of them, which is a difficult art requiring intelligence, experience, decision, and proportion. Compounded of tact and experience, proportion is one of the foremost attributes of the manager. There is no limit to the number of principles of management, every rule or managerial procedure which strengthens the body corporate or facilitates its functioning has a place among the principles so long, at least, as experience confirms its worthiness. A change in the state of affairs can be responsible for change of rules which had been engendered by that state.

I am going to review some of the principles of management which I have most frequently had to apply; viz.—

1. Division of work.
2. Authority and responsibility.
3. Discipline.
4. Unity of command.
5. Unity of direction.
6. Subordination of individual interest to the general interest.
7. Remuneration of personnel.
8. Centralization.
9. Scalar chain (line of authority).
10. Order.
11. Equity.
12. Stability of tenure of personnel.
13. Initiative.
14. Esprit de corps.

## 1. DIVISION OF WORK

Specialization belongs to the natural order; it is observable in the animal world, where the more highly developed the creature the more highly differentiated its organs; it is observable in human societies where the more important the body corporate[1] the closer is the relationship between structure and function. As society grows, so new organs develop destined to replace the single one performing all functions in the primitive state.

The object of division of work is to produce more and better work with the same effort. The worker always on the same part, the manager concerned always with the same matters, acquire an ability, sureness, and accuracy which increase their output. Each change of work brings in its train an adaptation which reduces output. Division of work permits reduction in the number of

Henri Fayol, *General and Industrial Management*, trans. Constance Storrs. (London: Pitman, 1949), 19–42 (originally published 1916).

objects to which attention and effort must be directed and has been recognized as the best means of making use of individuals and of groups of people. It is not merely applicable to technical work, but without exception to all work involving a more or less considerable number of people and demanding abilities of various types, and it results in specialization of functions and separation of powers. Although its advantages are universally recognized and although possibility of progress is inconceivable without the specialized work of learned men and artists, yet division of work has its limits which experience and a sense of proportion teach us may not be exceeded.

## 2. AUTHORITY AND RESPONSIBILITY

Authority is the right to give orders and the power to exact obedience. Distinction must be made between a manager's official authority deriving from office and personal authority, compounded of intelligence, experience, moral worth, ability to lead, past services, etc. In the make up of a good head personal authority is the indispensable complement of official authority. Authority is not to be conceived of apart from responsibility, that is apart from sanction—reward or penalty—which goes with the exercise of power. Responsibility is a corollary of authority, it is its natural consequence and essential counterpart, and wheresoever authority is exercised responsibility arises.

The need for sanction, which has its origin in a sense of justice, is strengthened and increased by this consideration, that in the general interest useful actions have to be encouraged and their opposite discouraged. Application of sanction to acts of authority forms part of the conditions essential for good management, but it is generally difficult to effect, especially in large concerns. First, the degree of responsibility must be established and then the weight of the sanction. Now, it is relatively easy to establish a workman's responsibility for his acts and a scale of corresponding sanctions; in the case of a foreman it is somewhat difficult, and proportionately as one goes up the scalar chain of businesses, as work grows more complex, as the number of workers involved increases, as the final result is more remote, it is increasingly difficult to isolate the share of the initial act of authority in the ultimate result and to establish the degree of responsibility of the manager. The measurement of this responsibility and its equivalent in material terms elude all calculation.

Sanction, then, is a question of kind, custom, convention, and judging it one must take into account the action itself, the attendant circumstances and potential repercussions. Judgment demands high moral character, impartiality, and firmness. If all these conditions are not fulfilled there is a danger that the sense of responsibility may disappear from the concern.

Responsibility valiantly undertaken and borne merits some consideration; it is a kind of courage everywhere much appreciated. Tangible proof of this exists in the salary level of some industrial leaders, which is much higher than that of civil servants of comparable rank but carrying no responsibility. Nevertheless, generally speaking, responsibility is feared as much as authority is sought after, and fear of responsibility paralyses much initiative and destroys many good qualities. A good leader should possess and infuse into those around him courage to accept responsibility.

The best safeguard against abuse of authority and against weakness on the part of a higher manager is personal integrity and particularly high moral character of such a manager, and this integrity, it is well known, is conferred neither by election nor ownership.

## 3. DISCIPLINE

Discipline is in essence obedience, application, energy, behaviour, and outward marks of respect observed in accordance with the standing agreements between the firm and its employees, whether these agreements have been freely debated or accepted without prior discussion, whether they be written or implicit, whether they derive from the wish of the parties to them or from rules and customs, it is these agreements which determine the formalities of discipline.

Discipline, being the outcome of different varying agreements, naturally appears under the most diverse forms; obligations of obedience, application, energy, behaviour, vary, in effect, from one firm to another, from one group of employees to another, from one time to another. Nevertheless, general opinion is deeply convinced that discipline is absolutely essential for the smooth running of business and that without discipline no enterprise could prosper.

This sentiment is very forcibly expressed in military hand-books, where it runs that "Discipline constitutes the chief strength of armies." I would approve unreservedly of this aphorism were it followed by this other, "Discipline is what leaders make it." The first one inspires respect for discipline, which is a good thing, but it tends to eclipse from view the responsibility of leaders, which is undesirable, for the state of discipline of any group of people depends essentially on the worthiness of its leaders.

When a defect in discipline is apparent or when relations between superiors and subordinates leave much to be desired, responsibility for this must not be cast heedlessly, and without going further afield, on the poor state of the team, because the ill mostly results from the ineptitude of the leaders. That, at all events, is what I have noted in various parts of France, for I have always found French workmen obedient and loyal provided they are ably led.

In the matter of influence upon discipline, agreements must set side by side with command. It is important that they be clear and, as far as possible, afford satisfaction to both sides. This is not easy. Proof of that exists in the great strikes of miners, railwaymen, and civil servants which, in these latter years, have jeopardized national life at home and elsewhere and which arose out of agreements in dispute or inadequate legislation.

For half a century a considerable change has been effected in the mode of agreements between a concern and its employees. The agreements of former days fixed by the employer alone are being replaced, in ever increasing measure, by understandings arrived at by discussion between an owner or group of owners and workers' associations. Thus each individual owner's responsibility has been reduced and is further diminished by increasingly frequent state intervention in labour problems. Nevertheless, the setting up of agreements binding a firm and its employees from which disciplinary formalities emanate, should remain one of the chief preoccupations of industrial heads.

The well-being of the concern does not permit, in cases of offence against discipline, of the neglect of certain sanctions capable of preventing or minimizing their recurrence. Experience and tact on the part of a manager are put to the proof in the choice and degree of sanctions to be used, such as remonstrances, warning, fines, suspensions, demotion, dismissal. Individual people and attendant circumstances must be taken into account. In fine, discipline is respect for agreements which are directed at achieving obedience, application, energy, and the outward marks of respect. It is incumbent upon managers at high levels as much as upon humble employees, and the best means of establishing and maintaining it are—

1. Good superiors at all levels.
2. Agreements as clear and fair as possible.
3. Sanctions (penalties) judiciously applied.

## 4. UNITY OF COMMAND

For any action whatsoever, an employee should receive orders from one superior only. Such is the rule of unity of command, arising from general and ever-present necessity and wielding an influence on the conduct of affairs, which to my way of thinking, is at least equal to any other principle whatsoever. Should it be violated, authority is undermined, discipline is in jeopardy, order disturbed and stability threatened. This rule seems fundamental to me and so I have given it the rank of principle. As soon as two superiors wield their authority over the same person or department, uneasiness makes itself felt and should the cause persist, the disorder increases, the malady takes on the appearance of an animal organism troubled by a foreign body, and the following consequences are to be observed: either the dual command ends in disappearance or elimination of one of the superiors and organic well being is restored, or else the organism continues to wither away. In no case is there adaptation of the social organism to dual command.

Now dual command is extremely common and wreaks havoc in all concerns, large or small, in home and in state. The evil is all the more to be feared in that it worms its way into the social organism on the most plausible pretexts. For instance—

(a) In the hope of being better understood or gaining time or to put a stop forthwith to an undesirable practice, a superior $S^2$ may give orders directly to an employee E without going via the superior $S^1$. If this mistake is repeated there is dual command with its consequences, *viz.*, hesitation on the part of the subordinate, irritation and dissatisfaction on the part of the superior set aside, and disorder in the work. It will be seen later that it is possible to bypass the scalar chain when necessary, whilst avoiding the drawbacks of dual command.

(b) The desire to get away from the immediate necessity of dividing up authority as between two colleagues, two friends, two members of one family, results at times in dual command reigning at the top of a concern right from the outset. Exercising the same powers and having the same authority over the same men, the two colleagues end up inevitably with dual command and its consequences. Despite harsh lessons, instances of this sort are still numerous. New colleagues count on their mutual regard, common interest, and good sense to save them from every conflict, every serious disagreement and, save for rare exceptions, the illusion is short-lived. First an awkwardness makes itself felt, then a certain irritation and, in time, if dual command exists, even hatred. Men cannot bear dual command. A judicious assignment of duties would have reduced the danger without entirely banishing it, for between two superiors on the same footing there must always be some question ill-defined. But it is riding for a fall to set up a business organization with two superiors on equal footing without assigning duties and demarcating authority.

(c) Imperfect demarcation of departments also leads to dual command: two superiors issuing orders in a sphere which each thinks his own, constitutes dual command.

(d) Constant linking up as between different departments, natural intermeshing of functions, duties often badly defined, create an ever present danger of dual command. If a knowledgeable superior does not put it in order, footholds are established which later upset and compromise the conduct of affairs.

In all human associations, in industry, commerce, army, home, state, dual command is a perpetual source of conflicts, very grave sometimes, which have special claim on the attention of superiors of all ranks.

## 5. UNITY OF DIRECTION

This principle is expressed as: one head and one plan for a group of activities having the same objective. It is the condition essential to unity of action, coordination of strength, and focusing of effort. A body with two heads is in the social as in the animal sphere a monster, and has difficulty in surviving. Unity of direction (one head one plan) must not be confused with unity of command (one employee to have orders from one superior only). Unity of direction is provided for by sound organization of the body corporate, unity of command turns on the functioning of the personnel. Unity of command cannot exist without unity of direction, but does not flow from it.

## 6. SUBORDINATION OF INDIVIDUAL INTEREST TO GENERAL INTEREST

This principle calls to mind the fact that in a business the interest of one employee or group of employees should not prevail over that of the concern, that the interest of the home should come before that of its members and that the interest of the state should have pride of place over that of one citizen or group of citizens.

It seems that such an admonition should not need calling to mind. But ignorance, ambition, selfishness, laziness, weakness, and all human passions tend to cause the general interest to be lost sight of in favour of individual interest and a perpetual struggle has to be waged against them. Two interests of a different order, but claiming equal respect, confront each other and means must be found to reconcile them. That represents one of the great difficulties of management. Means of effecting it are—

1. Firmness and good example on the part of superiors.
2. Agreements as fair as is possible.
3. Constant supervision.

## 7. REMUNERATION OF PERSONNEL

Remuneration of personnel is the price of services rendered. It should be fair and, as far as is possible, afford satisfaction both to personnel and firm (employee and employer). The rate of remuneration depends, firstly, on circumstances independent of the employer's will and employee's worth, viz. cost of living, abundance or shortage of personnel, general business conditions, the economic position of the business, and after that it depends on the value of the employee and mode of payment adopted. Appreciation of the factors dependent on the employer's will and on the value of employees, demands a fairly good knowledge of business, judgment,

and impartiality. Later on in connection with selecting personnel we shall deal with assessing the value of employees; here only the mode of payment is under consideration as a factor operation on remuneration. The method of payment can exercise considerable influence on business progress, so the choice of this method is an important problem. It is also a thorny problem which in practice has been solved in widely different ways, of which so far none has proved satisfactory. What is generally looked for in the method of payment is that—

1. It shall assure fair remuneration.
2. It shall encourage keenness by rewarding well-directed effort.
3. It shall not lead to overpayment going beyond reasonable limits.

I am going to examine briefly the modes of payment in use for workers, junior managers, and higher managers.

### Workers

The various modes of payment in use for workers are—

1. Time rates.
2. Job rates.
3. Piece rates.

These three modes of payment may be combined and give rise to important variations by the introduction of bonuses, profit-sharing schemes, payment in kind, and nonfinancial incentives.

**1. Time rates.** Under this system the workman sells the employer, in return for a predetermined sum, a day's work under definite conditions. This system has the disadvantage of conducing to negligence and of demanding constant supervision. It is inevitable where the work done is not susceptible to measurement and in effect it is very common.

**2. Job rates.** Here payment made turns upon the execution of a definite job set in advance and may be independent of the length of the job. When payment is due only on condition that the job be completed during the normal work spell, this method merges into time rate. Payment by daily job does not require as close a supervision as payment by the day, but it has the drawback of levelling the output of good workers down to that of mediocre ones. The good ones are not satisfied, because they feel that they could earn more; the mediocre ones find the task set too heavy.

**3. Piece rates.** Here payment is related to work done and there is no limit. This system is often used in workshops where a large number of similar articles have to be made, and is found where the product can be measured by weight, length, or cubic capacity, and in general is used wherever possible. It is criticized on the grounds of emphasizing quantity at the expense of quality and of provoking disagreements when rates have to be revised in the light of manufacturing improvements. Piecework becomes contract work when applied to an important unit of work. To reduce the contractor's risk, sometimes there is added to the contract price a payment for each day's work done.

Generally, piece rates give rise to increased earnings which act for some time as a stimulus, then finally a system prevails in which this mode of payment gradually approximates to time rates for a pre-arranged sum.

The above three modes of payment are found in all large concerns; sometimes time rates prevail, sometimes one of the other two. In a workshop the same workman may be seen working now on piece rates, not on time rates. Each one of these methods had its advantages and drawbacks, and their effectiveness depends on circumstances and the ability of superiors. Neither method nor rate of payment absolves management from competence and tact, and keenness of workers and peaceful atmosphere of the workshop depend largely upon it.

### Bonuses

To arouse the worker's interest in the smooth running of the business, sometimes an increment in the nature of a bonus is added to the time-, job-, or piece-rate: for good time keeping, hard work, freedom from machine breakdown output, cleanliness, etc. The relative importance, nature and qualifying conditions of these bonuses are very varied. There are to be found the small daily supplement, the monthly sum, the annual award, shares or portions of shares distributed to the most meritorious, and also even profit-sharing schemes such as, for example, certain monetary allocations distributed annually among workers in some large firms. Several French collieries started some years back the granting of a bonus proportional to profits distributed or to extra profits. No contract is required from the workers save that the earning of the bonus is subject to certain conditions, for instance, that there shall be no strike during the year, or that absenteeism shall not have exceeded a given number of days. This type of bonus introduced an element of profit-sharing into miners' wages without any prior discussion as between workers and employer. The workman did not refuse a gift, largely gratuitous, on the part of the employer, that is, the contract was a unilateral one. Thanks to a successful trading period the yearly wages have been appreciably increased by the operation of the bonus. But what is to happen in lean times? This interesting procedure is as yet too new to be judged, but obviously it is no general solution of the problem....

### Profit-Sharing

**1. Workers.** The idea of making workers share in profits is a very attractive one and it would seem that it is from there that harmony as between Capital and Labour should come. But the practical formula for such sharing has not yet been found. Workers' profit-sharing has hitherto come up against insurmountable difficulties of application in the case of large concerns. Firstly, let us note that it cannot exist in enterprises having no monetary objective (State services, religion, philanthropic, scientific societies) and also that it is not possible in the case of businesses running at a loss. Thus profit-sharing is excluded from a great number of concerns. There remain the prosperous business concerns and of these latter the desire to reconcile and harmonize workers' and employers' interests is nowhere so great as in French mining and metallurgical industries. Now, in these industries I know of no clear application of workers' profit-sharing, whence it may be concluded forthwith that the matter is difficult, if not impossible. It is very difficult indeed. Whether a business is making a profit or not the worker must have an immediate wage assured him, and a system which would make workers' payment depend entirely on eventual future profit is unworkable. But perhaps a part of wages might come from business profits. Let us see. Viewing all contingent factors, the workers' greater or lesser share of activity or ability in the final outcome of a large concern is impossible to assess and is, moreover, quite insignificant. The portion accruing to him of distributed dividend would at the most be a few centimes on a wage of five francs for instance, that is to say the smallest extra effort, the stroke of a pick or of a file operating directly on his wage, would prove of greater advantage to him. Hence the worker has no interest in being rewarded by a share in profits proportionate to the effect he has upon profits. It is worthy of note that, in most large concerns, wages increases, operative now for some twenty years, represent a total sum greater than the amount of capital shared out. In effect, unmodified real profit-sharing by workers of large concerns has not yet entered the sphere of practical business politics.

**2. Junior Managers.** Profit-sharing for foremen, superintendents, engineers, is scarcely more advanced than for workers. Nevertheless the influence of these employees on the results of a business is quite considerable, and if they are not consistently interested in profits the only reason is that the basis for participation is difficult to establish. Doubtless managers have no need of monetary incentive to carry out their duties, but they are not indifferent to material satisfactions and it must be acknowledged that the hope of extra profit is capable of arousing their enthusiasm. So employees at middle levels should, where possible, be induced to have an interest in profits. It is relatively easy in businesses which are starting out or on trial, where exceptional effort can yield outstanding results. Sharing may then be applied to overall business profits or merely to the running of the particular department of the employee in question. When the business is of long standing and well run the zeal of a junior manager is scarcely apparent in the general outcome, and it is very hard to establish a useful basis on which he may participate. In fact, profit-sharing among junior managers in France is very rare in large concerns. Production or workshop output bonuses—not to be confused with profit-sharing—are much more common.

**3. Higher Managers.** It is necessary to go right up to top management to find a class of employee with frequent interest in the profits of large-scale French concerns. The head of the business, in view of his knowledge, ideas, and actions, exerts considerable influence on general results, so it is quite natural to try and provide him with an interest in them. Sometimes it is possible to establish a close connection between his personal activity and its effects. Nevertheless, generally speaking, there exist other influences quite independent of the personal capability of the manager which can influence results to a greater extent than can his personal activity. If the manager's salary were exclusively dependent upon profits, it might at times be reduced to nothing. There are besides, businesses being built up, wound up, or merely passing through temporary crisis, wherein management depends no less on talent than in the case of prosperous ones, and wherein profit-sharing cannot be a basis for remuneration for the manager. In fine, senior civil servants cannot be paid on a profit-sharing basis. Profit-sharing, then, for either higher managers or workers is not a general rule of remuneration. To sum up, then: profit-sharing is a mode of payment capable of giving excellent results in certain cases, but is not a general rule. It does not seem to me possible, at least for the present, to count on this mode of payment for appeasing conflict between Capital and Labour. Fortunately, there are other means which hitherto have been sufficient to maintain relative social quiet. Such methods have not lost their power and it is up to managers to study them, apply them, and make them work well.

### *Payment in Kind, Welfare Work, Non-Financial Incentives*

Whether wages are made up of money only or whether they include various additions such as heating, light, housing, food, is of little consequence provided that the employee be satisfied.

From another point of view, there is no doubt that a business will be better served in proportion as its employees are more energetic, better educated, more conscientious and more permanent. The employer should have regard, if merely in the interests of the business, for the health, strength, education, morale, and stability of his personnel. These elements of smooth running are not acquired in the workshop alone, they are formed and developed as well, and particularly, outside it, in the home and school, in civil and religious life. Therefore, the employer comes to be concerned with his employees outside the works and here the question of proportion comes up again. Opinion is greatly divided on this point. Certain unfortunate experiments have resulted in some employers stopping short their interest, at the works gate and at the regulation of wages. The majority consider that the employer's activity may be used to good purpose outside the factory confines provided that there be discretion and prudence, that it be sought after rather than

imposed, be in keeping with the general level of education and taste of those concerned and that it have absolute respect for their liberty. It must be benevolent collaboration, not tyrannical stewardship, and therein lies an indispensable condition of success....

## 8. CENTRALIZATION

Like division of work, centralization belongs to the natural order; this turns on the fact that in every organism, animal or social, sensations converge toward the brain or directive part, and from the brain or directive part orders are sent out which set all parts of the organism in movement. Centralization is not a system of management good or bad of itself, capable of being adopted or discarded at the whim of managers or of circumstances; it is always present to a greater or less extent. The question of centralization or decentralization, is a simple question of proportion, it is a matter of finding the optimum degree for the particular concern. In small firms, where the manager's orders go directly to subordinates there is absolute centralization; in large concerns, where a long scalar chain is interposed between manager and lower grades, orders and counterinformation too, have to go through a series of intermediaries. Each employee, intentionally or unintentionally, puts something of himself into the transmission and execution of orders and of information received too. He does not operate merely as a cog in a machine. What appropriate share of initiative may be left to intermediaries depends on the personal character of the manager, on his moral worth, on the reliability of his subordinates, and also on the condition of the business. The degree of centralization must vary according to different cases. The objective to pursue is the optimum utilization of all faculties of the personnel.

If the moral worth of the manager, his strength, intelligence, experience, and swiftness of thought allow him to have a wide span of activities he will be able to carry centralization quite far and reduce his seconds in command to mere executive agents. If, conversely, he prefers to have greater recourse to the experience, opinions, and counsel of his colleagues whilst reserving to himself the privilege of giving general directives, he can effect considerable decentralization.

Seeing that both absolute and relative value of manager and employees are constantly changing, it is understandable that the degree of centralization or decentralization may itself vary constantly. It is a problem to be solved according to circumstances, to the best satisfaction of the interests involved. It arises, not only in the case of higher authority, but for superiors at all levels and not one but can extend or confine, to some extent, his subordinates' initiative.

The finding of the measure which shall give the best overall yield: that is the problem of centralization or decentralization. Everything which goes to increase the importance of the subordinate's role is decentralization, everything which goes to reduce it is centralization.

## 9. SCALAR CHAIN

The scalar chain is the chain of superiors ranging from the ultimate authority to the lowest ranks. The line of authority is the route followed—via every link in the chain—by all communications which start from or go to the ultimate authority. This path is dictated both by the need for some transmission and by the principle of unity of command, but it is not always the swiftest. It is even at times disastrously lengthy in large concerns, notably in governmental ones. Now, there are many activities whose success turns on speedy execution, hence respect for the line of authority must be reconciled with the need for swift action.

Let us imagine that section F has to be put into contact with section P in a business whose scalar chain is represented by the double ladder G-A-Q thus—

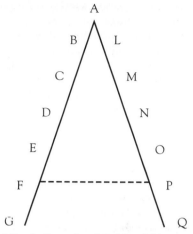

Henri Fayol, *General and Industrial Management,* trans. Constance Storrs (London: Pitman, 1949), 19–42; original work published 1916.

By following the line of authority the ladder must be climbed from F to A and then descended from A to P, stopping at each rung, then ascended again from P to A, and descended once more from A to F, in order to get back to the starting point. Evidently it is much simpler and quicker to go directly from F to P by making use of FP as a "gang plank" and that is what is most often done. The scalar principle will be safeguarded if managers E and O have authorized their respective subordinates F and P to treat directly, and the position will be fully regularized if F and P inform their respective superiors forthwith of what they have agreed upon. So long as F and P remain in agreement, and so long as their actions are approved by their immediate superiors, direct contact may be maintained, but from the instant that agreement ceases or there is no approval from the superiors direct contact comes to an end, and the scalar chain is straightway resumed. Such is the actual procedure to be observed in the great majority of businesses. It provides for the usual exercise of some measure of initiative at all levels of authority. In the small concern, the general interest, viz. that of the concern proper, is easy to grasp, and the employer is present to recall this interest to those tempted to lose sight of it. In government enterprise the general interest is such a complex, vast, remote thing, that it is not easy to get a clear idea of it, and for the majority of civil servants the employer is somewhat mythical and unless the sentiment of general interest be constantly revived by higher authority, it becomes blurred and weakened and each section tends to regard itself as its own aim and end and forgets that it is only a cog in a big machine, all of whose parts must work in concert. It becomes isolated, cloistered, aware only of the line of authority.

The use of the "gang plank" is simple, swift, sure. It allows the two employees F and P to deal at one sitting, and in a few hours, with some question or other which via the scalar chain would pass through twenty transmissions, inconvenience many people, involve masses of paper, lose weeks or months to get to a conclusion less satisfactory generally than the one which could have been obtained via direct contact as between F and P.

Is it possible that such practices, as ridiculous as they are devastating, could be in current use? Unfortunately there can be little doubt of it in government department affairs. It is usually acknowledged that the chief cause is fear of responsibility. I am rather of the opinion that it is insufficient executive capacity on the part of those in charge. If supreme authority A insisted that his assistants B and L made use of the "gang plank" themselves and made its use incumbent upon their subordinates C and M, the habit and courage of taking responsibility would be established and at the same time the custom of using the shortest path.

It is an error to depart needlessly from the line of authority, but it is an even greater one to keep to it when detriment to the business ensues. The latter may attain extreme gravity in certain conditions. When an employee is obliged to choose between the two practices, and it is impossible for him to take advice from his superior, he should be courageous enough and feel free enough to adopt the line dictated

by the general interest. But for him to be in this frame of mind there must have been previous precedent, and his superiors must have set him the example—for example must always come from above.

## 10. ORDER

The formula is known in the case of material things "A place for everything and everything in its place." The formula is the same for human order. "A place for everyone and everyone in his place."

### *Material Order*

In accordance with the preceding definition, so that material order shall prevail, there must be a place appointed for each thing and each thing must be in its appointed place. Is that enough? Is it not also necessary that the place shall have been well chosen? The object of order must be avoidance of loss of material, and for this object to be completely realized not only must things be in their place suitably arranged but also the place must have been chosen so as to facilitate all activities as much as possible. If this last condition be unfulfilled, there is merely the appearance of order. Appearance of order may cover over real disorder. I have seen a works yard used as a store for steel ingots in which the material was well stacked, evenly arranged and clean and which gave a pleasing impression of orderliness. On close inspection it could be noted that the same heap included five or six types of steel intended for different manufacture all mixed up together. Whence useless handling, lost time, risk of mistakes because each thing was not in its place. It happens, on the other hand, that the appearance of disorder may actually be true order. Such is the case with papers scattered about at a master's whim which a well-meaning but incompetent servant re-arranges and sticks in neat piles. The master can no longer find his way about them. Perfect order presupposes a judiciously chosen place and the appearance of order is merely a false or imperfect image of real order. Cleanliness is a corollary of orderliness, there is no appointed place for dirt. A diagram representing the entire premises divided up into as many sections as there are employees responsible facilitates considerably the establishing and control of order.

### Social Order

For social order to prevail in a concern there must, in accordance with the definition, be an appointed place for every employee and every employee be in his appointed place. Perfect order requires, further, that the place be suitable for the employee and the employee for the place—in English idiom, "The right man in the right place."

Thus understood, social order presupposes the successful execution of the two most difficult managerial activities: good organization and good selection. Once the posts essential to the smooth running of the business have been decided upon and those to fill such posts have been selected, each employee occupies that post wherein he can render most service. Such is perfect social order, "A place for each one and each one in his place." That appears simple, and naturally we are so anxious for it to be so that when we hear for the twentieth time a government departmental head assert this principle, we conjure up straightway a concept of perfect administration. This is a mirage.

Social order demands precise knowledge of the human requirements and resources of the concern and a constant balance between these requirements and resources. Now this balance is most difficult to establish and maintain and all the more difficult the bigger the business, and when it has been upset and individual interests resulted in neglect or sacrifice of the general interest, when ambition, nepotism, favouritism, or merely ignorance, has multiplied positions without good reason or filled them with incompetent employees, much talent and strength of will and more persistence than current instability of ministerial appointments

presupposes, are required in order to sweep away abuses and restore order....

## 11. EQUITY

Why equity and not justice? Justice is putting into execution established conventions, but conventions cannot foresee everything, they need to be interpreted or their inadequacy supplemented. For the personnel to be encouraged to carry out its duties with all the devotion and loyalty of which it is capable it must be treated with kindliness, and equity results from the combination of kindliness and justice. Equity excludes neither forcefulness nor sternness and the application of it requires much good sense, experience, and good nature.

Desire for equity and equality of treatment are aspirations to be taken into account in dealing with employees. In order to satisfy these requirements as much as possible without neglecting any principle or losing sight of the general interest, the head of the business must frequently summon up his highest faculties. He should strive to instill a sense of equity throughout all levels of the scalar chain.

## 12. STABILITY OF TENURE OF PERSONNEL

Time is required for an employee to get used to new work and succeed in doing it well, always assuming that he possesses the requisite abilities. If when he has got used to it, or before then, he is removed, he will not have had time to render worthwhile service. If this be repeated indefinitely the work will never be properly done. The undesirable consequences of such insecurity of tenure are especially to be feared in large concerns, where the settling in of managers is generally a lengthy matter. Much time is needed indeed to get to know men and things in a large concern in order to be in a position to decide on a plan of action, to gain confidence in oneself, and inspire it in others. Hence it has often been recorded that a mediocre manager who stays is infinitely preferable to outstanding managers who merely come and go.

Generally the managerial personnel of prosperous concerns is stable, that of unsuccessful ones is unstable. Instability of tenure is at one and the same time cause and effect of bad running. The apprenticeship of a higher manager is generally a costly matter. Nevertheless, changes of personnel are inevitable; age, illness, retirement, death, disturb the human make-up of the firm, certain employees are no longer capable of carrying out their duties, whilst others become fit to assume greater responsibilities. In common with all the other principles, therefore, stability of tenure and personnel is also a question of proportion.

## 13. INITIATIVE

Thinking out a plan and ensuring its success is one of the keenest satisfactions for an intelligent man to experience. It is also one of the most powerful stimulants of human endeavour. This power of thinking out and executing is what is called initiative, and freedom to propose and to execute belongs too, each in its way, to initiative. At all levels of the organizational ladder zeal and energy on the part of employees are augmented by initiative. The initiative of all, added to that of the manager, and supplementing it if need be, represents a great source of strength for businesses. This is particularly apparent at difficult times; hence it is essential to encourage and develop this capacity to the full.

Much tact and some integrity are required to inspire and maintain everyone's initiative, within the limits imposed, by respect for authority and for discipline. The manager must be able to sacrifice some personal vanity in order to grant this sort of satisfaction to subordinates. Other things being equal, moreover, a manager able to permit the exercise of initiative on the part of subordinates is infinitely superior to one who cannot do so.

## 14. ESPRIT DE CORPS

"Union is strength." Business heads would do well to ponder on this proverb. Harmony, union among the personnel of a concern, is great strength in that concern. Effort, then, should be made to establish it. Among the countless methods in use I will single out specially one principle to be observed and two pitfalls to be avoided. The principle to be observed is unity of command; the dangers to be avoided are (*a*) a misguided interpretation of the motto "divide and rule," (*b*) the abuse of written communications.

(a) **Personnel must not be split up.** Dividing enemy forces to weaken them is clever, but dividing one's own team is a grave sin against the business. Whether this error results from inadequate managerial capacity or imperfect grasp of things, or from egoism which sacrifices general interest to personal interest, it is always reprehensible because harmful to the business. There is no merit in sowing dissension among subordinates; any beginner can do it. On the contrary, real talent is needed to coordinate effort, encourage keenness, use each man's abilities, and reward each one's merit without arousing possible jealousies and disturbing harmonious relations.

(b) **Abuse of written communications.** In dealing with a business matter or giving an order which requires explanation to complete it, usually it is simpler and quicker to do so verbally than in writing. Besides, it is well known that differences and misunderstandings which a conversation could clear up, grow more bitter in writing. Thence it follows that, wherever possible, contacts should be verbal; there is a gain in speed, clarity and harmony. Nevertheless, it happens in some firms that employees of neighbouring departments with numerous points of contact, or even employees within a department, who could quite easily meet, only communicate with each other in writing. Hence arise increased work and complications and delays harmful to the business. At the same time, there is to be observed a certain animosity prevailing between different departments or different employees within a department. The system of written communications usually brings this result. There is a way of putting an end to this deplorable system and that is to forbid all communications in writing which could easily and advantageously be replaced by verbal ones. There again, we come up against a question of proportion....

There I bring to an end this review of principles, not because the list is exhausted—this list has no precise limits—but because to me it seems at the moment especially useful to endow management theory with a dozen or so well-established principles, on which it is appropriate to concentrate general discussion. The foregoing principles are those to which I have most often had recourse. I have simply expressed my personal opinion in connection with them. Are they to have a place in the management code which is to be built up? General discussion will show.

This code is indispensable. Be it a case of commerce, industry, politics, religion, war, or philanthropy, in every concern there is a management function to be performed, and for its performance there must be principles, that is to say acknowledged truths regarded as proven on which to rely. And it is the code which represents the sum total of these truths at any given moment.

Surprise might be expressed at the outset that the eternal moral principles, the laws of the Decalogue and Commandments of the Church are not sufficient guide for the manager, and that a special code is needed. The explanation is this: the higher laws of religious or moral order envisage the individual only, or else interests which are not of this world, whereas management principles aim at the success of associations of individuals and at the satisfying of economic interests. Given that the aim is different, it is not surprising that the means are not the same. There is no identity, so there is no contradiction. Without principles one is in darkness and chaos; interest, experience, and proportion are still very handicapped, even with the best principles. The principle is the lighthouse fixing the bearings, but it can only serve those who already know the way into port.

## NOTE

1. "*Body corporate.*" Fayol's term "corps social," meaning all those engaged in a given corporate activity in any sphere, is best rendered by this somewhat unusual term because (*a*) it retains his implied biological metaphor; (*b*) it represents the structure as distinct from the process of organization. The term will be retained in all contexts where these two requirements have to be met. (Translator's note.)

# 6

# The Principles of Scientific Management

*Frederick Winslow Taylor*

By far the most important fact which faces the industries of our country, the industries, in fact, of the civilized world, is that not only the average worker, but nineteen out of twenty workmen throughout the civilized world firmly believe that it is for their best interests to go slow instead of to go fast. They firmly believe that it is for their interest to give as little work in return for the money that they get as is practical. The reasons for this belief are twofold, and I do not believe that the workingmen are to blame for holding these fallacious views.

If you will take any set of workmen in your own town and suggest to those men that it would be a good thing for them in their trade if they were to double their output in the coming year, each man turn out twice as much work and become twice as efficient, they would say, "I don't know anything about other people's trades; what you are saying about increasing efficiency being a good thing may be good for other trades, but I know that the only result if you come to our trade would be that half of us would be out of a job before the year was out." That to the average workingman is an axiom; it is not a matter subject to debate at all. And even among the average business men of this country that opinion is almost universal. They firmly believe that that would be the result of a great increase in efficiency, and yet directly the opposite is true.

## THE EFFECT OF LABOR-SAVING DEVICES

Whenever any labor-saving device of any kind has been introduced into any trade—go back into the history of any trade and see it—even though that labor-saving device may turn out ten, twenty, thirty times that output that was originally turned out by men in that trade, the result has universally been to make work for more men in that trade, not work for less men.

Let me give you one illustration. Let us take one of the staple businesses, the cotton industry. About 1840 the power loom succeeded the old hand loom in the cotton industry. It was invented many years before, somewhere about 1780 or 1790, but it came in very slowly. About 1840 the weavers of Manchester, England, saw that the power loom was coming, and they knew it would turn out three times the yardage of cloth in a day that the hand loom turned out. And what did they do, these five thousand weavers of Manchester, England, who saw starvation staring them in the face? They broke into the establishments into which those machines were being introduced, they smashed them, they did everything possible to stop the introduction of the power loom. And the same result followed that follows every attempt to interfere with the introduction of any labor-saving device, if it is really a labor-saving device. Instead of stopping the introduction of the power loom, their opposition apparently accelerated it, just as opposition to scientific management all over the country, bitter labor opposition today, is accelerating the introduction of it instead of retarding it. History repeats itself in that respect. The power loom came right straight along.

And let us see the result in Manchester. Just what follows in every industry when any labor-saving device is introduced. Less

*Source: Bulletin of the Taylor Society* (December 1916). An abstract of an address given by Taylor to the Cleveland Advertising Club, March 3, 1915, two weeks before his death, and repeated the following day at Youngstown, Ohio. This presentation was Taylor's last public appearance.

than a century has gone by since 1840. The population of England in that time has now more than doubled. Each man in the cotton industry in Manchester, England, now turns out, at a restricted estimate ten yards of cloth for every yard of cloth that was turned out in 1840. In 1840 there were 5,000 weavers in Manchester. Now there are 265,000. Has that thrown men out of work? Has the introduction of labor-saving machinery, which has multiplied the output per man by tenfold, thrown men out of work?

What is the real meaning of this? All that you have to do is to bring wealth into this world and the world uses it. That is the real meaning. The meaning is that where in 1840 cotton goods were a luxury to be worn only by rich people when they were hardly ever seen on the street, now every man, woman, and child all over the world wears cotton goods as a daily necessity.

Nineteen-twentieths of the real wealth of this world is used by the poor people, and not the rich, so that the workingman who sets out as a steady principle to restrict output is merely robbing his own kind. That group of manufacturers which adopts as a permanent principle restriction of output, in order to hold up prices, is robbing the world. The one great thing that marks the improvement of this world is measured by the enormous increase in output of the individuals in this world. There is fully twenty times the output per man now than there was three hundred years ago. That marks the increase in the real wealth of the world; that marks the increase of the happiness of the world, that gives us the opportunity for shorter hours, for better education, for amusement, for art, for music, for everything that is worthwhile in this world—goes right straight back to this increase in the output of the individual. The workingmen of today live better than the king did three hundred years ago. From what does the progress the world has made come? Simply from the increase in the output of the individual all over the world.

## THE DEVELOPMENT OF SOLDIERING

The second reason why the workmen of this country and of Europe deliberately restrict output is a very simple one. They, for this reason, are even less to blame than they are for the other. If, for example, you are manufacturing a pen, let us assume for simplicity that a pen can be made by a single man. Let us say that the workman is turning out ten pens per day, and that he is receiving $2.50 a day for his wages. He has a progressive foreman who is up to date, and that foreman goes to the workman and suggests, "Here, John, you are getting $2.50 a day, and you are turning out ten pens. I would suggest that I pay you 25 cents for making that pen." The man takes the job, and through the help of his foreman, through his own ingenuity, through his increased work, through his interest in his business, through the help of his friends, at the end of the year he finds himself turning out twenty pens instead of ten. He is happy, he is making $5, instead of $2.50 a day. His foreman is happy because, with the same room, with the same men he had before, he has doubled the output of his department, and the manufacturer himself is sometimes happy, but not often. Then someone on the board of directors asks to see the payroll, and he finds that we are paying $5 a day where other similar mechanics are only getting $2.50, and in no uncertain terms he announces that we must stop ruining the labor market. We cannot pay $5 a day when the standard rate of wages is $2.50; how can we hope to compete with surrounding towns? What is the result? Mr. Foreman is sent for, and he is told that he has got to stop ruining the labor market of Cleveland. And the foreman goes back to his workman in sadness, in depression, and tells his workman, "I am sorry, John, but I have got to cut the price down for that pen; I cannot let you earn $5 a day; the board of directors has got on to it, and it is ruining the labor market; you ought to be willing to have the price reduced. You cannot earn more than

$3 or $2.75 a day, and I will have to cut your wages so that you will only get $3 a day." John, of necessity accepts the cut, but he sees to it that he never makes enough pens to get another cut.

## CHARACTERISTICS OF THE UNION WORKMAN

There seem to be two divergent opinions about the workmen of this country. One is that a lot of the trade unions' workmen, particularly in this country, have become brutal, have become dominating, careless of any interests but their own, and are a pretty poor lot. And the other opinion which those same trade unionists hold of themselves is that they are pretty close to little gods. Whichever view you may hold of the workingmen of this country, and my personal view of them is that they are a pretty fine lot of fellows, they are just about the same as you and I. But whether you hold the bad opinion or the good opinion, it makes no difference. Whatever the workingmen of this country are or whatever they are not, they are not fools. And all that is necessary is for a workingman to have but one object lesson, like that I have told you, and he soldiers for the rest of his life.

There are a few exceptional employers who treat their workmen differently, but I am talking about the rule of the country. Soldiering is the absolute rule with all workmen who know their business. I am not saying it is for their interest to soldier. You cannot blame them for it. You cannot expect them to be large enough minded men to look at the proper view of the matter. Nor is the man who cuts the wages necessarily to blame. It is simply a misfortune in industry.

## THE DEVELOPMENT OF SCIENTIFIC MANAGEMENT

There has been, until comparatively recently, no scheme promulgated by which

the evils of rate cutting could be properly avoided, so soldiering has been the rule.

Now the first step that was taken toward the development of those methods, of those principles, which rightly or wrongly have come to be known under the name of scientific management—the first step that was taken in an earnest endeavor to remedy the evils of soldiering; an earnest endeavor to make it unnecessary for workmen to be hypocritical in this way, to deceive themselves, to deceive their employers, to live day in and day out a life of deceit, forced upon them conditions—the very first step that was taken toward the development was to overcome that evil. I want to emphasize that, because I wish to emphasize the one great fact relating to scientific management, the greatest factor: namely, that scientific management is no new set of theories that has been tried on by any one at every step. Scientific management at every step has been an evolution, not a theory. In all cases the practice has preceded the theory, not succeeded it. In every case one measure after another has been tried out, until the proper remedy has been found. That series of proper eliminations, that evolution, is what is called scientific management. Every element of it has had to fight its way against the elements that preceded it, and prove itself better or it would not be there tomorrow.

All the men that I know of who are in any way connected with scientific management are ready to abandon any scheme, and theory in favor of anything else that could be found that is better. There is nothing in scientific management that is fixed. There is no one man, or group of men, who have invented scientific management.

What I want to emphasize is that all of the elements of scientific management are an evolution, not an invention. Scientific management is in use in an immense range and variety of industries. Almost every type of industry in this country has scientific management working successfully. I think I can safely say that on the average in those establishments in which scientific management has been introduced, the average workman is turning out double the output he was before. I think that is a conservative statement.

## THE WORKMEN: THE CHIEF BENEFICIARIES

Three or four years ago I could have said there were about fifty thousand men working under scientific management, but now I know there are many more. Company after company is coming under it, many of which I know nothing about. Almost universally they are working successfully. This increasing of the output per individual in the trade, results, of course, in cheapening the product; it results, therefore, in larger profit usually to the owners of the business; it results also, in many cases, in a lowering of the selling price, although that has not come to the extent it will later. In the end the public gets the good. Without any question, the large good which so far has come from scientific management has come to the worker. To the workmen has come, practically right off as soon as scientific management is introduced, an increase in wages amounting from 33 to 100 percent, and yet that is not the greatest good that comes to the workmen from scientific management. The great good comes from the fact that, under scientific management, they look upon their employers as the best friends they have in the world; the suspicious watchfulness which characterizes the old type management, the semi-antagonism, or the complete antagonism between workmen and employers is entirely superseded, and in its place comes genuine friendship between both sides. That is the greatest good that has come under scientific management. As a proof of this in the many businesses in which scientific management has been introduced, I know of not one single strike of workmen working under it after it had been introduced, and only two or three while it was in process of introduction. In this connection I must speak of the

fakers, those who have said they can introduce scientific management into a business in six months or a year. That is pure nonsense. There have been many strikes stirred up by that type of man. Not one strike has ever come, and I do not believe ever will come, under scientific management.

## WHAT SCIENTIFIC MANAGEMENT IS

What is scientific management? It is no efficiency device, nor is it any group of efficiency devices. Scientific management is no new scheme for paying men, it is no bonus system, no piecework system, no premium system of payment; it is no new method of figuring costs. It is no one of the various elements by which it is commonly known, by which people refer to it. It is not time study nor man study. It is not the printing of a ton or two of blanks and unloading them on a company and saying, "There is your system, go ahead and use it." Scientific management does not exist and cannot exist until there has been a complete mental revolution on the part of the workmen working under it, as to their duties toward themselves and toward their employers, and a complete mental revolution in the outlook for the employers, toward their duties, toward themselves, and toward their workmen. And until this great mental change takes place, scientific management does not exist. Do you think you can make a great mental revolution in a large group of workmen in a year, or do you think you can make it in a large group of foremen and superintendents in a year? If you do, you are very much mistaken. All of us hold mighty close to our ideas and principles in life, and we change very slowly toward the new, and very properly too.

Let me give you an idea of what I mean by this change in mental outlook. If you are manufacturing a hammer or a mallet, into the cost of that mallet goes a certain amount of raw materials, a certain amount of wood and metal. If you will take the cost of the raw materials and then add to it that cost which is frequently called by various names—overhead expenses, general expense, indirect expense; that is, the proper share of taxes, insurance, light, heat, salaries of officers, and advertising—and you have a sum of money. Subtract that sum from the selling price, and what is left over is called the surplus. It is over this surplus that all of the labor disputes in the past have occurred. The workman naturally wants all he can get. His wages come out of that surplus. The manufacturer wants all he can get in the shape of profits, and it is from the division of this surplus that all the labor disputes have come in the past—the equitable division.

The new outlook that comes under scientific management is this: The workmen, after many object lessons, come to see and the management come to see that this surplus can be made so great, providing both sides will stop their pulling apart, will stop their fighting and will push as hard as they can to get as cheap an output as possible, that there is no occasion to quarrel. Each side can get more than ever before. The acknowledgement of this fact represents a complete mental revolution....

## WHAT SCIENTIFIC MANAGEMENT WILL DO

I am going to try to prove to you that the old style of management has not a ghost of a chance in competition with the principles of scientific management. Why? In the first place, under scientific management, the initiative of the workmen, their hard work, their goodwill, their best endeavors are obtained with absolute regularity. There are cases all the time where men will soldier, but they become the exception, as a rule, and they give their true initiative under scientific management. That is the least of the two sources of gain. The greatest source of gain under scientific management comes from the new and almost unheard-of duties and burdens which are voluntarily

assumed, not by the workmen, but by the men on the management side. These are the things which make scientific management a success. These new duties, these new burdens undertaken by the management have rightly or wrongly been divided into four groups, and have been called the principles of scientific management.

The first of the great principles of scientific management, the first of the new burdens which are voluntarily undertaken by those on the management side is the deliberate gathering together of the great mass of traditional knowledge which, in the past, has been in the heads of the workmen, recording it, tabulating it, reducing it in most cases to rules, laws, and in many cases to mathematical formulae, which, with these new laws, are applied to the cooperation of the management to the work of the workmen. This results in an immense increase in the output, we may say, of the two. The gathering in of this great mass of traditional knowledge, which is done by the means of motion study, time study, can be truly called the science.

Let me make a prediction. I have before me the first book, so far as I know, that has been published on motion study and on time study. That is, the motion study and time study of the cement and concrete trades. It contains everything relating to concrete work. It is of about seven hundred pages and embodies the motions of men, the time and the best way of doing that sort of work. It is the first case in which a trade has been reduced to the same condition that engineering data of all kinds have been reduced, and it is this sort of data that is bound to sweep the world.

I have before me something which has been gathering for about fourteen years, the time or motion study of the machine shop. It will take probably four or five years more before the first book will be ready to publish on that subject. There is a collection of sixty or seventy thousand elements affecting machine-shop work. After a few years, say three, four or five years more, someone will be ready to publish the first book giving the laws of the movements of men in the machine shop—all the laws, not only a few of them. Let me predict, just as sure as the sun shines, that is going to come in every trade. Why? Because it pays, for no other reason. That results in doubling the output in any shop. Any device which results in an increased output is bound to come in spite of all opposition, whether we want it or not. It comes automatically.

## THE SELECTION OF THE WORKMAN

The next of the four principles of scientific management is the scientific selection of the workman, and then his progressive development. It becomes the duty under scientific management of not one, but of a group of men on the management side, to deliberately study the workmen who are under them; study them in the most careful, thorough and painstaking way; and not just leave it to the poor, overworked foreman to go out and say, "Come on, what do you want? If you are cheap enough I will give you a trial."

That is the old way. The new way is to take a great deal of trouble in selecting the workmen. The selection proceeds year after year. And it becomes the duty of those engaged in scientific management to know something about the workmen under them. It becomes their duty to set out deliberately to train the workmen in their employ to be able to do a better and still better class of work than ever before, and to then pay them higher wages than ever before. This deliberate selection of the workmen is the second of the great duties that devolve on the management under scientific management.

## BRINGING TOGETHER THE SCIENCE AND THE MAN

The third principle is the bringing together of this science of which I have spoken and the trained workmen. I say bringing because they don't come together unless someone

brings them. Select and train your workmen all you may, but unless there is someone who will make the men and the science come together, they will stay apart. The "make" involves a great many elements. They are not all disagreeable elements. The most important and largest way of "making" is to do something nice for the man whom you wish to make come together with the science. Offer him a plum, something that is worthwhile. There are many plums offered to those who come under scientific management—better treatment, more kindly treatment, more consideration for their wishes, and an opportunity for them to express their wants freely. That is one side of the "make." An equally important side is, whenever a man will not do what he ought, to either make him do it or stop it. If he will not do it, let him get out. I am not talking of any mollycoddle. Let me disabuse your minds of any opinion that scientific management is a mollycoddle scheme....

## THE PRINCIPLE OF THE DIVISION OF WORK

The fourth principle is the plainest of all. It involves a complete re-division of the work of the establishment. Under the old scheme of management, almost all of the work was done by the workmen. Under the new, the work of the establishment is divided into two large parts. All of that work which formerly was done by the workmen alone is divided into two large sections, and one of those sections is handed over to the management. They do a whole division of the work formerly done by the workmen. It is this real cooperation, this genuine division of the work between the two sides, more than any other element which accounts for the fact that there never will be strikes under scientific management. When the workman realizes that there is hardly a thing he does that does not have to be preceded by some act of preparation on the part of management, and when that workman realizes when the management falls down and does not do its part, that he is not only entitled to a kick, but that he can register that kick in the most forcible possible way, he cannot quarrel with the men over him. It is teamwork. There are more complaints made every day on the part of the workmen that the men on the management side fail to do their duties than are made by the management that the men fail. Every one of the complaints of the men have to be heeded, just as much as the complaints from the management that the workmen do not do their share. That is characteristic of scientific management. It represents a democracy, co-operation, a genuine division of work which never existed before in this world.

## THE PROOF OF THE THEORY

I am through now with the theory. I will try to convince you of the value of these four principles by giving you some practical illustrations. I hope that you will look for these four elements in the illustrations. I shall begin by trying to show the power of these four elements when applied to the greatest kind of work I know of that is done by man. The reason I have heretofore chosen pig-iron for an illustration is that it is the lowest form of work that is known.

A pig of iron weighs about ninety-two pounds on an average. A man stoops down and, with no other implement than his hands, picks up a pig of iron, walks a few yards with it, and drops it on a pile. A large part of the community has the impression that scientific management is chiefly handling pig-iron. The reason I first chose pig-iron for an illustration is that, if you can prove to any one the strength, the effect, of those four principles when applied to such rudimentary work as handling pig-iron, the presumption is that it can be applied to something better. The only way to prove it is to start at the bottom and show those four principles all along the line. I am sorry I cannot, because of the lack of time, give you the illustration of handling pig-iron.

Many of you doubt whether there is much of any science in it. I am going to try to prove later with a high class mechanic that the workman who is fit to work at any type of work is almost universally incapable of understanding the principles without the help of someone else. I will use shoveling because it is a shorter illustration, and I will try to show what I mean by the science of shoveling, and the power which comes to the man who knows the science of shoveling. It is a high art compared with pig-iron handling.

## THE SCIENCE OF SHOVELING

When I went to the Bethlehem Steel Works, the first thing I saw was a gang of men unloading rice coal. They were a splendid set of fellows, and they shoveled fast. There was no loafing at all. They shoveled as hard as you could ask any man to work. I looked with the greatest of interest for a long time, and finally they moved off rapidly down into the yard to another part of the yard and went right at handling iron ore. One of the main facts connected with that shoveling was that the work those men were doing was that, in handling the rice coal, they had on their shovels a load of 3¾ pounds, and when the same men went to handling ore with the same shovel, they had over 38 pounds on their shovels. Is it asking too much of anyone to inquire whether 3¾ pounds is the right load for a shovel, or whether 38 pounds is the right load for a shovel? Surely if one is right the other must be wrong. I think that is a self-evident fact, and yet I am willing to bet that that is what workmen are doing right now in Cleveland.

That is the old way. Suppose we notice that fact. Most of us do not notice it because it is left to the foreman. At the Midvale works, we had to find out these facts. What is the old way of finding them out? The old way was to sit down and write one's friends and ask them the questions. They got answers from contractors about what they thought it ought to be, and then they averaged them up, or took the most reliable man, and said

"That is all right; now we have a shovel load of so much." The more common way is to say, "I want a good shovel foreman." They will send for the foreman of the shovelers and put the job up to him to find what is the proper load to put on a shovel. He will tell you right off the bat. I want to show you the difference under scientific management.

Under scientific management you ask no one. Every little trifle—here is nothing too small—becomes the subject of experiment. The experiments develop into a law; they save money; they increase the output of the individual and make the thing worthwhile. How is this done? What we did in shoveling experiments was to deliberately select two first class shovelers, the best we knew how to get. We brought them into the office and said, "Jim and Mike, you two fellows are both good shovelers. I have a proposition to make to you. I am going to pay you double wages if you fellows will go out and do what I want you to do. There will be a young chap go along with you with a pencil and a piece of paper, and he will tell you to do a lot of fool things, and you will do them, and he will write down a lot of fool things, and you will think it is a joke, but it is nothing of the kind. Let me tell you one thing: if you fellows think that you can fool that chap you are very much mistaken, you cannot fool him at all. Don't get it through your heads you can fool him. If you take this double wages, you will be straight and do what you are told." They both promised and did exactly what they were told. What we told them was this: "We want you to start in and do whatever shoveling you are told to do and work at just the pace, all day long, that when it comes night you are going to be good and tired, but not tired out. I do not want you exhausted or anything like that, but properly tired. You know what a good day's work is. In other words, I do not want any loafing business or any overwork business. If you find yourself overworked and

getting too tired, slow down." Those men did that and did it in the most splendid kind of way day in and day out. We proved their cooperation because they were in different parts of the yard, and they both got near enough the same results. Our results were duplicated.

I have found that there are a lot of schemes among my working friends, but no more among them than among us. They are good, straight fellows if you only treat them right, and put the matter up squarely to them. We started in at a pile of material, with a very large shovel. We kept innumerable accurate records of all kinds, some of them useless. Thirty or forty different items were carefully observed about the work of those two men. We counted the number of shovelfuls thrown in a day. We found with a weight of between thirty-eight and thirty-nine pounds on the shovel, the man made a pile of material of a certain height. We then cut off the shovel, and he shoveled again and with a thirty-four pound load his pile went up and he shoveled more in a day. We again cut off the shovel to thirty pounds, and the pile went up again. With twenty-six pounds on the shovel, the pile again went up, and at twenty-one and one-half pounds the men could do their best. At twenty pounds the pile went down, at eighteen it went down, at fourteen it went down, so that they were at the peak of twenty-one and one-half pounds. There is a scientific fact. A first class shoveler ought to take twenty-one and one-half pounds on his shovel in order to work to the best possible advantage. You are not giving that man a chance unless you give him a shovel which will hold twenty-one pounds.

The men in the yard were run by the old fashioned foreman. He simply walked about with them. We at once took their shovels away from them. We built a large labor tool room which held ten to fifteen different kinds of shoveling implements so that for each kind of material that was handled in that yard, all the way from rice coals, ashes, coke, all the way up to ore, we would have a shovel that would just hold twenty-one pounds, or average twenty-one. One time it would hold eighteen, the next twenty-four, but it will average twenty-one.

When you have six hundred men laboring in the yard, as we had there, it becomes a matter of quite considerable difficulty to get, each day, for each one of those six hundred men, engaged in a line one and one-half to two miles long and a half mile wide, just the right shovel for shoveling material. That requires organization to lay out and plan for those men in advance. We had to lay out the work each day. We had to have large maps on which the movements of the men were plotted out a day in advance. When each workman came in the morning, he took out two pieces of paper. One of the blanks gave them a statement of the implements which they had to use, and the part of the yard in which they had to work. That required organization planning in advance.

One of the first principles we adopted was that no man in that labor gang could work on the new way unless he earned sixty percent higher wages than under the old plan. It is only just to the workman that he shall know right off whether he is doing his work right or not. He must not be told a week or month after, that he fell down. He must know it the next morning. So the next slip that came out of the pigeon hole was either a white or yellow slip. We used the two colors because some of the men could not read. The yellow slip meant that he had not earned his sixty percent higher wages. He knew that he could not stay in that gang and keep on getting yellow slips.

## TEACHING THE MEN

I want to show you again the totally different outlook there is under scientific management by illustrating what happened when that man got his yellow slips. Under the old scheme, the foreman could say to him, "You are no good, get out of this; no time for you, you cannot earn sixty percent higher wages; get out of this! Go!" It was not done politely, but the foreman had no

time to palaver. Under the new scheme what happened? A teacher of shoveling went down to see that man. A teacher of shoveling is a man who is handy with a shovel, who has made his mark in life with a shovel, and yet who is a kindly fellow and knows how to show the other fellow what he ought to do. When that teacher went there he said, "See here, Jim, you have a lot of those yellow slips, what is the matter with you? What is up? Have you been drunk? Are you tired? Are you sick? Anything wrong with you? Because if you are tired or sick we will give you a show somewhere else." "Well, no, I am all right." "Then if you are not sick, or there is nothing wrong with you, you have forgotten how to shovel. I showed you how to shovel. You have forgotten something, now go ahead and shovel and I will show you what is the matter with you." Shoveling is a pretty big science, it is not a little thing.

If you are going to use the shovel right you should always shovel off an iron bottom; if not an iron bottom, a wooden bottom; and if not a wooden bottom a hard dirt bottom. Time and again the conditions are such that you have to go right into the pile. When that is the case, with nine out of ten materials it takes more trouble and more time and more effort to get the shovel into the pile than to do all the rest of the shoveling. That is where the effort comes. Those of you again who have taught the art of shoveling will have taught your workmen to do this. There is only one way to do it right. Put your forearm down onto the upper part of your leg, and when you push into the pile, throw your weight against it. That relieves your arm of work. You then have an automatic push, we will say, about eighty pounds, the weight of your body thrown on to it. Time and again we would find men whom we had taught to shovel right were going at it in the same old way, and of course, they could not do a day's work. The teacher would simply stand over that fellow and say, "There is what is the matter with you, Jim, you have forgotten to shovel into the pile."

You are not interested in shoveling, you are not interested in whether one way or the other is right, but I do hope to interest you in the difference of the mental attitude of the men who are teaching under the new system. Under the new system, if a man falls down, the presumption is that it is our fault at first, that we probably have not taught the man right, have not given him a fair show, have not spent time enough in showing him how to do his work.

Let me tell you another thing that is characteristic of scientific management. In my day, we were smart enough to know when the boss was coming, and when he came up we were apparently really working. Under scientific management, there is none of that pretense. I cannot say that in the old days we were delighted to see the boss coming around. We always expected some kind of roast if he came too close. Under the new, the teacher is welcomed; he is not an enemy, but a friend. He comes there to try to help the man get bigger wages, to show him how to do something. It is the great mental change, the change in the outlook that comes, rather than the details of it.

## DOES SCIENTIFIC MANAGEMENT PAY?

It took the time of a number of men for about three years to study the art of shoveling in that yard at the Bethlehem Steel Works alone. They were carefully trained college men, and they were busy all the time. That costs money, the tool room costs money, the clerks we had to keep there all night figuring up how much the men did the day before cost money, the office in which the men laid out and planned the work cost money. The very fair and proper question, the only question to ask is "Does it pay?" because if scientific management does not pay in dollars and cents, it is the rankest kind of nonsense. There is nothing philanthropic about it. It has got to pay, because business which cannot be done on a profitable basis, ought not to be done on a philanthropic basis, for it will not last. At the end of three and one-half years we had a very good chance to know whether or not it paid.

Fortunately in the Bethlehem Steel Works they had records of how much it cost to handle the materials under the old system, where the single foreman led a group of men around the works. It costs them between seven and eight cents a ton to handle materials, on an average throughout the year. After paying for all this extra work I have told you about, it cost between three and four cents a ton to handle materials, and there was a profit of between seventy-five and eighty thousand dollars a year in that yard by handling those materials in the new way. What the men got out of it was this: Under the old system there were between four and six hundred men handling the material in that yard, and when we got through there were about one hundred and forty. Each one was earning a great deal more money. We made careful investigation and found they were almost all saving money, living better, happier; they are the most contented set of laborers to be seen anywhere. It is only by this kind of justification, justification of a profit for both sides, an advantage to both sides, that scientific management can exist.

I would like to give you one more illustration. I want to try to prove to you that even the highest class mechanic cannot possibly understand the philosophy of his work, cannot possibly understand the laws under which he has to operate. There is a man who has had a high school education, an ingenious fellow who courts variety in life, to whom it is pleasant to change from one kind of work to another. He is not a cheap man, he is rather a high grade man among the machinists of this country. The case of which I am going to tell you is one in which my friend Barth went to introduce scientific management in the works of an owner, who, at between 65 and 70 years of age, had built up his business from nothing to almost five thousand men. They had a squabble, and after they got through,

Mr. Barth made the proposition, "I will take any machine that you use in your shop, and I will show you that I can double the output of that machine." A very fair machine was selected. It was a lathe on which the workman had been working about twelve years. The product of that shop is a patented machine with a good many parts, 350 men working making those parts year in and year out. Each man had ten or a dozen parts a year.

The first thing that was done was in the presence of the foreman, the superintendent and the owner of the establishment. Mr. Barth laid down the way in which all of the parts were to be machined on that machine by the workman. Then Mr. Barth, with one of his small slide rules, proceeded to analyze the machine. With the aid of this analysis, which embodies the laws of cutting metals, Mr. Barth was able to take his turn at the machine; his gain was from two and one-half times to three times the amount of work turned out by the other man. This is what can be done by science as against the old rule of thumb knowledge. That is not exaggeration; the gain is as great as that in many cases.

Let me tell you something. The machines of this country, almost universally in the machine shops of our country, are speeded two or three hundred percent wrong. I made that assertion before the tool builders in Atlantic City. I said, "Gentlemen, in your own shops, many of your machines are two and three hundred percent wrong in speeds. Why? Because you have guessed at it." I am trying to show you what are the losses under the old opinions, the difference between knowledge on the one hand and guesswork on the other.

In 1882, at the end of a long fight with the machinists of the Midvale Steel Works, I went there as a laborer, and finally became a machinist after serving my apprenticeship outside. I finally got into the shop, and worked up to the place of a clerk who had something wrong with him. I then did a little bit more work than the others were doing, not too much. They came to me and said, "See here, Fred, you are not going to be a piecework hog." I said, "You fellows mean that you think I am not going to try to get any more work off these machines? I certainly am. Now I am on the other side, and I am going to be straight with you, and I will tell you so in advance." They said, "All right then, we will give you fair notice you will be outside the fence inside of six weeks." Let me tell you gentlemen, if any of you have been through a fight like that, trying to get workmen to do what they do not want to do, you will know the meanness of it, and you will never want to go into another one. I never would have gone into it if I had known what was ahead of me. After the meanest kind of a bitter fight, at the end of three years, we fairly won out and got a big increase in output. I had no illusion at the end of that time as to my great ability or anything else. I knew that those workmen knew about ten times as much as I did about doing the work. I set out deliberately to get on our side some of that knowledge that those workmen had.

Mr. William Sellers was the president, and he was a man away beyond his generation in progress. I went to him and said, "I want to spend quite a good deal of money trying to educate ourselves on the management side of our works. I do not know much of anything, and I am just about in the same condition as all the rest of the foremen around here." Very reluctantly, I may say, he allowed us to start to spend money. That started the study of the art of cutting metals. At the end of six months, from the standpoint of how to cut the metal off faster, the study did not amount to anything, but we unearthed a gold mine of information. Mr. Sellers laughed at me, but when I was able to show him the possibilities that lay ahead of us, the number of things we could find out, he said, "Go ahead." So until 1889, that experiment went straight ahead day in and day out. That was done because it paid in dollars and cents.

After I left the Midvale Steel Works, we had no means of figuring those experiments except the information which we had already gotten. Ten different machines were built to develop the art of cutting metals, so that almost continuously from 1882 for twenty-six years, all sorts of experiments went on to determine the twelve great elements that go to make up the art of cutting metals. I am trying to show you just what is going to take place in every industry throughout this world. You must know those facts if you are going to manufacture cheaply, and the only way to know them is to pay for them....

## THE EFFECT ON THE WORKMAN

Almost everyone says, "Why, yes, that may be a good thing for the manufacturer, but how about the workmen? You are taking all the initiative away from that workman, you are making a machine out of him; what are you doing for him? He becomes merely a part of the machine." That is the almost universal impression. Again let me try to sweep aside the fallacy of that view by an illustration. The modern surgeon without a doubt is the finest mechanic in the world. He combines the greatest manual dexterity with the greatest knowledge of implements and the greatest knowledge of materials on which he is working. He is a true scientist, and he is a very highly skilled mechanic.

How does the surgeon teach his trade to the young men who come to the medical school? Does he say to them, "Now, young men, we belong to an older generation than you do, but the new generation is going to far outstrip anything that has been done in our generation; therefore, what we want of you is your initiative. We must have your brains, your thought, with your initiative. Of course, you know we old fellows have certain prejudices. For example, if we were going to amputate a leg, when we come down to the bone we are accustomed to take a saw, and we use it in that way and saw the bone off. But, gentlemen, do not let that fact one minute interfere with your originality, with your initiative, if you prefer an axe or a hatchet." Does the surgeon say this? He does not. He says, "You young men are going to outstrip us, but we will show you how. You shall not use a single implement in a single way until you know just which one to use, and we will tell you which one to use, and until you know how to use it, we will tell you how to use that implement, and after you have learned to use that implement our way, if you then see any defects in the implements, any defects in the method, then invent; but, invent so that you can invent upwards. Do not go inventing things which we discarded years ago."

That is just what we say to our young men in the shops. Scientific management makes no pretense that there is any finality in it. We merely say that the collective work of thirty or forty men in this trade through eight or ten years has gathered together a large amount of data. Every man in the establishment must start that way, must start our way, then if he can show us any better way, I do not care what it is, we will make an experiment to see if it is better. It will be named after him, and he will get a prize for having improved on one of our standards. There is the way we make progress under scientific management. There is your justification for all this. It does not dwarf initiative, it makes true initiative. Most of our progress comes through our workmen, but comes in a legitimate way.

# 7
# Bureaucracy
*Max Weber*

## 1. CHARACTERISTICS OF BUREAUCRACY

Modern officialdom functions in the following specific manner:

*I. There is the principle of fixed and official jurisdictional areas, which are generally ordered by rules, that is, by laws or administrative regulations.*

1. The regular activities required for the purposes of the bureaucratically governed structure are distributed in a fixed way as official duties.

2. The authority to give the commands required for the discharge of these duties is distributed in a stable way and is strictly delimited by rules concerning the coercive means, physical, sacerdotal, or otherwise, which may be placed at the disposal of officials.

3. Methodical provision is made for the regular and continuous fulfillment of these duties and for the execution of the corresponding rights; only persons who have the generally regulated qualifications to serve are employed.

In public and lawful government these three elements constitute "bureaucratic authority." In private economic domination, they constitute bureaucratic "management." Bureaucracy, thus understood, is fully developed in political and ecclesiastical communities only in the modern state, and, in the private economy, only in the most advanced institutions of capitalism. Permanent and public office authority, with fixed jurisdiction, is not the historical rule but rather the exception. This is so even in large political structures such as those of the ancient Orient, the Germanic and Mongolian empires of conquest, or of many feudal structures of state. In all these cases, the ruler executes the most important measures through personal trustees, table-companions, or courtservants. Their commissions and authority are not precisely delimited and are temporarily called into being for each case.

*II. The principles of office hierarchy and of levels of graded authority mean a firmly ordered system of super- and subordination in which there is a supervision of the lower offices by the higher ones.* Such a system offers the governed the possibility of appealing the decision of a lower office to its higher authority, in a definitely regulated manner. With the full development of the bureaucratic type, the office hierarchy is monocratically organized. The principle of hierarchical office authority is found in all bureaucratic structures: in state and ecclesiastical structures as well as in large party organizations and private enterprises. It does not matter for the character of bureaucracy whether its authority is called "private" or "public."

When the principle of jurisdictional "competency" is fully carried through, hierarchical subordination—at least in public office—does not mean that the "higher" authority is simply authorized to take over the business of the "lower." Indeed, the opposite is the rule. Once established and

*Source: From Max Weber: Essays in Sociology* translated by Gerth and Mills (1973) 3259w from pp.196–204 © 1946, 1958, 1973 by H. H. Gerth and C. Wright Mills. By permission of Oxford University Press, USA.

having fulfilled its task, an office tends to continue in existence and be held by another incumbent.

**III. *The management of the modern office is based upon written documents ("the files"), which are preserved in their original or draught form.*** There is, therefore, a staff or subaltern officials and scribes of all sorts. The body of officials actively engaged in a "public" office, along with the respective apparatus of material implements and the files, make up a "bureau." In private enterprise, "the bureau" is often called "the office."

In principle, the modern organization of the civil service separates the bureau from the private domicile of the official, and, in general, bureaucracy segregates official activity as something distinct from the sphere of private life. Public monies and equipment are divorced from the private property of the official. This condition is everywhere the product of a long development. Nowadays, it is found in public as well as in private enterprises; in the latter, the principle extends even to the leading entrepreneur. In principle, the executive office is separated from the household, business from private correspondence, and business assets from private fortunes. The more consistently the modern type of business management has been carried through the more are these separations the case. The beginnings of this process are to be found as early as the Middle Ages.

It is the peculiarity of the modern entrepreneur that he conducts himself as the "first official" of his enterprise, in the very same way in which the ruler of a specifically modern bureaucratic state spoke of himself as "the first servant" of the state. The idea that the bureau activities of the state are intrinsically different in character from the management of private economic offices is a continental European notion and, by way of contrast, is totally foreign to the American way.

**IV. *Office management, at least all specialized office management—and such management is distinctly modern—usually presupposes thorough and expert training.*** This increasingly holds for the modern executive and employee of private enterprises, in the same manner as it holds for the state official.

**V. *When the office is fully developed, official activity demands the full working capacity of the official, irrespective of the fact that his obligatory time in the bureau may be firmly delimited.*** In the normal case, this is only the product of a long development, in the public as well as in the private office. Formerly, in all cases, the normal state of affairs was reversed: official business was discharged as a secondary activity.

**VI. *The management of the office follows general rules, which are more or less stable, more or less exhaustive, and which can be learned.*** Knowledge of these rules represents a special technical learning which the officials possess. It involves jurisprudence, or administrative or business management.

The reduction of modern office management to rules is deeply embedded in its very nature. The theory of modern public administration, for instance, assumes that the authority to order certain matters by decree—which has been legally granted to public authorities—does not entitle the bureau to regulate the matter by commands given for each case, but only to regulate the matter abstractly. This stands in extreme contrast to the regulation of all relationships through individual privileges and bestowals of favor, which is absolutely dominant in patrimonialism, at least in so far as such relationships are not fixed by sacred tradition.

## 2. THE POSITION OF THE OFFICIAL

All this results in the following for the internal and external position of the official:

*I. Office holding is a "vocation."* This is shown, first, in the requirement of a firmly prescribed course of training, which demands the entire capacity for work for a long period of time, and in the generally prescribed and special examinations which are prerequisites of employment. Furthermore, the position of the official is in the nature of a duty. This determines the internal structure of his relations, in the following manner: Legally and actually, office holding is not considered a source to be exploited for rents or emoluments, as was normally the case during the Middle Ages and frequently up to the threshold of recent times. Nor is office holding considered a usual exchange of services for equivalents, as is the case with free labor contracts. Entrance into an office, including one in the private economy, is considered an acceptance of a specific obligation of faithful management in return for a secure existence. It is decisive for the specific nature of modern loyalty to an office that, in the pure type, it does not establish a relationship to a person, like the vassal's or disciple's faith in feudal or in patrimonial relations of authority. Modern loyalty is devoted to impersonal and functional purposes. Behind the functional purposes, of course, "ideas of culture-values" usually stand. These are ersatz for the earthly or supra-mundane personal master: ideas such as "state," "church," "community," "party," or "enterprise" are thought of as being realized in a community; they provide an ideological halo for the master.

The political official—at least in the fully developed modern state—is not considered the personal servant of a ruler. Today, the bishop, the priest, and the preacher are in fact no longer, as in early Christian times, holders of purely personal charisma. The supra-mundane and sacred values which they offer are given to everybody who seems to be worthy of them and who asks for them. In former times, such leaders acted upon the personal command of their master; in principle, they were responsible only to him. Nowadays, in spite of the partial survival of the old theory, such religious leaders are officials in the service of a functional purpose, which in the present-day "church" has become routinized and, in turn, ideologically hallowed.

*II. The personal position of the official is patterned in the following way:*

1. Whether he is in a private office or a public bureau, the modern official always strives and usually enjoys a distinct *social esteem* as compared with the governed. His social position is guaranteed by the prescriptive rules of rank order and, for the political official, by special definitions of the criminal code against "insults of officials" and "contempt" of state and church authorities.

The actual social position of the official is normally highest where, as in old civilized countries, the following conditions prevail: a strong demand for administration by trained experts; a strong and stable social differentiation, where the official predominantly derives from socially and economically privileged strata because of the social distribution of power; or where the costliness of the required training and status conventions are binding upon him. The possession of educational certificates—to be discussed elsewhere—are usually linked with qualification for office. Naturally, such certificates or patents enhance the "status element" in the social position of the official. For the rest this status factor in individual cases is explicitly and impassively acknowledged; for example, in the prescription that the acceptance or rejection of an aspirant to an official career depends upon the consent ("election") of the members of the official body. This is the case in the German army with the officer corps. Similar phenomena, which promote this guild-like closure of officialdom, are typically found in patrimonial and, particularly, in prebendal officialdoms of the past. The desire to resurrect such phenomena in changed forms is by no means infrequent among modern bureaucrats. For instance, they have played a role among the demands of the quite proletarian and expert officials (the *tretyj* element) during the Russian revolution.

Usually the social esteem of the officials as such is especially low where the demand for expert administration and the dominance of status conventions are weak. This is especially the case in the United States; it is often the case in new settlements by virtue of their wide fields for profit-making and the great instability of their social stratification.

2. The pure type of bureaucratic official is *appointed* by a superior authority. An official elected by the governed is not a purely bureaucratic figure. Of course, the formal existence of an election does not by itself mean that no appointment hides behind the election—in the state, especially, appointment by party chiefs. Whether or not this is the case does not depend upon legal statutes but upon the way in which the party mechanism functions. Once firmly organized, the parties can turn a formally free election into the mere acclamation of a candidate designated by the party chief. As a rule, however, a formally free election is turned into a fight, conducted according to definite rules, for votes in favor of one of two designated candidates.

In all circumstances, the designation of officials by means of an election among the governed modifies the strictness of hierarchical subordination. In principle, an official who is so elected has an autonomous position opposite the superordinate official. The elected official does not derive his position "from above" but "from below," or at least not from a superior authority of the official hierarchy but from powerful party men ("bosses"), who also determine his further career. The career of the elected official is not, or at least not primarily, dependent upon his chief in the administration. The official who is not elected but appointed by a chief normally functions more exactly, from a technical point of view, because, all other circumstances being equal, it is more likely that purely functional points of consideration and qualities will determine

his selection and career. As laymen, the governed can become acquainted with the extent to which a candidate is expertly qualified for office only in terms of experience, and hence only after his service. Moreover, in every sort of selection of officials by election, parties quite naturally give decisive weight not to expert considerations but to the services a follower renders to the party boss. This holds for all kinds of procurement of officials by elections, for the designation of formally free, elected officials by party bosses when they determine the slate of candidates, or the free appointment by a chief who has himself been elected. The contrast, however, is relative: substantially similar conditions hold where legitimate monarchs and their subordinates appoint officials, except that the influence of the followings is then less controllable.

Where the demand for administration by trained experts is considerable, and the party followings have to recognize an intellectually developed, educated, and freely moving "public opinion," the use of unqualified officials falls back upon the party in power at the next election. Naturally, this is more likely to happen when the officials are appointed by the chief. The demand for a trained administration now exists in the United States, but in the large cities, where immigrant votes are "corralled," there is, of course, no educated public opinion. Therefore, popular elections of the administrative chief and also of his subordinate officials usually endanger the expert qualification of the official as well as the precise functioning of the bureaucratic mechanism. It also weakens the dependence of the officials upon the hierarchy. This holds at least for the large administrative bodies that are difficult to supervise. The superior qualification and integrity of federal judges, appointed by the President, as over against elected judges in the United States is well known, although both types of officials have been selected primarily in terms of party considerations. The great changes in American metropolitan administrations demanded by reformers have proceeded essentially from elected mayors working with an apparatus of officials who were appointed by them. These reforms have thus come about in a "Caesarist" fashion. Viewed technically, as an organized form of authority, the efficiency of "Caesarism," which often grows out of democracy, rests in general upon the position of the "Caesar" as a free trustee of the masses (of the army or of the citizenry), who is unfettered by tradition. The "Caesar" is thus the unrestrained master of a body of highly qualified military officers and officials whom he selects freely and personally without regard to tradition or to any other considerations. This "rule of the personal genius," however, stands in contradiction to the formally "democratic" principle of a universally elected officialdom.

3. Normally, the position of the official is held for life, at least in public bureaucracies; and this is increasingly the case for all similar structures. As a factual rule, *tenure for life* is presupposed, even where the giving of notice or periodic reappointment occurs. In contrast to the worker in a private enterprise, the official normally holds tenure. Legal or actual life-tenure, however, is not recognized as the official's right to the possession of office, as was the case with many structures of authority in the past. Where legal guarantees against arbitrary dismissal or transfer are developed, they merely serve to guarantee a strictly objective discharge of specific office duties free from all personal considerations. In Germany, this is the case for all juridical and, increasingly, for all administrative officials.

Within the bureaucracy, therefore, the measure of "independence," legally guaranteed by tenure, is not always a source of increased status for the official whose position is thus secured. Indeed, often the reverse holds, especially in old cultures and communities that are highly differentiated. In such communities, the stricter the subordination under the arbitrary rule of the master, the more it guarantees the maintenance of the conventional seigneurial style of living for the official. Because of the very absence of these legal guarantees of tenure, the conventional esteem for the official may rise in the same way as, during the Middle Ages, the esteem of the nobility of office rose at the expense of esteem for the freemen, and as the king's judge surpassed that of the people's judge. In Germany, the military officer or the administrative official can be removed from office at any time, or at least far more readily than the "independent judge," who never pays with loss of his office for even the grossest offense against the "code of honor" or against social conventions of the salon. For this very reason, if other things are equal, in the eyes of the master stratum the judge is considered less qualified for social intercourse than are officers and administrative officials, whose greater dependence on the master is a greater guarantee of their conformity with status conventions. Of course, the average official strives for a civil-service law, which would materially secure his old age and provide increased guarantees against his arbitrary removal from office. This striving, however, has its limits. A very strong development of the "right to the office" naturally makes it more difficult to staff them with regard to technical efficiency, for such a development decreases the career opportunities of ambitious candidates for office. This makes for the fact that officials, on the whole, do not feel their dependency upon those at the top. This lack of a feeling of dependency, however, rests primarily upon the inclination to depend upon one's equals rather than upon the socially inferior and governed strata. The present conservative movement among the Badenia clergy, occasioned by the anxiety of a presumably threatening separation of church and state, has been expressly determined by the desire not to be turned "from a master into a servant of the parish."

4. The official receives the regular *pecuniary* compensation of a normally fixed *salary* and the old age security provided by a pension. The salary is not measured like a wage in terms of work done, but according to "status," that is, according to the kind of function (the "rank") and, in addition, possibly, according to the length of service. The relatively great security of the official's income, as well as the rewards of social esteem, make the office a sought-after position, especially in countries which no longer provide opportunities for colonial profits. In such countries, this situation permits relatively low salaries for officials.

5. The official is set for a *"career"* within the hierarchical order of the public service. He moves from the lower, less important, and lower paid to the higher positions. The average official naturally desires a mechanical fixing of the conditions of promotion: if not of the offices, at least of the salary levels. He wants these conditions fixed in terms of "seniority," or possibly according to grades achieved in a developed system of expert examinations. Here and there, such examinations actually form a character *indelebilis* of the official and have lifelong effects on his career. To this is joined the desire to qualify the right to office and the increasing tendency toward status group closure and economic security. All of this makes for a tendency to consider the offices as "prebends" of those who are qualified by educational certificates. The necessity of taking general personal and intellectual qualifications into consideration, irrespective of the often subaltern character of the education certificate, has led to a condition in which the highest political offices, especially the positions of "ministers," are principally filled without reference to such certificates.

# 8

# Notes on the Theory of Organization

*Luther Gulick*

Every large-scale or complicated enterprise requires many men to carry it forward. Wherever many men are thus working together the best results are secured when there is a division of work among these men. The theory of organization, therefore, has to do with the structure of co-ordination imposed upon the work-division units of an enterprise. Hence it is not possible to determine how an activity is to be organized without, at the same time, considering how the work in question is to be divided. Work division is the foundation of organization; indeed, the reason for organization.

## 1. THE DIVISION OF WORK

It is appropriate at the outset of this discussion to consider the reasons for and the effect of the division of work. It is sufficient for our purpose to note the following factors.

### Why Divide Work?

Because men differ in nature, capacity, and skill, and gain greatly in dexterity by specialization; because the same man cannot be at two places at the same time; because the range of knowledge and skill is so great that a man cannot within his lifespan know more than a small fraction of it. In other words, it is a question of human nature, time, and space.

In a shoe factory it would be possible to have 1,000 men each assigned to making complete pairs of shoes. Each man would cut his leather, stamp in the eyelets, sew up the tops, sew on the bottoms, nail on the heels, put in the laces, and pack each pair in a box. It might take two days to do the job. One thousand men would make 500 pairs of shoes a day. It would also be possible to divide the work among these same men, using the identical hand methods, in an entirely different way. One group of men would be assigned to cut the leather, another to putting in the eyelets, another to stitching up the tops, another to sewing on the soles, another to nailing on the heels, another to inserting the laces and packing the pairs of shoes. We know from common sense and experience that there are two great gains in this latter process: first, it makes possible the better utilization of the varying skills and aptitudes of the different workmen, and encourages the development of specialization; and second, it eliminates the time that is lost when a workman turns from a knife, to a punch, to a needle and awl, to a hammer, and moves from table to bench, to anvil, to stool. Without any pressure on the workers, they could probably turn out twice as many shoes in a single day. There would be additional economies, because inserting laces and packing could be assigned to unskilled and low-paid workers. Moreover, in the cutting of the leather there would be less spoilage because the less skillful pattern cutters would be eliminated and assigned to other work. It would also be possible to cut a dozen shoe tops at the same time from the same pattern with little additional effort. All of these advances would follow, without the introduction of new labor saving machinery.

The introduction of machinery accentuates the division of work. Even such a

*Source: Papers on the Science of Administration*, ed. Luther Gulick and Lyndall Urwick. New York: Institute of Public Administration, 1937, 3–13.

simple thing as a saw, a typewriter, or a transit requires increased specialization, and serves to divide workers into those who can and those who cannot use the particular instrument effectively. Division of work on the basis of the tools and machines used in work rests no doubt in part on aptitude, but primarily upon the development and maintenance of skill through continued manipulation.

Specialized skills are developed not alone in connection with machines and tools. They evolve naturally from the materials handled, like wood, or cattle, or paint, or cement. They arise similarly in activities which center in a complicated series of interrelated concepts, principles, and techniques. These are most clearly recognized in the professions, particularly those based on the application of scientific knowledge, as in engineering, medicine, and chemistry. They are none the less equally present in law, ministry, teaching, accountancy, navigation, aviation, and other fields.

The nature of these subdivisions is essentially pragmatic, in spite of the fact that there is an element of logic underlying them. They are therefore subject to a gradual evolution with the advance of science, the invention of new machines, the progress of technology and the change of the social system. In the last analysis, however, they appear to be based upon differences in individual human beings. But it is not to be concluded that the apparent stability of "human nature," whatever that may be, limits the probable development of specialization. The situation is quite the reverse. As each field of knowledge and work is advanced, constituting a continually larger and more complicated nexus of related principles, practices and skills, any individual will be less and less able to encompass it and maintain intimate knowledge and facility over the entire area, and there will thus arise a more minute specialization because knowledge and skill advance while man stands still. Division of work and integrated organization are the bootstraps by which mankind lifts itself in the process of civilization.

## The Limits of Division

There are three clear limitations beyond which the division of work cannot to advantage go. The first is practical and arises from the volume of work involved in man-hours. Nothing is gained by subdividing work if that further subdivision results in setting up a task which requires less than the full time of one man. This is too obvious to need demonstration. The only exception arises where space interferes, and in such cases the part-time expert must fill in his spare time at other tasks, so that as a matter of fact a new combination is introduced.

The second limitation arises from technology and custom at a given time and place. In some areas nothing would be gained by separating undertaking from the custody and cleaning of churches, because by custom the sexton is the undertaker; in building construction it is extraordinarily difficult to redivide certain aspects of electrical and plumbing work and to combine them in a more effective way, because of the jurisdictional conflicts of craft unions; and it is clearly impracticable to establish a division of cost accounting in a field in which no technique of costing has yet been developed.

This second limitation is obviously elastic. It may be changed by invention and by education. If this were not the fact, we should face a static division of labor. It should be noted, however, that a marked change has two dangers. It greatly restricts the labor market from which workers may be drawn and greatly lessens the opportunities open to those who are trained for the particular specialization.

The third limitation is that the subdivision of work must not pass beyond physical division into organic division. It might seem far more efficient to have the front half of the cow in the pasture grazing and the rear half in the barn being milked all of the time, but this organic division would fail. Similarly there is no gain from splitting a single movement or gesture like licking an envelope, or tearing apart a series of intimately and intricately related activities.

It may be said that there is in this an element of reasoning in a circle; that the test here applied as to whether an activity is organic or not is whether it is divisible or not—which is what we set out to define. This charge is true. It must be a pragmatic test. Does the division work out? Is something vital destroyed and lost? Does it bleed?

### The Whole and the Parts

It is axiomatic that the whole is equal to the sum of its parts. But in dividing up any "whole," one must be certain that every part, including unseen elements and relationships, is accounted for. The marble sand to which the Venus de Milo may be reduced by a vandal does not equal the statue, though every last grain be preserved; nor is a thrush just so much feathers, bones, flesh, and blood; nor a typewriter merely so much steel, glass, paint, and rubber. Similarly a piece of work to be done cannot be subdivided into the obvious component parts without great danger that the central design, the operating relationships, the imprisoned idea, will be lost....

When one man builds a house alone he plans as he works; he decides what to do first and what next, that is, he "co-ordinates the work." When many men work together to build a house this part of the work, the co-ordinating, must not be lost sight of.

In the "division of the work" among the various skilled specialists, a specialist in planning and coordination must be sought as well. Otherwise, a great deal of time may be lost, workers may get in each other's way, material may not be on hand when needed, things may be done in the wrong order, and there may even be a difference of opinion as to where the various doors and windows are to go. It is self-evident that the more the work is subdivided, the greater is the danger of confusion, and the greater is the need of overall supervision and coordination. Co-ordination is not something that develops by accident. It must be won by intelligent, vigorous, persistent, and organized effort.

## 2. THE CO-ORDINATION OF WORK

If subdivision of work is inescapable, co-ordination becomes mandatory. There is, however, no one way to co-ordinate. Experience shows that it may be achieved in two primary ways. These are:

1. By organization, that is, by interrelating the subdivisions of work by allotting them to men who are placed in a structure of authority, so that the work may be co-ordinated by orders of superiors to subordinates, reaching from the top to the bottom of the entire enterprise.
2. By the dominance of an idea, that is, the development of intelligent singleness of purpose in the minds and wills of those who are working together as a group, so that each worker will of his own accord fit his task into the whole with skill and enthusiasm.

These two principles of co-ordination are not mutually exclusive, in fact, no enterprise is really effective without the extensive utilization of both.

Size and time are the great limiting factors in the development of co-ordination. In a small project, the problem is not difficult; the structure of authority is simple, and the central purpose is real to every worker. In a large complicated enterprise, the organization becomes involved, the lines of authority tangled, and there is danger that the workers will forget that there is any central purpose, and so devote their best energies only to their own individual advancement and advantage.

The interrelated elements of time and habit are extraordinarily important in co-ordination. Man is a creature of habit. When an enterprise is built up gradually from small beginnings the staff can be "broken in" step by step. And when difficulties develop, they can be ironed out, and the new method followed from that point on as a matter of habit, with the knowledge that that particular difficulty will not develop again. Routines may even be mastered by drill as they are in the army. When, however, a large new enterprise must be set up or altered overnight, then the real difficulties of coordination make their appearance. The factor of habit, which is thus an important foundation of co-ordination when time is available, becomes a serious handicap when time is not available, that is, when rules change. The question of co-ordination therefore must be approached with different emphasis in small and in large enterprises; in simple and in complex situations; in stable and in new or changing organizations.

### Co-ordination through Organization

Organization as a way of co-ordination requires the establishment of a system of authority whereby the central purpose or objective of an enterprise is translated into reality through the combined efforts of many specialists, each working in his own field at a particular time and place.

It is clear from long experience in human affairs that such a structure of authority requires not only many men at work in many places at selected times, but also a single directing executive authority.[1] The problem of organization thus becomes the problem of building up between the executive at the center and the subdivisions of work on the periphery of an effective network of communication and control.

The following outline may serve further to define the problem:

I. First Step: Define the job to be done, such as the furnishing of pure water to all of the people and industries within a given area at the lowest possible cost;

II. Second Step: Provide a director to see that the objective is realized;

III. Third Step: Determine the nature and number of individualized and specialized work units into which the job will have to be divided. As has been seen above, this subdivision depends partly upon the size of the job (no ultimate subdivision can generally be so small as to require less than the full time of one worker) and upon the status of technological and social development at a given time;

IV. Fourth Step: Establish and perfect the structure of authority between the director and the ultimate work subdivisions.

It is this fourth step which is the central concern of the theory of organization. It is the function of this organization (IV) to enable the director (II) to co-ordinate and energize all of the subdivisions of work (III) so that the major objective (I) may be achieved efficiently.

### The Span of Control

In this undertaking we are confronted at the start by the inexorable limits of human nature. Just as the hand of man can span only a limited number of notes on the piano, so the mind and will of man can span but a limited number of immediate managerial contacts. The problem has been discussed brilliantly by Graicunas in his paper included in this collection. The limit of control is partly a matter of the limits of knowledge, but even more is it a matter of the limits of time and of energy. As a result the executive of any enterprise can personally direct only a few persons. He must depend upon these to direct others, and upon them in turn to direct still others, until the last man in the organization is reached....

But when we seek to determine how many immediate subordinates the director of an enterprise can effectively supervise, we enter a realm of experience which has not been brought under sufficient scientific study to furnish a final answer. Sir Ian Hamilton says, "The nearer we approach the supreme head of the whole organization, the more we ought to work towards groups of three; the closer we get to the foot of the whole organization (the Infantry of the Line), the more we work towards groups of six."[2]

The British Machinery of Government Committee of 1918 arrived at the conclusions that "The Cabinet should be small in number—preferably ten or, at most, twelve."[3]

Henri Fayol said "[In France] a minister has twenty assistants, where the

Administrative Theory says that a manager at the head of a big undertaking should not have more than five or six."[4]

Graham Wallas expressed the opinion that the cabinet should not be increased "beyond the number of ten or twelve at which organized oral discussion is most efficient."[5]

Léon Blum recommended for France a prime minister with a technical cabinet modelled after the British War Cabinet, which was composed of five members.[6]

It is not difficult to understand why there is this divergence of statement among authorities who are agreed on the fundamentals. It arises in part from the differences in the capacities and work habits of individual executives observed, and in part from the noncomparable character of the work covered. It would seem that insufficient attention has been devoted to three factors: first, the element of diversification of function; second, the element of time; and third, the element of space. A chief of public works can deal effectively with more direct subordinates than can the general of the army, because all of his immediate subordinates in the department of public works will be in the general field of engineering, while in the army there will be many different elements, such as communications, chemistry, aviation, ordinance, motorized service, engineering, supply, transportation, etc., each with its own technology. The element of time is also of great significance as has been indicated above. In a stable organization the chief executive can deal with more immediate subordinates than in a new or changing organization. Similarly, space influences the span of control. An organization located in one building can be supervised through more immediate subordinates than can the same organization if scattered in several cities. When scattered there is not only need for more supervision, and therefore more supervisory personnel, but also for a fewer number of contacts with the chief executive because of the increased difficulty faced by the chief executive in learning sufficient details about a far-flung organization to do an intelligent job. The failure to attach sufficient importance to these variables has served to limit the scientific validity of the statements which have been made that one man can supervise but three, or five, or eight, or twelve immediate subordinates.

These considerations do not, however, dispose of the problem. They indicate rather the need for further research. But without further research we may conclude that the chief executive of an organization can deal with only a few immediate subordinates; that this number is determined not only by the nature of the work, but also by the nature of the executive; and that the number of immediate subordinates in a large, diversified and dispersed organization must be even less than in a homogeneous and unified organization to achieve the same measure of co-ordination.

### One Master

From the earliest times it has been recognized that nothing but confusion arises under multiple command. "A man cannot serve two masters" was adduced as a theological argument because it was already accepted as a principle of human relation in everyday life. In administration this is known as the principle of "unity of command."[7] The principle may be stated as follows: A workman subject to orders from several superiors will be confused, inefficient, and irresponsible; a workman subject to orders from but one superior may be methodical, efficient, and responsible. Unity of command thus refers to those who are commanded, not to those who issue the commands.[8]

The significance of this principle in the process of co-ordination and organization must not be lost sight of. In building a structure of co-ordination, it is often tempting to set up more than one boss for a man who is doing work which has more than one relationship. Even as great a philosopher of management as Taylor fell into this error in setting up separate foremen to deal with machinery, with materials, with speed, etc., each with the power of giving orders directly to the individual workman.[9] The rigid adherence to the principle of unity of command may have its absurdities; these are, however, unimportant in comparison with the certainty of confusion, inefficiency and irresponsibility which arise from the violation of the principle.

### Technical Efficiency

There are many aspects of the problem of securing technical efficiency. Most of these do not concern us here directly. They have been treated extensively by such authorities as Taylor, Dennison, and Kimball, and their implications for general organization by Fayol, Urwick, Mooney, and Reiley. There is, however, one efficiency concept which concerns us deeply in approaching the theory of organization. It is the principle of homogeneity.

It has been observed by authorities in many fields that the efficiency of a group working together is directly related to the homogeneity of the work they are performing, of the processes they are utilizing, and of the purposes which actuate them. From top to bottom, the group must be unified. It must work together.

It follows from this (1) that any organizational structure which brings together in a single unit work divisions which are non-homogeneous in work, in technology, or in purpose will encounter the danger of friction and inefficiency; and (2) that a unit based on a given specialization cannot be given technical direction by a layman.

In the realm of government it is not difficult to find many illustrations of the unsatisfactory results of non-homogeneous administrative combinations. It is generally agreed that agricultural development and education cannot be administered by the same men who enforce pest and disease control, because the success of the former rests upon friendly co-operation and trust of the farmers, while the latter engenders resentment and suspicion. Similarly, activities

like drug control established in protection of the consumer do not find appropriate homes in departments dominated by the interests of the producer. In the larger cities and in states it has been found that hospitals cannot be so well administered by the health department directly as they can be when set up independently in a separate department, or at least in a bureau with an extensive autonomy, and it is generally agreed that public welfare administration and police administration require separation, as do public health administration and welfare administration, though both of these combinations may be found in successful operation under special conditions. No one would think of combining water supply and public education, or tax administration and public recreation. In every one of these cases, it will be seen that there is some element either of work to be done, or of the technology used, or of the end sought which is non-homogeneous.

Another phase of the combination of incompatible functions in the same office may be found in the common American practice of appointing unqualified laymen and politicians to technical positions or to give technical direction to highly specialized services. As Dr. Frank J. Goodnow pointed out a generation ago, we are faced here by two heterogeneous functions, "politics" and "administration," the combination of which cannot be undertaken within the structure of the administration without producing inefficiency.

### Caveamus Expertum

At this point a word of caution is necessary. The application of the principle of homogeneity has its pitfalls. Every highly trained technician, particularly in the learned professions, has a profound sense of omniscience and a great desire for complete independence in the service of society. When employed by government he knows exactly what the people need better than they do themselves, and he knows how to render this service. He tends to be utterly oblivious of all other needs, because, after all, is not his particular technology the road to salvation? Any restraint applied to him is "limitation of freedom," and any criticism "springs from ignorance and jealousy." Every budget increase he secures is "in the public interest," while every increase secured elsewhere is "a sheer waste." His efforts and maneuvers to expand are "public education" and "civic organization," while similar efforts by others are "propaganda" and "politics."

Another trait of the expert is his tendency to assume knowledge and authority in fields in which he has no competence. In this particular, educators, lawyers, priests, admirals, doctors, scientists, engineers, accountants, merchants, and bankers are all the same—having achieved technical competence or "success" in one field, they come to think this competence is a general quality detachable from the field and inherent in themselves. They step without embarrassment into other areas. They do not remember that the robes of authority of one kingdom confer no sovereignty in another; but that there they are merely a masquerade.

The expert knows his "stuff." Society needs him, and must have him more and more as man's technical knowledge becomes more and more extensive. But history shows us that the common man is a better judge of his own needs in the long run than any cult of experts. Kings and ruling classes, priests and prophets, soldiers, and lawyers, when permitted to rule rather than serve mankind, have in the end done more to check the advance of human welfare than they have to advance it. The true place of the expert is, as A. E. said so well, "on tap, not on top." The essential validity of democracy rests upon this philosophy, for democracy is a way of government in which the common man is the final judge of what is good for him.

Efficiency is one of the things that is good for him because it makes life richer and safer. That efficiency is to be secured more and more through the use of technical

specialists. These specialists have no right to ask for, and must not be given freedom from supervisory control, but in establishing that control, a government which ignores the conditions of efficiency cannot expect to achieve efficiency.

## 3. ORGANIZATIONAL PATTERNS

### *Organization Up or Down?*

One of the great sources of confusion in the discussion of the theory of organization is that some authorities work and think primarily from the top down, while others work and think from the bottom up. This is perfectly natural because some authorities are interested primarily in the executive and in the problems of central management, while others are interested primarily in individual services and activities. Those who work from the top down regard the organization as a system of subdividing the enterprise under the chief executive, while those who work from the bottom up, look upon organization as a system of combining the individual units of work into aggregates which are in turn subordinated to the chief executive. It may be argued that either approach leads to a consideration of the entire problem, so that it is of no great significance which way the organization is viewed. Certainly it makes this very important practical difference: those who work from the top down must guard themselves from the danger of sacrificing the effectiveness of the individual services in their zeal to achieve a model structure at the top, while those who start from the bottom, must guard themselves from the danger of thwarting coordination in their eagerness to develop effective individual services.

In any practical situation the problem of organization must be approached from both top and bottom. This is particularly true in the reorganization of a going concern. May it not be that this practical necessity is likewise the sound process theoretically? In that case one would develop the plan of an organization or reorganization both from the top downward and from the bottom upward, and would reconcile the two at the center. In planning the first subdivisions under the chief executive, the principle of the limitation of the span of control must apply; in building up the first aggregates of specialized functions, the principle of homogeneity must apply. If any enterprise has such an array of functions that the first subdivisions from the top down do not readily meet the first aggregations from the bottom up, then additional divisions and additional aggregates must be introduced, but at each further step there must be a less and less rigorous adherence to the two conflicting principles until their juncture is effected....

### Organizing the Executive

The effect of the suggestion presented above is to organize and institutionalize the executive function as such so that it may be more adequate in a complicated situation. This is in reality not a new idea. We do not, for example, expect the chief executive to write his own letters. We give him a private secretary, who is part of his office and assists him to do this part of his job. This secretary is not a part of any department, he is a subdivision of the executive himself. In just this way, though on a different plane, other phases of the job of the chief executive may be organized.

Before doing this, however, it is necessary to have a clear picture of the job itself. This brings us directly to the question, "What is the work of the chief executive? What does he do?"

The answer is POSDCORB.

POSDCORB is, of course, a made-up word designed to call attention to the various functional elements of the work of a chief executive because "administration" and "management" have lost all specific content.[10] POSDCORB is made up of

the initials and stands for the following activities:

Planning, that is working out in broad outline the things that need to be done and the methods for doing them to accomplish the purpose set for the enterprise;

Organizing, that is the establishment of the formal structure of authority through which work subdivisions are arranged, defined, and co-ordinated for the defined objective;

Staffing, that is the whole personnel function of bringing in and training the staff and maintaining favorable conditions of work;

Directing, that is the continuous task of making decisions and embodying them in specific and general orders and instructions and serving as the leader of the enterprise;

Co-ordinating, that is the all important duty of interrelating the various parts of the work;

Reporting, that is keeping those to whom the executive is responsible informed as to what is going on, which thus includes keeping himself and his subordinates informed through records, research, and inspection;

Budgeting, with all that goes with budgeting in the form of fiscal planning, accounting, and control.

This statement of the work of a chief executive is adapted from the functional analysis elaborated by Henri Fayol in his "Industrial and General Administration." It is believed that those who know administration intimately will find in this analysis a valid and helpful pattern, into which can be fitted each of the major activities and duties of any chief executive.

If these seven elements may be accepted as the major duties of the chief executive, it follows that they *may* be separately organized as subdivisions of the executive. The need for such subdivision depends entirely on the size and complexity of the enterprise. In the largest enterprises, particularly where the chief executive is as a matter of fact unable to do the work that is thrown upon him, it may be presumed that one or more parts of POSDCORB should be suborganized.

## NOTES

1. i.e., when *organization is the basis of co-ordination*. Wherever the central executive authority is composed of several who exercise their functions jointly by majority vote, as on a board, this is from the standpoint of organization still a "single authority"; where the central executive is in reality composed of several men acting freely and independently, then organization cannot be said to be the basis of co-ordination; it is rather the dominance of an idea and falls under the second principle stated above.

2. Sir Ian Hamilton, "The Soul and Body of an Army." Arnold, London, 1921, p. 230.

3. Great Britain. Ministry of Reconstruction. Report of the Machinery of Government Committee. H. M. Stationery Office, London, 1918, p. 5.

4. Henri Fayol, "The Administrative Theory in the State." Address before the Second International Congress of Administrative Science at Brussels, September 13, 1923.

5. Graham Wallas, "The Great Society." Macmillan, London and New York, 1919, p. 264.

6. Léon Blum, "La Réforme Gouvernementale." Grasset, Paris, 1918. Reprinted in 1936, p. 59.

7. Henri Fayol, "Industrial and General Administration." English translation by J. A. Coubrough. International Management Association, Geneva, 1930.

8. Fayol terms the latter "unity of direction."

9. Frederick Winslow Taylor, "Shop Management." Harper and Brothers, New York and London, 1911, p. 99.

10. See Minutes of the Princeton Conference on Training for the Public Service, 1935, p. 35. See also criticism of this analysis in Lewis Meriam, "Public Service and Special Training." University of Chicago Press, 1936, pp. 1, 2, 10, and 15, where this functional analysis is misinterpreted as a statement of qualifications for appointment.

# CHAPTER 2

# *Neoclassical Organization Theory*

There is no precise definition of the term "neoclassical" in the context of organization theory. Basically, this theoretical perspective revises and/or criticizes classical organization theory—particularly for minimizing the humanness of organizational members, the coordination needs of administrative units, internal-external organizational relations, and decision-making processes. Most work in classical organization theory occurred before World War II. Neoclassical writers gained their reputations by attacking the classical organizational theorists from 1945 through the 1950s. Because classical theories were largely derived intellectually rather than empirically, their artificial assumptions left them vulnerable to attack. For example, classical theorists thought that organizations should be based on universally applicable scientific principles.

In spite of their frequent and vigorous attacks on the classicalists, the neoclassicalists did not develop a body of theory that could adequately replace the classical school. The neoclassicalists modified, added to, and somewhat extended classical theory. They attempted to blend assumptions of classical theory with concepts that were subsequently used by later organization theorists from all perspectives. The neoclassical school tried to save classical theory by introducing modifications based upon research findings in the behavioral sciences. It did not have a bona fide theory of its own. To a great extent, the neoclassisical school was an "anti-school," but it stopped short of seeking to destroy classical theory.

Despite its limitations, the neoclassical era was extremely important in the development of organization theory. But, like a rebellious teenager, neoclassical theory could not permanently stand on its own. It was a transitional, somewhat reactionary school, although important for several reasons. First, it moved away from the overly simplistic, mechanistic views of classical organization theory. The neoclassicalists challenged some of the basic tenets of the classical theories *head on*. And remember, the classical school was the only school in existence at that time. Organization theory and classical organization theory were virtually synonymous.

Second, in the process of challenging the classical theories, neoclassicalists raised issues and initiated theories that became central to most of the schools that have followed. The neoclassicalists were crucially important forerunners. Most of the serious post-1960 articles from *any* school of organization cite neoclassical theorists. All the neoclassical selections included in this chapter are important precursors of the human relations, "modern" structural, systems, power and politics, and organizational culture perspectives of organization theory.

In the opening chapter, Introduction to Organization Theory, we noted that most groupings of theories into schools or perspectives are based on two variables: shared views about organizations *and* the period in time during which the most important works were written. The giants of the neoclassical era include Chester Barnard, James March and his colleagues, Philip Selznick, and Herbert Simon. This does not mean, however, that their significance ended with their neoclassical-era work. These theorists have continued to make major contributions well into the twenty-first century—contributions that have extended beyond the neoclassical era and the neoclassical perspective.

Chester Barnard's purposes in writing *The Functions of the Executive* were ambitious. He sought to create a comprehensive theory of behavior in organizations. The primary responsibilities of an executive are (1) to create and maintain a sense of purpose and a *moral code* for the organization—a set of ethical visions that establish "*right* or *wrong* in a moral sense, of deep feeling, of innate conviction, not arguable; emotional, not intellectual in character" (1938, p. 266); (2) to establish systems of formal and informal communication; and (3) to ensure the willingness of people to cooperate. The need for people in organizations to cooperate—to enlist others to help accomplish tasks that individuals could not accomplish alone is paramount, and it is the executive's *moral imperative* to steer that cooperation.

Barnard argued that individuals must be induced to cooperate, because to do otherwise would result in dissolution of the organization or, at the least, in changes of organizational purpose. In "Chester I. Barnard and the Guardians of the Managerial State: The Moral Obligations of the Elite," reprinted in this chapter, William G. Scott explains why Barnard viewed the creation of a *moral code* as a *moral imperative* for executives—who are the "elites." In essence, executives are not accountable to anyone for their decisions.

> .... management accountability is a worrisome issue [for Barnard] ... Politically managers are not held accountable because there are no mechanisms ... to bring them to task for poor judgment or shaky performance....

> Finally, there is the language barrier. It ensures that no one in business, government, education or labor can articulate to anyone else how organizations work, how decisions are made, and why certain goals are selected and not others..... Therefore, it is no wonder that Barnard decided that management was mainly accountable to itself....

Thus, the moral imperative for executives is to create *moral codes* to provide direction for collective behavior in their organizations. Executives are the elites. They are accountable only to themselves. Without accountability to others, organizations are at risk of becoming immoral unless executives create moral codes.

Herbert A. Simon was one of the first neoclassicalists to raise serious challenges to classical organization theory. Simon didn't just criticize classical theory, he attacked it. In his widely quoted 1946 *Public Administration Review* article, "The Proverbs of Administration," Simon is devastating in his criticism of the classical approach to "general principles of management," such as those proposed by Fayol, Gulick, and others, as being inconsistent, conflicting, and inapplicable to many of the administrative situations facing managers. He argued persuasively that "principles" such as "span of control" and "unity of command" could, with equal logic, be applied in diametrically opposite ways to the same set of circumstances. Simon concluded that the so-called principles of administration were instead proverbs of administration. The basic themes of the article were incorporated in his landmark book, *Administrative Behavior*, originally published in 1947. The fourth edition (1997) is the most recent.

One of the major themes of neoclassical organization theorists was that organizations did not and could not exist as self-contained islands isolated from their environments. As might be expected, the first significant efforts to "open up" organizations (theoretically speaking) came from analysts whose professional identities required them to take a broad view of things: sociologists. One such sociologist, Philip Selznick, in his 1948 *American Sociological Review* article, "Foundations of the Theory of Organization" (reprinted here), asserted that while it is possible to describe and design organizations in a purely rational manner, such efforts can never hope to cope with the nonrational aspects of organizational behavior. Selznick maintained that organizations consist not simply of a number of positions for management to control, but of individuals, whose goals and aspirations might not coincide with the formal goals of the organization. Selznick is perhaps best known for his concept of "co-optation," which describes the organization's process of bringing and subsuming new elements into its policy-making process to prevent such factors from becoming a threat to the organization or its mission. The fullest account of Selznick's "co-optation" is found in *TVA and the Grass Roots*, his 1949 case study of how the Tennessee Valley Authority first gained local support for its programs. Selznick's approach to studying organizations and his intellectual distinction between the concepts of "organization" and "institution" have been held up as exemplary models of organizational theory's insightfulness and usefulness by writers on organizational culture (see Chapters 7 and 8).

Many other sociologists have made important contributions to the neoclassical school and to the general development of the field of organization theory:

- Melville Dalton (1950, 1959/2014) focused on structural frictions between line and staff units and between the central office of an organization and geographically dispersed facilities. His work drew attention to some universal conflict within organizations and to problems of educating and socializing managers.
- Talcott Parsons introduced the general theory of social systems as an approach to the analysis of formal organizations. In his 1956 article, "Suggestions for a Sociological Approach to the Theory of Organizations," Parsons defined an organization as a social system that focuses on the attainment of specific goals and contributes, in turn, to the accomplishment of goals of a more comprehensive system, such as the larger organization or even society itself.
- William F. Whyte (1948) studied human relations in the restaurant business to understand and describe stresses that result from interrelations and status differences in the workplace.

As we mentioned earlier, Herbert Simon and his associates at the Carnegie Institute of Technology (now Carnegie-Mellon University) also were major developers of theories of organizational decision making. Simon believed that decision making should be the focus of a new "administrative science." He asserted (1947) that organizational theory is, in fact, the theory of the bounded rationality of human beings who "satisfice" because they do not have the intellectual capacity to maximize. Simon (1960) also distinguished between "programmed" and "unprogrammed" organizational decisions and highlighted the importance of this distinction for management information systems. His work on administrative science and decision making went in two major directions. First, he was a pioneer in developing the "science" of improved organizational decision making through quantitative methods, such as operations research and computer technology. Second, and perhaps even more important, he was a leader in studying the processes by which administrative organizations make decisions. Herbert Simon's extensive contributions continue to influence the field of organization theory.

Thus, the neoclassical school played a very important role in the evolution of organization theory. Its writers provided the intellectual and empirical impetus to break the classicalists' simplistic, mechanically oriented, monopolistic dominance of the field. Neoclassicalists also paved the way and opened the door for the soon-to-follow explosions of thinking from the human relations, "modern" structural, systems, power and politics, and organizational culture perspectives of organizations.

## BIBLIOGRAPHY

Barnard, C. I. (1938, 1968). *The functions of the executive*. Cambridge, MA: Harvard University Press.

Cyert, R. M., & J. G. March (1959). Behavioral theory of organizational objectives. In M. Haire, ed., *Modern organization theory* (pp. 76–90). New York: Wiley.

Cyert, R. M., & J. G. March (1963). *A behavioral theory of the firm*. Englewood Cliffs, NJ: Prentice Hall.

Dalton, M. (1950, June). Conflicts between staff and line managerial officers. *American Sociological Review, 15*, 342–351.

Dalton, M. (1959). *Men who manage*. New York: Wiley. Republished in 2014 by Transaction Publishers, Piscataway, NJ.

Durkheim, E. (1947). *The division of labor in society*. Trans. George Simpson. New York: Free Press. (Originally published in 1893.)

Etzioni, A. (1961). *A comparative analysis of complex organizations*. New York: Free Press.

Etzioni, A. (1964). *Modern organizations*. Englewood Cliffs, NJ: Prentice-Hall, Inc.

Gabor, A., & J. T. Mahoney. (2010). *Chester Barnard and the Systems Approach to Nurturing Organizations*. College of Business working papers; 10-0102. Champaign, IL: College of Business, University of Illinois at Urbana-Champaign.

March, J. G., & H. A. Simon (1958). *Organizations*. New York: John Wiley. (Second edition, 1993. New York: John Wiley.)

Merton, R. K. (1957). Bureaucratic structure and personality. In R. K. Merton, eds., *Social Theory and Social Structure*, rev. and enl. ed. New York: Free Press. (A revised version of an article of the same title that appeared in *Social Forces, 18* [1940].)

Parsons, T. (1956). Suggestions for a sociological approach to the theory of organizations. *Administrative Science Quarterly, 1*, 63–85.

Scott, W. G. (1992). *Chester I. Barnard and the guardians of the managerial state*. Lawrence, KS: University Press of Kansas.

Selznick, P. (1984). *Leadership in administration: A sociological interpretation*. Berkley, CA: University of California Press.

Selznick, P. (1948). Foundations of the theory of organization. *American Sociological Review, 13*, 25–35.

Simon, H. A. (1946). The proverbs of administration. *Public Administration Review, 6*, 53–67.

Simon, H. A. (1947). *Administrative behavior*. New York: Macmillan.

Simon, H. A. (1960). *The new science of management decisions*. New York: Harper & Row.

Simon, H. A. (1997). *Administrative behavior*, 4th ed. New York: Free Press.

Whyte, W. F. (1948). *Human relations in the restaurant business*. New York: McGraw-Hill.

Wolf, W. B., & H. Iino., eds. (1986). *Philosophy for managers: Selected papers of Chester I. Barnard*. Ithaca, NY: ILR Press.

# 9

# Chester I. Barnard and the Guardians of the Managerial State: The Moral Obligations of the Elite

*William G. Scott*

One might think that as executive discretion increased, so should management accountability, certainly not absolutely proportionately but commensurately. However, such are not the ways of managerialism. Discretion and accountability are inversely related in managerial societies, confirming the King of Id's dictum, "He who has the gold rules." No immutable logic or deterministic social force compelled this to be the case. Rather it resulted from the conscious application of executive power to concentrate organizational control in management, and keep it there.

However, democracy imposes some inconveniences, such as the justification of power in institutions that are critical to public welfare and that embody esteemed social values. Therefore, from Barnard to the present-day discretionists,[1] the argument has been that executive power is legitimate because it is not absolute. Their litany of limitations,[2] intoned before the altar of legitimacy, repeats:

- legal mandates define management's fiduciary responsibilities toward property owners
- the court system provides legal oversight and review
- professional norms regulate practice, and management expertise is often self-justifying
- competition in free markets disciplines management, as do the countervailing interests of pluralistic groups.

This list contains enough truth to be compelling, if not altogether convincing. Consequently, the issue of legitimacy has not disappeared, perhaps because of the curious nature of executive power. It is at once subordinate to higher authorities and largely unaccountable to them. Thus, all of management's moral obligations stem from an ambiguous relationship in which executives are free and not free from accountability to the authorities (God, nature, the people, government, stockholders, creditors, etc.) that grant them the right to rule.[3] Therefore, when executives are freed from constraint to use their power, the public is compelled to trust in their skills, good character, and nobility of purposes for the assurance that right things will be done.

But this formula for noblesse oblige is not heartening in democratic societies. The critical legal scholar Gerald E. Frug, for instance, has argued at great length that the discretionists' litany of limitation was merely a fairy tale supporting the unsupportable. Without participatory democracy, Frug contends, organizations are unproductive of democracy's most important moral outcome: citizen virtue through self-government.[4] The shortcomings of the limitation argument were not lost on Barnard or the political scientist Harvey C. Mansfield, Jr. Both invoked another justification of executive power, the legitimizing potential of the moral virtues. Mansfield wrote, "The perceived need of executive power constitutes an admission of the need for virtue."[5]

William G. Scott (1992). *Chester I. Barnard and the Guardians of the Managerial State*, chapter 8, "The Leadership Attributes of the Management Elite," pp. 134 – 144. Lawrence, Kans.: University Press of Kansas)

Consequently, the present management surge toward ethics implies the need to elevate the virtue of practitioners. If this does not happen, then public uproar, translated into legal restrictions, will reduce executive discretion by increasing accountability. Barnard foresaw these threats and that led him to argue emphatically for management morality as the last, and most important, defense against the erosion of autonomous executive power.

Thus, management as a moral discipline occupied a critically important space in Barnard's thought. Barnard's basic opinions about theology and morality were consistent for most of his life. Having established his bona fides as an authority on ethics in his book, he became a natural source to whom John D. Rockefeller, Jr., and the Foundation's board of trustees could turn when deliberating the place of ethics and morals in its funding policies.

Barnard's last published words about the moral issues in management came six years after he retired as president of the RF (Rockefeller Foundation).[6] Thus, Barnard attended to the ethics and morals issue for two decades and searched for ways to bring the subject down to earth for practitioners. Nevertheless, during all this time he held firm to his beliefs in the essential morality of cooperation and management's obligation to achieve it.[7] Time and time again he returned to his testimony of faith found in the last paragraph of his book.

> I believe in the power of the cooperation of men of free will to make men free to cooperate; that only as they choose to work together can they achieve the fullness of personal development; that only as each accepts a responsibility for choice can they enter into that communion of men from which arise the higher purposes of individual and of cooperative behavior alike. I believe that the expansion of cooperation and the development of the individual are mutually dependent realities, and that a due proportion or balance between them is a necessary condition of human welfare.[8]

## BARNARD'S EXISTENTIALISM AND LEAP OF FAITH

Barnard believed that Christian ideals and values failed to provide moral guidelines for people in formal organizations. Lacking ethical criteria for resolving organizational dilemmas, such as conflicts in loyalties and moral codes, Christian principles did not suit the ambiguous and uncertain environment of modern times. Barnard attributed this lack to the origins of Christianity. "Christian ethics had developed in agricultural, pastoral, and nomadic societies and were chiefly expressed in terms intelligible to the people of such societies."[9] Bucolic metaphors had little meaning to urban dwellers. What did New Yorkers know, Barnard asked, about the "care of the flock, lost sheep, black sheep"?[10]

As an alternative to Christian values, Barnard turned to a moral perspective that was compatible with existential philosophy and his own Yankee deism. Although he never mentioned the existentialists, his beliefs were similar to many of theirs, relative to the freedom of individual choice and commensurate individual moral responsibility for the choices made.

Some existentialists believed that moral responsibility was "the dark side of freedom," and Barnard held a similar idea. He thought that the subjective and contingent qualities of individual decisionmaking limited freedom and made it impossible for an executive to know where moral responsibility lay or what was the right thing to do. The higher an individual rose in an organization, the greater this uncertainty.

Traditional laws and ethical rules offered little comfort, guidance, or even relevance to those who were forced to resolve moral conflicts in the organizations. This situation was generalized to the human condition by such extreme existentialists as Sartre and Camus, who contended that universal anguish would arise among the people as they "lucidly" recognized the absurdity of their lives in the absence of cosmic guarantees.

Barnard rejected this extreme, but he did go to another. His was a Kierkegaardian vision in which the experience of human interdependency in cooperative systems created the need for people to make a leap of faith that affirmed the morality of the organizations to which they belonged and in which they found the source of their own moral development. The closing paragraph of his book, quoted above, was a marvelously existential statement of faith.

Nevertheless, the type of cooperation that Barnard visualized posed a serious dilemma. While cooperation was, a priori, a moral enterprise, individual executive moral rectitude was not predetermined to be characteristic of their practice. Instead executives' acts of moral responsibility came from their will to be controlled by a personal code consistent with the cooperative code of the organization. In other words, managers must first be committed to cooperative principles, and then they must convert others to the same principles. Good management, thus, was an act of virtue if it flowed from the free will of individual managers to regulate their conduct to conform with organizational codes. Those managers who based their practices on this commitment became the moral exemplars of the organization.

However, cooperation was not so morally inexorable that it drove managers into this path of righteousness in spite of themselves. Self-interest always contended with the cooperative good. So Barnard argued that management was a calling, something akin to a religious conversion, requiring a life of selfless commitment to a profession of transcendent social importance. Managers who accepted this calling and regulated their conduct accordingly were those with highly developed moral characters.

The idea that managers' personal moral characters could be enhanced was in some ways similar to the tenets of some existential philosophers. As David Norton pointed out, the highest stage of moral development, in Kierkegaard's philosophy, was faith in God.[11] But for Kierkegaard's god, Barnard substituted faith in cooperation. However, Barnard did not suppose for one moment that people would follow those who defaulted on their avowed principles. Managers had to practice the cooperative virtues in order to lend credence to their claims of legitimacy. Once these claims were established, people then would be inspired to subordinate their individual interests to the welfare of the cooperative whole. Within the boundary of these semi-existential notions Barnard framed his practical moral philosophy.

The central question in moral philosophy for more than 2,500 years was, what are the requisite conditions of a worthy life? Traditional discourse in ethics pertained to character, integrity, education, and moral enlightenment. However, beginning with Hobbes, this discourse changed. Hobbesian problematics, otherwise known in management as contingency theories, required that ethics be approached from an "administrative point of view." Hobbes retreated from the morally enhanced self and reduced "ethics to a code of minimal standards of behavior ... that cannot be ignored without social disaster."[12]

Philosophical discourse thence turned from the virtues of character toward moral minimalism. It became less concerned with what constituted a worthy life and more interested in the diagnosis of ethical dilemmas, perplexities, and quandaries whose solutions were found in rule systems. Barnard exemplified this reductivism, and if present trends in the management field of business ethics are of any significance, morality has become equated with rule responsibility.

For instance the Bennis and Nanus slogan about leaders doing right things raises the obvious moral question of what is right. In modern management, that tends to be rules that ensure the collective well-being of the organization rather than what enhances the moral character of organizational members. Thus, ethics all too often heed organizational technicalities, legalities, and public relations and ignore employee moral development. This state of affairs grew directly from Barnard's approach to moral responsibility as instrumental practices that protected management's discretion.

Whether or not managers did right things depended on their moral status. And although an individual's moral codes might be high, if his or her behavior was not controlled by these codes, a person might be judged irresponsible, another way of saying that the road to hell is paved with good intentions. Therefore, both personal control and high moral status were necessary for responsible executive practice. In Barnard's opinion, the confluence of these conditions in an executive's behavior produced a moral exemplar, or a "qualified moral agent" in Aristotle's words.

These exemplary people were permitted to inculcate morals in others, elevating the role of management guardianship to a position that had previously been reserved for teachers, ministers, rabbis, and priests. Managers would emphasize "fundamental attitudes, loyalties to the organization or cooperative system, and to the system of objective authority," encouraging employees to subordinate their "individual interests and minor dictates of personal codes to the good of the cooperative whole."[13]

Barnard told a second story, presumably based on an actual incident, about a woman who worked as a telephone operator in a small exchange. Looking out of the window one day, she saw her nearby house, one she shared with her invalid mother, burning. Her mother was in it! Even so, she stuck to her switchboard, motivated, according to Barnard, by the "*moral* necessity of uninterrupted service."[14]

From the standpoint of the subordinate employee, conscientiousness coupled with obedience were the prime organizational virtues.

The importance of all of this was patently clear. The complexity of modern organization required the elaboration of rules to prevent breakdown and disorder. This in turn necessitated employing the type of person who would be rule responsible, as well as one who would not panic when confronted with a crisis of conscience. Since there is little in Barnard's writing that gives much weight to other virtues such as friendship, compassion, love, or sympathy, it must be concluded that conscientiousness was central to his moral philosophy.

Rule responsibility and rule creativeness were thus the quintessential tests of management morality. But because management was uniquely situated in organizations, it had to be the final and sole arbitrator of what was right and how to achieve it. Therefore, the amount of discretion needed to fulfill these moral obligations had to be considerable, and, as Barnard judged it, accountability to external sources for decisions about ethical quandaries only confused people and inhibited the successful performance of management functions.

## MORAL DEFICITS AND MANAGEMENT OBLIGATIONS

The moral deficit, while an infelicitous condition of civilization in general, was not an affliction of the leadership elite, or so it seemed in the rarified atmosphere of the RF boardroom. Barnard most assuredly believed that a morally superior management had the obligation to help humanity overcome this problem, and his twelve years with the Foundation sharpened this point of view.

But he was ambiguous toward the ethics and morals project. On the one hand, he was aligned in principle with the position of Fosdick, Willits, and Gifford, which opposed Foundation support of projects proposed by religious organizations. He agreed as well with John D. Rockefeller, Jr., that the Foundation's entry into ethics and morals should be on a practical level that promised tangible benefits for "all mankind." However, curing the world's moral sickness was of a different order than the prevention of malaria or the discovery of penicillin. Practicality in this area, as in the social sciences, was elusive but necessary to men of affairs. On the other hand, Barnard was sensitive to the moral deficit problem. He believed, as did the other people in his circle, that the war had created a sag in Americans' moral character and that the wealthy and powerful had an obligation to engage in its moral uplift; management after all was a moral discipline.

However, Foundation policy had to be circumspect, and in this regard he gave two pieces of advice: steer clear of entanglements with religious groups, and support noncontroversial empirical studies such as those in comparative values and conflicts in moral codes. Regarding the latter, Barnard referred to the memorandum he had written in 1946,[15] concerning the moral problems of organizations and the individual's relationship to them. Since there were few recognized moral codes (other than certain legal precepts) that defined these relationships, the definition of moral obligations of corporate management to employees and the community was open and researchable. This topic was proper to fund, as were more important issues concerning conflicts in loyalty that often arose between individual employees and the organization.

Barnard's Rockefeller years exemplified his remarkable consistency on philosophical issues. In his alliance with Hocking, Fosdick, Willits, and Gifford, he found support for his opinion that traditional Christianity offered little to people in organizations. His stand against Foundation grants to religious groups was, therefore, compatible with his more general evaluation of the inadequacy

of Christian values in the solution of moral quandaries. Their place had to be filled by the modern moral principle of cooperation.

So while Barnard disagreed with Dulles on how to spend Foundation money, and while he did not see eye to eye with John D. Rockefeller, Jr., on some Foundation policy goals, he was nevertheless in their camp with regard to the nature of the postwar world. It was an existential fact that society would be controlled by professional managers who represented the interests of the private sector elite. No leaders from other institutions could inspire the people's faith in cooperation as they were in the position to do.

Barnard's experience at the RF reinforced his belief that traditional religious institutions could not reconcile social harmony and material progress in modern managerial states. As president of the RF, Barnard found affirmation for his opinion of the essential morality of cooperation if it was pursued by a virtuous managerial elite. Given this perspective, it followed that management had to have maximum discretion. Anything less prevented the achievement of a cooperative commonwealth from which all would benefit. Therefore, the people had to have faith that executives did the right things with their vast discretionary power. To demonstrate that this faith was warranted became management's supreme moral obligation.

## NOTES

1. See, for example, Charles J. Fox and Clarke C. Cochran, "Discretion Advocacy in Public Administration Theory: Toward a Platonic Guardian Class?" *Administration and Society* 22 (August 1990): 249–271.

2. Gerald E. Frug identified five of these conditions as typical of the arguments for legitimizing management discretion. However, he did not notice the virtue argument

that Barnard heavily relied upon. See Frug, "The Ideology of Bureaucracy in American Law," *Harvard Law Review* 97 (Spring 1984): 1277–1388.

3. A theme eloquently argued by Harvey C. Mansfield, Jr., *Taming the Prince: The Ambivalence of Modern Executive Power* (New York: Free Press, 1989).

4. See Frug, "Ideology of Bureaucracy," pp. 1278, 1386–1388. Also see Carole Pateman, *Participation and Democratic Theory* (Cambridge: Cambridge University Press, 1990), and Frederick C. Thayer, *An End to Hierarchy and Competition* (New York: New Viewpoints, 1981).

5. Mansfield, *Taming the Prince*, p. 297.

6. Chester I. Barnard, "Elementary Conditions of Business Morals," *California Management Review* 1 (Fall 1958): 1–13.

7. The fundamental ideas in Barnard's moral philosophy were intact from 1938, when his book was published, until 1961 when he was interviewed by William B. Wolf. Barnard died two months after this interview. See William B. Wolf, *Conversations with Chester I. Barnard*, ILR Paperback No. 12 (Ithaca, NY: Cornell University, School of Industrial and Labor Relations, 1972).

8. Chester I. Barnard, *The Functions of the Executive* (Cambridge, MA: Harvard University Press, 1938), p. 296.

9. Barnard to F. Ernest Johnson, March 28, 1946, RAC Series 900, box 56, folder 303, p. 2.

10. Barnard, *Functions*, p. 296.

11. David L. Norton, *Personal Destinies* (Princeton: Princeton University Press, 1976), pp. 64–79.

12. Edmund L. Pincoffs, *Quandaries and Virtues: Against Reductivism in Ethics* (Lawrence: University Press of Kansas, 1986), p. 31.

13. Barnard, *Functions*, p. 279.

14. Ibid. (emphasis in the original), p. 269. This incident had a happy ending. "The mother was rescued," Barnard said in a laconic footnote.

15. Barnard, "Memorandum on Modern Problems of Morals and Ethics."

# 10

# The Proverbs of Administration

*Herbert A. Simon*

A fact about proverbs that greatly enhances their quotability is that they almost always occur in mutually contradictory pairs. "Look before you leap!"—but "He who hesitates is lost."

This is both a great convenience and a serious defect—depending on the use to which one wishes to put the proverbs in question. If it is a matter of rationalizing behavior that has already taken place or justifying action that has already been decided upon, proverbs are ideal. Since one is never at a loss to find one that will prove his point or the precisely contradictory point, for that matter—they are a great help in persuasion, political debate, and all forms of rhetoric.

But when one seeks to use proverbs as the basis of a scientific theory, the situation is less happy. It is not that the propositions expressed by the proverbs are insufficient; it is rather that they prove too much. A scientific theory should tell what is true but also what is false. If Newton had announced to the world that particles of matter exert either an attraction or a repulsion on each other, he would not have added much to scientific knowledge. His contribution consisted in showing that an attraction was exercised and in announcing the precise law governing its operation.

Most of the propositions that make up the body of administrative theory today share, unfortunately, this defect of proverbs. For almost every principle one can find an equally plausible and acceptable contradictory principle. Although the two principles of the pair will lead to exactly opposite organizational recommendations, there is nothing in the theory to indicate which is the proper one to apply.[1]

It is the purpose of this paper to substantiate this sweeping criticism of administrative theory, and to present some suggestions—perhaps less concrete than they should be—as to how the existing dilemma can be solved.

## SOME ACCEPTED ADMINISTRATIVE PRINCIPLES

Among the more common "principles" that occur in the literature of administration are these:

1. Administrative efficiency is increased by a specialization of the task among the group.
2. Administrative efficiency is increased by arranging the members of the group in a determinate hierarchy of authority.
3. Administrative efficiency is increased by limiting the span of control at any point in the hierarchy to a small number.
4. Administrative efficiency is increased by grouping the workers, for purposes of control, according to (a) purpose, (b) process, (c) clientele, or (d) place. (This is really an elaboration of the first principle but deserves separate discussion.)

Since these principles appear relatively simple and clear, it would seem that their application to concrete problems of administrative organization would be unambiguous and that their validity would be easily submitted to empirical test. Such, however, seems not to be the case. To show why it is

*Public Administration Review* (winter 1946): 6, 53–67. © 1946 by the American Society for Public Administration (ASPA), 1120 G. Street NW, Suite 700, Washington, DC 20005. Reprinted with permission. All rights reserved.

not, each of the four principles just listed will be considered in turn.

**Specialization.** Administrative efficiency is supposed to increase with an increase in specialization. But is this intended to mean that *any* increase in specialization will increase efficiency? If so, which of the following alternatives is the correct application of the principle in a particular case?

1. A plan of nursing should be put into effect by which nurses will be assigned to districts and do all nursing within that district, including school examinations, visits to homes of school children, and tuberculosis nursing.
2. A functional plan of nursing should be put into effect by which different nurses will be assigned to school examinations, visits to homes of school children, and tuberculosis nursing. The present method of generalized nursing by districts impedes the development of specialized skills in the three very diverse programs.

Both of these administrative arrangements satisfy the requirement of specialization—the first provides specialization by place; the second, specialization by function. The principle of specialization is of no help at all in choosing between the two alternatives.

It appears that the simplicity of the principle of specialization is a deceptive simplicity—a simplicity which conceals fundamental ambiguities. For "specialization" is not a condition of efficient administration; it is an inevitable characteristic of all group effort, however efficient or inefficient that effort may be. Specialization merely means that different persons are doing different things—and since it is physically impossible for two persons to be doing the same thing in the same place at the same time, two persons are always doing different things.

The real problem of administration, then, is not to "specialize," but to specialize in that particular manner and along those particular lines which will lead to administrative efficiency. But, in thus rephrasing this "principle" of administration, there

has been brought clearly into the open its fundamental ambiguity: "Administrative efficiency is increased by a specialization of the task among the group in the direction which will lead to greater efficiency."

Further discussion of the choice between competing bases of specialization will be undertaken after two other principles of administration have been examined.

**Unity of Command.** Administrative efficiency is supposed to be enhanced by arranging the members of the organization in a determinate hierarchy of authority in order to preserve "unity of command."

Analysis of this "principle" requires a clear understanding of what is meant by the term "authority." A subordinate may be said to accept authority whenever he permits his behavior to be guided by a decision reached by another, irrespective of his own judgment as to the merits of that decision.

In one sense the principle of unity of command, like the principle of specialization, cannot be violated; for it is physically impossible for a man to obey two contradictory commands—that is what is meant by "contradictory commands." Presumably, if unity of command is a principle of administration, it must assert something more than this physical impossibility. Perhaps it asserts this: that it is undesirable to place a member of an organization in a position where he receives orders from more than one superior. This is evidently the meaning that Gulick attaches to the principle when he says,

> The significance of this principle in the process of co-ordination and organization must not be lost sight of. In building a structure of co-ordination, it is often tempting to set up more than one boss for a man who is doing work which has more than one relationship. Even as great a philosopher of management as Taylor fell into this error in setting up separate foremen to deal with machinery, with materials, with speed, etc., each with the power of giving orders directly to the

individual workman. The rigid adherence to the principle of unity of command may have its absurdities; these are, however, unimportant in comparison with the certainty of confusion, inefficiency and irresponsibility which arise from the violation of the principle.[2]

Certainly the principle of unity of command, thus interpreted, cannot be criticized for any lack of clarity or any ambiguity. The definition of authority given above should provide a clear test whether, in any concrete situation, the principle is observed. The real fault that must be found with this principle is that it is incompatible with the principle of specialization. One of the most important uses to which authority is put in organization is to bring about specialization in the work of making decisions, so that each decision is made at a point in the organization where it can be made most expertly. As a result, the use of authority permits a greater degree of expertness to be achieved in decision making than would be possible if each operative employee had himself to make all the decisions upon which his activity is predicated. The individual fireman does not decide whether to use a two-inch hose or a fire extinguisher; that is decided for him by his officers, and the decision is communicated to him in the form of a command.

However, if unity of command, in Gulick's sense, is observed, the decisions of a person at any point in the administrative hierarchy are subject to influence through only one channel of authority; and if his decisions are of a kind that require expertise in more than one field of knowledge, then advisory and informational services must be relied upon to supply those premises which lie in a field not recognized by the mode of specialization in the organization. For example, if an accountant in a school department is subordinate to an educator, and if unity of command is observed, then the finance department cannot issue direct orders to him regarding the technical, accounting aspects of his work. Similarly, the director of motor vehicles in the public works department will be unable to issue

direct orders on care of motor equipment to the fire-truck driver.[3]

Gulick, in the statement quoted above, clearly indicates the difficulties to be faced if unity of command is not observed. A certain amount of irresponsibility and confusion are almost certain to ensue. But perhaps this is not too great a price to pay for the increased expertise that can be applied to decisions. What is needed to decide the issue is a principle of administration that would enable one to weigh the relative advantages of the two courses of action. But neither the principle of unity of command nor the principle of specialization is helpful in adjudicating the controversy. They merely contradict each other without indicating any procedure for resolving the contradiction....

The principle of unity of command is perhaps more defensible if narrowed down to the following: In case two authoritative commands conflict, there should be a single determinate person whom the subordinate is expected to obey; and the sanctions of authority should be applied against the subordinate only to enforce his obedience to that one person.

If the principle of unity of command is more defensible when stated in this limited form, it also solves fewer problems. In the first place, it no longer requires, except for settling conflicts of authority, a single hierarchy of authority. Consequently, it leaves unsettled the very important question of how authority should be zoned in a particular organization (i.e., the modes of specialization) and through what channels it should be exercised. Finally, even this narrower concept of unity of command conflicts with the principle of specialization, for whenever disagreement does occur and the organization members revert to the formal lines of authority, then only those types of specialization which are represented in the hierarchy of authority can impress themselves on decisions. If the training officer of a city exercises only functional supervisions over the police training officer, then in case of disagreement with the police chief, specialized knowledge of training problems will be subordinated or ignored. That this actually occurs is shown by the frustration so commonly expressed by functional supervisors at their lack of authority to apply sanctions.

**Span of Control.** Administrative efficiency is supposed to be enhanced by limiting the number of subordinates who report directly to any one administrator to a small number—say six. This notion that the "span of control" should be narrow is confidently asserted as a third incontrovertible principle of administration. The usual common-sense arguments for restricting the span of control are familiar and need not be repeated here. What is not so generally recognized is that a contradictory proverb of administration can be stated which, though it is not so familiar as the principle of span of control, can be supported by arguments of equal plausibility. The proverb in question is the following: Administrative efficiency is enhanced by keeping at a minimum the number of organizational levels through which a matter must pass before it is acted upon.

This latter proverb is one of the fundamental criteria that guide administrative analysis in procedures simplification work. Yet in many situations the results to which this principle leads are in direct contradiction to the requirements of the principle of span of control, the principle of unity of command, and the principle of specialization. The present discussion is concerned with the first of these conflicts. To illustrate the difficulty, two alternative proposals for the organization of a small health department will be presented—one based on the restriction of span of control, the other on the limitation of number of organization levels:

1.  The present organization of the department places an administrative overload on the health officer by reason of the fact that all eleven employees of the department report directly to him and the further fact that some of the staff lack adequate technical training. Consequently,

venereal disease clinic treatments and other details require an undue amount of the health officer's personal attention.

It has previously been recommended that the proposed medical officer be placed in charge of the venereal disease and chest clinics and all child hygiene work. It is further recommended that one of the inspectors be designated chief inspector and placed in charge of all the department's inspectional activities and that one of the nurses be designated as head nurse. This will relieve the health commissioner of considerable detail and will leave him greater freedom to plan and supervise the health program as a whole, to conduct health education, and to coordinate the work of the department with that of other community agencies. If the department were thus organized, the effectiveness of all employees could be substantially increased.

2.  The present organization of the department leads to inefficiency and excessive red tape by reason of the fact that an unnecessary supervisory level intervenes between the health officer and the operative employees, and that those four of the twelve employees who are best trained technically are engaged largely in "overhead" administrative duties. Consequently, unnecessary delays occur in securing the approval of the health officer on matters requiring his attention, and too many matters require review and re-review.

    The medical officer should be left in charge of the venereal disease and chest clinics and child hygiene work. It is recommended, however, that the position of chief inspector and head nurse be abolished and that the employees now filling these positions perform regular inspectional and nursing duties. The details of work scheduling now handled by these two employees can be taken care of more economically by the secretary to the health officer, and, since broader matters of policy have, in any event, always required the personal attention of the health officer, the abolition of these two positions will eliminate a wholly unnecessary step in review, will allow an expansion of inspectional and nursing services, and will permit at least a beginning to be made in the recommended program of health education. The number of persons reporting directly to the health officer will be increased to nine, but since there are few matters requiring the coordination of these employees, other than the work schedules and policy questions referred to above, this change will not materially increase his work load.

The dilemma is this: in a large organization with complex interrelations between members, a restricted span of control inevitably produces excessive red tape, for each contact between organization members must be carried upward until a common superior is found. If the organization is at all large, this will involve carrying all such matters upward through several levels of officials for decision and then downward again in the form of orders and instructions—a cumbersome and time-consuming process.

The alternative is to increase the number of persons who are under the command of each officer, so that the pyramid will come more rapidly to a peak, with fewer intervening levels. But this, too, leads to difficulty, for if an officer is required to supervise too many employees, his control over them is weakened.

If it is granted, then, that both the increase and the decrease in span of control has some undesirable consequences, what is the optimum point? Proponents of a restricted span of control have suggested three, five, even eleven, as suitable numbers, but nowhere have they explained the reasoning which led them to the particular number they selected. The principle as stated casts no light on this very crucial question. One is reminded of current arguments about the proper size of the national debt.

**Organization by Purpose, Process, Clientele, Place.** Administrative efficiency is supposed to be increased by grouping workers according to (a) purpose, (b) process, (c) clientele, or (d) place. But from the discussion of specialization it is clear that this principle is internally inconsistent; for purpose, process, clientele, and place are competing bases of organization, and at any given point of division the advantages of three must be sacrificed to secure the advantages of the fourth. If the major departments of a city, for example, are organized on the basis of major purpose, then it follows that all the physicians, all the lawyers, all the engineers, all the statisticians will not be located in a single department exclusively composed of members of their profession but will be distributed among the various city departments needing their services. The advantages of organization by process will thereby be partly lost.

Some of these advantages can be regained by organizing on the basis of process *within* the major departments. Thus there may be an engineering bureau within the public works department, or the board of education may have a school health service as a major division of its work. Similarly, within small units there may be division by area or by clientele: for example, a fire department will have separate companies located throughout the city, while a welfare department may have intake and case work agencies in various locations. Again, however, these major types of specialization cannot be simultaneously achieved, for at any point in the organization it must be decided whether specialization at the next level will be accomplished by distinction of major purpose, major process, clientele, or area.

The conflict may be illustrated by showing how the principle of specialization according to purpose would lead to a different result from specialization according to clientele in the organization of a health department.

1. Public health administration consists of the following activities for the prevention of disease and the maintenance of healthful conditions: (1) vital statistics; (2) child hygiene—prenatal, maternity, postnatal, infant, preschool, and school health programs; (3) communicable disease control; (4) inspection of milk, foods, and drugs; (5) sanitary inspection; (6) laboratory service; (7) health education.

One of the handicaps under which the health department labors is the fact that the department has no control over school health, that being an activity of the county board of education, and there is little or no coordination between that highly important part of the community health program and the balance of the program which is conducted by the city-county health unit. It is recommended that the city and county open negotiations with the board of education for the transfer of all school health work and the appropriation therefore to the joint health unit….

2. To the modern school department is entrusted the care of children during almost the entire period that they are absent from the parental home. It has three principal responsibilities toward them: (1) to provide for their education in useful skills and knowledge and in character; (2) to provide them with wholesome play activities outside school hours; (3) to care for their health and to assure the attainment of minimum standards of nutrition.

One of the handicaps under which the school board labors is the fact that, except for school lunches, the board has no control over child health and nutrition, and there is little or no coordination between that highly important part of the child development program and the balance of the program which is conducted by the board of education. It is recommended that the city and county open negotiations for the transfer of all health work for children of school age to the board of education.

Here again is posed the dilemma of choosing between alternative, equally plausible, administrative principles. But this is not the only difficulty in the present case, for a closer study of the situation shows there are fundamental ambiguities in the meanings of the key terms—"purpose," "process," "clientele," and "place."

"Purpose" may be roughly defined as the objective or end for which an activity is carried on; "process" as a means for accomplishing a purpose. Processes, then, are carried on in order to achieve purposes. But purposes themselves may generally be arranged in some sort of hierarchy. A typist moves her fingers in order to type; types in order to reproduce a letter; reproduces a letter in order that an inquiry may be answered. Writing a letter is then the purpose for which the typing is performed; while writing a letter is also the process whereby the purpose of replying to an inquiry is achieved. It follows that the same activity may be described as purpose or as process.

This ambiguity is easily illustrated for the case of an administrative organization. A health department conceived as a unit whose task it is to care for the health of the community is a purpose organization; the same department conceived as a unit which makes use of the medical arts to carry on its work is a process organization. In the same way, an education department may be viewed as a purpose (to educate) organization, or a clientele (children) organization; the forest service as a purpose (forest conservation), process (forest management), clientele (lumbermen and cattlemen utilizing public forests), or area (publicly owned forest lands) organization. When concrete illustrations of this sort are selected, the lines of demarcation between these categories become very hazy and unclear indeed.

"Organization by major purpose," says Gulick, "… serves to bring together in a single large department all of those who are at work endeavoring to render a particular service."[4] But what is a particular service? Is fire protection a single purpose, or is it merely a part of the purpose of public safety?—or is it a combination of purposes including fire prevention and fire fighting? It must be concluded that there is no such thing as a purpose, or a unifunctional (single-purpose) organization. What is to be considered a single function depends entirely on language and techniques.[5] If the English language has a comprehensive term which covers both of two subpurposes it is natural to think of the two together as a single purpose. If such a term is lacking, the two subpurposes become purposes in their own right. On the other hand, a single activity may contribute to several objectives, but since they are technically (procedurally) inseparable, the activity is considered a single function or purpose.

The fact, mentioned previously, that purposes form a hierarchy, each subpurpose contributing to some more final and comprehensive end, helps to make clear the relation between purpose and process. "Organization by major process," says Gulick, "... tends to bring together in a single department all of those who are at work making use of a given special skill or technology, or are members of a given profession."[6] Consider a simple skill of this kind—typing. Typing is a skill which brings about a means-end coordination of muscular movements, but a very low level in the means-end hierarchy. The content of the typewritten letter is indifferent to the skill that produces it. The skill consists merely in the ability to hit the letter "t" quickly whenever the letter "t" is required by the content and to hit the letter "a" whenever the letter "a" is required by the content.

There is, then, no essential difference between a "purpose" and a "process," but only a distinction of degree. A "process" is an activity whose immediate purpose is at a low level in the hierarchy of means and ends, while a "purpose" is a collection of activities whose orienting value or aim is at a high level in the means-end hierarchy.

Next consider "clientele" and "place" as bases of organization. These categories are really not separate from purpose, but a part of it. A complete statement of the purpose of a fire department would have to include the area served by it: "to reduce fire losses on property in the city of X." Objectives of an administrative organization are phrased in terms of a service to be provided and an area for which it is provided. Usually, the term "purpose" is meant to refer only to the first element, but the second is just as legitimately an aspect of purpose. Area of service, of course, may be a specified clientele quite as well as a geographical area. In the case of an agency which works on "shifts," time will be a third dimension of

purpose—to provide a given service in a given area (or to a given clientele) during a given time period.

With this clarification of terminology, the next task is to reconsider the problem of specializing the work of an organization. It is no longer legitimate to speak of a "purpose" organization, a "process" organization, a "clientele" organization, or an "area" organization. The same unit might fall into any one of these four categories, depending on the nature of the larger organizational unit of which it was a part. A unit providing public health and medical services for school-age children in Multnomah County might be considered (1) an "area" organization if it were part of a unit providing the same service for the state of Oregon; (2) a "clientele" organization if it were part of a unit providing similar services for children of all ages; (3) a "purpose" or a "process" organization (it would be impossible to say which) if it were part of an education department.

It is incorrect to say that Bureau A is a process bureau; the correct statement is that Bureau A is a process bureau *within* Department X.[7] This latter statement would mean that Bureau A incorporates all the processes of a certain kind in Department X, without reference to any special subpurposes, sub-areas, or subclientele of Department X. Now it is conceivable that a particular unit might incorporate all processes of a certain kind but that these processes might relate to only certain particular subpurposes of the department purpose. In this case, which corresponds to the health unit in an education department mentioned above, the unit would be specialized by both purpose and process. The health unit would be the only one in the education department using the medical art (process) and concerned with health (subpurpose).

Even when the problem is solved of proper usage for the terms "purpose," "process," "clientele," and "area," the principles of administration give no guide as to which of these four competing bases of specialization is applicable in any particular situation. The British Machinery of Government Committee had no doubts about the matter. It considered purpose and clientele as the two possible bases of organization and put its faith entirely in the former. Others have had equal assurance in choosing between purpose and process. The reasoning which leads to these unequivocal conclusions leaves something to be desired. The Machinery of Government Committee gives this sole argument for its choice:

> Now the inevitable outcome of this method of organization [by clientele] is a tendency to Lilliputian administration. It is impossible that the specialized service which each Department has to render to the community can be of as high a standard when its work is at the same time limited to a particular class of persons and extended to every variety of provision for them, as when the Department concentrates itself on the provision of the particular service only by whomsoever required, and looks beyond the interest of comparatively small classes.[8]

The faults in this analysis are obvious. First, there is no attempt to determine how a service is to be recognized. Second, there is a bald assumption, absolutely without proof, that a child health unit, for example, in a department of child welfare could not offer services of "as high a standard" as the same unit if it were located in a department of health. Just how the shifting of the unit from one department to another would improve or damage the quality of its work is not explained. Third, no basis is set forth for adjudicating the competing claims of purpose and process—the two are merged in the ambiguous term "service." It is not necessary here to decide whether the committee was right or wrong in its recommendation; the important point is that the recommendation represented a choice, without any apparent logical or empirical grounds, between contradictory principles of administration....

These contradictions and competitions have received increasing attention from students of administration during the past few years. For example, Gulick, Wallace, and Benson have stated certain advantages

and disadvantages of the several modes of specialization, and have considered the conditions under which one or the other mode might best be adopted.[9] All this analysis has been at a theoretical level—in the sense that data have not been employed to demonstrate the superior effectiveness claimed for the different modes. But though theoretical, the analysis has lacked a theory. Since no comprehensive framework has been constructed within which the discussion could take place, the analysis has tended either to the logical one-sidedness which characterizes the examples quoted above or to inconclusiveness.

**The Impasse of Administrative Theory.** The four "principles of administration" that were set forth at the beginning of this paper have now been subjected to critical analysis. None of the four survived in very good shape, for in each case there was found, instead of an unequivocal principle, a set of two or more mutually incompatible principles apparently equally applicable to the administrative situation.

Moreover, the reader will see that the very same objections can be urged against the customary discussions of "centralization" versus "decentralization," which usually conclude, in effect, that "on the one hand, centralization of decision-making functions is desirable; on the other hand, there are definite advantages in decentralization."

Can anything be salvaged which will be useful in the construction of an administrative theory? As a matter of fact, almost everything can be salvaged. The difficulty has arisen from treating as "principles of administration" what are really only criteria for describing and diagnosing administrative situations. Closet space is certainly an important item in the design of a successful house; yet a house designed entirely with a view to securing a maximum of closet space—all other considerations being forgotten—would be considered, to say the least, somewhat unbalanced. Similarly, unity of command, specialization by purpose, and decentralization are all items to be considered in the design of an efficient administrative organization. No single one of these items is of sufficient importance to suffice as a guiding principle for the administrative analyst. In the design of administrative organizations, as in their operation, overall efficiency must be the guiding criterion. Mutually incompatible advantages must be balanced against each other, just as an architect weighs the advantages of additional closet space against the advantages of a larger living room.

This position, if it is a valid one, constitutes an indictment of much current writing about administrative matters. As the examples cited in this chapter amply demonstrate, much administrative analysis proceeds by selecting a single criterion and applying it to an administrative situation to reach a recommendation; while the fact that equally valid, but contradictory, criteria exist which could be applied with equal reason, but with a different result, is conveniently ignored. A valid approach to the study of administration requires that *all* the relevant diagnostic criteria be identified; that each administrative situation be analyzed in terms of the entire set of criteria; and that research be instituted to determine how weights can be assigned to the several criteria when they are, as they usually will be, mutually incompatible.

## AN APPROACH TO ADMINISTRATIVE THEORY

This program needs to be considered step by step. First, what is included in the description of administrative situations for purposes of such an analysis? Second, how can weights be assigned to the various criteria to give them their proper place in the total picture?

**The Description of Administrative Situations.** Before a science can develop principles, it must possess concepts. Before a law of gravitation could be formulated, it was necessary to have the notions of "acceleration" and "weight." The first task of administrative theory is to develop a set of concepts that will permit the description in terms relevant to the theory of administrative situations. These concepts, to be scientifically useful, must be operational; that is, their meanings must correspond to empirically observable facts or situations. The definition of *authority* given earlier in this paper is an example of an operational definition.

What is a scientifically relevant description of an organization? It is a description that, so far as possible, designates for each person in the organization what decisions that person makes and the influences to which he is subject in making each of these decisions. Current descriptions of administrative organizations fall far short of this standard. For the most part, they confine themselves to the allocation of *functions* and the formal structure of *authority*. They give little attention to the other types of organizational influence or to the system of communications....[10]

Consider the term "centralization." How is it determined whether the operations of a particular organization are "centralized" or "decentralized"? Does the fact that field offices exist prove anything about decentralization? Might not the same decentralization take place in the bureaus of a centrally located office? A realistic analysis of centralization must include a study of the allocation of decisions in the organization and the methods of influence that are employed by the higher levels to affect the decisions at the lower levels. Such an analysis would reveal a much more complex picture of the decision-making process than any enumeration of the geographical locations of organizational units at the different levels.

Administrative description suffers currently from superficiality, oversimplification, lack of realism. It had confined itself too closely to the mechanism of authority and has failed to bring within its orbit the other, equally important, modes of influence on organizational behavior. It has refused to undertake the tiresome task of studying the actual allocation of decision-making functions. It has been satisfied to speak of "authority," "centralization," "span of control," "function," without seeking operational definitions of these terms. Until administrative description reaches a higher level of sophistication, there is little reason to hope that rapid progress will be made toward the identification and verification of valid administrative principles.

Does this mean that a purely formal description of an administrative organization is impossible—that a relevant description must include an account of the content of the organization's decisions? This is a question that is almost impossible to answer in the present state of knowledge of administrative theory. One thing seems certain: content plays a greater role in the application of administrative principles than is allowed for in the formal administrative theory of the present time. This is a fact that is beginning to be recognized in the literature of administration. If one examines the chain of publications extending from Mooney and Reilley, through Gulick and the President's Committee controversy, to Schuyler Wallace and Benson, he sees a steady shift of emphasis from the "principles of administration" themselves to a study of the *conditions* under which competing principles are respectively applicable. Recent publications seldom say that "organization should be by purpose," but rather that "under such and such conditions purpose organization is desirable." It is to these conditions which underlie the application of the proverbs of administration that administrative theory and analysis must turn in their search for really valid principles to replace the proverbs.

**The Diagnosis of Administrative Situations.** Before any positive suggestions can be made, it is necessary to digress a bit and to consider more closely the exact nature of the propositions of administrative theory. The theory of administration is concerned with how an organization should be constructed and operated in order to accomplish its work efficiently. A fundamental principle of administration, which follows almost immediately from the rational character of "good" administration, is that among several alternatives involving the same expenditure that one should always be selected which leads to the greatest accomplishment of administrative objectives; and among several alternatives that lead to the same accomplishment that one should be selected which involves the least expenditure. Since this "principle of efficiency" is characteristic of any activity that attempts rationally to maximize the attainment of certain ends with the use of scarce means, it is as characteristic of economic theory as it is of administrative theory. The "administrative man" takes his place alongside the classical "economic man."[11]

Actually, the "principle" of efficiency should be considered a definition rather than a principle: it is a definition of what is meant by "good" or "correct" administrative behavior. It does not tell *how* accomplishments are to be maximized, but merely states that this maximization is the aim of administrative activity, and that administrative theory must disclose under what conditions the maximization takes place.

Now what are the factors that determine the level of efficiency which is achieved by an administrative organization? It is not possible to make an exhaustive list of these but the principal categories can be enumerated. Perhaps the simplest method of approach is to consider the single member of the administrative organization and ask what the limits are to the quantity and quality of his output. These limits include (*a*) limits on his ability to perform and (*b*) limits on his ability to make correct decisions. To the extent that these limits are removed, the administrative organization approaches its goal of high efficiency. Two persons, given the same skills, the same objectives and values, the same knowledge and information, can rationally decide only upon the same course of action. Hence, administrative theory must be interested in the factory that will determine with what skills, values, and knowledge the organization member undertakes his work. These are the "limits" to rationality with which the principles of administration must deal.

On one side, the individual is limited by those skills, habits, and reflexes which are no longer in the realm of the conscious. His performance, for example, may be limited by his manual dexterity or his reaction time or his strength. His decision-making processes may be limited by the speed of his mental processes, his skill in elementary arithmetic, and so forth. In this area, the principles of administration must be concerned with the physiology of the human body and with the laws of skill-training and of habit. This is the field that has been most successfully cultivated by the followers of Taylor and in which has been developed time-and-motion study and the therblig.

On a second side, the individual is limited by his values and those conceptions of purpose which influence him in making decisions. If his loyalty to the organization is high, his decisions may evidence sincere acceptance of the objectives set for the organization; if that loyalty is lacking, personal motives may interfere with his administrative efficiency. If his loyalties are attached to the bureau by which he is employed, he may sometimes make decisions that are inimical to the larger unit of which the bureau is a part. In this area the principles of administration must be concerned with the determinants of loyalty and morale, with leadership and initiative, and with the influences that determine where the individual's organizational loyalties will be attached.

On a third side, the individual is limited by the extent of his knowledge of things relevant to his job. This applies both to the basic knowledge required in decision-making—a bridge designer must know the fundamentals of mechanics—and to the information that is required to make his decisions appropriate to the given situation. In this area, administrative theory is concerned with such fundamental questions as these: What are the limits on the mass of knowledge that human minds can accumulate and apply? How rapidly can knowledge be assimilated? How is specialization in the administrative organization to be related to the specializations of knowledge that are prevalent in the community's occupational

structure? How is the system of communication to channel knowledge and information to the appropriate decision-points? What types of knowledge can, and what types cannot, be easily transmitted? How is the need for intercommunication of information affected by the modes of specialization in the organization? This is perhaps the *terra incognita* of administrative theory, and undoubtedly its careful exploration will cast great light on the proper application of the proverbs of administration.

Perhaps this triangle of limits does not completely bound the area of rationality, and other sides need to be added to the figure. In any case, this enumeration will serve to indicate the kinds of considerations that must go into the construction of valid and noncontradictory principles of administration.

An important fact to be kept in mind is that the limits of rationality are variable limits. Most important of all, consciousness of the limits may in itself alter them. Suppose it were discovered in a particular organization, for example, that organizational loyalties attached to small units had frequently led to a harmful degree of intraorganizational competition. Then, a program which trained members of the organization to be conscious of their loyalties, and to subordinate loyalties to the smaller group to those of the large, might lead to a very considerable alteration of the limits in that organization.[12]

A related point is that the term "rational behavior" as employed here, refers to rationality when that behavior is evaluated in terms of the objectives of the larger organization; for, as just pointed out, the difference in direction of the individual's aims from those of the larger organization is just one of those elements of nonrationality with which the theory must deal.

A final observation is that, since administrative theory is concerned with the nonrational limits of the rational, it follows that the larger the area in which rationality has been achieved the less important is the exact form of the administrative organization. For example, the function of plan preparation, or design, if it results in a written plan that can be communicated interpersonally without difficulty, can be located almost anywhere in the organization without affecting results. All that is needed is a procedure whereby the plan can be given authoritative status, and this can be provided in a number of ways. A discussion, then, of the proper location for a planning or designing unit is apt to be highly inconclusive and is apt to hinge on the personalities in the organization and their relative enthusiasm, or lack of it, toward the planning function rather than upon any abstract principles of good administration.[13]

On the other hand, when factors of communication or faiths or loyalty are crucial to the making of a decision, the location of the decision in the organization is of great importance. The method of allocating decisions in the army, for instance, automatically provides (at least in the period prior to the actual battle) that each decision will be made where the knowledge is available for coordinating it with other decisions.

**Assigning Weights to the Criteria.** A first step, then, in the overhauling of the proverbs of administration is to develop a vocabulary, along the lines just suggested, for the description of administrative organization. A second step, which has also been outlined, is to study the limits of rationality in order to develop a complete and comprehensive enumeration of the criteria that must be weighed in evaluating an administrative organization. The current proverbs represent only a fragmentary and unsystematized portion of these criteria.

When these two tasks have been carried out, it remains to assign weights to the criteria. Since the criteria, or "proverbs," are often mutually competitive or contradictory, it is not sufficient merely to identify them. Merely to know, for example, that a specified change in organization will reduce the span of control is not enough to justify the change. This gain must be balanced against the possible resulting loss of contact between the higher and lower ranks of the hierarchy.

Hence, administrative theory must also be concerned with the question of the weights that are to be applied to these criteria—to the problems of their relative importance in any concrete situation. This question is not one that can be solved in a vacuum. Arm-chair philosophizing about administration—of which the present paper is an example—has gone about as far as it can profitably go in this particular direction. What is needed now is empirical research and experimentation to determine the relative desirability of alternative administrative arrangements.

The methodological framework for this research is already at hand in the principle of efficiency. If an administrative organization whose activities are susceptible to objective evaluation be subjected to study, then the actual change in accomplishment that results from modifying administrative arrangements in these organizations can be observed and analyzed.

There are two indispensable conditions to successful research along these lines. First, it is necessary that the objectives of the administrative organization under study be defined in concrete terms so that results, expressed in terms of these objectives, can be accurately measured. Second, it is necessary that sufficient experimental control be exercised to make possible the isolation of the particular effect under study from other disturbing factors that might be operating on the organization at the same time.

These two conditions have seldom been even partially fulfilled in so-called "administrative experiments." The mere fact that a legislature passes a law creating an administrative agency, that the agency operates for five years, that the agency is finally abolished, and that a historical study is then made of the agency's operations is not sufficient to make of that agency's history an "administrative experiment." Modern American legislation is full of such "experiments" which furnish orators in neighboring states with abundant ammunition when similar issues arise in their bailiwicks, but which provide the scientific investigator with little or nothing in the way of objective evidence, one way or the other....

Perhaps the program outlined here will appear an ambitious or even a quixotic one. There should certainly be no illusions, in undertaking it, as to the length and deviousness of the path. It is hard to see, however, what alternative remains open. Certainly neither the practitioner of administration nor the theoretician can be satisfied with the poor analytic tools that the proverbs provide him. Nor is there any reason to believe that a less drastic reconversion than that outlined here will rebuild those tools to usefulness.

It may be objected that administration cannot aspire to be a "science"; that by the nature of its subject it cannot be more than an "art." Whether true or false, this objection is irrelevant to the present discussion. The question of how "exact" the principles of administration can be made is one that only experience can answer. But as to whether they should be logical or illogical there can be no debate. Even an "art" cannot be founded on proverbs.

## NOTES

1. Lest it be thought that this deficiency is peculiar to the science—or "art"—of administration, it should be pointed out that the same trouble is shared by most Freudian psychological theories, as well as by some sociological theories.
2. Luther Gulick, "Notes on the Theory of Organization," in Luther Gulick and L. Urwick (eds.), *Papers on the Science of Administration* (Institute of Public Administration, Columbia University, 1937), p. 9.
3. This point is discussed in Herbert A. Simon, "Decision-Making and Administrative Organization," 4 *Public Administration Review* 20–21 (Winter, 1944).
4. Gulick and Urwick (eds.), *op. cit.*, p. 21.
5. If this is correct, then any attempt to prove that certain activities belong in a single department because they relate to a single purpose is doomed to fail. See, for example, John M. Gaus and Leon Wolcott, *Public Administration and the U.S. Department of*

*Agriculture* (Public Administration Service, 1940).
6. *Op. cit.*, p. 23.
7. This distinction is implicit in most of Gulick's analysis of specialization. However, since he cites as examples single departments within a city, and since he usually speaks of "grouping activities" rather than "dividing work," the relative character of these categories is not always apparent in this discussion (*op. cit.*, pp. 15–30).
8. *Report of the Machinery of Government Committee* (H. M. Stationery Office, 1918).
9. Gulick, "Notes on the Theory of Organization," pp. 21–30; Schuyler Wallace, *Federal Departmentalization* (Columbia University Press, 1941); George C. S. Benson, "International Administrative Organization," 1 *Public Administration Review* 473–486 (Autumn, 1941).
10. The monograph by Macmahon, Millett, and Ogden, *op. cit.*, perhaps approaches nearer than any other published administrative study to the sophistication required in administrative description. See, for example, the discussion on pp. 233–236 of headquarters-field relationships.
11. For an elaboration of the principle of efficiency and its place in administrative theory see Clarence E. Ridley and Herbert A. Simon, *Measuring Municipal Activities* (International City Managers' Association, 2nd ed., 1943), particularly Chapter 1 and the preface to the second edition.
12. For an example of the use of such training, see Herbert A. Simon and William Divine, "Controlling Human Factors in an Administrative Experiment," 1 *Public Administration Review* 487–492 (Autumn, 1941).
13. See, for instance, Robert A. Walker, *The Planning Function in Urban Government* (University of Chicago Press, 1941), pp. 166–175. Walker makes out a strong case for attaching the planning agency to the chief executive. But he rests his entire case on the rather slender reed that "as long as the planning agency is outside the governmental structure ... planning will tend to encounter resistance from public officials as an invasion of their responsibility and jurisdiction." This "resistance" is precisely the type of nonrational loyalty which has been referred to previously, and which is certainly a variable.

## 11

# Foundations of the Theory of Organization

*Philip Selznick*

Trades unions, governments, business corporations, political parties, and the like are formal structures in the sense that they represent rationally ordered instruments for the achievement of stated goals. "Organization," we are told, "is the arrangement of personnel for facilitating the accomplishment of some agreed purpose through the allocation of functions and responsibilities."[1] Or, defined more generally, formal organization is "a system of consciously coordinated activities or forces of two or more persons."[2] Viewed in this light, formal organization is the structural expression of rational action. The mobilization of technical and managerial skills requires a pattern of coordination, a systematic ordering of positions and duties which defines a chain of command and makes possible the administrative integration of specialized functions. In this context *delegation* is the primordial organization act, a precarious venture which requires the continuous elaboration of formal mechanisms of coordination and control. The security of all participants, and of the system as a whole, generates a persistent pressure for the institutionalization of relationships, which are thus removed from the uncertainties of individual fealty or sentiment. Moreover, it is necessary for the relations within the structure to be determined in such a way that individuals will be interchangeable and the organization will thus be free of dependence upon personal qualities.[3] In this way, the formal structure becomes subject to calculable manipulation, an instrument of rational action.

But as we inspect these formal structures we begin to see that they never succeed in conquering the nonrational dimensions of organizational behavior. The latter remain at once indispensable to the continued existence of the system of coordination and at the same time the source of friction, dilemma, doubt, and ruin. This fundamental paradox arises from the fact that rational action systems are inescapably imbedded in an institutional matrix, in two significant senses: (1) the action system—or the formal structure of delegation and control which is its organizational expression—is itself only an aspect of a concrete social structure made up of individuals who may interact as *wholes*, not simply in terms of their formal roles within the system; (2) the formal system, and the social structure within which it finds concrete existence, are alike subject to the pressure of an institutional environment to which some overall adjustment must be made. The formal administrative design can never adequately or fully reflect the concrete organization to which it refers, for the obvious reason that no abstract plan or pattern can—or may, if it is to be useful—exhaustively describe an empirical totality. At the same time, that which is not included in the abstract design (as reflected, for example, in a staff-and-line organization chart) is vitally relevant to the maintenance and development of the formal system itself.

Organization may be viewed from two standpoints which are analytically distinct but which are empirically united in a context of reciprocal consequences. On the

*Source: American Sociological Review* 13 (1948): 25–35.

one hand, any concrete organizational system is an economy; at the same time, it is an adaptive social structure. Considered as an economy, organization is a system of relationships which define the availability of scarce resources *and* which may be manipulated in terms of efficiency and effectiveness. It is the economic aspect of organization which commands the attention of management technicians and, for the most part, students of public as well as private administration.[4] Such problems as the span of executive control, the role of staff or auxiliary agencies, the relation of headquarters to field offices, and the relative merits of single or multiple executive boards are typical concerns of the science of administration. The coordinative scalar, and functional principles, as elements of the theory of organization, are products of the attempt to explicate the most general features of organization as a "technical problem" or, in our terms, as an economy.

Organization as an economy is, however, necessarily conditioned by the organic states of the concrete structure, outside of the systematics of delegation and control. This becomes especially evident as the attention of leadership is directed toward such problems as the legitimacy of authority and the dynamics of persuasion. It is recognized implicitly in action and explicitly in the work of a number of students that the possibility of manipulating the system of coordination depends on the extent to which that system is operating within an environment of effective inducement to individual participants and of conditions in which the stability of authority is assured. This is in a sense the fundamental thesis of Barnard's remarkable study, *The Functions of the Executive*. It is also the underlying hypothesis which makes it possible for Urwick to suggest that "proper" or formal channels in fact function to "confirm and record" decisions arrived at by more personal means.[5] We meet it again in the concept of administration as a process of education, in which the winning of consent and support is conceived to be a basic

function of leadership.[6] In short, it is recognized that control and consent cannot be divorced even within formally authoritarian structures.

The indivisibility of control and consent makes it necessary to view formal organizations as *cooperative* systems, widening the frame of reference of those concerned with the manipulation of organizational resources. At the point of action, of executive decision, the economic aspect of organization provides inadequate tools for control over the concrete structure. This idea may be readily grasped if attention is directed to the role of the individual within the organizational economy. From the standpoint of organization as a formal system, persons are viewed functionally, in respect to their *roles*, as participants in assigned segments of the cooperative system. But in fact individuals have a propensity to resist depersonalization, to spill over the boundaries of their segmentary roles, to participate as *wholes*. The formal systems (at an extreme, the disposition of "rifles" at a military perimeter) cannot take account of the deviations thus introduced, and consequently break down as instruments of control when relied upon alone. The whole individual raises new problems for the organization, partly because of the needs of his own personality, partly because he brings with him a set of established habits as well, perhaps, as commitments to special groups outside of the organization.

Unfortunately for the adequacy of formal systems of coordination, the needs of individuals do not permit a single-minded attention to the stated goals of the system within which they have been assigned. The hazard inherent in the act of delegation derives essentially from this fact. Delegation is an organizational act, having to do with formal assignments to functions and powers. Theoretically, these assignments are made to roles or official positions, not to individuals as such. In fact, however, delegation necessarily involves concrete individuals who have interests and goals which do not always coincide with the goals of the formal system. As a consequence, individual personalities may offer resistance to the demands made upon them by the official conditions of delegation. These resistances are not accounted for within the categories of coordination and delegation, so that when they occur they must be considered as unpredictable and accidental. Observations of this type of situation within formal structures are sufficiently commonplace. A familiar example is that of delegation to a subordinate who is also required to train his own replacement. The subordinate may resist this demand in order to maintain unique access to the "mysteries" of the job, and thus insure his indispensability to the organization.

In large organizations, deviations from the formal system tend to become institutionalized, so that "unwritten laws" and informal associations are established. Institutionalization removes such deviations from the realm of personality differences, transforming them into a persistent structural aspect of formal organizations.[7] These institutionalized rules and modes of informal cooperation are normally attempts by participants in the formal organization to control the group relations which form the environment of organizational decisions. The informal patterns (such as cliques) arise spontaneously, are based on personal relationships, and are usually directed to the control of some specific situation. They may be generated anywhere within a hierarchy, often with deleterious consequences for the formal goals of the organization, but they may also function to widen the available resources of executive control and thus contribute to rather than hinder the achievement of the stated objectives of the organization. The deviations tend to force a shift away from the purely formal system as the effective determinant of behavior to (1) a condition in which informal patterns buttress the formal, as through the manipulation of sentiment within the organization in favor of established authority; or (2) a condition wherein the informal controls

effect a consistent modification of formal goals, as in the case of some bureaucratic patterns.[8] This trend will eventually result in the formalization of erstwhile informal activities, with the cycle of deviation and transformation beginning again on a new level.

The relevance of informal structures to organizational analysis underlines the significance of conceiving of formal organizations as cooperative systems. When the totality of interacting groups and individuals becomes the object of inquiry, the latter is not restricted by formal, legal, or procedural dimensions. The *state of the system* emerges as a significant point of analysis, as when an internal situation charged with conflict qualifies and informs actions ostensibly determined by formal relations and objectives. A proper understanding of the organizational process must make it possible to interpret changes in the formal system—new appointments or rules or reorganizations—in their relation to the informal and unavowed ties of friendship, class loyalty, power cliques, or external commitment. This is what it means "to know the score." ...

To recognize the sociological relevance of formal structures is not, however, to have constructed a theory of organization. It is important to set the framework of analysis, and much is accomplished along this line when, for example, the nature of authority in formal organizations is reinterpreted to emphasize the factors of cohesion and persuasion as against legal or coercive sources.[9] This redefinition is logically the same as that which introduced the conception of the self as social. The latter helps make possible, but does not of itself fulfill, the requirements for a dynamic theory of personality. In the same way, the definition of authority as conditioned by sociological factors of sentiment and cohesion—or more generally the definition of formal organizations as cooperative systems—only sets the stage, as an initial requirement, for the formulation of a theory of organization.

## STRUCTURAL-FUNCTIONAL ANALYSIS

Cooperative systems are constituted of individuals interacting as wholes in relation to a formal system of coordination. The concrete structure is therefore a resultant of the reciprocal influences of the formal and informal aspects of organization. Furthermore, this structure is itself a totality, an adaptive "organism" reacting to influences upon it from an external environment. These considerations help to define the objects of inquiry; but to progress to a system of predicates *about* these objects it is necessary to set forth an analytical method which seems to be fruitful and significant. The method must have a relevance to empirical materials, which is to say, it must be more specific in its reference than discussions of the logic or methodology of social science.

The organon which may be suggested as peculiarly helpful in the analysis of adaptive structures has been referred to as "structural-functional analysis."[10] This method may be characterized in a sentence: *Structural-functional analysis relates contemporary and variable behavior to a presumptively stable system of needs and mechanisms.* This means that a given empirical system is deemed to have basic needs, essentially related to self-maintenance; the system develops repetitive means of self-defense; and day-to-day activity is interpreted in terms of the function served by that activity for the maintenance and defense of the system. Put thus generally, the approach is applicable on any level in which the determinate "states" of empirically isolable systems undergo self-impelled and repetitive transformations when impinged upon by external conditions. This self-impulsion suggests the relevance of the term "dynamic," which is often used in referring to physiological, psychological, or social systems to which this type of analysis has been applied.[11]

It is a postulate of the structural-functional approach that the basic need of all empirical systems is the maintenance of the integrity and continuity of the system itself.

Of course, such a postulate is primarily useful in directing attention to a set of "derived imperatives" or needs which are sufficiently concrete to characterize the system at hand.[12] It is perhaps rash to attempt a catalogue of these imperatives for formal organizations, but some suggestive formulation is needed in the interests of setting forth the type of analysis under discussion. In formal organizations, the "maintenance of the system" as a generic need may be specified in terms of the following imperatives:

1. *The security of the organization as a whole in relation to social forces in its environment.* This imperative requires continuous attention to the possibilities of encroachment and to the forestalling of threatened aggressions or deleterious (though perhaps unintended) consequences from the actions of others.
2. *The stability of the lines of authority and communication.* One of the persistent reference-points of administrative decision is the weighing of consequences for the continued capacity of leadership to control and to have access to the personnel or ranks.
3. *The stability of informal relations within the organization.* Ties of sentiment and self-interest are evolved as unacknowledged but effective mechanisms of adjustment of individuals and subgroups to the conditions of life within the organization. These ties represent a cementing of relationships which sustains the formal authority in day-to-day operations and widens opportunities for effective communication.[13] Consequently, attempts to "upset" the informal structure, either frontally or as an indirect consequence of formal reorganization, will normally be met with considerable resistance.
4. *The continuity of policy and of the sources of its determination.* For each level within the organization, and for the organization as a whole, it is necessary that there be a sense that action taken in the light of a given policy will not be placed in continuous jeopardy. Arbitrary or unpredictable changes in policy undermine the significance of (and therefore the attention to) day-to-day action by injecting a note of capriciousness. At the same time, the

organization will seek stable roots (or firm statutory authority or popular mandate) so that a sense of the permanency and legitimacy of its acts will be achieved.

5. *A homogeneity of outlook with respect to the meaning and role of the organization.* The minimization of disaffection requires a unity derived from a common understanding of what the character of the organization is meant to be. When this homogeneity breaks down, as in situations of internal conflict over basic issues, the continued existence of the organization is endangered. On the other hand, one of the signs of "healthy" organization is the ability to effectively orient new members and readily slough off those who cannot be adapted to the established outlook.

This catalogue of needs cannot be thought of as final, but it approximates the stable system generally characteristic of formal organizations. These imperatives are derived, in the sense that they represent the conditions for survival or self-maintenance of cooperative systems of organized action. An inspection of these needs suggests that organizational survival is intimately connected with the struggle for relative prestige, both for the organization and for elements and individuals within it. It may therefore be useful to refer to a *prestige-survival motif* in organizational behavior as a shorthand way of relating behavior needs, especially when the exact nature of the needs remains in doubt. However, it must be emphasized that prestige-survival in organizations does not derive simply from like motives in individuals. Loyalty and self-sacrifice may be individual expressions of organizational or group egotism and self-consciousness.

The concept of organizational need directs analysis to the *internal relevance* of organizational behavior. This is especially pertinent with respect to discretionary action undertaken by agents manifestly in pursuit of formal goals. The question then becomes one of relating the specific act of discretion to some presumptively stable organizational need. In other words, it is not simply action plainly oriented internally (such as in-service training) but also action

presumably oriented externally which must be inspected for its relevance to internal conditions. This is of prime importance for the understanding of bureaucratic behavior, for it is of the essence of the latter that action formally undertaken for substantive goals be weighed and transformed in terms of its consequences for the position of the officialdom....

The setting of structural-functional analysis as applied to organizations requires some qualification, however. Let us entertain the suggestion that the interesting problem in social science is not so much why men act the way they do as why men in certain circumstances *must* act the way they do. This emphasis upon constraint, if accepted, releases us from an ubiquitous attention to behavior in general, and especially from any undue fixation upon statistics. On the other hand, it has what would seem to be a salutary consequence of focusing inquiry upon certain necessary relationships of the type "if ... then," for example: If the cultural level of the rank and file members of a formally democratic organization is below that necessary for participation in the formulation of policy, then there will be pressure upon the leaders to use the tools of demagogy.

Is such a statement universal in its applicability? Surely not in the sense that one can predict without remainder the nature of all or even most political groups in a democracy. Concrete behavior is a resultant, a complex vector, shaped by the operation of a number of such general constraints. But there is a test of general applicability: it is that of noting whether the relation made explicit must be *taken into account* in action. This criterion represents an empirical test of the significance of social generalizations. If a theory is significant it will state a relation which will either (1) be taken into account as an element of achieving control; or (2) be ignored only at the risk of losing control and will evidence itself in a ramification of objective or unintended consequences.[14] It is a corollary of this principle of significance that investigation must search out the underlying factors in organizational action, which requires a kind of intensive analysis of the same order as psychoanalytic probing.

A frame of reference which invites attention to the constraints upon behavior will tend to highlight tensions and dilemmas, the characteristic paradoxes generated in the course of action. The dilemma may be said to be the handmaiden of structural-functional analysis, for it introduces the concept of *commitment* or *involvement* as fundamental to organizational analysis. A dilemma in human behavior is represented by an inescapable commitment which cannot be reconciled with the needs of the organism or the social system. There are many spurious dilemmas which have to do with verbal contradictions, but inherent dilemmas to which we refer are of a more profound sort, for they reflect the basic nature of the empirical system in question. An economic order committed to profit as its sustaining incentive may, in Marxist terms, sow the seed of its own destruction. Again, the anguish of man, torn between finitude and pride, is not a matter of arbitrary and replaceable assumptions but is a reflection of the psychological needs of the human organism, and is concretized in his commitment to the institutions which command his life; he is in the world and of it, inescapably involved in its goals and demands; at the same time, the needs of the spirit are compelling, proposing modes of salvation which have continuously disquieting consequences for worldly involvements. In still another context, the need of the human organism for affection and response necessitates a commitment to elements of the culture which can provide them; but the rule of the super-ego is uncertain since it cannot be completely reconciled with the need for libidinal satisfaction....

Organizational analysis, too, must find its selective principle; otherwise the indiscriminate attempts to relate activity functionally to needs will produce little in the way of significant theory. Such a principle might read as follows: *Our frame of reference is to select out those needs which cannot be fulfilled within approved avenues of expression and thus must have recourse to such adaptive mechanisms as ideology and to the manipulation of formal processes and structures in terms of informal goals.* This formulation has many difficulties, and is not presented as conclusive, but it suggests the kind of principle which is likely to separate the quick and the dead, the meaningful and the trite, in the study of cooperative systems in organized action.[15]

The frame of reference outlined here for the theory of organization may now be identified as involving the following major ideas: (1) the concept of organizations as cooperative systems, adaptive social structures, made up of interacting individuals, subgroups, and informal plus formal relationships; (2) structural-functional analysis, which relates variable aspects of organization (such as goals) to stable needs and self-defensive mechanisms; (3) the concept of recalcitrance as a quality of the tools of social action, involving a break in the continuum of adjustment and defining an environment of constraint, commitment, and tension. This frame of reference is suggested as providing a specifiable *area of relations* within which predicates in the theory of organization will be sought, and at the same time setting forth principles of selection and relevance in our approach to the data of organization.

It will be noted that we have set forth this frame of reference within the overall context of social action. The significance of events may be defined by their place and operational role in a means-end scheme. If functional analysis searches out the elements important for the maintenance of a given structure, and that structure is one of the materials to be manipulated in action, then that which is functional in respect to the structure is also functional in respect to the action system. This provides a ground for the significance of functionally derived theories. At the same time, relevance to control in action is the empirical test of their applicability or truth.

## CO-OPTATION AS A MECHANISM OF ADJUSTMENT

The frame of reference stated above is in fact an amalgam of definition, resolution, and substantive theory. There is an element of *definition* on conceiving of formal organizations as cooperative systems, though of course the interaction of informal and formal patterns is a question of fact; in a sense, we are *resolving* to employ structural-functional analysis on the assumption that it will be fruitful to do so, though here, too, the specification of needs or derived imperatives is a matter for empirical inquiry; and our predication of recalcitrance as a quality of the tools of action is itself a *substantive theory*, perhaps fundamental to a general understanding of the nature of social action.

A theory of organization requires more than a general frame of reference, though the latter is indispensable to inform the approach of inquiry to any given set of materials. What is necessary is the construction of generalizations concerning transformations within and among cooperative systems. These generalizations represent, from the standpoint of particular cases, possible predicates which are relevant to the materials as we know them in general, but which are not necessarily controlling in all circumstances. A theory of transformations in organization would specify those states of the system which resulted typically in predictable, or at least understandable, changes in such aspects of organization as goals, leadership, doctrine, efficiency, effectiveness, and size. These empirical generalizations would be systematized as they were related to the stable needs of the cooperative system.

Changes in the characteristics of organizations may occur as a result of many different conditions, not always or necessarily related to the processes of organization as such. But the theory of organization must be selective, so that explanations of transformations will be sought within its own assumptions or frame of reference. Consider the question of size. Organizations may expand for many reasons—the availability of markets, legislative delegations, the swing of opinion—which may be accidental from the point of view of the organizational process. To explore changes in size (as of, say, a trades union) as related to changes in nonorganizational conditions may be necessitated by the historical events to be described, but it will not of itself advance the frontiers of the theory of organization. However, if "the innate propensity of all organizations to expand" is asserted as a function of "the inherent instability of incentives"[16] then transformations have been stated within the terms of the theory of organization itself. It is likely that in many cases the generalization in question may represent only a minor aspect of the empirical changes, but these organizational relations must be made explicit if the theory is to receive development.

In a frame of reference which specifies needs and anticipates the formulation of a set of self-defensive responses or mechanisms, the latter appear to constitute one kind of empirical generalization or "possible predicate" within the general theory. The needs of organizations (whatever investigation may determine them to be) are posited as attributes of all organizations, but the responses to disequilibrium will be varied. The mechanisms used by the system in fulfillment of its needs will be repetitive and thus may be described as a specifiable set of assertions within the theory of organization, but any given organization may or may not have recourse to the characteristic modes of response. Certainly no given organization will employ all of the possible mechanisms which are theoretically available. When Barnard speaks of an "innate propensity of organization to expand," he is in fact formulating one of the general mechanisms, namely, expansion, which is a characteristic mode of response available to an organization under pressure from within. These responses necessarily involve a transformation (in this case, size) of some structural aspect of the organization.

Other examples of the self-defensive mechanisms available to organizations may derive primarily from the response of these organizations to the institutional environments in which they live. The tendency to construct ideologies, reflecting the need to come to terms with major social forces, is one such mechanism. Less well understood as a mechanism of organizational adjustment is what we may term *co-optation*. Some statement of the meaning of this concept may aid in clarifying the foregoing analysis.

Co-optation is the process of absorbing new elements into the leadership or policy-determining structure of an organization as a means of averting threats to its stability or existence. This is a defensive mechanism, formulated as one of a number of possible predicates available for the interpretation of organizational behavior. Co-optation tells us something about the process by which an institutional environment impinges itself upon an organization and effects changes in its leadership and policy. Formal authority may resort to co-optation under the following general conditions:

1. When there exists a hiatus between consent and control, so that the legitimacy of the formal authority is called into question. The "indivisibility" of consent and control refers, of course, to an optimum situation. Where control lacks an adequate measure of consent, it may revert to coercive measures or attempt somehow to win the consent of the governed. One means of winning consent is to co-opt elements into the leadership or organization, usually elements which in some way reflect the sentiment, or possess the confidence of the relevant public or mass. As a result, it is expected that the new elements will lend respectability or legitimacy to the organs of control and thus reestablish the stability of formal authority. This process is widely used, and in many different contexts. It is met in colonial countries, where the organs of alien control reaffirm their legitimacy by co-opting native leaders into the colonial administration. We find it in the phenomenon of "crisis-patriotism" wherein formally disfranchised groups are temporarily given representation in the councils of government in order to win their solidarity in a time of national stress. Co-optation is presently being considered by the United States Army in its study of proposals to give enlisted personnel representation in the court-martial machinery—a clearly adaptive response to stresses made explicit during the war, the lack of confidence in the administration of army justice. The "unity" parties of totalitarian states are another form of co-optation; company unions or some employee representation plans in industry are still another. In each of these cases, the response of formal authority (private or public, in a large organization or a small one) is an attempt to correct a state of imbalance by *formal* measures. It will be noted, moreover, that what is shared is the *responsibility* for power rather than power itself. These conditions define what we shall refer to as *formal co-optation*.

2. Co-optation may be a response to the pressure of specific centers of power. This is not necessarily a matter of legitimacy or of a general and diffuse lack of confidence. These may be well established; and yet organized forces which are able to threaten the formal authority may effectively shape its structure and policy. The organization in respect to its institutional environment—or the leadership in respect to its ranks—must take these forces into account. As a consequence, the outside elements may be brought into the leadership or policy-determining structure, may be given a place as a recognition of and concession to the resources they can independently command. The representation of interests through administrative constituencies is a typical example of this process. Or, within an organization, individuals upon whom the group is dependent for funds or other resources may insist upon and receive a share in the determination of policy. This form of cooperation is typically expressed in informal terms, for the problem is not one of responding to a state of imbalance with respect to the "people as a whole" but rather one of meeting the pressure of specific individuals or interest-groups which are in a position to enforce demands. The latter are interested in the

substance of power and not its forms. Moreover, an open acknowledgement of capitulation to specific interests may itself undermine the sense of legitimacy of the formal authority within the community. Consequently, there is a positive pressure to refrain from explicit recognition of the relationship established. This form of the co-optative mechanism, having to do with the sharing of power as a response to specific pressures, may be termed *informal co-optation*.

Co-optation reflects a state of tension between formal authority and social power. The former is embodied in a particular structure and leadership, but the latter has to do with subjective and objective factors which control the loyalties and potential manipulability of the community. Where the formal authority is an expression of social power, its stability is assured. On the other hand, when it becomes divorced from the sources of social power its continued existence is threatened. This threat may arise from the sheer alienation of sentiment or from the fact that other leaderships have control over the sources of social power. Where a formal authority has been accustomed to the assumption that its constituents respond to it as individuals, there may be a rude awakening when organization of those constituents on a nongovernmental basis creates nuclei of power which are able effectively to demand a sharing of power.[17]

The significance of co-optation for organizational analysis is not simply that there is a change in or a broadening of leadership, and that this is an adaptive response, but also that *this change is consequential for the character and role of the organization*. Co-optation involves commitment, so that the groups to which adaptation has been made constrain the field of choice available to the organization or leadership in question. The character of the co-opted elements will necessarily shape (inhibit or broaden) the modes of action available to the leadership which has won adaptation and security at the price of commitment. The concept of co-optation thus implicitly

sets forth the major points of the frame of reference outlined above: it is an adaptive response of a cooperative system to a stable need, generating transformations which reflect constraints enforced by the recalcitrant tools of action.

## NOTES

1. John M. Gaus, "A Theory of Organization in Public Administration," in *The Frontiers of Public Administration* (Chicago: University of Chicago Press, 1936), p. 66.

2. Chester I. Barnard, *The Functions of the Executive* (Cambridge: Harvard University Press, 1938), p. 73.

3. cf. Talcott Parsons' generalization (after Max Weber) of the "law of the increasing rationality of action systems," in *The Structure of Social Action* (New York: McGraw-Hill, 1937), p. 752.

4. See Luther Gulick and Lydall Urwick (eds.), *Papers on the Science of Administration* (New York: Institute of Public Administration, Columbia University, 1937); Lydall Urwick, *The Elements of Administration* (New York: Harper, 1943); James D. Mooney and Alan C. Reiley, *The Principles of Organization* (New York: Harper, 1939); H. S. Dennison, *Organization Engineering* (New York: McGraw-Hill, 1931).

5. Urwick, *The Elements of Administration*, *op. cit.*, p. 47.

6. See Gaus, *op. cit.* Studies of the problem of morale are instances of the same orientation, having received considerable impetus in recent years from the work of the Harvard Business School group.

7. The creation of informal structures within various types of organizations has received explicit recognition in recent years. See F. J. Roethlisberger and W. J. Dickson, *Management and the Worker* (Cambridge: Harvard University Press, 1941), p. 524; also Barnard, *op. cit.*, c. ix; and Wilbert E. Moore, *Industrial Relations and the Social Order* (New York: Macmillan, 1946), chap. xv.

8. For an analysis of the latter in these terms, see Philip Selznick, "An Approach to a Theory of Bureaucracy," *American Sociological Review* 8 (February, 1943).

9. Robert Michels, "Authority," *Encyclopedia of the Social Sciences* (New York: Macmillan, 1931), pp. 319 ff.; also Barnard, *op. cit.*, c. xii.

10. For a presentation of this approach having a more general reference than the study of formal organizations, see Talcott Parsons, "The Present Position and Prospects of Systematic Theory in Sociology," in Georges Gurvitch and Wilbert E. Moore (ed.), *Twentieth Century Sociology* (New York: The Philosophical Library, 1945).

11. "Structure" refers to both the relationships within the system (formal plus informal patterns in organization) and the set of needs and modes of satisfaction which characterize the given type of empirical system. As the utilization of this type of analysis proceeds, the concept of "need" will require further clarification. In particular, the imputation of a "stable set of needs" to organizational systems must not function as a new instinct theory. At the same time, we cannot avoid using these inductions as to generic needs, for they help us to stake out our area of inquiry. The author is indebted to Robert K. Merton who has, in correspondence, raised some important objections to the use of the term "need" in this context.

12. For "derived imperative" see Bronislaw Malinowski, *The Dynamics of Culture Change* (New Haven: Yale University Press, 1945), pp. 44 ff. For the use of "need" in place of "motive" see the same author's *A Scientific Theory of Culture* (Chapel Hill: University of North Carolina Press, 1944), pp. 89–90.

13. They may also *destroy* those relationships, as noted above, but the need remains, generating one of the persistent dilemmas of leadership.

14. See R. M. MacIver's discussion of the "dynamic assessment" which "brings the external world selectively into the subjective realm, conferring on it subjective significance for the ends of action." *Social Causation* (Boston: Ginn, 1942), chaps. 11 and 12. The analysis of this assessment within the context of organized action yields the implicit knowledge which guides the choice among alternatives. See also Robert K. Merton, "The Unanticipated Consequences of Purposive Social Action," *American Sociological Review* 1 (December, 1936).

15. This is not meant to deprecate the study of organizations as *economies* or formal systems. The latter represent an independent level, abstracted from organizational structures as cooperative or adaptive systems ("organisms").

16. Barnard, *op. cit.*, pp. 158–159.

17. It is perhaps useful to restrict the concept of co-optation to formal organizations, but in fact it probably reflects a process characteristic of all group leaderships. This has received some recognition in the analysis of class structure, wherein the ruling class is interpreted as protecting its own stability by absorbing new elements. Thus Michels made the point that "an aristocracy cannot maintain an enduring stability by sealing itself off hermetically." See Robert Michels, *Umschichtungen in den herrschenden Klassen nach dem Kriege* (Stuttgart: Kohlhammer, 1934), p. 39; also Gaetano Mosca, *The Ruling Class* (New York: McGraw-Hill, 1939), pp. 413 ff. The alliance or amalgamation of classes in the face of a common threat may be reflected in formal and informal cooptative responses among formal organizations sensitive to class pressures. In a forthcoming volume, *TVA and the Grass Roots*, the author has made extensive use of the concept of co-optation in analyzing some aspects of the organizational behavior of a government agency.

# CHAPTER 3

# *Human Resource Theory, or the Organizational Behavior Perspective*

Students and practitioners of management have always been interested in and concerned with the behavior of people in organizations. But fundamental assumptions about the behavior of people at work did not change dramatically from the beginning of humankind's attempts to organize until only a few decades ago. Using the traditional "the boss knows best" mindset (set of assumptions), Hugo Münsterberg (1863–1916), the German-born psychologist whose work at Harvard would earn him the title "father of industrial or applied psychology," pioneered the application of psychological findings from laboratory experiments to practical matters. He sought to match the abilities of new hires with a company's work demands, to positively influence employee attitudes toward their work and their company, and to understand the impact of psychological conditions on employee productivity (H. Münsterberg, 1913; M. Münsterberg, 1922). Münsterberg's approach characterized how the behavioral sciences tended to be applied in organizations well into the 1950s. During and following World War II, the armed services were particularly active in conducting and sponsoring research into how the military could best *find and shape people to fit its needs*.

In contrast to the Münsterberg-type perspective on organizational behavior, in the post-1950s, applied behavioral scientists have sought to answer questions such as how organizations could and should allow and encourage their people to grow and develop. From this perspective, it is *assumed* that organizational creativity, flexibility, and prosperity flow naturally from employee growth and development. The essence of the relationship between organizations and people is redefined from dependence to codependence or interdependence. People are considered to be as important as or more important than the organization itself. Current organizational behavior approaches and techniques could not have been used in Hugo Münsterberg's days *because at that time, it was not believed (not assumed) that codependence or interdependence was the "right" relationship between an organization and its employees*.

Therefore, although practitioners and researchers have always been interested in the behavior of people inside organizations, it has only been since about 1960 that our basic assumptions about the relationship between organizations and people truly began to change, and the organizational behavior perspective, or human resource theory of organization, came into being. Those who see organizations through the lenses of the organizational behavior perspective focus on people, groups, and the relationships among them and the organizational environment. Because the organizational behavior perspective places a very high value on humans as individuals, things typically are done openly, including providing employees with information they need to make informed decisions with free will about their future (Argyris, 1970).

Human resource theory draws on an extensive body of research and theory built around the following assumptions:

1. Organizations exist to serve human needs (not the reverse).
2. Organizations and people need each other. Organizations need ideas, energy, and talent; people need careers, salaries, and work opportunities.
3. When the fit between the individual and the organization is poor, one or both suffer. Individuals will be exploited, or will seek to exploit the organization, or both.
4. A good fit between individual and organization benefits both. Humans find meaningful and satisfying work, and organizations get the human talent and energy that they need (Bolman & Deal, 2013).

It should be evident that human resource organization theory is an enormous field of study supported by a large body of literature because it both addresses numerous subfields and has so much research available for use. In this chapter, we can introduce only a few of its most important ideas and best-known authors. For a more thorough presentation, we suggest the fourth edition of the anthology compiled by Ott, Parkes, and Simpson (2008), *Classic Readings in Organizational Behavior*.

Ott, Parkes, and Simpson group the literature of human resource theory by its most pervasive themes:

- leadership
- motivation
- individuals in teams and groups
- effects of the work environment
- power and influence
- organizational change

Unquestionably, Mary Parker Follett authored one of the two most significant pre-1960s theories of organizational behavioral. Follett was a truly pioneering theorist who articulated the situational or contingency approach to leadership in 1926 – while classical organization theory still was still unchallenged orthodoxy. In "The Giving of Orders," Follett argued for a participatory leadership style, in which employees and employers cooperate to assess the situation and decide what should be done at that moment in that situation. Once the "law" of the situation is discovered, "the employee can issue it to the employer as well as employer to employee." This manner of giving orders facilitates better attitudes within an organization because nobody is necessarily under another person; rather, all take their cues from the situation. We, the editors of this volume, believe Mary Parker Follett deserves special acknowledgment as a courageous ground-breaker in the developmental history of organization theory.

Along with Mary Parker Follett's "The Giving of Orders," the other most significant set of events that preceded and presaged a conscious theory (and field) of organizational behavior was the multiyear work done by the Elton Mayo team at the Hawthorne plant of the Western Electric Company beginning in 1927 (Mayo, 1933; Roethlisberger & Dickson, 1939). Interestingly, the Mayo team began its work trying to fit into the mold of classical organization theory thinking. The team phrased its questions in the language and concepts that industry was accustomed to using in order to see and explain problems such as productivity in relation to such factors as the amount of light, the rate of flow of materials, and alternative wage payment plans. According to human resource theory, the organization is not the independent variable to be manipulated in order to change behavior (as a dependent variable), even though organizations pay employees to help them achieve organizational goals. Instead, the organization must be seen as the context in which behavior occurs. It is both an independent and a dependent variable. The organization influences human behavior just as behavior shapes the organization. The interactions shape conceptualizations of jobs, human communication and interaction in work groups, the impact of participation in decisions about one's own work in general, and the roles of leaders in particular.

In 1924, a team of researchers went to the Hawthorne plant of the Western Electric Company, near Chicago, under the aegis of the National Academy of Sciences' National Research Council to study ways for improving productivity. The research team began its work from the perspective of scientific management. Scientific investigative procedures were used to find and identify environmental changes that would increase worker productivity. The investigations focused on room temperature, humidity, and illumination levels. By 1927, the results were so snarled that Western Electric and the National Research Council were ready to abandon the entire endeavor. In that year, however, George Pennock, Western Electric's superintendent of inspection, heard Harvard professor Elton Mayo speak at a meeting and invited him to take a team to Hawthorne. Team members eventually included Frederick (Fritz) Roethlisberger, George Homans, and T. N. Whitehead.

The Mayo team made significant breakthroughs in understanding only after it redefined the Hawthorne problems as social psychological problems—problems conceptualized in such terms as interpersonal relations in groups, group norms, control over one's own environment, and personal recognition. Once the Mayo team achieved this breakthrough understanding, the "Hawthorne studies" became legendary and eventually the "grandfather"—the direct precursor—of the field of organizational behavior and human resource theory. We feel obligated, however, to report recent research that appears to invalidate core findings from the Hawthorne Studies (Levitt & List, 2009). Levitt and List claim,

> Our research has uncovered [data from the illumination experiments that]… were never formally analyzed and were thought to have been destroyed.… We find that existing descriptions of supposedly remarkable data patterns [from the Hawthorne Studies] prove to be entirely fictional.

On the other hand, according to Levitt and List, "There are, however, hints of more subtle manifestations of a Hawthorne effect in the original data."

Subsequently, several articles have cast doubt on the validity of the Hawthorne Studies, asserting that data were manipulated in order to find relationships that the team wanted to find (Gale, 2004 and especially Levitt & List, 2009). Whether or not these accusations are warranted, the Hawthorne studies laid the foundation for a set of assumptions that would be fully articulated and would displace the assumptions of classical organization theory. The experiments were the emotional and intellectual wellspring of the organizational behavior perspective and modern theories of motivation; they showed that complex, interacting variables make the difference in motivating people—things like attention paid to workers as individuals, workers' control over their own work, differences between individuals' needs, management's willingness to listen, group norms, and direct feedback.

The three most cited accounts of the Hawthorne studies are Fritz Roethlisberger's retrospective studies, *Management and Morale* (1941) and *Management and the Worker* (1939, with William J. Dickson), and Elton Mayo's earlier and more formative, *The Human Problems of an Industrial Civilization* (1933). In recent editions of *Classics of Organization Theory*, we have included a chapter from Roethlisberger's *Management and Morale*. For this edition, we decided to reprint a chapter from Elton Mayo's *The Human Problems of an Industrial Civilization* titled "The Hawthorne Experiment. Western Electric Company." In this chapter, Mayo obviously is still attempting to assess the significance of the team's experiments and findings. Writing six and nine years before Roethlisberger, Mayo is far less convinced of what his team was observing.

All discussions of motivation start with Abraham Maslow. His hierarchy of needs stands alongside the Hawthorne experiments and Douglas McGregor's Theory X and Theory Y as the points of departure for studying motivation in organizations. An overview of Maslow's basic theory of needs is presented here from his 1943 *Psychological Review* article, "A Theory of Human Motivation." Maslow's theoretical premises can be summarized in a few phrases:

- All humans have needs that underlie their motivational structure.
- As lower levels of needs are satisfied, they no longer "drive" behavior.
- Satisfied needs are not motivators.
- As lower-level needs of workers become satisfied, higher-order needs take over as the motivating forces.

Maslow's theory has been attacked frequently. Few empirical studies have supported it, and it oversimplifies the complex structure of human needs and motivations. Several modified needs hierarchies have been proposed that are reportedly better able to withstand empirical testing (for example, Alderfer, 1969). Despite the criticisms and the continuing advances across the spectrum of applied behavioral sciences, Abraham Maslow's theory continues to occupy a most honored and prominent place in organizational behavior and management textbooks.

While a handful of early breakthrough studies and theories, such as the Hawthorne studies and Maslow's hierarchy of needs, served as important precursors to the organizational behavior perspective, this perspective actually exploded onto the organization scene between 1957 and 1960 (Heil, Bennis, & Stephens, 2000). On April 9, 1957, Douglas M. McGregor delivered the fifth anniversary convocation address to the School of Industrial Management at the Massachusetts Institute of Technology (MIT). In his address titled "The Human Side of Enterprise," McGregor expanded his talk into some of the most influential articles and books in the history of organizational behavior and organization theory (McGregor 1957a, 1957b, 1960). "The Human Side of Enterprise" explained how managerial assumptions about employees become self-fulfilling prophecies. McGregor labeled his two sets of contrasting assumptions Theory X and Theory Y, but they are more than just theories. McGregor articulated the basic assumptions of the organizational behavior perspective and contrasted them with the tenets of classical organization theory.

Theory X and Theory Y are contrasting basic managerial assumptions about employees. According to McGregor, managerial assumptions *cause* employee behavior. Theory X and Theory Y are ways of seeing and thinking about people that, in turn, affect their behavior. Thus, "The Human Side of Enterprise" (1957b), which is reprinted in this chapter, is a landmark theory of motivation.

Theory X assumptions restate the tenets of the scientific management movement in the era of classical organization theory. Theory X holds that human beings inherently dislike work and will avoid it if possible. Most people must be coerced, controlled, directed, or threatened with punishment to get them to work toward the achievement of organizational objectives. In addition, humans prefer to be directed and to avoid responsibility and will seek security above all else.

These assumptions serve as polar opposites to McGregor's Theory Y. In contrast, Theory Y assumes that people do not inherently dislike work; rather, people can find work to be a source of satisfaction. People will exercise self-direction and self-control if they are committed to organization objectives. People are willing to seek and to accept responsibility; avoidance of responsibility is not natural—it is a consequence of experiences. The intellectual potential of most humans is only partially utilized at work.

Irving Janis' 1971 article, "Groupthink," is a study of pressures for conformance—the reasons that social conformity is frequently encountered and expected in groups. Janis examines high-level decision makers and policy decision making during times of major U.S. fiascoes: the 1962 Bay of Pigs in particular, and also the Johnson administration's decision to escalate the Vietnam War, and the 1941 failure to prepare for the attack on Pearl Harbor. Groupthink is "the mode of thinking that persons engage in when *concurrence seeking* becomes so dominant in a cohesive in-group that it tends to override realistic appraisal of alternative courses of action … the desperate drive for consensus at any cost that suppresses dissent among the mighty in the corridors of power." Janis identifies eight symptoms of groupthink that are relatively easy to observe:

- an illusion of invulnerability
- collective construction of rationalizations that permit group members to ignore warnings or other forms of negative feedback
- unquestioning belief in the morality of the in-group
- strong, negative, stereotyped views about the leaders of enemy groups
- rapid application of pressure against group members who express even momentary doubts about virtually any illusions the group shares
- careful, conscious, personal avoidance of deviation from what appears to be a group consensus
- shared illusions of unanimity of opinion
- establishment of *mindguards*—people who "protect the leader and fellow members from adverse information that might break the complacency they shared about the effectiveness and morality of past decisions."

Janis concludes with an assessment of the negative influence of groupthink on executive decision making, including overestimation of the group's capability and self-imposed isolation from new or opposing information and points of view, as well as several preventive and remedial steps for preventing and dealing with groupthink.

The steady evolution over the past two decades from *organizations as places* where people work in face-to-face contact with supervisors, peers, and subordinates, to *organizations as the center of networks*, often virtual networks, has produced significant new challenges for the organizational behavior perspective. How do people develop the relationships and trust that permit leadership, group and team norms, and loyalty to others and an organization to emerge when their colleagues may be physically located on a different continent and may be connected to the organization by contract rather than an employer-employee relationship? What types of relationships and trust can be reasonably expected to form through only electronic connections? Which long-standing principles of organizational behavior apply when organizations and relationships are electronic and/or virtual (Lipnack, J. and Stamps, J. 2000)? Has technology advanced enough to allow feelings and relationships to develop between people who are connected only electronically?

The organizational behavior perspective is the most optimistic of all perspectives or schools of organization theory. Building from Douglas McGregor's Theory X and Theory Y assumptions, organizational behavior has assumed that under the right circumstances, people and organizations will grow and prosper together. The ultimate worth of people is an overarching value of the human relations movement, a worthy end in and of itself—not simply a means or process for achieving a higher-order organizational end. Individuals and organizations are not necessarily antagonists. Managers can learn to unleash previously stifled energies and creativity. The beliefs, values, and tenets of organizational behavior are noble, uplifting, and exciting. They hold a promise for humankind, especially those who will spend their lives working in organizations.

As one would expect of a very optimistic and humanistic set of assumptions and values, they (and the strategies of organizational behavior) became strongly normative (prescriptive). For many organizational behavior practitioners especially in the 1960s— and up through the 1990s—this perspective's assumptions and methods became a cause. It is hoped that through the choices of articles and this Introductions to the chapter, we have communicated these optimistic tenets and values and articulated the logical and emotional reasons that the organizational behavior perspective developed into a movement. This is the true essence of *organizational behavior*.

## BIBLIOGRAPHY

Alderfer, J. S. (1969). An empirical test of a new theory of human needs. *Organizational Behavior and Human Performance, 4*, 142–175.

Argyris, C. (1962). *Interpersonal competence and organizational effectiveness*. Homewood, IL: Dorsey Press and Richard D. Irwin.

Argyris, C. (1970). *Intervention theory and method*. Reading, MA: Addison-Wesley.

Argyris, C. (2012). *Organizational traps: Leadership, culture, organizational design*. New York: Oxford University Press.

Bennis, W. G. (1989). *Why leaders can't lead: The unconscious conspiracy continues*. San Francisco: Jossey-Bass.

Bennis, W. G. (2009). *On becoming a leader*. New York: Basic Books.

Blanchard, K. (2009). *Leading at a higher level* (revised and expanded ed.). Upper Saddle River, NJ: FT Press.

Bolman, L. G., & T. E. Deal (2013). *Reframing organizations: Artistry, choice, and leadership*, 5th ed. San Francisco: Jossey-Bass/Wiley.

Bolman, L. G., & T. E. Deal (2011). *Leading with soul: An uncommon journey of spirit*. San Francisco: Jossey-Bass/Wiley.

Chemers, M. M. (2002). Efficacy and effectiveness: Integrating models of leadership and intelligence. In R. E. Riggio, S. E. Murphy, & F. J. Pirozzlo, eds., *Multiple intelligences and leadership*. Mahwah, NJ: Lawrence Erlbaum.

Cohen, A. R., & D. L. Bradford (2005). *Influence without authority*. Hoboken, NJ: John Wiley.

Cohen, A. R., & S. L. Fink (2003). *Effective behavior in organizations*, 7th ed. Boston: McGraw-Hill/Irwin.

Cooperrider, D. L., & D. Whitney (2005). *Appreciative inquiry: A positive revolution in change*. San Francisco: Berrett-Koehler.

Follett, M. P. (1926). The giving of orders. In H. C. Metcalf, ed., *Scientific foundations of business administration*. Baltimore, MD: Williams & Wilkins.

French, W. L., C. H. Bell Jr., & R. Zawacki (2004). *Organization development and transformation: Managing effective change*, 6th ed. Boston: McGraw-Hill/Irwin.

Gale, E. A. M. (2004). The Hawthorne studiesa fable for our times? *Quarterly Journal of Medicine*, 97(7), 439–449.

Haire, M. (1954). Industrial social psychology. In G. Lindzey, ed., *Handbook of social psychology, vol. 2: Special fields and applications* (pp. 1104–1123). Reading, MA: Addison-Wesley.

Heil, G., W. Bennis, & D. C. Stephens. (2000). *Douglas McGregor, revisited: Managing the human side of enterprise*. Hoboken, NJ: Wiley

Hersey, P., & K. H. Blanchard (1982). *Management of organizational behavior: Utilizing human resources*, 4th ed. Englewood Cliffs, NJ: Prentice Hall.

Janis, I. L. (1971). Groupthink. *Psychology Today*, 5, 44–76.

Levitt, S. D., and J. A. List (May 2009). Was there really a Hawthorne effect at the Hawthorne plant? An analysis of the original illumination experiments. Cambridge, MA: National Bureau of Economic Research Working Paper 15016, http://www.nber.org/papers/w15016

Lewin, K. (1947). Frontiers in group dynamics: Concept, method and reality in social science: Social equilibrium and social change. *Human Relations*, 1, 5–41.

Lewin, K. (1948). *Resolving social conflicts*. New York: Harper.

Lipnack, J. and Stamps, J. (2000). *Virtual Teams: People Working across Boundaries with Technology*, John Wiley & Sons, New York, NY.

Locke, E. A., & G. P. Latham. (2013). *New developments in goal setting and task performance*. New York: Routledge.

Maslow, A. H. (1943). A theory of human motivation. *Psychological Review*, 50, 370–396.

Maslow, A. H. (1998). *Maslow on management*. Hoboken, NJ: Wiley.

Mayo, G. E. (1933). *The human problems of an industrial civilization*. Boston: Harvard Business School, Division of Research.

Mayo, E. (1945). *The social problems of an industrial civilization*. Cambridge, MA: Harvard University Press.

McGregor, D. M. (1957a). The human side of enterprise. Address to the fifth anniversary convocation of the School of Industrial Management, Massachusetts Institute of Technology. In *Adventure in thought and action*. Cambridge, MA: MIT School of Industrial Management, 1957. Reprinted in W. G. Bennis, E. H. Schein, & C. McGregor, eds. (1966). *Leadership and motivation: Essays of Douglas McGregor* (pp. 3–20). Cambridge, MA: MIT Press.

McGregor, D. M. (1957b). The human side of enterprise. *Management Review*, 46, 22–28, 88–92.

McGregor, D. M. (1960). *The human side of enterprise*. New York: McGraw-Hill.

Morgan, G. (2006). *Images of organization* (updated ed.). Newbury Park, CA: Sage.

Münsterberg, H. (1913). *Psychology and industrial efficiency*. Boston, MA: Houghton Mifflin.

Münsterberg, M. (1922). *Hugo Münsterberg: His life and work*. New York: Appleton.

Northouse, P. G. (2012). *Leadership: Theory and practice*, 6th ed. Thousand Oaks, CA: Sage.

Ott, J. S., S. J. Parkes, & R. B. Simpson, eds. (2008). *Classic readings in organizational behavior*, 4th ed. Belmont, CA: Wadsworth/Perseus Books.

Porter, L. W., E. E. Lawler III, & J. R. Hackman (1975). *Behavior in organizations* (pp. 403–422). New York: McGraw-Hill.

Roethlisberger, F. J. (1941). *Management and morale*. Cambridge, MA: Harvard University Press.

Roethlisberger, F. J., & W. J. Dickson (1939). *Management and the worker*. Cambridge, MA: Harvard University Press.

Schermerhorn, J., R. N. Osborn, M. Uhl-Bien, & J. G. Hunt. (2012). *Organizational behavior*, 12th ed. Hoboken, NJ: John Wiley.

Scott, W. G. (1992). *Chester I. Barnard and the guardians of the managerial state*. Lawrence, KS: University Press of Kansas.

Senge, Peter M. (2006). *The fifth discipline: The art & practice of the learning organization* (revised ed.). New York: Doubleday.

Wheatley, M. (2007). *Leadership and the new science: Discovering order in a chaotic world* (rev. ed.). San Francisco: Jossey-Bass.

Wolf, W. B, & H. Iino, eds., (1986). *Philosophy for managers: Selected papers of Chester I. Barnard*. Ithaca, NY: ILR Press.

## 12

# The Hawthorne Experiment. Western Electric Company

*Elton Mayo*

At the time of which I speak, the year 1926, L. J. Henderson and the Harvard Fatigue Laboratory had empirically discovered that one may organize, and apparently scientifically, a carefully contrived inquiry into a human industrial problem and yet fail completely to elucidate the problem in any particular. Acting in collaboration with the National Research Council, the Western Electric Company had for three years been engaged upon an attempt to assess the effect of illumination upon the worker and his work. No official report of these experiments has yet been published, and it is consequently impossible to quote chapter and verse as to the methods employed and the results obtained. I can, however, state with confidence that the inquiry involved in one phase the segregation of two groups of workers, engaged upon the same task, in two rooms equally illuminated. The experimental diminution of the lighting, in ordered quantities, in one room only, gave no sufficiently significant difference, expressed in terms of measured output, as compared with the other still fully illuminated room. Somehow or other that complex of mutually dependent factors, the human organism, shifted its equilibrium and unintentionally defeated the purpose of the experiment.

There were many concrete questions of high importance to which the executive authority desired objective answers, independent of executive opinion. Fatigue, monotony, and their effects upon work and worker were topics of much contemporary discussion. Was it possible to demonstrate clearly the part played by these in industrial situations? Furthermore, any company controlling many thousand workers tends naturally to develop its own methods or "policies," but tends also to lack any satisfactory criterion of the actual value of its methods of dealing with people. Whereas a machine will in some way reveal an inefficiency, a method of handling human situations will rarely reveal that it is rooted in mere custom and use rather than wisdom. These various considerations led to the institution of a second inquiry or series of inquiries in April 1927.

In the institution of this second inquiry full heed was paid to the lesson of the first experiment. A group of workers was segregated for observation of the effect of various changes in the conditions of work. No attempt was made to "test for the effect of single variables." Where human beings are concerned one cannot change one condition without inadvertently changing other—so much the illumination experiment had shown. The group was kept small—six operatives—because the company officers had become alert to the possible significance for the inquiry of changes of mental attitude; it was believed that such changes were more likely to the noticed by the official observers if the group were small. Arrangements were made to measure accurately all changes in output; this also meant that the group must be small. An accurate record of output was desired for two reasons: first, changes in production

Elton Mayo, *The Human Problems of an Industrial Civilization*, chapter III, "The Hawthorne Experiment: Western Electric Company," pgs. 55-76. Originally published in 1933 by Macmillan Co. Republished in 2003 by Routledge. © 1933 The Estate of George Elton Mayo.

differ from many other human changes in that they lend themselves to exact and continuous determination; second, variations in output do effectively show "the combined effect" of all the conditions affecting a group. The work of Vernon and Wyatt[1] supports the view than an output curve does indicate the relative equilibrium or disequilibrium of the individual and the group.

The operation selected was that of assembling telephone relays. The operation ranks as repetitive; it is performed by women. A standard assembly bench with places for five workers and the appropriate equipment were put into one of the experimental rooms. This room was separated from the main assembly department by a ten-foot wooden partition. The bench was well illuminated; arrangements were made for observation of temperature and humidity changes. An attempt was made to provide for the observation of other changes and especially of unanticipated changes as well as those experimentally introduced. This again reflected the experience gained in the illumination experiments. Thus constituted, presumably for a relatively short period of observation, the experimental room actually ran on from April, 1927, to the middle of 1932, a period of over five years.

Six female operatives were chosen, five to work at the bench, one to procure and distribute parts for those engaged in assembly. Within the first year the two operatives first chosen—numbers one and two at the outset—dropped out, and their places were taken by two other workers of equal or superior skill who remained as numbers one and two until the end. The original number five left the Hawthorne Works for a time in the middle period but subsequently returned to her place in the group. In effect, then, there exist continuous records of the output of five workers for approximately five years. These records were obtained by means of a specially devised apparatus which, as each relay was completed, punched a hole in a moving tape. The tape moved at a constant speed, approximately one-quarter of an inch per minute; it punched five rows of holes, one row for each worker. At the right of each worker's place at the bench was a chute within which was an electric gate. When the worker finished a relay she placed it in the chute; as it passed through, it operated the electric gate and the punching apparatus duly recorded the relay. By measuring the distance on the tape between one hole and the next it is possible to calculate the time elapsing between the completion of one relay and another. The Company thus has a record of every relay assembled by every operative in the experimental room for five years and in almost every instance has also a record of the time taken to assemble it.

The transfer of the five workers into the experimental room was carefully arranged. For two weeks before the five operatives were moved into the special room, a record was kept of the production of each one without her knowledge. This is stated as the base output from which she starts. After this, the girls were moved into the experimental room and again for five weeks their output was recorded without the introduction of any change of working conditions or procedures. This, it was assumed, would sufficiently account for any changes incidental to the transfer. In the third period, which lasted for eight weeks, the experimental change introduced was a variation in method of payment. In the department the girls had been paid a group piece rate as members of a group of approximately one hundred workers. The change in the third period was to constitute the five a unitary group for piece-rate payment. "This meant that each girl would earn an amount more nearly in proportion to her individual effort since she was paid with a group of five instead of a group of one hundred."[2] It also meant that each girl was given a strong, though indirect, interest in the achievement of the group.

In the fourth experimental period the group was given two rest-pauses of five minutes each, beginning at 10:00 in the mid-morning and at 2:00 in the afternoon respectively. The question had been discussed beforehand with the operatives—as all subsequent changes were—and the decision had been in favor of a five minute rather than a ten or fifteen minute pause partly because there was some feeling that, if the break were longer, the lost time would perhaps not be made up. This was continued for five weeks at which time it was clear that just as total output had increased perceptibly after the constitution of the workers as

a group for payment, so also had it definitely risen again in response to the rests. The alternative of the original proposals, two ten-minute rest-pauses, was therefore adopted as the experimental change in period five. This change was retained for four weeks, in which time both the daily and weekly output of the group showed a greater rise than for any former change. In the sixth period the group was given six five-minute rests for four weeks. The girl operatives expressed some dislike of the constant interruption and the output curve showed a small recession.

The seventh experimental period was destined to become standard for the remaining years of the experiment. Period seven was originally intended to discover the effect of giving some refreshment—coffee or soup and a sandwich—to the workers

## FIGURE 12.1

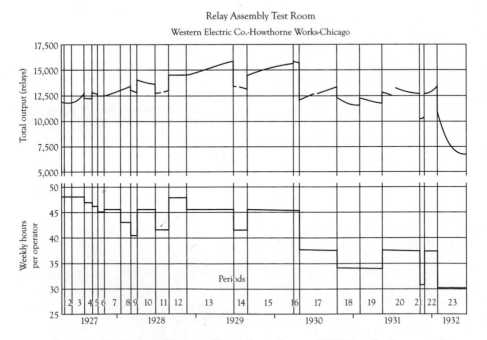

Relay Assembly Test Room

Western Electric Co.-Howthorne Works-Chicago

Elton Mayo, The Hawthorne Experiment. Western Electric Company, © 1933 Macmillan Company, p. 61

in the mid-morning period. The observers in charge had, in process of talking with the girls, found out that they frequently came to work in the morning after little or no breakfast. They became hungry long before lunch and it was thought that there was an indication of this in a downward trend of the output record before the midday break. It was therefore decided that the Company should supply each member of the group with adequate refection in the middle of the working morning and perhaps some slighter refreshment in the mid-afternoon. The refreshment provided, however, made necessary some extension of the morning break. Period seven accordingly is characterized by a mid-morning break of fifteen minutes (9:30 a.m.) with lunch and a mid-afternoon break of ten minutes (2:30 p.m.).

In the second phase of experimentation, periods eight to eleven inclusive, the conditions of period seven are held constant and other changes are introduced. In period eight the group stopped work half an hour earlier every day—at 4:30 p.m. This was attended with a remarkable rise in both daily and weekly output. This continued for seven weeks until the tenth of March 1928. In the ninth period the working day was shortened still further and the group stopped at 4:00 p.m. daily. This lasted for four weeks and in that time there was slight fall both in daily and weekly output—although the average hourly output rose. In the tenth period the group returned to the conditions of work of period seven—fifteen-minute morning rest-pause with refreshment, ten-minute rest-pause in mid-afternoon and a full working day to five o'clock. This period lasted for twelve weeks and in that time the group in respect of its recorded daily and weekly output achieved and held a production very much higher than at any previous time. It was, perhaps, this "high" of production which brought to expression certain grave doubts which had been growing in the minds of the Company

officers responsible for the experiment. Many changes other than those in production had been observed to be occurring; up to this time it had been possible to assume for practical purposes that such changes were of the nature of adaptation to special circumstance and not necessarily otherwise significant. Equally it had been possible to assume that the changes recorded in output were, at least for the most part, related to the experimental changes in working conditions—rest-pauses or what-not—singly and successively imposed. At this stage these assumptions had become untenable—especially in the light of the previously expressed determination "not to test for single variables" but to study the situation.

Period eleven was a concession to the workers, at least in part. It had already been agreed between the workers and the officers in charge that the next experiment, twelve, should be the restoration of the original conditions of work—no rest–pauses, on lunch, no shortened day or week. In period eleven—the shortened week in summer—the daily output continued to increase; it did not, however, increase sufficiently to compensate for the loss of Saturday morning's work, consequently the weekly output shows small recession.

September, 1928, was an important month in the development of the inquiry. In this period, as I have said, the group returned to the conditions of work which obtained in period three at the beginning of the inquiry; rest–periods, special refreshments, and other concessions were all abolished for approximately three months. In September, 1928, also began that extension of the inquiry known as "The Interview Programme." Both of these events must be regarded as having strongly influenced the course of the inquiry.

The history of the twelve-week return to the so-called original conditions of work is soon told. The daily and weekly output rose to a point higher than at any other time and in the whole period "there was no downward trend." At the end of twelve weeks, in period thirteen, the group returned, as had been arranged, to the conditions of period seven with the sole difference that whereas the Company continued to supply coffee or other beverage for the mid-morning lunch, the girls now provided their won food. This arrangement lasted for thirty-one weeks—much longer than any previous change. Whereas in period twelve the group's output had exceeded that of all the other performances, in period thirteen, with rest-pauses and refreshment restored, their output rose once again to even greater heights. It had become clear that the itemized changes experimentally imposed, although they could perhaps be used to account for minor differences between one period and another, yet could not be used to explain the major change—the continually increasing production. This steady increase as represented by all the contemporary records seemed to ignore the experimental changes in its upward development.

The fourteenth experimental period was a repetition of period eleven; it permitted the group to given up work on Saturday between the first of July and the thirty-first of August, 1929. The fifteenth period returned again to the conditions of the thirteenth, and at this point we may regard the conditions of period seven as the established standard for the group.

It had been the habit of the officers in charge to issue reports of the progress of the experiment from time to time. These reports were published privately to the Western Electric Company and certain of its officers. From these documents one can gain some idea of the contemporary attitude to the inquiry of those who were directing it. The fourth was issued on May 11, 1929, and in it one finds interesting discussion of the events I have just described. The first allusion to the problem is a remark to the effect that "although periods seven, ten, and thirteen involve the same

length working day, the upward trend has continued through all three of these periods" (p. 34). Later the report says: "The increased production during the test has taken the operators from an average weekly output of about 2,400 relays (each) at the beginning to a present average weekly output of about 3,000 relays. (Period 13, which lasted until the end of June, 1929.) Periods seven, ten, and thirteen had the same working conditions; namely, a fifteen-minute rest and lunch in the morning and a ten-minute rest in the afternoon. Yet the average weekly output for the group in period seven was a little over 2,500 relays each, for period ten it was a little over 2,800 relays, and for period thirteen it was about 3,000 relays. Furthermore, period twelve was like period three in working conditions requiring a full day's work without any lunch or rest. Yet the average output for period three was less than 2,500 relays a week and that for period twelve was more than 2,900 relays a week. Period twelve was continued for twelve weeks and there was no downward trend. ... The hourly output rate was distinctly higher during the full working day of period twelve than during the full working day of period three. Between the comparable periods seven, ten, and thirteen the rate of production also increased" (p. 84).

As instances of the "outcome" of the experiment the report mentions the interviewing programme, also the fact that the rest-pause system had been extended to about 3,000 employees in various departments (p. 125). From the "conclusions" I select the following passages:

"(b) There has been a continual upward trend in output which has been independent of the changes in rest-pauses. This upward trend has continued too long to be ascribed to an initial stimulus from the novelty of starting a special study."

"(c) The reduction of muscular fatigue has not been the primary factor in increasing output. Cumulative fatigue is not present."

"(f) There has been an important increase in contentment among the girls working under test-room conditions."

"(g) There has been a decrease in absences of about 80 per cent among the girls since entering the test-room group. Test-room operators have had approximately one-third as many sick absences as the regular department during the last six months" (p. 126).

"(v) Output is more directly related to the type of working day than to the number of (working) days in the week…" (p. 127).

"(y) Observations of operators in the relay assembly test room indicate that their health is being maintained or improved and that they are working within their capacity…" (p. 129).

The following conclusions in former reports are reaffirmed:

"(n) The changed working conditions have resulted in creating an eagerness on the part of operators to come to work in the morning" (p. 130).

"(s) Important factors in the production of a better mental attitude and greater enjoyment of work have been the greater freedom, less strict supervision and the opportunity to vary from a fixed pace without reprimand from a gang boss."

"The operators have no clear idea as to why they are able to produce more in the test room; but as shown in the replies to questionnaires … there is the feeling that better output is in some way related to the distinctly pleasanter, freer, and happier working conditions" (p. 131).

The report proceeds to remark that "much can be gained industrially by carrying greater personal consideration to the lowest levels of employment."

Mr. G. A. Pennock in a paper read before a conference of the Personnel Research Federation on September 15, 1929, in New York says: "…this unexpected and continual upward trend in productivity throughout the periods, even in period twelve when the girls were put on a full forty-eight hour week with no rest period or lunch, led us to seek some explanation or analysis." He goes on to mention three possibilities: first, fatigue which he finds it easy to exclude on the medical evidence, on the basis of certain physiological findings, and on the obvious ground that the "gradually rising production over a period of two years" precludes such a possibility. He considers that the payment incentive of the higher group earnings may play some small part, but proceeds to state his conviction that the results are mainly due to changes in mental attitude. He proceeds to cite evidence to show the extent of this change.

It will be remembered that one of the avowed intentions of this inquiry was to observe as well as might be the unanticipated changes, including changes of mental attitude. The method overtly adopted at the beginning of the inquiry is stated in an early report as follows:

## *"C. Pertinent Records*

Other records pertinent to the test and of value as an aid in interpreting results and psychological effects are maintained as follows:

1. The temperature and relative humidity, which are recorded each hour and then averaged, are plotted on the daily average hourly curve.

2. A complete report of the daily happenings (history sheets) of the test is made and this records what changes are made; what transpires during the day; operators' remarks; our own observations; and anything that will assist as an explanation when rationalizing the performance curve.

3. A "Log Sheet" is maintained on each operator upon which her starting and finishing time is entered, and the time at which changes from one type to another are made; also all intervals, or non-productive time, such as personal time out, changes in

type, repairs, and anything detracting from the actual production time.

4. An original hospital report, or record of physical examination, is kept. This has been supplemented each time the group is reexamined which occurs periodically every five or six weeks....

5. An attempt was made to discover the home and social environs of each girl worker....

6. Data have been gathered in the attempt to reflect what in the judgment of the operators themselves is the reason why they do better work under test-room conditions...."[3]

These original provisions were effective largely because the experimental room was in charge of an interested and sympathetic chief observer. He understood clearly from the first that any hint of "the supervisor" in his methods might be fatal to the interests of the inquiry.

In the early stages of development, it was inevitable that the group should become interested in its achievement and should to some extent enjoy the reflected glory of the interest the inquiry attracted. As the years passed this abated somewhat, but all the evidence— including the maintenance of a high output— goes to show that something in the reconditioning of the group must be regarded as a permanent achievement. At no time in the five-year period did the girls feel that they were working under pressure; on the contrary they invariably cite the absence of this as their reason for preferring the "test room."

The reason, then, for Mr. Pennock's claim is plain. Undoubtedly, there had been a remarkable change of mental attitude in the group. This showed in their recurrent conferences with high executive authorities. At first shy and uneasy, silent and perhaps somewhat suspicious of the Company's intention, later their attitude is marked by confidence and candor. Before every change of programme, the group is consulted. Their comments are

listened to and discussed; sometimes their objections are allowed to negative a suggestion. The group unquestionably develops a sense of participation in the critical determinations and becomes something of a social unit. This developing social unity is illustrated by the entertainment of each other in their respective homes, especially operatives one, two, three, and four.

How can a change such as this be assessed? It is a change of mental attitude; it is also far more. The institution of rest-pauses is probably the only major change and it takes time for those secondary changes to be effected which finally show in increased output—amongst other effects. By "secondary changes" I mean those secondary effects of rest-pauses such as diminished discontent with work and working conditions and all that may imply in human thought.

The most significant change that the Western Electric Company introduced onto its "test room" bore only a casual relation to the experimental changes. What the Company actually did for the group was to reconstruct entirely its whole industrial situation. Miss May Smith has wisely observed that the repetition work is "a thread of the total pattern," but "is not the total pattern." The Company, in the interest of developing a new form of scientific control—namely, measurement and accurate observation—incidentally altered the total pattern, in Miss Smith's analogy, and then experimented with that thread which, in this instance, was the work of assembling relays. The consequence was that there was a period during which the individual workers and the group had to re-adapt themselves to a new industrial milieu, a milieu in which their own self-determination and their social well-being ranked first and the work was incidental. The experimental changes—rest-pauses, food, and talk at appropriate intervals— perhaps operated at first mainly to convince them of the major change and to assist the re-adaptation. But once the new orientation had been established, it became proof against the minor experimental changes. At Hawthorne as the situation developed the experimental changes became minor matters in actuality—whatever the operatives thought. With respect to period twelve any theory that there was "a return to original conditions" is nonsensical. At that time the new industrial milieu, the new "total pattern," had been sufficiently established and the repetition work, "the thread," ran true to this, its chief determinant.

It must not be supposed that the abandonment of rest-pauses and other concessions in period twelve was without effect. But these minor consequences were obscured by the major achievement, the capacity of the group—unsuspected even by themselves— to ignore an interference and continue their response to the major change—the novel industrial milieu. All this is, of course, mere description of an empirical kind antecedent to analysis. The analysis proceeds and will at some later time be reported. In the meantime it is of interest to observe the manner in which the Western Electric experiment echoes the biological findings of Cyril Burt and May Smith, of L. J. Henderson and his colleagues of the Fatigue Laboratory. May Smith quotes Cyril Burt's apt description of "multiple determination" in his discussion of juvenile delinquency. "A particular result is not caused by some one factor operating equally on all people, so that the presence of this factor invariably would produce the same results. Rather is it that there are several factors which together, operating on a particular temperament, will produce the result." The Western Electric experiment was primarily directed not to the external condition but to the inner organization. By strengthening the "temperamental" inner equilibrium of the workers, the Company enabled them to achieve a mental

"steady state" which offered a high resistance to a variety of external conditions.

I have said that this is merely descriptive and is no more than a first step toward the requisite analysis. T. N. Whitehead, by a fortunate use of mathematics, has embarked upon an analysis of the records of output which promises to be of the highest interest. I cannot present his work, nor shall I attempt to anticipate his illuminating findings. I shall merely indicate one or two of the directions in which his work is leading—this by way of arousing some alertness to what is to come. For example, he tends to the view that learning and skill are not capacities which are achieved once and for all time by a given individual. On the contrary the individual's skill is reachieved each day and consequently depends in some degree upon the external conditions of that day and inner equilibrium. While this would probably be admitted at once by any neurologist, its demonstration from a work-curve is unusual. He finds also that in a group such as that described the determination of muscular movement is partly socially and partly individually conditioned. The gross muscular movements seem to be determined by one's neighbors after some years of association; the manipulative movements appear to be more individual. This has an effect both on output and on accidents because both are products of the relation between the speed and dexterity of gross muscular and of manipulative movement.

## NOTES

1. Industrial Fatigue Research Board, No. 25, H. M. Vernon, T. Bedford, S. Wyatt; No. 26, H. M. Vernon, S. Wyatt, A.D. Ogden.
2. *Personnel Journal*, 1. Vol. VIII, No. 5.
3. Third Report, Western Electric Company, pp. 2, 3.

# 13

# A Theory of Human Motivation

*Abraham H. Maslow*

## I. INTRODUCTION

In a previous paper [11] various propositions were presented which would have to be included in any theory of human motivation that could lay claim to being definitive. These conclusions may be briefly summarized as follows:

1. The integrated wholeness of the organism must be one of the foundation stones of motivation theory.
2. The hunger drive (or any other physiological drive) was rejected as a centering point or model for a definitive theory of motivation. Any drive that is somatically based and localizable was shown to be atypical rather than typical in human motivation.
3. Such a theory should stress and center itself upon ultimate or basic goals rather than partial or superficial ones, upon ends rather than means to these ends. Such a stress would imply a more central place for unconscious than for conscious motivations.
4. There are usually available various cultural paths to the same goal. Therefore conscious, specific, local-cultural desires are not as fundamental in motivation theory as the more basic, unconscious goals.
5. Any motivated behavior, either preparatory or consummatory, must be understood to be a channel through which many basic needs may be simultaneously expressed or satisfied. Typically an act has *more* than one motivation.
6. Practically all organismic states are to be understood as motivated and as motivating.
7. Human needs arrange themselves in hierarchies of prepotency. That is to say, the appearance of one need usually rests on the prior satisfaction of another, more pre-potent need. Man is a perpetually wanting animal. Also no need or drive can be treated as if it were isolated or discrete; every drive is related to the state of satisfaction or dissatisfaction of other drives.
8. Lists of drives will get us nowhere for various theoretical and practical reasons. Furthermore any classification of motivations must deal with the problem of levels of specificity or generalization of the motives to be classified.
9. Classifications of motivations must be based upon goals rather than upon instigating drives or motivated behavior.
10. Motivation theory should be human-centered rather than animal-centered.
11. The situation or the field in which the organism reacts must be taken into account but the field alone can rarely serve as an exclusive explanation for behavior. Furthermore the field itself must be interpreted in terms of the organism. Field theory cannot be a substitute for motivation theory.
12. Not only the integration of the organism must be taken into account, but also the possibility of isolated, specific, partial or segmental reactions.

It has since become necessary to add to these another affirmation.

13. Motivation theory is not synonymous with behavior theory. The motivations are only one class of determinants of behavior. While behavior is almost always motivated, it is also almost always biologically, culturally and situationally determined as well.

The present paper is an attempt to formulate a positive theory of motivation which will satisfy these theoretical demands and

*Source: Psychological Review* 50 (1943): 370–396.

at the same time conform to the known facts, clinical and observational as well as experimental. It derives most directly, however, from clinical experience. This theory is, I think, in the functionalist tradition of James and Dewey, and is fused with the holism of Wertheimer [15], Goldstein [5], and Gestalt Psychology, and with the dynamicism of Freud [3] and Adler [1]. This fusion or synthesis may arbitrarily be called a "general-dynamic" theory.

It is far easier to perceive and to criticize the aspects in motivation theory than to remedy them. Mostly this is because of the very serious lack of sound data in this area. I conceive this lack of sound facts to be due primarily to the absence of a valid theory of motivation. The present theory then must be considered to be a suggested program or framework for future research and must stand or fall, not so much on facts available or evidence presented, as upon researches yet to be done, researches suggested perhaps, by the questions raised in this paper.

## II. THE BASIC NEEDS

**The "Physiological" Needs.** The needs that are usually taken as the starting point for motivation theory are the so-called physiological drives. Two recent lines of research make it necessary to revise our customary notions about these needs, first, the development of the concept of homeostasis, and second, the finding that appetites (preferential choices among foods) are a fairly efficient indication of actual needs or lacks in the body.

Homeostasis refers to the body's automatic efforts to maintain a constant, normal state of the blood stream. Cannon [2] has described this process for (1) the water content of the blood, (2) salt content, (3) sugar content, (4) protein content, (5) fat content, (6) calcium content, (7) oxygen content, (8) constant hydrogen-ion level (acid-base balance), and (9) constant temperature of the blood. Obviously this list can be extended to include other minerals, the hormones, vitamins, etc.

Young in a recent article [16] has summarized the work on appetite in its relation to body needs. If the body lacks some chemical, the individual will tend to develop a specific appetite or partial hunger for that food element....

It should be pointed out again that any of the physiological needs and the consummatory behavior involved with them serve as channels for all sorts of other needs as well. That is to say, the person who thinks he is hungry may actually be seeking more for comfort, or dependence, than for vitamins or proteins. Conversely, it is possible to satisfy the hunger need in part by other activities such as drinking water or smoking cigarettes. In other words, relatively isolable as these physiological needs are, they are not completely so.

Undoubtedly these physiological needs are the most prepotent of all needs. What this means specifically is that, in the human being who is missing everything in life in an extreme fashion, it is most likely that the major motivation would be the physiological needs rather than any others. A person who is lacking food, safety, love, and esteem would most probably hunger for food more strongly than for anything else.

If all the needs are unsatisfied, and the organism is then dominated by the physiological needs, all other needs may become simply nonexistent or be pushed into the background.... For the man who is extremely and dangerously hungry, no other interests exist but food. He dreams food, he remembers food, he thinks about food, he emotes only about food, he perceives only food, and he wants only food. The more subtle determinants that ordinarily fuse with the physiological drives in organizing even feeding, drinking, or sexual behavior, may not be so completely overwhelmed as to allow us to speak at this time (but *only* at this time) of pure hunger drive and behavior, with the one unqualified aim of relief.

Another peculiar characteristic of the human organism when it is dominated by a certain need is that the whole philosophy of the future tends also to change. For our chronically and extremely hungry man, Utopia can be defined very simply as a place where there is plenty of food. He tends to think that, if only he is guaranteed food for the rest of his life, he will be perfectly happy and will never want anything more. Life itself tends to be defined in terms of eating. Anything else will be defined as unimportant. Freedom, love, community feeling, respect, philosophy, may all be waved aside as fripperies which are useless since they fail to fill the stomach. Such a man may fairly be said to live by bread alone.

It cannot possibly be denied that such things are true but their *generality* can be denied. Emergency conditions are, almost by definition, rare in the normally functioning peaceful society....

*At once other (and "higher") needs emerge* and these, rather than physiological hungers, dominate the organism. And when these in turn are satisfied, again new (and still "higher") needs emerge and so on. This is what we mean by saying that the basic human needs are organized into a hierarchy of relative prepotency.

One main implication of this phrasing is that gratification becomes as important a concept as deprivation in motivation theory, for it releases the organism from the domination of a relatively more physiological need, permitting thereby the emergence of other more social goals. The physiological needs, along with their partial goals, when chronically gratified cease to exist as active determinants or organizers of behavior. They now exist only in a potential fashion in the sense that they may emerge again to dominate the organism if they are thwarted. But a want that is satisfied is no longer a want. The organism is dominated and its behavior organized only by unsatisfied needs. If hunger is satisfied, it becomes unimportant in the current dynamics of the individual....

**The Safety Needs.** If the physiological needs are relatively well gratified, there then emerges a new set of needs, which we may categorize roughly as the safety needs. All that has been said of the physiological needs is equally true, although in lesser degree, of these desires. The organism may equally well be wholly dominated by them. They may serve as the almost exclusive organizers of behavior, recruiting all the capacities of the organism in their service, and we may then fairly describe the whole organism as a safety-seeking mechanism. Again we may say of the receptors, the effectors, of the intellect and the other capacities that they are primarily safety-seeking tools. Again, as in the hungry man, we find that the dominating goal is a strong determinant not only of his current world-outlook and philosophy but also of his philosophy of the future. Practically everything looks less important than safety (even sometimes the physiological needs which being satisfied, are now underestimated). A man, in this state, if it is extreme enough and chronic enough, may be characterized as living almost for safety alone.

Although in this paper we are interested primarily in the needs of the adult, we can approach an understanding of his safety needs perhaps more efficiently by observation of infants and children, in whom these needs are much more simple and obvious. One reason for the clearer appearance of the threat or danger reaction in infants is that they do not inhibit this reaction at all, whereas adults in our society have been taught to inhibit it at all costs. Thus even when adults do feel their safety threatened we may not be able to see this on the surface. Infants will react in a total fashion and as if they were endangered, if they are disturbed or dropped suddenly, startled by loud noises, flashing light, or other unusual sensory stimulation, by rough handling, by general loss of support in the mother's arms, or by inadequate support.[1]

In infants we can also see a much more direct reaction to bodily illnesses of various kinds. Sometimes these illnesses seem to be immediately and *per se* threatening and seem to make the child feel unsafe. For instance, vomiting, colic or other sharp pains seem to make the child look at the whole world in a different way. At such a moment of pain, it may be postulated that, for the child, the appearance of the whole world suddenly changes from sunniness to darkness, so to speak, and becomes a place in which anything at all might happen, in which previously stable things have suddenly become unstable. Thus a child who because of some bad food is taken ill may, for a day or two, develop fear, nightmares, and a need for protection and reassurance never seen in him before his illness.

Another indication of the child's need for safety is his preference for some kind of undisrupted routine or rhythm. He seems to want a predictable, orderly world. For instance, injustice, unfairness, or inconsistency in the parents seems to make a child feel anxious and unsafe. This attitude may be not so much because of the injustice *per se* or any particular pains involved, but rather because this treatment threatens to make the world look unreliable, or unsafe, or unpredictable. Young children seem to thrive better under a system which has at least a skeletal outline of rigidity, in which there is a schedule of a kind, some sort of routine, something that can be counted upon, not only for the present but also far into the future. Perhaps one could express this more accurately by saying that the child needs an organized world rather than an unorganized or unstructured one....

From these and similar observations, we may generalize and say that the average child in our society generally prefers a safe, orderly, predictable, organized world, which he can count on, and in which unexpected, unmanageable or other dangerous things do not happen, and in which, in any case, he has all-powerful parents who protect and shield him from harm.

That these reactions may so easily be observed in children is in a way a proof of the fact that children in our society feel too unsafe (or, in a word, are badly brought up). Children who are reared in an unthreatening, loving family do *not* ordinarily react as we have described above [14]. In such children the danger reactions are apt to come

mostly to objects or situations that adults too would consider dangerous.[2]

The healthy, normal, fortunate adult in our culture is largely satisfied in his safety needs. The peaceful, smoothly running, "good" society ordinarily makes its members feel safe enough from wild animals, extremes of temperature, criminals, assault and murder, tyranny, etc. Therefore, in a very real sense, he no longer has any safety needs as active motivators. Just as a sated man no longer feels hungry, a safe man no longer feels endangered. If we wish to see these needs directly and clearly we must turn to neurotic or near-neurotic individuals, and to the economic and social underdogs. In between these extremes, we can perceive the expressions of safety needs only in such phenomena as, for instance, the common preference for a job with tenure and protection, the desire for a savings account, and for insurance of various kinds (medical, dental, unemployment, disability, old age).

Other broader aspects of the attempt to seek safety and stability in the world are seen in the very common preference for familiar rather than unfamiliar things, or for the known rather than the unknown. The tendency to have some religion or worldphilosophy that organizes the universe and the men in it into some sort of satisfactorily coherent, meaningful whole is also in part motivated by safety-seeking. Here too we may list science and philosophy in general as partially motivated by the safety needs (we shall see later that there are also other motivations to scientific, philosophical, or religious endeavor).

Otherwise the need for safety is seen as an active and dominant mobilizer of the organism's resources only in emergencies, *e.g.*, war, disease, natural catastrophes, crime waves, societal disorganization, neurosis, brain injury, chronically bad situation....

The neurosis in which the search for safety takes its clearest form is in the compulsiveobsessive neurosis. Compulsive-obsessives try frantically to order and stabilize the world so that no unmanageable, unexpected or unfamiliar dangers will ever appear [12]. They hedge themselves about with all sorts of ceremonials, rules, and formulas so that every possible contingency may be provided for and so that no new contingencies may appear. They are much like the brain injured cases, described by Goldstein [5], who manage to maintain their equilibrium by avoiding everything unfamiliar and strange and by ordering their restricted world in such a neat, disciplined, orderly fashion that everything in the world can be counted upon....

**The Love Needs.** If both the physiological and the safety needs are fairly well gratified, then there will emerge the love and affection and belongingness needs, and the whole cycle already described will repeat itself with this new center. Now the person will feel keenly, as never before, the absence of friends, or a sweetheart, or a wife, or children. He will hunger for affectionate relations with people in general, namely, for a place in his group, and he will strive with great intensity to achieve this goal. He will want to attain such a place more than anything else in the world and may even forget that once, when he was hungry, he sneered at love....

One thing that must be stressed at this point is that love is not synonymous with sex. Sex may be studied as a purely physiological need. Ordinarily sexual behavior is multi-determined, that is to say, determined not only by sexual but also by other needs chief among which are the love and affection needs. Also not to be overlooked is the fact that the love needs involve both giving *and* receiving love.[3]

**The Esteem Needs.** All people in our society (with a few pathological exceptions) have a need or desire for a stable, firmly based, (usually) high evaluation of themselves, for self-respect, or self-esteem, and for the esteem of others. By firmly based self-esteem, we mean that which is soundly based upon real capacity, achievement, and respect from others. These needs may be classified into two subsidiary sets. These are, first, the desire for strength, for achievement, for adequacy, for confidence in the face of the world, and for independence and freedom.[4] Secondly, we have what we may call the desire for reputation or prestige (defining it as respect or esteem from other people), recognition, attention, importance, or appreciation.[5] These needs have been relatively stressed by Alfred Adler and his followers, and have been relatively neglected by Freud and the psychoanalysts. More and more today however there is appearing widespread appreciation of their central importance.

Satisfaction of the self-esteem need leads to feelings of self-confidence, worth, strength, capability, and adequacy of being useful and necessary in the world. But thwarting of these needs produces feelings of inferiority, of weakness, and of helplessness. These feelings in turn give rise to either basic discouragement or else compensatory or neurotic trends. An appreciation of the necessity of basic self-confidence and an understanding of how helpless people are without it, can be easily gained from a study of severe traumatic neurosis [6].[6]

**The Need for Self-Actualization.** Even if all these needs are satisfied, we may still often (if not always) expect that a new discontent and restlessness will soon develop unless the individual is doing what he is fitted for. A musician must make music, an artist must paint, a poet must write, if he is to be ultimately happy. What a man can be, he must be. This need we may call self-actualization.

This term, first coined by Kurt Goldstein, is being used in this paper in a much more specific and limited fashion. It refers to the desire for self-fulfillment, namely, to the tendency for him to become actualized in what he is potentially. This tendency might be phrased as the desire to become more and more what one is, to become everything that one is capable of becoming.

The specific form that these needs will take will of course vary greatly from person to person. In one individual it may take the form of the desire to be an ideal mother, in another it may be expressed athletically, and in still another it may be expressed in painting pictures or in inventions. It is not necessarily a creative urge although in people who have any capacities for creation it will take this form.

The clear emergence of these needs rests upon prior satisfaction of the physiological, safety, love, and esteem needs. We shall call people who are satisfied in these needs, basically satisfied people, and it is from these that we may expect the fullest (and healthiest) creativeness.[7] Since, in our society, basically satisfied people are the exception, we do not know much about self-actualization, either experimentally or clinically. It remains a challenging problem for research.

**The Preconditions for the Basic Need Satisfactions.** There are certain conditions which are immediate prerequisites for the basic need satisfactions. Danger to these is reacted to almost as if it were a direct danger to the basic needs themselves. Such conditions as freedom to speak, freedom to do what one wishes so long as no harm is done to others, freedom to express one's self, freedom to investigate and seek for information, freedom to defend one's self, justice, fairness, honesty, orderliness in the group are examples of such preconditions for basic need satisfactions. Thwarting in these freedoms will be reacted to with a threat or emergency response. These conditions are not ends in themselves but they are *almost* so since they are so closely related to the basic needs, which are apparently the only ends in themselves. These conditions are defended because without them the basic satisfactions are quite impossible, or at least, very severely endangered.

If we remember that the cognitive capacities (perceptual, intellectual, learning) are a set of adjustive tools, which have, among other functions, that of satisfaction of our basic needs, then it is clear that any danger to them, any deprivation or blocking of their free use, must also be indirectly threatening to the basic needs themselves. Such a

statement is a partial solution of the general problems of curiosity, the search for knowledge, truth, and wisdom, and the ever-persistent urge to solve the cosmic mysteries.

We must therefore introduce another hypothesis and speak of degrees of closeness to the basic needs, for we have already pointed out that *any* conscious desires (partial goals) are more or less important as they are more or less close to the basic needs. The same statement may be made for various behavior acts. An act is psychologically important if it contributes directly to satisfaction of basic needs. The less directly it so contributes, or the weaker this contribution is, the less important this act must be conceived to be from the point of view of dynamic psychology. A similar statement may be made for the various defense or coping mechanisms. Some are very directly related to the protection or attainment of the basic needs, others are only weakly and distantly related. Indeed if we wished, we could speak of more basic and less basic defense mechanisms, and then affirm that danger to the more basic defenses is more threatening than danger to less basic defenses (always remembering that this is so only because of their relationship to the basic needs)....

## III. FURTHER CHARACTERISTICS OF THE BASIC NEEDS

**The Degree of Fixity of the Hierarchy of Basic Needs.** We have spoken so far as if this hierarchy were a fixed order but actually it is not nearly as rigid as we may have implied. It is true that most of the people with whom we have worked have seemed to have these basic needs in about the order that has been indicated. However, there have been a number of exceptions.

(1) There are some people in whom, for instance, self-esteem seems to be more important than love. This most common reversal in the hierarchy is usually due to the development of the notion that the

person who is most likely to be loved is a strong or powerful person, one who inspires respect or fear, and who is self-confident or aggressive. Therefore such people who lack love and seek it, may try hard to put on a front of aggressive, confident behavior. But essentially they seek high self-esteem and its behavior expressions more as a means-to-an-end than for its own sake; they seek self-assertion for the sake of love rather than for self-esteem itself.

(2) There are other, apparently innately creative people in whom the drive to creativeness seems to be more important than any other counter-determinant. Their creativeness might appear not as self-actualization released by basic satisfaction, but in spite of lack of basic satisfaction.

(3) In certain people the level of aspiration may be permanently deadened or lowered. That is to say, the less prepotent goals may simply be lost, and may disappear forever, so that the person who has experienced life at a very low level, i.e., chronic unemployment, may continue to be satisfied for the rest of his life if only he can get enough food.

(4) The so-called "psychopathic personality" is another example of permanent loss of the love needs. These are people who, according to the best data available [7], have been starved for love in the earliest months of their lives and have simply lost forever the desire and the ability to give and to receive affection (as animals lose sucking or pecking reflexes that are not exercised soon enough after birth).

(5) Another cause of reversal of the hierarchy is that when a need has been satisfied for a long time, this need may be underevaluated....

(6) Another partial explanation of *apparent* reversals is seen in the fact that we have been talking about the hierarchy of prepotency in terms of consciously felt wants or desires rather than behavior. Looking at behavior itself may give us the wrong impression. What we have claimed is that the person will *want* the more basic of two needs when deprived in both. There is no necessary implication here that he will act upon his desires. Let us say again that

there are many determinants of behavior other than the needs and desires.

(7) Perhaps more important than all these exceptions are the ones that involve ideals, high social standards, high values, and the like. With such values people become martyrs; they will give up everything for the sake of a particular ideal, or value. These people may be understood, at least in part, by reference to one basic concept (or hypothesis) which may be called "increased frustration-tolerance through early gratification." People who have been satisfied in their basic needs throughout their lives, particularly in their earlier years, seem to develop exceptional power to withstand present or future thwarting of these needs simply because they have strong, healthy character structure as a result of basic satisfaction. They are the "strong" people who can easily weather disagreement or opposition, who can swim against the stream of public opinion and who can stand up for the truth at great personal cost. It is just the ones who have loved and been well loved, and who have had many deep friendships who can hold out against hatred, rejection or persecution.

I say all this in spite of the fact that there is a certain amount of sheer habituation which is also involved in any full discussion of frustration-tolerance. For instance, it is likely that those persons who have been accustomed to relative starvation for a long time, are partially enabled thereby to withstand food deprivation. What sort of balance must be made between these two tendencies, of habituation on the one hand, and of past satisfaction breeding present frustration-tolerance on the other hand, remains to be worked out by further research. Meanwhile we may assume that they are both operative, side by side, since they do not contradict each other. In respect to this phenomenon of increased frustration-tolerance, it seems probable that the most important gratifications come in the first two years of life. That is to say, people who have been made secure and strong in the earliest years tend to remain secure and strong thereafter in the face of whatever threatens.

**Degrees of Relative Satisfaction.** So far, our theoretical discussion may have given the impression that these five sets of needs are somehow in a step-wise, all-or-none relationship to each other. We have spoken in such terms as the following: "If one need is satisfied, then another emerges." This statement might give the false impression that a need must be satisfied 100 percent before the next need emerges. In actual fact, most members of our society who are normal, are partially satisfied in all their basic needs and partially unsatisfied in all their basic needs at the same time. A more realistic description of the hierarchy would be in terms of decreasing percentages of satisfaction as we go upon the hierarchy of prepotency. For instance, if I may assign arbitrary figures for the sake of illustration, it is as if the average citizen is satisfied perhaps 85 percent in his physiological needs, 70 percent in his safety needs, 50 percent in his love needs, 40 percent in his self-esteem needs, and 10 percent in his self-actualization needs.

As for the concept of emergence of a new need after satisfaction of the prepotent need, this emergence is not a sudden, salutatory phenomenon but rather a gradual emergence by slow degrees from nothingness. For instance, if prepotent need A is satisfied only 10 percent then need B may not be visible at all. However, as this need A becomes satisfied 25 percent, need B may emerge 5 percent, as need A becomes satisfied 75 percent need B may emerge 90 percent, and so on.

**Unconscious Character of Needs.** These needs are neither necessarily conscious nor unconscious. On the whole, however, in the average person, they are more often unconscious rather than conscious....

**Cultural Specificity and Generality of Needs.** This classification of basic needs makes some attempt to take account of the relative unity behind the superficial differences in specific desires from one culture to another. Certainly in any particular culture an individual's conscious motivational content will usually be extremely different from the conscious motivational content of an individual in another society. However, it is the common experience of anthropologists that people, even in different societies, are much more alike than we would think from our first contact with them, and that as we know them better we seem to find more and more of this commonness....

**Multiple Motivations of Behavior.** These needs must be understood *not* to be *exclusive* or single determiners of certain kinds of behavior. An example may be found in any behavior that seems to be physiologically motivated, such as eating, or sexual play or the like. The clinical psychologists have long since found that any behavior may be a channel through which flow various determinants. Or to say it in another way, most behavior is multi-motivated. Within the sphere of motivational determinants any behavior tends to be determined by several or *all* of the basic needs simultaneously rather than by only one of them. The latter would be more an exception than the former. Eating may be partially for the sake of filling the stomach, and partially for the sake of comfort and amelioration of other needs. One may make love not only for pure sexual release, but also to convince one's self of one's masculinity, or to make a conquest, to feel powerful, or to win more basic affection. As an illustration, I may point out that it would be possible (theoretically if not practically) to analyze a single act of an individual and see in it the expression of his physiological needs, his safety needs, his love needs, his esteem needs, and self-actualization. This contrasts sharply with the more naive brand of trait psychology in which one trait or one motive accounts for a certain kind of act, *i.e.*, an aggressive act is traced solely to a trait of aggressiveness.

**Multiple Determinants of Behavior.** Not all behavior is determined by the basic needs. We might even say that not all behavior is motivated. There are many determinants of behavior other than motives.[8] For instance, one other important class of determinants is the so-called "field" determinants. Theoretically, at least, behavior may be determined completely by the field, or even by specific isolated external stimuli, as in association of ideas, or certain conditioned reflexes. If in response to the stimulus word "table," I immediately perceive a memory image of a table, this response certainly has nothing to do with my basic needs.

Secondly, we may call attention again to the concept of "degree of closeness to the basic needs" or "degree of motivation." Some behavior is highly motivated, other behavior is only weakly motivated. Some is not motivated at all (but all behavior is determined).

Another important point[9] is that there is a basic difference between expressive behavior and coping behavior (functional striving, purposive goal seeking). An expressive behavior does not try to do anything; it is simply a reflection of the personality. A stupid man behaves stupidly, not because he wants to, or tries to, or is motivated to, but simply because he *is* what he is. The same is true when I speak in a bass voice rather than tenor or soprano. The random movements of a healthy child, the smile on the face of a happy man even when he is alone, the springiness of the healthy man's walk, and the erectness of his carriage are other examples of expressive, non-functional behavior. Also the *style* in which a man carries out almost all his behavior, motivated as well as unmotivated, is often expressive.

We may then ask, is *all* behavior expressive or reflective of the character structure? The answer is "No." Rote, habitual, automatized, or conventional behavior may or may not be expressive. The same is true for most "stimulus-bound" behaviors.

It is finally necessary to stress that expressiveness of behavior, and goal-directedness of behavior are not mutually exclusive categories. Average behavior is usually both.

**Goals as Centering Principle in Motivation Theory.** It will be observed that the basic principle in our classification has been neither the instigation nor the motivated behavior but rather the functions, effects, purposes, or goals of the behavior. It has been proven sufficiently by various people that this is the most suitable point for centering any motivation theory.[10]

**Animal- and Human-Centering.** This theory starts with the human being rather than any lower and presumably "simpler" animal. Too many of the findings that have been made in animals have been proven to be true for animals but not for the human being. There is no reason whatsoever why we should start with animals in order to study human motivation....

**Motivation and the Theory of Psychopathogenesis.** The conscious motivational content of everyday life has, according to the foregoing, been conceived to be relatively important or unimportant accordingly as it is more or less closely related to the basic goals. A desire for an ice cream cone might actually be an indirect expression of a desire for love. If it is, then this desire for the ice cream cone becomes extremely important motivation. If, however, the ice cream is simply something to cool the mouth with, or a casual appetitive reaction, then the desire is relatively unimportant. Everyday conscious desires are to be regarded as symptoms, as *surface indicators of more basic needs*. If we were to take these superficial desires at their face value we would find ourselves in a state of complete confusion which could never be resolved, since we would be dealing seriously with symptoms rather than with what lay behind the symptoms.

Thwarting of unimportant desires produces no psychopathological results; thwarting of a basically important need does produce such results. Any theory of psychopathogenesis must then be based on a sound theory of motivation. A conflict or a frustration is not necessarily pathogenic. It becomes so only when it threatens or thwarts the basic needs, or partial needs that are closely related to the basic needs [8].

**The Role of Gratified Needs.** It has been pointed out above several times that our needs usually emerge only when more prepotent needs have been gratified. Thus gratification has an important role in motivation theory. Apart from this, however, needs cease to play an active determining or organizing role as soon as they are gratified.

What this means is that, *e.g.*, a basically satisfied person no longer has the needs for esteem, love, safety, etc....

It is such considerations as these that suggest the bold postulation that a man who is thwarted in any of his basic needs may fairly be envisaged simply as a sick man. This is a fair parallel to our designation as "sick" of the man who lacks vitamins or minerals. Who is to say that a lack of love is less important than a lack of vitamins? Since we know the pathogenic effects of love starvation, who is to say that we are invoking value-questions in an unscientific or illegitimate way, any more than the physician does who diagnoses and treats pellagra or scurvy? If I were permitted this usage, I should then say simply that a healthy man is primarily motivated by his needs to develop and actualize his fullest potentialities and capacities. If a man has any other basic needs in any active, chronic sense, then he is simply an unhealthy man. He is as surely sick as if he had suddenly developed a strong salt-hunger or calcium hunger.[11]

If this statement seems unusual or paradoxical the reader may be assured that this is only one among many such paradoxes that will appear as we revise our ways of looking at man's deeper motivations. When we ask what man wants of life, we deal with his very essence.

## IV. SUMMARY

(1) There are at least five sets of goals, which we may call basic needs. These are briefly physiological, safety, love, esteem, and self-actualization. In addition, we are motivated by the desire to achieve or maintain the various conditions upon which these basic satisfactions rest and by certain more intellectual desires.

(2) These basic goals are related to each other, being arranged in a hierarchy of prepotency. This means that the most prepotent goal will monopolize consciousness and will tend of itself to organize the recruitment of the various capacities of the organism. The less prepotent needs are minimized, even forgotten or denied. But when a need is fairly well satisfied, the next prepotent ("higher") need emerges, in turn to dominate the conscious life and to serve as the center of organization of behavior, since gratified needs are not active motivators.

Thus man is a perpetually wanting animal. Ordinarily the satisfaction of these wants is not altogether mutually exclusive, but only tends to be. The average member of our society is most often partially satisfied and partially unsatisfied in all of his wants. The hierarchy principle is usually empirically observed in terms of increasing percentages of nonsatisfaction as we go up the hierarchy. Reversals of the average order of the hierarchy are sometimes observed. Also it has been observed that an individual may permanently lose the higher wants in the hierarchy under special conditions. There are not only ordinarily multiple motivations for usual behavior, but in addition many determinants other than motives.

(3) Any thwarting or possibility of thwarting of these basic human goals, or danger to the defenses which protect them, or to the conditions upon which they rest, is considered to be a psychological threat. With a few exceptions, all psychopathology may be partially traced to such threats. A basically thwarted man may actually be defined as a "sick" man, if we wish.

(4) It is such basic threats which bring about the general emergency reactions....

## NOTES

1. As the child grows up, sheer knowledge and familiarity as well as better motor development make these "dangers" less and less dangerous and more and more

manageable. Throughout life it may be said that one of the main conative functions of education is this neutralizing of apparent dangers through knowledge, e.g., I am not afraid of thunder because I know something about it.

2. A "test battery" for safety might be confronting the child with a small exploding firecracker, or with a bewhiskered face, having the mother leave the room, putting him upon a high ladder, a hypodermic injection, having a mouse crawl up to him, etc. Of course I cannot seriously recommend the deliberate use of such "tests" for they might very well harm the child being tested. But these and similar situations come up by the score in the child's ordinary day-to-day living and may be observed. There is no reason why these stimuli should not be used with, for example, young chimpanzees.

3. For further details see [10].

4. Whether or not this particular desire is universal we do not know. The crucial question, especially important today, is "Will men who are enslaved and dominated inevitably feel dissatisfied and rebellious?" We may assume on the basis of commonly known clinical data that a man who has known true freedom (not paid for by giving up safety and security but rather built on the basis of adequate safety and security) will not willingly or easily allow his freedom to be taken away from him. But we do not know that this is true for the person born into slavery. The events of the next decade should give us our answer. See discussion of this problem in [4].

5. Perhaps the desire for prestige and respect from others is subsidiary to the desire for self-esteem or confidence in oneself. Observation of children seems to indicate that this is so, but clinical data give no clear support for such a conclusion.

6. For more extensive discussion of normal self-esteem, as well as for reports of various researchers, see [9].

7. Clearly creative behavior, like painting, is like any other behavior in having multiple determinants. It may be seen in "innately creative" people whether they are satisfied or not, happy or unhappy, hungry or sated.

Also it is clear that creative activity may be compensatory, ameliorative or purely economic. It is my impression (as yet unconfirmed) that it is possible to distinguish the artistic and intellectual products of basically satisfied people from those of basically unsatisfied people by inspection alone. In any case, here too we must distinguish, in a dynamic fashion, the overt behavior itself from its various motivations or purposes.

8. I am aware that many psychologists and psychoanalysts use the term "motivated" and "determined" synonymously, *e.g.*, Freud. But I consider this an obfuscating usage. Sharp distinctions are necessary for clarity of thought, and precision in experimentation.

9. To be discussed fully in a subsequent publication.

10. The interested reader is referred to the very excellent discussion of this point in Murray's *Explorations in Personality* [13].

11. If we were to use the word "sick" in this way, we should then also have to face squarely the relations of man to his society. One clear implication of our definition would be that (1) since a man is to be called sick who is basically thwarted, and (2) since such basic thwarting is made possible ultimately only by forces outside the individual, then (3) sickness in the individual must come ultimately from a sickness in the society. The "good" or healthy society would then be defined as one that permitted man's highest purposes to emerge by satisfying all his prepotent basic needs.

## REFERENCES

1. Adler, A. *Social interest*. London: Faber & Faber, 1938.

2. Cannon, W. B. *Wisdom of the body*. New York: Norton, 1932.

3. Freud, S. *New introductory lectures on psychoanalysis*. New York: Norton, 1933.

4. Fromm, E. *Escape from freedom*. New York: Farrar and Rinehart, 1941.

5. Goldstein, K. *The organism*. New York: American Book Co., 1939.

6. Kardiner, A. *The traumatic neuroses of war.* New York: Hoeber, 1941.

7. Levy, D. M. Primary effect of hunger. *Amer. J. Psychiat.*, 1937, 94, 643–652.

8. Maslow, A. H. Conflict, frustration, and the theory of threat. *J. abnorm. (soc.) Psychol.*, 1943, 38, 81–86.

9. _____. Dominance, personality and social behavior in women. *J. soc. Psychol.*, 1939, 10, 3–39.

10. _____. The dynamics of psychological security-insecurity. *Character & Pers.*, 1942, 10, 331–344.

11. _____. A preface to motivation theory. *Psychosomatic Med.*, 1943, 5, 85–92.

12. Maslow, A.H, & Mittlemann, B. *Principles of abnormal psychology.* New York: Harper & Bros., 1941.

13. Murray, H. A., *et al. Explorations in personality.* New York: Oxford University Press, 1938.

14. Shirley, M. Children's adjustments to a strange situation. *J. abnorm. (soc.) Psychol.*, 1942, 37, 201–217.

15. Wertheimer, M. Unpublished lectures at the New School for Social Research.

16. Young, P. T. *Motivation of behavior.* New York: Wiley, 1936.

17. _____. The experimental analysis of appetite. *Psychol. Bull.*, 1941, 38, 129–164.

## 14
# The Human Side of Enterprise

*Douglas Murray McGregor*

It has become trite to say that industry has the fundamental know-how to utilize physical science and technology for the material benefit of mankind, and that we must now learn how to utilize the social sciences to make our human organizations truly effective.

To a degree, the social sciences today are in a position like that of the physical sciences with respect to atomic energy in the thirties. We know that past conceptions of the nature of man are inadequate and, in many ways, incorrect. We are becoming quite certain that, under proper conditions, unimagined resources of creative human energy could become available within the organizational setting....

## MANAGEMENT'S TASK: THE CONVENTIONAL VIEW

The conventional conception of management's task in harnessing human energy to organizational requirements can be stated broadly in terms of three propositions. In order to avoid the complications introduced by a label, let us call this set of propositions "Theory X":

1. Management is responsible for organizing the elements of productive enterprise—money, materials, equipment, people—in the interest of economic ends.
2. With respect to people, this is a process of directing their efforts, motivating them, controlling their actions, modifying their behavior to fit the needs of the organization.

3. Without this active intervention by management, people would be passive—even resistant—to organizational needs. They must therefore be persuaded, rewarded, punished, controlled—their activities must be directed. This is management's task. We often sum it up by saying that management consists of getting things done through other people.

Behind this conventional theory there are several additional beliefs—less explicit, but widespread:

4. The average man is by nature indolent—he works as little as possible.
5. He lacks ambition, dislikes responsibility, prefers to be led.
6. He is inherently self-centered, indifferent to organizational needs.
7. He is by nature resistant to change.
8. He is gullible, not very bright, the ready dupe of the charlatan and the demagogue.

The human side of economic enterprise today is fashioned from propositions and beliefs such as these. Conventional organization structures and managerial policies, practices, and programs reflect these assumptions.

In accomplishing its task—with these assumptions as guides—management has conceived of a range of possibilities.

At one extreme, management can be "hard" or "strong." The methods for directing behavior involve coercion and threat (usually disguised), close supervision, tight controls over behavior. At the other extreme, management can be "soft" or "weak." The methods for directing behavior involve being permissive, satisfying people's demands, achieving harmony. Then they will be tractable, accept direction.

This range has been fairly completely explored during the past half century, and management has learned some things from the exploration. There are difficulties in the "hard" approach. Force breeds counterforces: restriction of output, antagonism, militant unionism, subtle but effective sabotage of management objectives. This "hard" approach is especially difficult during times of full employment.

There are also difficulties in the "soft" approach. It leads frequently to the abdication of management—to harmony, perhaps, but to indifferent performance. People take advantage of the soft approach. They continually expect more but they give less and less.

Currently, the popular theme is "firm but fair." This is an attempt to gain the advantages of both the hard and the soft approaches. It is reminiscent of Teddy Roosevelt's "speak softly and carry a big stick."

## IS THE CONVENTIONAL VIEW CORRECT?

...The social scientist does not deny that human behavior in industrial organization today is approximately what management perceives it to be. He has, in fact, observed it and studied it fairly extensively. But he is pretty sure that this behavior is *not* a consequence of man's inherent nature. It is a consequence rather of the nature of industrial organizations, of management philosophy, policy, and practice. The conventional approach of Theory X is based on mistaken notions of what is cause and what is effect.

Perhaps the best way to indicate why the conventional approach of management

is inadequate is to consider the subject of motivation.

## PHYSIOLOGICAL NEEDS

Man is a wanting animal—as soon as one of his needs is satisfied, another appears in its place. This process is unending. It continues from birth to death....

*A satisfied need is not a motivator of behavior!* This is a fact of profound significance that is regularly ignored in the conventional approach to the management of people. Consider your own need for air: Except as you are deprived of it, it has no appreciable motivating effect upon your behavior.

## SAFETY NEEDS

When the physiological needs are reasonably satisfied, needs at the next higher level begin to dominate man's behavior—to motivate him. These are called *safety needs*. They are needs for protection against danger, threat, deprivation. Some people mistakenly refer to these as needs for security. However, unless man is in a dependent relationship where he fears arbitrary deprivation, he does not demand security. The need is for the "fairest possible break." When he is confident of this, he is more than willing to take risks. But when he feels threatened or dependent, his greatest need is for guarantees, for protection, for security.

The fact needs little emphasis that, since every industrial employee is in a dependent relationship, safety needs may assume considerable importance. Arbitrary management actions, behavior which arouses uncertainty with respect to continued employment or which reflects favoritism or discrimination, unpredictable administration of policy—these can be powerful motivators of the safety needs in the employment relationship *at every level,* from worker to vice president.

## SOCIAL NEEDS

When man's physiological needs are satisfied and he is no longer fearful about his physical welfare, his *social needs* become important motivators of his behavior—needs for belonging, for association, for acceptance by his fellows, for giving and receiving friendship and love.

Management knows today of the existence of these needs, but it often assumes quite wrongly that they represent a threat to the organization. Many studies have demonstrated that the tightly knit, cohesive work group may, under proper conditions, be far more effective than an equal number of separate individuals in achieving organization goals.

Yet management, fearing group hostility to its own objectives, often goes to considerable lengths to control and direct human efforts in ways that are inimical to the natural "groupiness" of human beings. When man's social needs—and perhaps his safety needs, too—are thus thwarted, he behaves in ways which tend to defeat organizational objectives. He becomes resistant, antagonistic, uncooperative. But this behavior is a consequence, not a cause.

## EGO NEEDS

Above the social needs—in the sense that they do not become motivators until lower needs are reasonably satisfied—are the needs of greatest significance to management and to man himself. They are the *egoistic needs*, and they are of two kinds:

1. Those needs that relate to one's self-esteem—needs for self-confidence, for independence, for achievement, for competence, for knowledge.
2. Those needs that relate to one's reputation—needs for status, for recognition, for appreciation, for the deserved respect of one's fellows.

Unlike the lower needs, these are rarely satisfied: man seeks indefinitely for more satisfaction of these needs once they have become important to him. But they do not appear in any significant way until physiological, safety, and social needs are all reasonably satisfied.

The typical industrial organization offers few opportunities for the satisfaction of these egoistic needs to people at lower levels in the hierarchy. The conventional methods of organizing work, particularly in mass-production industries, give little heed to these aspects of human motivation. If the practices of scientific management were deliberately calculated to thwart these needs, they could hardly accomplish this purpose better than they do.

## SELF-FULFILLMENT NEEDS

Finally—a capstone, as it were, on the hierarchy of man's needs—there are what we may call the *needs for self-fulfillment*. These are the needs for realizing one's own potentialities, for continued self-development, for being creative in the broadest sense of that term.

It is clear that the conditions of modern life give only limited opportunity for these relatively weak needs to obtain expression. The deprivation most people experience with respect to other lower-level needs diverts their energies into the struggle to satisfy *those* needs, and the needs for self-fulfillment remain dormant.

## MANAGEMENT AND MOTIVATION

We recognize readily enough that a man suffering from a severe-dietary deficiency is sick. The deprivation of physiological needs has behavioral consequences. The same is true—although less well recognized—of deprivations of higher-level needs. The man whose needs for safety, association, independence, or status are thwarted is sick just as surely as the man who has rickets. And his sickness will have behavioral consequences. We will be mistaken if we attribute his resultant passivity, his hostility, his refusal to accept responsibility to his inherent "human nature." These forms of behavior are *symptoms* of illness—of deprivation of his social and egoistic needs.

The man whose lower-level needs are satisfied is not motivated to satisfy those needs any longer. For practical purposes they exist no longer. Management often asks, "Why aren't people more productive? We pay good wages, provide good working conditions, have excellent fringe benefits and steady employment. Yet people do not seem to be willing to put forth more than minimum effort."

The fact that management has provided for these physiological and safety needs has shifted the motivational emphasis to the social and perhaps to the egoistic needs. Unless there are opportunities *at work* to satisfy these higher-level needs, people will be deprived; and their behavior will reflect this deprivation. Under such conditions, if management continues to focus its attention on physiological needs, its efforts are bound to be ineffective.

People *will* make insistent demands for more money under these conditions. It becomes more important than ever to buy the material goods and services which can provide limited satisfaction of the thwarted needs. Although money has only limited value in satisfying many higher-level needs, it can become the focus of interest if it is the *only* means available.

## THE CARROT-AND-STICK APPROACH

The carrot-and-stick theory of motivation (like Newtonian physical theory) works reasonably well under certain circumstances. The *means* for satisfying man's physiological

and (within limits) his safety needs can be provided or withheld by management. Employment itself is such a means, and so are wages, working conditions, and benefits. By these means the individual can be controlled so long as he is struggling for subsistence.

But the carrot-and-stick theory does not work at all once man has reached an adequate subsistence level and is motivated primarily by higher needs. Management cannot provide a man with self-respect, or with the respect of his fellows, or with the satisfaction of needs for self-fulfillment. It can create such conditions that he is encouraged and enabled to seek such satisfactions for *himself,* or it can thwart him by failing to create those conditions.

But this creation of conditions is not "control." It is not a good device for directing behavior. And so management finds itself in an odd position. The high standard of living created by our modern technological know-how provides quite adequately for the satisfaction of physiological and safety needs. The only significant exception is where management practices have not created confidence in a "fair break"— and thus where safety needs are thwarted. But by making possible the satisfaction of low-level needs, management has deprived itself of the ability to use as motivators the devices on which conventional theory has taught it to rely—rewards, promises, incentives, or threats and other coercive devices.

The philosophy of management by direction and control—*regardless of whether it is hard or soft*—is inadequate to motivate because the human needs on which this approach relies are today unimportant motivators of behavior. Direction and control are essentially useless in motivating people whose important needs are social and egoistic. Both the hard and the soft approach fail today because they are simply irrelevant to the situation.

People, deprived of opportunities to satisfy at work the needs which are now important to them, behave exactly as we might predict—with indolence, passivity, resistance to change, lack of responsibility, willingness to follow the demagogue, unreasonable demands for economic benefits. It would seem that we are caught in a web of our own weaving.

## A NEW THEORY OF MANAGEMENT

For these and many other reasons, we require a different theory of the task of managing people based on more adequate assumptions about human nature and human motivation. I am going to be so bold as to suggest the broad dimensions of such a theory. Call it "Theory Y," if you will.

1. Management is responsible for organizing the elements of productive enterprise— money, materials, equipment, people—in the interest of economic ends.
2. People are *not* by nature passive or resistant to organizational needs. They have become so as a result of experience in organizations.
3. The motivation, the potential for development, the capacity for assuming responsibility, the readiness to direct behavior toward organizational goals are all present in people. Management does not put them there. It is a responsibility of management to make it possible for people to recognize and develop these human characteristics for themselves.
4. The essential task of management is to arrange organizational conditions and methods of operation so that people can achieve their own goals *best* by directing *their own* efforts toward organizational objectives.

This is a process primarily of creating opportunities, releasing potential, removing obstacles, encouraging growth, providing guidance. It is what Peter Drucker has called "management by objectives" in contrast to "management by control." It does *not* involve the abdication of management, the absence

of leadership, the lowering of standards, or the other characteristics usually associated with the "soft" approach under Theory X.

## SOME DIFFICULTIES

It is no more possible to create an organization today which will be a full, effective application of this theory than it was to build an atomic power plant in 1945. There are many formidable obstacles to overcome.

The conditions imposed by conventional organization theory and by the approach of scientific management for the past half century have tied men to limited jobs which do not utilize their capabilities, have discouraged the acceptance of responsibility, have encouraged passivity, have eliminated meaning from work. Man's habits, attitudes, expectations—his whole conception of membership in an industrial organization— have been conditioned by his experience under these circumstances.

People today are accustomed to being directed, manipulated, controlled in industrial organizations and to finding satisfaction for their social, egoistic, and self-fulfillment needs away from the job. This is true of much of management as well as of workers. Genuine "industrial citizenship"—to borrow again a term from Drucker—is a remote and unrealistic idea, the meaning of which has not even been considered by most members of industrial organizations.

Another way of saying this is that Theory X places exclusive reliance upon external control of human behavior, while Theory Y relies heavily on self-control and self-direction. It is worth noting that this difference is the difference between treating people as children and treating them as mature adults. After generations of the former, we cannot expect to shift to the latter overnight.

## STEPS IN THE RIGHT DIRECTION

Before we are overwhelmed by the obstacles, let us remember that the application of theory is always slow. Progress is usually achieved in small steps. Some innovative ideas which are entirely consistent with Theory Y are today being applied with some success.

### Decentralization and Delegation

These are ways of freeing people from the too-close control of conventional organization, giving them a degree of freedom to direct their own activities, to assume responsibility, and, importantly, to satisfy their egoistic needs. In this connection, the flat organization of Sears, Roebuck and Company provides an interesting example. It forces "management by objectives," since it enlarges the number of people reporting to a manager until he cannot direct and control them in the conventional manner.

### Job Enlargement

This concept, pioneered by I.B.M. and Detroit Edison, is quite consistent with Theory Y. It encourages the acceptance of responsibility at the bottom of the organization; it provides opportunities for satisfying social and egoistic needs. In fact, the reorganization of work at the factory level offers one of the more challenging opportunities for innovation consistent with Theory Y.

### Participation and Consultative Management

Under proper conditions, participation and consultative management provide encouragement to people to direct their creative energies toward organizational objectives, give them some voice in decisions that affect them, provide significant opportunities for the satisfaction of social and egoistic needs....

### Performance Appraisal

Even a cursory examination of conventional programs of performance appraisal within the ranks of management will reveal how completely consistent they are with Theory X. In fact, most such programs tend to treat the individual as though he were a product under inspection on the assembly line.

A few companies—among them General Mills, Ansul Chemical, and General Electric—have been experimenting with approaches which involve the individual in setting "targets" or objectives *for himself* and in a *self*-evaluation of performance semi-annually or annually. Of course, the superior plays an important leadership role in this process—one, in fact, which demands substantially more competence than the conventional approach. The role is, however, considerably more congenial to many managers than the role of "judge" or "inspector" which is usually forced upon them. Above all, the individual is encouraged to take a greater responsibility for planning and appraising his own contribution to organizational objectives; and the accompanying effects on egoistic and self-fulfillment needs are substantial.

## APPLYING THE IDEAS

The not infrequent failure of such ideas as these to work as well as expected is often attributable to the fact that a management has "bought the idea" but applied it within the framework of Theory X and its assumptions.

Delegation is not an effective way of exercising management by control.

Participation becomes a farce when it is applied as a sales gimmick or a device for kidding people into thinking they are important. Only the management that has confidence in human capacities and is itself directed toward organizational objectives rather than toward the preservation of personal power can grasp the implications of this emerging theory. Such management will find and apply successfully other innovative ideas as we move slowly toward the full implementation of a theory like Y.

## THE HUMAN SIDE OF ENTERPRISE

...The ingenuity and the perseverance of industrial management in the pursuit of economic ends have changed many scientific and technological dreams into commonplace realities. It is now becoming clear that the application of these same talents to the human side of enterprise will not only enhance substantially these materialistic achievements, but will bring us one step closer to "the good society."

## 15

# Groupthink: The Desperate Drive for Consensus at Any Cost

*Irving L. Janis*

"How could we have been so stupid?" President John F. Kennedy asked after he and a close group of advisers had blundered into the Bay of Pigs invasion. For the last two years I have been studying that question, as it applies not only to the Bay of Pigs decision-makers but also to those who led the United States into such other major fiascoes as the failure to be prepared for the attack on Pearl Harbor, the Korean War stalemate, and the escalation of the Vietnam War.

Stupidity certainly is not the explanation. The men who participated in making the Bay of Pigs decision, for instance, comprised one of the greatest arrays of intellectual talent in the history of American Government—Dean Rusk, Robert McNamara, Douglas Dillon, Robert Kennedy, McGeorge Bundy, Arthur Schlesinger Jr., Allen Dulles, and others.

It also seemed to me that explanations were incomplete if they concentrated only on disturbances in the behavior of each individual within a decision-making body: temporary emotional states of elation, fear, or anger that reduce a man's mental efficiency, for example, or chronic blind spots arising from a man's social prejudices or idiosyncratic biases.

I preferred to broaden the picture by looking at the fiascoes from the standpoint of group dynamics as it has been explored over the past three decades, first by the great social psychologist Kurt Lewin and later in many experimental situations by myself and other behavioral scientists. My conclusion after poring over hundreds of relevant documents—historical reports about formal group meetings and informal conversations among the members—is that the groups that committed the fiascoes were victims of what I call "groupthink."

**Groupy.** In each case study, I was surprised to discover the extent to which each group displayed the typical phenomena of social conformity that are regularly encountered in studies of group dynamics among ordinary citizens. For example, some of the phenomena appear to be completely in line with findings from social-psychological experiments showing that powerful social pressures are brought to bear by the members of a cohesive group whenever a dissident begins to voice his objections to a group consensus. Other phenomena are reminiscent of the shared illusions observed in encounter groups and friendship cliques when the members simultaneously reach a peak of "groupy" feelings.

Above all, there are numerous indications pointing to the development of group norms that bolster morale at the expense of critical thinking. One of the most common norms appears to be that of remaining loyal to the group by sticking with the policies to which the group has already committed itself, even when those policies are obviously working out badly and have unintended consequences that disturb the conscience of each member. This is one of the key characteristics of groupthink.

**1984.** I use the term groupthink as a quick and easy way to refer to the mode of thinking that persons engage in when *concurrence-seeking* becomes so dominant in a cohesive ingroup that it tends to override realistic appraisal of alternative courses of action. Groupthink is a term of the same order as the words in the newspeak vocabulary George Orwell used in his dismaying world of 1984. In that context, groupthink takes on an invidious connotation. Exactly such a connotation is intended, since the term refers to a deterioration in mental efficiency, reality testing, and moral judgments as a result of group pressures.

The symptoms of groupthink arise when the members of decision-making groups become motivated to avoid being too harsh in their judgments of their leaders' or their colleagues' ideas. They adopt a soft line of criticism, even in their own thinking. At their meetings, all the members are amiable and seek complete concurrence on every important issue, with no bickering or conflict to spoil the cozy, "we-feeling" atmosphere.

**Kill.** Paradoxically, soft-headed groups are often hard-hearted when it comes to dealing with outgroups or enemies. They find it relatively easy to resort to dehumanizing solutions—they will readily authorize bombing attacks that kill large numbers of civilians in the name of the noble cause of persuading an unfriendly government to negotiate at the peace table. They are unlikely to pursue the more difficult and controversial issues that arise when alternatives to a harsh military solution come up for discussion. Nor are they inclined to raise ethical issues that carry the implication that *this fine group of ours, with its humanitarianism and its high-minded principles, might be capable of adopting a course of action that is inhumane and immoral.*

**Norms.** There is evidence from a number of social-psychological studies that as the members of a group feel more accepted by the others, which is a central feature of increased group cohesiveness, they display less overt conformity to group norms. Thus

we would expect that the more cohesive a group becomes, the less the members will feel constrained to censor what they say out of fear of being socially punished for antagonizing the leader or any of their fellow members.

In contrast, the groupthink type of conformity tends to increase as group cohesiveness increases. Groupthink involves non-deliberate suppression of critical thoughts as a result of internalization of the group's norms, which is quite different from deliberate suppression on the basis of external threats of social punishment. The more cohesive the group, the greater the inner compulsion on the part of each member to avoid creating disunity, which inclines him to believe in the soundness of whatever proposals are promoted by the leader or by a majority of the group's members.

In a cohesive group, the danger is not so much that each individual will fail to reveal his objections to what the others propose but that he will think the proposal is a good one, without attempting to carry out a careful, critical scrutiny of the pros and cons of the alternatives. When groupthink becomes dominant, there also is considerable suppression of deviant thoughts, but it takes the form of each person's deciding that his misgivings are not relevant and should be set aside, that the benefit of the doubt regarding any lingering uncertainties should be given to the group consensus.

**Stress.** I do not mean to imply that all cohesive groups necessarily suffer from groupthink. All ingroups may have a mild tendency toward groupthink, displaying one or another of the symptoms from time to time, but it need not be so dominant as to influence the quality of the group's final decision. Neither do I mean to imply that there is anything necessarily inefficient or harmful about group decisions in general. On the contrary, a group whose members have properly defined roles, with traditions concerning the procedures to follow in pursuing a critical inquiry, probably is capable of making better decisions than any individual group member working alone.

The problem is that the advantages of having decisions made by groups are often lost because of powerful psychological pressures that arise when the members work closely together, share the same set of values and, above all, face a crisis situation that puts everyone under intense stress.

The main principle of groupthink, which I offer in the spirit of Parkinson's Law, is this: *The more amiability and esprit de corps there is among the members of a policy-making ingroup, the greater the danger that independent critical thinking will be replaced by groupthink, which is likely to result in irrational and dehumanizing actions directed against outgroups.*

**Symptoms.** In my studies of high-level governmental decision-makers, both civilian and military, I have found eight main symptoms of groupthink.

**1.** *Invulnerability.* Most or all of the members of the ingroup share an illusion of invulnerability that provides for them some degree of reassurance about obvious dangers and leads them to become over-optimistic and willing to take extraordinary risks. It also causes them to fail to respond to clear warnings of danger.

The Kennedy ingroup, which uncritically accepted the Central Intelligence Agency's disastrous Bay of Pigs plan, operated on the false assumption that they could keep secret the fact that the United States was responsible for the invasion of Cuba. Even after news of the plan began to leak out, their belief remained unshaken. They failed even to consider the danger that awaited them: a worldwide revulsion against the United States.

A similar attitude appeared among the members of President Lyndon B. Johnson's ingroup, the "Tuesday Cabinet," which kept escalating the Vietnam War despite repeated setbacks and failures. "There was a belief," Bill Moyers commented after he resigned, "that if we indicated a willingness to use our power, they [the North Vietnamese] would get the message and back away from an all-out confrontation.... There was a confidence—it was never bragged about, it was just there—that when the chips were really down, the other people would fold."

A most poignant example of an illusion of invulnerability involves the ingroup around Admiral H. E. Kimmel, which failed to prepare for the possibility of a Japanese attack on Pearl Harbor despite repeated warnings. Informed by his intelligence chief that radio contact with Japanese aircraft carriers had been lost, Kimmel joked about it: "What, you don't know where the carriers are? Do you mean to say that they could be rounding Diamond Head (at Honolulu) and you wouldn't know it?" The carriers were in fact moving full-steam toward Kimmel's command post at the time. Laughing together about a danger signal, which labels it as a purely laughing matter, is a characteristic manifestation of groupthink.

**2.** *Rationale.* As we see, victims of groupthink ignore warnings; they also collectively construct rationalizations in order to discount warnings and other forms of negative feedback that, taken seriously, might lead the group members to reconsider their assumptions each time they recommit themselves to past decisions. Why did the Johnson ingroup avoid reconsidering its escalation policy when time and again the expectations on which they based their decisions turned out to be wrong? James C. Thomson, Jr., a Harvard historian who spent five years as an observing participant in both the State Department and the White House, tells us that the policymakers avoided critical discussion of their prior decisions and continually invented new rationalizations so that they could sincerely recommit themselves to defeating the North Vietnamese.

In the fall of 1964, before the bombing of North Vietnam began, some of the policymakers predicted that six weeks of air strikes would induce the North Vietnamese to seek peace talks. When someone asked, "What if they don't?" the answer was that another four weeks certainly would do the trick....

**3.** *Morality.* Victims of groupthink believe unquestioningly in the inherent morality of their ingroup; this belief inclines the members to ignore the ethical or moral consequences of their decisions.

Evidence that this symptom is at work usually is of a negative kind—the things that are left unsaid in group meetings. At least two influential persons had doubts about the morality of the Bay of Pigs adventure. One of them, Arthur Schlesinger, Jr., presented his strong objections in a memorandum to President Kennedy and Secretary of State Rusk but suppressed them when he attended meetings of the Kennedy team. The other, Senator J. William Fulbright, was not a member of the group, but the President invited him to express his misgivings in a speech to the policymakers. However, when Fulbright finished speaking the President moved on to other agenda items without asking for reactions of the group.

David Kraslow and Stuart H. Loory, in *The Secret Search for Peace in Vietnam*, report that during 1966 President Johnson's ingroup was concerned primarily with selecting bomb targets in North Vietnam. They based their selections on four factors—the military advantage, the risk to American aircraft and pilots, the danger of forcing other countries into the fighting, and the danger of heavy civilian casualties. At their regular Tuesday luncheons, they weighed these factors the way school teachers grade examination papers, averaging them out. Though evidence on this point is scant, I suspect that the group's ritualistic adherence to a standardized procedure induced the members to feel morally justified in their destructive way of dealing with the Vietnamese people—after all, the danger of heavy civilian casualties from U.S. air strikes was taken into account on their checklists.

**4.** *Stereotypes.* Victims of groupthink hold stereotyped views of the leaders of enemy groups: they are so evil that genuine attempts at negotiating differences with them are unwarranted, or they are too weak or too stupid to deal effectively with whatever attempts the ingroup makes to defeat their purposes, no matter how risky the attempts are.

Kennedy's groupthinkers believed that Premier Fidel Castro's air force was so ineffectual that obsolete B-26's could knock it out completely in a surprise attack before the invasion began. They also believed that Castro's army was so weak that a small Cuban-exile brigade could establish a well-protected beachhead at the Bay of Pigs. In addition, they believed that Castro was not smart enough to put down any possible internal uprisings in support of the exiles. They were wrong on all three assumptions. Though much of the blame was attributable to faulty intelligence, the point is that none of Kennedy's advisers even questioned the CIA planners about these assumptions.

The Johnson advisers' sloganistic thinking about "the Communist apparatus" that was "working all around the world" (as Dean Rusk put it) led them to overlook the powerful nationalistic strivings of the North Vietnamese government and its efforts to ward off Chinese domination. The crudest of all stereotypes used by Johnson's inner circle to justify their policies was the domino theory ("If we don't stop the Reds in South Vietnam, tomorrow they will be in Hawaii and next week they will be in San Francisco," Johnson once said). The group so firmly accepted this stereotype that it became almost impossible for any adviser to introduce a more sophisticated viewpoint.

In the documents on Pearl Harbor, it is clear to see that the Navy commanders stationed in Hawaii had a naive image of Japan as a midget that would not dare to strike a blow against a powerful giant.

**5.** *Pressure.* Victims of groupthink apply direct pressure to any individual who momentarily expresses doubts about any of the group's shared illusions or who questions the validity of the arguments supporting a policy alternative favored by the majority. This gambit reinforces the concurrence-seeking norm that loyal members are expected to maintain.

President Kennedy probably was more active than anyone else in raising skeptical questions during the Bay of Pigs meetings, and yet he seems to have encouraged the group's docile, uncritical acceptance of defective arguments in favor of the CIA's plan. At every meeting, he allowed the CIA representatives to dominate the discussion. He permitted them to give their immediate refutations in response to each tentative doubt that one of the others expressed, instead of asking whether anyone shared the doubt or wanted to pursue the implications of the new worrisome issue that had just been raised. And at the most crucial meeting, when he was calling on each member to give his vote for or against the plan, he did not call on Arthur Schlesinger, the one man there who was known by the President to have serious misgivings.

Historian Thomson informs us that whenever a member of Johnson's ingroup began to express doubts, the group used subtle social pressures to "domesticate" him. To start with, the dissenter was made to feel at home provided that he lived up to two restrictions: (1) that he did not voice his doubts to outsiders, which would play into the hands of the opposition; and (2) that he kept his criticisms within the bounds of acceptable deviation, which meant not challenging any of the fundamental assumptions that went into the group's prior commitments. One such "domesticated dissenter" was Bill Moyers. When Moyers arrived at a meeting, Thomson tells us, the President greeted him with, "Well, here comes Mr. Stop-the-Bombing."

**6.** *Self-Censorship.* Victims of groupthink avoid deviating from what appears to be group consensus; they keep silent about their misgivings and even minimize to themselves the importance of their doubts.

As we have seen, Schlesinger was not at all hesitant about presenting his strong objections to the Bay of Pigs plan in a memorandum to the President and the Secretary of State. But he became keenly aware of his tendency to suppress objections at the White House meetings. "In the months after the Bay of Pigs, I bitterly reproached myself for having kept so silent during those crucial discussions in the cabinet room," Schlesinger writes in *A Thousand Days*, "I can only explain my failure to do more than raise a few timid questions by reporting that one's impulse to blow the whistle on this nonsense was simply undone by the circumstances of the discussion."

**7.** *Unanimity.* Victims of groupthink share an illusion of unanimity within the group concerning almost all judgments expressed by members who speak in favor of the majority view. This symptom results partly from the preceding one, whose effects are augmented by the false assumption that any individual who remains silent during any part of the discussion is in full accord with what the others are saying.

When a group of persons who respect each other's opinions arrives at a unanimous view, each member is likely to feel that the belief must be true. This reliance on consensual validation within the group tends to replace individual critical thinking and reality testing, unless there are clear-cut disagreements among the members. In contemplating a course of action such as the invasion of Cuba, it is painful for the members to confront disagreements within their group, particularly if it becomes apparent that there are widely divergent views about whether the preferred course of action is too risky to undertake at all. Such disagreements are likely to arouse anxieties about making a serious error. Once the sense of unanimity is shattered, the members no longer can feel complacently confident about the decision they are inclined to make. Each man must then face the annoying realization that there are troublesome uncertainties and he must diligently seek out the best information he can get in order to decide for himself exactly how serious the risks might be. This is one of the unpleasant consequences of being in a group of hardheaded, critical thinkers.

To avoid such an unpleasant state, the members often become inclined, without quite realizing it, to prevent latent disagreements from surfacing when they are about to initiate a risky course of action. The group leader and the members support each other in playing up the areas of convergence in their thinking, at the expense of fully exploring divergencies that might reveal unsettled issues. . . .

**8.** *Mindguards.* Victims of groupthink sometimes appoint themselves as mindguards to protect the leader and fellow members from adverse information that might break the complacency they shared about the effectiveness and morality of past decisions. At a large birthday party for his wife, Attorney General Robert F. Kennedy, who had been constantly informed about the Cuban invasion plan, took Schlesinger aside and asked him why he was opposed. Kennedy listened coldly and said, "You may be right or you may be wrong, but the President has made his mind up. Don't push it any further. Now is the time for everyone to help him all they can."

Rusk also functioned as a highly effective mindguard by failing to transmit to the group the strong objections of three "outsiders" who had learned of the invasion plan—Undersecretary of State Chester Bowles, USIA Director Edward R. Murrow, and Rusk's intelligence chief, Roger Hilsman. Had Rusk done so, their warnings might have reinforced Schlesinger's memorandum and jolted some of Kennedy's ingroup, if not the President himself, into reconsidering the decision.

**Products.** When a group of executives frequently displays most or all of these interrelated symptoms, a detailed study of their deliberations is likely to reveal a number of immediate consequences. These consequences are, in effect, products of poor decision-making practices because they lead to inadequate solutions to the problems under discussion.

First, the group limits its discussions to a few alternative courses of action (often only two) without an initial survey of all the alternatives that might be worthy of consideration.

Second, the group fails to reexamine the course of action initially preferred by the majority after they learn of risks and drawbacks they had not considered originally.

Third, the members spend little or no time discussing whether there are nonobvious gains they may have overlooked or ways of reducing the seemingly prohibitive costs that made rejected alternatives appear undesirable to them.

Fourth, members make little or no attempt to obtain information from experts within their own organizations who might be able to supply more precise estimates of potential losses and gains.

Fifth, members show positive interest in facts and opinions that support their preferred policy, and they tend to ignore facts and opinions that do not.

Sixth, members spend little time deliberating about how the chosen policy might be hindered by bureaucratic inertia, sabotaged by political opponents, or temporarily derailed by common accidents. Consequently, they fail to work out contingency plans to cope with foreseeable setbacks that could endanger the overall success of their chosen course.

**Support.** The search for an explanation of why groupthink occurs has led me through a quagmire of complicated theoretical issues in the murky area of human motivation. My belief, based on recent social psychological research, is that we can best understand the various symptoms of group-think as a mutual effort among the group members to maintain self-esteem and emotional equanimity by providing social support to each other, especially at times when they share responsibility for making vital decisions.

Even when no important decision is pending, the typical administrator will begin to doubt the wisdom and morality of his past decisions each time he receives information about setbacks, particularly if the information is accompanied by negative feedback from prominent men who originally had been his supporters. It should not be surprising, therefore, to find that individual members strive to develop unanimity and esprit de corps that will help bolster each other's morale, to create an optimistic outlook about the success of pending decisions, and to reaffirm the positive value of past policies to which all of them are committed.

**Pride.** Shared illusions of invulnerability, for example, can reduce anxiety about taking risks. Rationalizations help members believe that the risks are really not so bad after all. The assumption of inherent morality helps the members to avoid feelings of shame or guilt. Negative stereotypes function as stress-reducing devices to enhance a sense of moral righteousness as well as pride in a lofty mission.

The mutual enhancement of self-esteem and morale may have functional value in enabling the members to maintain their capacity to take action, but it has maladaptive consequences insofar as concurrence-seeking tendencies interfere with critical, rational capacities and lead to serious errors of judgment.

While I have limited my study to decision-making bodies in government, groupthink symptoms appear in business, industry and any other field where small, cohesive groups make the decisions. It is vital, then, for all sorts of people—and especially group leaders—to know what steps they can take to prevent groupthink.

**Remedies.** To counterpoint my case studies of the major fiascoes, I have also investigated two highly successful group enterprises, the formulation of the Marshall Plan in the Truman Administration and the handling of the Cuban missile crisis by President Kennedy and his advisers. I have found it instructive to examine the

steps Kennedy took to change his group's decision-making processes. These changes ensured that the mistakes made by his Bay of Pigs ingroup were not repeated by the missile-crisis ingroup, even though the membership of both groups was essentially the same.

The following recommendations for preventing groupthink incorporate many of the good practices I discovered to be characteristic of the Marshall Plan and missile crisis groups:

1. The leader of a policy-forming group should assign the role of critical evaluator to each member, encouraging the group to give high priority to open airing of objections and doubts. This practice needs to be reinforced by the leader's acceptance of criticism of his own judgments in order to discourage members from soft-pedaling their disagreements and from allowing their striving for concurrence to inhibit critical thinking.

2. When the key members of a hierarchy assign a policy-planning mission to any group within their organization, they should adopt an impartial stance instead of stating preferences and expectations at the beginning. This will encourage open inquiry and impartial probing of a wide range of policy alternatives.

3. The organization routinely should set up several outside policy-planning and evaluation groups to work on the same policy question, each deliberating under a different leader. This can prevent the insulation of an ingroup.

4. At intervals before the group reaches a final consensus, the leader should require each member to discuss the group's deliberations with associates in his own unit of the organization—assuming that those associates can be trusted to adhere to the same security regulations that govern the policy-makers—and then to report back their reactions to the group.

5. The group should invite one or more outside experts to each meeting on a staggered basis and encourage the experts to challenge the views of the core members.

6. At every general meeting of the group, whenever the agenda calls for an evaluation of policy alternatives, at least one

member should play devil's advocate, functioning as a good lawyer in challenging the testimony of those who advocate the majority position.

7. Whenever the policy issue involves relations with a rival nation or organization, the group should devote a sizable block of time, perhaps an entire session, to a survey of all warning signals from the rivals and should write alternative scenarios on the rivals' intentions.

8. When the group is surveying policy alternatives for feasibility and effectiveness, it should from time to time divide into two or more subgroups to meet separately, under different chairmen, and then come back together to hammer out differences.

9. After reaching a preliminary consensus about what seems to be the best policy, the group should hold a "second-chance" meeting at which every member expresses as vividly as he can all his residual doubts, and rethinks the entire issue before making a definitive choice.

**How.** These recommendations have their disadvantages. To encourage the open airing of objections, for instance, might lead to prolonged and costly debates when a rapidly growing crisis requires immediate solution. It also could cause rejection, depression and anger. A leader's failure to set a norm might create cleavage between leader and members that could develop into a disruptive power struggle if the leader looks on the emerging consensus as anathema. Setting up outside evaluation groups might increase the risk of security leakage. Still, inventive executives who know their way around the organizational maze probably can figure out how to apply one or another of the prescriptions successfully, without harmful side effects.

They also could benefit from the advice of outside experts in the administrative and behavioral sciences. Though these experts have much to offer, they have had few chances to work on policy-making machinery within large organizations. As matters now stand, executives innovate only when they need new procedures to avoid repeating serious errors that have deflated their self-images.

In this era of atomic warheads, urban disorganization and ecocatastrophes, it seems to me that policymakers should collaborate with behavioral scientists and give top priority to preventing groupthink and its attendant fiascoes.

# CHAPTER 4

# *"Modern" Structural Organization Theory*

Usually when we refer to the structure of an organization, we are talking about the relatively stable relationships among the positions, groups of positions (units), and work processes that make up the organization. Structural organization theory is concerned with vertical differentiations—hierarchical levels of organizational authority and coordination, and horizontal differentiations between organizational units—such as those between product or service lines, geographical areas, or skills. The organization chart is the ever-present tool of a structural organization theorist.

Why then do we use the word "modern" with "structural organization theory"? It is because most organizational theories and theorists from the classical school (see Chapter 1) also were structural. They focused on the structure—or design—of organizations and their production processes. Examples of a few classical structural theories reprinted in Chapter 1 include works by Adam Smith, Henri Fayol, Daniel McCallum, Frederick Winslow Taylor, and Max Weber. Thus, we add the word "modern" in quotation marks to differentiate between the pre–World War II classical school structuralists and the structural organization theorists from the second half of the twentieth century and the first two decades of the twenty-first century.

The "modern" structural theories are concerned with many of the same issues as the classical structural theories. "Modern" structuralists are grounded in the thinking of Fayol, Taylor, Gulick, and Weber, and their underlying tenets are quite similar: Organizational efficiency is the essence of organizational rationality, and the goal of rationality is to increase the production of wealth in terms of real goods and services. "Modern" structural theories, however, were also informed and influenced substantially by more recent schools of organization theory. Bolman and Deal (2013) identify the basic assumptions of the structural perspective:

1. Organizations are rational institutions whose primary purpose is to accomplish established objectives; rational organizational behavior is achieved best through systems of defined rules and formal authority. Organizational control and coordination are key for maintaining organizational rationality.

2. There is a "best" structure for any organization, or at least a most appropriate structure in light of its given objectives, the environmental conditions surrounding it (for example, its markets, the competition, and the extent of government regulation), the nature of its products and/or services (the "best" structure for a management consulting firm probably differs substantially from that for a certified public accounting firm), and the technology of the production processes (a coal mining company has a different "best structure" than the high-tech manufacturer of computer microcomponents).

3. Specialization and the division of labor increase the quality and quantity of production, particularly in highly skilled operations and professions.

4. Most problems in an organization result from structural flaws and can be solved by changing the structure.

What sorts of practical issues are addressed by "modern" structural organization theory? Is it useful? The issue is the design of an organization—its structure—and how well the structure will help an organization deal with the most common structural questions of specialization, departmentalization, span of control, and the coordination and control of specialized units.

Burns and Stalker (1961) provided an excellent example of a "modern" structural theory commonly known now as simply "mechanistic–organic system theory." Burns and Stalker determined that stable conditions may suggest the use of a mechanistic form of organization where a traditional pattern of hierarchy, reliance on formal rules and regulations, vertical communications, and structured decision making is possible and desirable. However, more dynamic conditions—situations in which the environment changes rapidly—require the use of an organic form of organization where there is less rigidity, more participation, and more reliance on workers to define and redefine their positions and relationships. Obviously, the impacts of these two organizational forms on operations and individuals are quite different.

The first reading reprinted in this chapter, "The Concept of Formal Organization," from Peter M. Blau and W. Richard Scott's 1962 book, *Formal Organizations: A Comparative Approach*, provides another excellent example of a "modern" structural theory. The authors assert that all organizations include both a formal and an informal dimension of structure. The informal organization by its nature is rooted in the formal structure and supports its formal organization by establishing norms for the operation of the organization that cannot always be spelled out by rules and policies. For these reasons, Blau and Scott maintain that it is impossible to know and understand the true structure of a formal organization without a similar understanding of its parallel informal organization. Clearly, Blau and Scott were influenced by Chester Barnard's, *The Functions of the Executive* (1938) (see Reading 9 in Chapter 2):

> ... informal organization, although comprising the processes of society which are unconscious as contrasted with those of formal organizations which are conscious, has two important classes of effects: (a) it establishes certain attitudes, understandings, customs, habits, [and] institutions, and (b) it creates the condition under which formal organization may arise.

In 1776, Adam Smith first advocated the division of labor to increase the effectiveness of the factory system of production. In 1922, Max Weber described two strong and opposing forces that have an impact on all organizations: the need for division of labor and specialization and the need for centralizing authority. Division of labor is an inevitable consequence of specialization by skills, products, or processes. Most "modern" structuralists use the word *differentiation*, which means essentially the same thing as specialization but also reflects increased appreciation of the myriad and rapidly changing external environmental forces with which organizations interact (for example, different markets, sociopolitical cultures, regulatory environments, technologies, competition, and the economy). Thus, complex differentiation is also essential for organizational effectiveness as well as efficiency. However, differentiation means diverse forces that "pull organizations apart." Differentiation increases the need for organizational coordination and control that, in the language of "modern" structuralists, is labeled "integration."

In their 1968 *Harvard Business Review* article, "Organizational Choice: Product vs. Function," Arthur H. Walker and Jay W. Lorsch grapple with an aspect of differentiation and integration that poses one of the more difficult decisions facing those who would design organizations: Should an organization be structured according to product or function? "Should all specialists in a given function be grouped under a common boss, regardless of differences in products they are involved in, or should the various functional specialists working on a single product be grouped together under the same superior?" Walker and Lorsch tackle this problem by examining two firms in the same industry—one organized by product and the other by function. They conclude that either structural arrangement can be appropriate, depending upon the organization's environment and the nature of the organization itself.

Henry Mintzberg has been one of the most widely respected management and organizational theorists in the second half of the twentieth century and the early years of the twenty-first century. Mintzberg began compiling a comprehensive theory of management policy in the 1960s—a field of management and organization theory that had been largely overlooked. His influence on the field is in part because he has synthesized many schools of organization and management theory—and has done so with coherence. His 1980 article, "Structure in 5's: A Synthesis of the Research on Organization Design," is reprinted in this chapter. In it, Mintzberg asserts that elements of organizational structure "show a curious tendency to appear in five's—suggesting a typology of five basic configurations: Simple Structure, Machine Bureaucracy, Professional Bureaucracy, Divisionalized Form, and Adhocracy." These five elements include the five basic parts of the organization, five basic mechanisms of coordination, five design parameters, and five primary contingency or context factors.Mintzberg's 1983 book, *Power In and Around Organizations* addresses aspects of the second component of his model, mechanisms of coordination. A chapter is reprinted as Reading 18 in Chapter 6, "Power and Politics Organization Theory."

## BIBLIOGRAPHY

Barnard, C. I. (1938). *The functions of the executive*. Cambridge, MA: Harvard University Press.

Bennis, W. G. (1966). *Changing organizations*. New York: McGraw-Hill.

Blau, P. M., & W. R. Scott (1962). *Formal organizations: A comparative approach*. San Francisco, CA: Jossey-Bass.

Bolman, L. G., & T. E. Deal (2013). *Reframing organizations: Artistry, choice, and leadership*, 4th ed. San Francisco, CA: Jossey-Bass.

Burns, T., & G. M. Stalker (1961). *The management of innovation*. London: Tavistock Publications.

Burton, R. M., & B. Obel. (1998). *Strategic organizational diagnosis and design: Developing theory for application*, 2nd ed. Boston, MA: Kluwer Academic.

Crozier, M. (1964). *The bureaucratic phenomenon*. Chicago, IL: University of Chicago Press.

Davis, S. M., & P. R. Lawrence (1977). *Matrix*. Reading, MA: Addison-Wesley.

Drucker, P. F. (1988, January–February). The coming of the new organization. *Harvard Business Review*, 66(1), 45–53.

Etzioni, A. (1961). *A comparative analysis of complex organizations*. Englewood Cliffs, NJ: Prentice Hall.

Fulk, J., & DeSanctis, G. (1999). Articulation of communication technology and organizational form. In G. DeSanctis & J. Fulk, eds., *Shaping organization form: Communication, connection, and community* (pp. 5–32). Thousand Oaks, CA: Sage.

Galbraith, J. R. (1974). Organization design: An information processing view. *Interfaces, 4,* 28–36.

Handy, C. (1990). *The Age of Unreason.* Boston, MA: Harvard Business School Press.

Jaques, E. (1990). In praise of hierarchy. *Harvard Business Review,* 68(1), 127–133.

Kaufman, H. (1977). *Red tape.* Washington, DC: Brookings Institution.

Lawrence, P. R., & J. W. Lorsch (1969). *Developing organizations.* Reading, MA: Addison-Wesley.

Mintzberg, H. (1979). *The structuring of organizations.* Englewood Cliffs, NJ: Prentice Hall.

Mintzberg, H. (1980). Structure in 5's: A synthesis of the research on organization design. *Management Science,* 26(3), 322–341.

Mintzberg, H. (1983). *Power in and around organizations.* Englewood Cliffs, NJ: Prentice Hall.

Perrow, C. (1967). A framework for the comparative analysis of organization. *American Sociological Review, 32,* 144–208.

Schein, E. H. (1989, Winter). Reassessing the "divine rights" of managers. *Sloan Management Review, 30,* 63–68.

Scott, W. R., & G. F. Davis. (2007). *Organizations: Rational, natural and open systems perspectives.* Upper Saddle River, NJ: Pearson.

Thompson, J. D. (1967). *Organizations in action.* New York: McGraw-Hill.

Thompson, V. A. (1961). *Modern organization.* New York: Knopf.

Walker, A. H., & J. W. Lorsch (1968). Organizational choice: Product vs. function. *Harvard Business Review, 46,* 129–138.

Woodward, J. (1965). *Industrial organization theory and practice.* Oxford: Oxford University Press.

# 16

# The Concept of Formal Organization

*Peter M. Blau & W. Richard Scott*

## SOCIAL ORGANIZATION AND FORMAL ORGANIZATIONS

Although a wide variety of organizations exists, when we speak of an organization it is generally quite clear what we mean and what we do not mean by this term. We may refer to the American Medical Association as an organization, or to a college fraternity; to the Bureau of Internal Revenue, or to a union; to General Motors, or to a church; to the Daughters of the American Revolution, or to an army. But we would not call a family an organization, nor would we so designate a friendship clique, or a community, or an economic market, or the political institutions of a society. What is the specific and differentiating criterion implicit in our intuitive distinction of organizations from other kinds of social groupings or institutions? It has something to do with how human conduct becomes socially organized, but it is not, as one might first suspect, whether or not social controls order and organize the conduct of individuals, since such social controls operate in both types of circumstances.

Before specifying what is meant by formal organization, let us clarify the general concept of social organization. "Social organization" refers to the ways in which human conduct becomes socially organized, that is, to the observed regularities in the behavior of people that are due to the social conditions in which they find themselves rather than to their physiological or psychological characteristics as individuals. The many social conditions that influence the conduct of people can be divided into two main types, which constitute the two basic aspects of social organizations: (1) the structure of social relations in a group or larger collectivity of people, and (2) the shared beliefs and orientations that unite the members of the collectivity and guide their conduct.

The conception of structure or system implies that the component units stand in some relation to one another and, as the popular expression "The whole is greater than the sum of its parts" suggests, that the relations between units add new elements to the situation.[1] This aphorism, like so many others, is a half-truth. The sum of fifteen apples, for example, is no more than fifteen times one apple. But a block of ice is more than the sum of the atoms of hydrogen and oxygen that compose it. In the case of the apples, there exist no linkages or relations between the units comprising the whole. In the case of the ice, however, specific connections have been formed between H and O atoms and among $H_2O$ molecules that distinguish ice from hydrogen and oxygen, on the one hand, and from water, on the other. Similarly, a busload of passengers does not constitute a group, since no social relations unify individuals into a common structure.[2] But a busload of club members on a Sunday outing is a group, because a network of social relations links the members into a social structure, a structure which is an emergent characteristic of the collectivity that cannot be reduced to the attributes of its individual members. In short, a network of social relations transforms an aggregate of individuals into a group (or an aggregate of groups into a larger social structure), and the group is more than the sum of the individuals composing it since the structure of social relations is an emergent element that influences the conduct of individuals.

To indicate the nature of social relations, we can briefly dissect this concept. Social relations involve, first, patterns of social interaction: the frequency and duration of the contacts between people, the tendency to initiate these contacts, the direction of influence between persons, the degree of cooperation, and so forth. Second, social relations entail people's sentiments to one another, such as feelings of attraction, respect, and hostility. The differential distribution of social relations in a group, finally, defines its status structure. Each member's status in the group depends on his relations with the others—their sentiments toward and interaction with him. As a result, integrated members become differentiated from isolates, those who are widely respected from those who are not highly regarded, and leaders from followers. In addition to these relations between individuals within groups, relations also develop between groups, relations that are a source of still another aspect of social status, since the standing of the group in the larger social system becomes part of the status of any of its members. An obvious example is the significance that membership in an ethnic minority, say, Puerto Rican, has for an individual's social status.

The networks of social relations between individuals and groups, and the status structure defined by them, constitute the core of the social organization to a collectivity, but not the whole of it. The other main dimension of social organization is a system of shared beliefs and orientations, which serve as standards for human conduct. In the course of social interaction common

notions arise as to how people should act and interact and what objectives are worthy of attainment. First, common values crystallize, values that govern the goals for which men strive—their ideals and their ideas of what is desirable—such as our belief in democracy or the importance financial success assumes in our thinking. Second, social norms develop—that is, common expectations concerning how people ought to behave—and social sanctions are used to discourage violations of these norms. These socially sanctioned rules of conduct vary in significance from moral principles or mores, as Sumner calls them, to mere customs or folkways. If values define the ends of human conduct, norms distinguish behavior that is a legitimate means for achieving these ends from behavior that is illegitimate. Finally, aside from the norms to which everybody is expected to conform, differential role expectations also emerge, expectations that become associated with various social positions. Only women in our society are expected to wear skirts, for example. Or, the respected leader of a group is expected to make suggestions, and the other members will turn to him in times of difficulties, whereas group members who have not earned the respect of others are expected to refrain from making suggestions and generally to participate little in group discussions.

These two dimensions of social organization—the networks of social relations and the shared orientations—are often referred to as the social structure and the culture, respectively.[3] Every society has a complex social structure and a complex culture, and every community within a society can be characterized by these two dimensions of social organization, and so can every group within a community (except that the specific term "culture" is reserved for the largest social systems). The prevailing cultural standards and the structure of social relations serve to organize human conduct in the collectivity. As people conform more or less closely to the expectations of their fellows, and as the degree of their conformity in turn influences their relations with others and their social status, and as their status in further turn affects their inclinations to adhere to social norms and their chances to achieve valued objectives, their patterns of behavior become socially organized.

In contrast to the social organization that emerges whenever men are living together, there are organizations that have been deliberately established for a certain purpose.[4] If the accomplishment of an objective requires collective effort, men set up an organization designed to coordinate the activities of many persons and to furnish incentives for others to join them for this purpose. For example, business concerns are established in order to produce goods that can be sold for a profit, and workers organize unions in order to increase their bargaining power with employers. In these cases, the goals to be achieved, the rules the members of the organization are expected to follow, and the status structure that defines the relations between them (the organizational chart) have not spontaneously emerged in the course of social interaction but have been consciously designed a priori to anticipate and guide interaction and activities. Since the distinctive characteristic of these organizations is that they have been formally established for the explicit purpose of achieving certain goals, the term "formal organization" is used to designate them. And this formal establishment for an explicit purpose is the criterion that distinguishes our subject matter from the study of social organization in general.

## FORMAL ORGANIZATION AND INFORMAL ORGANIZATION

The fact that an organization has been formally established, however, does not mean that all activities and interactions of its members conform strictly to the official blueprint. Regardless of the time and effort devoted by management to designing a rational organization chart and elaborate procedure manuals, this official plan can never completely determine the conduct and social relations of the organization's members. Stephen Vincent Benét illustrates this limitation when he contrasts the military blueprint with military action:

> If you take a flat map
> And move wooden blocks upon it strategically,
> The thing looks well, the blocks behave as they should.
> The science of war is moving live men like blocks.
> And getting the blocks into place at a fixed moment.
> But it takes time to mold your men into blocks
> And flat maps turn into country where creeks and gullies
> Hamper your wooden squares. They stick in the brush,
> They are tired and rest, they straggle after ripe blackberries.
> And you cannot lift them up in your hand and move them.[5]

In every formal organization there arise informal organizations. The constituent groups of the organization, like all groups, develop their own practices, values, norms, and social relations as their members live and work together. The roots of these informal systems are embedded in the formal organization itself and nurtured by the very formality of its arrangements. Official rules must be general to have sufficient scope to cover the multitude of situations that may arise. But the application of these general rules to particular cases often poses problems of judgment, and informal practices tend to emerge that provide solutions for these problems. Decisions not anticipated by official regulations must frequently be made, particularly in times of change, and here again unofficial practices are likely to furnish guides for decisions long before the formal rules have been adapted to the changing circumstances. Moreover, unofficial norms are apt to develop that regulate performance and productivity. Finally, complex networks of social relations and informal status structures emerge, within groups and between them, which are influenced by many factors besides the organizational chart, for example by the background characteristics of various persons, their abilities, their willingness to help others, and their conformity to group norms. But to say that these informal structures are not completely determined by the formal institutions is not to say that they are entirely independent of it. For informal organizations develop in response to the opportunities created and the problems posed by their environment, and the formal organization constitutes the immediate environment of the groups within it.

When we speak of formal organizations in this book, we do not mean to imply that attention is confined to formally instituted patterns; quite the contrary. It is impossible to understand the nature of a formal organization without investigating the networks of informal relations and the unofficial norms as well as the formal hierarchy of authority and the official body of rules, since the formally instituted and the informally emerging patterns are inextricably intertwined. The distinction between the formal and the informal aspects of organizational life is only an analytical one and should not be reified; there is only one actual organization. Note also that one does not speak of the informal organization of a family or of a community. The term "informal organization" does not refer to all types of emergent patterns of social life but only to those that evolve within the framework of a formally established organization. Excluded from our purview are social institutions that have evolved without explicit design; included

are the informally emerging as well as the formally instituted patterns within formally established organizations.

The decision of the members of a group to formalize their endeavors and relations by setting up a specific organization, say, a social and athletic club, is not fortuitous. If a group is small enough for all members to be in direct social contact, and if it has no objectives that require coordination of activities, there is little need for explicit procedures or a formal division of labor. But the larger the group and the more complex the task it seeks to accomplish, the greater are the pressures to become explicitly organized.[6] Once a group of boys who merely used to hang around a drugstore decide to participate in the local baseball league, they must organize a team. And the complex coordination of millions of soldiers with thousands of specialized duties in a modern army requires extensive formalized procedures and a clear-cut authority structure.

Since formal organizations are often very large and complex, some authors refer to them as "large-scale" or as "complex" organizations. But we have eschewed these terms as misleading in two respects. First, organizations vary in size and complexity, and using these variables as defining criteria would result in such odd expressions as "a small large-scale organization" or "a very complex complex organization." Second, although formal organizations often become very large and complex, their size and complexity do not rival those of the social organization of a modern society, which includes such organizations and their relations with one another in addition to other nonorganizational patterns. (Perhaps the complexity of formal organizations is so much emphasized because it is man-made whereas the complexity of societal organization has slowly emerged, just as the complexity of modern computers is more impressive than that of the human brain. Complexity by design may be more conspicuous than complexity by growth or evolution.)

The term "bureaucratic organization" which also is often used, calls attention to the fact that organizations generally possess some sort of administrative machinery. In an organization that has been formally established, a specialized administrative staff usually exists that is responsible for maintaining the organization as a going concern and for coordinating the activities of its members. Large and complex organizations require an especially elaborate administrative apparatus. In a large factory, for example, there is not only an industrial work force directly engaged in production but also an administration composed of executive, supervisory, clerical, and other staff personnel. The case of a government agency is more complicated, because such an agency is part of the administrative arm of the nation. The entire personnel of, say, a law-enforcement agency is engaged in administration, but administration of different kinds; whereas operating officials administer the law and thereby help maintain social order in the society, their superiors and the auxiliary staff administer agency procedures and help maintain the organization itself.

One aspect of bureaucratization that has received much attention is the elaboration of detailed rules and regulations that the members of the organization are expected to faithfully follow. Rigid enforcement of the minutiae of extensive official procedures often impedes effective operations. Colloquially, the term "bureaucracy" connotes such rule-encumbered inefficiency. In sociology, however, the term is used neutrally to refer to the administrative aspects of organizations. If bureaucratization is defined as the amount of effort devoted to maintaining the organization rather than to directly achieving its objectives, all formal organizations have at least a minimum of bureaucracy— even if this bureaucracy involves no more than a secretary-treasurer who collects dues.

But wide variations have been found in the degree of bureaucratization in organizations, as indicated by the amount of effort devoted to administrative problems, the proportion of administrative personnel, the hierarchical character of the organization, or the strict enforcement of administrative procedures and rigid compliance with them.

## NOTES

1. For a discussion of some of the issues raised by this assertion, see Ernest Nagel, "On the Statement 'The Whole Is More Than the Sum of Its Parts'," Paul F. Lazarsfeld and Morris Rosenberg, eds., *The Language of Social Research*, Glencoe, IL: Free Press, 1955, pp. 519–527.

2. A purist may, concededly, point out that all individuals share the role of passenger and so are subject to certain generalized norms, courtesy for example.

3. See the recent discussion of these concepts by Kroeber and Parsons, who conclude by defining culture as "transmitted and created content and patterns of values, ideas, and other symbolic meaningful systems" and social structure or system as "the specifically relational system of interaction among individuals and collectivities." A. L. Kroeber and Talcott Parsons, "The Concepts of Culture and of Social System," *American Sociological Review, 23* (1958), p. 583.

4. Sumner makes this distinction between, in his terms, *crescive* and *enacted* social institutions. William Graham Sumner, *Folkways*, Boston: Ginn, 1907, p. 54.

5. From *John Brown's Body*. Holt, Rinehart &Winston, Inc. Copyright, 1927, 1928, by Stephen Vincent Benét. Copyright renewed, 1955, 1956, by Rosemary Carr Benét.

6. For a discussion of size and its varied effects on the characteristics of social organization, see Theodore Caplow, "Organizational Size," *Administrative Science Quarterly, 1* (1957), pp. 484–505.

# 17

# Organizational Choice:
# Product versus Function

*Arthur H. Walker & Jay W. Lorsch*

Of all the issues facing a manager as he thinks about the form of his organization, one of the thorniest is the question of whether to group activities primarily by product or by function. Should all specialists in a given function be grouped under a common boss, regardless of differences in products they are involved in, or should the various functional specialists working on a single product be grouped together under the same superior?

In talks with managers we have repeatedly heard them anguishing over this choice. For example, recently a divisional vice president of a major U.S. corporation was contemplating a major organizational change. After long study, he made this revealing observation to his subordinate managers:

> We still don't know which choice will be the best one. Should the research, engineering, marketing, and production people be grouped separately in departments for each function? Or would it be better to have them grouped together in product departments, each department dealing with a particular product group?
>
> We were organized by product up until a few years ago. Then we consolidated our organization into specialized functional departments, each dealing with all of our products. Now I'm wondering if we wouldn't be better off to divide our operations again into product units. Either way I can see advantages and disadvantages, trade-offs. What criteria should I use? How can we predict what the outcomes will be if we change?

Companies that have made a choice often feel confident that they have resolved this dilemma. Consider the case of a large advertising agency that consolidated its copy, art, and television personnel into a "total creative department." Previously they had reported to group heads in their areas of specialization. In a memo to employees the company explained the move:

> Formation of the "total creative" department completely tears down the walls between art, copy, and television people. Behind this move is the realization that for best results all creative people, regardless of their particular specialty, must work together under the most intimate relationship as total advertising people, trying to solve creative problems together from start to finish.
>
> The new department will be broken into five groups reporting to the senior vice president and creative director, each under the direction of an associate creative director. Each group will be responsible for art, television, and copy in their accounts.

But our experience is that such reorganizations often are only temporary. The issues involved are so complex that many managements oscillate between these two choices or try to effect some compromise between them.

In this article we shall explore—from the viewpoint of the behavioral scientist—some of the criteria that have been used in the past to make these choices, and present ideas from recent studies that suggest more relevant criteria for making the decision. We hope to provide a way of thinking about these problems that will lead to the most sensible decisions for the accomplishment of organizational goals.

The dilemma of products versus function is by no means new; managers have been facing the same basic question for decades. As large corporations like Du Pont and General Motors grew, they found it necessary to divide their activities among product divisions.[1] Following World War II, as companies expanded their sales of existing products and added new products and businesses, many of them implemented a transition from functional organizations handling a number of different products to independently managed product divisions. These changes raised problems concerning divisionalization, decentralization, corporate staff activities, and the like.

As the product divisions grew and prospered, many companies extended the idea of product organization further down in their organizations under such labels as "the unit management concept." Today most of the attention is still being directed to these changes and innovations *within* product or market areas below the divisional level.

We are focusing therefore on these organizational issues at the middle and lower echelons of management, particularly on the crucial questions being faced by managers today within product divisions. The reader should note, however, that a discussion of these issues is immensely complicated by the fact that a choice at one level of the corporate structure affects the choices and criteria for choice at other levels. Nonetheless, the ideas we suggest in this article are directly relevant to organizational choice at any level.

## ELEMENTS TO CONSIDER

To understand more fully the factors that make these issues so difficult, it is useful to review the criteria often relied on in making this decision. Typically, managers have used technical and economic criteria. They ask themselves, for instance, "Which choice will minimize payroll costs?" Or, "Which will best utilize equipment and specialists?" This approach not only makes real sense in the traditional logic of management, but it has strong support from the classical school of organization theorists. Luther Gulick, for example, used it in arguing for organization by function:

> It guarantees the maximum utilization of up-to-date technical skill and ... makes it possible in each case to make use of the most effective divisions of work and specialization.... [It] makes possible also the economies of the maximum use of labor-saving machinery and mass production.... [It] encourages coordination in all of the technical and skilled work of the enterprise.... [It] furnishes an excellent approach to the development of central coordination and control.[2]

In pointing to the advantages of the product basis of organization, two other classical theorists used the same approach:

> Product or product line is an important basis for departmentalizing, because it permits the maximum use of personal skills and specialized knowledge, facilitates the employment of specialized capital and makes easier a certain type of coordination.[3]

In sum, these writers on organization suggested that the manager should make the choice based on three criteria:

1. Which approach permits maximum use of special technical knowledge?
2. Which provides the most efficient utilization of machinery and equipment?
3. Which provides the best hope of obtaining the required control and coordination?

There is nothing fundamentally wrong with these criteria as far as they go, and, of course, managers have been using them. But they fail to recognize the complex set of trade-offs involved in these decisions. As a consequence, managers make changes that produce unanticipated results and may even reduce the effectiveness of their organization. For example:

> A major manufacturer of corrugated containers a few years ago shifted from a product basis to a functional basis. The rationale for the decision was that it would lead to improved control of production costs and efficiencies in production and marketing. While the

organization did accomplish these aims, it found itself less able to obtain coordination among its local sales and production units. The functional specialists now reported to the top officers in charge of production and sales, and there was no mechanism for one person to coordinate their work below the level of division management. As a result, the company encountered numerous problems and unresolved conflicts among functions and later returned to the product form.

This example pinpoints the major tradeoff that the traditional criteria omit. Developing highly specialized functional units makes it difficult to achieve coordination or integration among these units. On the other hand, having product units as the basis for organization promotes collaboration between specialists, but the functional specialists feel less identification with functional goals.

## BEHAVIORISTS' FINDINGS

We now turn to some new behavioral science approaches to designing organization structure.... Studies[4] have highlighted three other important factors about specialization and coordination:

- As we have suggested, the classical theorists saw specialization in terms of grouping similar activities, skills, or even equipment. They did not look at its psychological and social consequences.... Behavioral scientists (including the authors) have found that there is an important relationship between a unit's or individual's assigned activities and the unit members' patterns of thought and behavior. Functional specialists tend to develop patterns of behavior and thought that are in tune with the demands of their jobs and their prior training, and as a result these specialists (e.g., industrial engineers and production supervisors) have different ideas and orientation about what is important in getting the job done. This is called *differentiation*, which simply means the differences in behavior and thought patterns that develop among different specialists in relation to their respective tasks. Differentiation is

necessary for functional specialists to perform their jobs effectively.

- Differentiation is closely related to achievement of coordination, or what behavioral scientists call *integration*. This means collaboration between specialized units or individuals. Recent studies have demonstrated that there is an inverse relationship between differentiation and integration: the more two functional specialists (or their units) differ in their patterns of behavior and thought, the more difficult it is to bring about integration between them. Nevertheless, this research has indicated, achievement of both differentiation and integration is essential if organizations are to perform effectively.
- While achievement of both differentiation and integration is possible, it can occur only when well-developed means of communication among specialists exist in the organization and when the specialists are effective in resolving the inevitable cross-functional conflicts.

These recent studies, then, point to certain related questions that managers must consider when they choose between a product or functional basis of organization.

1. How will the choice affect differentiation among specialists? Will it allow the necessary differences in viewpoint to develop so that specialized tasks can be performed effectively?
2. How does the decision affect the prospects of accomplishing integration? Will it lead, for instance, to greater differentiation, which will increase the problems of achieving integration?
3. How will the decision affect the ability of organization members to communicate with each other, resolve conflicts, and reach the necessary joint decisions?

There appears to be a connection between the appropriate extent of differentiation and integration and the organization's effectiveness in accomplishing its economic goals. What the appropriate pattern is depends on the nature of external factors—markets, technology, and so on—facing the organization, as well as the goals themselves. The question of how the organizational pattern will affect individual members is equally complex. Management must consider how much stress will be associated with a certain pattern and whether such stress should be a serious concern.

To explore in more detail the significance of modern approaches to organizational structuring, we shall describe one recent study conducted in two manufacturing plants—one organized by *product*, the other on a *functional* basis.[5]

## PLANT F AND PLANT P

The two plants where this study was conducted were selected because they were closely matched in several ways. They were making the same product; their markets, technology, and even raw materials were identical. The parent companies were also similar: both were large, national corporations that developed, manufactured, and marketed many consumer products. In each case divisional and corporate headquarters were located more than 100 miles from the facilities studied. The plants were separated from other structures at the same site, where other company products were made.

Both plants had very similar management styles. They stressed their desire to foster employees' initiative and autonomy and placed great reliance on selection of well-qualified department heads. They also identified explicitly the same two objectives. The first was to formulate, package, and ship the products in minimum time at specified levels of quality and at minimum costs—that is, within existing capabilities. The second was to improve the capabilities of the plant.

In each plant there were identical functional specialists involved with the manufacturing units and packing unit, as well as quality control, planning and scheduling, warehousing, industrial engineering, and plant engineering. In Plant F (with the *functional* basis of organization), only the manufacturing departments and the planning and scheduling function reported to the plant manager responsible for the

product (see Figure 17.1). All other functional specialists reported to the staff of the divisional manufacturing manager, who was also responsible for plants manufacturing other products. At Plant P (with the *product* basis of organization), all functional specialists with the exception of plant engineering reported to the plant manager (see Figure 17.2).

### *State of Differentiation*

In studying differentiation, it is useful to focus on the functional specialists' differences in outlook in terms of: orientation toward goals, orientation toward time, and perception of the formality of organization.

**Goal Orientation.** The bases of organization in the two plants had a marked effect on the specialists' differentiated goal orientations. In Plant F they focused sharply on their specialized goals and objectives. For example, quality control specialists were concerned almost exclusively with meeting quality standards, industrial engineers with methods improvements and cost reduction, and scheduling specialists with how to meet requirements. An industrial engineer in Plant F indicated this intensive interest in his own activity:

> We have 150 projects worth close to a million dollars in annual savings. I guess I've completed some that save as much as $90,000 a year. Right now I'm working on cutting departmental costs. You need a hard shell in this work. No one likes to have his costs cut, but that is my job.

That these intense concerns with specialized objectives were expected is illustrated by the apologetic tone of a comment on production goals by an engineering supervisor at Plant F:

> At times we become too much involved in production. It causes a change in heart. We are interested in production, but not at the expense of our own standards of performance. If we get too much involved, then we may become compromised.

## FIGURE 17.1 • ORGANIZATIONAL CHART AT PLANT F

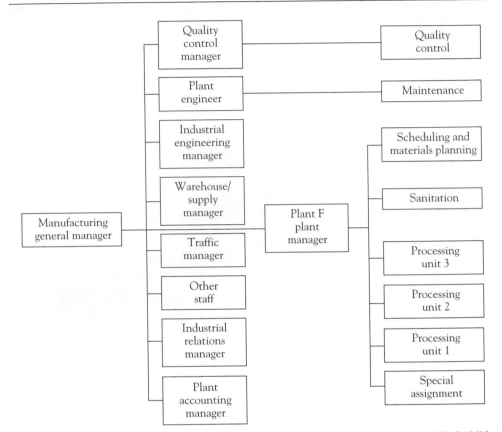

A final illustration is when production employees stood watching while members of the maintenance department worked to start a new production line, and a production supervisor remarked:

> I hope that they get that line going soon. Right now, however, my hands are tied. Maintenance has the job. I can only wait. My people have to wait, too.

This intense concern with one set of goals is analogous to a rifle shot; in a manner of speaking, each specialist took aim at one set of goals and fired at it. Moreover, the specialists identified closely with their counterparts in other plants and at divisional headquarters. As one engineer put it:

We carry the ball for them (the central office). We carry a project through and get it working right.

At Plant P the functional specialists' goals were more diffuse—like buckshot. Each specialist was concerned not only with his own goals, but also with the operation of the entire plant. For example, in contrast to the Plant F production supervisor's attitude about maintenance, a Plant P maintenance manager said, under similar circumstances:

> We're all interested in the same thing. If I can help, I'm willing. If I have a mechanical problem, there is no member of the operating department who wouldn't go out of his way to solve it.

## FIGURE 17.2 • ORGANIZATIONAL CHART AT PLANT P

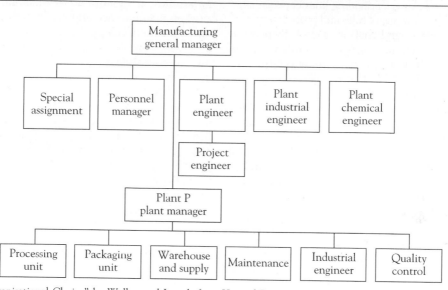

Additional evidence of this more diffuse orientation toward goals is provided by comments such as these which came from Plant P engineers and managers:

> We are here for a reason—to run this place the best way we know how. There is no reluctance to be open and frank despite various backgrounds and ages.
>
> The changeovers tell the story. Everyone shows willingness to dig in. The whole plant turns out to do cleaning up.

Because the functional specialists at Plant F focused on their individual goals, they had relatively wide differences in goals and objectives. Plant P's structure, on the other hand, seemed to make functional specialists more aware of common product goals and reduced differences in goal orientation. Yet, as we shall see, this lesser differentiation did not hamper their performance.

**Time Orientation.** The two organizational bases had the opposite effect, however, on the time orientation of functional managers. At Plant F, the specialists shared a concern with short-term issues (mostly daily problems). The time orientation of specialists at Plant P was more differentiated. For example, its production managers concentrated on routine matters, while planning and industrial engineering focused on issues that needed solution within a week, and quality control specialists worried about even longer-term problems.

The reason is not difficult to find. Since Plant P's organization led its managers to identify with product goals, those who could contribute to the solution of longer-term problems became involved in these activities. In Plant F, where each unit focused on its own goals, there was more of a tendency to worry about getting daily progress. On the average, employees of Plant P reported devoting 30 percent of their time to daily problems, while at Plant F this figure was 49 percent. We shall have more to say shortly about how these factors influenced the results achieved in the two plants.

**Organizational Formality.** In the study, the formality of organizational structure in each functional activity was measured by three criteria: clarity of definition of job responsibilities, clarity of dividing lines between jobs, and importance of rules and procedures.

It was found that at Plant F there were fewer differences among functional activities in the formality of organization structure than at Plant P. Plant F employees reported that a uniform degree of structure existed across functional specialties; job responsibilities were well defined, and the distinctions between jobs were clear. Similarly, rules and procedures were extensively relied on. At Plant P, on the other hand, substantial differences in the formality of organization existed. Plant engineers and industrial engineers, for example, were rather vague about their responsibilities and about the dividing line between their jobs and other jobs. Similarly, they reported relatively low reliance on rules and procedures. Production managers, on the other hand, noted that their jobs were well defined and that rules and procedures were more important to them.

The effects of these two bases of organization on differentiation along these three dimensions are summarized in Table 17.1. Overall, differentiation was greater between functional specialists at Plant P than at Plant F.

### Integration Achieved

While the study found that both plants experienced some problems in accomplishing integration, these difficulties were more noticeable at Plant F. Collaboration between maintenance and production personnel and between production and scheduling was a problem there. In Plant P the only relationship where integration was unsatisfactory was that between production and quality control specialists. Thus Plant P seemed to be getting slightly better integration in spite of the greater differentiation among specialists in that organization. Since differentiation and integration are basically antagonistic, the only way managers at Plant P could get both was by being effective at communication and conflict resolution. They were better at this than were managers at Plant F.

**Communication Patterns.** In Plant P, communication among employees was more frequent, less formal, and more often of a face-to-face nature than was the case with Plant F personnel. One Plant P employee volunteered:

> Communications are no problem around here. You can say it. You can get an answer.

Members of Plant F did not reflect such positive feelings. They were heard to say:

> Why didn't they tell me this was going to happen? Now they've shut down the line.
> When we get the information, it is usually too late to do any real planning. We just do our best.

### TABLE 17.1 • DIFFERENTIATION IN PLANTS F AND P

| Dimensions of Differentiation | Plant F | Plant P |
|---|---|---|
| Goal orientation | More differentiated and focused | Less differentiated and more diffuse |
| Time orientation | Less differentiated and shorter term | More differentiated and longer term |
| Formality of structure | Less differentiated, with more formality | More differentiated, with less formality |

The formal boundaries outlining positions that were more prevalent at Plant F appeared to act as a damper on communication. The encounters observed were often a succession of two-man conversations, even though more than two may have been involved in a problem. The telephone and written memoranda were more often employed than at Plant P, where spontaneous meetings involving several persons were frequent, usually in the cafeteria.

**Dealing with Conflict.** In both plants, *confrontation* of conflict was reported to be more typical than either the use of power to force one's own position or an attempt to *smooth* conflict by "agreeing to disagree." There was strong evidence, nevertheless, that in Plant P managers were coming to grips with conflicts more directly than in Plant F. Managers at Plant F reported that more conflicts were being smoothed over. They worried that issues were often not getting settled. As they put it:

> We have too many nice guys here.
>
> If you can't resolve an issue, you go to the plant manager. But we don't like to bother him often with small matters. We should be able to settle them ourselves. The trouble is we don't. So it dies.

Thus, by ignoring conflict in the hope it would go away, or by passing it to a higher level, managers at Plant F often tried to smooth over their differences. While use of the management hierarchy is one acceptable way to resolve conflict, so many disagreements at Plant F were pushed upstairs that the hierarchy became overloaded and could not handle all the problems facing it. So it responded by dealing with only the more immediate and pressing ones.

At Plant P the managers uniformly reported that they resolved conflicts themselves. There was no evidence that conflicts were being avoided or smoothed over. As one manager said:

> We don't let problems wait very long. There's no sense to it. And besides, we get together frequently and have plenty of chances to discuss differences over a cup of coffee.

As this remark suggests, the quicker resolution of conflict was closely related to the open and informal communication pattern prevailing at Plant P. In spite of greater differentiation in time and orientation and structure, then, Plant P managers were able to achieve more satisfactory integration because they could communicate and resolve conflict effectively.

### Performance and Attitudes

Before drawing some conclusions from the study of these two plants, it is important to make two more relevant comparisons between them—their effectiveness in terms of the goals set for them and the attitudes of employees.

**Plant Performance.** As we noted before, the managements of the two plants were aiming at the same two objectives: maximizing current output within existing capabilities and improving the capabilities of the plant. Of the two facilities, Plant F met the first objective more effectively; it was achieving a higher production rate with greater efficiency and at less cost than was Plant P. In terms of the second objective, however, Plant P was clearly superior to Plant F; the former's productivity had increased by 23 percent from 1963 to 1966 compared with the latter's increment of only 3 percent. One key manager at Plant F commented:

> There has been a three- or four-year effort to improve our capability. Our expectations have simply not been achieved. The improvement in performance is just not there. We are still where we were three years ago. But our targets for improvements are realistic.

By contrast, a key manager at Plant P observed:

> Our crews have held steady, yet our volume is up. Our quality is consistently better too.

Another said:

> We are continuing to look for and find ways to improve and consolidate jobs.

**Employee Attitudes.** Here, too, the two organizations offer a contrast, but the contrast presents a paradoxical situation. Key personnel at Plant P appeared to be more deeply involved in their work than did managers at Plant F, and they admitted more often to feeling stress and pressure than did their opposite numbers at Plant F. But Plant F managers expressed more satisfaction with their work than did those at Plant P; they liked the company and their jobs more than did managers at Plant P.

Why Plant P managers felt more involved and had a higher level of stress, but were less satisfied than Plant F managers, can be best explained by linking these findings with the others we have reported.

### Study Summary

The characteristics of these two organizations are summarized in Table 17.2. The nature of the organization at Plant F seemed to suit its stable but high rate of efficiency. Its specialists concentrated on their own goals and performed well, on the whole. The jobs were well defined and managers worked within procedures and rules. The managers

were concerned primarily with short-term matters. They were not particularly effective in communicating with each other and in resolving conflict. But this was not very important to achieve steady, good performance, since the coordination necessary to meet this objective could be achieved through plans and procedures and through the manufacturing technology itself.

As long as top management did not exert much pressure to improve performance dramatically, the plant's managerial hierarchy was able to resolve the few conflicts arising from daily operations. And as long as the organization avoided extensive problem solving, a great deal of personal contact was not very important. It is not surprising therefore that the managers were satisfied and felt relatively little pressure. They attended strictly to their own duties, remained uninvolved, and got the job done. For them, this combination was satisfying. And higher management was pleased with the facility's production efficiency.

The atmosphere at Plant P, in contrast, was well suited to the goal of improving plant capabilities, which it did very well. There was less differentiation between goals, since the functional specialists to a

### TABLE 17.2 • OBSERVED CHARACTERISTICS OF THE TWO ORGANIZATIONS

| Characteristics | Plant F | Plant P |
|---|---|---|
| Differentiation | Less differentiation except in goal orientation | Greater differentiation in structure and time orientation |
| Integration | Somewhat less effective | More effective |
| Conflict management | Confrontation, but also "smoothing over" and avoidance; rather restricted communication pattern | Confrontation of conflict; open, face-to-face communication |
| Effectiveness | Efficient, stable production; but less successful in improving plant capabilities | Successful in improving plant capabilities, but less effective in stable production |
| Employee attitudes | Prevalent feeling of satisfaction, but less feeling of stress and involvement | Prevalent feeling of stress and involvement, but less satisfaction |

degree shared the product goals. Obviously, one danger in this form of organization is the potential attraction of specialist managers to total goals to the extent that they lose sight of their particular goals and become less effective in their jobs. But this was not a serious problem at Plant P.

Moreover, there was considerable differentiation in time orientation and structure; some specialists worked at the routine and programmed tasks in operating the plant, while others concentrated on longer-term problems to improve manufacturing capability. The latter group was less constrained by formal procedures and job definitions, and this atmosphere was conducive to problem solving. The longer time orientation of some specialists, however, appeared to divert their attention from maintaining schedules and productivity. This was a contributing factor to Plant P's less effective current performance.

In spite of the higher degree of differentiation in these dimensions, Plant P managers were able to achieve the integration necessary to solve problems that hindered plant capability. Their shared goals and a common boss encouraged them to deal directly with each other and confront their conflicts. Given this pattern, it is not surprising that they felt very involved in their jobs. Also they were under stress because of their great involvement in their jobs. This stress could lead to dissatisfaction with their situation. Satisfaction for its own sake, however, may not be very important; there was no evidence of higher turnover of managers at Plant P.

Obviously, in comparing the performance of these two plants operating with similar technologies and in the same market, we might predict that, because of its greater ability to improve plant capabilities, Plant P eventually will reach a performance level at least as high as Plant F's. While this might occur in time, it should not obscure one important point: The functional organization seems to lead to better results in a situation where stable performance of a routine task is desired, while the product organization leads to better results in situations where the task is less predictable and requires innovative problem solving.

## CLUES FOR MANAGERS

How can the manager concerned with the function versus product decision use these ideas to guide him in making the appropriate choice? The essential step is identifying the demands of the task confronting the organization.

Is it a routine, repetitive task? Is it one where integration can be achieved by plan and conflict managed through the hierarchy? This was the way the task was implicitly defined at Plant F. If this is the nature of the task, or, to put it another way, if management is satisfied with this definition of the task, then the functional organization is quite appropriate. While it allows less differentiation in time orientation and structure, it does encourage differentiation in goal orientation. This combination is important for specialists to work effectively in their jobs.

Perhaps even more important, the functional structure also seems to permit a degree of integration sufficient to get the organization's work done. Much of this can be accomplished through paper systems and through the hardware of the production line itself. Conflict that comes up can more safely be dealt with through the management hierarchy, since the difficulties of resolving conflict are less acute. This is so because the tasks provide less opportunity for conflict and because the specialists have less differentiated viewpoints to overcome. This form of organization is less psychologically demanding for the individuals involved.

On the other hand, if the task is of a problem-solving nature, or if management defines it this way, the product organization seems to be more appropriate. This is especially true where there is a need for tight integration among specialists. As illustrated at Plant P, the product organization form allows the greater differentiation in time orientation and structure that specialists need to attack problems. While encouraging identification with superordinate goals, this organizational form does allow enough differentiation in goals for specialists to make their contributions.

Even more important, to identify with product ends and have a common boss encourages employees to deal constructively with conflict, communicate directly and openly with each other, and confront their differences, so they can collaborate effectively. Greater stress and less satisfaction for the individual may be unavoidable, but it is a small price to pay for the involvement that accompanies it.

The manager's problem in choosing between product and functional forms is complicated by the fact that in each organization there are routine tasks and tasks requiring problem solving, jobs requiring little interdependence among specialists and jobs requiring a great deal. Faced with these mixtures, many companies have adopted various compromises between product and functional bases. They include (in ascending order of structural complexity):

1. *The use of cross-functional teams to facilitate integration.* These teams provide some opportunity for communication and conflict resolution and also a degree of the common identification with product goals that characterizes the product organization. At the same time, they retain the differentiation provided by the functional organization.

2. *The appointment of full-time integrators or coordinators around a product.* These product managers or project managers encourage the functional specialists to become committed to product goals and help resolve conflicts between them. The specialists still retain their primary identification with their functions.[6]

3. *The "matrix" or grid organization, which combines the product and functional forms by overlaying them.* Some managers wear functional hats and are involved in the day-to-day, more routine activities. Naturally, they identify with functional goals. Others, wearing product or project hats, identify with total product goals and are more involved in the problem-solving activity required to cope with long-range issues and to achieve cross-functional coordination.

These compromises are becoming popular because they enable companies to deal with multiple tasks simultaneously. But we do not propose them as a panacea, because they make sense only for those situations where the differentiation and integration required by the sum of all the tasks make a middle approach necessary. Further, the complexity of interpersonal plus organizational relationships in these forms and the ambiguity associated with them make them difficult to administer effectively and psychologically demanding on the persons involved.

In our view, the only solution to the product versus function dilemma lies in analysis of the multiple tasks that must be performed, the differences between specialists, the integration that must be achieved, and the mechanisms and behavior required to resolve conflict and arrive at these states of differentiation and integration. This analysis provides the best hope of making a correct product or function choice or of arriving at some appropriate compromise solution.

## NOTES

1. For a historical study of the organizational structure of U.S. corporations, see Alfred D. Chandler, Jr., *Strategy and Structure*, Cambridge: The M.I.T. Press, 1962.

2. Luther Gulick, "Notes on the Theory of Organization," in *Papers on the Science of Administration*, edited by Luther Gulick and Lyndall F. Urwick, New York Institute of Public Administration, 1917, pp. 23–24.

3. Harold D. Koontz and C. J. O'Donnell, *Principles of Management*, New York, McGraw-Hill, 2nd ed. 1959, p. 111.

4. See Paul R. Lawrence and Jay W. Lorsch, *Organization and Environment*, Boston, Division of Research, Harvard Business School, 1967; and Eric J. Miller and A. K. Rice, *Systems of Organization*, London, Tavistock Publications, 1967.

5. Arthur H. Walker, *Behavioral Consequences of Contrasting Patterns of Organization*, Boston, Harvard Business School, unpublished doctoral dissertation, 1967.

6. See Paul R. Lawrence and Jay W. Lorsch, "New Management Job: The Integrator," *HBR* November–December 1967, p. 142.

## 18

# Structure in 5's: A Synthesis of the Research on Organization Design

*Henry Mintzberg*

### The Design Parameters

The literature on organizational structuring focuses on a number of mechanisms organizations are able to use to design their structures—in effect, the levers they can turn to effect the division of labor and coordination. Among the most commonly researched are the nine discussed below.

- *Job specialization*, the chief parameter for determining the division of labor, concerns the number of tasks and the breadth of each in a given position (horizontal job specialization) and the incumbent's control over these tasks (vertical job specialization). Highly specialized jobs in both horizontal and vertical senses usually fall into the category called *unskilled*, those specialized horizontally but "enlarged" vertically are usually referred to as *professional*.

- *Behavior formalization* is the design parameter by which work processes are standardized, through rules, procedures, policy manuals, job descriptions, work instructions, and so on. Hickson [29] has pointed out that this one parameter of organizational design has dominated the writings on management throughout this century. It is typically the unskilled jobs that are the most highly formalized. Structures that rely on standardization for coordination (whether of work process or otherwise) are generally referred to as *bureaucratic*; those

that rely on direct supervision or mutual adjustment, as *organic*.

- *Training and indoctrination* is the design parameter by which skills and knowledge are standardized, through extensive educational programs, usually outside the organization and before the individual begins his job (particularly in the case of training). This is a key design parameter in all work that is professional.

Two design parameters are associated with the design of the superstructure:

- *Unit grouping*, the design parameter by which direct supervision is most importantly effected (and one used also to influence mutual adjustment), deals with the bases by which positions are clustered into units and units into ever more comprehensive units, until all are clustered together under the strategic apex. The various possible bases for grouping—by skill, knowledge, work process, business function, product, service client, place—can be consolidated into two basic ones: by *function*, that is, by the means the organization uses to produce its products and services, and by *market*, that is, by ends, by the characteristics of the ultimate markets the organization serves.

- *Unit size* (usually called span of control) deals with the number of positions, or subunits, that are grouped into a single unit. The literature suggests that the greater the reliance on standardization for coordination (whether by work process, output, or skill), the larger the size of the unit, simply because there is less need for direct supervision, so more positions or units can be grouped under a single manager; it also suggests that a reliance on mutual adjustment keeps unit size small, because informal communication requires a small work group (Ouchi and Dowling; Filley et al. [pp. 417–418]).

Two design parameters are associated with the design of lateral linkages to flesh out the superstructure:

- *Planning and control systems* constitute the design parameter by which outputs are standardized in the organization. These systems may be considered to be two types. *Action planning* focuses on the predetermination of the outputs of specific decisions or actions, for example, that holes be drilled with two centimeter diameters or that new products be introduced in September. *Performance control* focusses on the after-the-fact measurement of performance of all the decisions or actions of a given position or unit over a given period of time, for example, of the sales growth of a division in the first quarter of the year.

- The *liaison devices* are the means by which the organization encourages mutual adjustment across units. As Galbraith has shown, these can be placed along a rough continuum of increasing elaboration and formality, from liaison positions and then task forces and standing committees, which establish informational connections across units, through integrating managers who are given some (limited) measure of formal authority over the decisions of the units they connect, to fully developed matrix structures which sacrifice the classical principle of unity of command in favor of the joint responsibility of two or more managers or units over the making of certain decisions.

Finally, there are the parameters associated with the design of the decision making system, generally referred to as ones of *decentralization* (which we define as the extent to which power over decision making in the organization is dispersed among its members). We find it convenient to divide these into two groups:

- *Vertical decentralization* refers to the extent to which formal decision making power is "delegated" down to the chain of line authority.

- *Horizontal decentralization* refers to the extent to which power flows informally outside this chain of line authority (that is, to analysts, support staffers, and operators in the operating core).[1] Combining these two design parameters with two other types of decentralization—*selective*, in which power is dispersed to different places for different decision processes, and *parallel*, in which power over various decisions is dispersed to the same place—yields five different kinds of decentralization, shown symbolically on Figure 18.1. In *vertical and horizontal centralization*, formal and informal power remains "primarily at the strategic apex." In *limited horizontal decentralization*, informal power flows selectively to the analysts of the technostructure who play major roles in standardizing everyone else's work, while formal power remains at the strategic apex. In *limited vertical decentralization*, much formal power is delegated in parallel to the managers of market-based line units, usually called "divisions." (As shown in Figure 18.1, some horizontal decentralization takes place here as well, to the analysts who design

## FIGURE 18.1 • THE FIVE TYPES OF DECENTRALIZATION

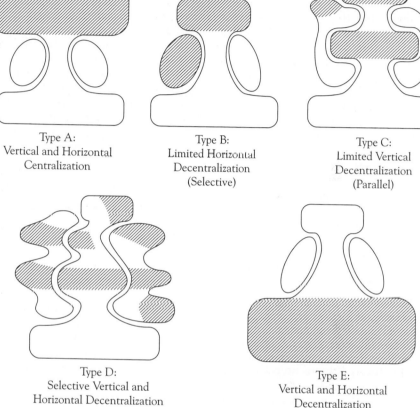

Type A:
Vertical and Horizontal
Centralization

Type B:
Limited Horizontal
Decentralization
(Selective)

Type C:
Limited Vertical
Decentralization
(Parallel)

Type D:
Selective Vertical and
Horizontal Decentralization

Type E:
Vertical and Horizontal
Decentralization

the performance control systems used to monitor the results of these divisions.) In *horizontal and vertical decentralization*, power flows, largely in parallel, all the way down the line of authority and then out at the bottom to the operators of the operating core. And in *selective decentralization* (horizontal and vertical), decision making power is diffused widely in the organization, to "work constellations" at various levels and containing various mixtures of line managers and staff and operating specialists.

### The Contingency Factors

The thrust of research on organizational structuring in the last twenty years has been toward assessing the effects of various so-called *contingency factors* on these design parameters. This research has been based on what might be called the *congruence* hypothesis, that effective structuring requires a close fit between contingency factor and design parameter, more specifically, that structure must reflect situation. Four sets of contingency factors have received the most attention.

- *Age and Size* have both been shown in the research to have important effects on structure. In particular, the older and/or the larger an organization, the more formalized its behavior (Inkson et al. Samuel and Mannheim; Pugh et al.; Udy). Moreover it has been found that the larger the organization, the larger the size of its average unit (Dale; Blau and Schoenherr) and the more elaborate its structure, that is, the more specialized its tasks, the more differentiated its units, and the more developed its administrative component of middle line and technostructure (Blau et al.; Reimann; Pugh et al.). Finally, Stinchcombe has shown that the structure of an organization often reflects the age of founding of its industry.

- *Technical System* has also been found to affect certain design parameters significantly. For one thing, the more regulating the technical system—in other words, the more it controls the work of the operators—the more formalized is their work and the more bureaucratic is the structure of the operating core (Woodward; Pugh et al.; Hickson et al.; Inkson et al.; Child and Mansfield). And the more sophisticated the technical system— that is, the more difficult it is to understand—the more elaborate the administrative structure, specifically, the larger and more professional the support staff, the greater the selective decentralization (of technical decisions to that staff), and the greater the use of liaison devices (to coordinate the work of that staff) (Woodward; Khandwalla Udy; Hunt; Hickson et al.). Finally Woodward has shown how the automation of the work of the operating core tends to transform a bureaucratic administrative structure into an organic one.

- *Environment* is another major contingency factor discussed in the literature. Dynamic environments have been identified with organic structures (Duncan Burns and Stalker; Burns; Harvey; Lawrence and Lorsch), and complex environments with decentralized ones (Hage and Aiken; Pennings). However, laboratory evidence suggests that hostile environments might lead organizations to centralize their structures temporarily (Hamblin). And disparaties in the environment appear to encourage selective decentralization to differentiated work constellations (Hlavacek and Thompson; Khandwalla; Lawrence and Lorsch). Finally, there is a good deal of evidence that diversification of the organization's markets encourage the use of market bases for grouping at high levels, assuming favorable economies of scale (Chandler; Wrigley; Rumelu; Channon; Dyas and Thanheiser).

- *Power* factors have also been shown to have selective effects on structure. Most importantly, external control of organizations appears to increase formalization and centralization (Samuel and Mannheim; Heydebrand; Holdaway et al.; Pugh et al.; Reimann; Pondy). The need for power of the various members can influence the distribution of decision making authority, especially in the case of a chief executive whose strong need for power tends to increase centralization (Dill). And fashion has been shown to have an influence on structure, sometimes driving organizations to favor inappropriate though fashionable structures (Woodward; Lawrence and Lorsch; Rumelt; Franko; Child and Keiser; Azuni and McMillan).

## THE CONFIGURATIONS OF STRUCTURE

The congruence hypothesis relates organizational effectiveness to the fit between a given design parameter and a given contingency factor. But a second hypothesis is also possible—what can be called the *configuration* hypothesis—that effective structuring requires an internal consistency among the design parameters.

In fact, we can combine our two hypotheses to propose a third, combined one, that we can call the *extended configuration* hypothesis: effective structuring requires a consistency among the design parameters and the contingency factors. In other words, we can search for natural clusters or configurations of the design parameters together with the contingency factors. Implicit in this hypothesis is the notion that the two sets of factors merge into interactive systems, that the design parameters "cause" the so-called contingency factors just as much as the contingency factors influence the choice of design parameters. An organization may become more bureaucratic as it grows, but bureaucracies also have a habit of trying to grow larger; dynamic environments may call for organic structures, but organizations with organic structures also seek out dynamic environments, where they can outmaneuver the bureaucracies. Our sets of elements provide us with enough detail to begin to speculate about what some of those configurations might be.

Let us return to that number five. It must surely be more than coincidental that we have five coordinating mechanisms, five parts of the organization, five kinds of decentralization. In fact, in searching for ways to combine our various elements into configurations, five of these too emerged as most obvious. And this naturally led to a consideration of the correspondences among all these quintets. In fact, these proved to be obvious ones. It turned out that in each configuration a different coordinating mechanism dominated, a different part of the organization was key, and a different one of the five types of decentralization was used. This can be explained by considering the organization as being pulled in five different directions, by each of its parts. Most organizations experience all five of these pulls; however, to the extent that conditions favor one over the others, the organization is drawn to structure itself as one of the configurations.

- The strategic apex exerts a pull for centralization, by which it can retain control over decision making. This it achieves when direct supervision is relied upon for coordination. To the extent that conditions favor this pull, the configuration called *Simple Structure* emerges.
- The technostructure exerts its pull for standardization—notably for that of work processes, the tightest form—because the design of the standards is its raison d'etre. This amounts to a pull for limited horizontal decentralization. To the extent that conditions favor this pull, the organization structures itself as a *Machine Bureaucracy*.
- In contrast, the members of the operating core seek to minimize the influence of the administrators—managers as well as analysts—over their work. That is, they promote horizontal and vertical decentralization. When they succeed, they work relatively autonomously, achieving whatever coordination is necessary through the standardization of skills. Thus, the operators exert a pull for professionalism, that is, for a reliance on outside training that enhances their skills. To the extent that conditions favor this pull, the organization structures itself as a *Professional Bureaucracy*.

- The managers of the middle line also seek autonomy but must achieve it in a very different way—by drawing power down from the strategic apex and, if necessary, up from the operating core, to concentrate it in their own units. In effect, they favor limited vertical decentralization. As a result, they exert a pull to Balkanize the structure, to split it into market-based units which can control their own decisions, coordination being restricted to the standardization of their outputs. To the extent that conditions favor this pull, the *Divisionalized Form* results.
- Finally, the support staff gains the most influence in the organization not when it is autonomous but when its collaboration is called for in decision making, owing to its expertise. This happens when the organization is structured into work constellations to which power is decentralized selectively and which are free to coordinate within and between themselves by mutual adjustment. To the extent that conditions favor this pull to collaborate, the organization adopts the *Adhocracy* configuration.

These five configurations consititute a typology of "ideal" or "pure" types. The central purpose of this article is to present this typology, and in so doing to make the case that it brings together the various elements of structuring discussed in the literature and also encompasses many of the major findings of the research. As such, it is hoped that the typology will be viewed as a framework useful for comprehending and analyzing the behavior of organizations. Table 18.1 shows how the various elements we have been discussing are incorporated into the typology of the five configurations. The remainder of this article is devoted to a description of the five configurations.

### The Simple Structure

The Simple Structure is characterized, above all, by what it is not—elaborated. Typically it has little or no technostructure, few support staffers, a loose division of labor, minimal differentiation among its units, and a small middle line hierarchy. Little of its behavior is formalized, and it makes minimal use of planning, training, or the liaison devices. It is, above all, organic. Its coordination is effected largely by direct supervision. Specifically, power over all important decisions tends to be centralized in the hands of the chief executive officer. Thus, the strategic apex emerges as the key part of the structure; indeed, the structure often consists of little more than a one-person strategic apex and an organic operating core. Grouping into units—if it exists at all—more often than not is on a loose functional basis. Likewise, communication flows informally in this structure, most of it between the chief executive and everyone else. Likewise, decision making is informal, with the centralization of power allowing for rapid response.

Above all, the environment of the Simple Structure tends to be at one and the same time simple and dynamic. A simple environment can be comprehended by a single individual, and so allows decision making to be controlled by that individual. And a dynamic environment means organic structure: because the future state of the environment cannot be predicted, the organization cannot effect coordination by standardization. Another condition common to Simple Structure is a technical system that is neither sophisticated nor regulating. A sophisticated one would require an elaborate support structure, to which power over technical decisions would have to be delegated, while a regulating one would call for bureaucratization of the operating core. Young organizations and small organizations also tend to use the Simple Structure,

**TABLE 18.1 • ELEMENTS OF THE FIVE STRUCTURAL CONFIGURATIONS**

| | Simple Structure | Machine Bureaucracy | Professional Bureaucracy | Divisionalized Form | Adhocracy |
|---|---|---|---|---|---|
| Key coordinating mechanism: | Direct Supervision | Standardization of work | Standardization of skills | Standardization of outputs | Mutual Adjustment |
| **Design parameters:** | | | | | |
| Specialization of jobs: | | | | | |
| -horizontal | low | high | high | some (between HQ and divisions) | high |
| -vertical | high | high | low | some | low |
| Training | low | low | high | some (for division managers) | high |
| Indoctrination | low | low | high (retraining) | some | varies |
| Formalization of behavior | low | high | low | high (within divisions) | low |
| Bureaucratic/organic | organic | bureaucratic | bureaucratic | bureaucratic | organic |
| Grouping | usually functional | usually functional | functional and market | market | function and market |
| Unit Size | large | large (at bottom, narrow elsewhere) | large (at bottom, narrow elsewhere) | large (between HQ and divisions) | small (throughout) |
| Planning and control systems | little | action planning | little | perf. control | limited action pl. (esp. in Adm. Ad.) |
| Liaison devices | few | few | some in administration | few | many throughout |
| Decentralization | centralization | limited horizontal decentralization | horizontal and vertical decentralization | limited vertical decentralization | selective decentralization |
| **Contingency factors:** | | | | | |
| Age (typically) | young | old | varies | old | young (Op. Ad.) |
| Size (typically) | small | large | varies | very large | varies |

**TABLE 18.1** (*continued*)

| | Simple Structure | Machine Bureaucracy | Professional Bureaucracy | Divisionalized Form | Adhocracy |
|---|---|---|---|---|---|
| **Technical system** | | | | | |
| -regulation | low | high | low | high | low |
| -complexity | low | low | Low | Low | low/high (Op./Adm. Ad.) |
| -automated | no | no | no | no | no/often (Op./Adm. Ad.) |
| **Environment** | | | | | |
| -complexity | low | low | high | low | high |
| -dynamism | High (sometimes hostile) | low | low | Low (diversified markets) | High (sometimes disparate) |
| **Power** | | | | | |
| -focus | strategic apex | technostructure, often external | professional operators | middle line | experts |
| -fashionable | no | no | yes | yes | especially |

because they have not yet had the time, or yet reached the scale of operations, required for bureaucratization. Finally extreme hostility in their environments force most organizations to use the Simple Structure, no matter how they are normally organized. To deal with crises, organizations tend to centralize at the top temporarily, and to suspend their standard operating procedures.

The classic case of the Simple Structure is, of course, the entrepreneurial firm. The firm is aggressive and often innovative, continually searching for risky environments where the bureaucracies hesitate to operate. But it is also careful to remain in a market niche that its entrepreneur can fully comprehend. Entrepreneurial firms are usually small, so that they can remain organic and their entrepreneurs can retain tight control. Also they are often young, in part because the attrition rate among entrepreneurial firms is so high, and in part because those that survive tend to make the transition to bureaucracy as they age. Inside the structure, all revolves around the entrepreneur. Its goals are his goals, its strategy his vision of its place in the world. Most entrepreneurs loathe bureaucratic procedures as impositions on their flexibility. Their unpredictable maneuvering keeps their structures lean, flexible, organic.

### The Machine Bureaucracy

A second clear configuration of the design parameters has held up consistently in the research: highly specialized, routine operating tasks, very formalized procedures and large-sized units in the operating core, reliance on the functional basis for grouping tasks throughout the structure, little use made of training and of the liaison devices, relatively centralized power for decision making with some use of action planning systems, and an elaborate administrative structure with a sharp distinction between line and staff.

Despite its sharp distinction between line and staff, because the machine bureaucracy depends above all on standardization of work processes for coordination, the technostructure—which houses the many analysts who do the standardizing—emerges as the key part of the structure. Consequently, these analysts develop some informal power, with the result that the organization can be described as having limited horizontal decentralization. The analysts gain their power largely at the expense of the operators, whose work they formalize to a high degree, and of the first-line managers, who would otherwise supervise the operators directly. But the emphasis on standardization extends well above the operating core, and with it follows the analysts' influence. Rules and regulations—an obsession with control—permeate the entire structure; formal communication is favored at all levels; decision making tends to follow the formal chain of authority. Only at the strategic apex are the different functional responsibilities brought together; therefore, only at that level can the major decisions be made, hence the centralization of the structure in the vertical dimension.

The Machine Bureaucracy is typically associated with environments that are both simple and stable. The work of complex environments cannot be rationalized into simple operating tasks, while that of dynamic environments cannot be predicted, made repetitive, and so standardized. Thus the Machine Bureaucracy responds to a simple, stable environment, and in turn seeks to insure that its environment remains both simple and stable. In fact, this helps to explain the large size of the support staff in the Machine Bureaucracy. To ensure stability, the Machine Bureaucracy prefers to make rather than buy—to supply own support services wherever possible so that it can closely control them. In addition, the Machine Bureaucracy is typically found in the mature organization, large enough to have the scale of operations that allows for repetition and standardization, and old enough to have been able to settle on the standards it wishes to use. Machine Bureaucracies also tend to be identified with regulating technical systems, since these routinize work and so enable that work to be standardized. But it is not typically found with sophisticated or automated technical systems because, as noted earlier, one disperses power to the support staff and the other calls for organic structure in administration, thereby driving the organization to a different configuration. Finally, the Machine Bureaucracy is often associated with external control. As noted earlier, the greater the external control of an organization, the more its structure tends to be centralized and formalized, the two prime design parameters of the Machine Bureaucracy.

Typical examples of organizations drawn to the Machine Bureaucracy configuration are mass production firms, service firms with simple, repetitive work such as insurance and telephone companies, government agencies with similar work such as post offices and tax collection departments, and organizations that have special needs for safety, such as airlines and fire departments.

### The Professional Bureaucracy

Organizations can be bureaucratic without being centralized, that is their behavior can be standardized by a coordinating mechanism that allows for decentralization. That coordinating mechanism is the standardization of skills, a reliance on which gives rise to the configuration called Professional Bureaucracy, found typically in school systems, social work agencies, accounting firms, and craft manufacturing firms. The organization hires highly trained specialists—called professionals—in its operating core, and then gives them considerable autonomy in their work. In other words, they work relatively freely not only of the administrative hierarchy but also of their own colleagues. Much of the necessary coordination is achieved by design—by the standard skills that predetermine behavior. And this autonomy in the operating core means that the operating units are typically very large and that the structure is decentralized in both the vertical and horizontal dimensions. In other words, much of the formal and informal power of the Professional Bureaucracy rests in its operating core, clearly its key part. Not only do the professionals control their own work, but they also tend to maintain collective control of the administrative apparatus of the organization. Managers of the middle line, in order to have power in the Professional Bureaucracy, must be professionals themselves, and must maintain the support of the professional operators. Moreover, they typically share the administrative tasks with the operating professionals. At the administrative level, however, in contrast with the operating level, tasks require a good deal of mutual adjustment, achieved in large part through standing committees, task forces, and other liaison devices.

The technostructure is minimal in this configuration, because the complex work of the operating professionals cannot easily be formalized, or its outputs standardized by action planning and performance control systems. The support staff is, however, highly elaborated but largely to carry out the simpler, more routine work and to back-up the high-priced professionals in general. As a result, the support staff tend to work in a machine bureaucratic pocket off to one side of the Professional Bureaucracy. For the support staff of these organizations, there is no democracy, only the oligarchy of the professionals. Finally, a curious feature of this configuration is that it uses the functional and market bases for grouping concurrently in its operating core. That is, clients are categorized and served in terms of functional specialties—chemistry students by the chemistry department in the university, cardiac patients by the cardiac department in the hospital.

The Professional Bureaucracy typically appears in conjunction with an environment that is both complex and stable. Complexity demands the use of skills and knowledge that can be learned only in extensive training programs, while stability ensures that these skills settle down to become the standard operating procedures of the organization. Age and size are not important factors in this configuration: the organization tends to use the same standard skills no matter how small or young it is because its professionals bring these skills with them when they first join the organization. So unlike the Machine Bureaucracy, which must design its own standards, in the Professional Bureaucracy no time is lost and no scale of operations is required to establish standards. Technical system is of importance in this configuration only for what it is not—neither regulating, or sophisticated, nor automated. Any one of these characteristics would destroy individual operator autonomy in favor of administrative or peer group influence, and so drive the organization to a different configuration. Finally, fashion is a factor, simply because it has proven to the advantage of all kinds of operator groups to have their work defined as professional; this enables them to demand influence and autonomy in the organization. For this reason, Professional Bureaucracy is a highly fashionable structure today.

### The Divisionalized Form

The Divisionalized Form is not so much a complete structure as the superimposition of one structure on others. This structure can be described as a market-based one, with a central headquarters overseeing a set of divisions, each charged with serving its own markets. In this way there need be little interdependence between the divisions (beyond that Thompson refers to as the "pooled" type), and little in the way of close coordination. Each division is thus given a good deal of autonomy. The result is the limited, parallel form of vertical decentralization,[2] with the middle line emerging as the key part of the organization. Moreover, without the need for close coordination, a large number of divisions can report up to the one central headquarters. The main concern of that headquarters then becomes to find a mechanism to coordinate the goals of the divisions with its own, without sacrificing divisional autonomy. And that it does by standardizing the outputs of the divisions—specifically, by relying on performance control systems to impose performance standards on the divisions and then monitor their results. Hence Figure 18.2 shows a small headquarters technostructure, which is charged with designing and operating the performance control system. Also shown is a small headquarters support staff. Included here are those units that serve all of the divisions (e.g., legal counsel), with other support units dispersed to the divisions serve their particular needs (e.g., industrial relations).

## FIGURE 18.2 • THE DIVISIONALIZED FORM

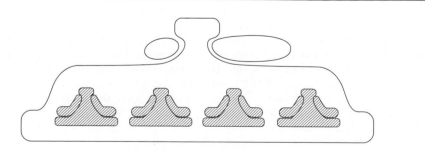

Finally there arises the question of what structure is found in the divisions themselves. Although in principle the Divisionalized Form is supposed to work with any kind of structure in the divisions, in fact there is reason to believe that the divisions are driven to use the Machine Bureaucracy. The Divisionalized Form requires the establishment for each division of clearly defined performance standards, the existence of which depend on two major assumptions. First, each division must be treated as a single integrated system with a single, consistent set of goals. In other words, while the divisions may be loosely coupled with each other, the assumption is that each is tightly coupled within. Second, those goals must be operational ones, in other words, lend themselves to quantitative measures of performance control. And these two assumptions hold only in one configuration, the one that is both bureaucratic (i.e., operates in a stable enough environment to be able to establish performance standards) and integrated, in other words, in Machine Bureaucracy. Moreover, as noted earlier, external control drives organizations toward Machine Bureaucracy; here the headquarters constitutes external control of the divisions.

One factor above all encourages the use of the Divisionalized Form—market diversity, specifically, that of products and services. (Diversity only in region or client leads, as Channon has shown, to an incomplete form of divisionalization, with certain "critical" functions concentrated at headquarters, as in the case of purchasing in a regionally diversified retailing chain.) But by the same token, it has also been found that divisionalization encourages further diversification (Rumelt, pp. 76–77]; Fouraker and Stopford), headquarters being encouraged to do so by the ease with which it can add divisions and by the pressures from the corps of aggressive general managers trained in the middle lines of such structures. Otherwise, as befits a structure that houses Machine Bureaucracies, the Divisionalized Form shares many of their conditions—an environment that is neither very complex nor very dynamic, and an organization that is typically large and mature. In effect, the Divisionalized Form is the common structural response to an integrated Machine Bureaucracy that has diversified its product or service lines horizontally (i.e., in conglomerate fashion).

The Divisionalized Form is very fashionable in industry, found in pure or partial form among the vast majority of America's largest corporations, the notable exceptions being those with giant economies of scale in their traditional businesses (Wrigley; Rumelt). It is also found outside the sphere of business (in the form of multiverities, conglomerate unions, and government itself), but often in impure form due to the difficulty of developing relevant performance measures.

### The Adhocracy

Sophisticated innovation requires a fifth and very different structural configuration, one that is able to fuse experts drawn from different specialties into smoothly functioning project teams. Adhocracy is such a configuration, consisting of organic structure with little formalization of behavior; extensive horizontal job specialization based on formal training; a tendency to group the professional specialists in functional units for housekeeping purposes but to deploy them in small market-based teams to do their project work; a reliance on the liaison devices to encourage mutual adjustment—the key coordinating mechanism—within and between these teams; and selective decentralization to these teams, which are located at various places in the organization and involve various mixtures of line managers and staff and operating experts. Of all the configurations, Adhocracy shows the least reverance for the classical principles of management. It gives quasi-formal authority to staff personnel, thereby blurring the line-staff distinction, and it relies extensively on matrix structure, combining functional and market bases for grouping concurrently and thereby dispensing with the principle of unity of command.

Adhocracies may be divided into two main types. In the *Operating Adhocracy*, the innovation is carried out directly on behalf of the clients, as in the case of consulting firms, advertising agencies, and film companies. In effect, there corresponds to every Professional Bureaucracy an Operating Adhocracy that does similar work but with a broader orientation. For the consulting firm that seeks to pigeonhole each client problem into the most relevant standard skill within its given repertoire, there exists another that treats that problem as a unique challenge requiring a creative solution. The former, because of its standardization, can allow its professional operators to work on their own; the latter, in order to achieve innovation, must group its professionals in multidisciplinary teams so as to encourage mutual adjustment. In the Operating Adhocracy, the administrative and operating work tend to blend into a single effort. In other words, ad hoc project work does not allow a sharp differentiation of the planning and design of the work from its actual execution.

In the *Administrative Adhocracy*, the project work serves the organization itself, as in the case of chemical firms and space agencies. And here the administrative and operating components are sharply differentiated: in fact, the operating core is typically truncated from the rest of the organization—set up as a separate structure, contracted out, or automated—so that the administrative component is free to function as an Adhocracy.

Adhocracy is clearly positioned in environments that are both dynamic and complex. These are the ones that demand sophisticated innovation, the kind of innovation that calls for organic structure with a good deal of decentralization. Disparate forces in the environment, by encouraging selective decentralization to differentiated work constellations, as noted earlier, also encourage use of Adhocracy, notably the Administrative kind. Age—or at least youth—is another condition associated with Adhocracy, because time encourages an organization to bureaucratize, for example, by settling on the set of skills it performs best and so converting itself from an Operating Adhocracy into a Professional Bureaucracy. Moreover, because Operating Adhocracies in particular are such vulnerable structures—they can never be sure where their next project will come from— they tend to be very young on average: many of them either die early or else shift to bureaucratic configurations to escape the uncertainty.

Adhocracies of the Administrative kind are also associated with technical systems that are sophisticated and automated. Sophistication requires that power over decisions concerning the technical system be given to specialists in the support staff, thereby creating selective decentralization to a work constellation that makes heavy use of the liaison devices. And automation in the operating core transforms a bureacratic administrative structure into an organic one, because it frees the organization of the need to control operators by technocratic standards. The standards are built right into the machines. In effect, the support staff, being charged with the selection and engineering of the automated equipment, takes over the function of designing the work of the operating core. The result is the Adhocracy configuration.

Finally, fashion is an important factor, because every characteristic of Adhocracy is very much in vogue today—emphasis on expertise, organic and matrix structure, teams and task forces, decentralization without power concentration, sophisticated and automated technical systems, youth, and complex, dynamic environments. In fact, perhaps the best support for Stinchcombe's claim, cited earlier, that structure reflects the age of founding of the industry, comes from the observation that while Adhocracy seems to be used in few industries that were fully developed before World War II, it found extensively in virtually every one that developed since that time. Adhocracy seems clearly to be the structure of *our* age.

## BEYOND FIVE

Our five configurations have been referred to repeatedly in this article as ideal or pure types. The question then arises as to where—or whether—they can be found. It is clear that each configuration is a simplification, understating the true complexity of all but the simplest organizational structures. In that sense, every sentence in our description of the configurations has been an overstatement (including this one!). And yet our reading of the research literature suggests that in many cases one of the five pulls discussed earlier dominates the other four in an organization, with the result that its structure is drawn toward one of the configurations. It is presumably its search for harmony in structure and situation that causes an organization to favor one of the pure types.

Other structures of course emerge differently. Some appear to be in transition from one pure type to another, in response to a changed situation. Others exhibit structures that can be described as hybrids of the configurations, perhaps because different forces pull them toward different pure types. The symphony orchestra, for example, seems to use a combination of Simple Structure and Professional Bureaucracy: it hires highly trained musicians and relies largely on their standardized skills to produce its music, yet it also requires a strong, sometimes autocratic, leader to weld them into a tightly coordinated unit. Other hybrids seem to be dysfunctional, as in the case of the organization that no sooner gives its middle managers autonomy subject to performance control, as in the Divisionalized Form, than it takes it away by direct supervision, as in the Simple Structure. School systems, police forces, and the like are often forced to centralize power inappropriately because of the external controls imposed upon them. Would-be Professional Bureaucracies become Machine Bureaucracies, to the regret of operator and client alike.

The point to be emphasized is not that the five configurations represent some hard and fast typology but that together as a set they represent a conceptual framework which can be used to help us comprehend organizational behavior—how structures emerge, how and why they change over time, why certain pathologies plague organizational design.

### *Finally ....*

Is there a sixth structural configuration? Well, the rainbow still has only five colors. But the planets turned out to number more than five. We even seem to be on the verge of recognizing a sixth sense. So why not a sixth configuration. As long, of course, as it maintains the harmony of the theory: it must have its own unique coordinating mechanism, and a new, sixth part of the organization must dominate it.

We do, in fact, have a candidate for that sixth configuration. It relies for coordination on socialization—in effect, the standardization of norms; it uses indoctrination as its main design parameter; and its dominant part is ideology, a sixth part, in fact, of every organization, representing a pull toward a sense of mission. Perhaps the *Missionary Configuration* will emerge as the fashionable structure of the post-adhocratic age.[3]

## NOTES

1. A third use of the term decentralization relates to the physical dispersal of services. Since this has nothing to do with the dispersal of decision making power per se, it is not considered here to be a type of decentralization. The term "concentration" is used instead, and is associated with unit grouping (i.e., the determination of where the support units are grouped).

2. "Limited" means that the equating of divisionalization with "decentralization," as is done in so much of the literature, is simply not correct. In fact, as Perrow [p. 38] points out, the most famous example of divisionalization—that of General Motors in the 1920s—was clearly one of the relative *centralization* of the structure.

3. This paper draws on *The Structuring of Organizations: A Synthesis of the Research* (Prentice-Hall, 1979). The author wishes to express his appreciation to Andy Van de Ven who commented extensively and very helpfully on an earlier version of this paper, and to Arie Lewin, because hard working editors seldom get the recognition they deserve.

## REFERENCES

Azuni, K. and McMillan, C. J., "Culture and Organizational Structure: A Comparison of Japanese and British Organizations," *International Studies of Management and Organization,* 1975, pp. 35–47.

Blau, P. M. and Schoenherr, P. A., *The Structure of Organizations,* Basic Books, New York, 1971.

———, Falbe, C. M., McKinley, W. and Tracy, D. K., "Technology and Organization in Manufacturing," *Admin. Sci. Quart.* (1976), pp. 20–40.

Burns, T., "The Comparative Study of Organization," in V. Vroom (ed.), *Methods of Organizational Research,* Univ. of Pittsburgh Press, Pittsburgh, Penn., 1967.

———and Stalker, G. M., *The Management of innovation,* 2nd ed., Tavistock, 1966.

Chandler, A. D., *Strategy and Structure,* MIT Press, Cambridge, Mass., 1962.

Channon, D. F., *The Strategy and Structure of British Enterprise,* Division of Research Harvard Graduate School of Business Administration, 1973.

Child, J. and Kieser, A., "Organization and Managerial Roles in British and West German Companies—An Examination of the Culture-Free Thesis," in C. J. Lamers and D. J. Hickson (eds.), *Organizations Alike and Unlike,* Routledge and Kegan Paul, 1978.

——— and Mansfield, R., "Technology, Size and Organization Structure," *Sociology* (1972), pp. 369–393.

Dale, E., *Planning and Developing the Company Organization Structure,* American Management Association, 1952.

Dill, W. R., "Business Organizations," in J. G. March (ed.), *The Handbook of Organizations,* Rand McNally, 1965, Chapter 25.

Duncan, R. B., "Multiple Decision-Making Structures in Adapting to Environmental Uncertainty: The Impact on Organizational Effectiveness," *Human Relations* (1973), pp. 273–291.

Dyas, G. P. and Thanheiser, H. T., *The Emerging European Enterprise: Strategy and Structure in French and German Industry,* Macmillan, London, 1976.

Filley, A. C. and House, R. J., *Managerial Process and Organizational Behaviour,* Scott,

Foresman, Glenview, Ill., 1969; also second edition with S. Kerr, 1976.

Fouraker, L. E. and Stopford, J. M., "Organizational Structure and the Multinational Strategy," *Admin. Sci. Quart.* (1968), pp. 47–64.

Franko, L. G., "The Move Toward a Multidivisional Structure in European Organizations," *Admin. Sci. Quart.* (1974), pp. 493–506.

Galbraith, J. R., *Designing Complex Organizations*, Addison-Wesley, Reading, Mass., 1973.

Hage, J. and Aiken, M., "Relationship of Centralization to Other Structural Properties," *Admin. Sci. Quart.* (1967), pp. 72–92.

Hamblin, R. L., "Leadership and Crises," *Sociometry* (1958), pp. 322–335.

Harvey, E., "Technology and the Structure of Organization," *Amer. Sociological Rev.* (1968), pp. 247–259.

Heydebrand, W. V., "Autonomy, Complexity, and Non-bureaucratic Coordination in Professional Organization," in W. V. Heydebrand (ed.) *Comparative Organizations*, Prentice-Hall, Englewood Cliffs, N.J., 1973, pp. 158–189.

Hickson, D. J., "A Convergence in Organization Theory," *Admin. Sci. Quart.* (1966–1967), pp. 224–237.

———, Pugh, D. S. and Pheysey, D. C., "Operations Technology and Organization Structure: An Empirical Reappraisal," *Admin. Sci. Quart.* (1969), pp. 378–379.

Hlavacek, J. D. and Thompson, V. A., "Bureaucracy and New Product Innovation," *Acad. Management J.* (1973), pp. 361–372.

Holdaway, E. A., Newberry, J. F., Hickson, D. J. and Heron, R. P., "Dimensions or Organizations in Complex Societies: The Educational Sector," *Admin. Sci. Quart.* (1975), pp. 37–58.

Hunt, R. G., "Technology and Organization," *Acad. Management J.* (1970), pp. 235–252.

Inkson, J. H. K., Pugh, D. S. and Hickson, D. J., "Organization, Context and Structure: An Abbreviated Replication," *Admin. Sci. Quart.* (1970), pp. 318–329.

Khandwalla, P. N., "Effect of Competition on the Structure of Top Management Control," *Acad. Management J.* (1973), pp. 481–495.

———, "Mass Output Orientation of Operations Technology and

Organizational Structure," *Admin. Sci. Quart.* (1974), pp. 74–97.

Lawrence, P. R. and Lorsch, J. W., *Organization and Environment*, Irwin, Homewood, Ill., 1967.

Ouchi, W. G. and Dowling, J. B., "Defining the Span of Control," *Admin. Sci. Quart.* (1974), pp. 357–365.

Pennings, J. M., "The Relevance of the Structural-Contingency Model for Organizational Effectiveness," *Admin. Sci. Quart.* (1975), pp. 393–410.

Pondy, L. R., "Effects of Size, Complexity, and Ownership on Administrative Intensity," *Admin. Sci. Quart.* (1969), pp. 47–60

Pugh, D. S., Hickson, D. J., Hinings, C. R. and Turner, C., "Dimensions of Organizatioon Structure," *Admin. Sci. Quart.* (1968), pp. 65–105.

———, ———, ——— and Turner, C., "The Context of Organization Structures," *Admin. Sci. Quart.* (1969), pp. 91–114.

Reimann, B. C., "On the Dimensions of Bureaucratic Structure: An Empirical Reappraisal," *Admin. Sci. Quart.* (1973), pp. 462–476.

Rumelt, R. P., *Strategy, Structure, and Economic Performance*, Division of Research, Graduate School of Business Administration, Harvard University, 1974.

Samuel, Y. and Mannheim, B. F., "A Multidimensional Approach Toward a Typology of Bureaucracy," *Admin. Sci. Quart.* (1970), pp. 216–228.

Stinchcombe, A. L., "Social Structure and Organizations," in J. G. March (ed.), *Handbook of Organizations*, Rand McNally, 1965, Chapter 4.

Thompson, J. D., *Organizations in Action*, McGraw-Hill, New York, 1967.

Udy, S. H., *Organizations of Work*, HRAF Press, New Haven, Conn., 1959.

Udy, S. J., Jr., "The Comparative Analysis of Organization," In J. G. March (ed.), *Handbook of Organizations*, Rand McNally, 1965, Chapter 16.

Woodward, J., *Industrial Organization: Theory and Practice*, Oxford Univ. Press, 1965.

Wrigley, L., *Diversification and Divisional Autonomy*, D. B. A. thesis, Harvard Business School, 1970.

# CHAPTER 5

# *Organizational Economics Theory*

Organizational economists use concepts and tools mostly from the field of micro-economics to study the internal processes and structures of the firm. They ask questions such as "Why do organizations exist?" "What determines the size, scope, and structure of a firm?" "Why are some workers paid hourly rates while others receive salaries?" and "What factors determine organizational survival and growth?" Most development in this field occurred in the second half of the twentieth century, including the introduction of important ideas associated with, for example, agency theory, behavioral theory, incomplete contract theory, transaction cost economics, and game theory (Augier, Kreiner, & March, 2000).

The recognized field of organizational economics originated with a 1937 article by Ronald H. Coase, "The Nature of the Firm." Coase asked a framing question: "Why would firms exist if market and price systems worked perfectly?" His answer was that in some situations, the cost of using market and price mechanisms exceeded the cost of using a firm. Thus, establishing a firm—creating a hierarchy—was more profitable. Therefore, the discipline of economics could not rely on price theory alone to explain behavior in and of firms. Although price theory often could adequately explain some resource allocation decisions, a second coordinating mechanism—hierarchy—also had to be considered.

The interests and concerns of organizational economics have expanded greatly since 1937. Some of the key questions organizational economists have addressed over the past 70 years have included the contractual nature of firms, bounded rationality, the significance of investment in specific assets, the distinction between specific rights and residual rights, and the effects of imperfect information. These different approaches to organizational economics share a common attention to explaining the emergence and expansion of organizations—hierarchies—given the existence of costs associated with uncertainties, information asymmetries, bounded rationality, and cognitive barriers.

Three articles are reprinted here that introduce the essence of organizational economics and its core theory components: transaction cost, principal-agent relations, the theory of property rights, and common-pool resources, "The Economics of Organization: The Transaction Cost Approach" by Oliver E. Williamson (1981); "Learning from Organizational Economics," by Jay Barney and William Ouchi (1986); and "An Institutional Approach to the Study of Self-Organization and Self-Governance," by Elinor Ostrom (1990). Williamson's "The Economics of Organization: The Transaction Cost Approach" sketches the basic themes and research agendas in the field of organizational economics. Barney and Ouchi's "Learning from Organizational Economics" provides an integrative overview of the central themes that organizational economists have contributed to organization theory. Ostrom, in "An Institutional Approach to the Study of Self-Organization and Self-Governance," introduces the concept of "common pool resource"

(CPR) and highlights the role of self-governing cooperative institutions as a way to manage CPRs effectively.

*Transaction cost theory* provides a general framework for understanding the origin of organizations as mechanisms to reduce transaction costs and support management decisions under conditions of high uncertainty and opportunism. The typical neoclassical economic models see organizations as systems for managing production costs and schedules. Oliver E. Williamson was among the first economists to shift attention from production to transactions. In "The Economics of Organization: The Transaction Cost Approach," Williamson (1981) explains that a transaction occurs "when a good or service is transferred across a technologically separable interface." Simple transactions take place in "on-the-spot" situations and are conducted in the free marketplace where price systems work reasonably well. In recent decades, however, simple exchange relations have been replaced by more complex and uncertain situations. The environment in which transactions occur has become increasingly uncertain and trust in relationships more problematic, and thus, transaction costs have increased markedly. According to Williamson's transaction cost model, organizations are superior to markets in managing complex and uncertain economic exchanges because they reduce the cost of transactions.

According to the transaction cost model, the major challenge to doing business is making certain that business partners cooperate and abide by the terms of exchange. The costs of managing the challenge include obtaining information about the service quality of partners and alternatives, negotiating and policing agreements, and settling and preventing disputes. Williamson argues that the emergence of hierarchies and the expansion of organizations are consequences.

By converting exchange relations into hierarchical sub-elements, for example, by *making* instead of *buying* components of final products, behaviors of transaction partners can be better monitored through direct supervision, auditing, and other organizational control mechanisms. Transaction costs are thereby reduced or at least controlled by the presence of the hierarchy. Under highly complex and uncertain situations, organizations (hierarchies) are likely to be viewed as attractive alternatives to market-mediated transactions. Organizations help to solve the problems of opportunism among potential exchange partners whose trustworthiness is unknown.

*Agency theory* defines managers and other employees as "agents" of owners ("principals") who must delegate some authority to agents out of necessity. *Price theory* is concerned with how to structure organizations for the free interplay of markets among agents and principals. As Donaldson (1990) queries, "Why should not all economic activity be arranged as free contracts [including the pricing structure needed to keep agents working in the best interests of principals]?" However, price theory falls short because the interests of the principal and agent tend to diverge, and agents do not always act in the best interests of principals. Like everyone else, agents are utility maximizers who tend to act in their *own* best interests. *Agency theory* thus examines the use of price theory mechanisms (for example, incentives) *and* hierarchy mechanisms (for example, monitoring) by principals "to limit the aberrant activities of the agent" (Jensen & Meckling, 1976, p. 308).

The *theory of property rights* addresses the allocation of costs and rewards among the participants in an organization and, for example, how "claims on the assets and cash flows of the organization … can generally be sold without permission of the other contracting individuals" (Jensen & Meckling, 1976, p. 311). An organization is a form of legal fiction. It is a "multitude of complex relationships (such as contracts) between the legal fiction (the firm) and the owners of labor, material and capital inputs and the consumers of output" (Jensen & Meckling, 1976, p. 311). The intellectual heritage of property rights theory can be traced to John Locke's *Two Treatises of Government* (1967) and, to a lesser extent, Jean-Jacques Rousseau's "The Social Contract" (1947). In this century, Richard Cyert and James March's seminal book, *A Behavioral Theory of the Firm* (1963), describes organizations as coalitions of self-interested participants.

*Common pool resource* refers to a type of good consisting of "a natural or man-made resource system that is sufficiently large as to make it costly (but not impossible) to exclude potential beneficiaries from obtaining benefits from its use" (Ostrom, 1990, p. 30). Unlike pure public goods, common pool resources are often in danger of depletion and misuse because they are subtractable.

*Common pool resource theory* (CPR) is concerned with "how a group of principals who are in an interdependent situation can organize and govern themselves to obtain continuing joint benefits when all face temptations to free-ride, shirk, or otherwise act opportunistically" (Ostrom 1990, p. 29). Analyzing a wide variety of cases with regard to the common use of resources, Ostrom puts forth *cooperative self-governing institution* as an alternative solution to market and government for solving "the tragedy of commons," a situation where rational independent individuals behave against the long-term best interests of the collective and misuse and deplete common resources by pursuing each one's self-interest.

There are two common ways to manage the problems of common pool resources; one is to leave them to the market, and the other is government regulation. Ostrom, on the other hand, used empirical analyses in several different countries to suggest another approach to successful CPR management: *cooperative institutions*, which are community-based, autonomous, governing entities. Around the world, Ostrom found that common pool problems oftentimes are solved more effectively by voluntary self-governing organizations rather than by a coercive state or a rational market.

Ostrom argues collective action is possible only when individuals are rational enough to act to advance the broader public interests rather than their own, but in reality people are quite irrational. As a result, building trust between the members is more important than any other measures suggested by rational theories, such as *prisoner's dilemma* or collective action. Eventually, trust building among self-governing institutions will reduce the divergence of opinions between the agents and the principals and result in decreased transaction costs. However, a collective action approach does not mean the complete exclusion of government interventions or market mechanisms. Rather, she emphasizes the efficacy of cooperation, which has not been fully explored in previous major rational approaches.

In sum, organizational economics deals with a fundamental and universal problem of organizations: How to induce managers and other employees to act in the best interests of those who control ownership or, in the case of government agencies and nonprofit organizations, those who have the authority to control policy and resource allocation decisions. Management theorists who advocate devolution, outsourcing, and employee and group empowerment approaches must address the types of issues that the organizational economists have been wrestling with at least since 1937. In addition, more recent theories of organizational economics go a step farther from the relatively simple dichotomy between public and private solution approaches between a principal and an agent or between a government and the market. They now also pay attention to cooperative self-governing institutions as effective alternatives for reducing transaction costs and solving common pool resource problems.

## BIBLIOGRAPHY

Augier, M., K. Kreiner, & J. G. March (2000). Introduction: Some roots and branches of organizational economics. *Industrial and Corporate Change*, 9(4): 555–565.

Baldwin, R, M. Cave, & M. Lodge. (eds.). (2010). *The Oxford handbook of regulation*. Oxford, UK: Oxford University Press.

Barney, J. B., & W. G. Ouchi (1986). *Organizational economics*. San Francisco, CA: Jossey-Bass.

Boyes, W. (2012). *Managerial economics: Markets and the firm*. Mason, OH: South-Western/Cengage Learning.

Coase, R. H. (1937). The nature of the firm. *Economica [new series]*, 4: 386–405.

Cyert, R. M., & J. G. March (1963). *A behavioral theory of the firm*. Englewood Cliffs, NJ: Prentice Hall.

Donaldson, L. (1990). The ethereal hand: Organizational economics and management theory. *Academy of Management Review*, 15(3): 369–381.

Foss, N. J. (2006). *Strategy, economic organization, and the knowledge economy: The coordination of firms and resources*. New York: Oxford University Press.

Furubotn, E. G., & R. Richter (1991). The new institutional economics: An assessment. In E. G. Furubotn and R. Richter (eds.), *The new institutional economics: A collection of articles from the Journal of Institutional and Theoretical Economics* (pp. 1–32). Tubingen: Mohr (Siebeck).

Gibbons, R., & J. Roberts. (eds.). (2013). *The handbook of organizational economics*. Princeton, NJ: Princeton University Press.

Hart, O. D., & B. Holmstrom (1987). The theory of contracts. In T. F. Bewley (ed.), *Advances in economic theory: 5th World Congress* (pp. 71–155). New York: Cambridge University Press.

Hodgson, G. M. (2000). What is the essence of institutional economics? *Journal of Economic Issues*, 34: 317–329.

Hodgson, G. M. (2002). The legal nature of the firm and the myth of the firm-market hybrid. *International Journal of the Economics of Business*, 9(1): 37–60.

Holmstrom, B. & J. Tirole (1989). The theory of the firm. In R. Schmalensee & R. D. Willig (eds.), *Handbook of industrial organization* (pp. 61–133). New York: Elsevier Science.

Jensen, M. C., & W. H. Meckling (1976). Theory of the firm: Managerial behavior, agency costs, and ownership structure. *Journal of Financial Economics*, 3: 305–360.

Jones, G. R. (1987). Organization-client transactions and organizational governance structures. *Academy of Management Journal*, 30(2): 197–218.

Jones, S. R. H. (1997). Transaction costs and the theory of the firm: The scope and limitations of the new institutional approach. *Business History*, 39(4): 9–25.

Levinthal, D. (1988). A survey of agency models of organization. *Journal of Economic Behavior and Organization*, 9(2): 153–186.

Lim, S., & A. Prakash. (2014). Voluntary regulations and innovation: The case of ISO 14001. *Public Administration Review* 74(2): 233–244.

Locke, J. (1967). *Two treatises of government*, 2nd ed. P. Lastett, ed. London: Cambridge University Press. (Originally published in 1690.)

Morroni, M. (2006). *Knowledge, scale and transactions in the theory of the firm*. New York: Cambridge University Press.

Ostrom, E. (1990). *Governing the commons: The evolution of institutions for collective action.* New York: Cambridge University Press.

Ostrom, E., R. Gardner, & J. Walker. (1994). *Rules, games, and common-pool resources.* Ann Arbor, MI: University of Michigan Press.

Ouchi, W. G. (1980). Markets, bureaucracies, and clans. *Administrative Science Quarterly, 25*(1): 129–141.

Perry, M. (1989). Vertical integration: Determinants and effects. In R. Schmalensee & R. D. Willig (eds.), *Handbook of industrial organization* (pp. 183–255). New York: Elsevier Science.

Reed, O. L., M. Pagnattaro, D. Cahoy, P. Shedd, & J. Morehead. (2012). *The legal and regulatory environment of business.* New York: McGraw-Hill/Irwin.

Rindfleisch, A., & J. B. Heide (1997). Transaction cost analysis: Past, present, and future applications. *Journal of Marketing, 61*(October): 30–54.

Robins, J. A. (1987). Organizational economics: Notes on the use of transaction-cost theory in the study of organizations. *Administrative Science Quarterly, 32*(1): 68–86.

Rousseau, J. J. (1947). The social contract. In E. Barker (ed.), *Social contract* (pp. 167–307). London: Oxford University Press. (Originally published in 1762.)

Rubin, P. H. (1990). *Managing business transactions.* New York: Free Press.

Shelanski, H., & P. G. Klein (1995). Empirical research in transaction cost economics: A review and assessment. *Journal of Law, Economics, and Organization, 11*(2): 335–361.

Simon, H. A. (1957). *Models of man.* New York: Wiley.

Walker, G., & L. Poppo (1991). Profit centers, single-source suppliers, and transaction costs. *Administrative Science Quarterly, 36*: 66–87.

Wall, D. (2014). *The sustainable economics of Elinor Ostrom: Commons, contestation and craft.* New York: Routledge.

Wiggins, S. N. (1991). The economics of the firm and contracts: A survey. *Journal of Institutional and Theoretical Economics, 147*: 603–661.

Williamson, O. E. (1975). *Markets and hierarchies.* New York: Free Press.

Williamson, O. E. (1979). Transaction-cost economics: The governance of contractual relations, *Journal of Law and Economics, 22*(2): 233–261.

Williamson, O. E. (1981). The economics of organization: The transaction cost approach. *American Journal of Sociology, 87*: 548–577.

Williamson, O. E. (1994). Transaction cost economics and organization theory. In N. J. Smelser and R. Swedberg (eds.), *The handbook of economic sociology* (pp. 77–107). Princeton, NJ: Princeton University Press.

Williamson, O. E. (2014). *The transaction cost economics project: The theory and practice of the governance of contractual relations.* Northampton, MA: Edward Elgar.

# 19

# The Economics of Organization: The Transaction Cost Approach

*Oliver E. Williamson*

The proposition that the firm is a production function to which a profit-maximization objective has been assigned has been less illuminating for organization theory purposes than for economics. Even within economics, however, there is a growing realization that the neoclassical theory of the firm is self-limiting. A variety of economic approaches to the study of organization have recently been proposed in which the importance of internal organization is acknowledged. The one described here emphasizes transaction costs and efforts to economize thereon. More than most economic approaches, it makes allowance for what Frank Knight (1965, p. 270) has felicitously referred to as "human nature as we know it." Economic approaches to the study of organization, transaction cost analysis included, generally focus on efficiency. To be sure, not every interesting organizational issue can be usefully addressed, except perhaps in minor way, in efficiency terms. A surprisingly large number can, however, especially if transaction cost aspects are emphasized. This is accomplished by making the transaction—rather than commodities—the basic unit of analysis and by assessing governance structures, of which firms and markets are the leading alternatives, in terms of their capacities to economize on transaction costs.

The transaction cost approach to the study of organizations has been applied at three levels of analysis. The first is the overall structure of the enterprise. This takes the scope of the enterprise as given and asks how the operating parts should be related one to another. Unitary, holding company, and multidivisional forms come under scrutiny when these issues are addressed. The second or middle level focuses on the operating parts and asks which activities should be performed within the firm, which outside it, and why. This can be thought of as developing the criteria for and defining the "efficient boundaries" of an operating unit. The third level of analysis is concerned with the manner in which human assets are organized. The object here is to match internal governance structures with the attributes of work groups in a discriminating way....

## I. ANTECEDENTS

The transaction cost approach to the study of organizations relates to three relatively independent literatures.... Considering that economizing is central to the transaction cost approach, it is not surprising that an economics literature is among the antecedents. Also, inasmuch as internal organizational issues are featured, the organization theory literature makes an expected appearance. The third literature is less obvious: this is the contract law literature in which contract is addressed as a governance issue.

...The proposition that the transaction is the basic unit of economic analysis was advanced by John R. Commons in 1934. He recognized that there were a variety of governance structures with which to mediate the exchange of goods or services between technologically separable entities.

Williamson, O.E. (1981). The Economics of Organization: The Transaction Cost Approach. *American Journal of Sociology* 87: 548–577. Reprinted by permission of The University of Chicago Press.

Assessing the capacities of different structures to harmonize relations between parties and recognizing that new structures arose in the service of these harmonizing purposes were central to the study of institutional economics as he conceived it.

Ronald Coase posed the problem more sharply in his classic 1937 paper, "The Nature of the Firm." He, like others, observed that the production of final goods and services involved a succession of early stage processing and assembly activities. But whereas others took the boundary of the firm as a parameter and examined the efficacy with which markets mediated exchange in intermediate and final goods markets, Coase held that the boundary of the firm was a decision variable for which an economic assessment was needed. What is it that determines when a firm decides to integrate and when instead it relies on the market?

Friedrich Hayek's 1945 article, "The Use of Knowledge in Society," shed further insight. He observed that the economic problem is relatively uninteresting except when economic events are changing and sequential adaptations to these changes are needed. What distinguishes a high performance economy is its capacity to adapt efficiently to uncertainty. Although he did not state the issues in transaction-cost-economizing terms, such terms are implicit in much of the argument.

The postwar market failure literature helped better to define some of the "failures" with markets that common ownership (the firm) served to overcome. It was not until 1969, however, that the underlying difficulties with markets were unambiguously traced to transaction cost origins. As Kenneth Arrow put it: "Market failure is not absolute; it is better to consider a broader category, that of transaction costs, which in general impede and in particular cases completely block the formation of markets" (1969, p. 48).

The appearance of Chester Barnard's book *The Functions of the Executive* in 1938 and of Herbert Simon's explication of the Barnard thesis in *Administrative Behavior* in 1947 are widely recognized as significant events in the organization theory field. Purposive organization was emphasized, but the limits of human actors in bounded rationality respects and the importance of informal organization were prominently featured.

This stream of research was further developed by the "Carnegie School" (March and Simon 1958; Cyert and March 1963). Hierarchical organization and associated controls are traced to the limited capacities of human actors to cope with the complexity and uncertainty with which they are confronted. The organization is essentially viewed as a "problem-facing and problem-solving" entity (Thompson 1967, p. 9). But organizational efforts are often myopic, and demands for control can and often do give rise to dysfunctional outcomes.

Although Alfred Chandler's remarkable book, *Strategy and Structure* (1962), had its origins in business history rather than organization theory, in many respects this historical account of the origins, diffusion, nature, and importance of the multidivisional form of organization ran ahead of contemporary economic and organization theory. The mistaken notion that economic efficiency was substantially independent of internal organizational structure was no longer tenable after this book appeared.

James Thompson built on all of the foregoing in fashioning his classic statement of the organizational problem in 1967. Both uncertainty and bounded rationality were featured. Moreover, implicitly, and sometimes explicitly attention was fixed on efforts to economize on transaction costs. Core technologies, domains (or boundaries) of organized action, and the powers and limits of market and hierarchical modes are all recognized.

The legal literature to which I refer is concerned with contracting—especially the distinction between "hard contracting" (or black-letter law) and "soft contracting" in which the contract serves mainly as framework.... This is especially true where continuity of the exchange relation between the parties is highly valued.

...By the early 1970s it was becoming clear that the study of organizations was a comparative institutional undertaking in which alternative governance structures—both within and between firms and markets—required explicit attention.... Transaction cost economizing needs to be located within a larger economizing framework and the relevant trade-offs need to be recognized.

## II. SOME RUDIMENTS

A transaction occurs when a good or service is transferred across a technologically separable interface. One stage of activity terminates and another begins. With a well-working interface, as with a well-working machine, these transfers occur smoothly. In mechanical systems we look for frictions: do the gears mesh, are the parts lubricated, is there needless slippage or other loss of energy? The economic counterpart of friction is transaction cost: do the parties to the exchange operate harmoniously, or are there frequent misunderstandings and conflicts that lead to delays, breakdowns, and other malfunctions? Transaction cost analysis supplants the usual preoccupation with technology and steady-state production (or distribution) expenses with an examination of the comparative costs of planning, adapting, and monitoring task completion under alternative governance structures.

Some transactions are simple and easy to mediate. Others are difficult and require a good deal more attention. Can we identify the factors that permit transactions to be classified as one kind or another? Can we identify the alternative governance structures within which transactions can be organized? And can we match governance structures with transactions in a discriminating (transaction-cost-economizing) way? These are the neglected issues with which organizational design needs to come

to grips. These are the issues for which transaction cost analysis promises to offer new insights.

### Behavioral Assumptions

It is widely recognized... that complex contracts are costly to write and enforce.... The two behavioral assumptions on which transaction cost analysis relies that both add realism and distinguish this approach from neoclassical economics are (1) the recognition that human agents are subject to bounded rationality and (2) the assumption that at least some agents are given to opportunism.

...Unlike "economic man," to whom hyperrationality is often attributed, "organization man" is endowed with less powerful analytical and data-processing apparatus. Such limited competence does not, however, imply irrationality. Instead, although boundedly rational agents experience limits in formulating and solving complex problems and in processing (receiving, storing, retrieving, transmitting) information (Simon 1957), they otherwise remain "intendedly rational."

But for bounded rationality, all economic exchange could be efficiently organized by contract... Given bounded rationality, however, it is impossible to deal with complexity in all contractually relevant respects. As a consequence, incomplete contracting is the best that can be achieved.

Ubiquitous, albeit incomplete, contracting would nevertheless be feasible if human agents were not given to opportunism. Thus, if agents, though boundedly rational, were fully trustworthy, comprehensive contracting would still be feasible..., [I]f some economic actors (either principals or agents) are dishonest (or, more generally, disguise attributes or preferences, distort data, obfuscate issues, and otherwise confuse transactions), and it is very costly to distinguish opportunistic from nonopportunistic types ex ante.

...Thus, whereas economic man engages in simple self-interest seeking, opportunism makes provision for self-interest seeking with guile.... That economic agents are simultaneously subject to bounded rationality and (at least some) are given to opportunism does not by itself, however, vitiate autonomous trading. On the contrary, when effective ex ante and ex post competition can both be presumed, autonomous contracting will be efficacious.... Whether ex post competition is equally efficacious or breaks down as a result of contract execution depends on the characteristics of the transactions in question, which brings us to the matter of dimensionalizing.

### Dimensionalizing

As set out elsewhere (Williamson 1979), the critical dimensions for describing transactions are (1) uncertainty, (2) the frequency with which transactions recur, and (3) the degree to which durable, transaction-specific investments are required to realize least cost supply. Only recurrent transactions are of interest for the purposes of this paper; hence attention will hereafter be focused on uncertainty and asset specificity, especially the latter.

Asset specificity is both the most important dimension for describing transactions and the most neglected attribute in prior studies of organization. The issue is less whether there are large fixed investments, though this is important, than whether such investments are specialized to a particular transaction. Items that are unspecialized among users pose few hazards, since buyers in these circumstances can easily turn to alternative sources and suppliers can sell output intended for one buyer to other buyers without difficulty....

Asset specificity can arise in any of three ways: site specificity, as when successive stations are located in cheek-by-jowl relation to each other so as to economize on inventory and transportation expenses; physical asset specificity, as where specialized dies are required to produce a component; and human asset specificity that arises from learning by doing. The reason

asset specificity is critical is that, once an investment has been made, buyer and seller are effectively operating in a bilateral (or at least quasi-bilateral) exchange relation for a considerable period thereafter.... Accordingly, where asset specificity is great, buyer and seller will make special efforts to design an exchange that has good continuity properties.

The site-specific assets referred to here appear to correspond with those Thompson describes as the "core technology" (1967, pp. 19–23). Indeed, the common ownership of site-specific stations is thought to be so "natural" that alternative governance structures are rarely considered. In fact, however, the joining of separable stations—for example, blast furnace and rolling mill, thereby to realize thermal economies—under common ownership is not technologically determined but instead reflects transaction-cost-economizing judgments. It will nevertheless be convenient, for the purposes of this paper, to assume that all site-specific stations constitute a technological core the common ownership of which will be taken as given.... The efficient governance structure for these turns on physical asset and human asset specificity....

## III. EFFICIENT BOUNDARIES

... Only two organizational alternatives are considered: either a firm makes a component itself or it buys it from an autonomous supplier.... The object is to describe how the economizing decisions which define the outer boundaries of this division are made.

### A Simple Model

The crucial issue is how the choice between firm and market governance structures for decisions ... are made. Transaction cost reasoning is central to this analysis, but trade-offs between production cost economies (in which the market may be presumed to enjoy certain advantages) and governance cost economies (in which the advantages may shift to internal organization) need to be recognized

...If assets are nonspecific, markets enjoy advantages in both production cost and governance cost respects: static scale economies can be more fully exhausted by buying instead of making; markets can also aggregate uncorrelated demands, thereby realizing risk-pooling benefits; and external procurement avoids many of the hazards to which internal procurement is subject. As assets become more specific, however, the aggregation benefits of markets in the first two respects are reduced and exchange takes on a progressively stronger bilateral character. The governance costs of markets escalate as a result and internal procurement supplants external supply for this reason. Thus, the governance of recurrent transactions for which uncertainty is held constant (in intermediate degree) will vary as follows: classical market contracting will be efficacious whenever assets are nonspecific to the trading parties; bilateral or obligational market contracting will appear as assets become semispecific; and internal organization will displace markets as assets take on a highly specific character.

The advantages of firms over markets in harmonizing bilateral exchange are three. First, common ownership reduces the incentives to suboptimize. Second, and related, internal organization is able to invoke fiat to resolve differences, whereas costly adjudication is needed when an impasse develops between autonomous traders. Third, internal organization has easier and more complete access to the relevant information when dispute settling is needed....

...Similarly, the decision to integrate forward into distribution reflects the fact that the product cannot be marketed effectively through standard channels, presumably because specialized human assets are needed to sell and service the product and a bilateral employment relation develops as a consequence....

## IV. MANAGING HUMAN ASSETS: THE EMPLOYMENT RELATION

... The same general principles apply to the governance of human assets as apply to the efficient organization of transactions in general.... The discussion is in two parts. The first addresses the organization of human assets at the staff level. The second deals with union organization, which applies primarily at the production level.

### Governance, General

Recall that transactions are described in terms of three attributes: frequency, uncertainty, and asset specificity. The assets of interest here involve a continuing supply of services, whence frequency aspects will be suppressed and attention focused on the internal organizational aspects of uncertainty and asset specificity.

It will facilitate the argument to assume that transfers of goods and services across interfaces are not at issue. Internal governance is thus concerned entirely with intrastage activity. Inasmuch as physical assets are nonvolitional, transactions assigned to internal organization pose problems only in conjunction with human asset specificity.

Note in this connection that skill acquisition is a necessary but not a sufficient condition for a human asset governance problem to arise. The nature of the skills also matters; the distinction between transaction-specific and nonspecific human assets is crucial. Thus, physicians, engineers, lawyers, etc., possess valued skills for which they expect to be compensated, but such skills do not by themselves pose a governance issue. Unless these skills are deepened and specialized to a particular employer, neither employer nor employee has a special interest in maintaining a continuing employment relation. The employer can easily hire a substitute and the employee can move to alternative employment without loss of productive value.

Mere deepening of skills through job experience does not by itself pose a problem either. Thus, typing skills may be enhanced by practice, but if they are equally valued by current and potential employers there is no need to devise special protection for an ongoing employment relation. Knowledge of a particular firm's filing system, in contrast, may be highly specific (nontransferable). Continuity of the employment relation in the latter case is a source of added value.

Thus to the neoclassical proposition that the acquisition of valued skills leads to greater compensation, transaction cost reasoning adds the following proposition: skills acquired in a learning-by-doing fashion and imperfectly transferable across employers need to be embedded in a protective governance structure, lest productive values be sacrificed if the employment relation is unwittingly severed.... This poses a problem in the degree to which assets are firm-specific.

The internal organizational counterpart for uncertainty is the ease with which the productivity of human assets can be evaluated.... [F]irms arise when tasks are technologically nonseparable, the standard example being manual freight loading.... "Two men jointly lift cargo into trucks. Solely by observing the total weight loaded per day, it is impossible to determine each person's marginal productivity.... The output is yielded by a team, by definition, and it is not a sum of separable outputs of each of its members."

When tasks are nonseparable in this sense, individual productivity cannot be assessed by measuring output—an assessment of inputs is needed. Sometimes productivity may be inferred by observing the intensity with which an individual works; ...Human assets can thus be described in terms of (1) the degree to which they are firm-specific and (2) the ease with which productivity can be metered.... Letting $H_1$ and $H_2$ represent low and high degrees of human asset specificity and $M_1$ and $M_2$ represent easy and difficult conditions of meterability, the following four-way classification of internal governance structures is tentatively proposed:

1. $H_1$, $M_1$: *internal spot market.*—Human assets that are nonspecific and for which metering is easy are essentially meeting market tests continuously for their jobs. Neither workers nor firms have an efficiency interest in maintaining the association.... Hence no special governance structure is devised to sustain the relation. Instead, the employment relation is terminated when either party is sufficiently dissatisfied. An internal spot market labor relation may be said to exist. Examples include migrant farm workers, and professional employees whose skills are nonspecific....

2. $H_1$, $M_2$: *primitive team.*—Although the human assets here are nonspecific, the work cannot be metered easily.... Although the membership of such teams can be altered without loss of productivity, compensation cannot easily be determined on an individual basis. The manual freight loading example would appear to qualify....

3. $H_2$, $M_1$: *obligational market.*—There is a considerable amount of firm-specific learning here, but tasks are easy to meter ...Both firm and workers have an interest in maintaining the continuity of such employment relations. Procedural safeguards will thus be devised to discourage arbitrary dismissal. And nonvested retirement and other benefits will accrue to such workers so as to discourage unwanted quitting....

4. $H_2$, $M_2$: *relational team.*—The human assets here are specific to the firm and very difficult to meter. This appears to correspond with the "clan" form of organization to which William Ouchi (1980) has referred.... [E]mployees understand and are dedicated to the purposes of the firm, and employees will be provided with considerable job security, which gives them assurance against exploitation....

### Some Remarks on Union Organization

The foregoing discussion of internal governance structures refers mainly to staff rather than production-level employees. Since it is among the latter that union organization appears, the question arises as to whether transaction cost reasoning has useful applications to the study of collective organization. To the extent that it does, further confidence in the power of the approach is presumably warranted.

...[T]he transaction cost approach to the study of unionization yields testable implications that do not derive from more familiar theories of unionization that rely on power or politics to drive the analysis (Freeman and Medoff, 1979). The principal implications are: (1) the incentive to organize production workers within a collective governance structure increases with the degree of human asset specificity; and (2) the degree to which an internal governance structure is elaborated will vary directly with the degree of human asset specificity...

The transaction cost hypothesis does not deny the possibility that unions will appear in settings where human asset specificity is slight. Where this occurs, however, the presumption is that these outcomes are driven more by power than by efficiency considerations. Employers in these circumstances will thus be more inclined to resist unionization; successful efforts to achieve unionization will often require the assistance of the political process; and, since power rather than efficiency is at stake, the resulting governance structure will be relatively primitive.

## VI. CONCLUDING REMARKS

Transaction cost analysis is an interdisciplinary approach to the study of organizations that joins economics, organization theory, and aspects of contract law. It provides a unified interpretation for a disparate set of organizational phenomena. Although applications additional to those set out here have been made, the limits of transaction cost analysis have yet to be reached. Indeed, there is reason to believe that the surface has merely been scratched.

Transaction cost reasoning probably has greater relevance for studying commercial than noncommercial enterprise, since natural selection forces operate with greater assurance in the former. Transaction cost economizing is nevertheless important to all forms of organization. Accordingly, the following proposition applies quite generally: governance structures that have better transaction cost economizing properties will eventually displace those that have worse, *ceteris paribus*. The *cetera*, however, are not always *paria*, whence the governance implications of transaction cost analysis will be incompletely realized in noncommercial enterprises in which transaction cost economizing entails the sacrifice of other valued objectives (of which power will often be one; the study of these trade-offs is an important topic on the future research agenda)....

While it is injudicious to claim too much for the transaction cost approach, neither do I want to claim too little. At present, it is probably under- rather than overapplied to organization theory. In contrast with the highly microanalytic approach to the study of organizations, in which personalities and detailed organizational procedures are scrutinized, and the highly aggregative approach to organizations employed in mainline economics, the transaction cost approach employs a semimicroanalytic level of analysis. This appears to be a level of analysis at which sociologists and other students of organization enjoy a comparative advantage. Facility with the apparatus, however, requires that an irreducible minimal investment in transaction cost reasoning be made. This paper attempts both to supply requisite background and to make substantive headway on some of the governance issues of common interest to economics, law, and sociology.

## REFERENCES

Arrow, Kenneth J. 1969. "The Organization of Economic Activity." The Analysis and Evaluation of Public Expenditure: The PPB System. Joint Economic Committee, 91st Cong., 1st sess., pp. 59–73.

Barnard, Chester I. 1938. *The Functions of the Executive.* Cambridge, Mass.: Harvard University Press.

Coase, Ronald H. (1937) 1952. "The Nature of the Firm." pp. 386–405 in *Readings in Price Theory,* edited by G. J. Stigler and K. E. Boulding. Homewood, Ill.: Irwin.

Commons, John R. 1934. *Institutional Economics.* Madison: University of Wisconsin Press.

Cyert, Richard M., and James G. March. 1963. *A Behavioral Theory of the Firm.* Englewood Cliffs, N.J.: Prentice-Hall.

Freeman, Richard B., and James L. Medoff. 1979. "The Two Faces of Unionism." *Public Interest* (Fall), pp. 69–93.

Fuller, Lon L. 1964. *The Morality of Law.* New Haven, Conn.: Yale University Press.

Hayek, Friedrich. 1945. "The Use of Knowledge in Society." *American Economic Review* 35(September): 519–530.

Knight, Frank H. 1965. *Risk, Uncertainty and Profit.* New York: Harper & Row.

March, James G., and Herbert A. Simon. 1958. *Organizations.* New York: Wiley.

Ouchi, William G. 1980. "Markets, Bureaucracies, and Clans." *Administrative Science Quarterly* 25(March): 129–142.

Pfeffer, Jeffrey. 1978. *Organizational Design.* Northbrook, Ill.: AHM.

Porter, Glenn, and Harold C. Livesay. 1971. *Merchants and Manufacturers.* Baltimore: Johns Hopkins University Press.

Radner, Roy. 1968. "Competitive Equilibrium under Uncertainty." *Econometrica* 36 (January): 31–58.

Simon, Herbert A. 1957. *Models of Man.* New York: Wiley.

Simon, Herbert A. 1961 (1945). *Administrative Behavior.* 2nd ed. New York: Macmillan.

Thompson, James D. 1967. *Organizations in Action.* New York: McGraw-Hill.

Weick, K. E. 1969. *The Social Psychology of Organizing.* Reading, Mass.: Addison-Wesley.

Williamson, Oliver E. 1979. "Transaction Cost Economics: The Governance of Contractual Relations." *Journal of Law and Economics* 22(October): 233–261.

## 20

# Learning from Organizational Economics

*Jay B. Barney & William G. Ouchi*

...Much of what organization theorists can learn from organizational economics has less to do with specific applications of concepts or models, and more to do with a way of thinking about organizations and about organizational phenomena. Incorporating these ways of thinking into organization theory is likely to have as important an impact on organization theory as would incorporating any particular model or concept taken from organizational economics. We next consider three specific aspects of this economic way of thinking and their implications for organization theory.

### Equilibrium Analysis

...Equilibrium reasoning has a soiled reputation among many organization theorists, because this form of reasoning is often associated with the abstractions of neoclassical price theory. Organization theorists might question spending so much time and energy attempting to characterize intra- and inter-organizational equilibria when it is obvious that real organizations are never in such states.

But, in many ways, this question misses the point about equilibrium reasoning. First, equilibrium reasoning is not the same as neoclassical price theory. One does not need to assume perfect information, zero transaction costs, homogeneous products and firms, and so on in order to use equilibrium reasoning. Rather, the focus is on underlying processes within and between organizations and on the stable state to which those processes will evolve if left alone....

Second, the criticism that equilibrium arguments waste intellectual energy describing results that will never exist misses the importance of such arguments in suggesting why these states never develop. In fact, the strength of the equilibrium form of reasoning rests in its ability to highlight the reasons why equilibrium states do not actually develop....

A final strength of equilibrium analyses lies in their inherently dynamic form. Equilibrium analysis does not stop at: the actions of firm A engender the actions of firm B. Rather, it tells us that the actions of A lead to the actions of B, which in turn lead to more responses by A (and by other firms, C and D), and so on. This multistage dynamic stands in contrast to what is seen in most organization theory models, where behavior A leads to behavior B, and that is the end of it. This limitation in the reasoning used by most organization theorists has already been pointed out in the case of resource dependence theory (Pfeffer and Salancik, 1978), where an equilibrium analysis of resource dependence logic suggests that industries characterized by any uncertainty will be dominated by a small number of large, vertically integrated firms. Since this is not the case in most industries, the question that resource dependence theory should ask but has yet to is: why not? What constraints face firms seeking to reduce their dependence to zero? What constraints prevent the equilibrium that is the result of following resource dependence logic to its conclusion?

### The Transaction as the Unit of Analysis

In organization theory and organizational behavior, there is a widespread belief that research on organization needs to go forward on multiple levels of analysis simultaneously. The levels of analysis cited most commonly are the individual, the group, inter-group relations, the organization, inter-organizational relations, and, finally, organization-environment relations. The discipline bases of these units of analysis also increase in scope from psychology to social psychology to sociology and political science. Recently, anthropology has begun to reemerge as an important discipline in understanding inter-group and organizational phenomena.

While research conducted at multiple levels of analysis is not unknown, it is nevertheless relatively rare. The reasons for this are clear. Each level of analysis has associated with it different disciplines, although they overlap to some extent. The theoretical content of these disciplines is typically based on different sets of assumptions and beliefs. Developing single frameworks to deal with multilevel phenomena requires at least a partial integration of theories based on different disciplines. Such "general social theories" tend to be very abstract indeed, often divorced from the empirical reality. Perhaps the best example of the pitfalls of such multilevel general social theories can be found in the highly abstract, and no longer influential, work of Talcott Parsons (1951). Thus, rather than fall subject to these abstractions, research in organization theory has tended to retreat to single levels of analysis, only rarely venturing forth to multiple levels and then only in a tentative way.

Much of the theory of organizational economics overcomes the liabilities of multiple levels of analysis by positing the existence of only one appropriate level: the transaction. A transaction, as defined by Williamson (1981), is simply an exchange between technologically separable entities. In this way, the definition of a transaction is closely related to exchange theory as it has been developed in sociology and social psychology (Blau, 1964; Homans, 1958). And even though the language is not used universally among organizational economists, such concepts as "the nexus of contracts" and "inter-specific human capital" as used by property rights, agency, and transaction-costs theorists all build on this single unit of analysis.

Organizational sociologists, in particular, are likely to find the abandonment of multiple levels of analysis particularly troubling, since they often see in this abandonment the destruction of their discipline. Ever since Durkheim (1966), sociologists have specialized in arguing that there is something distinctly different about sociological phenomena, that it requires a separate unit of analysis for explanation.

Adoption of the transaction as the single unit of analysis in organization theory would have important implications for research and teaching in the field. Many old and familiar concepts suddenly disappear. For example, there is no such thing as an "organizational boundary," at least as it has been defined; that is, there is no longer a clear inside and outside to a firm. Some economic exchanges occur between separate legal entities but are long-lasting and cooperative. What meaning does the concept of a boundary have for these exchanges?

By implication, then, there is no such thing as an "organizational environment." Rather, firms face hundreds of microenvironments for each of the different transactions in which they engage. Some of these may be uncertain and complex, while others may be certain and simple. Overall characterizations of environments as uncertain or turbulent or complex or simple become meaningless in this context. Also, there is no such thing as an "organization's structure," at least as this concept traditionally has been used. Rather, exchanges are governed in a wide variety of ways, using competition or cooperation, rules or trust, and bureaucracies or clans, all simultaneously. Obviously, characterizing a structure as centralized or decentralized when it might be both simultaneously is misleading.

All this is not to suggest that macroorganizational analyses are impossible when using the transaction as the unit of analysis. Indeed, Williamson's (1975) M-form hypothesis is just such an analysis. However, by adopting the transaction as the unit of analysis, careful attention must be focused on important questions about: the process of aggregating individual transactions into bundles of transactions to discuss groups; aggregating groups to discuss inter-group relations (that is, transactions between groups); aggregating even further to focus on firms and firm structure; and, finally, aggregating transactions to the point where inter-firm relations can be discussed. In other words, adopting the transaction as the unity of analysis, and then proceeding to conduct a macroanalysis of organizations necessitates multiple levels of analysis and cross-discipline research.

### The Concept of Organization

Finally, organizational economists have been able to point to a fundamental ambiguity at the heart of organization theory. This ambiguity lies in what does and does not constitute organization. For organizational economists, an event or process is organized if it exhibits regular patterns and structures. Thus, market exchanges, because they exhibit such regular patterns, are organized social events, subject to study and analysis (Hirshleifer, 1980). Also, the structure of events inside firms can be organized and is subject to similar forms of analysis (Hoenack, 1983).

For organization theorists, on the other hand, organization is typically meant to include activities within and between what might be called firms (both for profit and nonprofit) and within and between government bureaucracies. This concept of organization is much more narrow and restrictive than what would be accepted by organizational economists.

One of the liabilities of adopting this narrow definition of organization is that it unrealistically restricts the range of phenomena that can be studied by organization theorists. One of the common themes running throughout organizational economics is comparing the efficiency characteristics of a hierarchy to those of a market in governing specific economic transactions. In this sense, hierarchies, markets, and intermediate market forms are specific alternatives among which managers can choose when deciding how to govern transactions. In organization theory, several of these alternatives are often omitted. Research is artificially restricted to considering one of several types of hierarchical responses. Markets and quasi-market alternatives are thereby excluded, perhaps prematurely.

There is, of course, a political and value laden side to including markets as transaction governance mechanisms within a broader redefined organization theory. Indeed, the neoconservative political leanings of many economists are well known (Friedman, 1970). Indeed, the organization theorist's emphasis on hierarchical governance may reflect underlying value preferences for the use of centralized control to resolve economic exchange problems or a preference for exposing the abuse of power in hierarchies. Nevertheless, as Williamson (1975) and others have shown, it is possible to separate the value and political questions from the efficiency questions of transaction governance mechanisms.

Perhaps organization theorists balk at generalizing the definition of the concept of organization to include market and quasi-market phenomena out of fear of academic incursions by economists into their protected domain. Without this broader definition, organization theory becomes just part of a general framework for analyzing economic transactions, a specialty that focuses on the more behavioral aspects of exchange. Perhaps this is appropriate. Perhaps organization theory will ultimately find itself integrated into this larger framework, its distinctiveness lost. Is this a bad thing? If, after all, the nature of the phenomena being studied requires this integration, is it not appropriate to attempt to accomplish it?

## LEARNING FROM ORGANIZATION THEORY

But the learning between organizational economics and organization theory has not been one-way. Organization theory has had and continues to have important implications for organizational economics. Incorporating these points of view into organizational economics almost certainly will improve the analyses, explanations, and predictions of organizational economists.

### Organizational Influences on Rational Decision Making

One of the most important contributions of organization theory to organizational economics has been recognition of the extrarational aspects of decision making. For most organizational economists, decision making is characterized by boundedly rational—but intentionally rational—utility maximizing information collectors and analyzers. While this is a description of decision making that applies in some settings, including perhaps the making of certain investment decisions, it is certainly not complete. For example, it probably does not describe how organizational economists, themselves, make a large number of decisions about their lives or careers.

Organization theorists also acknowledge bounded rationality and self-interest (Simon, 1961); but organizational research has shown that so-called rational decision making is affected by many other factors. These include the age and sex of those making decisions (Elder, 1975; Kanter, 1977), the nature of intergroup conflicts in an organization (Alderfer, 1977), the number and types of individuals making a decision (Kanter, 1977), the abilities of senior managers to encourage open discussion (Ouchi, 1981; Vroom and Yetton, 1973), and a host of other factors. Note that these factors do not create a situation in which individuals make irrational decisions, but rather a situation in which that which is rational changes in stable and predictable ways. That is, what is rational for a woman in a large organization may not be rational for a man in that same organization. What is rational when one is twenty-five is not rational, perhaps, at age thirty or at midlife. The level of open discussion that is rational in a participatively managed firm may not be rational in an autocratically managed firm.

Including these other factors in describing decision making by organization participants will almost certainly improve the predictive capabilities of economic models. It is also likely to substantially alter the structure of those models and introduce a level of complexity and subtlety that has yet to be characteristic of organizational economics.

### Empirical Research

The other major tradition in organization theory that should influence organizational economists lies in the role and use of empirical research. Organization theory is characterized by a rich tradition of both qualitative and quantitative research. Beginning with the Hawthorne studies (Roethlisberger and Dickson, 1939), this work has not only been used to test theories deductively, but also to develop concepts and ideas inductively. The number of qualitatively rich descriptions of actual organizational processes has been and continues to be a resource pool of empirical phenomena against which many theories in organization behavior and theory have been judged (Christensen and others, 1982).

In organizational economics, quantitative and qualitative empirical research has been the exception rather than the rule....

On the one hand, this lack of empirical research suggests a strong theoretical focus among organizational economists, a focus which certainly can be applauded. It also reflects a level of confidence in theory that organization theorists would probably find overstated. On the other hand, this paucity of empirical research leaves much of the ultimate potential of this approach unexamined. There is, within organizational economics, a large number of interesting ideas. Whether they help explain actual organizational phenomena unfortunately remains a largely unanswered question.

...It is interesting to note ... that most of the current empirical research in organizational economics, including Walker and Weber (1984), Barney (1986), and others has been conducted by organization theorists, with the important exception of Teece and his associates (Armour and Teece, 1978; Monteverde and Teece, 1982), marketing specialists, and other noneconomists. This suggests that, despite the difficulty of empirical work in this area, the paucity of such work done by economists reflects their interests and tastes as much as it does the difficulty of the research....

## REFERENCES

Alderfer, C. P. "Improving Organizational Communication Through Long-term Intergroup Intervention." *Journal of Applied Behavioral Science*, 1977, *13*, 193–210.

Armour, H. O., and Teece, D. J. "Organization Structure and Economic Performance: A Test of the Multidivisional Hypothesis." *Bell Journal of Economics*, 1978, *9*, 106–122.

Barney, J. B. "The Organization of Capital Acquisition." Unpublished manuscript, Graduate School of Management, University of California, Los Angeles, 1986.

Blau, P. M. *Exchange and Power in Social Life*. New York: Wiley, 1964.

Christensen, C. R., and others. *Business Policy*. Homewood, Ill.: Irwin, 1982.

Durkheim, E. *The Rules of the Sociological Method*, 8th ed. New York: Free Press, 1966.

Elder, G. H., Jr. "Age Differentiation and Life Course." In A. Inkeles, J. Coleman, and N. Smelser (eds.), *Annual Review of Sociology, 1975*, vol. 1. Palo Alto, Calif.: Annual Review, 1975.

Friedman, M. "The Social Responsibility of Business Is To Increase Its Profits." *New York Times Magazine*, Sept. 13, 1970.

Hirshleifer, J. *Price Theory and Applications*, 2nd ed. Englewood Cliffs, N.J.: Prentice-Hall, 1980.

Hoenack, S. A. *Economic Behavior Within Organizations*. New York: Cambridge University Press, 1983.

Homans, G. C. "Social Behavior as Exchange." *American Journal of Sociology*, 1958, *63*, 597–606.

Kanter, R. *Men and Women of the Corporation*. New York: Basic, 1977.

Monteverde, K., and Teece, D. J. "Supplier Switching Costs and Vertical Integration." *Bell Journal of Economics*, 1982, *13*, 206–213.

Ouchi, W. G. *Theory Z*. Reading, Mass.: Addison-Wesley, 1981.

Parsons, T. *The Social System*. New York: Free Press, 1951.

Pfeffer, J., and Salancik, G. R. *The External Control of Organizations: A Resource Dependence Perspective*. New York: Harper & Row, 1978.

Roethlisberger, F. J., and Dickson, W. J. *Management and the Worker*. Cambridge, Mass.: Harvard University Press, 1939.

Simon, H. A. *Administrative Behavior*, 2nd ed. New York: Wiley, 1961.

Vroom, V., and Yetton, P. *Leadership and Decision Making*. Pittsburgh, Penn.: University of Pittsburgh Press, 1973.

Walker, G., and Weber, D. "A Transaction Cost Approach to Make-or-Buy Decisions." *Administrative Science Quarterly*, 1984, *29*, 373–391.

Williamson, O. E. *Markets and Hierarchies: Analysis and Antitrust Implications*. New York: Free Press, 1975.

Williamson, O. E. "Transaction-Cost Economics: The Governance of Contractual Relations." *Journal of Law and Economics*, 1979, *22*, 233–261.

Williamson, O. E. "The Modern Corporation: Origins, Evolution, Attributes." *Journal of Economic Literature*, 1981, *19*, 1537–1568.

# 21

# An Institutional Approach to the Study of Self-Organization and Self-Governance

*Elinor Ostrom*

The central question in this study is how a group of principals who are in an interdependent situation can organize and govern themselves to obtain continuing joint benefits when ail face temptations to free-ride, shirk, or otherwise act opportunistically. Parallel questions have to do with the combinations of variables that will (1) increase the initial likelihood of self-organization, (2) enhance the capabilities of individuals to continue self-organized efforts over time, or (3) exceed the capacity of self-organization to solve CPR problems without external assistance of some form.

This chapter has several objectives. First, I define what I mean by CPRs and how I view individual behaviors in complex and uncertain CPR situations. Then I examine the general problem facing individuals in CPR situations: how to organize to avoid the adverse outcomes of independent action. This general problem is solved by external agents in two well-accepted theories: the theory of the firm and the theory of the state. These explain how new institutions are supplied, how commitments are obtained, and how the actions of agents and subjects are monitored effectively, using in one case the firm, and in the other state, as an organizational device. How a group of principals – a community of citizens – can organize themselves to solve the problems of institutional supply, commitment, and monitoring is still a theoretical puzzle. Given that some individuals solve this puzzle, whereas others do not, a study of successful and unsuccessful efforts to

solve CPR problems should address important issues related to the theory of collective action and the development of better policies related to CPRs. Many efforts to analyze collective-action problems have framed the analysis by presuming that all such problems can be represented as prisoner's dilemma (PD) games, that a single level of analysis is sufficient, and that transactions costs are insignificant and can be ignored. In the last section of this chapter, I propose assumptions that are alternatives to those that normally frame the analysis of collective action.

## THE CPR SITUATION

### CPRs and resource units

The term "common-pool resource" refers to a natural or man-made resource system that is sufficiently large as to make it costly (but not impossible) to exclude potential beneficiaries from obtaining benefits from its use. To understand the processes of organizing and governing CPRs, it is essential to distinguish between the *resource system* and the flow of *resource units* produced by the system, while still recognizing the dependence of the one on the other.

Resource systems are best thought of as stock variables that are capable, under favorable conditions, of producing a maximum quantity of a flow variable without harming the stock or the resource system itself. Examples of resource systems include fishing grounds, groundwater basins,

Elinor Ostrom (1990). *Governing the Commons: The Evolution of Institutions for Collective Action.* Cambridge Univ. Press. Chapter 2, "An Institutional Approach to the study of Self-Organization and Self-Governance in CPR Situations," pp. 29–57. Reprinted with the permission of Cambridge University Press.

grazing areas, irrigation canals, bridges, parking garages, mainframe computers, and streams, lakes, oceans, and other bodies of water. Resource units are what individuals appropriate or use from resource systems. Resource units are typified by the tons of fish harvested from a fishing ground, the acre-feet or cubic meters of water withdrawn from a groundwater basin or an irrigation canal, the tons of fodder consumed by animals from a grazing area, the number of bridge crossings used per year by a bridge, the parking spaces filled, the central processing units consumed by those sharing a computer system, and the quantity of biological waste absorbed per year by a stream or other waterway. The distinction between the resource as *a stock* and the harvest of use units as a *flow* is especially useful in connection with *renewable* resources, where it is possible to define a replenishment rate. As long as the average rate of withdrawal does not exceed the average rate of replenishment, a renewable resource is sustained over time.[1]

Access to a CPR can be limited to a single individual or firm or to multiple individuals or teams of individuals who use the resource system at the same time. The CPRs studied in this volume are used by multiple individuals or firms. Following Plott and Meyer (1975), I call the process of withdrawing resource units from a resource system "appropriation." Those who withdraw such units are called "appropriators."[2] One term – "appropriator" – can thus be used to refer to herders, fishers, irrigators, commuters, and anyone else who appropriates resource units from some type of resource system. In many instances appropriators use or consume the resource units they withdraw (e.g., where fishers harvest primarily for consumption). Appropriators also use resource units as inputs into production processes (e.g., irrigators apply water to their fields to produce rice). In other instances, the appropriators

immediately transfer ownership of resource units to others, who are then the users of the resource units (e.g., fishers who sell their catch as soon as possible after arrival at a port).

The term I use to refer to those who arrange for the provision of a CPR is "providers." I use the term "producer" to refer to anyone who actually constructs, repairs, or takes actions that ensure the long-term sustenance of the resource system itself. Frequently, providers and producers are the same individuals, but they do not have to be (V. Ostrom, Tiebout, and Warren 1961). A national government may provide an irrigation system in the sense of arranging for its financing and design. It may then arrange with local farmers to produce and maintain it. If local farmers are given the authority to arrange for maintenance, then they become both the providers and the producers of maintenance activities related to a CPR.

A resource system can be jointly provided and/or produced by more than one person or firm. The actual process of appropriating resource units from the CPR can be undertaken by multiple appropriators simultaneously or sequentially. The resource units, however, *are not subject to joint use or appropriation*. The fish harvested by one boat are not there for someone else. The water spread on one farmer's fields cannot be spread onto someone else's fields. Thus, the resource units are not jointly used, but the resource system is subject to joint use. Once multiple appropriators rely on a given resource system, improvements to the system are simultaneously available to all appropriators. It is costly (and in some cases infeasible) to exclude one appropriator of a resource system from improvements made to the resource system itself. All appropriators benefit from maintenance performed on an irrigation canal, a bridge, or a computer system whether they contribute or not.

## *Rational appropriators in complex and uncertain situations*

The decisions and actions of CPR appropriators to appropriate from and provide a CPR are those of broadly rational individuals who find themselves in complex and uncertain situations. An individual's choice of behavior in any particular situation will depend on how the individual learns about, views, and weighs the benefits and costs of actions and their perceived linkage to outcomes that also involve a mixture of benefits and costs.[3]

Organizing appropriators for collective action regarding a CPR is usually an uncertain and complex undertaking. Uncertainty has many external sources: the quantity and timing of rainfall, the temperature and amount of sunlight, the presence or absence of disease-bearing vectors, and the market prices of various inputs or final products. Other sources of uncertainty are internal to the CPR and the appropriators using the CPR. A major source of uncertainty is lack of knowledge. The exact structure of the resource system itself – its boundary and internal characteristics – must be established. Ascertaining the structure of the resource system may come about as a by-product of extended use and careful observation, as in the case of appropriating from a fishing ground or grazing range. Moreover, this folk knowledge must be preserved and passed along from one generation to the next. For a groundwater basin, on the other hand, the discovery of the internal structure may require a major investment in research by geologists and engineers.

How appropriators' actions affect the resource system, the yield of resource units, and each other's outcomes must also be ascertained.[4] It is not immediately apparent, for example, how one irrigator's forbearance in taking water from a canal will affect the yield obtained by that farmer or by other farmers. In some cases, a farmer located near the head of a system may be able to curtail his water use substantially without a major impact on his own yield, while substantially enhancing the yields of downstream farmers. In other cases, the excess water taken by the farmer located near the headworks may subsequently also flow to farmers located lower in the system. Restraint by the farmer located higher in the system may not increase total yield. Uncertainties stemming from lack of knowledge may be reduced over time as a result of skillful pooling and blending of scientific knowledge and local time-and-place knowledge. Uncertainty reduction is costly and never fully accomplished. The uncertainty stemming from strategic behavior by the appropriators remains even after one acquires considerable knowledge about the resource system itself.

Given these levels of uncertainty about the basic structure of the problems appropriators face, the only reasonable assumption to make about the discovery and calculation processes employed is that appropriators engage in a considerable amount of trial-and-error learning. Many actions are selected without full knowledge of their consequences. Some dams wash out after the first heavy rains. Some rules cannot be enforced because no one is able to monitor conformance to them. By definition, trial-and-error methods involve error, perhaps even disasters. Over time, appropriators gain a more accurate understanding of the physical world and what to expect from the behavior of others.

Collective-action problems related to the provision of CPRs and appropriation from CPRs extend over time. Individuals attribute less value to benefits that they expect to receive in the distant future, and more value to those expected in the immediate future. In other words, individuals discount future benefits – how severely depends on several factors. Time horizons are affected by whether or not individuals expect that they or their children will be present to reap these benefits, as well as by opportunities they may have for more rapid returns in other settings. The discount rates applied to future yields derived from a particular CPR may differ substantially across various types of appropriators. In a fishery, for example the discount rates of local fishers who live in nearby villages will differ from the discount rates of those who operate the larger trawlers, who may fish anywhere along a coastline. The time horizons of the local fishers, in relation to the yield of the inshore fishery, extend far into the future. They hope that their children and their children's children can make a living in the same location. More mobile fishers, on the other hand, can go on to other fishing grounds when local fish are no longer available.

Discount rates are affected by the levels of physical and economic security faced by appropriators. Appropriators who are uncertain whether or not there will be sufficient food to survive the year will discount future returns heavily when traded off against increasing the probability of survival during the current year. Similarly, if a CPR can be destroyed by the actions of others, no matter what local appropriators do, even those who have constrained their harvesting from a CPR for many years will begin to heavily discount future returns, as contrasted with present returns.[5] Discount rates are also affected by the general norms shared by the individuals living in a particular society, or even a local community, regarding the relative importance of the future as compared with the present.

Discount rates are not the only aspects of human choice that are affected by shared norms of behavior. Although I stress the importance that the expected consequences will have on one's decisions, individuals vary in regard to the importance they place on acting in ways that they and others view as right and proper. Norms of behavior reflect valuations that individuals place on actions or strategies in and of themselves, not as they are connected to immediate consequences.[6] When an individual has strongly internalized a norm related to keeping promises, for example, the individual suffers shame and guilt when a personal promise is broken. If the norm is shared with others, the individual is also subject to considerable social censure for taking an action considered to be wrong by others.

Norms of behavior therefore affect the way alternatives are perceived and weighed. For many routine decisions, actions that are considered wrong among a set of individuals interacting together over time will not even be included in the set of strategies contemplated by the individual. If the individual's attention is drawn to the possibility of taking such an action by the availability of a very large payoff for doing so, the action may be included in the set of alternatives to be considered, but with a high cost attached. Actions that are strongly proscribed among a set of individuals will occur less frequently (even though they promise to yield high net payoffs to individuals) than will those same actions in a community that does not censure such actions.

The most important impact that the type and extent of shared norms will have on the Strategies available to individuals has to do with the level of opportunistic behavior that appropriators can expect from other appropriators. Opportunism is defined as "self-interest with guile" (Williamson 1975). In a setting in which few individuals share norms about the impropriety of breaking promises, refusing to do one's share, shirking, or taking other opportunistic actions, each appropriator must expect all other appropriator to act opportunistically whenever they have the chance. In such a setting it is difficult to develop stable, long-term commitments. Expensive monitoring and sanctioning mechanisms may be needed. Some long-term arrangements that once were productive are no longer feasible given their costs of enforcement. In a setting in which there are strong norms against opportunistic behavior, each appropriator will be less wary about the dangers of opportunism.

Shared norms that reduce the cost monitoring and sanctioning activities can be viewed as social capital to be utilized in solving CPR problems.

Because CPR settings extend over time, and individuals adopt internal norms, it is possible for individuals to utilize contingent strategies, not simply independent strategies, in relating to one another. By "contingent strategies" I mean a whole class of planned actions that are contingent on conditions in the world. The contingent strategy that has been the object of the most scholarly attention is tit for tat in a two-person game in which an individual adopts a cooperative action in the first round and then mimics the action of the opponent in future rounds (Axelrod 1981, 1984). There are many other contingent strategies that can be adopted; they vary

in terms of the level of initial cooperation extended and the actions of others required for switching for switching behavioral patterns. That individuals utilize contingent strategies in many complex and uncertain field settings is an important foundation for later analysis.

Thus, I use a very broad conception of rational action, rather than a narrowly defined conception. The internal world of individual choice that I use is illustrated in Figure 21.1. Four internal variables – expected benefits, expected costs, internal norms, and discount rates – affect an individual's choice of strategies. Individuals selecting strategies jointly produce outcomes in an external world that impinge on future expectations concerning the benefits and costs of actions. What types of internal norms an individual possesses are affected by the shared norms held by others in regard to particular types of situations. Similarly, internal discount rates are affected by the range of opportunities that an individual has outside any particular situation.

## FIGURE 21.1 • THE INTERNAL WORLD OF INDIVIDUAL CHOICE

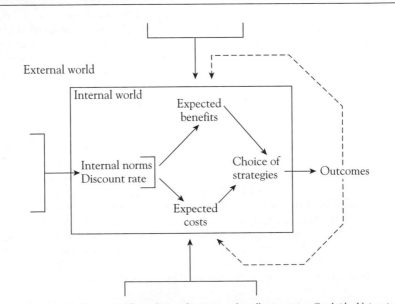

Governing the Commons: The evolution of institutions for collective action. Cambridge University Press, p. 37

## INTERDEPENDENCE, INDEPENDENT ACTION, AND COLLECTIVE ACTION

When multiple appropriators are dependent on a given CPR as a source of economic activity, they are jointly affected by almost everything they do. Each individual must take into account the choices of others when assessing personal choices. If one fisher occupies a good fishing site, a second fisher arriving at the same location must invest more resources to travel to another site, or else fight for the first site. If one irrigator allocates time and materials to repairing a broken control gate in an irrigation canal, all other irrigators using that canal are affected by that action, whether or not they want the control gate fixed and whether or not they contribute anything to the repair. The key fact of life for coappropriators is that they are tied together in a lattice of interdependence so long as they continue to share a single CPR. The physical interdependence does not disappear when effective institutional rules are utilized in the governance and management of the CPR. The physical interdependence remains; what changes is the result the appropriators obtain.

When appropriators act independently in relationship to a CPR generating scarce resource units, the total net benefits they obtain usually will be less than could have been achieved if they had coordinated their strategies in some way. At a minimum, the returns they receive from their appropriation efforts will be lower when decisions are made independently than they would have been otherwise. At worst, they can destroy the CPR itself. As long as the appropriators stay "unorganized," they cannot achieve a joint return as high as they could have received if they had organized in some way to undertake collective action.

Prisoners who have been placed in separate cells and cannot communicate with one another are also in an interdependent situation in which they must act independently. Acting independently in this situation is the result of coercion, not its absence. The herders in Hardin's model also act independently. Each decides on the number of animals to put on the meadow without concern for how that will affect the actions chosen by others.

At the most general level, the problem facing CPR appropriators is one of organizing: how to change the situation from one in which appropriators act independently to one in which they adopt coordinated strategies to obtain higher joint benefits or reduce their joint harm. That does not necessarily mean creating an organization. Organizing is a process; an organization is the result of that process. An organization of individuals who constitute an ongoing enterprise is only one form of organization that can result from the process of organizing.

The core of organization involves changes that order activities so that sequential, contingent, and frequency-dependent decisions are introduced where simultaneous, noncontingent, and frequency-independent actions had prevailed.[7] Almost all organization is accomplished by specifying a sequence of activities that must be carried out in a particular order.[8] Because of the repeated situations involved in most organized processes, individuals can use contingent strategies in which cooperation will have a greater chance of evolving and surviving. Individuals frequently are willing to forgo immediate returns in order to gain larger joint benefits when they observe many others following the same strategy. By requiring the participation of a minimal set of individuals, organizations can draw on this frequency-dependent behavior to obtain willing contributions on the part of many others. Changing the positive and negative inducements associated with particular actions and outcomes and the levels and types of information available can also encourage coordination of activities.[9]

Unlike prisoners, most CPR appropriators are not coerced into acting independently. Making the switch, however, from independent to coordinated or collective action is a nontrivial problem. The costs involved in transforming a situation from one in which individuals act independently to one in which they coordinate activities can be quite high. And the benefits produced are shared by all appropriators, whether or not they share any of the costs of transforming the situation. The theory of the firm and the theory of the state can each provide an explanation for one way in which collective action can be achieved. Each involves the creation of a new institutional arrangement in which the rules in use are fundamentally different from those that structure independent action. Let us briefly and in a stylized fashion consider how each theory can "solve" the problem of independent action in an interdependent situation. By doing this, we can better illustrate the absence of a similar theory that would identify the mechanisms by which a group of individuals could organize themselves.

### The theory of the firm

In the theory of the firm, an entrepreneur recognizes an opportunity to increase the return that can be achieved when individuals are potentially involved in an interdependent relationship.[10] The entrepreneur then negotiates a series of contracts with various participants that specify how they are to act in a coordinated, rather than independent, fashion. Each participant voluntarily chooses whether or not to join the firm, but gives up to the entrepreneur discretion over some range of choices. The participants become the agents of the entrepreneur. After paying each of the agents, the entrepreneur retains residual profits (or absorbs losses).

Consequently, the entrepreneur is highly motivated to organize the activity in a manner as efficient as possible. The entrepreneur attempts to craft contracts with agents that will induce them to act so as to increase the returns to the entrepreneur, and the entrepreneur monitors the agents' performances. The entrepreneur can terminate the contract of an agent who does not perform to the satisfaction of the entrepreneur. Because agents freely decide whether or not to accept the terms of the entrepreneur's contract, the organization is considered private, voluntary, and, at least by some individuals, nonexploitative. If there are large residuals to be obtained, however, it is the entrepreneur, not the agents, who receives them.[11] When a firm is located in an open market, one can presume that external competition will pressure the entrepreneur toward developing efficient internal institutions.

### The theory of the state

The theory of the state can also be presented in a brief and stylized version. Instead of an entrepreneur, we posit a ruler who recognizes that substantial benefits can be obtained by organizing some activities. As Hobbes first formulated the theory, individuals who independently engage in protection activities overinvest in weapons and surveillance and consequently live in constant fear. If a ruler gains a monopoly on the use of force, the ruler can use coercion as the fundamental mechanism to organize a diversity of human activities that will produce collective benefits. The ruler obtains taxes, labor, or other resources from subjects by threatening them with severe sanctions if they do not provide the resources.

The "wise" ruler uses the resources thus obtained to increase the general level of economic well-being of the subjects to a degree sufficient that the ruler can increase tax revenues while being able to reduce the more oppressive uses of coercion. Rulers, like entrepreneurs, keep the residuals. Subjects, like agents, may be substantially better off as a result of subjecting themselves to the coercion exercised by rulers. If the effort is highly successful, the ruler captures a substantial portion of the surplus.[12] There is no mechanism, such as a competitive market, that would exert pressure on the ruler to design efficient institutions. The ruler may face rebellion if the measures selected are too repressive, or military defeat if the realm is not adequately organized to do well in warfare.

In both the theory of the firm and the theory of the state, the burden of organizing collective action is undertaken by one individual, whose returns are directly related to the surplus generated. Both involve an outsider taking primary responsibility for supplying the needed changes in institutional rules to coordinate activities. The entrepreneur or the ruler makes credible commitments to punish anyone who does not follow the rules of the firm or the state. Because they gain the residuals, it is in their interest to punish nonconformance to their rules if they are confronted with nonconformance. Consequently, their threats to punish are credible (Schelling 1960; Williamson 1983). It is also in their interest to monitor the actions of agents and subjects to be sure they conform to prior agreements. Both theories thus address how a new institutional arrangement can come about, how credible commitments can be made, and why monitoring must be supplied.[13]

## THREE PUZZLES: SUPPLY, COMMITMENT, AND MONITORING

Although the theory of the firm and the theory of the state can resolve these problems, no equivalently well developed and generally accepted theory provides a coherent account for how a set of principals, faced with a collective-action problem, can solve (1) the problem of supplying a new set of institutions, (2) the problem of making credible commitments, and (3) the problem of mutual monitoring.

### The problem of supply

In a recent commentary on contractarianism and the new institutionalism, Robert Bates (1988) raises the issue that modern institutional theories do not adequately address the problem of supply. As he points out, "the new institutionalism is contractarian in spirit. Institutions are demanded because they enhance the welfare of rational actors. The problem is: Why are they supplied?" Bates first examines assurance games, where supplying new rules is considered easier to accomplish than it is in PD games, because there are mutually beneficial outcomes that are potential equilibria in the sense that once reached, no one has an incentive independently to switch strategies. Equilibria in assurance games do not, however, necessarily reward participants equally. Participants prefer a set of rules that will give them the most advantageous outcome. Although all will prefer a new institution that will enable them to coordinate their activities to achieve one of these equilibria, in contrast to continuing their independent actions, a fundamental disagreement is likely to arise among participants regarding which institution to choose. "The proposed solution to coordination – or assurance – games thus itself constitutes a collective dilemma" (Bates 1988, p. 394).[14]

Bates then turns to problems faced by a set of symmetric principals facing a collective dilemma in which all would benefit from a change in rules. Because supplying a new set of rules is the equivalent of providing another public good, the problem faced by a set of principals is that obtaining these new rules is a second-order collective dilemma.

> Even if the payoffs were symmetric and all persons were made [equally] better off from the introduction of the institutions, there would still be a failure of supply, since the institution would provide a collective good and rational individuals would seek to secure its benefits for free. The incentives to free-ride would undermine the incentives to organize a solution to the collective dilemma. It is subject to the very incentive problems it is supposed to resolve. (Bates 1988, pp. 394–5)

Because Bates presumes that the second-order dilemma is no easier to solve than the initial dilemma, he concludes that a new set of rules to solve the collective dilemma will not be provided by a set of principals (M. Taylor 1987).

Bates finds this deeply puzzling as it is obvious to him that some individuals in field settings *do* solve the problem of supply. Kreps and associates (1982) have demonstrated that in a finitely repeated PD game, some uncertainty about the exact payoff to a player can produce cooperative equilibria, as well as many other equilibria. Given this, it will pay one player to signal to other players an intention to cooperate, in the hope that they will reciprocate for a series of mutually productive plays. Thus, establishing trust and establishing a sense of community are, in Bates's view, mechanisms for solving the problem of supplying new institutions.

> Driven by a concern with institutions, we re-enter the world of the behavioralists. But we do so not in protest against the notion of rational choice, but rather in an effort to understand how rationality on the part of individuals leads to coherence at the level of society. (Bates 1988, p. 399)

### The problem of credible commitment
A second puzzle to be solved in explaining how a set of principals can organize themselves to obtain long-term collective

benefits is the problem of commitment.[15] To understand the heart of the "commitment" problem, let us consider a highly simplified picture of the choices available to appropriators in CPR situations.[16] In all cases in which individuals have organized themselves to solve CPR problems, rules have organized themselves to solve GPR problems, rules have been established by the appropriators that have severely constrained the authorized actions available to them. Such rules specify, for example, how many resource units an individual can appropriate, when, where, and how they can be appropriated, and the amounts of labor, materials, or money that must be contributed to various provisioning activities. If everyone, or almost everyone, follows these rules, resource units will be allocated more predictably and efficiently, conflict levels will be reduced, and the resource system itself will be sustained over time.

During an initial time period, an appropriator, calculating his or her estimated future flow of benefits if most appropriators agree to follow a proposed set of rules, may agree to abide by the set of rules in order to get others to agree. During later time periods, the immediate return to the appropriator for breaking one or another of the rules frequently can be high. When an irrigator's crops are severely stressed, the financial benefit of taking water "out of turn" can be substantial. Breaking the rules may save an entire crop from drought. On many occasions after an initial agreement to a set of rules, each appropriator must make further choices. Minimally, the choice at each decision time subsequent to the agreement can be thought of as the choice between complying to a set of rules, $C_n$ or breaking the set of rules in some fashion, $B_t$. On many occasions, $B_t$ will generate a higher immediate return for the appropriator than will $C_n$ unless $B_t$ is detected and a sanction, $S$, is imposed that makes $C_t > B_t - S$.[17]

External coercion is a frequently cited theoretical solution to the problem of commitment (Schelling 1984). The presumption is made that if individuals commit themselves to a contract whereby a stiff sanction ($S > B_{max}$) will be imposed by an external enforcer to ensure compliance during all future time periods, then each can make a credible commitment and obtain benefits that would not otherwise be attainable. That is not, however, the issue at hand; it will be discussed later. The immediate issue is that a self-organized group must solve the commitment problem without an external enforcer. They have to motivate themselves (or their agents) to monitor activities and be willing to impose sanctions to keep conformance high.

These puzzles cumulate. Even if one appropriator took the time and effort to analyze the problems they faced and to devise a set of rules that could improve their joint returns, the effort at supply would be pointless unless the appropriators could commit themselves to follow the rules. Unless the monitoring problem can be solved, credible commitments cannot be made. So let us now address the problem of mutual monitoring.

### The problem of mutual monitoring

The question of how a set of principals can engage in mutual monitoring of conformance to a set of their own rules is not easily addressed within the confines of collective-action theory. In fact, the usual theoretical prediction is that they will not do so. The usual presumption that individuals will not themselves monitor a set of rules, even if they have devised those rules themselves, was summarized by Jon Elster in a recent discussion of the motivations for workers to monitor each other's participation in a union:

> Before a union can force or induce workers to join it must overcome a free-rider problem in

the first place. To assume that the incentives are offered in a decentralized way, by mutual monitoring, gives rise to a second-order free-rider problem. Why, for instance, should a rational, selfish worker ostracize or otherwise punish those who don't join the union? What's in it for him? True, it may be better for all members if all punish non-members than if none do, but for each member it may be even better to remain passive. Punishment almost invariably is costly to the punisher, while the benefits from punishment are diffusely distributed over the members. It is, in fact, a public good; to provide it, one would need second-order selective incentives which would, however, run into a third-order free-rider problem (Elster 1989, pp. 40–1).[18]

Dilemmas nested inside dilemmas appear to be able to defeat a set of principals attempting to solve collective-action problems through the design of new institutions to alter the structure of the incentives they face. Without monitoring, there can be no credible commitment; without credible commitment, there is no reason to propose new rules. The process unravels from both ends, because the problem of supply is presumed unsolvable in the first place. But some individuals have created institutions, committed themselves to follow rules, and monitored their own conformance to their agreements, as well as their conformance to the rules in a CPR situation. Trying to understand how they have done this is the challenge of this study.

## FRAMING INQUIRY

Scholars addressing the problem of collective action frequently presume (1) that the underlying structure is always that of a PD [prisoners dilemma] game and (2) that one level of analysis is sufficient. When CPR problems are conceptualized as collective-action problems – a useful way to think of them – these same presumptions continue to frame the analyses, leading to policy prescriptions.

Consequently, part of the strategy pursued in this inquiry is to start from an alternative set of initial presumptions:

1  Appropriators in CPR situations face a variety of appropriation and provision problem whose structures vary from one setting to another, depending on the values of underlying parameters.
2  Appropriators must switch back and forth across arenas and levels of analysis.

These presumptions lead me to examine questions in a manner somewhat different from that of an analyst using the "normal" presuppositions of collective-action theory, although I still rely heavily on the work of other scholars.

### Appropriation and provision problems

Although some interdependent CPR situations have the structure of a PD game, many do not. Several scholars have shown how some simple situations facing appropriators may be better characterized as "assurance" games and as the game known as "chicken" (Runge 1981, 1984a).

In many irrigation systems, the fundamental choices facing appropriators are whether or not to steal water and whether or not to monitor the behaviors of others who might be stealing. The resulting game structure is complex and does not reduce down to any simple game. It does not have a single equilibrium. The amounts of stealing and monitoring that occur will depend on the values of parameters such as the number of appropriators, the cost of monitoring, the benefit from stealing, the punishment imposed when stealing is discovered, and the reward that a monitor receives for detecting a rule-breaker (Weissing and E. Ostrom 1990).

Consequently, instead of presuming that all CPR situations involve one underlying structure, I presume that the appropriators relying on any CPR face a variety of problems to be solved. The structure of

these problems will depend on the values of underlying parameters, such as the value and predictability of the flow of resource units, the ease of observing and measuring appropriator activities, and so forth. In an effort to develop a unified framework within which to organize the analysis of CPR situations using the tools of game theory and institutional analysis and the findings from empirical studies in laboratory and field settings, Roy Gardner, James Walker, and I have found it most useful to cluster the problems facing CPR appropriators into two broad classes: appropriation problems and provision problems (Gardner et al. 1990).

When appropriators face appropriation problems, they are concerned with the effects that various methods of allocating a fixed, or time-independent, quantity of resource units will have on the net return obtained by the appropriators. Provision problems concern the effects of various ways of assigning responsibility for building, restoring, or maintaining the resource system over time, as well as the well-being of the appropriators. Appropriation problems are concerned with the allocation of the flow; provision problems are concerned with the stock. Appropriation problems are time-independent; provision problems are time-dependent. Both types of problems are involved in every CPR to a greater or lesser extent, and thus the solutions to one problem must be congruent with solutions to the other. The structure of an appropriation problem or a provision problem will depend on the particular configuration of variables related to the physical world, the rules in use, and the attributes of the individuals involved in a specific setting.

*Appropriation problems.* In regard to appropriation, the key problem in a CPR environment is how to allocate a fixed, time-independent quantity of resource units so as to avoid rent dissipation and reduce uncertainty and conflict over the assignment of rights. Rents are dissipated whenever the marginal returns from an appropriation process are smaller than the marginal costs of* appropriation. Rent dissipation can occur because too many individuals are allowed to appropriate from the resource, because appropriators are allowed to withdraw more than the economically optimal quantity of resource units, or because appropriators overinvest in appropriation equipment (e.g., fishing gear).

In an open-access[19] CPR, in which no limit is placed on who can appropriate, the time-independent appropriation process frequently can be characterized as a PD game.[20] Rent dissipation is likely to be endemic. No appropriator has any incentive to leave any resource units for other appropriators to harvest (Gordon 1954; Scott 1955). In a limited-access CPR, in which a well-defined group of appropriators must jointly rely on a CPR for access to resource units, the incentives facing the appropriators will depend on the rules governing the quantity, timing, location, and technology of appropriation and how these are monitored and enforced. The structure of a limited-access CPR is not a PD game (Dasgupta and Heal 1979, p. 59) and lacks a dominant strategy for each participant. The incentives of appropriators who act independently, however, will lead them to over-invest in any input factor that is not constrained under the current rules (Townsend and Wilson 1987).

A second type of appropriation problem relates to assignment of spatial or temporal access to the resource. This occurs because spatial and temporal distributions of resource units frequently are heterogeneous and uncertain. Many fishing grounds, such as Alanya, are characterized by "fishing sites" that vary in their productivity. In grazing areas, one region may be drowned out in one year, but lush with growth in another year. Farmers who extract water from the head of an irrigation system can obtain more water than farmers who are located at the tail end. The risks associated with geographic or temporal uncertainty can be very high. Physical works, particularly those with storage, involve somewhat reduced risks, but well-enforced rules to allocate time or location of use or the quantity of resource units to specific users can reduce risks still further if the rules are well crafted to fit the physical attributes of the resource system. If risks are sufficiently reduced, appropriators can invest in productive enterprises that would not otherwise be economically viable. Physical violence occurring among the users of fisheries and irrigation systems is symptomatic of inadequate assignments of spatial or temporal slots to appropriators. When appropriators consider the assignment of access rights and duties to be unfair uneconomic, uncertain, or inappropriately enforced, that can adversely affect their willingness to invest in provision activities. The particular rules used to regulate appropriation will affect monitoring and policing costs and the type of strategic behavior that will occur between appropriators and monitors (the detection/deterrence game).[21]

*Provision problems.* Analyses of provision problems focus on the time-dependent, productive nature of investment in the resource itself. Provision problems may occur on the supply side, on the demand side, or on both sides. The supply-side problem faced in a CPR environment is related to the construction of the resource itself and its maintenance. Construction problems are like any long-term investment in capital infrastructure. Maintenance problems involve determining the type and level of regular maintenance (and reserves for emergency repair) that will sustain the resource system over time. Given that an investment in maintenance will affect the future rate at which a capital infrastructure will deteriorate, decisions about these activities are difficult to make even when a single entrepreneur makes them. When this difficult long-term problem is combined with the free-riding incentives of multiple appropriators, we see that organizing to maintain a system is a challenging task.

Demand-side-provision problems involve regulating withdrawal rates so that they do not adversely affect the resource itself. Many of the dynamic models of "rent dissipation" in the fisheries literature (Clark 1980; Clark, Munro, and Charles 1985) have focused on the time-dependent relationship between current withdrawals and future yields. The same rules that affect the allocation of this year's resource units will have an impact on the availability of resource units next year and the years thereafter.

The underlying uniformities of all CPR situations relate to the non-separability of one's choice of strategy and the choices made by others, as well as the fact that solving provision problems depends on achieving adequate solutions to appropriation problems, not the particular game-theoretical representations for these commonalities.[22] Many factors affect the strategic structure of a particular appropriation or provision problem, including the physical structure of a particular CPR, the technology available to the appropriators, the economic environment, and the sets of rules that affect the incentives that appropriators face.

### Multiple levels of analysis

Most current analyses of CPR problems and related collective-action problems focus on a single level of analysis – what can be called the operational level of analysis (Kiser and E. Ostrom 1982). At the operational level of analysis, one assumes that both the rules of the game and the physical, technological constraints are given and will not change

during the time frame of analysis: The actions of individuals in an operational situation directly affect the physical world. Resource units are withdrawn from a CPR. Inputs are transformed into outputs. Goods are exchanged. Appropriation and provision problems occur at an operational level. When doing an analysis of an operational situation, it is necessary for the analyst to assume that the technology and the institutional rules are known and unchanging. Both technology and rules, are, however, subject to change over time. Analysis of technological changes has proved to be far more difficult than analysis of production and consumption decisions within a fixed technology (Dosi 1988; Nelson and Winter 1982). Analysis of institutional change is also far more difficult than analysis of operational decisions within a fixed set of rules.[23] The rules affecting operational choice are made within a set of collective-choice rules. The constitutional-choice rules for a micro-setting are affected by collective-choice and constitutional-choice rules for larger jurisdictions. Individuals who have self-organizing capabilities switch back and forth between operational-, collective-, and constitutional-choice arenas, just as managers of production firms switch back and forth between producing products within a set technology, introducing a new technology, and investing resources in technology development. Given that CPR appropriators in some of the cases to be discussed in this volume do switch back and forth between arenas, we must drop the framing assumption that analysis at a single level will be sufficient. It is also essential to clarify what is meant by "institutions" in the first place.

"Institutions" can be defined as the sets of working rules that are used to determine who is eligible to make decisions in some arena, what actions are allowed or constrained, what aggregation rules will be used, what procedures must be followed, what information must or must not be provided, and what payoffs will be assigned to individuals dependent on their actions (E. Ostrom 1986a). All rules contain prescriptions that forbid, permit, or require some action or outcome. Working rules are those actually used, monitored, and enforced when individuals make choices about the actions they will take (Commons 1957). Enforcement may be undertaken by others directly involved, agents they hire, external enforcers, or any combination of these enforcers. One should not talk about a "rule" unless most people whose strategies are affected by it know of its existence and expect others to monitor behavior and to sanction nonconformance. In other words, working rules are common knowledge and are monitored and enforced. Common knowledge implies that every participant knows the rules, and knows that others know the rules, and knows that they also know that the participant knows the rules.[24] Working rules are always monitored and enforced, to some extent at least, by those directly involved. In any repetitive situation, one can assume that individuals come to know, through experience, good approximations of the levels of monitoring and enforcing involved.

Working rules may or may not closely resemble the formal laws that are expressed in legislation, administrative regulations, and court decisions. Formal law obviously is a major source of working rules in many settings, particularly when conformance to them is actively monitored and sanctions for noncompliance are enforced. When one speaks about a system that is governed by a "rule of law," this expresses the idea that formal laws and working rules are closely aligned and that enforcers are held accountable to the rules as well as others. In many CPR settings, the working rules used by appropriators may differ considerably from legislative, administrative, or court regulations (Wade 1988). The difference

between working rules and formal laws may involve no more than filling in the lacunae left in a general system of law. More radically, operational rules may assign de facto rights and duties that are contrary to the de jure rights and duties of a formal legal system. My primary focus in this study will be on the de facto rules actually used in CPR field settings, in an effort to understand the incentives and consequences they produce.

All rules are nested in another set of rules that define how the first set of rules can be changed.[25] This nesting of rules within rules at several levels is similar to the nesting of computer languages at several levels. What can be done at a higher level will depend on the capabilities and limits of the software (rules) at that level, on the software (rules) at a deeper level, and on the hardware (the CPR). Whenever one addresses questions about *institutional change*, as contrasted to action within institutional constraints, it is essential to recognize the following:

1 Changes in the rules used to order action at one level occur within a currently "fixed" set of rules at a deeper level.
2 Changes in deeper-level rules usually are more difficult and more costly to accomplish, thus increasing the stability of mutual expectations among individuals interacting according to a set of rules.

It is useful to distinguish three levels of rules that cumulatively affect the actions taken and outcomes obtained in using CPRs (Kiser and E. Ostrom 1982). *Operational rules* directly affect the day-to-day decisions made by appropriators concerning when, where, and how to withdraw resource units, who should monitor the actions of others and how, what information must be exchanged or withheld, and what rewards or sanctions will be assigned to different combinations of actions and outcomes. *Collective-choice rules* indirectly affect operational choices. These are the rules that are used by appropriators, their officials, or external authorities in making policies – the operational rules – about how a CPR should be managed. *Constitutional-choice rules* affect operational activities and results through their effects in determining who is eligible and determining the specific rules to be used in crafting the set of collective-choice rules that in turn affect the set of operational rules. One can think of the linkages among these rules and the related level of analysis at which humans make choices and take actions, as shown in Figure 21.2. The processes of appropriation, provision, monitoring, and enforcement occur at the operational level. The processes of policy-making, management, and adjudication of policy decisions occur at the collective-choice level. Formulation, governance, adjudication, and modifications of constitutional decisions occur at the constitutional level.[26]

This nesting of rules within rules is the source of considerable confusion and debate. Making the choice of operational-level rules endogenous does not imply making the choice of collective-choice or constitutional-choice rules endogenous at the same time. For purposes of analysis, the theorist has to assume that some rules already exist and are exogenous for purposes of a particular analysis. The fact that they are held constant and unchanging during

analysis, however, does not mean that they cannot be changed. Those very same rules may themselves be the objects of choice in a separate analysis or in the context of a different area of choice. At the end of every season, for example, intercollegiate sports leagues consider whether or not to alter the rules of the game for the next season.

On the other hand, rules are changed less frequently than are the strategies that individuals adopt within the rules. Changing the rules at any level of analysis will increase the uncertainty that individuals will face. Rules provide stability of expectations, and efforts to change rules can rapidly reduce that stability. Further, it is usually the case that operational rules are easier to change than collective-choice rules, and collective-choice rules are easier to change than constitutional-choice rules. Analyses of deeper layers of rules are more difficult for scholars and participants to make. Deciding whether an irrigation association should use a legislative body of five or nine members will depend on the physical and historical environment and, the analyst's speculation about different outcomes at several levels.[26]

When doing analysis at any one level, the analyst keeps the variables of a deeper level fixed for the purpose of analysis. Otherwise, the structure of the problem

**FIGURE 21.2 • LINKAGES AMONG RULES AND LEVELS OF ANALYSIS**

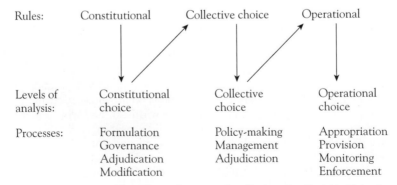

Governing the Commons: The evolution of institutions for collective action. Cambridge University Press, p. 53

would unravel. But self-organizing and self-governing individuals trying to cope with problems in field settings go back and forth across levels as a key strategy for solving problems. Individuals who have no self-organizing and self-governing authority are stuck in a single-tier world. The structure of their problems is given to them. The best they can do is to adopt strategies within the bounds that are given.

At each level of analysis there may be one or more arenas in which the types of decisions made at that level will occur. The concept of an "arena" does not imply a formal setting, but can include such formal settings as legislatures and courts. An arena is simply the situation in which a particular type of action occurs. Policy-making regarding the rules that will be used to regulate operational-level choices is carried out in one or more collective-choice arenas. If the appropriators using a CPR change at least some of the working rules used to organize appropriation and provision, the arena in which collective-choice decisions will be made may be a local coffeehouse, the meetings of a producers' co-op, or the meetings of an organization that has been set up specifically for the purpose of managing and governing

this CPR and possibly others related to it. If the appropriators using a CPR cannot change the rules used to organize operational choices, then the only arenas for collective choice are external to the CPR appropriators. In such cases, choices about the rules to be used will be made by government officials in bureaucratic structures, by elected representatives in local or national legislatures, and by judges in judicial arenas.

The relationships among arenas and rules rarely involve a single arena related to a single set of rules. Most frequently, several collective-choice arenas affect the set of operational rules actually used by appropriators for making choices about harvesting and investment strategies in a CPR. Decisions made in national legislatures and courts concerning access to all resources of particular types, when given legitimacy in a local setting and enforced, are likely to affect the operational rules actually used in particular locations. The relationships among formal and informal collective-choice arenas and the resulting operational rules are illustrated in Figure 21.3. Similarly, formal and informal constitutional-choice processes may occur in local, regional, and/or national arenas.

## FIGURE 21.3 • RELATIONSHIPS OF FORMAL AND INFORMAL COLLECTIVE-CHOICE ARENAS AND CPR OPERATIONAL RULES

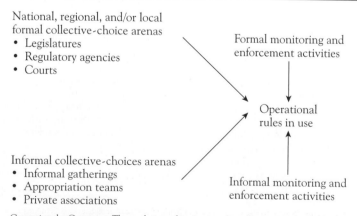

National, regional, and/or local formal collective-choice arenas
• Legislatures
• Regulatory agencies
• Courts

Formal monitoring and enforcement activities

Operational rules in use

Informal collective-choices arenas
• Informal gatherings
• Appropriation teams
• Private associations

Informal monitoring and enforcement activities

Governing the Commons: The evolution of institutions for collective action. Cambridge University Press, p. 53

That the working rules used by appropriators may have multiple sources, and may include de facto as well as de jure rules, greatly complicates the problem of understanding behaviors and outcomes in particular locations and the problem of improving outcomes. The absence of national, formal laws regulating the appropriation from and provision of a CPR is not equivalent to the absence of effective rules. Over a long period of time, local appropriators may have developed working rules that constrain the entry to and use of a CPR. Such rules may or may not lead appropriators to manage their resource efficiently and fairly, but they will affect the strategies that appropriators perceive to be available to them and the resulting outcomes.

## NOTES

1. For physical resources, this translates into the relation between usage-neutral deterioration, on the one hand, and investments made in maintain and repair, on the other hand (E. Ostrom, Schroeder, and Wynne 1993).

2. Let me state at this point that the term "appropriator" is used in some level systems to denote a person who has a particular legal claim to withdraw resource units.

3. See Radnitzky (1987) and Stroebe and Frey (1980) for a similar approach.

4. The concept of average yield may not be meaningful in regard to all biological resources (Schlager 1989).

5. See Berkes (1989) for a description of the strategies temporarily adopted by the Cree Indians near Hudson's Bay when an influx of nonnative trappers threatened the beaver stock. Legislation passed in 1930 legally recognized American Indian, communal and family territories, allowing the. Cree to anticipate long-term survival for a key CPR. Since 1930, the Cree have successfully managed the beaver stock using the rules that had been tested by centuries of trial and error prior to the arrival of Europeans on the North American continent.

6. See Coleman (1987, 1990) and Opp (1979, 1982, 1986) for extended analyses of the relationship between norms and rational-choice theory.

7. Sequential, contingent, and frequency-dependent behaviors may, of course, occur in unorganized settings. Some very interesting game-theoretical results have relied on the potentialities of individuals to rely on such forms of coordinated activities, alone, without changing the underlying structures (Kreps et al. 1982; Levhari and Mirman 1980; Scheiling 1978).

8. An important aspect of organizing a legislative process, for example, is the set of rules that specify the steps through which a bill must be processed before it becomes a law.

9. Changing the positive and negative inducements is the type of intervention that has received the most mention in the social sciences.

10. Alchian and Dèmsetz ( 1972) overtly posit that key problem underlying reliance on a firm to organize behavior, rather than reliance on the independent actions of buyers and sellers in a market institution, is that of an interdependent production function. When the production function is interdependent, the marginal contribution of any one owner of an input factor will depend on the level of other inputs. One cannot tell from an examination of outputs alone how much any individual contributed. Rewarding inputs requires high levels of monitoring that are not needed, when factors are combined additively. Williamson (1975), drawing inspiration from Coase (1937), argues that is only one source of the need for organized firms. Williamson relies more on the costs of transacting in a market in, which all act independently, as contrasted with a firm in which individuals agree ex ante to coordinate their activities ex post.

11. This stylized version does not do full justice to the extensive work of the theory of

the firm, and I certainly do not recommend any policy prescriptions on the basis of this sketch. Because my purpose is only to show how the theory solves the collective-action problem, I am presenting only this barebones outline. Readers are advised to see the work of Cease (1937), Alchian and Densetz (1972), and Williamson (1975, 1985).

12. This discussion of the theory of the state draws most heavily on the work of scholars who base their theory of the state on Hobbes; it does not reflect the full range of debate about the theory of the state (Breton 1974; M. Taylor 1987).

13. Both are also subject to limits imposed by span-of-control problems: The cost of monitoring increases with the size and diversity of a firm or a state.

14. See Feeny (1988b) for an insightful discussion of the supply of institution.

15. See, for example, the studies by Schelling (1960), Elster (1979), Brennan and Buchanan (1985), Levi (1988a,b), Shepsle (1989a), North and Weingast (1989), and Williamson (1985).

16. Reading a working paper by Shepsle (1989a) made me recognize how important this problem is to understanding CPR problems, as well as many other problems of interest to an institutional analyst.

17. This is how the literature on the "economics of crime" models the decision to comply or not (Becker 1968; Ehrlich 1973; Ehrlich and Brower 1987); for an insightful critique, see Tsebelis (1989).

18. Elster is not completely sure that the dilemma of mutual monitoring is always "decisive." He points to the possibility that tasks may be organized so the monitoring can be done without additional effort.

19. Ciriacy-Wantrup and Bishop (1975) carefully distinguished between an open access CPR, in which no one has any property rights, and a closed-access CPR in which a well-defined group owns property in common. "Common-property resources" is a term that is still used inappropriately in many instances to refer to both open-access and closed-access CPRs.

20. Exactly how one models this depends on many underlying parameters. One that is essential to the production of full rent dissipation is that the underlying appropriation function (usually called a production function in this literature) is characterized by diminishing returns (Dasgupta and Heal 1979, p. 25).

21. A third appropriation problem has to do with technological externalities. Because none of the cases in this volume clearly illustrates this problem, I do not discuss it here, see Gardner, E. Ostrom, and Walker (1990).

22. This intimate relationship between solving appropriation problems and solving provision problems has frequently been ignored by contemporary designers of large-scale irrigation systems.

23. See Frey (1988), Brennan and Buchanan (1985), Buchanan (1977), and Buchanan and Tullock (1962).

24. "Common knowledge" is an important assumption frequently used in game theory and essential for most analyses of equilibrium. It implies that all participants know $x$, that the participants know that each of the others knows $x$, and that the participants know that each of the others know that each of the others knows $x$ (Aumann 1976).

25. Heckathorn (1984) models this as a series of nested games.

26. These levels exist whether the organized human activity is public or private. See Boudreaux and Holcombe (1989) for a discussion of the constitutional rules of homeowner associations, condominiums, and some types of housing developments.

27. In designing the constitution of an irrigation community, for example, setting up a legislative body requires determining how many representatives there should be. Determining the number of representatives will be affected by the physical layout. If there are 5 canals, having one representative from each canal may work well. If there are 50 canals, the participant may want to cluster canals into branches in order to select representatives. Whatever constitutional-choice is made about how many (and how to select) representatives,

the effects on appropriation practices will come about as a result of decisions made at both a collective-choice level and an operational level. It is extremely difficult to predict these with any exactitude prior to experience in a particular setting.

# REFERENCES

Alchian, A., and H. Demsetz. 1973. The Property Rights Paradigm. *Journal of Economic History* 33: 16–27.

Aumann, R. J. 1976. Agreeing to Disagree. *Annals of Statistics* 4: 1236–9.

Aumann, R. J. 1987. Correlated Equilibrium as an Expression of Bayesian Rationality. *Econometrica* 55: 1–18.

Axelrod, R. 1981. The Emergence of Cooperation Among Egoists. *American Political Science Review* 75: 306–18.

Axelrod, R. 1984, *The Evolution of Cooperation*, New York: Basic Books.

Bates, R. H. 1988. Contra Contractarianism: Some Reflections on the New Institutionalism. *Politics and Society* 16: 387–401.

Becker, G. S. 1968. Crime and Punishment: An Economic Approach. *Journal of Political Economy* 76: 169–217.

Berkes, F., ed. 1989. *Common Property Resources. Ecology and Community-Based Sustainable Development.* London: Belhaven Press.

Boudreaux, D. J., and R. G. Holcombe. 1989. Government by Contract. *Public Finance Quarterly* 17: 264–80.

Brennan, G., and J. Buchanan. 1985. *The Reason of Rules.* Cambridge University Press.

Breton, A. 1974. *The Economic Theory of Representative Government.* Chicago: Aldine.

Buchanan, J. M. 1977. *Freedom in Constitutional Contract. Perspectives of a Political Economist.* College Station: Texas A&M University Press.

Buchanan, J. M., and G. Tullock. 1962. *The Calculus of Consent: Logical Foundations of Constitutional Democracy.* Ann Arbor: University of Michigan Press.

Ciriacy-Wantrup, S. V., and R. C. Bishop. 1975. "Common Property" as a Concept in Natural Resource Policy. *Natural Resources Journal.* 15: 713–27.

Clark, C. W., G. Munro, and A. Charles. 1985. *Fisheries: Dynamics, and Use certainty, in Progress in Natural Resource Economics,* ed. A. Scott, pp. 99–119. Oxford University Press (Clarendon Press).

Coase, R. H. 1937. The Nature of the Firm. *Economica* 4: 386–405.

Coleman, J. S. 1987. Norms as Social Capital. In *Economic Imperialism, The Economic Approach Applied Outside the Field of Economics,* eds. G. Radnitzky and P. Bernholz, pp. 133–55. New York: Paragon House.

Coleman, J. S. 1990. *Foundations of Social Theory,* Cambridge, Mass.: Harvard University Press.

Commons, J. R. 1957. *Legal Foundations of Capitalism.* Madison: University of Wisconsin Press.

Dasgupta, P. S., and G. M. Heal. 1979. *Economic Theory and Exhaustible Resources.* Cambridge University Press.

Dosi, G. 1988. Technical Change, Institutional Processes and Economic Dynamics: Some Tentative Propositions and a Research Agenda. Working paper, Department of Economics, University of Rome.

Ehrlich, I. 1973. Participation in illegitimate Activities: A Theoretical and Empirical Investigation. *Journal of Political Economy* 81: 521–64.

Ehrlich, I., and G. D. Brower. 1987. On the Issue of Causality in the Economic Model of Crime and Law Enforcement: Some Theoretical Considerations and Experimental Evidence. *American Economic Review* 77: 99–106.

Elster, J. 1979. *Ulysses and the Sirens: Studies in Rationality and Irrationality.* Cambridge University Press.

Elster, J. 1989. *The Cement of Society. A Study of Social Order.* Cambridge University Press.

Frey, B. S. 1988. Political Economy and Institutional Choice. *European Journal of Political Economy* 4: 349–66

Gardner, R., E. Ostrom, and J. M. Walker 1990. The Nature of Common-Pool Resource Problems. *Rationality and Society* 2: 335–58.

Gordon, H. S. 1954. The Economic Theory of a Common-Property Resource: The Fishery. *Journal of Political Economy* 62: 124–42.

Hechter, M. 1984. When Actors Comply: Monitoring Costs and the Production of Social Order. *Acta Sociologica* 27: 161–83.

Kiser, L. L., and E. Ostrom. 1982. The Three Worlds of Action. A Metatheoretical Synthesis of Institutional Approaches. In *Strategies of Political Inquiry*, ed. E. Ostrom, pp. 179–222. Beverly Hills: Sage.

Kreps, D. M., P. Milgrom, J. Roberts, and R. Wilson. 1982. Rational Cooperation in the Finitely Repeated Prisoner's Dilemma. *Journal of Economic Theory* 27: 245–52.

Levhari, D., and L. H. Mirman. 1980. The Great Fish War: An Example Using a Dynamic Cournot-Nash Solution. *Bell Journal of Economics* 11: 322–34.

Levi, M. 1988a. *Of Rule and Revenue*. Berkeley: University of California Press.

Levi, M. 1988b. The Transformation of Agrarian Institutions: An Introduction and Perspective. *Politics and Society* 18: 159–70.

Nelson, R., and S. Winter. 1982. *An Evolutionary Theory of Economic Change*. Cambridge, Mass.: Harvard University Press.

Niskanen, W. 1971. *Bureaucracy and Representative Government*. Chicago: Aldine-Atherton.

North, D. C., and B. R. Weingast. 1989. Constitutions and Commitment: The Evolution of Institutions Governing Public Choice in 17th Century England. St. Louis: Washington University, Center in Political Economy.

Opp, K. D. 1979. The Emergence and Effects of Social Norms. *Kyklos*. 32: 775–801.

Opp, K. D. 1982. The Evolutionary Emergence of Norms. *British Journal of Social Psychology* 21: 139–49.

Opp, K. D. 1986. The Evolution of a Prisoner's Dilemma in the Market. In *Paradoxical Effects of Social Behavior*, eds. A. Diekmann and P. Mitter, pp. 149–68. Vienna: Physica-Verlag.

Ostrom, E. 1986. An Agenda for the Study of Institutions. *Public Choice* 48: 3–25.

Ostrom, E., L. Schroeder, and S. Wynne. 1993. *Institutional Incentives and Sustainable Development: Infrasuructure Policies in Perspective*, Boulder, CO: Westview Press.

Ostrom, V., C. M. Tiebour, and R. Warren, 1961. The Organization of Government in Metropolitan Areas: A Theortical Inquiry. *American Political Science Review* 55: 831–42.

Plott, C. R., and R. A. Meyer. 1975. The Technology of Public Goods, Externalities, and the Exclusion Principle. In *Economic Analysis of Environmental Problems*, ed. E. S. Mills, pp. 65–94. New York: Columbia University Press.

Radnitzky, G. 1987. Cost-Benefit Thinking in the Methodology of Research: The "Economic Approach" Applied to Key Problems of the Philosophy of Science, In *Economic Imperialism. The Economic Approach Applied Outside the Field of Economic*, eds. G. Radnitzky and P. Bernholz, pp. 283–331. New York: Paragon House.

Runge, C. F. 1981. Common Property Externalities: Isolation, Assurance and Resource Depletion in an Traditional Grazing Context. *American Journal of Agricultural Economics* 63: 595–606.

Schelling, T. C. 1960. *The Strategy of Conflict*. Cambridge, Mass. Harvard University Press (Cambridge, Mass.).

Schelling, T. C. 1978. *Micromotives and Macrobehavior*. New York: Norton.

Schelling, T. C. 1984. *Choice and Consequence: Perspectives of an Errant Economist*. Cambridge, Mass.: Harvard University Press.

Schlager, E. 1989. Bounding Unboundable Resource: An Empirical Analysis of Property Rights and Rules in Coastal Fisheries. Working paper, Workshop in Political Theory and Policy Analysis, Indiana University.

Scott, A. D. 1955. The Fishery: The Objectives of Sole Ownership. *Journal of Political Economy* 63: 116–24.

Shepsle, K. A. 1989a. Discretion, Institutions, and the Problem of Government Commitment, Working paper, Cambridge, Mass.: Harvard University, Department of Government.

Stroebe, W., and B. S. Frey. 1980. In Defense of Economic Man: Towards an Integration of Economics and Psychology. *Zeitschrift für Volkswirtschaft and Statistik* 2: 119–48.

Taylor, M. 1987. *The Possibility of Cooperation.* Cambridge, UK.

Townsend, R., and J. A. Wilson. 1987. An Economic View of the Commons. In *The Question of the Commons*, eds. B J. McCay and J. M. Acheson, pp. 311–26. Tucson: University of Arizona Press.

Wade, R. 1988. *Village Republics: Economic Conditions for Collective Action in South India.* Cambridge, UK.

Weissing, F., and E. Ostrom. 1990. Irrigation Institutions and the Games Irrigators Play. In *Game Equilibrium Models. Vol. II: Methods, Morals, and Markets*, ed. R., Selten. Berlin: Springer-Verlag.

Williamson, O. E. 1975. *Market and Hierarchies: Analysis and Antitrust Implications.* New York: Free Press.

Williamson, O. E. 1983. Credible Commitments: Using Hostages to Support Exchange. *American Economic Review* 83: 519–40.

Williamson, O. E. 1985. *The Economic Institutions of Capitalism: Firms, Markets, Relational Contracting.* New York: Free Press.

# CHAPTER 6

# *Power and Politics Organization Theory*

The neatest thing about power is that we all understand it. We may have first discovered power as children when our mothers said, "Don't do that!" We learn about power in organizations as soon as we go to school. Most of us have a good intuitive grasp of the basic concepts of organizational power by the time we reach third grade. So, the newest thing about power in organizations is not our understanding of it, but rather our intellectualizing about it.

Ordinary people as well as scholars hesitate to talk about power. First, for many, power is not a subject for polite conversation. We often equate power with force, brutality, unethical behavior, manipulation, connivance, and subjugation. Rosabeth Moss Kanter (1979) contends that "power is America's last dirty word. It is easier to talk about money—and much easier to talk about sex—than it is to talk about power." Besides, power doesn't fit well with our Western notion of rationality in business and government. Thus, relatively few people have been exposed to analyses of organizational power. So it will be useful to start our introduction to the power and politics perspective on organization theory by contrasting some of its basic assumptions with those of the more rational classical, neoclassical, "modern" structural, organizational economics, and organizations/environment perspectives as in our Chapters 1, 2, 4, 5, and 8.

In the classical, neoclassical, "modern" structural, organizational economics, and systems/environment theories of organization, organizations are assumed to be rational institutions—institutions whose primary purpose is to accomplish established goals. People in positions of formal authority set goals. In these schools of thought, the primary questions for organization theory involve how best to design and manage organizations so they achieve their declared purposes effectively and efficiently. The personal preferences of organizational members are restrained by systems of formal rules, authority, and norms of rational behavior.

The power and politics school rejects these assumptions about organizations as naive and unrealistic, and therefore of limited practical value. Instead, organizations are viewed as complex systems of individuals and coalitions, each having its own interests, beliefs, values, preferences, perspectives, and perceptions. Coalitions continuously compete with each other for scarce organizational resources. Conflict is inevitable. Influence—as well as the power and political activities through which influence is acquired and maintained—is the primary "weapon" for use in competition and conflicts. Thus, power, politics, and influence are essential and permanent facts of organizational life.

Organizational goals result from ongoing maneuvering and bargaining among individuals and coalitions. Most coalitions are transitory: They shift with issues and often cross vertical and horizontal organizational boundaries. They may, for example, include key stakeholders outside the organization as well as people at several levels in the organizational hierarchy and from different product, functional, and/or geographical divisions or departments. Organizations have many conflicting goals, and different sets of goals take priority as the balance of power shifts among coalitions—as different coalitions gain and use enough power to control the organization (Baldridge, 1971). Why then are organizational goals so important in the theory of organizational power and politics? The answer is essential for understanding this perspective on organization theory—*because they provide the official rationale and the legitimacy for allocating and reallocating scarce organizational resources.*

Power relations are permanent features of organizations primarily because specialization and the division of labor result in the creation of many interdependent organization units with varying degrees of importance to the well-being of the organization. The units compete with each other for scarce resources as well as with the transitory coalitions. As James D. Thompson pointed out in 1967 (Reading 30 in Chapter 8), a lack of balance in the interdependence among units sets the stage for the use of power relations. Jeffrey Pfeffer emphasizes: "Those persons and those units that have the responsibility for performing the more critical tasks in the organization have a natural advantage in developing and exercising power in the organization. ... Power is first and foremost a structural phenomenon, and should be understood as such" (1981).

The more rational theories of organization place high importance on "legitimate authority" (authority that flows down through the organizational hierarchy) and formal rules (promulgated and enforced by those in authority) to ensure that organizational behavior is directed toward the attainment of established organizational goals. For example, these theories tend to define power synonymously with authority. In contrast, power and politics theorists note the gap in today's organizations between the power one needs to get the job done and the power that comes with the job (authority). Unlike the more rational theories, authority in power and politics theory is only one of the many sources of organizational power available, and power is aimed in *all* directions—not just down through the hierarchy.

According to power and politics theory, other forms of power and influence may prevail over authority-based power. Several of this chapter's selections identify different sources of power in organizations, so we list only a few here as examples:

- Control over scarce resources (for example, office space, discretionary funds, current and accurate information, and time and skill to work on projects)
- Access to others who are perceived as having power (for example, important customers or clients, members of the board of directors, or someone else with formal authority or who controls scarce resources)
- A central place in a potent coalition, ability to "work the organizational rules" (knowing how to get things done or to prevent others from getting things done), and credibility (for example, trustworthiness)

Many definitions of "power" have been proposed over the years. Our preferred one blends definitions offered by Gerald Salancik and Jeffrey Pfeffer (1977) and Robert Allen and Lyman Porter (1983): "Power is the ability to get things done the way one wants them done; it is the latent ability to influence people." This definition offers several advantages for understanding organizations. First, it emphasizes the relativity of power. A person is not powerful or powerless in general, but has power only with respect to others in specific social relationships (Pfeffer, 1981). In other words, power is specific to the context and the relationship.

Second, the phrase "the way one wants them done" is a potent reminder that conflict and the use of power often occur because of disagreement about the choice of methods, means, approaches, and/or "turf." They are not limited to battles about outcomes. This point is important because power is primarily a structural phenomenon, a consequence of the division of labor and specialization. For example, competing organizational coalitions often form around professions: hospital nurses versus paramedics, sociologists versus mathematicians in a college of arts and sciences, business school-educated staff specialists versus generalists from the "school of hard knocks" in a production unit, or social workers versus educators in a center for incarcerated youth. Organizational conflicts among people representing different professions, educational backgrounds, genders, and ages frequently do not involve goals. They center on questions about *the right* of a profession, academic discipline, or sex or age group to exercise its perception of its *professional rights*, to control the way things will be done, or to protect its turf and status. This point is crucially important because it reemphasizes that organizational behavior and decisions are frequently not rational—as the word is used to mean "directed toward the accomplishment of established organizational goals" by the classical, neoclassical, "modern" structural, organizational economics, and the systems/environment theorists. Our preferred definition of power highlights the primary reason why the power and politics theories reject the basic assumptions of the more rational theorists as being naive and unrealistic.

"The Bases of Social Power," by John R. P. French, Jr. and Bertram Raven (1959), reprinted here, was one of the earliest looks at the use of power in organizations and its ethical limits. French and Raven start from the premise that power and influence involve relations between at least two agents (they limit their definition of agents to individuals) and theorizes that the reaction of the *recipient agent* is the more useful focus for explaining the phenomena of social influence and power. The core of French and Raven's chapter is their identification of five bases or sources of social power: reward power, the perception of coercive power, legitimate power (organizational authority), referent power (through association with others who possess power), and expert power (power of knowledge or ability).

"The Bases of Social Power" identifies two categories of *effects of power* derived from these five different sources: *attraction* (the recipient's sentiment toward the agent who uses power) and *resistance* to the use of power. Use of power from the different bases has different consequences. For example, coercive power typically decreases attraction and causes high resistance, whereas reward power increases attraction and creates minimal levels of resistance. French and Raven conclude that "the more legitimate the coercion [is perceived to be], the less it will produce resistance and decreased attraction."

James March's essay "The Power of Power" is not limited to power inside organizations. March reviews alternative definitions, concepts, and approaches for empirically studying social power in organizations and communities. Therefore, "The Power of Power" has particular applicability for open system organization theories. His observations about "community power" are more than tangentially germane to organization theory because of the current enthusiasm for "boundaryless organizations," "virtual organizations," and networks, as are described in Chapters 8 and 9. March discusses the advantages and limitations of three approaches to the study of power: experimental studies, community studies, and institutional studies. "The third alternative approach … is the analysis of the structure of institutions to determine the power structure within them." March assesses the usefulness of six types of models of social choice for arriving at empirically meaningful predictions about power. March concludes: "Although power and influence are useful concepts for many kinds of situations, they have not greatly helped us to understand many of the natural social-choice mechanisms to which they have traditionally been applied …. On the whole, … power is a disappointing concept" for social science research.

In her 1979 *Harvard Business Review* article, "Power Failure in Management Circuits," which is reprinted here, Rosabeth Moss Kanter argues that executive and managerial power is a necessary ingredient for moving organizations toward their goals. "Power can mean efficacy and capacity" for organizations. The ability of managers to lead effectively cannot be predicted by studying their styles or traits; it requires knowledge of a leader's real power sources. Kanter identifies three groups of positions within organizations that are particularly susceptible to powerlessness: first-line supervisors, staff professionals, and top executives. However, she carefully distinguishes between "power" and "dominance, control, and oppression." Her primary concern is that at higher organizational levels, the power to "punish, to prevent, to sell off, to reduce, to fire, all without appropriate concern for consequences" grows, but the power needed for positive accomplishments does not. Managers who perceive themselves as being powerless and who think their subordinates are discounting them tend to use more dominating or punishing forms of influence. Thus, in larger organizations, powerlessness (or perceived powerlessness) can be a more substantive problem than possession of power. By empowering others, leaders can actually acquire more "productive power"—the power needed to accomplish organizational goals. "Power Failure in Management Circuits" also contains an embedded subarticle on the particular problems that power poses for women managers.

Henry Mintzberg describes his 1983 book, *Power in and around Organizations*, as a discussion of a theory of organizational power. Organizational behavior is viewed as a power game. The "players" are "influencers" with varying personal needs who attempt to control organizational decisions and actions. "Thus, to understand the behavior of the organization, it is necessary to understand which influencers are present, what needs each seeks to fulfill in the organization, and how each is able to exercise power to fulfill them." His chapter, "The Power Game and the Players," which is reprinted here, focuses on the "influencers," who they are, and where their power comes from. Eleven groups of possible influencers are listed: five are in the "external coalition" and six in the "internal coalition." The external coalition consists of the owners, "associates" (suppliers, clients, trading partners, and competitors), employee associations (unions and professional associations), the organization's various publics (at large), and the corporate directors (which include representatives from the other four groups in the external coalition and also some internal influencers). The internal coalition is composed of the chief executive officer, operators (the organization's "producers"), line managers, analysts (staff specialists), the support staff, and—the final "actor" in Mintzberg's internal coalition—the ideology of the organization, that is, "the set of beliefs shared by its internal influencers that distinguishes it from other organizations." As it happens, ideology plays an important role in organizational culture, which is the topic of the next chapter.

# REFERENCES

Akella, D. (2003). *Unlearning the fifth discipline: Power, politics and control in organizations*. Thousand Oaks, CA: Sage.

Allen, R. W., & L. W. Porter (1983). *Organizational influence processes*. Glenview, IL: Scott, Foresman.

Baldridge, J. V. (1971). *Power and conflict in the university*. New York: Wiley.

Broom. M. F. (2011). *The infinite organization: Celebrating the positive use of power in organizations*. Baltimore, MD: Center for Human Systems.

Buchanan, D. A., & R. J. Badham.(2009). *Power, politics, and organizational change*. Thousand Oaks, CA: Sage.

Cialdini, R. B. (2009). *Influence: Science and practice*, 5th ed. Boston: Pearson Education.

Clegg, S., D., Courpasson, & N. Phillips (2006). *Power and organizations*. Thousand Oaks, CA: Sage.

Cobb, A. T., & N. Margulies (1981). Organization development: A political perspective. *Academy of Management Review*, 6, 49–59.

Cohen, A. R., & D. L. Bradford (1990). *Influence without authority*. New York: Wiley.

Cohen, M. D., & J. G. March (1974). *Leadership and ambiguity: The American college president*. New York: McGraw-Hill.

Cross, R., & A. Parker (2004). *The hidden power of social networks: Understanding how work really gets done in organizations*. Boston: Harvard Business School Press.

Cyert, R. M., & J. G. March (1963). *A behavioral theory of the firm*. Englewood Cliffs, NJ: Prentice Hall.

French, J. R. P., Jr., & B. Raven (1959). The bases of social power. In D. P. Cartwright, ed., *Studies in social power* (pp. 150–167). Ann Arbor, MI: University of Michigan, Institute for Social Research.

Hagberg, J. O. (2003). *Real power: Stages of personal power in organizations*, 3rd ed. Salem, WI: Sheffield.

Hardy, C., ed. (1995). *Power and politics in organizations*. Aldershot, UK: Dartmouth.

Jay, A. (1967). *Management and Machiavelli*. New York: Holt, Rinehart & Winston.

Kanter, R. M. (1979, July–August). Power failure in management circuits. *Harvard Business Review*, 57, 65–75.

Kaufman, H. (1964, March). Organization theory and political theory. *American Political Science Review*, 58, 5–14.

Korda, M. (1975). *Power! How to get it, how to use it*. New York: Random House.

Kotter, J. P. (1977). Power, dependence, and effective management. *Harvard Business Review*, 55, 125–136.

Kotter, J. P. (1994). *Managing with power: Politics and influence in organizations*. Boston, MA: Harvard Business School Press.

Kotter, J. P. (2009). *Power and influence: Beyond formal authority*, New York: Free Press.

March, J. G. (1966). The power of power. In David Easton, ed., *Varieties of political theory* (pp. 39–70). Englewood Cliffs, NJ: Prentice Hall.

Mechanic, D. (1962). Sources of power of lower participants in complex organizations. *Administrative Science Quarterly*, 7, 349–364.

Michels, R. (1962). Political parties: A sociological study of the oligarchical tendencies of modern democracy (Eden and Cedar Paul, trans.). New York: Free Press. Originally published in German in 1915.

Mintzberg, H. (1983). *Power in and around organizations*. Englewood Cliffs, NJ: Prentice Hall.

Mintzberg, H. (1985). The organization as political arena. *Journal of Management Studies*, 22(2), 133–154.

Ott, J. S., S. J. Parkes, & R. B. Simpson, eds. (2008). *Classic readings in organizational behavior.* 4th ed. Belmont, CA: Thomson-Wadsworth.

Pfeffer, J. (1981). *Power in organizations.* Boston: Pitman.

Pfeffer, J. (1992). *Managing with power: Politics and influence in organizations.* Boston: Harvard Business School Press.

Pfeffer, J. (2011). *Power: Why some people have it and others don't.* New York: HarperBusiness.

Pfeffer, J., & G. Salancik. (2003). *The external control of organizations: A resource dependence perspective.* Stanford, CA: Stanford Business Books.

Porter, L. W., R. W. Allen, & H. L. Angle (1981). The politics of upward influence in organizations. In L. L. Cummings & B. M. Staw, eds., *Research in organizational behavior,* vol. 3 (pp. 408–422). Greenwich, CT: JAI Press.

Salancik, G. R., & J. Pfeffer (1977). Who gets power—and how they hold on to it: A strategic-contingency model of power. *Organizational Dynamics,* 5, 2–21.

Siu, R. G. H. (1979). *The craft of power.* New York: Wiley.

Thompson, J. D. (1967). *Organizations in action.* New York: McGraw-Hill.

Tushman, M. L. (1977, April). A political approach to organizations: A review and rationale. *Academy of Management Review,* 2, 206–216.

Vecchio, R. P. ed. (2007). *Leadership: Understanding the dynamics of power and influence in organizations,* 2nd ed. South Bend, IN: University of Notre Dame Press.

Yates, D., Jr. (1985). *The politics of management.* San Francisco, CA: Jossey-Bass.

Zaleznik, A., & M. F. R. Kets de Vries (1985). *Power and the corporate mind.* Chicago, IL: Bonus Books.

## 22

# The Bases of Social Power

*John R. P. French Jr. & Bertram Raven*

The processes of power are pervasive, complex, and often disguised in our society. Accordingly, one finds in political science, in sociology, and in social psychology a variety of distinctions among different types of social power or among qualitatively different processes of social influence (1, 6, 14, 20, 23, 29, 30, 38, 41). Our main purpose is to identify the major types of power and to define them systematically so that we may compare them according to the changes which they produce and the other effects which accompany the use of power. The phenomena of power and influence involve a dyadic relation between two agents which may be viewed from two points of view: (a) What determines the behavior of the agent who exerts power? (b) What determines the reactions of the recipient of this behavior? We take this second point of view and formulate our theory in terms of the life space of P, the person upon whom the power is exerted. In this way we hope to define basic concepts of power which will be adequate to explain many of the phenomena of social influence, including some which have been described in other less genotypic terms....

## POWER, INFLUENCE, AND CHANGE

### Psychological Change

Since we shall define power in terms of influence, and influence in terms of psychological change, we begin with a discussion of change. We want to define change at a level of generality which includes changes in behavior, opinions, attitudes, goals, needs, values and all other aspects of the person's psychological field. We shall use the word "system" to refer to any such part of the life space.[1] Following Lewin (26, p. 305), the state of a system at time 1 will be noted $s_1(a)$.

Psychological change is defined as any alteration of the state of some system $a$ over time. The amount of change is measured by the size of the difference between the states of the system $a$ at time 1 and at time 2: ch (a) 5 $s_2$(a) 2 $s_1$(a).

Change in any psychological system may be conceptualized in terms of psychological forces. But it is important to note that the change must be coordinated to the resultant force of all the forces operating at the moment. Change in an opinion, for example, may be determined jointly by a driving force induced by another person, a restraining force corresponding to anchorage in a group opinion, and an own force stemming from the person's needs.

### Social Influence

Our theory of social influence and power is limited to influence on the person, P, produced by a social agent, O, where O can be either another person, a role, a norm, a group or a part of a group. We do not consider social influence exerted on a group.

The influence of O on system $a$ in the life space of P is defined as the resultant force on system $a$ which has its source in an act of O. This resultant force induced by O consists of two components: a force to change the system in the direction induced

John R. P. French Jr. and Bertram Raven, "The Bases of Social Power," in *Studies in Social Power*, ed. Dorwin P. Cartwright. Ann Arbor, MI: Institute for Social Research, University of Michigan, 1959, pp. 150–167. Reprinted by permission of the publisher.

by O and an opposing resistance set up by the same act of O.

By this definition the influence of O does not include P's own forces nor the forces induced by other social agents. Accordingly the "influence" of O must be clearly distinguished from O's "control" of P. O may be able to induce strong forces on P to carry out an activity (i.e., O exerts strong influence on P); but if the opposing forces induced by another person or by P's own needs are stronger, then P will locomote in an opposite direction (i.e., O does not have control over P). Thus psychological change in P can be taken as an operational definition of the social influence of O on P only when the effects of other forces have been eliminated.

Commonly, social influence takes place through an intentional act on the part of O. However, we do not want to limit our definition of "act" to such conscious behavior. Indeed, influence might result from the passive presence of O, with no evidence of speech or overt movement. A policeman's standing on a corner may be considered an act of an agent for the speeding motorist. Such acts of the inducing agent will vary in strength, for O may not always utilize all of his power. The policeman, for example, may merely stand and watch or act more strongly by blowing his whistle at the motorist.

The influence exerted by an act need not be in the direction intended by O. The direction of the resultant force on P will depend on the relative magnitude of the induced force set up by the act of O and the resisting force in the opposite direction which is generated by that same act. In cases where O intends to influence P in a given direction, a resultant force in the same direction may be termed positive influence whereas a resultant force in the opposite direction may be termed negative influence....

### Social Power

The strength of power of O/P in some system $a$ is defined as the maximum potential ability of O to influence P in $a$.

By this definition influence is kinetic power, just as power is potential influence. It is assumed that O is capable of various acts which, because of some more or less enduring relation to P, are able to exert influence on P.[2] O's power is measured by his maximum possible influence, though he may often choose to exert less than his full power.

An equivalent definition of power may be stated in terms of the resultant of two forces set up by the act of O: one in the direction of O's influence attempt and another resisting force in the opposite direction. Power is the maximum resultant of these two forces:

$$\text{Power of O/P}(a)\ 5\ (f_{a,x} - f_{\overline{a,x}})^{\max}$$

where the source of both forces is an act of O.

Thus, the power of O with respect to system $a$ of P is equal to the maximum resultant force of two forces set up by any possible act of O: (a) the force which O can set up on the system $a$ to change in the direction x, (b) the resisting force,[3] in the opposite direction. Whenever the first component force is greater than the second, positive power exists; but if the second component force is greater than the first, then O has negative power over P.

For certain purposes it is convenient to define the range of power as the set of all systems within which O has power of strength greater than zero. A husband may have a broad range of power over his wife, but a narrow range of power over his employer. We shall use the term "magnitude of power" to denote the summation of O's power over P in all systems of his range.

### The Dependence of s(a) on O

We assume that any change in the state of a system is produced by a change in some factor upon which it is functionally dependent. The state of an opinion, for example, may change because of a change either in some internal factor such as a need or in some external factor such as the arguments of O. Likewise the maintenance of the same state of a system is produced by the stability or lack of change in the internal and external factors. In general, then, psychological change and stability can be conceptualized in terms of dynamic dependence. Our interest is focused on the special case of dependence on an external agent, O (31).

In many cases the initial state of the system has the character of a quasi-stationary equilibrium with a central force field around $s_1(a)$ (26, p. 106). In such cases we may derive a tendency toward retrogression to the original state as soon as the force induced by O is removed....

Consider the example of three separated employees who have been working at the same steady level of production despite normal, small fluctuations in the work environment. The supervisor orders each to increase his production, and the level of each goes up from 100 to 115 pieces per day. After a week of producing at the new rate of 115 pieces per day, the supervisor is removed for a week. The production of employee A immediately returns to 100 but B and C return to only 110 pieces per day. Other things being equal, we can infer that A's new rate was completely dependent on his supervisor whereas the new rate of B and C was dependent on the supervisor only to the extent of 5 pieces. Let us further assume that when the supervisor returned, the production of B and of C returned to 115 without further orders from the supervisor. Now another month goes by during which B and C maintain a steady 115 pieces per day. However, there is a difference between them: B's level of production still depends on O to the extent of 5 pieces whereas C has come to rely on his own sense of obligation to obey the order of his legitimate supervisor rather than on the supervisor's external pressure for the maintenance of his 115 pieces per day. Accordingly, the next time the supervisor departs, B's production again drops to 110 but C's remains at 115 pieces per day. In cases like employee B, the degree of dependence is contingent on the perceived probability that O will observe the state of the system and note P's

conformity (5, 6, 11, 12, 23). The level of observability will in turn depend on both the nature of the system (e.g., the difference between a covert opinion and overt behavior) and on the environmental barriers to observation (e.g., O is too far away from P)....

## THE BASES OF POWER

By the basis of power we mean the relationship between O and P which is the source of that power. It is rare that we can say with certainty that a given empirical case of power is limited to one source. Normally, the relation between O and P will be characterized by several qualitatively different variables which are bases of power.... Although there are undoubtedly many possible bases of power which may be distinguished, we shall here define five which seem especially common and important. These five bases of O's power are: (1) reward power, based on P's perception that O has the ability to mediate rewards for him; (2) coercive power, based on P's perception that O has the ability to mediate punishments for him; (3) legitimate power, based on the perception by P that O has a legitimate right to prescribe behavior for him; (4) referent power, based on P's identification with O; (5) expert power, based on the perception that O has some special knowledge or expertness....

### Reward Power

Reward power is defined as power whose basis is the ability to reward. The strength of the reward power of O/P increases with the magnitude of the rewards which P perceives that O can mediate for him. Reward power depends on O's ability to administer positive valences and to remove or decrease negative valences. The strength of reward power also depends upon the probability that O can mediate the reward, as perceived by P. A common example of reward power is the addition of a piece-work rate in the factory as an incentive to increase production.

The new state of the system induced by a promise of reward (for example, the factory worker's increased level of production) will be highly dependent on O. Since O mediates the reward, he controls the probability that P will receive it. Thus P's new rate of production will be dependent on his subjective probability that O will reward him for conformity minus his subjective probability that O will reward him even if he returns to his old level. Both probabilities will be greatly affected by the level of observability of P's behavior....

The utilization of actual rewards (instead of promises) by O will tend over time to increase the attraction of P toward O and therefore the referent power of O over P. As we shall note later, such referent power will permit O to induce changes which are relatively independent. Neither rewards nor promises will arouse resistance in P, provided P considers it legitimate for O to offer rewards.

The range of reward power is specific to those regions within which O can reward P for conforming. The use of rewards to change systems within the range of reward power tends to increase reward power by increasing the probability attached to future promises. However, unsuccessful attempts to exert reward power outside the range of power would tend to decrease the power; for example, if O offers to reward P for performing an impossible act, this will reduce for P the probability of receiving future rewards promised by O.

### Coercive Power

Coercive power is similar to reward power in that it also involves O's ability to manipulate the attainment of valences. Coercive power of O/P stems from the expectation on the part of P that he will be punished by O if he fails to conform to the influence attempt. Thus, negative valences will exist in given regions of P's life space, corresponding to the threatened punishment by O. The strength of coercive power depends on the magnitude of the negative valence of the threatened punishment multiplied by the perceived probability that P can avoid the punishment by conformity, i.e., the probability of punishment for nonconformity minus the probability of punishment for conformity (11). Just as an offer of a piece-rate bonus in a factory can serve as a basis for reward power, so the ability to fire a worker if he falls below a given level of production will result in coercive power.

Coercive power leads to dependent change also, and the degree of dependence varies with the level of observability of P's conformity. An excellent illustration of coercive power leading to dependent change is provided by a clothes presser in a factory observed by Coch and French (3). As her efficiency rating climbed above average for the group the other workers began to "scapegoat" her. That the resulting plateau in her production was not independent of the group was evident once she was removed from the presence of the other workers. Her production immediately climbed to new heights.[5] ...

The distinction between these two types of power is important because the dynamics are different. The concept of "sanctions" sometimes lumps the two together despite their opposite effects. While reward power may eventually result in an independent system, the effects of coercive power will continue to be dependent. Reward power will tend to increase the attraction of P toward O; coercive power will decrease this attraction (11, 12). The valence of the region of behavior will become more negative, acquiring some negative valence from the threatened punishment. The negative valence of punishment would also spread to other regions of the life space. Lewin (25) has pointed out this distinction between the effects of rewards and punishment. In the case of threatened punishment, there will be a resultant force on P to leave the field entirely. Thus, to achieve conformity, O must not only place a strong negative valence in certain regions through threat of punishment, but O must also introduce restraining forces, or other strong valences, so as to prevent P from withdrawing completely from O's range of coercive power. Otherwise the probability of receiving the punishment, if P does not conform, will be too low to be effective.

### Legitimate Power

... There has been considerable investigation and speculation about socially prescribed behavior, particularly that which is specific to a given role or position. Linton (29) distinguishes group norms according to whether they are universals for everyone in the culture, alternatives (the individual having a choice as to whether or not to accept them), or specialties (specific to given positions). Whether we speak of internalized norms, role prescriptions and expectations (34), or internalized pressures (15), the fact remains that each individual sees certain regions toward which he should locomote, some regions toward which he should not locomote, and some regions toward which he may locomote if they are generally attractive for him. This applies to specific behaviors in which he may, should, or should not engage; it applies to certain attitudes or beliefs which he may, should, or should not hold. The feeling of "oughtness" may be an internalization from his parents, from his teachers, from his religion, or may have been logically developed from some idiosyncratic system of ethics. He will speak of such behaviors with expressions like "should," "ought to," or "has a right to." In many cases, the original source of the requirement is not recalled.

Though we have oversimplified such evaluations of behavior with a positive-neutral-negative trichotomy, the evaluation of behaviors by the person is really more one of degree. This dimension of evaluation, we shall call "legitimacy." Conceptually, we may think of legitimacy as a valence in a region which is induced by some internalized norm or value. This value has the same conceptual property as power,

namely an ability to induce force fields (26, p. 40–41)....

Legitimate power of O/P is here defined as that power which stems from internalized values in P which dictate that O has a legitimate right to influence P and that P has an obligation to accept this influence. We note that legitimate power is very similar to the notion of legitimacy of authority which has long been explored by sociologists, particularly by Weber (42), and more recently by Goldhammer and Shils (14). However, legitimate power is not always a role relation: P may accept an induction from O simply because he had previously promised to help O and he values his word too much to break the promise. In all cases, the notion of legitimacy involves some sort of code or standard, accepted by the individual, by virtue of which the external agent can assert his power. We shall attempt to describe a few of these values here.

**Bases for Legitimate Power.** Cultural values constitute one common basis for the legitimate power of one individual over another. O has characteristics which are specified by the culture as giving him the right to prescribe behavior for P, who may not have these characteristics. These bases, which Weber (42) has called the authority of the "eternal yesterday," include such things as age, intelligence, caste, and physical characteristics. In some cultures, the aged are granted the right to prescribe behavior for others in practically all behavior areas. In most cultures, there are certain areas of behavior in which a person of one sex is granted the right to prescribe behavior for the other sex.

Acceptance of the social structure is another basis for legitimate power. If P accepts as right the social structure of his group, organization, or society, especially the social structure involving a hierarchy of authority, P will accept the legitimate authority of O who occupies a superior office in the hierarchy. Thus legitimate power in a formal organization is largely a relationship between offices rather than between persons. And the acceptance of an office as *right* is a basis for legitimate power—a judge has a right to levy fines, a foreman should assign work, a priest is justified in prescribing religious beliefs, and it is the management's prerogative to make certain decisions (10). However, legitimate power also involves the perceived right of the person to hold the office.

Designation by a legitimizing agent is a third basis for legitimate power. An influencer O may be seen as legitimate in prescribing behavior for P because he has been granted such power by a legitimizing agent whom P accepts. Thus a department head may accept the authority of his vice-president in a certain area because that authority has been specifically delegated by the president. An election is perhaps the most common example of a group's serving to legitimize the authority of one individual or office for other individuals in the group. The success of such legitimizing depends upon the acceptance of the legitimizing agent and procedure. In this case it depends ultimately on certain democratic values concerning election procedures. The election process is one of legitimizing a person's right to an office which already has a legitimate range of power associated with it.

**Range of Legitimate Power of O/P.** The areas in which legitimate power may be exercised are generally specified along with the designation of that power. A job description, for example, usually specifies supervisory activities and also designates the person to whom the job holder is responsible for the duties described. Some bases for legitimate authority carry with them a very broad range. Culturally derived bases for legitimate power are often especially broad. It is not uncommon to find cultures in which a member of a given caste can legitimately prescribe behavior for all members of lower castes in practically all regions. More common, however, are instances of legitimate power where the range is specifically and narrowly prescribed. A sergeant in the army is given a specific set of regions within which he can legitimately prescribe behavior for his men.

The attempted use of legitimate power which is outside of the range of legitimate power will decrease the legitimate power of the authority figure. Such use of power which is not legitimate will also decrease the attractiveness of O (11, 12, 36).

**Legitimate Power and Influence.** The new state of the system which results from legitimate power usually has high dependence on O though it may become independent. Here, however, the degree of dependence is not related to the level of observability. Since legitimate power is based on P's values, the source of the forces induced by O include both these internal values and O. O's induction serves to activate the values and to relate them to the system which is influenced, but thereafter the new state of the system may become directly dependent on the values with no mediation by O. Accordingly this new state will be relatively stable and consistent across varying environmental situations since P's values are more stable than his psychological environment....

### Referent Power

The referent power of O/P has its basis in the identification of P with O. By identification, we mean a feeling of oneness of P with O, or a desire for such an identity. If O is a person toward whom P is highly attracted, P will have a feeling of membership or a desire to join. If P is already closely associated with O he will want to maintain this relationship (39, 41). P's identification with O can be established or maintained if P behaves, believes, and perceives as O does. Accordingly O has the ability to influence P, even though P may be unaware of this referent power. A verbalization of such power by P might be, "I am like O, and therefore I shall behave or believe as O does," or "I want to be like O, and I will be more like O if I behave or believe as O does." The stronger the identification of P with O the greater the referent power of O/P....

We must try to distinguish between referent power and other types of power which might be operative at the same time. If a member is attracted to a group and he conforms to its norms only because he fears ridicule or expulsion from the group for nonconformity, we would call this coercive power. On the other hand if he conforms in order to obtain praise for conformity, it is a case of reward power.... Conformity with majority opinion is sometimes based on a respect for the collective wisdom of the group, in which case it is expert power. It is important to distinguish these phenomena, all grouped together elsewhere as "pressures toward uniformity," since the type of change which occurs will be different for different bases of power.

The concepts of "reference group" (40) and "prestige suggestion" may be treated as instances of referent power. In this case, O, the prestigeful person or group, is valued by P; because P desires to be associated or identified with O, he will assume attitudes or beliefs held by O. Similarly a negative reference group which O dislikes and evaluates negatively may exert negative influence on P as a result of negative referent power.

It has been demonstrated that the power which we designate as referent power is especially great when P is attracted to O (2, 7, 8, 9, 13, 23, 30). In our terms, this would mean that the greater the attraction, the greater the identification, and consequently the greater the referent power. In some cases, attraction or prestige may have a specific basis, and the range of referent power will be limited accordingly: a group of campers may have great referent power over a member regarding campcraft, but considerably less effect on other regions (30). However, we hypothesize that the greater the attraction of P toward O, the broader the range of referent power of O/P....

### Expert Power

The strength of the expert power of O/P varies with the extent of the knowledge or perception which P attributes to O within a given area. Probably P evaluates O's expertness in relation to his own knowledge as well as against an absolute standard. In any case expert power results in primary social influence on P's cognitive structure and probably not on other types of systems. Of course changes in the cognitive structure can change the direction of forces and hence of locomotion, but such a change of behavior is secondary social influence. Expert power has been demonstrated experimentally (8, 33). Accepting an attorney's advice in legal matters is a common example of expert influence; but there are many instances based on much less knowledge, such as the acceptance by a stranger of directions given by a native villager.

Expert power, where O need not be a member of P's group, is called "informational power" by Deutsch and Gerard (4). This type of expert power must be distinguished from influence based on the content of communication as described by Hovland et al. (17, 18, 24). The influence of the content of a communication upon an opinion is presumably a secondary influence produced after the *primary* influence (i.e., the acceptance of the information). Since power is here defined in terms of primary changes, the influence of the content on a related opinion is not a case of expert power as we have defined it, but the initial acceptance of the validity of the content does seem to be based on expert power or referent power ....

The range of expert power, we assume, is more delimited than that of referent power. Not only is it restricted to cognitive systems but the expert is seen as having superior knowledge or ability in very specific areas, and his power will be limited to these areas, though some "halo effect" might occur. Recently, some of our renowned physical scientists have found quite painfully that their expert power in physical sciences does not extend to regions involving international politics. Indeed, there is some evidence that the attempted exertion of expert power outside of the range of expert power will reduce that expert power. An undermining of confidence seems to take place.

## SUMMARY

We have distinguished five types of power: referent power, expert power, reward power, coercive power, and legitimate power. These distinctions led to the following hypotheses.

1. For all five types, the stronger the basis of power, the greater the power.
2. For any type of power the size of the range may vary greatly, but in general referent power will have the broadest range.
3. Any attempt to utilize power outside the range of power will tend to reduce the power.
4. A new state of a system produced by reward power or coercive power will be highly dependent on O, and the more observable P's conformity the more dependent the state. For the other three types of power, the new state is usually dependent, at least in the beginning, but in any case the level of observability has no effect on the degree of dependence.
5. Coercion results in decreased attraction of P toward O and high resistance; reward power results in increased attraction and low resistance.
6. The more legitimate the coercion, the less it will produce resistance and decreased attraction.

## NOTES

1. The word "system" is here used to refer to a whole or to a part of the whole.
2. The concept of power has the conceptual property of *potentiality*; but it seems useful to restrict this potential influence to more or less enduring power relations between O and P by excluding from the definition of power those cases where the potential influence is so momentary or so changing that it cannot be predicted from the existing relationship. Power is a useful concept for describing social structure only if it has a certain stability over time; it is useless if every momentary social stimulus is viewed as actualizing social power.
3. We define resistance to an attempted induction as a force in the opposite direction which is set up by the same act of O. It must be distinguished from opposition which is defined as existing opposing forces which do not have their source in the same act of O. For example, a boy might resist his mother's order to eat spinach because of the manner of the induction attempt, and at the same time he might oppose it because he didn't like spinach.
4. Miller (32) assumes that all living systems have this character. However, it may be that some systems in the life space do not have this elasticity.
5. Though the primary influence of coercive power is dependent, it often produces secondary changes which are independent. Brainwashing, for example, utilizes coercive power to produce many primary changes in the life space of the prisoner, but these dependent changes can lead to identification with the aggressor and hence to secondary changes in ideology which are independent.

## REFERENCES

1. Asch, S. E. *Social psychology*. New York: Prentice-Hall, 1952.
2. Back, K. W. Influence through social communication. *J. Abnorm. Soc. Psychol.*, 1951, 46, 9–23.
3. Coch, L., & French, J. R. P., Jr. Overcoming resistance to change. *Hum. Relat.*, 1948, 1, 512–532.
4. Deutsch, M., & Gerard, H. B. A study of normative and informational influences upon individual judgment. *J. Abnorm. Soc. Psychol.*, 1955, 51, 629–636.
5. Dittes, J. E., & Kelley, H. H. Effects of different conditions of acceptance upon conformity to group norms. *J. Abnorm. Soc. Psychol.*, 1956, 53, 100–107.
6. Festinger, L. An analysis of compliant behavior. In Sherif, M., & Wilson, M. O., eds., *Group relations at the crossroads*. New York: Harper, 1953, 232–256.
7. Festinger, L. Informal social communication. *Psychol. Rev.*, 1950, 57, 271–282.

8. Festinger, L., Gerard, H. B., Hymovitch, B., Kelley, H. H., & Raven, B. H. The influence process in the presence of extreme deviates. *Hum. Relat.*, 1952, 5, 327–346.

9. Festinger, L., Schachter, S., & Back, K. The operation of group standards. In Cartwright, D., & Zander, A. *Group dynamics: research and theory.* Evanston: Row, Peterson, 1953, 204–223.

10. French, J. R. P., Jr., Israel, Joachim & Ås, Dagnn. "Arbeidernes medvirkning i industribedriften. En eksperimentell undersøkelse." Institute for Social Research, Oslo, Norway, 1957.

11. French, J. R. P., Jr., Levinger, G., & Morrison, H. W. The legitimacy of coercive power. In preparation.

12. French, J. R. P., Jr., & Raven, B. H. An experiment in legitimate and coercive power. In preparation.

13. Gerard, H. B. The anchorage of opinions in face-to-face groups. *Hum. Relat.*, 1954, 7, 313–325.

14. Goldhammer, H., & Shils, E. A. Types of power and status. *Amer. J. Sociol.*, 1939, 45, 171–178.

15. Herbst, P. G. Analysis and measurement of a situation. *Hum. Relat.*, 1953, 2, 113–140.

16. Hochbaum, G. M. Self confidence and reactions to group pressures. *Amer. Soc. Rev.*, 1954, 19, 678–687.

17. Hovland, C. I., Lumsdaine, A. A., & Shefeld, F. D. *Experiments on mass communication.* Princeton: Princeton Univer. Press, 1949.

18. Hovland, C. I., & Weiss, W. The influence of source credibility on communication effectiveness. *Publ. Opin. Quart.*, 1951, 15, 635–650.

19. Jackson, J. M., & Saltzstein, H. D. The effect of person-group relationships on conformity processes. *J. Abnorm. Soc. Psychol.*, 1958, 57, 17–24.

20. Jahoda, M. Psychological issues in civil liberties. *Amer. Psychologist*, 1956, 11, 234–240.

21. Katz, D., & Schank, R. L. *Social psychology.* New York: Wiley, 1938.

22. Kelley, H. H., & Volkart, E. H. The resistance to change of group-anchored attitudes. *Amer. Soc. Rev.*, 1952, 17, 453–465.

23. Kelman, H. Three processes of acceptance of social influence: compliance, identification and internalization. Paper read at the meetings of the American Psychological Association, August 1956.

24. Kelman, H., & Hovland, C. I. "Reinstatement" of the communicator in delayed measurement of opinion change. *J. Abnorm. Soc. Psychol.*, 1953, 48, 327–335.

25. Lewin, K. *Dynamic theory of personality.* New York: McGraw-Hill, 1935, 114–170.

26. Lewin, K. *Field theory in social science.* New York: Harper, 1951.

27. Lewin, K., Lippitt, R., & White, R. K. Patterns of aggressive behavior in experimentally created social climates. *J. Soc. Psychol.*, 1939, 10, 271–301.

28. Lasswell, H. D., & Kaplan, A. *Power and society: A framework for political inquiry.* New Haven: Yale Univer. Press, 1950.

29. Linton, R. *The cultural background of personality.* New York: Appleton-Century-Crofts, 1945.

30. Lippitt, R., Polansky, N., Redl, F., & Rosen, S. The dynamics of power. *Hum. Relat.*, 1952, 5, 37–64.

31. March, J. G. An introduction to the theory and measurement of influence. *Amer. Polit. Sci. Rev.*, 1955, 49, 431–451.

32. Miller, J. G. Toward a general theory for the behavioral sciences. *Amer. Psychologist*, 1955, 10, 513–531.

33. Moore, H. T. The comparative influence of majority and expert opinion. *Amer. J. Psychol.*, 1921, 32, 16–20.

34. Newcomb, T. M. *Social psychology.* New York: Dryden, 1950.

35. Raven, B. H. The effect of group pressures on opinion, perception, and communication. Unpublished doctoral dissertation, University of Michigan, 1953.

36. Raven, B. H., & French, J. R. P., Jr. Group support, legitimate power, and social influence. *J. Person.*, 1958, 26, 400–409.

37. Rommetveit, R. *Social norms and roles.* Minneapolis: Univer. Minnesota Press, 1953.

38. Russell, B. *Power: A new social analysis.* New York: Norton, 1938.

39. Stotland, E., Zander, A., Burnstein, E., Wolfe, D., & Natsoulas, T. Studies on

the effects of identification. University of Michigan, Institute for Social Research. Forthcoming.

40. Swanson, G. E., Newcomb, T. M., & Hartley, E. L. *Readings in social psychology.* New York: Henry Holt, 1952.

41. Torrance, E. P., & Mason, R. Instructor effort to influence: An experimental evalu-

ation of six approaches. Paper presented at USAF-NRC Symposium on Personnel, Training, and Human Engineering. Washington, D.C., 1956.

42. Weber, M. *The theory of social and economic organization.* Oxford: Oxford Univer. Press, 1947.

## 23

# The Power of Power

*James G. March*

## 1.0 INTRODUCTION

*Power* is a major explanatory concept in the study of social choice. It is used in studies of relations among nations, of community decision making, of business behavior, and of small-group discussion. Partly because it conveys simultaneously overtones of the cynicism of *Realpolitik*, the glories of classical mechanics, the realism of elite sociology, and the comforts of anthropocentric theology, *power* provides a prime focus for disputation and exhortation in several social sciences.

Within this galaxy of nuances, I propose to consider a narrowly technical question: To what extent is one specific concept of power useful in the empirical analysis of mechanisms for social choice? ...

The specific concept of power I have in mind is the concept used in theories having the following general assumptions:

1. The choice mechanism involves certain basic components (individuals, groups, roles, behaviors, labels, etc.).
2. Some amount of power is associated with each of these components.
3. The responsiveness (as measured by some direct empirical observation) of the mechanism to each individual component is monotone increasing with the power associated with the individual component....

In order to explore the power of power in empirical theories of social choice, I propose to do two things: First, I wish to identify three different variations in this basic approach to power as an intervening variable to suggest the kinds of uses of *power*

with which we will be concerned. Second, I wish to examine six different classes of models of social choice that are generally consistent with what at least one substantial group of students means by *social power*....

## 2.0 THREE APPROACHES TO THE STUDY OF POWER

### 2.1 The Experimental Study

... This brief introduction is intended simply to provide a relatively coherent characterization of a class of approaches to the study of power....

**Conceptual Basis.** The experimental studies of power are generally Newtonian. Many of them are directly indebted to Lewin, who defined the power of *b* over *a* "as the quotient of the maximum force which *b* can induce on *a*, and the maximum resistance which *a* can offer."[1] In general, the experimental studies assume that the greater the power of the individual, the greater the changes induced (with given resistance) and the more successful the resistance to changes (with given pressure to change).

The experimental studies tend to be reductionist. Although they are ultimately (and sometimes immediately) interested in the power of one individual over another, they usually seek to reduce that relationship to more basic components. Thus, we distinguish between the power of behavior and the power of roles, and characterize specific individuals as a combination of behavior and roles.[2] Or, we distinguish factors

J. G. March, "The Power of Power," in *Varieties of Political Theory*, ed. David Easton. Englewood Cliffs, NJ: Prentice-Hall, 1966, pp. 39–70. Reprinted by permission of the author.

affecting the agent of influence, the methods of influence, and the agent subjected to influence.[3] ...

**Procedures.** The procedures used in this class of experimental studies are the classic ones. We determine power by some a priori measure or experimental manipulation, use a relatively simple force model to generate hypotheses concerning differences in outcomes from different treatments, and compare the observed outcomes with the predicted outcomes.…

**Results.** ... For present purposes, two general results are particularly germane:

(1) It is possible to vary power of a specific subject systematically and (within limits) arbitrarily in an experimental setting. This can be done by manipulating some elements of his reputation[4] or by manipulating some elements of his power experience.[5] This apparently innocuous—and certainly minimal—result is in fact not so unimportant. It permits us to reject certain kinds of social-choice models for certain kinds of situations.

(2) The effectiveness of a priori power (i.e., manipulated, or a priori measured power) in producing behavior change is highly variable. Although there are indications that some kinds of leadership behavior are exhibited by some people in several different groups,[6] most studies indicate that the effectiveness of specific individuals, specific social positions, and specific behaviors in producing behavior change varies with respect to the content and relevancy of subject matter,[7] group identifications,[8] and power base.[9] ...

### 2.2 The Community Study

A second major approach to the study of power can be called *the community power approach*; it is typical of, but not limited to, community studies.[10] ...

**Conceptual    Basis.** The    conceptual definition of power implicit (and often explicit) in the community studies is clearly

Newtonian. The first two "laws" of social choice form a simple definition:

1. Social choice will be a predictable extension of past choices unless power is exerted on the choice.
2. When power is exerted, the modification of the choice will be proportional to the power.

... The community power studies generally assume that the decisions made by the community are a function of the power exerted on the community by various power holders. They assume some kind of "power field" in which individual powers are summed to produce the final outcome.

The community studies are analytic in the sense that they attempt to infer the power of individuals within the community by observing (either directly or indirectly) their net effects on community choice. That is, they assume that a decision is some function of individual powers and the individual preferences. Hence, they observe the decision outcome and the preferences, and estimate the powers.

The community studies are personal in the sense that power is associated with specific individuals. The estimation procedures are designed to determine the power of an individual. This power, in turn, is viewed as some function of the resources (economic, social, etc.), position (office, role, etc.), and skill (choice of behavior, choice of allies, etc.); but the study and the analysis assume that it is meaningful to aggregate resource power, position power, and skill power into a single variable associated with the individual.

**Procedures.** ... The procedure most generally used involves some variation of asking individuals within the community to assess the relative power of other individuals in the community. Essentially the panel is given the following task: On the basis of past experience (both your own and that of other people with whom you have communicated), estimate the power of the following individuals.[11] ...

A second procedure involves the direct observation of decision outcomes and prior preferences over a series of decisions.[12] Essentially, we define a model relating power to decisions, draw a sample of observations, and estimate the power of individuals on the basis of that model and those observations....

**Results.** At a general level, the results of the community studies can be described in terms of three broad types of interests. First, we ask how power is distributed in the community. Second, we ask what relation exists between power and the possession of certain other socioeconomic attributes. Third, we ask how power is exerted.

With respect to the distribution of power, most studies indicate that most people in most communities are essentially powerless. They neither participate in the making of decisions directly nor accumulate reputations for power. Whatever latent control they may have, it is rarely exercised....

With respect to the exercise of power, the studies have focused on specialization, activation, and unity of power holders. Most studies have identified significant specialization in power: Different individuals are powerful with respect to different things. But most studies also have shown "general leaders": Some individuals have significant power in several areas. Some studies have reported a significant problem associated with power activation: the more powerful members of the community are not necessarily activated to use their power, while less powerful members may be hyperactivated.... Some studies indicate a network of associations, consultations, and agreements among the more powerful; other studies indicate rather extensive disagreement among the more powerful.[13]

### 2.3 The Institutional Study

The third alternative approach to the study of power is in one sense the most common of all. It is the analysis of the structure of institutions to determine the power structure within them. Such studies are the basis of much of descriptive political science. Systematic attempts to derive quantitative indices of power from an analysis of institutional structure are limited, however. The approach will be characterized here in terms of the game-theory version....

**Conceptual Basis.** ... We assume the general von Neumann concept of a game: There are $n$ players, each with a well-defined set of alternative strategies. Given the choice of strategies by the player (including the mutual choice of coalitions), there is a well-defined set of rules for determining the outcome of the game. The outcomes are evaluated by the individual players in terms of the individual orderings of preference. The Shapley value for the game to an individual player (or coalition of players) has several alternative intuitive explanations. It can be viewed as how much a rational person would be willing to pay in order to occupy a particular position in the game rather than some other position. It can be viewed as the expected marginal contribution of a particular position to a coalition if all coalitions are considered equally likely and the order in which positions are added to the coalition is random. It can be viewed as how much a rational player would expect to receive from a second rational player in return for his always selecting the strategy dictated by the second player. Or, it can be viewed simply as a computational scheme with certain desirable properties of uniqueness.

The Shapley value is impersonal. It is associated not with a specific player but rather with a specific position in the game. It is not conceived to measure the power of President Kennedy or President Eisenhower; it is conceived to measure the power of the Presidency....

... In the standard Newtonian versions of power, power is that which induces a modification of choice by the system. Quite commonly, we measure the power by the extent to which the individual is able to induce the system to provide resources of value to him. We are aware that power, in this sense, is a function of many variables; we suspect that informal alliances and allegiances influence behavior; and we commonly allege that power is dependent on information and intelligence as well as formal position.

Suppose that we want to assess the contribution to power of formal position alone. One way to do so would be an empirical study in which we would consider simultaneously all of the various contributing factors, apply some variant of a multiple regression technique, and determine the appropriate coefficients for the position variables. A second way would be an experimental study in which nonposition factors are systematically randomized. A third way would be the one taken by Shapley and Shubik. We can imagine a game involving position variables only (e.g., the formal legislative scheme), and we can assume rationality on the part of the participants and ask for the value of each position under that assumption. Since this value is a direct measure of the resources the individual can obtain from the system by virtue of his position in the game alone, it is a reasonable measure of the power of that position. Alternatively, we can view the resources themselves as power.[14]

**Procedures.** There are two main ways in which we can use the Shapley-Shubik index in an empirical study: (1) We can construct some sort of empirical index of power, make some assumptions about the relation between the empirical and a priori measures, and test the consistency of the empirical results with the a priori measures. Thus, we might assume that the empirical measure consists of the a priori measure plus an error term representing various other (non-position) factors. If we can make some assumptions about the nature of the "error," we can test the consistency. Or, (2), we can deduce some additional propositions from the model underlying the index and test those propositions....

**Results.** ... Riker has applied the basic Shapley-Shubik measure to the French Assembly to derive changes in power indices for the various parties in the French Assembly during the period 1953–54, as thirty-four migrations from one party to another produced sixty-one individual changes in affiliation.[15] ... The data did not support the hypothesis. In subsequent work, Riker has almost entirely abandoned the Shapley-Shubik approach.[16]

## 3.0 SIX MODELS OF SOCIAL CHOICE AND THE CONCEPT OF POWER

The three general approaches described above illustrate the range of possible uses of the concept of power, and include most of the recent efforts to use the concept in empirical research or in empirically oriented theory. I wish to use these three examples as a basis for exploring the utility of the concept of power in the analysis of systems for social choice....

I shall now consider six types of models of social choice, evaluate their consistency with available data, and consider the problems of the concept of power associated with them. By a *model*, I mean a set of statements about the way in which individual choices (or behavior) are transformed into social choices, and a procedure for using those statements to derive some empirically meaningful predictions. The six types of models are as follows:

1. Chance models, in which we assume that choice is a chance event, quite independent of power.
2. Basic force models, in which we assume that the components of the system exert all their power on the system with choice being a direct resultant of those powers.
3. Force activation models, in which we assume that not all the power of every component is exerted at all times.
4. Force-conditioning models, in which we assume that the power of the components is modified as a result of the outcome of past choices.

5. Force depletion models, in which we assume that the power of the components is modified as a result of the exertion of power on past choices.
6. Process models, in which we assume that choice is substantially independent of power but not a chance event....

## 3.1 Chance Models

Let us assume that there are no attributes of human beings affecting the output of a social-choice mechanism. Further, let us assume that the only factors influencing the output are chance factors, constrained perhaps by some initial conditions. There are a rather large number of such models, but it will be enough here to describe three in skeleton form.

*The Unconstrained Model.* We assume a set of choice alternatives given to the system. These might be all possible bargaining agreements in bilateral bargaining, all possible appropriations in a legislative scheme, or all experimentally defined alternatives in an experimental setting. Together with this set of alternatives, we have a probability function....

*The Equal-Power Model.* We assume a set of initial positions for the components of the system and some well-defined procedures for defining a social choice consistent with the assumption of equal power. For example, the initial positions might be arranged on some simple continuum. We might observe the initial positions with respect to wage rates in collective bargaining, with respect to legislative appropriations for space exploration, or with respect to the number of peas in a jar in an experimental group. A simple arithmetic mean of such positions is a social choice consistent with the assumption of equal power. In this chance model, we assume that the social choice is the equal-power choice plus some error term....

*The Encounter Model.* We assume only two possible choice outcomes: We can win or lose; the bill can pass or fail; we will take the left or right branch in the maze. At each encounter (social choice), there are two opposing teams. The probability of choosing a given alternative if the teams have an equal number of members is 0.5....

What are the implications of such models? Consider the encounter model. Suppose we imagine that each power encounter occurs between just two people chosen at random from the total population of the choice system. Further, assume that at each encounter we will decide who prevails by flipping a coin.[17]... A model of this general class has been used by Deutsch and Madow to generate a distribution of managerial performance and reputations.[18]

Similar kinds of results can be obtained from the unconstrained-chance model. If we assume that social choice is equi-probable among the alternatives and that individual initial positions are equi-probable among the alternatives, the only difference is that the number of alternatives is no longer necessarily two. In general, there will be more than two alternatives; as a result the probability of success will be less than 0.5 on every trial and the probability of a long-run record of spectacular success correspondingly less. For example, if we assume a dozen trials with ten alternatives, the probability of failing no more than once drops to about $10^{-10}$ (as compared with about 0.0032 in the two alternative cases).

Finally, generally similar results are obtained from the equal-power model.... Our measures of success now become not the number (or proportion) of successes but rather the mean deviation of social choices from individual positions, and we generate from the model a distribution of such distances for a given number of trials.[19] ...

To what extent is it possible to reject the chance models in studies of social choice? ... The answer depends on an evaluation of four properties of the chance models that are potentially inconsistent with data either from field studies or from the laboratory.

First, we ask whether power is stable over time. With most of the chance models, knowing who won in the past or who had a reputation for winning in the past would not help us to predict who would win in the future. Hence, if we can predict the outcome of future social choices by weighting current positions with weights derived from past observations or from a priori consider-ations, we will have some justification for rejecting the chance model. Some efforts have been made in this direction, but with mixed results.[20] ...

Second, we ask whether power is stable over subject matter. Under the chance models, persons who win in one subject-matter area would be no more likely to win in another area than would people who lost in the first area. Thus, if we find a greater-than-chance overlap from one area to another, we would be inclined to reject the chance model. The evidence on this point is conflicting....

Third, we ask whether power is cor-related with other personal attributes.... Without any exception of which I am aware, the studies do show a greater-than-chance relation between power and such personal attributes as economic status, political office, and ethnic group. We can-not account under the simple chance model for the consistent underrepresentation of the poor, the unelected, and the Negro.

And fourth, we ask whether power is *susceptible to experimental manipulation.* If the chance model were correct, we could not systematically produce variations in who wins by manipulating power. Here the experimental evidence is fairly clear. It is possible to manipulate the results of choice mechanisms by manip-ulating personal attributes or personal reputations....

Chance models are extremely naïve; they are the weakest test we can imagine. Yet we have had some difficulty in rejecting them, and in some situations it is not clear that we can reject them.... Possibly, how-ever, our difficulty is not with the amount of order in the world, but with the concept of power....

### 3.2 Basic Force Models
Suppose we assume that power is real and controlling, and start with a set of mod-els that are closely linked with classical mechanics although the detailed form is somewhat different from mechanics. In purest form, the simple force models can be represented in terms of functions that make the resultant social choice a weighted aver-age of the individual initial positions—the weights being the power attached to the various individuals....

The force models... are reasonably well-defined and pose no great technical prob-lems, and the estimation procedures are straightforward. The observations required are no more than the observations required by any model that assumes some sort of power. What are the implications of the models? First, unless combined with a set of constraints (such as the power-structure constraints of the French and Harary formu-lation), the models say nothing about the distribution of power in a choice system. Thus, there is no way to test their appar-ent plausibility by comparing actual power distributions with derived distributions.

Second, in all of the models, the distance between the initial position of the indi-vidual and the social choice (or expected social choice) is inversely proportional to the power when we deal with just two individuals.... With more than two indi-viduals, the relation between distance and power becomes more complex, depend-ing on the direction and magnitude of the various forces applied to the system. Since the models are directly based on the ideas of center of mass, these results are not sur-prising. Given these results, we can evalu-ate the models if we have an independent measure of power, such as the Shapley-Shubik measure. Otherwise, they become, as they frequently have, simply a definition of power.

Third, we can evaluate the reasonable-ness of this class of models by a few general implications....

Insofar as the determinate models are concerned, both experimental and field observations make it clear that the models are not accurate portrayals of social choice. In order for the models to be accepted, the $m_i$ (as defined in the models) must be stable. As far as I know, no one has ever reported data suggesting that the $m_i$ are stable in a determinate model....

The basis for rejecting the simple force models ... is twofold:

(1) There seems to be general consensus that either potential power is different from actually exerted power or that actually exerted power is variable. If, while potential power is stable, there are some unknown factors that affect the actual exercise of power, the simple force models will not fit; they assume power is stable, but they also assume that power exerted is equal to power. If actually exerted power is unstable, the simple force models will fit only if we can make some plausible assertions about the nature of the instability....

(2) There appears to be ample evidence that power is not strictly exogenous to the exercise of power and the results of that exercise. Most observers would agree that present reputations for power are at least in part a function of the results of past encounters. Although the evidence for the proposition is largely experimental, most observers would probably also agree that power reputation, in turn, affects the results of encounters. If these assertions are true, the simple force model will fit in the case of power systems that are in equilibrium, but it will not fit in other systems.

These objections to the simple force model are general; we now need to turn to models that attempt to deal with endogenous shifts in power and with the problem of power activation or exercise.... We will consider three classes of models, all of which are elaborations of the simple force models. The first class can be viewed as *activation models*. They assume that power is a potential and that the exercise of power involves some mechanism of activation. The second class can be described as *conditioning models*. They assume that power is partly endogenous—specifically that apparent power leads to actual power. The third class can be classified as *depletion models*. They assume that power is a stock, and that exercise of power leads to a depletion of the stock.

### 3.3 Force Activation Models

All of the models considered thus far accept the basic postulate that all power is exerted all of the time. In fact, few observers of social-choice systems believe this to be true, either for experimental groups or for natural social systems. With respect to the latter, Schulze argues that "the Cibola study appears to document the absence of any neat, constant, and direct relationship between *power as a potential for determinative action*, and *power as determinative action itself*."[21] ...

Consider the problem of relating the activation models to observations of reality....

Suppose, for example, that we have some measures of the activation of individual members of a modern community. One such measure might be the proportion of total time devoted by the individual to a specific issue of social choice. We could use such a measure, observations of initial positions and social choices, and one of the basic force models to assign power indices (potential power) to the various individuals in the community. Similarly, if we took a comparable measure in an experimental group (e.g., some function of the frequency of participation in group discussions), we could determine some power indices. Because direct observational measures of the degree of power utilization are not ordinarily the easiest of measurements to take, the partition version of the model has an important comparative advantage from the point of view of estimation problems.... We need only observe whether the individual involved did or did not participate in a choice, rather than the degree of his participation.

If we are unable or do not choose to observe the extent of utilization directly, we can, at least in principle, estimate it from other factors in the situation. For example, if we can determine the opportunity costs[22] to the individual of the exercise of power, we might be able to assume that the individual will exercise power only up to the point at which the marginal cost equals the marginal gain. If we can further assume something about the relation between the exercise of power and the return from that exercise, we can use the opportunity costs to estimate the power of utilization. The general idea of opportunity costs, or subjective importance,[23] as a dimension of power has considerable intuitive appeal....

The second major alternative, given the assumption of constant potential power, is also to assume a constant utilization of power over all choices.... If both utilization and potential power are constant, we are back to the simple force model and can estimate the product ... in the same way we previously established the $m_i$. Under such circumstances, the introduction of the concepts of power utilization and power potential is unnecessary and we can deal directly with power exercised as the core variable.[24]

The force activation model has been compared with empirical data to a limited extent. Hanson and Miller undertook to determine independently the potential power and power utilization of community members and to predict from those measures the outcome of social choices.[25] Potential power was determined by a priori theory; utilization was determined by interviews and observation. The results, as previously noted, were consistent not only with the force activation model but also with a number of other models. The French and Harary graph theory models are essentially activation force models (with activation associated with a communication structure) and they have been compared generally with experimental data for the equal potential power case. The comparison suggests a general consistency of the data with several alternate models....

It is clear from a consideration both of the formal properties of activation models and of the problems observers have had with such models that they suffer from their excessive a posteriori explanatory power. If we observe that power exists and is stable and if we observe that sometimes weak people seem to triumph over strong people, we are tempted to rely on an activation hypothesis to explain the discrepancy.

But if we then try to use the activation hypothesis to predict the results of social-choice procedures, we discover that the data requirements of "plausible" activation models are quite substantial. As a result, we retreat to what are essentially degenerate forms of the activation model—retaining some of the form but little of the substance. This puts us back where we started, looking for some device to explain our failures in prediction. Unfortunately, the next two types of models simply complicate life further rather than relieve it.

### 3.4 Force-Conditioning Models

The conditioning models take as given either the basic force model or the force activation model. The only modification is to replace a constant power resource with a variable power resource. The basic mechanisms are simple: (1) People have power because they are believed to have power. (2) People are believed to have power because they have been observed to have power....

Furthermore, it is clear that if power is accurately specified by observations and if social choices are precisely and uniquely specified by the power distribution, then the conditioning models are relatively uninteresting. They become interesting because of non-uniqueness in the results of the exercise of power or because of non-uniqueness in the attributions of power....

Models of this general class have not been explored in the power literature. Experimental studies have demonstrated the realism of each of the two mechanisms—success improves reputation, reputation improves success. As a result, conditioning models cannot be rejected out of hand. Moreover, they lead directly to some interesting and relevant predictions.

In most of the literature on the measurement of power, there are two nagging problems—the problem of the chameleon who frequently jumps in and agrees with an already decided issue and the satellite who, though he himself has little power, is highly correlated with a high-power person. Since these problems must be at least as compelling for the individual citizen as they are for the professional observer, they have served as a basis for a number of strong attacks on the reputational approach to the attribution of power. But the problem changes somewhat if we assume that reputations affect outcomes. Now the chameleon and the satellite are not measurement problems but important phenomena. The models will predict that an association with power will lead to power. Whether the association is by chance or by deliberate imitation, the results are substantially the same.

To the best of my knowledge, no formal efforts have been made to test either the satellite prediction in a real-world situation, or to test some of its corollaries, which include:

1. Informal power is unstable. Let the king-maker beware of the king.
2. Unexercised power disappears. Peace is the enemy of victory.
3. Undifferentiated power diffuses. Beware of your allies lest they become your equals....

### 3.5 Force Depletion Models

Within the conditioning models, success breeds success. But there is another class of plausible models in which success breeds failure. As in the conditioning models, we assume that power varies over time. As in the force activation models, we assume that not all power is exercised at every point in time.

The basic idea of the model is plausible. We consider power to be a resource. The exercise of power depletes that resource. Subject to additions to the power supply, the more power a particular component in the system exercises, the less power there is available for that component to use....

Under this scheme, it is quite possible for power to shift as a result of variations in the rates of power utilization. So long as additions to the power supply are independent of the exercise of power, the use of power today means that we will have less to use

tomorrow. We can show various conditions for convergence and divergence of power resources or exercised power. We can also generate a set of aphorisms parallel to—but somewhat at variance with—the conditioning model aphorisms:

1. Formal power is unstable. Let the king beware of the kingmaker.
2. Exercised power is lost. Wars are won by neutrals.
3. Differentiation wastes power. Maintain the alliance as long as possible....

Some of the studies of interpersonal relations in organizations indicate that the exercise of power is often dysfunctional with regard to the effective exercise of power in the future. In those cases, the mechanism ordinarily postulated involves the impact of power on sentiments[26] rather than our simple resource notion. Nonetheless, the grosser attributes of observed behavior in such studies are consistent with the gross predictions of models that view power as a stock....

... From a simple concept of power in a simple force model, we have moved to a concept of power that is further and further removed from the basic intuitive notions captured by the simple model, and to models in which simple observations of power are less and less useful. It is only a short step from this point to a set of models that are conceptually remote from the original conception of a social-choice system.

### 3.6 Process Models

Suppose that the choice system we are studying is not random. Suppose further that power really is a significant phenomenon in the sense that it can be manipulated systematically in the laboratory and can be used to explain choice in certain social-choice systems. I think that both those suppositions are reasonable. But let us further suppose that there is a class of social-choice systems in which power is insignificant. Unless we treat *power* as true by definition, I think that suppression is reasonable.

If we treat *power* as a definition, I think it is reasonable to suppose there is a class of social-choice systems in which power measurement will be unstable and useless.

Consider the following process models of social choice as representative of this class:

*An Exchange Model.* We assume that the individual components in the system prefer certain of the alternative social choices, and that the system has a formal criterion for making the final choices (e.g., majority vote, unanimity, clearing the market). We also assume that there is some medium of exchange by which individual components seek to arrange agreements (e.g., exchanges of money or votes) that are of advantage to themselves. These agreements, plus the formal criterion for choice, determine the social decision. This general type of market system is familiar enough for economic systems and political systems.[27] It is also one way of viewing some modern theories of interpersonal influence[28] in which sentiments on one dimension ("I like you") are exchanged for sentiments on another ("You like my pots") in order to reach a social choice ("We like us and we like my pots").

*A Problem-Solving Model.* We assume that each of the individual components in the system has certain information and skills relevant to a problem of social choice, and that the system has a criterion for solution. We postulate some kind of process by which the system calls forth and organizes the information and skills so as systematically to reduce the difference between its present position and a solution. This general type of system is familiar to students of individual and group problem solving.[29]

*A Communication-Diffusion Model.* We assume that the components in the system are connected by some formal or informal communication system by which information is diffused through the system. We postulate some process by which the information is sent and behavior modified, one component at a time, until a social position is reached. This general type of system is familiar to many students of individual behavior in a social context.[30]

*A Decision-Making Model.* We assume that the components in the system have preferences with respect to social choices, and that the system has a procedure for rendering choices. The system and the components operate under two limitations:

1. Overload: They have more demands on their attention than they can meet in the time available.
2. Undercomprehension: The world they face is much more complicated than they can handle.

Thus, although we assume that each of the components modifies its behavior and its preferences over time in order to achieve a subjectively satisfactory combination of social choices, it is clear that different parts of the system contribute to different decisions in different ways at different times. This general type of system is a familiar model of complex organizations.[31]

In each of these process models, it is possible to attribute power to the individual components. We might want to say that a man owning a section of land in Iowa has more power in the economic system than a man owning a section of land in Alaska. We might want to say that, in a pot-selling competition, a man with great concern over his personal status has less power than a man with less concern. We might want to say that a man who knows Russian has more power than a man who does not in a group deciding the relative frequency of adjectival phrases in Tolstoi and Dostoievski. Or, we might want to say that, within an organization, a subunit that has problems has more power than a subunit that does not have problems. But I think we would probably not want to say any of these things. The concept of power does not contribute much to our understanding of systems that can be represented in any of these ways.

I am impressed by the extent to which models of this class seem to be generally consistent with the reports of ...[32] students of political systems and other relatively large (in terms of number of people involved) systems of social choice. "Observation of certain local communities makes it appear that inclusive over-all organization for many general purposes is weak or nonexistent," Long writes. "Much of what occurs seems to just happen with accidental trends becoming cumulative over time and producing results intended by nobody. A great deal of the communities' activities consist of undirected cooperation of particular social structures, each seeking particular goals and, in doing so, meshing with the others."[33]

Such descriptions of social choice have two general implications. On the one hand, if a system has the properties suggested by such students as Coleman, Long, Riesman, Lindblom, and Dahl, power will be a substantially useless concept. In such systems, the measurement of power is feasible, but it is not valuable in calculating predictions....

On the other hand, the process models—and particularly the decision-making process models—look technically more difficult with regard to estimation and testing than the more complex modifications of the force model. We want to include many more discrete and nominal variables, many more discontinuous functions, and many more rare combinations of events....

## 4.0 THE POWER OF POWER

... Although *power* and *influence* are useful concepts for many kinds of situations, they have not greatly helped us to understand many of the natural social-choice mechanisms to which they have traditionally been applied.

The extent to which we have used the concept of power fruitlessly is symptomatic of three unfortunate temptations associated with power:

*Temptation No. 1: The Obviousness of Power.* To almost anyone living in contemporary society, power is patently real. We can scarcely talk about our daily life or major political and social phenomena without talking about power. Our discussions of political machinations consist largely of stories of negotiations among the influentials. Our analyses of social events are punctuated with calculations of power. Our interpretations of organizational life are built on evaluations of who does and who does not have power. Our debates of the grand issues of social, political,

and economic systems are funneled into a consideration of whether *i* has too little power and *j* has too much.

Because of this ubiquity of power, we are inclined to assume that it is real and meaningful. There must be some fire behind the smoke. "I take it for granted that in every human organization some individuals have more influence over key decisions than do others."[34] Most of my biases in this regard are conservative, and I am inclined to give some credence to the utility of social conceptual validation. I think, however, that we run the risk of treating the social validation of power as more compelling than it is simply because the social conditioning to a simple force model is so pervasive.

*Temptation No. 2: The Importance of Measurement.* The first corollary of the obviousness of power is the importance of the measurement problem. Given the obviousness of power, we rarely reexamine the basic model by which social choice is viewed as some combination of individual choices, the combination being dependent on the power of the various individuals. Since we have a persistent problem discovering a measurement procedure that consistently yields results which are consistent with the model, we assert a measurement problem and a problem of the concept of power. We clarify and reclarify the concept, and we define and redefine the measures....

Although I have some sympathy with these efforts, I think our perseveration may be extreme. At the least, we should consider whether subsuming all our problems under the rubric of conceptual and measurement problems may be too tempting. I think we too often ask *how* to measure power when we should ask *whether* to measure power. The measurement problem and the model problem have to be solved simultaneously.

*Temptation No. 3: The Residual Variance.* The second corollary of the obviousness of power is the use of *power* as a residual category for explanation. We always have some unexplained variance in our data—results that simply cannot be explained within the theory. It is always tempting to give that residual variance some name. Some of us are inclined to talk about God's will; others talk about errors of observation; still others talk about some named variable (e.g., power, personality, extrasensory perception). Such naming can be harmless; we might just as well have some label for our failures. But where the unexplained variance is rather large, as it often is when we consider social-choice systems, we can easily fool ourselves into believing that we know something simply because we have a name for our errors. In general, I think we can roughly determine the index of the temptation to label errors by computing the ratio of uses of the variable for prediction to the uses for a posteriori explanation. On that calculation, I think power exhibits a rather low ratio, even lower than such other problem areas as personality and culture....

I have tried to suggest that the power of power depends on the extent to which a predictive model requires and can make effective use of such a concept. Thus, it depends on the kind of system we are confronting, the amount and kinds of data we are willing or able to collect, and the kinds of estimation and validation procedures we have available to us. Given our present empirical and test technology, power is probably a useful concept for many short-run situations involving the direct confrontations of committed and activated participants. Such situations can be found in natural settings, but they are more frequent in the laboratory. Power is probably not a useful concept for many long-run situations involving problems of component-overload and undercomprehension. Such situations can be found in the laboratory but are more common in natural settings. Power may become more useful as a concept if we can develop analytic and empirical procedures for coping with the more complicated forms of force models, involving activation, conditioning, and depletion of power.

Thus, the answer to the original question is tentative and mixed. Provided some rather restrictive assumptions are met, the concept of power and a simple force model represent a reasonable approach to the study of social choice. Provided some rather substantial estimation and analysis problems can be solved, the concept of power and more elaborate force models represent a reasonable approach. On the whole, however, power is a disappointing concept. It gives us surprisingly little purchase in reasonable models of complex systems of social choice.

## NOTES

1. Kurt Lewin, *Field Theory in Social Science* (New York: Harper & Row, Publishers, 1951), p. 336.

2. See J. G. March, "Measurement Concepts in the Theory of Influence," *Journal of Politics*, 14 (1957), 202–26.

3. Dorwin Cartwright, "Influence, Leadership, Control," in *Handbook of Organizations*, ed. J. G. March (Chicago: Rand McNally & Co., 1965).

4. See C. I. Hovland, I. L. Janis, and H. H. Kelley, *Communication and Persuasion* (New Haven: Yale University Press, 1953).

5. See B. Mausner, "The Effect of Prior Reinforcement on the Interaction of Observer Pairs," *Journal of Abnormal and Social Psychology*, 49 (1954), 65–68, and "The Effects of One Partner's Success or Failure in a Relevant Task on the Interaction of Observer Pairs," *Journal of Abnormal and Social Psychology*, 49 (1954), 577–60.

6. See E. F. Borgatta, A. S. Couch, and R. F. Bales, "Some Findings Relevant to the Great Man Theory of Leadership," *American Sociological Review*, 19 (1954), 755–59.

7. J. G. March, "Influence Measurement in Experimental and Semi-Experimental Groups," Sociometry, 19 (1956), 260–71.

8. Cartwright, *Studies in Social Power.*

9. Cartwright, *Studies in Social Power.*

10. For reviews of the literature, see P. H. Rossi, "Community Decision Making," *Administrative Science Quarterly*, 1 (1957), 415–43; and L. J. R. Henson, "In the Footsteps of Community Power," American Political Science Review, 55 (1961), 817–30.

11. See F. Hunter, *Community Power Structures* (Chapel Hill: University of North Carolina Press, 1953).

12. See R. A. Dahl, *Who Governs?* (New Haven: Yale University Press, 1961).

13. See W. H. Form and W. V. D'Antonio, "Integration and Cleavage among Community Influentials in Two Border Cities," *American Sociological Review*, 24 (1959), 804–14; and H. Scoble, "Leadership Hierarchies and Political Issues in a New England Town," in *Community Political Systems*, ed. Morris Janowitz (New York: Free Press of Glencoe, Inc., 1961).

14. See R. D. Luce, "Further Comments on Power Distributions for a Stable Two-Party Congress," Paper read at American Political Science Association meetings (1956); and W. H. Riker, "A Test of the Adequacy of the Power Index," *Behavioral Science, 9* (1959), 276–90.

15. Riker, "A Test of the Adequacy of the Power Index."

16. W. H. Riker, *The Theory of Political Coalitions* (New Haven: Yale University Press, 1962).

17. See H. White, "Uses of Mathematics in Sociology," in Mathematics and the Social Sciences, ed. J. C. Charlesworth (Philadelphia: American Academy of Political and Social Science, 1963).

18. K. W. Deutsch and W. G. Madow, "A Note on the Appearance of Wisdom in Large Organizations," *Behavioral Science, 6* (1961), 72–78.

19. See D. MacRae, Jr., and H. D. Price, "Scale Positions and 'Power' in the Senate," *Behavioral Science, 4* (1959), 212–18.

20. See, for example, Hanson, "Predicting a Community Decision: A Test of the Miller-Form Theory," *American Sociological Review, 24* (1959), 662–71.

21. R. O. Schulze, "The Role of Economic Dominants in Community Power Structure," *American Sociological Review, 23* (1958), 9.

22. See J. C. Harsanyi, "Measurement of Social Power, Opportunity Costs, and the Theory of Two-Person Bargaining Games," *Behavioral Science, 7* (1962), 67–80.

23. See R. Dubin, "Power and Union-Management Relations," *Administrative Science Quarterly,* II (1957), 60–81; and A. S. Tannenbaum, "An Event Structure Approach to Social Power and to the Problem of Power Comparability," *Behavioral Science, 7* (1962), 315–31.

24. See Dahl, *Who Governs?* and R. E. Wolfinger, "Reputation and Reality in the Study of 'Community Power,' " *American Sociological Review, 25* (1960), 636–44.

25. Hanson, "Predicting a Community Decision"; D. C. Miller, "The Prediction of Issue Outcome in Community Decision-Making," *Research Studies of the State College of Washington, 25* (1957), 137–47.

26. See W. G. Bennis, "Effecting Organizational Change: A New Role for the Behavioral Sciences," *Administrative Science Quarterly, 8* (1963).

27. See, for example, Anthony Downs, An *Economic Theory of Democracy* (New York: Harper & Row, Publishers, 1957); J. M. Buchanan and Gordon Tullock, *The Calculus of Consent* (Ann Arbor: University of Michigan Press, 1962); and W. H. Riker, *The Theory of Political Coalitions* (New Haven, CT: Yale University Press, 1967).

28. Dale Carnegie, *How to Win Friends and Influence People* (New York: Simon and Schuster, Inc., 1936); Leon Festinger, *A Theory of Cognitive Dissonance* (New York: Harper & Row, Publishers, 1957).

29. See, for example, A. Newell, J. C. Shaw, and H. A. Simon, "Elements of a Theory of Human Problem Solving," *Psychological Review, 65* (1958), 151–66; and D. W. Taylor, James G. March, ed. Skokie, IL: Rand McNally, 1965 in *Handbook of Organizations,* ed. March.

30. See, for example, Elihu Katz and P. F. Lazarsfeld, *Personal Influence* (New York: Free Press of Glencoe, Inc., 1955); and Angus Campbell, Philip Converse, W. E. Miller, and Donald Stokes, *The American Voter* (New York: John Wiley & Sons, Inc., 1960).

31. See C. E. Lindblom, "The Science of Muddling Through," *Public Administration Review, 19* (1959), 79–88; and R. M. Cyert and J. G. March, *A Behavioral Theory of the Firm* (Englewood Cliffs, NJ: Prentice-Hall, Inc., 1963).

32. For example, David Riesman, *The Lonely Crowd* (New Haven: Yale University Press, 1951).

33. N. E. Long, "The Local Community as an Ecology of Games," *American Journal of Sociology, 44* (1958), 252.

34. R. A. Dahl, "A Critique of the Ruling Elite Model," *American Political Science Review, 52* (1958).

## 24
# Power Failure in Management Circuits

*Rosabeth Moss Kanter*

Power is America's last dirty word. It is easier to talk about money—and much easier to talk about sex—than it is to talk about power. People who have it deny it; people who want it do not want to appear to hunger for it; and people who engage in its machinations do so secretly.

Yet, because it turns out to be a critical element in effective managerial behavior, power should come out from undercover. Having searched for years for those styles or skills that would identify capable organization leaders, many analysts, like myself, are rejecting individual traits or situational appropriateness as key and finding the sources of a leader's real power.

Access to resources and information and the ability to act quickly make it possible to accomplish more and to pass on more resources and information to subordinates. For this reason, people tend to prefer bosses with "clout." When employees perceive their manager as influential upward and outward, their status is enhanced by association and they generally have high morale and feel less critical or resistant to their boss.[1] More powerful leaders are also more likely to delegate (they are too busy to do it all themselves), to reward talent, and to build a team that places subordinates in significant positions.

Powerlessness, in contrast, tends to breed bossiness rather than true leadership. In large organizations, at least, it is powerlessness that often creates ineffective, desultory management and petty, dictatorial, rules-minded managerial styles.

Accountability without power—responsibility for results without the resources to get them—creates frustration and failure. People who see themselves as weak and powerless and find their subordinates resisting or discounting them tend to use more punishing forms of influence. If organizational power can "ennoble," then, recent research shows, organizational powerlessness can (with apologies to Lord Acton) "corrupt."[2]

So perhaps power, in the organization at least, does not deserve such a bad reputation. Rather than connoting only dominance, control, and oppression, *power* can mean efficacy and capacity—something managers and executives need to move the organization toward its goals. Power in organizations is analogous in simple terms to physical power: it is the ability to mobilize resources (human and material) to get things done. The true sign of power, then, is accomplishment—not fear, terror, or tyranny. Where power is "on," the system can be productive; where the power is "off," the system bogs down....

## WHERE DOES POWER COME FROM?

The effectiveness that power brings evolves from two kinds of capacities: first, access to resources, information, and support necessary to carry out a task; and, second, ability to get cooperation in doing what is necessary. (Table 24.1 identifies some symbols of an individual manager's power.) ...

Rosabeth Moss Kanter, "Power Failure in Management Circuits," *Harvard Business Review* (July–August 1979).

## TABLE 24.1 • SOME COMMON SYMBOLS OF A MANAGER'S ORGANIZATIONAL POWER (INFLUENCE UPWARD AND OUTWARD)

*To What Extent a Manager Can—*

Intercede favorably on behalf of someone in trouble with the organization.

Get a desirable placement for a talented subordinate.

Get approval for expenditures beyond the budget.

Get above-average salary increases for subordinates.

Get items on the agenda at policy meetings.

Get fast access to top decision makers.

Get regular, frequent access to top decision makers.

Get early information about decisions and policy shifts.

Rosabeth Moss Kanter, "Power Failure in Management Circuits," *Harvard Business Review* (July-August 1979). © 1979 by the President and Fellows of Harvard College. Reprinted by permission of Harvard Business Review. All rights reserved.

We can regard the uniquely organizational sources of power as consisting of three "lines":

1. *Lines of Supply*. Influence outward, over the environment, means that managers have the capacity to bring in the things that their own organizational domain needs— materials, money, resources to distribute as rewards, and perhaps even prestige.
2. *Lines of Information*. To be effective, managers need to be "in the know" in both the formal and the informal sense.
3. *Lines of Support*. In a formal framework, a manager's job parameters need to allow for nonordinary action, for a show of discretion or exercise of judgment. Thus managers need to know that they can assume innovative, risk-taking activities without having to go through the stifling multilayered approval process. And, informally, managers need the backing of other important figures in the organization whose tacit approval becomes another resource they bring to their own work unit as well as a sign of the manager's being "in."

Note that productive power has to do with *connections* with other parts of a system. Such systemic aspects of power derive from two sources—job activities and political alliances:

1. Power is most easily accumulated when one has a job that is designed and located to allow discretion (nonroutinized action permitting flexible, adaptive, and creative contributions), recognition (visibility and notice), and relevance (being central to pressing organizational problems).
2. Power also comes when one has relatively close contact with sponsors (higher-level people who confer approval, prestige, or backing), peer networks (circles of acquaintanceship that provide reputation and information, the grapevine often being faster than formal communication channels), and subordinates (who can be developed to relieve managers of some of their burdens and to represent the manager's point of view).

When managers are in powerful situations, it is easier for them to accomplish more. Because the tools are there, they are likely to be highly motivated and, in turn, to be able to motivate subordinates. Their activities are more likely to be on target and to net them successes. They can flexibly interpret or shape policy to meet the needs of particular areas, emergent situations, or sudden environmental shifts. They gain the respect and cooperation that attributed power brings. Subordinates' talents are resources rather than threats. And, because powerful managers have so many lines of connection and thus are oriented outward, they tend to let go of control downward, developing more independently functioning lieutenants.

The powerless live in a different world. Lacking the supplies, information, or support to make things happen easily, they may

## TABLE 24.2 • WAYS ORGANIZATIONAL FACTORS CONTRIBUTE TO POWER OR POWERLESSNESS

| Factors | Generates Power When Factor Is | Generates Powerlessness When Factor Is |
|---|---|---|
| Rules inherent in the job | few | many |
| Predecessors in the job | few | many |
| Established routines | few | many |
| Task variety | high | low |
| Rewards for reliability/predictability | few | many |
| Rewards for unusual performance/innovation | many | few |
| Flexibility around use of people | high | low |
| Approvals needed for nonroutine decisions | few | many |
| Physical location | central | distant |
| Publicity about job activities | high | low |
| Relation of tasks to current problem areas | central | peripheral |
| Focus of tasks | outside work unit | inside work unit |
| Interpersonal contact in the job | high | low |
| Contact with senior officials | high | low |
| Participation in programs, conferences, meetings | high | low |
| Participation in problem-solving task forces | high | low |
| Advancement prospects of subordinates | high | low |

turn instead to the ultimate weapon of those who lack productive power—oppressive power: holding others back and punishing with whatever threats they can muster.

Table 24.2 summarizes some of the major ways in which variables in the organization and in job design contribute to either power or powerlessness.

## POSITIONS OF POWERLESSNESS

Understanding what it takes to have power and recognizing the classic behavior of the powerless can immediately help managers make sense out of a number of familiar organizational problems that are usually attributed to inadequate people:

The ineffectiveness of first-line supervisors.
The petty interest protection and conservatism of staff professionals.
The crises of leadership at the top.

Instead of blaming the individuals involved in organizational problems, let us look at the positions people occupy....

### First-line Supervisors

Because an employee's most important work relationship is with his or her supervisor, when many of them talk about "the company," they mean their immediate boss. Thus a supervisor's behavior is an important determinant of the average employee's relationship to work and is in itself a critical link in the production chain.

Yet I know of no U.S. corporate management entirely satisfied with the performance of its supervisors. Most see them as supervising too closely and not training their people. In one manufacturing company where direct laborers were asked on a survey how they learned their job, on a list of seven possibilities "from my supervisor" ranked next to last. (Only company training programs ranked worse.) Also, it is said that supervisors do not translate company policies into practice—for instance, that they do not carry out the right of every employee to frequent performance reviews or to career counseling.

In court cases charging race or sex discrimination, first-line supervisors are frequently cited as the "discriminating official."[3] And, in studies of innovative work redesign and quality of work life projects, they often appear as the implied villains; they are the ones who are said to undermine the program or interfere with its effectiveness. In short, they are often seen as "not sufficiently managerial." ...

A large part of the problem lies in the position itself—one that almost universally creates powerlessness.

First-line supervisors are "people in the middle," and that has been seen as the source of many of their problems.[4] But by recognizing that first-line supervisors are caught between higher management and workers, we only begin to skim the surface of the problem. There is practically no other organizational category as subject to powerlessness.

First, these supervisors may be at a virtual dead end in their careers. Even in companies where the job used to be a stepping stone to higher-level management jobs, it is now common practice to bring in MBAs from the outside for those positions. Thus, moving from the ranks of direct labor into supervision may mean, essentially, getting "stuck" rather than moving upward. Because employees do not perceive supervisors as eventually joining the leadership circles of the organization, they may see them as lacking the high-level contacts needed to have clout. Indeed, sometimes turnover among supervisors is so high that workers feel they can outwait—and outwit—any boss.

Second, although they lack clout, with little in the way of support from above, supervisors are forced to administer programs or explain policies that they have no hand in shaping. In one company, as part of a new personnel program supervisors were required to conduct counseling interviews with employees. But supervisors were not trained to do this and were given no incentives to get involved. Counseling was just another obligation. Then managers suddenly encouraged the workers to bypass their supervisors or to put pressure on them. The personnel staff brought them together and told them to demand such interviews as a basic right. If supervisors had not felt powerless before, they did after that squeeze from below, engineered from above.

The people they supervise can also make life hard for them in numerous ways. This often happens when a supervisor has himself or herself risen up from the ranks. Peers that have not made it are resentful or derisive of their former colleague, whom they now see as trying to lord it over them. Often it is easy for workers to break the rules and let a lot of things slip.

Yet first-line supervisors are frequently judged according to rules and regulations while being limited by other regulations in what disciplinary actions they can take. They often lack the resources to influence or reward people; after all, workers are guaranteed their pay and benefits by someone other than their supervisors. Supervisors cannot easily control events; rather, they must react to them....

It is not surprising, then, that supervisors frequently manifest symptoms of powerlessness: overly close supervision, rules-mindedness, and a tendency to do the job themselves rather than to train their people (since job skills may be one of the few remaining things they feel good about). Perhaps this is why they sometimes stand as roadblocks between their subordinates and the higher reaches of the company.

## Women Managers Experience Special Power Failures

The traditional problems of women in management are illustrative of how formal and informal practices can combine to engender powerlessness. Historically, women in management have found their opportunities in more routine, low-profile jobs. In staff positions, where they serve in support capacities to line managers but have no line responsibilities of their own, or in supervisory jobs managing "stuck" subordinates, they are not in a position either to take the kinds of risks that build credibility or to develop their own team by pushing bright subordinates.

Such jobs, which have few favors to trade, tend to keep women out of the mainstream of the organization. This lack of clout, coupled with the greater difficulty anyone who is "different" has in getting into the information and support networks, has meant that merely by organizational situation, women in management have been more likely than men to be rendered structurally powerless. This is one reason those women who have achieved power have often had family connections that put them in the mainstream of the organization's social circles.

A disproportionate number of women managers are found among first-line supervisors or staff professionals; and they, like men in those circumstances, are likely to be organizationally powerless. But the behavior of other managers can contribute to the powerlessness of women in management in a number of less obvious ways.

One way other managers can make a woman powerless is by patronizingly overprotecting her: putting her in "a safe job," not giving her enough to do to prove herself, and not suggesting her for high-risk, visible assignments. This protectiveness is sometimes born of "good" intentions to give her every chance to succeed (why stack the deck against her?). Out of managerial concerns, out of awareness that a woman may be up against situations that men simply do not have to face, some very well-meaning managers protect their female managers ("It's a jungle, so why send her into it?").

Overprotectiveness can also mask a manager's fear of association with a woman should she fail. One senior bank official at a level below vice president told me about his concerns with respect to a high-performing, financially experienced woman reporting to him. Despite *his* overwhelmingly positive work experiences with her, he was still afraid to recommend her for other assignments because he felt it was a personal risk. "What if other managers are not as accepting of women as I am?" he asked. "I know I'd be sticking my neck out; they would take her more because of my endorsement than her qualifications. And what if she doesn't make it? My judgment will be on the line."

Overprotection is relatively benign compared with rendering a person powerless by providing obvious signs of lack of managerial support. For example, allowing someone supposedly in authority to be bypassed easily means that no one else has to take him or her seriously. If a woman's immediate supervisor or other managers listen willingly to criticism of her and show they are concerned every time a negative comment comes up and that they assume she must be at fault, then they are helping to undercut her. If managers let other people know that they have concerns about this person or that they are testing her to see how she does, then they are inviting other people to look for signs of inadequacy or failure.

Furthermore, people assume they can afford to bypass women because they "must be uninformed" or "don't know the ropes." Even though women may be respected for their competence or expertise, they are not necessarily seen as being informed beyond the technical requirements of the job. There may be a grain of historical truth in this. Many women come to senior management positions as "outsiders" rather than up through the usual channels.

Also, because until very recently men have not felt comfortable seeing women as businesspeople (business clubs have traditionally excluded women), they have tended to seek each other out for informal socializing. Anyone, male or female, seen as organizationally naive and lacking sources of "inside dope" will find his or her own lines of information limited.

Finally, even when women are able to achieve some power on their own, they have not necessarily been able to translate such personal credibility into an organizational power base. To create a network of supporters out of individual clout requires that a person pass on and share power, that subordinates and peers be empowered by virtue of their connection with that person. Traditionally, neither men nor women have seen women as capable of sponsoring others, even though they may be capable of achieving and succeeding on their own. Women have been viewed as the *recipients of sponsorship rather than as the sponsors themselves....*

Viewing managers in terms of power and powerlessness helps explain two familiar stereotypes about women and leadership in organizations: that no one wants a woman boss (although studies show that anyone who has ever had a woman boss is likely to have had a positive experience), and that the reason no one wants a woman boss is that women are "too controlling, rules-minded, and petty."

The first stereotype simply makes clear that power is important to leadership. Underneath the preference for men is the assumption that, given the current distribution of people in organizational leadership positions, men are more likely than women to be in positions to achieve power and, therefore, to share their power with others. Similarly, the "bossy woman boss" stereotype is a perfect picture of powerlessness. All of those traits are just as characteristic of men who are powerless, but women are slightly more likely, because of circumstances I have mentioned, to find themselves powerless than are men. Women with power in the organization are just as effective—and preferred—as men.

Recent interviews conducted with about 600 bank managers show that, when a woman exhibits the petty traits of powerlessness, people assume that she does so "because she is a woman." A striking difference is that, when a man engages in the same behavior, people assume the behavior is a matter of his own individual style and characteristics and do not conclude that it reflects on the suitability of men for management.

---

### Staff Professionals

Also working under conditions that can lead to organizational powerlessness are the staff specialists. As advisers behind the scenes, staff people must sell their programs and bargain for resources, but unless they get themselves entrenched in organizational power networks, they have little in the way of favors to exchange. They are seen as useful adjuncts to the primary tasks of the organization but inessential in a day-to-day operating sense. This disenfranchisement occurs particularly when staff jobs consist of easily routinized administrative functions which are out of the mainstream of the currently relevant areas and involve little innovative decision making.

Furthermore, in some organizations, unless they have had previous line experience, staff people tend to be limited in the number of jobs into which they can move. Specialists' ladders are often very short, and professionals are just as likely to get "stuck" in such jobs as people are in less prestigious clerical or factory positions.

Staff people, unlike those who are being groomed for important line positions, may be hired because of a special expertise or particular background. But management rarely pays any attention to developing them into more general organizational resources. Lacking growth prospects themselves and working alone or in very small teams, they are not in a position to develop others or pass on power to them. They miss out on an important way that power can be accumulated....

Staff people tend to act out their powerlessness by becoming turf-minded. They create islands within the organization. They set themselves up as the only ones who can control professional standards and judge their own work. They create sometimes false distinctions between themselves as experts (no one else could possibly do what they do) and lay people, and this continues to keep them out of the mainstream.

One form such distinctions take is a combination of disdain when line managers attempt to act in areas the professionals think are their preserve and of subtle refusal to support the managers' efforts. Or staff groups battle with each other for control of new "problem areas," with the result that no one really handles the issue at all. To cope with their essential powerlessness, staff groups may try to elevate their own status and draw boundaries between themselves and others.

When staff jobs are treated as final resting places for people who have reached their level of competence in the organization—a good shelf on which to dump managers who are too old to go anywhere but too young to retire—then staff groups can also become pockets of conservatism, resistant to change. Their own exclusion from the risk-taking action may make them resist *anyone's* innovative proposals. In the past, personnel departments, for example, have sometimes been the last in their organization to know about innovations in human resource development or to be interested in applying them.

### Top Executives

Despite the great resources and responsibilities concentrated at the top of an organization, leaders can be powerless for reasons that are not very different from those that affect staff and supervisors: lack of supplies, information, and support.

We have faith in leaders because of their ability to make things happen in the larger world, to create possibilities for everyone else, and to attract resources to the organization. These are their supplies. But influence outward—the source of much credibility downward—can diminish as environments change, setting terms and conditions out of the control of the leaders. Regardless of top management's grand plans for the organization, the environment presses. At the very least, things going on outside the organization can deflect a leader's attention and drain energy. And more detrimental, decisions made elsewhere can have severe consequences for the organization and affect top management's sense of power and thus its operating style inside....

As powerlessness in lower levels of organizations can manifest itself in overly routinized jobs where performance measures are oriented to rules and absence of change, so it can at upper levels as well. Routine work often drives out nonroutine work. Accomplishment becomes a question of nailing down details. Short-term results provide immediate gratifications and satisfy stockholders or other constituencies with limited interests.

It takes a powerful leader to be willing to risk short-term deprivations in order to bring about desired long-term outcomes. Much as first-line supervisors are tempted to focus on daily adherence to rules, leaders are tempted to focus on short-term fluctuations and lose sight of long-term objectives. The dynamics of such a situation are self-reinforcing. The more the long-term goals go unattended, the more a leader feels powerless and the greater the scramble to prove that he or she is in control of daily events at least. The more he is involved in the organization as a short-term Mr. Fix-it, the more out of control of long-term objectives he is, and the more ultimately powerless he is likely to be.

Credibility for the top executives often comes from doing the extraordinary: exercising discretion, creating, inventing, planning, and acting in nonroutine ways. But since routine problems look easier and more manageable, require less change and consent on the part of anyone else, and lend themselves to instant solutions that can make any leader look good temporarily, leaders may avoid the risk by taking over what their subordinates should be doing. Ultimately, a leader may succeed in getting all the trivial problems dumped on his or her desk. This can establish expectations even for leaders attempting more challenging tasks. When Warren Bennis was president of the University of Cincinnati, a professor called him when the heat was down in a classroom. In writing about this incident, Bennis commented, "I suppose he expected me to grab a wrench and fix it."[5]

People at the top need to insulate themselves from the routine operations of the organization in order to develop and exercise power. But this very insulation can lead to another source of powerlessness—lack of information. In one multinational corporation, top executives who are sealed off in a large, distant office, flattered and virtually babied by aides, are frustrated by their distance from the real action.[6]

At the top, the concern for secrecy and privacy is mixed with real loneliness. In one bank, organization members were so accustomed to never seeing the top leaders that when a new senior vice president went to the branch offices to look around, they had suspicion, even fear, about his intentions.

Thus leaders who are cut out of an organization's information networks understand neither what is really going on at lower levels nor that their isolation may be having negative effects. All too often top executives design "beneficial" new employee programs or declare a new humanitarian policy (e.g., "Participatory management is now our style") only to find the policy ignored or mistrusted because it is perceived as coming from uncaring bosses.

The information gap has more serious consequences when executives are so insulated from the rest of the organization or from other decision makers that, as Nixon so dramatically did, they fail to see their own impending downfall. Such insulation is partly a matter of organizational position and, in some cases, of executive style.

For example, leaders may create closed inner circles consisting of "doppelgängers," people just like themselves, who are their principal sources of organizational information and tell them only what they want to know. The reasons for the distortions are varied: key aides want to relieve the leader of burdens, they think just like the leader, they want to protect their own positions of power, or the familiar "kill the messenger" syndrome makes people close to top executives reluctant to be the bearers of bad news.

Finally, just as supervisors and lower-level managers need their supporters in order to be and feel powerful, so do top executives. But for them sponsorship may not be so much a matter of individual endorsement as an issue of support by larger sources of legitimacy in the society. For top executives the

problem is not to fit in among peers; rather, the question is whether the public at large and other organization members perceive a common interest which they see the executives as promoting....

When common purpose is lost, the system's own politics may reduce the capacity of those at the top to act. Just as managing decline seems to create a much more passive and reactive stance than managing growth, so does mediating among conflicting interests. When what is happening outside and inside their organizations is out of control, many people at the top turn into decline managers and dispute mediators. Neither is a particularly empowering role.

Thus when top executives lose their own lines of supply, lines of information, and lines of support, they too suffer from a kind of powerlessness. The temptation for them then is to pull in every shred of power they can and to decrease the power available to other people to act. Innovation loses out in favor of control. Limits rather than targets are set. Financial goals are met by reducing "overhead" (people) rather than by giving people the tools and discretion to increase their own productive capacity. Dictatorial statements come down from the top, spreading the mentality of powerlessness farther until the whole organization becomes sluggish and people concentrate on protecting what they can....

## TO EXPAND POWER, SHARE IT

In no case am I saying that people in the three hierarchical levels described are always powerless, but they are susceptible to common conditions that can contribute to powerlessness. Table 24.3 summarizes the most common symptoms of powerlessness for each level and some typical sources of that behavior....

The absence of ways to prevent individual and social harm causes the polity to feel it must surround people in power with constraints, regulations, and laws that limit the arbitrary use of their authority. But if oppressive power corrupts, then so does

**TABLE 24.3 • COMMON SYMPTOMS AND SOURCES OF POWERLESSNESS FOR THREE KEY ORGANIZATIONAL POSITIONS**

| Position | Symptoms | Sources |
|---|---|---|
| First-line supervisors | Close, rules-minded supervision | Routine, rules-minded jobs with little control over lines of supply |
| | Tendency to do things oneself, blocking of subordinates' development and information | Limited lines of information |
| | Resistant, underproducing subordinates | Limited advancement or involvement prospects for oneself/subordinates |
| Staff professionals | Turf protection, information control | Routine tasks seen as peripheral to "real tasks" of line organization |
| | Retreat into professionalism | Blocked careers |
| | Conservative resistance to change | Easy replacement by outside experts |
| Top executives | Focus on internal cutting, short-term results, "punishing" | Uncontrollable lines of supply because of environmental changes |
| | Dictatorial top-down communications | Limited or blocked lines of information about lower levels of organization |
| | Retreat to comfort of like-minded lieutenants | Diminished lines of support because of challenges to legitimacy (e.g., from the public or special interest groups) |

the absence of productive power. In large organizations, powerlessness can be a bigger problem than power....

Organizational power can grow, in part, by being shared. We do not yet know enough about new organizational forms to say whether productive power is infinitely expandable or where we reach the point of diminishing returns. But we do know that sharing power is different from giving or throwing it away. Delegation does not mean abdication.

Some basic lessons could be translated from the field of economics to the realm of organizations and management. Capital investment in plants and equipment is not the only key to productivity. The productive capacity of nations, like organizations, grows if the skill base is upgraded. People with the tools, information, and support to make more informed decisions and act more quickly can often accomplish more. By empowering others, a leader does not decrease his power; instead he may increase it—especially if the whole organization performs better....

Also, if the powerless bosses could be encouraged to share some of the power they do have, their power would grow. Yet, of course, only those leaders who feel secure about their own power outward—their lines of supply, information, and support—can see empowering subordinates as a gain rather than as a loss. The two sides of power (getting it and giving it) are closely connected.

There are important lessons here for both subordinates and those who want to change organizations, whether executives or change agents. Instead of resisting or criticizing a powerless boss, which only increases the boss's feeling of powerlessness and need to control, subordinates instead might concentrate on helping the boss become more powerful. Managers might make pockets of ineffectiveness in the organization more productive not by training or replacing individuals but by structural solutions such as opening supply and support lines.

Similarly, organizational change agents who make a new program or policy to succeed should make sure that the change itself does not render any other level of the organization powerless. In making changes, it is wise to make sure that the key people in the level or two directly above and in neighboring functions are sufficiently involved, informed, and taken into account, so that the program can be used to build their own sense of power also. If such involvement is impossible, then it is better to move these people out of the territory altogether than to leave behind a group from whom some power has been removed and who might resist and undercut the program.

In part, of course, spreading power means educating people to this new definition of it. But words alone will not make the difference; managers will need the real experience of a new way of managing....

Naturally, people need to have power before they can learn to share it. Exhorting managers to change their leadership styles is rarely useful by itself. In one large plant of a major electronics company, first-line production supervisors were the source of numerous complaints from managers who saw them as major roadblocks to overall plant productivity and as insufficiently skilled supervisors. So the plant personnel staff undertook two pilot programs to increase the supervisor's effectiveness. The first program was based on a traditional competency and training model aimed at teaching the specific skills of successful supervisors. The second program, in

contrast, was designed to empower the supervisors by directly affecting their flexibility, access to resources, connections with higher-level officials, and control over working conditions....

One might wonder why more organizations do not adopt such empowering strategies. There are standard answers: that giving up control is threatening to people who have fought for every shred of it; that people do not want to share power with those they look down on; that managers fear losing their own place and special privileges in the system; that "predictability" often rates higher than "flexibility" as an organizational value; and so forth.

But I would also put skepticism about employee abilities high on the list. Many modern bureaucratic systems are designed to minimize dependence on individual intelligence by making routine as many decisions as possible. So it often comes as a genuine surprise to top executives that people doing the more routine jobs could, indeed, make sophisticated decisions or use resources entrusted to them in intelligent ways....

## NOTES

1. Donald C. Pelz, "Influence: A Key to Effective Leadership in the First-Line Supervisor," *Personnel*, November 1952, p. 209.

2. See my book, *Men and Women of the Corporation* (New York: Basic Books, 1977), pp. 164–205; and David Kipnis, *The Powerholders* (Chicago: University of Chicago Press, 1976).

3. William E. Fulmer, "Supervisory Selection: The Acid Test of Affirmative Action," *Personnel*, November–December 1976, p. 40.

4. See my chapter (coauthor, Barry A. Stein), "Life in the Middle: Getting In, Getting Up, and Getting Along," in *Life in Organizations*, eds. Rosabeth M. Kanter and Barry A. Stein (New York: Basic Books, 1979).

5. Warren Bennis, *The Unconscious Conspiracy: Why Leaders Can't Lead* (New York: AMACOM, 1976).

6. See my chapter, "How the Top Is Different," in *Life in Organizations*.

## 25

# The Power Game and the Players

*Henry Mintzberg*

The core of this book is devoted to the discussion of a theory of organizational power. It is built on the premise that organizational behavior is a power game in which various players, called *influencers*, seek to control the organization's decisions and actions. The organization first comes into being when an initial group of influencers join together to pursue a common mission. Other influencers are subsequently attracted to the organization as a vehicle for satisfying some of their needs. Since the needs of influencers vary, each tries to use his or her own levers of power—*means or systems of influence*—to control decisions and actions. How they succeed determines what configuration of organizational power emerges. Thus, to understand the behavior of the organization, it is necessary to understand which influencers are present, what needs each seeks to fulfill in the organization, and how each is able to exercise power to fulfill them.

Of course, much more than power determines what an organization does. But our perspective in this book is that power is what matters, and that, if you like, everyone exhibits a lust for power (an assumption, by the way, that I do not personally favor, but that proves useful for the purposes of this book). When our conclusions here are coupled with those of the first book in this series, *The Structuring of Organizations* (Mintzberg 1979a, which will subsequently be referred to as the *Structuring book*), a more complete picture of the behavior of organizations emerges.

## THE EXERCISE OF POWER

Hirschman (1970) notes in a small but provocative book entitled *Exit, Voice, and Loyalty*, that the participant in any system has three basic options:

> To stay and contribute as expected, which Hirschman calls *loyalty* (in the vernacular, "Shut up and deal")
>
> To leave, which Hirschman calls *exit* ("Take my marbles and go")
>
> To stay and try to change the system, which Hirschman refers to as *voice* ("I'd rather fight than switch")

Should he or she choose voice, the participant becomes what we call an influencer...[1] Those who exit—such as the client who stops buying or the employee who seeks work elsewhere—cease to be influencers, while those who choose loyalty over voice—the client who buys without question at the going rate, the employees who do whatever they are told quietly—choose not to participate as active influencers (other than to support implicitly the existing power structure).

> To resort to voice, rather than exit, is for the customer or member to make an attempt at changing the practices, policies, and outputs of the firm from which one buys or of the organization to which one belongs. Voice is here defined as any attempt at all to change, rather than to escape from, an objectionable state of affairs....(Hirschman 1970, p. 30)[2]

For those who stay and fight, what gives power to their voice? Essentially the influencer requires (1) some source or basis of

Henry Mintzberg, *Power in and Around Organizations* (Englewood Cliffs, NJ: Prentice-Hall, 1983), pp. 22–30.

power, coupled with (2) the expenditure of energy in a (3) politically skillful way when necessary. These are the three basic conditions for the exercise of power. In Allison's concise words, "Power ... is an elusive blend of ... bargaining advantages, skill and will in using bargaining advantages...." (1971, p. 168).

## The General Bases of Power

In the most basic sense, the power of the individual in or over the organization reflects some *dependency* that it has—some gap in its own power as a system, in Crozier's view, an "uncertainty" that the organization faces (Crozier 1964; also Crozier and Friedberg 1977). This is especially true of three of the five bases of power we describe here.[3] Three prime bases of power are control of (1) a resource, (2) a technical skill, or (3) a body of knowledge, any one critical to the organization. For example, a monopolist may control the raw material supply to an organization, while an expert may control the repair of important and highly complex machinery. To serve as a basis of power, a resource, skill or body of knowledge must first of all be *essential* to the functioning of the organization. Second, it must be *concentrated*, in short supply or else in the hands of one person or a small number of people who cooperate to some extent. And third it must be *nonsubstitutable*, in other words, irreplaceable. These three characteristics create the dependency—the organization needs something, and it can get it only from the few people who have it.

A fourth general basis of power stems from legal prerogatives—exclusive rights or privileges to impose choices. Society, through its governments and judicial system, creates a whole set of legal prerogatives which grant power—*formal power*—to various influencers. In the first place, governments reserve for themselves the power to authorize the creation of the organization and thereafter impose regulations of various sorts on it. They also vest owners and/or the directors of the organization with certain powers, usually including the right to hire and fire the top executives. And these executives, in turn, usually have the power to hire and perhaps fire the rest of the employees, and to issue orders to them, tempered by other legal prerogatives which grant power to employees and their associations.

The fifth general basis of power derives from access to those who can rely on the other four. That access may be personal. For example, the spouses and friends of government regulators and of chief executives have power by virtue of having the ear of those who exercise legal prerogatives. The control of an important constituency which itself has influence—the customers who buy or the accountants who control the costs—can also be an important basis for power. Likewise power flows to those who can sway other influencers through the mass media—newspaper editors, TV commentators, and the like.

Sometimes access stems from favors traded: Friends and partners grant each other influence over their respective activities. In this case, power stems not from dependency but from *reciprocity*, the gaining of power in one sphere by the giving up of power in another. As we shall see in many examples in this book, the organizational power game is characterized as much by reciprocal as by dependency—one-sided, or "asymmetrical"—relationships.[4]

## Will and Skill

But having a basis for power is not enough. The individual must act in order to become an influencer, he or she must expend energy, use the basis for power. When the basis is formal, little effort would seem to be required to use it. But many a government has passed legislation that has never been respected, in many cases because it did not bother to establish an agency strong enough to enforce it. Likewise, managers often find that their power to give orders means little when not backed up by the effort to ensure that these are in fact carried out. On the other hand, when the basis of power is informal, much effort would seem to be required to use it. If orders cannot be given, battles will have to be won. Yet here too, sometimes the reverse is true. In universities, for example, power often flows to those who take the trouble to serve on the committees. As two researchers noted in one study: "Since few people were involved and those who were involved wandered in and out, someone who was willing to spend time being present could often become influential" (March and Romelaer 1976, p. 272). In the game of power, it is often the squeaky wheel that gets the grease.

In effect, the requirement that energy be expected to achieve outcomes, and the fact that those with the important bases of power have only so much personal energy to expend, means that power gets distributed more widely than our discussions of the bases of power would suggest. Thus, one article shows how the attendants in a mental hospital, at the bottom of the formal hierarchy, could block policy initiatives from the top because collectively they were willing and able to exert far more effort than could the administrators and doctors (Scheff 1961). What this means is that influencers pick and choose their issues, concentrating their efforts on the ones most important to them, and, of course, those they think they can win. Thus, Patchen (1974) finds that each influencer stakes out those areas that affect him or her most, deferring elsewhere to other influencers.

Finally, the influencer must not only have some basis for power and expend some energy, but often he or she must also do it in a clever manner, with political skill. Much informal and even formal power backed by great effort has come to naught because of political ineptness. Managers, by exploiting those over whom they have formal power, have often provoked resistance and even mutiny; experts regularly lose reasonable issues in meetings because they fail to marshal adequate support. Political skill means the ability to use the bases of power effectively—to convince those to whom one has access, to use one's resources, information, and technical skills to their fullest in bargaining, to exercise formal power with a sensitivity to the feelings of others, to know where to concentrate one's energies, to sense what is possible, to organize the necessary alliances.

Related to political skill is a set of intrinsic leadership characteristics—charm, physical strength, attractiveness, what Kipnis calls "personal resources" (1974, p. 88). *Charisma* is the label for that mystical quality that attracts followers to an individual. Some people become powerful simply because others support them; the followers pledge loyalty to a single voice.

Thus power derives from some basis for it is coupled with the efforts and the abilities to use the basis. We shall assume this in the rest of the book, and look more concretely at the channels through which power is exercised, what we call the *means* and *the systems of influence*—the specific instruments influencers are able to use to effect outcomes.

## THE CAST OF PLAYERS IN ORDER OF APPEARANCE

Who are these influencers to whom we have referred? We can first distinguish *internal* from *external* influencers. The internal influencers are the full-time employees who use voice, those people charged with making the decision and taking the actions on a permanent, regular basis; it is they who determine the outcomes, which express the goals pursued by the organization. The external influencers are nonemployees who use their bases of influence to try to affect the behavior of the employees.[5] The first two sections of our theory, on the elements of power, describe respectively the *External Coalition*, formed by the external influencers, and the *Internal Coalition*, formed by the internal influencers.

As the word *coalition* was retained in this book only after a good deal of consideration, it is worth explaining here why it was chosen. In general, an attempt was made to avoid jargon whenever it was felt to be possible—for example, employing "chief executive officer" instead of "peak coordinator." "Coalition" proved to be a necessary exception. Because there are no common labels—popular or otherwise—to distinguish the power in from that around the organization, one had to be selected. But why *coalition*? Because it seems to fit best, even though it may be misleading to the reader at first. The word *coalition* is normally used for a group of people who band together to win some issue. As the Hickson research team at the University of Bradford notes, it has the connotation of "engineered agreements and alliances" (Astley et al. 1980, p. 21). Ostensibly, we are not using the word in this sense, at least not at first. We use it more in the sense that Cyert and March (1963) introduced it, as a set of people who bargain among themselves to determine a certain distribution of organizational power. But as we proceed in our discussion, the reader will find the two meanings growing increasingly similar. For one thing, in the External or Internal Coalition, the various influencers band together around or within the same organization to satisfy their needs. They do form some sort of "coalition." As Hickson et al. note in an earlier publication, "it is their coalition of interests that sustains (or destroys) [the] organization" (1976, p. 9).[6] More importantly, we shall see that the external and internal influencers each typically form rather stable systems of power,

usually focused in nature. These become semi-permanent means to distribute benefits, and so resemble coalitions in the usual meaning of the term.

Our power play includes ten groups of possible influencers, listed below in order of appearance. The first four are found in the External Coalition:

- First are the owners, who hold the legal title to the organization. Some of them perhaps conceived the idea of founding the organization in the first place and served as brokers to bring the initial influencers together.
- Second are the *associates*, the suppliers of the organization's input resources, the clients for its output products and services, as well as its trading partners and competitors. It should be noted that only those associates who resort to voice—for example, who engage in contacts of other than a purely economic nature—are counted as influencers in the External Coalition.
- Third are the *employee associations*, that is, unions and professional associations. Again, these are included as influencers to the extent that they seek to influence the organization in other than purely economic ways, that is, to use voice to affect decisions and actions directly. Such employee associations see themselves as representatives of more than simple suppliers of labor resources. Note that employee associations are themselves considered *external* influencers, even though they represent people who can be internal influencers. Acting collectively, through their representatives, the employees choose to exert their influence on the organization from outside of its regular decision-making and action-taking channels, much as do owners and clients. (Singly, or even collectively but in different ways, the employees can of course bring their influence to bear directly on these processes, as internal influencers. Later, we shall in fact see that it is typically their impotence in the Internal Coalition that causes them to act collectively in the External Coalition.)
- A fourth category comprises the organization's various *publics*, groups representing

special or general interests of the public at large. We can divide these into three: (1) such general groups as families, opinion leaders, and the like; (2) special interest groups such as conservation movements or local community institutions; and (3) government in all of its forms—national, regional, local, departments and ministries, regulatory agencies, and so on.

- Another group of influencers, which is really made up of representatives from among the other four, as well as from the internal influencers, are the *directors* of the organization. These constitute a kind of "formal coalition." This group stands at the interface of the External and Internal Coalitions, but because it meets only intermittently,... it is treated as part of the External Coalition.

The Internal Coalition comprises six groups of influencers:

- First is the top or general management of the organization, Papandreou's peak coordinator. We shall refer to this by the single individual at the top of the hierarchy of authority, in standard American terminology, the *chief executive officer*, or CEO.[7]
- Second are the *operators*, those workers who actually produce the products and services, or who provide the direct support to them, such as the machine operators in the manufacturing plant or the doctors and nurses in the hospital.
- Third are the managers who stand in the hierarchy of line authority from the CEO down to the first-line supervisors to whom the operators formally report. We shall refer to these simply as the *line managers*.
- Fourth are the *analysts of the technostructure*, those staff specialists who concern themselves with the design and operation of the systems for planning and for formal control, people such as work study analysts, cost accountants, and long-range planners.
- Fifth is the *support staff*, comprising those staff specialists who provide indirect support to the operators and the rest of the organization, in a business firm, for example, the mailroom staff, the chef in the

cafeteria, the researchers, the public relation officers, and the legal counsel.[8]

- Finally, there is an eleventh actor in the organizational power system, one that is technically inanimate but in fact shows every indication of having a life of its own, namely the *ideology* of the organization— the set of beliefs shared by its internal influencers that distinguishes it from other organizations.

Figure 25.1 shows the position of each of these eleven groups schematically. The Internal Coalition is shown in the center, with the Chief Executive Officer at the top, followed, according to the formal hierarchy of authority, by the line managers and then the operators. (In some parts of the discussion, we shall accept these notions of formal authority, in others, we shall not. For now, we retain them.) Shown at either side to represent their roles as staff members are the analysts and the support staff. Above the CEO is shown the board of directors to which the CEO formally reports. And emanating from the organization is a kind of aura to represent its ideology. Surrounding all this are the various groups of the External Coalition. The owners are shown closest to the top of the hierarchy, and to the board of directors, where they are often inclined to exert their influence. The associates are shown surrounding the operating core where the operators work, the suppliers on the left (input) side and the clients on the right (output) side, with the partners and competitors in between. The employee associations are shown closest to the operators, whom they represent, while the various publics are shown to form a ring around the entire power system, in effect influencing every part of it. Thus the organization of Figure 25.1 can be seen to exist in a complex field of influencer forces.

Each of these eleven groups of players in the organizational power game will be discussed in turn, together with the means of influence they have at their disposal.

## FIGURE 25.1 • THE CAST OF PLAYERS

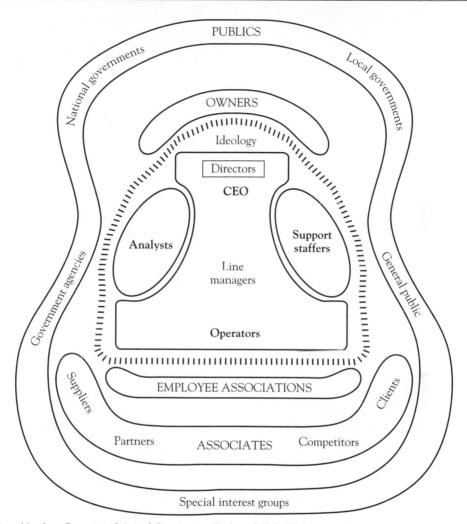

Henry Mintzberg, Power in and Around Organizations (Englewood Cliffs, NJ: Prentice-Hall, 1983), pp. 22–30. © 1983 by Prentice Hall. Reprinted by permission of SAGE.

We assume in this discussion that each is driven by the needs inherent in the roles they play. For example, owners will be described as owners, not as fathers, or Episcopalians, or power-hungry devils. People are of course driven by a variety of needs—by intrinsic values such as the need for control or autonomy, or in Maslow's (1954) needs hierarchy theory, by physiological, safety, love, esteem, and self-actualization needs; by the values instilled in them as children or developed later through socialization and various identifications; by the need to exploit fully whatever skills and abilities they happen to have; by their desire to avoid repetition of painful experiences or to repeat successful ones; by opportunism, the drive to exploit whatever opportunities happen to present themselves. All of these needs contribute to the makeup of each influencer and lead to an infinite variety of behaviors. All are, therefore, important to understand. But they are beyond the scope of this book. Here we focus on those behaviors that are dictated strictly by role. We assume throughout that each group discussed above is driven to gain power in or over the organization—in other words, is an influencer; our discussion then focuses on what ends each seeks to attain, what means or systems of influence each has at its disposal, and how much power each tends to end up with by virtue of the role it plays in the power coalition to which it happens to belong. This is the point of departure for the discussion of our theory.

## NOTES

1. Some writers call the influencer a "stakeholder," since he or she maintains a stake in the organization the way a shareholder maintains shares. Others use the term "claimant," in that he or she has a claim on the organization's benefits. Both these terms, however, would include those who express loyalty as well as voice.

2. There are some interesting linkages among these three options, as Hirschman points out. Exit is sometimes a last resort for frustrated voice, or in the case of a strike (temporary exit), a means to supplement voice. The effect of exit can be "galvanizing" when voice is the norm, or vice versa, as in the case of Ralph Nader who showed consumers how to use voice instead of exit against the automobile companies (p. 125). Of course, an inability to exit forces the disgruntled individual to turn to voice. Hirschman also makes the intriguing point

that exit belongs to the study of economics, voice to that of political science. In economic theory, the customer or employee dissatisfied with one firm is supposed to shift to another: " ... one either exits or one does not; it is impersonal" (p. 15). In contrast, voice is "a far more 'messy' concept because it can be graduated, all the way from hint grumbling to violent protest ... voice is political action par excellence" (p. 16). But students of political science also have a "blind spot": " ... exit has often been branded as *criminal*, for it has been labelled desertion, defection, and treason" (p. 17).

3. Related discussions of bases of power can be found in Allison (1971), Crozier and Friedberg (1977), Jacobs (1974), Kipnis (1974), Mechanic (1962), and Pfeffer and Salancik (1978).

4. French and Raven's (1959) five categories of power, as perhaps the most widely quoted typology of power, should be related to these five bases of power. Their "reward" and "coercive" power are used formally by those with legal prerogatives and may be used informally by those who control critical resources, skills, or knowledge (for example, to coerce by holding these back). Their "legitimate" power corresponds most closely to our legal prerogatives and their "expert" power to our critical skills and knowledge. Their fifth category, "referent" power, is not discussed here.

5. As we shall soon see, there are some circumstances in which external influencers can impose decisions directly on the organization, and others in which full-time employees acting in concert through their associations behave as external influencers by trying to affect the behavior of the senior managers. As Pfeffer and Salancik (1978, p. 30) point out, actors can be part of the organization as well as its environment. Nevertheless, the distinction between full-time employees—those individuals with an intensive and regular commitment to the organization—and others will prove to be a useful and important one in all that follows.

6. It might be noted that the Hickson group in the 1980 publication cited earlier (as Astley et al.) decided to replace the word *coalition* by *constellation*. That was tried in this book, but dropped as not having quite the right ring to it.

7. An alternate term which appears frequently in the more recent literature is *dominant coalition*. But we have no wish to prejudice the discussion of the power of one of our groups of influencers by the choice of its title.

8. For a more elaborate description of each of these five groups as well as clarification of the differences between technocratic and support staff and of line and staff in general, see Chapter 2 of the *Structuring* book [Mintzberg, 1979a].

## REFERENCES

Allison, G. T. (1971). *Essence of decision: Explaining the Cuban missile crisis.* Boston: Little, Brown.

Astley, W. G., Axelsson, R., Butler, R. J., Hickson, D. J., & Wilson, D. C. (1980). Decision making: Theory III. Working Paper, University of Bradford Management Centre.

Crozier, M. (1974). Why is France blocked? In H. J. Leavitt, L. Pinfield, & E. J. Webb (Eds.). *Organizations of the future: Interaction with the external environment.* New York: Praeger.

___, & Friedberg, E. (1977). *L'acteur et le système.* Paris: Editions du Seuil.

Cyert, R. M., & March, J. G. (1963). *A behavioral theory of the firm.* Englewood Cliffs, NJ: Prentice-Hall.

French, J. R. P., Jr., & Raven, B. (1959). The bases of social power. In D. Cartwright (Ed.). *Studies in social power* (pp. 150–167). Ann Arbor: Institute for Social Research, University of Michigan.

Hickson, D. J., Butler, R. J., Axelsson, R., & Wilson, D. (1976). Decisive coalitions. Paper presented to International Conference on Coordination and Control of Group and Organizational Performance, Munich, West Germany.

Hirschman, A. O. (1970). *Exit, voice, and loyalty: Responses to decline in firms, organizations, and states.* Cambridge, MA: Harvard University Press.

Jacobs, D. (1974). Dependency and vulnerability: An exchange approach to the control of organizations. *Administrative Science Quarterly,* 45–59.

Kipnis, D. (1974). The powerholder. In J. T. Tedeschi (Ed.), *Perspectives on social power* (pp. 82–122). Chicago: Aldine.

March, J. G., & Romelaer, P. J. (1976). Position and presence in the drift of decisions. In J. G. March & J. P. Olsen (Eds.), *Ambiguity and choice in organizations.* Bergen, Norway: Universitetsforlaget.

Maslow, A. H. (1954). *Motivation and personality.* New York: Harper & Row.

Mechanic, D. (1962). Sources of power of lower participants in complex organizations. *Administrative Science Quarterly,* 349–364.

Mintzberg, H. (1979a). *The structuring of organizations: A synthesis of the research.* Englewood Cliffs, NJ: Prentice-Hall.

Patchen, M. (1974). The locus and basis of influence on organizational decisions. *Organizational Behavior and Human Performance,* 195–221.

Pfeffer, N., and Salancik, G. R. (1978). *The external control of organizations: A resource dependence perspective.* New York: Harper & Row.

Scheff, T. J. (1961). Control over policy by attendants in a mental hospital. *Journal of Health and Human Behavior,* 93–105.

# CHAPTER 7

# *Theories of Organizational Culture and Change*

Organizational culture is the culture that exists in an organization, something akin to a societal culture. It is composed of many intangible phenomena, such as values, beliefs, assumptions, perceptions, behavioral norms, artifacts, and patterns of behavior. It is the unseen and unobservable force that is always behind the organizational activities that can be seen and observed. According to Kilmann and his colleagues (1985), "Culture is to the organization what personality is to the individual—a hidden, yet unifying theme that provides meaning, direction, and mobilization."

Since the 1980s, the literature on organizational change has had a dominant theme—*lasting organizational reform requires changes in organizational culture.* Organizational cultures that reflect unwanted values, such as hierarchy, rigidity, homogeneity, power based on authority and associations in closed networks, and reliance on rules restrict flexibility and can be formidable barriers to effecting lasting change (Cameron & Quinn, 2011). Organizational members often hang onto familiar "tried and true" beliefs, values, policies, and practices of the organizational culture even when these "old ways" have ceased to serve the organization well. The task is to replace these with cultures where horizontal relations, open and accessible networks, flexibility, responsiveness, individual and group empowerment, diversity, and customer service are valued. Advocates and advisers of organizational reform have shared a commitment to increase organizational effectiveness, competitiveness, flexibility, and responsiveness by changing organizational cultures. "Command-and-control" cultures must be replaced with cultures that encourage and support an increasingly diverse workforce and employee participation and empowerment approaches for individuals in work teams.

Therefore, understanding and appreciating the theory of organizational culture—the *organizational culture perspective*—as well as the existing culture of a particular organization, is necessary for effecting lasting organizational change.

## THE ORGANIZATIONAL CULTURE PERSPECTIVE

The organizational culture perspective is a set of theories with their own assumptions about organizational realities and relationships. It is yet another way of viewing, thinking about, studying, and trying to understand organizations. Like power and politics organization theory (Chapter 6), the assumptions, units of analysis, research methods, and approaches of the organizational culture perspective differ markedly from those of the rational, "modern" structural, organizational economics, and systems/environment theories.

The organizational culture perspective challenges the basic views of these more rational perspectives about, for example, how organizations make decisions and how and why organizations—and people in organizations—act as they do.

In the classical, neoclassical, "modern" structural, organizational economics, and systems/environment theories of organization, organizations are assumed to be rational-utilitarian institutions whose primary purpose is to accomplish established goals. People in positions of formal authority set goals. The primary questions for organization theory thus involve how best to design and manage organizations so they achieve their declared purposes effectively and efficiently. The personal preferences of organizational members are restrained by systems of formal rules, authority, and norms of rational behavior. In a 1982 *Phi Delta Kappan* article, however, Karl Weick argued that four organizational conditions must exist for the basic assumptions of the rational theories to be valid:

1. a self-correcting system of interdependent people;
2. consensus on objectives and methods;
3. coordination achieved through sharing information; and
4. predictable organizational problems and solutions.

But, Weick concludes, these conditions seldom if ever exist in large modern organizations.

The organizational culture perspective thus assumes that many organizational behaviors and decisions are not determined by rational analysis. Instead, they are, in effect, predetermined by the deep patterns of basic assumptions held by members of an organization. These patterns of assumptions continue to exist and influence behaviors in an organization because they have repeatedly led people to make decisions that worked in the past. With repeated use, the assumptions slowly drop out of people's consciousness but continue to influence organizational decisions and behaviors even when the environment changes and different decisions are needed. They become the underlying, unquestioned, but largely forgotten, reasons for "the way we do things here"—even when the ways may no longer be appropriate. They are so basic, so ingrained, and so completely accepted that no one thinks about or remembers them—thereby our claim that organizational culture can be a formidable barrier to effecting lasting organizational change.

A strong organizational culture can exert considerable influence on organizational behavior; for example, an organizational culture can block an organization from making changes that are needed to adapt to new market dynamics or new information technologies. From the organizational culture perspective, systems of formal rules, authority, and norms of rational behavior do not restrain the personal preferences of organizational members. Instead, they are controlled by cultural norms, values, beliefs, and assumptions. To understand or predict how an organization will behave under varying circumstances, one must know and understand the organization's patterns of basic assumptions—its organizational culture.

Organizational cultures differ for several reasons. First, what has worked repeatedly for one organization may not work for another, so basic assumptions may differ. Second, an organization's culture is shaped by many factors, including, for example, the societal culture in which it resides; its technologies, markets, and competition; the profession of many employees and executives, and the personality of its founder(s) or dominant early leaders. Some organizational cultures are more distinctive than others; some organizations have strong, unified, pervasive cultures, whereas others have weaker or less pervasive ones; some organizational cultures are quite pervasive, whereas others may have many *subcultures* existing in different functional or geographical areas (Ott, 1989, Chapter 4).

Knowledge of an organization's structure, information systems, strategic planning processes, markets, technology, goals, and so forth can provide clues about an organization's culture, but not accurately or reliably. As a consequence, an organization's behavior cannot be understood or predicted by studying only its structure and systems; its organizational culture must be studied. And the positivist, quantitative, quasi-experimental research methods favored by the "modern" structural, organizational economics, and systems/environment schools cannot identify or measure unconscious, virtually forgotten basic assumptions. Yet, quantitative research using quasi-experimental designs, control groups, computers, multivariate analyses, heuristic models, and the like are the essential tools of the rational schools. The organizational culture theories (along with theories from the power and politics school) have principally relied on qualitative research methods such as ethnography and participant observation (Schein, 2006). In sum, the organizational culture perspective believes that the "modern" structural, organizational economics, and systems/environment schools of organization theory are using the wrong tools (or the wrong "lenses") to look at the wrong organizational elements in their attempts to understand and predict organizational behavior.

## ORIGINS OF THE ORGANIZATIONAL CULTURE PERSPECTIVE

Essentially all the literature about the organizational culture perspective has been published since 1980. Although phrases such as *organizational culture* and *culture of a factory* can be found in a few books on management written as early as the 1950s (for example, Elliott Jaques's 1951 book, *The Changing Culture of a Factory*, and William H. Whyte Jr.'s 1956 book about conformity in business, *The Organization Man*), few students of management or organizations paid attention to the nature and content of organizational culture until the 1980s.

During the 1960s and early 1970s, several books and articles on organizational and professional socialization processes received wide attention. As useful as these earlier works were, they *assumed* the presence of organizational or professional cultures and proceeded to examine issues involving the match between individuals and cultures. Some of the more widely known of these included Becker, Geer, Hughes, and Strauss's analysis of the processes used to socialize students into the medical profession, *Boys in White* (1961); Herbert Kaufman's groundbreaking study of how the U.S. Forest Service developed the "will and capacity to conform" among its remotely stationed rangers, the 1960 study, *The Forest Ranger* (1960); Edgar H. Schein's "Organizational Socialization and the Profession of Management" (1968); and John Van Maanen's "Police Socialization" (1975) and "Breaking In: Socialization to Work" (1976).

## ORGANIZATIONAL CULTURE AND SYMBOLIC MANAGEMENT

The *symbolic frame* or *symbolic management*—an approach to cultures in organizations—that had roots in Berger and Luckmannn's highly influential, *Social Construction of Reality* (1967), started to appear in the organization theory literature during the late 1970s and reached full-bloom in the mid-1980s. Bolman and Deal (2013) identify the basic tenets of symbolic management as follows:

1. The meaning or the interpretation of what is happening in organizations is more important than what is actually happening.
2. Ambiguity and uncertainty, which are prevalent in most organizations, preclude rational problem-solving and decision-making processes.
3. People use symbols to reduce ambiguity and to gain a sense of direction when they are faced with uncertainty.

In *The Social Construction of Reality*, Berger and Luckmann defined meanings as "socially constructed realities" and thereby paved the way for the symbolic frame. Things are not real in and of themselves; the perceptions of them are, in fact, reality. As W. I. Thomas (1923) wrote, "If people believe things are real, they are real in their consequences." According to the organizational culture perspective, meaning (reality) is established by and among the people in organizations—by the organizational culture. Experimenters have shown that there is a strong relationship between culturally determined values and the perception of symbols. People will distort the perceptions of symbols according to the need for what is symbolized (Davis, 1963). Thus, organizational symbolism is an integral part of the organizational culture perspective.

The turning point in the acceptance of the organizational culture/symbolic management perspective emerged suddenly and swiftly between 1980 and 1984. Organizational culture and symbolism became hot topics in publications aimed at management practitioners and academicians, including Thomas Peters and Robert Waterman Jr.'s 1982 best seller, *In Search of Excellence* and its sequels; Terrence Deal and Allan Kennedy's 1982 *Corporate Cultures*; *Organizational Symbolism*, by Pondy, Frost, Morgan, and Dandridge; *Fortune* magazine's 1983 story "The Corporate Culture Vultures"; and *Business Week's* May 14, 1984, cover story, "Changing a Corporate Culture."

The first comprehensive, theoretically based, integrative writings on organizational culture were published between 1984 and 1986, including Thomas Sergiovanni and John Corbally's *Leadership and Organizational Culture* (1984); Edgar Schein's pioneering *Organizational Culture and Leadership* (1985); Vijay Sathe's *Culture and Related Corporate Realities* (1985); the first of Ralph Kilmann's books, *Gaining Control of the Corporate Culture* (1985); and the first edition of Gareth Morgan's highly influential book on organizational metaphors, *Images of Organization* (1986).

## REFORM MOVEMENTS REQUIRE CHANGES IN ORGANIZATIONAL CULTURE

Many of the best-known organizational and management reform movements of the past 35 years *required* changes in organizational culture. A few notable examples include:

- Total Quality Management (TQM) (Crosby, 1979, 1984; Deming, 1986, 1993; Juran, 1992; Walton, 1986);
- Japanese Management (Ouchi, 1981; Pascale & Athos, 1981);
- The Search for Excellence (Peters & Waterman, 1982; Peters, 1987);

- Sociotechnical Systems or Quality of Work Life (QWL) (Weisbord, 1991);
- Learning Organizations (Argyris, 1999; Cohen & Sproull, 1996; Cook & Yanow, 1993; Senge, 1990);
- Productivity Measurement/Balanced Scorecard (Berman, 2006; Eccles, 1991; Kaplan & Norton, 1992, 1993, 1996);
- Reinventing Government (Gore, 1993; Osborne & Gaebler, 1992);
- Reengineering, Process Reengineering, or Business Reengineering (Hammer & Champy, 1993);
- New Public Management (NPM) (Fattore, Dubois, & Lapenta, 2012; Kearney & Hays, 1998; Lane, 2000; Lynn, 2006; Patrick & French, 2011; Pollitt, C. & G. Bouckaert, 2012);
- Performance Management (Berman, 2006; Koliba, Campbell & Zia, 2011; Kotter & Heskett, 2011; Newcomer & Caudle, 2011; Poister, Pasha, & Edwards, 2013; Pollitt & Dan, 2013);
- Appreciative Inquiry (Bushe, 1995; Cooperrider & Whitney, 2005)

All these reform movements have sought to increase performance, productivity, flexibility, responsiveness, accountability, and customer service by reshaping organizational cultures. Empowered employees, work teams, and outsourced contractors are granted autonomy and discretion to make decisions. Work teams coordinate tasks and discipline their own members. Policies, procedures, and layers of hierarchy are eliminated. Accountability to bosses is replaced by primary accountability to customers or clients. Data-based information systems provide the information needed to coordinate and correct actions in real time. Levels of middle managers and supervisors are eliminated because they are not needed, do not add value, cost too much, and get in the way of empowered workers.

## READINGS REPRINTED IN THIS CHAPTER

The first selection reprinted here is a chapter from the fourth edition of Edgar H. Schein's *Organizational Culture and Leadership* (2011), "The Concept of Organizational Culture: Why Bother?" Schein articulates a formal definition of organizational culture that has gained wide—but not universal—acceptance. His definition consists of a model with three levels of culture that is particularly useful for sorting through myriad methodological and substantive problems associated with identifying an organizational culture. Schein also takes a unique stand on behalf of using a "clinical" rather than an "ethnographic" perspective for gaining knowledge about an organization's culture. He argues that an ethnographer seeks to understand an organizational culture for "intellectual and scientific" reasons, and organization members "have no particular stake in the intellectual issues that may have motivated the study." Thus, the ethnographer must work to obtain cooperation. In contrast, when clients call in an "outsider" (a consultant) to help solve problems, "the nature of the psychological contract between client and helper is completely different from that between researcher and subject, leading to a different kind of relationship between them, the revelation of different kinds of data, and the use of different criteria for when enough has been 'understood' to terminate the inquiry."

"Pyramids, Machines, Markets, and Families: Organizing Across Nations," by Geert Hofstede, Gert Jan Hofstede, and Michael Minkov explains how organizational culture is influenced by and partially reflects dimensions of national cultures and how nationality affects organizational rationality.

[Organization] theories, models, and practices are basically culture specific: they may apply across [national] borders, but this should always be proved. The naïve assumption that management ideas are universals is not found in popular literature: in scholarly journals ... the silent assumption of universal validity of culturally restricted findings is frequent. Hofstede, Hofstede, and Minkov caution against trying to export organization and management practices and approaches without understanding important dimensions of the national culture of the receiving organization.

In the final reading reprinted in this chapter, "Appreciative Inquiry" (2005), David Cooperrider and Diana Whitney assert that Appreciative Inquiry (AI)

turns the practice of change management inside out. It proposes, quite bluntly, that organizations are not, at their core, problems to be solved.... Organizations are centers of vital connections and life-giving potentials: relationships, partnerships, alliances, and ever-expanding webs of knowledge and action that are capable of harnessing the power of combinations of strengths.... AI offers a positive, strengths-based approach to organization development and change management.

Successful organizational improvement requires organizational culture changes. The AI approach to organizational development and change represents a conceptual reconfiguration of action research (McNiff & Whitehead, 2006) based on a socio-rationalist view of science that engages organizational members in a process of appreciating and valuing "what could be" rather than focusing on fixing existing problems and their causes.

## BIBLIOGRAPHY

Alvesson, M. (2002). *Understanding organizational culture*. Thousand Oaks, CA: Sage.

Argyris, C. (1999). *On organizational learning*, 2nd ed. Hoboken, NJ: Wiley-Blackwell.

Argyris, C. (2012). *Organizational traps: Leadership, culture, organizational design*. New York: Oxford University Press.

Becker, H. S., B. Geer, E. C. Hughes, & A. L. Strauss (1961). *The boys in white: Student culture in medical school*. Chicago, IL: University of Chicago Press.

Berger, P. L., & T. Luckman (1967). *The social construction of reality*. Garden City, NY: Doubleday Anchor.

Bergquist, W. H. (1992). *The four cultures of the academy*. San Francisco: Jossey-Bass.

Bergquist, W. H., & K. Pawlak. (2008). *Engaging the six cultures of the academy*, rev. ed. San Francisco: Jossey-Bass

Berman, E. M. (2006). *Performance and productivity in public and nonprofit organizations*, 2nd ed. Armonk, NY: M. E. Sharpe.

Bolman, L. G., & T. E. Deal (2013). *Reframing organizations: Artistry, choice, and leadership*, 5th ed. San Francisco: Jossey-Bass/Wiley.

Bushe, G. R. (1995). Advances in Appreciative Inquiry as an organization development intervention. *Organization Development Journal*, 13(3), 14–22.

*Business Week* (May 14, 1984). Changing a corporate culture: Can J&J move from Band-aids to high tech? 130–138.

Calas, M. B., & L. Smircich (2006). From the 'woman's point of view' ten years later: Towards a feminist organization studies. In S. R. Clegg, C. Hardy, T. Lawrence, & W R. Nord, eds. *The Sage handbook of organization studies*, 2nd ed. (pp. 284–346). Thousand Oaks, CA: Sage.

Cameron, K. S., & R. E. Quinn (2011). *Diagnosing and changing organizational culture*, 3rd ed. San Francisco: Jossey-Bass/Wiley.

Cohen, M. D., & L. S. Sproull, eds. (1996). *Organizational learning*. Thousand Oaks, CA: Sage.

Cook, S. D. N., & D. Yanow (1993). Culture and organizational learning. *Journal of Management Inquiry, 2*(4), 373–390.

Cooper, C. L., S. Cartwright, & P. C. Earley, eds. (2001). *The international handbook of organizational culture and climate*. New York: Wiley.

Cooperrider, D. L., & Whitney, D. (2005). *Appreciative Inquiry: A positive revolution in change*. San Francisco: Berrett-Koehler.

Crosby, P. B. (1979). *Quality is free*. New York: McGraw-Hill.

Crosby, P. B. (1984). *Quality without tears*. New York: McGraw-Hill..

Czarniawska-Joerges, B. (1992). *Exploring complex organizations: A cultural perspective*. Newbury Park, CA: Sage.

Deal, T. E., & A. A. Kennedy (2000). *Corporate cultures: The rites and rituals of corporate life*. New York: Basic Books.

Deming, W. E. (1986). *Out of the crisis*. Cambridge, MA: MIT Press.

Deming, W. E. (1993). *The new economics*. Cambridge, MA: MIT Press.

Durand, R., & Calori, R. (2006). Sameness, otherness? Enriching organizational change theories with philosophical considerations on the same and the other. *Academy of Management Review, 66*(2), 1–25.

Eccles, R. G. (1991). The performance measurement manifesto. *Harvard Business Review*, 131–137.

Eismore, P. J. A. (2001). *Organisational culture: Organisational change?* Aldershot, UK: Ashgate.

Fattore, G., H. F. W. Dubois, & A. Lapenta (2012). Measuring New Public Management and governance in political debate. *Public Administration Review, 72*(2), 218–227.

*Fortune* (October 17, 1983). The corporate culture vultures, 66–71.

Gore, A. (1993). *The Gore report on reinventing government*. New York: Times Books.

Hammer, M., & J. Champy (1993). *Reengineering the corporation*. New York: Harper-Business.

Handy, C. (1978). *The Gods of management: Who they are, how they work, and why they fail*. London: Souvenir Press.

Hatch, M. J., & A. L. Cunliffe (2013). *Organization theory: Modern, symbolic, and postmodern*. Oxford, UK: Oxford University Press.

Hofstede, G., G. J. Hofstede, & M. Minkov (2010). *Cultures and organizations: Software of the mind: Intercultural cooperation and its importance for survival*. New York: McGraw-Hill.

Hummel, R. P. (1991). Stories managers tell: Why they are as valid as science. *Public Administration Review, 51*, 31–41.

Ingersoll, V. H., & G. B. Adams (1992). *The tacit organization*. Greenwich, CT: JAI Press.

Jaques, E. (1951). *The changing culture of a factory*. London: Tavistock Institute.

Juran, J. M. (1992). *Juran on quality by design*. New York: Free Press.

Kaplan, R. S., & D. P. Norton (1992). The balanced scorecard: Measures that drive performance. *Harvard Business Review*, 71–79.

Kaplan, R. S., & D. P. Norton (1993). Putting the balanced scorecard to work. *Harvard Business Review*, 134–147.

Kaplan, R. S., & D. P. Norton (1996). Using the balanced scorecard as a strategic management system. *Harvard Business Review*, 75–85.

Kaufman, H. (1960). *The forest ranger*. Baltimore, MD: Johns Hopkins University Press.

Kearney, R. C., & S. W. Hays (1998). Reinventing government, the new public management and civil service systems in international perspective. *Review of Public Personnel Administration, 18*(4), 39–54.

Khademian, A. M. (2002). *Working with culture: The way the job gets done in public programs*. Washington, DC: CQ Press.

Kilmann, R. H., M. J. Saxton, & R. Serpa, eds. (1985). *Gaining control of the corporate culture*. San Francisco: Jossey-Bass.

Koliba, C., E. Cambell, & A. Zia (2011). Performance management systems of congestion management networks: Evidence from four cases. *Public Performance & Management Review, 34*(4), 520–548.

Kotter, J. P., & J. L. Heskett (2011). *Corporate culture and performance.* New York: Free Press.

Lane, J-E. (2000). *New Public Management: An introduction.* London, UK: Routledge.

Light, P. C. (1998). *The tides of reform: Making government work 1945–1995.* New Haven, CT: Yale University Press.

Louis, M. R. (1983). Organizations as culture-bearing milieux. In L. R. Pondy, P. J. Frost, G. Morgan, & T. C. Dandridge, eds., *Organizational symbolism* (pp. 39–54). Greenwich, CT: JAI Press.

Lynn, L. E. (2006). *Public management: Old and new.* London, UK: Routledge.

Martin, J. (1992). *Cultures in organizations: Three perspectives.* New York: Oxford University Press.

Martin, J. (2002). *Organizational culture: Mapping the terrain.* Thousand Oaks, CA: Sage.

McGuire, J. B., & G. B. Rhodes (2009). *Transforming your leadership culture.* San Francisco: Jossey-Bass/Wiley.

Morgan, G. (1986, 2006). *Images of organization,* rev. ed. Thousand Oaks, CA: Sage.

Nadler, D. A., M. S. Gerstein, & R. B. Shaw, eds. (1992). *Organizational architecture: Designs for changing organizations.* San Francisco: Jossey-Bass.

Newcomer, K., & S. Caudle (2011). Public performance management systems: Embedding practices for improved success. *Public Performance & Management Review, 35*(1), 108–132

Osborne, D., & T. Gaebler (1992). *Reinventing government.* Reading, MA: Addison-Wesley.

Ott, J. S. (1989). *The organizational culture perspective.* Fort Worth, TX: Harcourt Brace.

Ott, J. S., & A. M. Baksh (2010). Understanding organizational climate and culture. In S. E. Condrey, ed., *Handbook of human resource management in government,* 3rd ed. San Francisco: Jossey-Bass/Wiley.

Ott, J. S., S. J. Parkes, & R. B. Simpson, eds. (2008). *Classic readings in organizational behavior,* 4th ed. Belmont, CA: Wadsworth/Thomson.

Ouchi, W. G. (1981). *Theory Z: How American business can meet the Japanese challenge.* Reading, MA: Addison-Wesley.

Pascale, R. T., & A. G. Athos (1981). *The art of Japanese management: Applications for American executives.* New York: Simon & Schuster.

Patrick, B. A., & P. E. French (2011). Assessing New Public Management's focus on performance measurement in the public sector. *Public Performance and Management Review, 35*(2), 340–369.

Pearson, C. (2003). *Introduction to archetypes in organizational settings: A guide to interpreting the organizational and team culture instrument.* Gainsville, FL: Center for Applications of Psychological Type.

Pedersen, J. S., & J. S. Sorensen (1989). *Organisational cultures in theory and practice.* Aldershot, UK: Gower.

Peters, T. J. (1987). *Thriving on chaos.* New York: Knopf.

Peters, T. J., & R. H. Waterman Jr. (1982). *In search of excellence: Lessons from America's best-run companies.* New York: Harper & Row.

Pheysey, D. C. (1993). *Organizational cultures: Types and transformations.* London: Routledge.

Poister, T. H., O. Q. Pasha, & L. H. Edwards (2013). Does performance management lead to better outcomes? Evidence from the U.S. public transportation industry. *Public Administration Review,73*(4), 625–635.

Pollitt, C., & G. Bouckaert (2012). *Public management reform: A comparative analysis – New Public Management, governance, and the neo-Weberian state.* New York: Oxford University Press.

Pollitt, C., & S. Dan. (2013). Searching for impacts in performance-oriented management reform: A review of the European literature. *Public Performance & Management Review, 37*(1), 7–32.

Pondy, L. R., P. J. Frost, G. Morgan, & T. C. Dandridge, eds. (1983). *Organizational symbolism.* Greenwich, CT: JAI Press.

Sackman, S. A., ed. (1997). *Cultural complexity in organizations*. Thousand Oaks, CA: Sage.

Sathe, V. (1985). *Culture and related corporate realities*. Homewood, IL: Richard D. Irwin.

Schein, E. H. (1968). Organizational socialization and the profession of management. *Industrial Management Review, 9*, 1–15.

Schein, E. H. (1985; 1993; 2004; 2011). *Organizational culture and leadership*. San Francisco: Jossey-Bass.

Schein, E. H. (2006). So how can you assess your corporate culture? In J. V. Gallos, ed., *Organization development* (pp. 614–633). San Francisco: Jossey-Bass/Wiley.

Schein, E. H. (2010). *The corporate culture survival guide: Sense & nonsense about culture change* (rev. ed). San Francisco: Jossey-Bass.

Schultz, M. (1995). *On studying organizational cultures: Diagnosis and understanding*. Berlin: de Gruyter.

Senge, P. M. (1990). *The fifth discipline: The art and practice of the learning organization*. New York: Doubleday Currency.

Sergiovanni, T. J., & J. E. Corbally, eds. (1984). *Leadership and organizational culture*. Urbana, IL: University of Illinois Press.

Siehl, C., & J. Martin (1984). The role of symbolic management: How can managers effectively transmit organizational culture? In J. G. Hunt, D. M. Hosking, C. A. Schriesheim, & R. Stewart, eds., *Leaders and managers* (pp. 227–239). New York: Pergamon.

Thomas, W. I. (1923). *The unadjusted girl*. New York: Harper Torchbooks, 1967.

Tichy, N. M., & D. O. Ulrich (1984). The leadership challenge: A call for the transformational leader. *Sloan Management Review, 26*(1), 59–68.

Trice, H. M., & J. M. Beyer (1993). *The cultures of work organizations*. Englewood Cliffs, NJ: Prentice Hall.

Van Maanen, J. (1975). Police socialization. *Administrative Science Quarterly, 20*, 207–228.

Van Maanen, J. (1976). Breaking in: Socialization to work. In R. Dubin, ed., *Handbook of work, organization, and society* (pp. 67–130). Chicago: Rand McNally.

Walton, M. (1986). *The Deming management method*. New York: Putnam.

Weick, K. E. (1982). Administering education in loosely-coupled schools. *Phi Delta Kappan, 63*(10), 673–676.

Weisbord, M. R. (1991). *Productive workplaces: Organizing and managing for dignity, meaning, and community*. San Francisco: Jossey-Bass.

Whyte, W. H., Jr. (1956). *The organization man*. New York: Simon & Schuster.

# 26

# The Concept of Organizational Culture: Why Bother?

*Edgar H. Schein*

Culture is an abstraction, yet the forces that are created in social and organizational situations that derive from culture are powerful. If we don't understand the operation of these forces, we become victim to them. To illustrate how the concept of culture helps to illuminate organizational situations, I will begin by describing several situations I have encountered in my experience as a consultant.

## FOUR BRIEF EXAMPLES

In the first case, that of Digital Equipment Corporation (DEC), I was called in to help a management group improve its communication, interpersonal relationships, and decision making. After sitting in on a number of meetings, I observed, among other things, (1) high levels of interrupting, confrontation, and debate; (2) excessive emotionality about proposed courses of action; (3) great frustration over the difficulty of getting a point of view across; and (4) a sense that every member of the group wanted to win all the time.

Over a period of several months, I made many suggestions about better listening, less interrupting, more orderly processing of the agenda, the potential negative effects of high emotionality and conflict, and the need to reduce the frustration level. The group members said that the suggestions were helpful, and they modified certain aspects of their procedure; for example, they scheduled more time for some of their meetings. However, the basic pattern did not change. No matter what kind of intervention I attempted, the basic style of the group remained the same.

In the second case, that of the Ciba-Geigy Company—a large multinational chemical and pharmaceutical company located in Basel, Switzerland—I was asked, as part of a broader consultation project, to help create a climate for innovation in an organization that felt a need to become more flexible in order to respond to its increasingly dynamic business environment. The organization consisted of many different business units, geographical units, and functional groups. As I got to know more about these units and their problems, I observed that some very innovative things were going on in many places in the company. I wrote several memos that described these innovations and presented other ideas from my own experience. I gave the memos to my contact person in the company with the request that he distribute them to the various geographic and business unit managers who needed to be made aware of these ideas.

After some months, I discovered that those managers to whom I had personally given the memo thought it was helpful and on target, but rarely, if ever, did they pass it on, and none were ever distributed by my contact person. I also suggested meetings of managers from different units to stimulate lateral communication, but found no support at all for such meetings. No matter what I did, I could not seem to

*Organizational Culture and Leadership* (3rd. ed.), E. H. Schein San Francisco: Jossey-Bass, pp. 3–23. Copyright © 2004 John Wiley & Sons, Inc. Reproduced with permission of John Wiley & Sons Inc.

get information flowing, especially laterally across divisional, functional, or geographical boundaries. Yet everyone agreed in principle that innovation would be stimulated by more lateral communication and encouraged me to keep on "helping." ...

I did not really understand the forces operating in ... these cases until I began to examine my own assumptions about how things should work in these organizations and began to test whether my assumptions fitted those operating in my client's systems. This step—examining the shared assumptions in the organization or group one is dealing with and comparing them to one's own—takes one into cultural analysis and will be the focus from here on.

It turned out that at DEC, an assumption was shared by senior managers and most of the other members of the organization: that one cannot determine whether or not something is "true" or "valid" unless one subjects the idea or proposal to intensive debate; and further, that only ideas that survive such debate are worth acting on, and only ideas that survive such scrutiny will be implemented. The group assumed that what they were doing was discovering truth, and in this context being polite to each other was relatively unimportant. I became more helpful to the group when I realized this and went to the flip chart and just started to write down the various ideas they were processing. If someone was interrupted, I could ask them to restate their point instead of punishing the interrupter. The group began to focus on the items on the chart and found that this really did help their communication and decision process. I had finally understood and entered into an essential element of *their* culture instead of imposing my own.

At Ciba-Geigy I eventually discovered that there was a strong shared assumption that each manager's job was his or her private "turf," not to be infringed on. The strong impression was communicated that

one's job is like one's home, and if someone gives one unsolicited information, it is like walking into one's home uninvited. Sending memos to people implies that they do not already know what is in the memo, and that is potentially insulting. In this organization, managers prided themselves on knowing whatever they needed to know to do their job. Had I understood this, I would have asked for a list of the names of the managers and sent the memo directly to them. They would have accepted it from me because I was the paid consultant and expert....

To make sense of such situations requires taking a cultural perspective; learning to see the world through *cultural lenses*; becoming competent in cultural analysis—by which I mean being able to perceive and decipher the cultural forces that operate in groups, organizations, and occupations. Once we learn to see the world through cultural lenses, all kinds of things begin to make sense that initially were mysterious, frustrating, or seemingly stupid.

## CULTURE: AN EMPIRICALLY BASED ABSTRACTION

Culture as a concept has had a long and checkered history. It has been used by the layman as a word to indicate sophistication, as when we say that someone is very "cultured." It has been used by anthropologists to refer to the customs and rituals that societies develop over the course of their history. In the last several decades, it has been used by some organizational researchers and managers to refer to the climate and practices that organizations develop around their handling of people, or to the espoused values and credo of an organization.

In this context, managers speak of developing the "right kind of culture," a "culture of quality" or a "culture of customer service," suggesting that culture has to do with certain values that managers are trying to inculcate in their organizations. Also implied in this usage is the assumption that there are better or worse cultures and stronger or weaker cultures, and that the "right" kind of culture will influence how effective the organization is. In the managerial literature there is often the implication that having a culture is necessary for effective performance, and that the stronger the culture, the more effective the organization.

Researchers have supported some of these views by reporting findings that cultural "strength" or certain kinds of cultures correlate with economic performance (Denison, 1990; Kotter and Heskett, 1992; Sorensen, 2002). Consultants have touted "culture surveys" and have claimed that they can improve organizational performance by helping organizations create certain kinds of cultures, but these claims are based on very different definitions of culture than what I will be arguing for here. As we will see, many of these usages of the word *culture* display not only a superficial and incorrect view of culture, but also a dangerous tendency to evaluate particular cultures in an absolute way and to suggest that there actually are "right" cultures for organizations. As we will also see, whether or not a culture is "good" or "bad," "functionally effective" or not, depends not on the culture alone, but on the relationship of the culture to the environment in which it exists.

Perhaps the most intriguing aspect of culture as a concept is that it points us to phenomena that are below the surface, that are powerful in their impact but invisible and to a considerable degree unconscious. In that sense, culture is to a group what personality or character is to an individual. We can see the behavior that results, but often we cannot see the forces underneath that cause certain kinds of behavior. Yet, just as our personality and character guide and constrain our behavior, so does culture guide and constrain the behavior of members of

a group through the shared norms that are held in that group.

To complicate matters further, one can view personality and character as the accumulation of cultural learning that an individual has experienced in the family, the peer group, the school, the community, and the occupation. In this sense, culture is within us as individuals and yet constantly evolving as we join and create new groups that eventually create new cultures. Culture as a concept is thus an abstraction but its behavioral and attitudinal consequences are very concrete indeed.

If an abstract concept is to be useful to our thinking, it should be observable and also increase our understanding of a set of events that are otherwise mysterious or not well understood. From this point of view, I will argue that we must avoid the superficial models of culture and build on the deeper, more complex anthropological models. Culture as a concept will be most useful if it helps us to better understand the hidden and complex aspects of life in groups, organizations, and occupations, and we cannot obtain this understanding if we use superficial definitions.

## WHAT NEEDS TO BE EXPLAINED?

Most of us, in our roles as students, employees, managers, researchers, or consultants, work in and have to deal with groups and organizations of all kinds. Yet we continue to find it amazingly difficult to understand and justify much of what we observe and experience in our organizational life. Too much seems to be bureaucratic or political or just plain irrational—as in the four cases that I described at the beginning of this chapter.

People in positions of authority, especially our immediate bosses, often frustrate us or act incomprehensibly; those we consider the leaders of our organizations often disappoint us. When we get into arguments or negotiations with others, we often cannot understand how our opponents could take such ridiculous positions. When we observe other organizations, we often find it incomprehensible that smart people could do such dumb things. We recognize cultural differences at the ethnic or national level, but find them puzzling at the group, organizational, or occupational level.

As managers, when we try to change the behavior of subordinates, we often encounter resistance to change to an extent that seems beyond reason. We observe departments in our organization that seem to be more interested in fighting with each other than getting the job done. We see communication problems and misunderstandings between group members that should not be occurring between reasonable people. We explain in detail why something different must be done, yet people continue to act as if they had not heard us.

As leaders who are trying to get our organizations to become more effective in the face of severe environmental pressures, we are sometimes amazed at the degree to which individuals and groups in the organization will continue to behave in obviously ineffective ways, often threatening the very survival of the organization. As we try to get things done that involve other groups, we often discover that they do not communicate with each other and that the level of conflict between groups in organizations and in the community is often astonishingly high.

As teachers, we encounter the sometimes mysterious phenomenon that different classes behave completely differently from each other, even though our material and teaching style remains the same. As employees considering a new job, we realize that companies differ greatly in their approach, even in the same industry and geographic locale. We feel these differences even as we walk through the doors of different organizations, such as restaurants, banks, stores, or airlines.

As members of different occupations, we are aware that being a doctor, lawyer, engineer, accountant, or other professional involves not only the learning of technical skills but also the adoption of certain values and norms that define our occupation. If we violate some of these norms we can be thrown out of the occupation. But where do these come from and how do we reconcile the fact that each occupation considers its norms and values to be the correct ones?

The concept of culture helps to explain all of these phenomena and to normalize them. If we understand the dynamics of culture, we will be less likely to be puzzled, irritated, and anxious when we encounter the unfamiliar and seemingly irrational behavior of people in organizations, and we will have a deeper understanding not only of why various groups of people or organizations can be so different, but also why it is so hard to change them. Even more important, if we understand culture better we will better understand ourselves—better understand the forces acting within us that define who we are, that reflect the groups with which we identify and to which we want to belong.

## CULTURE AND LEADERSHIP

When we examine culture and leadership closely, we see that they are two sides of the same coin; neither can really be understood by itself. On the one hand, cultural norms define how a given nation or organizations will define leadership—who will get promoted, who will get the attention of followers. On the other hand, it can be argued that the only thing of real importance that leaders do is to create and manage culture; that the unique talent of leaders is their ability to understand and work with culture; and that it is an ultimate act of leadership to destroy culture when it is viewed as dysfunctional.

If one wishes to distinguish leadership from management or administration, one can argue that leadership creates and changes cultures, while management and administration act within a culture. By defining leadership in this manner, I am not implying that culture is easy to create or change, or that formal leaders are the only determiners of culture. On the contrary,... culture refers to those elements of a group or organization that are most stable and least malleable.

Culture is the result of a complex group learning process that is only partially influenced by leader behavior. But if the group's survival is threatened because elements of its culture have become maladapted, it is ultimately the function of leadership at all levels of the organization to recognize and do something about this situation. It is in this sense that leadership and culture are conceptually intertwined.

## TOWARD A FORMAL DEFINITION OF CULTURE

When we apply the concept of culture to groups, organizations, and occupations, we are almost certain to have conceptual and semantic confusion, because such social units are themselves difficult to define unambiguously. I will use as the critical defining characteristic of a *group* the fact that its members have a shared history. Any social unit that has some kind of shared history will have evolved a culture, with the strength of that culture dependent on the length of its existence, the stability of the group's membership, and the emotional intensity of the actual historical experiences they have shared. We all have a commonsense notion of this phenomenon, yet it is difficult to define it abstractly. In talking about organizational culture with colleagues and members of organizations, I often find that we agree that "it" exists and that it is important in its effects, but when we try to define it, we have completely different ideas of what "it" is.

To make matters worse, the concept of culture has been the subject of considerable

academic debate in the last twenty-five years and there are various approaches to defining and studying culture (for example, those of Hofstede, 1991; Trice and Beyer, 1993; Schultz, 1995; Deal and Kennedy, 1999; Cameron and Quinn, 1999; Ashkanasy, Wilderom, and Peterson, 2000; and Martin, 2002). This debate is a healthy sign in that it testifies to the importance of culture as a concept, but at the same time it creates difficulties for both the scholar and the practitioner if definitions are fuzzy and usages are inconsistent.... I will give only a quick overview of this range of usage and then offer a precise and formal definition that makes the most sense from my point of view....

Commonly used words relating to culture emphasize one of its critical aspects—the idea that certain things in groups are shared or held in common. The major categories of observables that are associated with culture in this sense are shown in Exhibit 26.1.

All of these concepts relate to culture or reflect culture in that they deal with things that group members *share* or hold in common, but none of them can usefully be thought of as "the culture" of an organization or group. If one asks why we need the word *culture* at all when we have so many other concepts—such as norms, values, behavior patterns, rituals, traditions, and so on—one recognizes that the word *culture* adds several other critical elements to the concept of sharing: structural stability, depth, breadth, and patterning or integration.

### Structural Stability

*Culture* implies some level of structural stability in the group. When we say that something is "cultural," we imply that it is not only shared, but also stable, because it defines the group. Once we achieve a sense of group identity, it is our major stabilizing force and will not be given up easily. Culture survives even when some members of the organization depart. Culture is hard to change

## EXHIBIT 26.1 VARIOUS CATEGORIES USED TO DESCRIBE CULTURE.

*Observed behavioral regularities when people interact*: the *language* they use, the *customs* and *traditions* that evolve, and the *rituals* they employ in a wide variety of situations (Goffman, 1959, 1967; Jones, Moore, and Snyder, 1988; Trice and Beyer, 1993, 1985; Van Maanen, 1979b).

*Group norms*: the implicit standards and values that evolve in working groups, such as the particular norm of "a fair day's work for a fair day's pay" that evolved among workers in the Bank Wiring Room in the Hawthorne studies (Homans, 1950; Kilmann and Saxton, 1983).

*Espoused values*: the articulated, publicly announced principles and values that the group claims to be trying to achieve, such as "product quality" or "price leadership" (Deal and Kennedy, 1982, 1999).

*Formal philosophy*: the broad policies and ideological principles that guide a group's actions toward stockholders, employees, customers, and other stakeholders, such as the highly publicized "HP Way" of Hewlett-Packard (Ouchi, 1981; Pascale and Athos, 1981; Packard, 1995).

*Rules of the game*: the implicit, unwritten rules for getting along in the organization; "the ropes" that a newcomer must learn in order to become an accepted member; "the way we do things around here" (Schein, 1968, 1978; Van Maanen, 1979a, 1979b; Ritti and Funkhouser, 1987).

*Climate*: the feeling that is conveyed in a group by the physical layout and the way in which members of the organization interact with each other, with customers, or other outsiders (Ashkanasy, Wilderom, and Peterson, 2000; Schneider, 1990; Tagiuri and Litwin, 1968).

*Embedded skills*: the special competencies displayed by group members in accomplishing certain tasks, the ability to make certain things that gets passed on from generation to generation without necessarily being articulated in writing (Argyris and Schön, 1978; Cook and Yanow, 1993; Henderson and Clark, 1990; Peters and Waterman, 1982).

*Habits of thinking, mental models, and linguistic paradigms*: the shared cognitive frames that guide the perceptions, thought, and language used by the members of a group and taught to new members in the early socialization process (Douglas, 1986; Hofstede, 2001; Van Maanen, 1979b; Senge and others, 1994).

*Shared meanings*: the emergent understandings created by group members as they interact with each other (as in Geertz, 1973; Smircich, 1983; Van Maanen and Barley, 1984; Weick, 1995).

*"Root metaphors" or integrating symbols*: the ways in which groups evolve to characterize themselves, which may or may not be appreciated consciously but become embodied in buildings, office layout, and other material artifacts of the group. This level of the culture reflects the emotional and aesthetic response of members as contrasted with the cognitive or evaluative response (as in Gagliardi, 1990; Hatch, 1990; Pondy, Frost, Morgan, and Dandridge, 1983; Schultz, 1995).

*Formal rituals and celebrations*: the ways in which a group celebrates key events that reflect important values or important "passages" by members, such as promotion, completion of important projects, and milestones (as in Deal and Kennedy, 1982, 1999; Trice and Beyer, 1993).

---

because group members value stability in that it provides meaning and predictability.

### Depth
Culture is the deepest, often unconscious part of a group and is, therefore, less tangible and less visible than other parts. From this point of view, most of the concepts reviewed above can be thought of as manifestations of culture,

but they are not the essence of what we mean by culture. Note that when something is more deeply embedded it also gains stability.

### Breadth
A third characteristic of culture is that once it has developed, it covers *all* of a group's functioning. Culture is pervasive; it influences all aspects of how an organization

deals with its primary task, its various environments, and its internal operations. Not all groups have cultures in this sense, but the concept connotes that when we refer to the culture of a group we are referring to all of its operations.

### *Patterning or Integration*

The fourth characteristic that is implied by the concept of culture and that further lends stability is patterning or integration of the elements into a larger paradigm or "gestalt" that ties together the various elements and that lies at a deeper level. Culture somehow implies that rituals, climate, values, and behaviors tie together into a coherent whole; this patterning or integration is the essence of what we mean by "culture." Such patterning or integration ultimately derives from the human need to make our environment as sensible and orderly as we can (Weick, 1995). Disorder or senselessness makes us anxious, so we will work hard to reduce that anxiety by developing a more consistent and predictable view of how things are and how they should be. Thus "organizational cultures, like other cultures, develop as groups of people struggle to make sense of and cope with their worlds" (Trice and Beyer, 1993, p. 4).

How then should we think about the "essence" of culture and how should we formally define it? The most useful way to arrive at a definition of something as abstract as culture is to think in dynamic evolutionary terms. If we can understand where culture comes from and how it evolves, then we can grasp something that is abstract; that exists in a group's unconscious, yet that has powerful influences on a group's behavior.

## HOW DOES CULTURE FORM?

Culture forms in two ways. [S]pontaneous interaction in an unstructured group gradually leads to patterns and norms of behavior

that become the culture of that group—often within just hours of the group's formation. In more formal groups an individual creates the group or becomes its leader. This could be an entrepreneur starting a new company, a religious person creating a following, a political leader creating a new party, a teacher starting a new class, or a manager taking over a new department of an organization. The individual founder—whether an entrepreneur or just the convener of a new group—will have certain personal visions, goals, beliefs, values, and assumptions about how things should be. He or she will initially impose these on the group and/or select members on the basis of their similarity of thoughts and values.

We can think of this imposition as a primary act of leadership, but it does not automatically produce culture. All it produces is compliance in the followers to do what the leader asks of them. Only if the resulting behavior leads to "success"—in the sense that the group accomplishes its task and the members feel good about their relationships to each other—will the founder's beliefs and values be confirmed and reinforced, and, most important, come to be recognized as *shared*. What was originally the founder's *individual* view of the world leads to shared action, which, if successful, leads to a *shared* recognition that the founder "had it right." The group will then act again on these beliefs and values and, if it continues to be successful, will eventually conclude that it now has the "correct" way to think, feel, and act.

If, on the other hand, the founder's beliefs and values do not lead to success, the group will fail and disappear or will seek other leadership until someone is found whose beliefs and values will lead to success. The culture formation process will then revolve around that new leader. With continued reinforcement, the group will become less and less conscious of these beliefs and values, and it will begin to treat them more and more as nonnegotiable assumptions. As this process continues, these assumptions will gradually drop out of awareness and come to be taken for granted. As assumptions come to be taken for granted they become part of the identity of the group; are taught to newcomers as the way to think, feel, and act; and, if violated, produce discomfort, anxiety, ostracism, and eventually excommunication. This concept of assumptions, as opposed to beliefs and values, implies nonnegotiability. If we are willing to argue about something, then it has not become taken for granted. Therefore, definitions of culture that deal with *values* must specify that culture consists of *nonnegotiable values*—which I am calling *assumptions*.

In summary, we can think of culture as the accumulated shared learning of a given group, covering behavioral, emotional, and cognitive elements of the group members' total psychological functioning. For such shared learning to occur, there must be a history of shared experience that, in turn, implies some stability of membership in the group. Given such stability and a shared history, the human need for stability, consistency, and meaning will cause the various shared elements to form into patterns that eventually can be called a culture.

## CULTURE FORMALLY DEFINED

The culture of a group can now be defined as a pattern of shared basic assumptions that was learned by a group as it solved its problems of external adaptation and internal integration, that has worked well enough to be considered valid and, therefore, to be taught to new members as the correct way to perceive, think, and feel in relation to those problems.

I am not arguing that all groups evolve integrated cultures in this sense. We all know of groups, organizations, and societies in which certain beliefs and values work at cross purposes with other beliefs and values, leading to situations full of conflict and ambiguity (Martin, 2002). This may result from insufficient stability of membership, insufficient shared history of experience, or the presence of many subgroups with different kinds of shared experiences. Ambiguity and conflict also result from the fact that each of us belongs to many groups, so that what we bring to any given group is influenced by the assumptions that are appropriate to our other groups.

But if the concept of culture is to have any utility, it should draw our attention to those things that are the product of our human need for stability, consistency, and meaning. Culture formation is always, by definition, a striving toward patterning and integration, even though in many groups their actual history of experiences prevents them from ever achieving a clear-cut, unambiguous paradigm.

If a group's culture is the result of that group's accumulated learning, how do we describe and catalogue the content of that learning? All group and organizational theories distinguish two major sets of problems that all groups, no matter what their size, must deal with: (1) survival, growth, and adaptation in their environment; and (2) internal integration that permits daily functioning and the ability to adapt and learn. Both of these areas of group functioning will reflect the larger cultural context in which the group exists and from which are derived broader and deeper basic assumptions about the nature of reality, time, space, human nature, and human relationships....

At this point, it is important to discuss several other elements that are important to our formal definition of culture.

### The Process of Socialization

Once a group has a culture, it will pass elements of this culture on to new generations of group members (Louis, 1980; Schein, 1968; Van Maanen, 1976; Van Maanen and Schein, 1979). Studying what new members of groups are taught is, in fact, a good way to discover some of the elements of a culture; however, by this means one only learns about surface aspects of the culture—especially because much of what is at the heart of a culture will not be revealed in the rules of behavior taught to newcomers. It will only be revealed to members as they gain permanent status and are allowed into the inner circles of the group in which group secrets are shared.

On the other hand, how one learns and the socialization processes to which one is subjected may indeed reveal deeper assumptions. To get at those deeper levels one must try to understand the perceptions and feelings that arise in critical situations, and one must observe and interview regular members or "old-timers" to get an accurate sense of the deeper-level assumptions that are shared.

Can culture be learned through anticipatory socialization or self-socialization? Can new members discover for themselves what the basic assumptions are? Yes and no. We certainly know that one of the major activities of any new member when she enters a new group is to decipher the operating norms and assumptions. But this deciphering can be successful only through the feedback that is meted out by old members to new members as they experiment with different kinds of behavior. In this sense, there is always a teaching process going on, even though it may be quite implicit and unsystematic.

If the group does not have shared assumptions, as will sometimes be the case, the new member's interaction with old members will be a more creative process of building a culture. But once shared assumptions exist, the culture survives through teaching them to newcomers. In this regard, culture is a mechanism of social control and can be the basis for explicitly manipulating members into perceiving, thinking, and feeling in certain ways (Van Maanen and Kunda, 1989; Kunda, 1992; Schein, 1968)....

### Behavior is Derivative, Not Central

This formal definition of culture does not include overt behavior patterns (although some such behavior—particularly formal rituals—does reflect cultural assumptions). Instead, it emphasizes that the critical assumptions deal with how we perceive, think about, and feel about things. Overt behavior is always determined both by the cultural predisposition (the perceptions, thoughts, and feelings that are patterned) and by the situational contingencies that arise from the immediate external environment.

Behavioral regularities can occur for reasons other than shared culture. For example, if we observe that all members of a group cower in the presence of a large, loud leader, this could be based on biological, reflex reactions to sound and size, or on individual or shared learning. Such a behavioral regularity should not, therefore, be the basis for defining culture—though we might later discover that, in a given group's experience, cowering is indeed a result of shared learning and, therefore, a manifestation of deeper shared assumptions. To put it another way, when we observe behavior regularities, we do not know whether or not we are dealing with a cultural manifestation. Only after we have discovered the deeper layers that I define as the essence of culture can we specify what is and what is not an artifact that reflects the culture.

### Can a Large Organization or Occupation Have One Culture?

My formal definition does not specify the size of social unit to which it can legitimately be applied. Our experience with large organizations tells us that at a certain size the variations among the subgroups is substantial, suggesting that it might not be appropriate to talk of the culture of an IBM or a General Motors or Shell. In the evolution of DEC over its thirty-five-year history one can see both a strong overall corporate culture and the growth of powerful subcultures that reflected the larger culture but also differed in important ways (Schein, 2003). In fact, the growing tensions among the subcultures were partly the reason why DEC as an economic entity ultimately failed to survive.

### Do Occupations Have Cultures?

If an occupation involves an intense period of education and apprenticeship, there will certainly be a shared learning of attitudes, norms, and values that eventually will become taken-for-granted assumptions for the members of those occupations. It is assumed that the beliefs and values learned during this time will remain stable as assumptions even though the person may not always be in a group of occupational peers. But reinforcement of those assumptions occurs at professional meetings and continuing education sessions, and by virtue of the fact that the practice of the occupation often calls for teamwork among several members of the occupation, who reinforce each other. One reason why so many occupations rely heavily on peer-group evaluation is that this process preserves and protects the culture of the occupation.

Determining which sets of assumptions apply to a whole society, or a whole organization, or a whole subgroup within an organization or occupation, should be done empirically. I have found all kinds of combinations; their existence is one reason why some theorists emphasize that organizational cultures can be integrated, differentiated, or fragmented (Martin, 2002). But for the purpose of defining culture, it is important to recognize that a fragmented or differentiated organizational culture usually reflects a multiplicity of subcultures, and within those subcultures there are shared assumptions.

### Are Some Assumptions More Important than Others?

…[O]rganizations do seem to function primarily in terms of some core of assumptions, some smaller set that can be thought of as the cultural paradigm or the governing assumptions, or as critical "genes" in the "cultural DNA." For the researcher, the problem is that different organizations will have different paradigms with different core assumptions. As a result, cultural typologies can be very misleading. One could measure many organizations on the same core dimensions, but in some of those organizations a particular dimension could be central to the paradigm, whereas in others its influence on the organization's behavior could be quite peripheral.

If the total set of shared basic assumptions of a given organizational culture can be thought of as its DNA, then we can examine some of the individual genes in terms of their centrality or potency in forcing certain kinds of growth and behavior, and other genes in terms of their power to inhibit or prevent certain kinds of behavior. We can then see that certain kinds of cultural evolution are determined by the "genetic structure," the kind of "autoimmune system" that the organization generates, and the impact of "mutations and hybridization."

## SUMMARY AND CONCLUSIONS

…[A]ny group with a stable membership and a history of shared learning will have developed some level of culture, but a group that has had either considerable turnover of members and leaders or a history lacking in any kind of challenging events may well lack any shared assumptions. Not every collection of people develops a culture; in fact, we tend to use the term *group* rather than, say, *crowd* or *collection* of people only when there has been enough of a shared history for some degree of culture formation to have taken place.

Once a set of shared assumptions has come to be taken for granted, it determines much of the group's behavior, and the rules and norms are taught to newcomers in a socialization process that is itself a reflection of culture. To define culture one must go below the behavioral level, because behavioral regularities can be caused by forces other than culture. Even large organizations and entire occupations can have a common culture if there has been enough of a history of shared experience. Finally, I noted that the shared assumptions will form a paradigm, with more or less central or governing assumptions driving the system, much as certain genes drive the genetic structure of human DNA.

Culture and leadership are two sides of the same coin, in that leaders first create cultures when they create groups and organizations. Once cultures exist, they determine the criteria for leadership and thus determine who will or will not be a leader. But if elements of a culture become dysfunctional, it is the unique function of leadership to be able to perceive the functional and dysfunctional elements of the existing culture and to manage cultural evolution and change in such a way that the group can survive in a changing environment.

The bottom line for leaders is that if they do not become conscious of the cultures in which they are embedded, those cultures will manage them. Cultural understanding is desirable for all of us, but it is essential to leaders if they are to lead....

## REFERENCES

Argyris, C., & Schön, D. A. (1978). *Organizational learning.* Reading, MA: Addison-Wesley.

Ashkanasy, N. M., Wilderom, C. P. M., & Peterson, M. F., eds. (2000). *Handbook of organizational culture and climate.* Thousand Oaks, CA: Sage.

Cameron, K. S., & Quinn, R. E. (1999). *Diagnosing and changing organizational culture.* Reading, MA: Addison-Wesley.

Cook, S. D. N., & Yanow, D. (1993). Culture and organizational learning. *Journal of Management Inquiry,* 2(4), 373–390.

Deal, T. E., & Kennedy, A. A. (1982). *Corporate cultures.* Reading, MA: Addison-Wesley.

Deal, T. E., & Kennedy, A. A. (1999). *The new corporate cultures.* New York: Perseus.

Denison, D. R. (1990). *Corporate culture and organizational effectiveness.* New York: Wiley.

Douglas, M. (1986). *How institutions think.* Syracuse, NY: Syracuse University Press.

Gagliardi, P. (Ed.) (1990). *Symbols and artifacts: Views of the corporate landscape.* New York: Walter de Gruyter.

Geertz, C. (1973). *The interpretation of cultures.* New York: Basic Books.

Goffman, E. (1959). *The presentation of self in everyday life.* New York: Doubleday.

Goffman, E. (1961). *Asylums.* New York: Doubleday Anchor.

Goffman, E. (1967). *Interaction ritual.* Hawthorne, NY: Aldine.

Hatch, M. J. (1990). The symbolics of office design. In P. Gagliardi, ed., *Symbols and artifacts.* New York: Walter de Gruyter.

Havrylyshyn, B. (1980). *Road maps to the future.* Oxford, England: Pergamon Press.

Henderson, R. M., & Clark, K. B. (1990). Architectural innovation: The reconfiguration of existing product technologies and the failure of established firms. *Administrative Science Quarterly,* 35, 9–30.

Hofstede, G. (1991). *Cultures and organizations.* London: McGraw-Hill.

Hofstede, G. (2001). *Culture's consequences,* 2nd ed. Thousand Oaks, CA: Sage (1st ed. 1980).

Homans, G. (1950). *The human group.* New York: Harcourt Brace Jovanovich.

Jaques, E. (1982). *The forms of time.* London: Heinemann.

Jaques, E. (1989). *Requisite organization.* Arlington, VA: Cason Hall.

Jones, M. O., Moore, M. D., & Snyder, R. C. (Eds.) (1988). *Inside organizations.* Thousand Oaks, CA: Sage.

Kets de Vries, M. F. R., & Miller, D. (1984). *The neurotic organization: Diagnosing and changing counterproductive styles of management.* San Francisco: Jossey-Bass.

Kilmann, R. H., & Saxton, M. J. (1983). *The Kilmann-Saxton culture gap survey.* Pittsburgh, PA: Organizational Design Consultants.

Kotter, J. P., & Heskett, J. L. (1992). *Culture and performance.* New York: Free Press.

Kunda, G. (1992). *Engineering culture.* Philadelphia, PA: Temple University Press.

Louis, M. R. (1980). Surprise and sense making. *Administrative Science Quarterly, 25,* 226–251.

Louis, M. R. (1981). A cultural perspective on organizations. *Human Systems Management, 2,* 246–258.

Martin, J. (2002). *Organizational culture: Mapping the terrain.* Thousand Oaks, CA: Sage.

Martin, J., & Powers, M. E. (1983). Truth or corporate propaganda: The value of a good war story. In L. R. Pondy & others, eds., *Organizational symbolism.* Greenwich, CT: JAI Press.

Ouchi, W. G. (1981). *Theory Z.* Reading, MA: Addison-Wesley.

Ouchi, W. G., & Johnson, J. (1978). Types of organizational control and their relationship to emotional well-being. *Administrative Science Quarterly, 23,* 293–317.

Packard, D. (1995). *The HP way.* New York: HarperCollins.

Pascale, R. T., & Athos, A. G. (1981). *The art of Japanese management.* New York: Simon & Schuster.

Peters, T. J. (1987). *Thriving on chaos.* New York: Knopf.

Peters, T. J., & Waterman, R. H., Jr. (1982). *In search of excellence.* New York: HarperCollins.

Pettigrew, A. M. (1979). On studying organizational cultures. *Administrative Science Quarterly, 24,* 570–581.

Pheysey, D. C. (1993). *Organizational cultures: Types and transformations.* London, UK: Routledge.

Pondy, L. R., Frost, P. J., Morgan, G., & Dandridge, T., eds. (1983). *Organizational symbolism.* Greenwich, CT: JAI Press.

Ritti, R. R., & Funkhouser, G. R. (1987). *The ropes to skip and the ropes to know.* Columbus, OH: Grid (3rd ed.; 1st ed. 1982).

Schein, E. H. (1968). Organizational socialization and the profession of management. *Industrial Management Review, 9,* 1–15.

Schein, E. H. (1969). *Process consultation: Its role in organization development.* Reading, MA: Addison-Wesley.

Schein, E. H. (1978). *Career dynamics: Matching individual and organizational needs.* Reading, MA: Addison-Wesley.

Schein, E. H. (1980). *Organizational psychology,* 3rd ed. Englewood Cliffs, NJ: Prentice Hall (1st ed. 1965).

Schein, E. H. (2003). *DEC is dead; long live DEC.* San Francisco: Berrett-Koehler.

Schein, E. H., & Bennis, W. G. (1965). *Personal and organizational change through group methods.* New York: Wiley.

Schneider, B. (Ed.) (1990). *Organizational climate and culture.* San Francisco: Jossey-Bass.

Schultz, M. (1995). *On studying organizational cultures.* New York: Walter de Gruyter.

Senge, P. M., Roberts, C., Ross, R. B., Smith, B. J., & Kleiner, A. (1994). *The fifth discipline field book.* New York: Doubleday Currency.

Sergiovanni, T. J., & J. E. Corbally, eds. (1984). *Leadership and organizational culture.* Urbana and Chicago, IL: University of Illinois Press.

Smircich, L. (1983). Concepts of culture and organizational analysis. *Administrative Science Quarterly, 28,* 339–358.

Sorensen, J. B. (2002). The strength of corporate culture and the reliability of firm performance. *Administrative Science Quarterly, 47,* 70–91.

Steward, J. H. (1955). *Theory of culture change.* Urbana: University of Illinois Press.

Tagiuri, R., & Litwin, G. H., eds. (1968). *Organizational climate: Exploration of a concept.* Boston: Division of Research, Harvard Graduate School of Business.

Trice, H. M., & Beyer, J. M. (1984). Studying organizational cultures through rites and ceremonials. *Academy of Management Review, 9,* 653–669.

Trice, H. M., & Beyer, J. M. (1985). Using six organizational rites to change culture. In R. H. Kilmann, M. J. Saxton, R. Serpa, and associates. *Gaining control of the corporate culture.* San Francisco: Jossey-Bass, 370–399.

Trice, H. M., & Beyer, J. M. (1993). *The cultures of work organizations.* Englewood Cliffs, NJ: Prentice Hall.

Van Maanen, J. (1976). Breaking in: Socialization at work. In R. Dubin, ed., *Handbook of work organization and society.* Skokie, IL: Rand McNally.

Van Maanen, J. (1977). Experiencing organizations. In J. Van Maanen, ed., *Organizational careers: Some new perspectives.* New York: Wiley.

Van Maanen, J. (1979a). The fact of fiction in organizational ethnography. *Administrative Science Quarterly,* 24, 539–550.

Van Maanen, J. (1979b). The self, the situation, and the rules of interpersonal relations. In W. Bennis and others, *Essays in interpersonal dynamics.* Florence, KY: Dorsey Press.

Van Maanen, J. (1988). *Tales of the field: On writing ethnography.* Chicago: University of Chicago Press.

Van Maanen, J., & Barley, S. R. (1984). Occupational communities: Culture and control in organizations. In B. M. Staw & L. L. Cummings, eds., *Research in organizational behavior* (Vol. 6). Greenwich, CT: JAI Press.

Van Maanen, J., & Kunda, G. (1989). Real feelings: Emotional expression and organizational culture. In B. Staw, ed., *Research in organizational behavior* (Vol. 11). Greenwich, CT: JAI Press.

Van Maanen, J., & Schein, E. H. (1979). Toward a theory of organizational socialization. In B. M. Staw & L. L. Cummings, eds., *Research in organizational behavior* (Vol. 1). Greenwich, CT: JAI Press.

Weick, K. (1995). *Sensemaking in organizations.* Thousand Oaks, CA: Sage.

Wilkins, A. L. (1983). Organizational stories as symbols which control the organization. In L. R. Pondy and others, eds., *Organizational symbolism.* Greenwich, CT: JAI Press.

# 27

# Cultures and Organizations: Pyramids, Machines, Markets, and Families: Organizing Across Nations

*Geert Hofstede, Gert Jan Hofstede, & Michael Minkov*

Somewhere in Western Europe a middle-sized textile printing company struggled for survival. Cloth, usually imported from Asian countries, was printed in multicolored patterns according to the desires of customers, firms producing fashion clothing for the local market. The company was run by a general manager, to whom three functional managers reported: one for design and sales, one for manufacturing, and one for finance and personnel. The total workforce numbered about 250.

The working climate in the firm was often disturbed by conflicts between the sales manager and the manufacturing manager. The manufacturing manager had an interest, as manufacturing managers have the world over, in maintaining a smooth production process with minimal product changes. He preferred grouping customer orders into large batches. Changing colors and/or designs involved cleaning the machines, which cut into productive time and also wasted costly dyestuffs. The worst was changing from a dark color set into a light one, because every bit of dark-colored dye left would show on the cloth and spoil the product quality. Therefore, the manufacturing planners tried to start on a clean machine with the lightest shades and gradually move toward darker ones, postponing the need for an overall cleaning round as long as possible.

The design and sales manager tried to satisfy his customers in a highly competitive market. These fashion clothing firms were notorious for short-term planning changes. As their supplier, the printing company often got requests for rush orders. Even when these orders were small and unlikely to be profitable, the sales manager hated to say no; the customer might go to a competitor, and then the printing firm would miss out on that big order that the sales manager was sure would come afterward. The rush orders, however, usually upset the manufacturing manager's schedules and forced him to print short runs of dark color sets on a beautifully clean machine, thus forcing the production operators to start cleaning all over again.

There were frequent disagreements between the two managers over whether a certain rush order should or should not be taken into production. The conflict was not limited to the department heads: production personnel publicly expressed doubts about the competence of the salespeople, and vice versa. In the cafeteria the production workers and salespeople would not sit together, although they had known each other for years.

## IMPLICIT MODELS OF ORGANIZATIONS

This story describes a banal problem of a kind that occurs regularly in all types of organizations. As with most other organization

Geert Hofstede, Gert Jan Hofstede, and Michael Minkov (2010). *Cultures and Organizations: Software of the Mind.* Selected sections from chapter 9, "Pyramids, Machines, Markets, and Families: Organizing Across Nations": 301–312; 315–331; 337–340. Reprinted with permission from Geert Hofstede.

problems, it has both structural and human aspects. The people involved react according to their mental software. Part of this mental software consists of people's ideas about what an organization should be like.

Organizing always requires answering two questions: (1) who has the power to decide what? and (2) what rules or procedures will be followed to attain the desired ends? The answer to the first question is influenced by cultural norms of power distance; the answer to the second question, by cultural norms about uncertainty avoidance. The remaining two dimensions, individualism and masculinity, affect our thinking about people in organizations, rather than about organizations themselves.

Power distance (PDI) and uncertainty avoidance (UAI) have been plotted against each other in Figure 27.1 and if the preceding analysis is correct, the position of a country in this diagram should tell us something about the country's way of solving organizational problems.

There is empirical evidence for the relationship between a country's position within the PDI-UAI matrix and models of organizations implicit in the minds of people from those countries that affect the way problems are tackled. In the 1970s Owen James Stevens, an American professor at INSEAD business school in Fontainebleau, France, used as an examination assignment for his organizational behavior course a case study very similar to the one presented at the beginning of this chapter. This case, too, dealt with a conflict between two department heads within a company. Among the INSEAD M.B.A. (master of business administration) students taking the exam, the three largest national contingents were the French, the Germans, and the British. In Figure 27.1, we find their countries in the lower right, lower left, and upper left quadrants, respectively.

Stevens had noticed earlier that the students' nationality seemed to affect their way of handling this case. He had kept a file of the examination work of about two hundred students, in which, with regard to the case in question, the students had written down, individually, (1) their diagnosis of the problem and (2) their suggested solution. Stevens had sorted these exams by the nationality of the author, and he separately reviewed all French, all German, and all British answers.

The results were striking. The majority of the French students diagnosed the case as negligence by the general manager to whom the two department heads reported. The solution preferred by the French was for the opponents to take the conflict to their common boss, who would issue orders for settling such dilemmas in the future. Stevens interpreted the implicit organization model of the French as a "pyramid of people": the general manager at the top of the pyramid and each successive level at its proper place below.

The majority of the Germans diagnosed the case as a lack of structure. The scope of responsibility of the two conflicting department heads had never been clearly laid down. The solution preferred by the Germans was the establishment of procedures. Possible ways to develop these procedures included calling in a consultant, nominating a task force, and asking the common boss. The Germans, Stevens felt, saw an organization ideally as a "well-oiled machine" in which management intervention is limited to exceptional cases because the rules should settle all daily problems.

The majority of the British diagnosed the case as a human relations problem. The two department heads were poor negotiators, and their skills in this respect should be developed by sending them to a management course, preferably together. The implicit model of an organization in the minds of the British, Stevens thought, was a "village market" in which neither hierarchy nor rules but rather the demands of the situation determine what will happen.

## FIGURE 27.1 • POWER DISTANCE VERSUS UNCERTAINTY AVOIDANCE

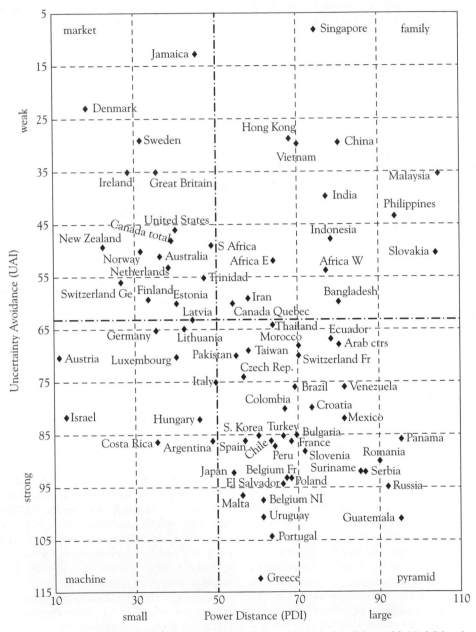

Geert Hofstede, Gert Jan Hofstede, and Michael Minkov (2010). *Cultures and Organizations: Software of the Mind.* Selected sections from chapter 9, "Pyramids, Machines, Markets, and Families: Organizing Across Nations." p. 303

Stevens's experience happened to coincide with the discovery, in the context of the IBM research project, of power distance and uncertainty avoidance as dimensions of country cultures. These two dimensions resembled those found a few years earlier through a piece of academic research commonly known as the Aston Studies. From 1961 through 1973, the University of Aston, in Birmingham, England, hosted an Industrial Administration Research Unit.[1] The Aston Studies represented a large-scale attempt to assess quantitatively—that is, to measure—key aspects of the structure of different organizations. The principal conclusion from the Aston Studies was that the two major dimensions along which structures of organizations differ are concentration of authority and structuring of activities. It did not take much imagination to associate the first with power distance and the second with uncertainty avoidance.

The Aston researchers had tried to measure the "hard" aspects of organization structure: *objectively* assessable characteristics. Power-distance and uncertainty-avoidance indexes measure soft, *subjective* characteristics of the people within a country. A link between the two would mean that organizations are structured in order to meet the subjective cultural needs of their members. Stevens's (1973) implicit models of organization in fact provided the proof. French INSEAD M.B.A. students with their "pyramid of people" model, coming from a country with large power distance *and* strong uncertainty avoidance, advocated measures to concentrate the authority *and* structure the activities. Germans with their "well-oiled *machine*" model, coming from a country with strong uncertainty avoidance but small power distance, wanted to structure the activities *without* concentrating the authority. British INSEAD M.B.A. students with a "village market" model, and with a national culture characterized by small power distant and weak uncertainty

avoidance, advocated neither concentrating authority nor structuring activities. And all of them were dealing with the same case study. People with international business experience have confirmed many times over that, other things being equal, French organizations concentrate authority more, German ones *do* need more structure, and people in British ones *do* believe more in resolving problems ad hoc.

A discussion of Stevens' models with Indian and Indonesian colleagues led to the suggestion that the equivalent implicit model of an organization in these countries is the (extended) "family," in which the owner-manager is the almighty (grand) father. It corresponds to large power distance but weak uncertainty avoidance, a situation in which people would resolve the conflict we pictured by permanent referral to the boss: concentration of authority without structuring of activities. Anant Negandhi and S. Benjamin Prasad, two Americans originally from India, quoted a senior Indian executive with a Ph.D. from a prestigious American university:

> What is most important for me and my department is not what I do or achieve for the company, but whether the Master's favor is bestowed on me.... This I have achieved by saying "yes" to everything the Master says or does..... To contradict him is to look for another job ... I left my freedom of thought in Boston.[2]

More recently, psychologist Jan Pieter van Oudenhoven, of Holland, collected spontaneous descriptions of local organizations from more than seven hundred business administration students in ten countries.[3] The students were asked to describe a company they knew well in a number of freely chosen adjectives. The way these students described organizations in their respective countries reflected aspects of their national culture.

A network of political scientists coordinated by Poul Erik Mouritzen, of Denmark, and James Svara, of the United States, studied local government administration in more than four thousand municipalities covering fourteen Western democracies. Among other things, they collected scores on national cultures, through survey answers by the top civil servant in each municipal administration. They distinguished four ways in which local government was organized, dividing roles between elected political leaders and appointed civil servants:

1. The *strong-mayor form*, in which an elected mayor controls the majority of the city council and is in charge of all executive functions. The top civil servant serves at the mayor's will. This form was found in France, Italy, Portugal, and Spain, as well as in major cities in the United States.
2. The *council-manager form*, in which all executive functions are in the hands of the top civil servant, who is appointed by an elected council that has responsibility for setting policies but not for their execution. This form was found in Australia, Finland, Ireland, and Norway and in the smaller municipalities in the United States.
3. The *committee-leader form*, in which the executive functions are shared by standing committees composed of elected politicians, the political leader (with or without the title of mayor), and the top civil servant. This form was found in Denmark, Sweden, and the United Kingdom.
4. The *collective form*, in which all executive functions are in the hands of an executive committee of elected politicians presided over by an appointed mayor, to whom the top civil servant reports. This form was found in Belgium and the Netherlands.[4]

The researchers relate these forms to the national cultural dimensions of power distance and uncertainty avoidance, as measured by the top civil servant's answers on the culture survey. On this basis and within this group of fourteen countries, the strong-mayor form was found where uncertainty avoidance was relatively strong. The council-manager form was found where uncertainty avoidance was relatively weak and power distance medium. The committee-leader form was found where uncertainty avoidance was relatively weak and power distance small.[5]

## Management Professors Are Human

Not only organizations are culture bound; theories about organizations are equally culture bound. The professors who wrote the theories are children of a culture; they grew up in families, went to schools, worked for employers. Their experiences represent the material on which their thinking and writing have been based. Scholars are as human and as culturally biased as other mortals.

For each of the four corners of Figure 27.1, we selected a classical author who described organizations in terms of the model belonging to his corner of the diagram: the pyramid, the machine, the market, or the family. The four are approximate contemporaries; all were born in the mid-nineteenth century.

Henri Fayol (1841–1925) was a French engineer whose management career culminated in the position of *président-directeur-général* of a mining company. After his retirement, he formulated his experiences in a ground-breaking text on organization: *Administration industrielle et générate* (1916). On the issue of the exercise of authority, Fayol wrote:

> We distinguish in a manager his statutory authority which is in the office, and his personal authority which consists of his intelligence, his knowledge, his experience, his moral value, his leadership, his service record, etc. For a good manager, personal authority is the indispensable complement to statutory authority.[6]

In Fayol's conception, the authority is both in the person *and in* the rules (the statute). We recognize the model of the organization as a pyramid of people with both personal power *and* formal rules as principles of coordination.

Max Weber (1864–1920) was a German academic with university training in law and some years' experience as a civil servant. He became a professor of economics and a founder of German sociology. Weber quotes a seventeenth-century Puritan Protestant Christian textbook about "the sinfulness of the belief in authority, which is only permissible in the form of an impersonal authority."[7] In his own design for an organization, Weber describes the *bureaucracy*. The word was originally a joke, a classic Greek ending grafted on a modern French stem. Nowadays, it has a distinctly negative connotation, but to Weber it represented the ideal type for any large organization. About the authority in a bureaucracy, Weber wrote:

> *The authority to give the commands required for the discharge of (the assigned) duties should be exercised in a stable way. It is strictly delimited by rules concerning the coercive means … which may be placed at the disposal of officials.*[8]

In Weber's conception the real authority is in the rules. The power of the "officials" is strictly delimited by these rules. We recognize the model of the organization as a well-oiled machine that runs according to the rules.

Frederick Winslow Taylor (1857–1915) was an American engineer who, contrary to Fayol, had started his career in industry as a worker. He attained his academic qualifications through evening studies. From chief engineer in a steel company, he became one of the first management consultants. Taylor was not really concerned with the issue of authority at all; his focus was on efficiency. He proposed splitting the task of the first-line boss into eight specialties, each exercised by a different person. Thus, each worker would have eight bosses, each with a different responsibility. This part of Taylor's ideas was never completely implemented, although we find elements of it in the modern *matrix organization*, in which an employee has two (or even three) bosses, usually one concerned with productivity and one with technical expertise.

Taylor's book *Shop Management* (1903) appeared in a French translation in 1913, and Fayol read it and devoted six full pages of his own 1916 book to Taylor's ideas. Fayol shows himself generally impressed but shocked by Taylor's "denial of the principle of the Unity of Command" in the case of the eight-boss system. "For my part," Fayol writes, "I do not believe that a department could operate in flagrant violation of the Unity of Command principle. Still, Taylor has been a successful manager of large organizations. How can we explain this contradiction?"[9] Fayol's rhetorical question had been answered by his compatriot Blaise Pascal two and a half centuries before: there are truths in one country that are falsehoods in another.

In a 1981 article, André Laurent, another of Fayol's compatriots, demonstrated that French managers in a survey reacted very strongly against a suggestion that one employee could report to two different bosses, while Swedish and U.S. managers, among others, in the same survey, showed fewer misgivings in this respect.[10] Matrix organization has never become as popular in France as it has in the United States. It is amusing to read Laurent's suggestion that in order to make matrix organizations acceptable in France, they should be translated into hierarchical terms—that is, one real boss plus one or more staff experts. Exactly the same solution was put forward by Fayol in his 1916 discussion of the Taylor system; in fact, Fayol writes that he supposes this is how the Taylor system really worked in Taylor's companies.

Whereas Taylor dealt only implicitly with the exercise of authority in organizations, another American pioneer of organization theory, Mary Parker Follett (1868–1933), did address the issue squarely. She wrote:

*How can we avoid the two extremes: too great bossism in giving orders, and practically no orders given? ... My solution is to depersonalize the giving of orders, to unite all concerned in a study of the situation, to discover the law of the situation and to obey that.... One person should not give orders to another person, but both should agree to take their orders from the situation.*[11]

In the conception of Taylor and Follett, the authority is neither in the person nor in the rules but rather, as Follett puts it, in the situation. We recognize the model of the organization as a market, in which market conditions dictate what will happen.

Sun Yat-sen (1867–1925), from China, was a scholar from the fourth corner of the power distance–uncertainty avoidance diagram. He received a Western education in Hawaii and Hong Kong and became a political revolutionary. As China started industrialization much later than the West, there is no indigenous theorist of industrial organization contemporary with Fayol, Weber, and Taylor. However, Sun was concerned with organization, albeit political. He wanted to replace the ailing government of the Manchu emperors by a modern Chinese state. He eventually became, for a short period, nominally the first president of the Chinese Republic. Sun's design for a Chinese form of government represents an integration of Western and traditional Chinese elements. From the West, he introduced Montesquieu's *trias politica*: the executive, legislative, and judicial branches. Unlike in the West, though, all three are placed under the authority of the president. Two more branches are added, both derived from Chinese tradition—the examination branch (determining access to the civil service) and the control branch, supposed to audit the government—bringing the total up to five.[12]

This remarkable mix of two systems is formally the basis of the present government structure of Taiwan, which has inherited Sun's ideas through the Kuomintang party. It stresses the authority of the president (large power distance): the legislative and judicial powers, which in the West are meant to guarantee government by law, are made dependent on the ruler and paralleled by the examination and control powers, which are based on government of man (weak uncertainty avoidance). It is the family model, with the ruler as the country's father and with whatever structure there is based on personal relationships.

Paradoxically, in the other China (which expelled the Kuomintang), the People's Republic, the 1966–1976 Cultural Revolution experiment can also be interpreted as an attempt to maintain the authority of the ruler (in this case Chairman Mao Zedong, 1893–1976) while rejecting the authority of the rules, which were felt to suffocate the modernization of the minds. The Cultural Revolution is now publicly recognized as a disaster. What passed for modernization may in fact have been a revival of centuries-old unconscious fears.

In the previous paragraphs the models of organization in different cultures have been related to the theories of the founding fathers (including one founding mother) of organization theory. The different models can also be recognized in more recent theories.

In the United States in the 1970s and 1980s, it became fashionable to look at organizations from the point of view of transaction costs. Economist Oliver Williamson opposed hierarchies to markets.[13] The reasoning is that human social life consists of economic transactions between individuals. These individuals will form hierarchical organizations when the cost of the economic transactions (such as getting information or finding out whom to trust) is lower in a hierarchy than if all transactions took place on a free market. What is interesting about this theory from a cultural point of view is that *the "market" is the point of departure or base model*, and the organization is explained from market failure. A culture that produces such a theory is likely to prefer organizations that internally resemble markets to organizations that internally resemble more structured models, such as pyramids. The ideal principle of control in organizations in the "market" philosophy is *competition* between individuals.

Williamson's colleague William Ouchi, an American of Japanese descent, has suggested two alternatives to markets: "bureaucracies" and "clans"; they come close to what earlier in this chapter we called the "machine" model and the "family" model, respectively.[14] If we take Williamson's and Ouchi's ideas together, we find all four organizational models described. The market, however, takes a special position as the theory's starting point, and this can be explained by the nationality of the authors.

In the work of both German and French organization theorists, markets play a modest role. German books tend to focus on formal systems—on the running of the machine.[15] The ideal principle of control in organizations is a system of *formal rules* on which everybody can rely. French books usually stress the exercise of power and sometimes the defenses of the individual against being crushed by the pyramid.[16] The principle of control is *hierarchical authority*, there is a system of rules, but contrary to the German case, the personal authority of the superiors prevails over the rules.

In China, in the days of Mao and the Cultural Revolution, it was neither markets nor rules nor hierarchy but *indoctrination* that was the attempted principle of control in organizations, in line with a national tradition that for centuries used comparative examinations as a test of adequate indoctrination.

Models of organizations in people's minds vary also *within* countries. In any given country, banks will function more like pyramids, post offices like machines, advertising agencies like markets, and orchestras like (autocratically led) families. We expect such differences, but when we cross national borders, we run into differences in organizational models that were not expected.

## CULTURE AND ORGANIZATIONAL STRUCTURE: ELABORATING ON MINTZBERG

Henry Mintzberg, from Canada, is one of today's leading authorities on organizational structure, at least in the English-speaking world. His chief merit has been to summarize the academic state of the art into a small number of concepts that are highly practical and easy to understand.

To Mintzberg, all good things in organizations come in fives.[17] Organizations in general contain up to five distinct parts:

1. The operating core (the people who do the work)
2. The strategic apex (the top management)
3. The middle line (the hierarchy in between)
4. The technostructure (people in staff roles supplying ideas)
5. The support staff (people in staff roles supplying services)

Organizations in general use one or more of five mechanisms for coordinating activities:

1. Mutual adjustment (of people through informal communication)
2. Direct supervision (by a hierarchical superior)
3. Standardization of work processes (specifying the contents of work)
4. Standardization of outputs (specifying the desired results)
5. Standardization of skills (specifying the training required to perform the work)

Most organizations show one of five typical configurations:

1. **The simple structure.** Key part: the strategic apex. Coordinating mechanism: direct supervision.

2. **The machine bureaucracy.** Key part: the technostructure. Coordinating mechanism: standardization of work processes.

3. **The professional bureaucracy.** Key part: the operating core. Coordinating mechanism: standardization of skills.

4. **The divisionalized form.** Key part: the middle line. Coordinating mechanism: standardization of outputs.

5. **The adhocracy.** Key part: the support staff (sometimes with the operating core). Coordinating mechanism: mutual adjustment.

Mintzberg recognized the role of values in the choice of coordinating mechanisms. For example, about formalization of behavior within organizations (a part of the standardization of work processes), he wrote:

> Organizations formalize behavior to reduce its variability, ultimately to predict and control it … to coordinate activities … to ensure the machine-like consistency that leads to efficient production … to ensure fairness to clients …. Organizations formalize behavior for other reasons as well, of more questionable validity. Formalization may, for example, reflect an arbitrary desire for order …. The highly formalized structure is above all the neat one; it warms the heart of people who like to see things orderly.[18]

Mintzberg's reference to "questionable validity" obviously represents his own values choice. He did not go as far as recognizing the link between values and nationality. The IBM research has demonstrated to what extent values about the desirability of centralization (reflected in power distance) and formalization (reflected in uncertainty avoidance) affect the implicit models of organizations in people's minds and to what extent these models differ from one country to another. This suggests that it should

be possible to link Mintzberg's typology of organizational configurations to national culture profiles. The link means that, other factors being equal, people from a particular national background will prefer a particular configuration because it fits their implicit model and that otherwise similar organizations in different countries will resemble different Mintzberg configuration types because of different cultural preferences.

The link between Mintzberg's five configurations and the quadrants of the power distance–uncertainty avoidance diagram is easy to make; it is presented in Figure 27.2.

Mintzberg uses the term *machine* in a different sense from that used by Stevens and by us: in his machine bureaucracy Mintzberg stresses the role of the technostructure (that is, the higher–educated specialists) but not the role of the highly trained workers who belong to his operating core. Therefore, Mintzberg's machine bureaucracy corresponds not with Stevens's machine but rather with his pyramid. In order to avoid confusion, in Figure 27.2 we have renamed it "full bureaucracy." This is the term used for a very similar configuration in the Aston Studies, referenced earlier in this chapter.

The adhocracy corresponds with the "village market" implicit organization model; the professional bureaucracy corresponds with the "well-oiled machine" model; the full (machine) bureaucracy corresponds with the "pyramid" model; and the simple structure corresponds with the "family" model, while the divisionalized form takes a middle position on both culture dimensions, containing elements of all four models. A typical country near the center of the diagram in Figure 27.2 is the United States, where the divisionalized form has been developed and enjoys much popularity.

Figure 27.2 explains a number of national characteristics known from the professional

## FIGURE 27.2 • MINTZBERG'S FIVE PREFERRED CONFIGURATIONS
OF ORGANIZATIONS

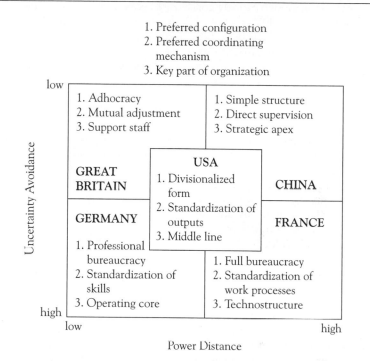

Geert Hofstede, Gert Jan Hofstede, and Michael Minkov (2010). *Cultures and Organizations: Software of the Mind.* Selected sections from chapter 9, "Pyramids, Machines, Markets, and Families: Organizing Across Nations." p. 314

and anecdotal literature about organizations; these are especially clear in the preferred coordination mechanisms. *Mutual adjustment* fits the market model of organizations and the stress on ad hoc negotiation in the Anglo countries. *Standardization of skills* explains the traditional emphasis in countries such as Germany and Switzerland on the professional qualification of workers and the high status in these countries of apprentice systems. *Standardization of work processes* fits the French concept of bureaucracy.[19] *Direct supervision* corresponds to Chinese organizations, including those outside mainland China, which emphasize coordination through personal intervention of the owner and his relatives.

*Standardization of outputs* is very much the preferred philosophy in the United States, even in cases in which outputs are difficult to assess.

## CORPORATE GOVERNANCE AND BUSINESS GOALS

Traditionally, patterns of *corporate governance*, the ownership and control of corporations, differ vastly among countries. A study across twelve European countries, published in 1997,[20] showed that while in Britain sixty-one of the hundred largest companies had dispersed shareholders (no single owner holding more than 20 percent), in

Austria and Italy no large companies at all had this ownership type. The percentages of dispersed, ownership were significantly correlated with individualism (IDV).[21]

Capitalism is historically linked to individualism. The United Kingdom inherited the ideas formulated by a Scot, Adam Smith (1723–90), about the market as an invisible hand. In the individualist value pattern, the relationship between the individual and the organization is *calculative* both for the owners and for the employees; it is based on enlightened self-interest. In more collectivist societies, in comparison, the link between individuals and their organizations is *moral* by tradition. A hire-and-fire approach, as with a buy-and-sell approach, is considered immoral or indecent. Sometimes firing employees is even prohibited by law. If it is not, selling companies and firing redundant employees still carry a high cost in terms of loss of public image and of goodwill with authorities. Differences in power distance also affect corporate governance. Across the same twelve European countries, dominant ownership of the hundred largest companies (one person, family, or company owning between 20 and 50 percent) was positively correlated with power distance.[22] In high-PDI France, banking, the development of large companies, and foreign trade were historically strongly directed and controlled by the state according to the principle of mercantilism; other fairly large companies continue to be family owned.

In the Nordic countries of Denmark, Finland, Norway, and Sweden, but also in Austria, ten or more of the hundred largest corporations were owned by a cooperative; in Britain and Italy, virtually none. The share of cooperatively owned corporations was negatively correlated with masculinity.[23] Cooperatives appeal to the need for cooperation in a feminine society.

A Russian economist, Radislav Semenov, compared (in 2000) the systems of corporate governance in seventeen Western countries and showed that culture scores explained their differences better than any of the economic variables suggested in the literature.[24] By a combination of power distance, uncertainty avoidance, and masculinity, he was able to classify countries in terms of market, bank, or other control; concentration of ownership; mind-sets of politicians, directors, employees, and investors; formation and implementation of economic policy; and industrial relations. In a separate analysis he studied ownership of firms across forty-four countries worldwide; this time he found a significant relationship with uncertainty avoidance only. His study shows the importance of cultural considerations when exporting one country's solutions to another, as was frequently tried in Eastern Europe in the 1990s.

Corporate governance is also related to corporate financial goals. It is a naive assumption that such goals are culture free. In interviews by the Dutch researcher Jeroen Weimer with Dutch, German, and U.S. business executives, besides the subject of making profits, the Dutch talked about assets, the Germans about independence from banks, and the Americans about shareholder value.[25] This diversity reflects the institutional differences among the countries (the strong role of banks in Germany, for example) as well as the prevailing ideologies (the shareholder as a culture hero in the United States).

Personal goals of top business executives are not limited to financial matters, of course, but how to find out what they really are is problematic. Asking the executives themselves will predictably produce self-serving, politically correct answers. Geert resolved this dilemma by asking junior managers and professionals enrolled in part-time M.B.A. courses to rate the goals of successful business leaders in their country. With the help of an international network of colleagues, Geert and three coauthors polled more than 1,800 M.B.A. students—part-timers or others with work experience—at twenty-one local universities in fifteen countries (later extended to seventeen), using a list of fifteen potential goals.[26] These goals and their average attributed order of priority across all seventeen countries are listed in Table 27.1.

The top five goals focus on immediate interests of the company—growth, continuity, and short-term profits—and on the leader's ego, represented by personal wealth and power. The middle five deal with stakeholder relationships and the future: reputation, creativity, long-term profits, legitimacy, and employee interests. The bottom five deal with spiritual and special interests: individual and societal ethics, game spirit, nation, and family.

Attributions within individual countries, however, differed considerably from this average. Using the ranking in Table same as a baseline, we computed country profiles, showing for each country the goals on which it deviated most (plus or minus) from this ranking.

Table 27.2 shows the profiles for five important economies: the United States, India, Brazil, China, and Germany. The scores for the United States were produced by M.B.A. students from five universities in different regions of the country; the five produced almost identical goal rankings. Their consensus ranking closely resembled the seventeen-country average from Table same; none of the other sixteen countries came closer.

The two most notable differences between the U.S. ranking and the overall average are continuity of the business,

## TABLE 27.1 • OVERALL ORDER OF PRIORITY OF 15 POTENTIAL BUSINESS GOALS ATTRIBUTED TO THEIR COUNTRY'S BUSINESS LEADERS BY PART-TIME M.B.A. STUDENTS FROM 17 COUNTRIES

### TOP FIVE

1. *Growth of the business*
2. *Continuity of the business*
3. *This year's profits*
4. *Personal wealth*
5. *Power*

### MIDDLE FIVE

6. Honor, face, reputation
7. Creating something new
8. Profits ten years from now
9. Staying within the law
10. Responsibility toward employees

### BOTTOM FIVE

11. *Respecting ethical norms*
12. *Responsibility toward society in general*
13. *Game and gambling spirit*
14. *Patriotism, national pride*
15. *Family interests (e.g., jobs for relatives)*

Geert Hofstede, Gert Jan Hofstede, and Michael Minkov (2010). Cultures and Organizations: Software of the Mind. Selected sections from chapter 9, "Pyramids, Machines, Markets, and Families: Organizing Across Nations": 322. Reprinted with permission from Geert Hofstede.

which U.S. M.B.A.s rated less important than their colleagues from any other country, and respecting ethical norms, internationally among the bottom five but rated quite important in the United States. What is considered ethical may differ from one country to the next. Across the seventeen countries, ratings for respecting ethical

TABLE 27.2 • PERCEIVED BUSINESS GOALS PRIORITIES IN FIVE COUNTRIES,
COMPARED WITH THE 17-COUNTRY AVERAGE

International top five in bold; international bottom five in *italics*.

### UNITED STATES

| More important | Less important |
|---|---|
| *Growth of the business* | *Profits ten years from now* |
| *Respecting ethical norms* | *Responsibility toward employees* |
| **Personal wealth** | *Family interests* |
| **This year's profits** | *Creating something new* |
| Power | **Continuity of the business** |

### INDIA

| More important | Less important |
|---|---|
| **Continuity of the business** | *Family interests* |
| *Patriotism, national pride* | **Staying within the law** |
| Power | *Game and gambling spirit* |
| Growth of the business | **This year's profits** |
| Profits ten years from now | *Respecting ethical norms* |

### BRAZIL

| More important | Less important |
|---|---|
| *Game and gambling spirit* | *Patriotism, national pride* |
| Power | **Creating something new** |
| This year's profits | *Responsibility toward society* |
| Continuity of the business | **Profits ten years from now** |
| *Family interests* | **Responsibility toward employees** |

### CHINA

| More important | Less important |
|---|---|
| *Respecting ethical norms* | *Family interests* |
| *Patriotism, national pride* | *Game and gambling spirit* |
| Power | **This year's profits** |
| **Honor, face, reputation** | **Personal wealth** |
| *Responsibility toward society* | Staying within the law |

### GERMANY

| More important | Less important |
|---|---|
| *Responsibility toward society* | Power |
| **Responsibility toward employees** | *Patriotism, national pride* |
| **Creating something new** | **Personal wealth** |
| **Profits ten years from now** | Growth of the business |
| *Respecting ethical norms* | This year's profits |

norms tended to correlate with ratings for staying within the law and for honor, face, and reputation.

The countries next most similar to the international average were India and Brazil, also shown in Table 27.2. In India, continuity of the business came out on top. Notable differences from the international average were patriotism, internationally near the bottom but in India much more important than average, and profits ten years from now, which replaced this year's profits among India's top five.

Brazil's profile gave game and gambling spirit and family interests much more importance than the average; creating something new, profits ten years from now, and responsibility toward employees were rated equally as unimportant as responsibility toward society in general and patriotism. Our first article about the business goals project described Brazilian business leaders as family entrepreneurs; to a greater degree than their colleagues in most other countries, they focused on their own inner circle, without much concern for other stakeholders, the longer-term future, society, and nation.

The two other countries in Table 27.2, China and Germany, were the most *dissimilar* from the international average. China's profile nevertheless resembled India's in a number of respects. Both China and India put patriotism much higher than average, together with power, and both rated this year's profits and staying within the law less important than average. Notable differences between China and India were that China placed respecting ethical norms even higher than the United States, while India put it at the bottom. China also rated responsibility toward society in general much more important than average, as well as face (the Chinese term for honor and reputation); face surpassed personal wealth, which was rated much less important.

Germany's profile represents almost a reversal of the international ranking in Table 27.1. In Germany four of the five international top goals were rated less important, and responsibility toward society in general was rated even higher than in China. As in India (and China), profits ten years from now were rated more important than this year's profits.

The fifteen goals were, naturally, not entirely independent of each other. Statistically,[27] they split into five clusters, which can be seen as dilemmas: (1) continuity and power versus honor, laws, and ethics; (2) wealth and family versus responsibility toward employees; (3) game and creativity versus patriotism; (4) short-term profits versus long-term profits; and (5) growth versus responsibility toward society.

As could be predicted, cluster 4, the relative importance of this year's profits over profits ten years from now, reflected a country's *long-term orientation* score.[28]

Cluster 5 opposes growth to responsibility toward society in general. Table 27.1; shows that in the average ranking, growth was strongly dominant. In fact, the extent to which responsibility toward society in general was balanced against growth in a country turned out to be the main determinant of how much that country deviated from the overall average.[29] Scores on cluster 5 showed that the United States, Australia, and Hong Kong most strongly focused on growth; the Netherlands, Germany, toward society in general.

Around 2000 many people assumed that globalization and the acquisition of companies across borders would wipe out differences like those in Table 27.2 and that all business leaders would acquire the American profile. The 2008 economic crisis and the fact that national goal profiles reflect national cultures with centuries-old roots make that assumption unlikely. Goal conflicts between leaders from different countries, as well as between expatriate leaders and their local personnel, are predictable.

The 2008 recession started as a financial crisis in the United States. Irresponsible practices had put U.S. banks on a disaster track, and the interdependence of the modern global economy spread the damage worldwide.

Our country-by-country comparison from around 1998 had pictured U.S. business leaders as—even more than their counterparts elsewhere—fascinated by bigness, greedy, short-term oriented, and out for power. They were seen as less interested than their foreign colleagues the longer-term future, taking less responsibility for their employees, less innovative, and caring less for the continuity of their businesses.

Aspects of the U.S. national culture described in various chapters of this book reinforced this pattern—in particular, strong individualism, masculinity, and short-term orientation. Until the 1980s, crisis checks and balances in U.S. legislation, introduced after the 1929 crisis, had prevented abusive business practices, but successive presidencies released controls, lowered business taxes, and opened the gates for a race to get bigger and wealthier in ways that had been closed before. This process led to giant deficits in the U.S. national budget and to astronomical self-payments by business leaders, plus a number of outright scandals, which also spread to other countries.

In hindsight, the 2008 financial crisis could have been predicted from our 1998 business goals study. Subsequent to the crisis, national governments stepped in, trying at considerable cost to repair the damage by rebalancing the interests of society, wage earners, and clients with those of shareholders. In the present financial reshuffling, top leaders from other parts of the world such as the European Union, China, India, and Brazil play an increasingly important role. Whoever owns the resources sets the

goals, so global business objectives will very likely shift in the direction of their values.

This scenario presupposes that economists get rid of the shibboleth of undisputed economic growth. In the goals attributed to business leaders, a fixation on growth opposed a sense of responsibility toward society in general. Nothing can grow forever—management is the art of balancing.

Different national business goals limit the exportability of "agency theory." *Agency* refers to the delegation of discretionary power by a principal to an agent, and since the 1980s the term has in particular been applied to the delegation by owners to managers. Agency theories are based on implicit assumptions about societal order, contractual relationships, and motivation. Such assumptions are bounded by national borders.

## LEADERSHIP, DECISION MAKING, AND EMPOWERMENT

Leadership and subordinateship in a country are inseparable. Vertical relations in organizations are based on the common values of superiors *and* subordinates. Beliefs about leadership reflect the dominant culture of a country. Asking people to describe the qualities of a good leader is a way of asking them to describe their culture. The leader is a culture hero, in the sense of being a model for behavior.

Authors from individualist countries tend to treat leadership as an independent characteristic that a person can acquire, without reference to its context. In the management literature from individualist, masculine cultures such as Australia, Britain, and the United States, romanticized descriptions of masculine leaders are popular. They describe what the readers would like to be and to believe. What really happens depends on leaders, on followers, and very much on the situation.

Feminine cultures believe in modest leaders. A prestigious U.S. consulting firm was once asked to analyze decision making in a leading Dutch corporation. The firm's report criticized the corporation's decision-making style for being, among other things, "intuitive" and "consensus-based."[30]

Two U.S. researchers, Ellen Jackofsky and John Slocum (1988), analyzed descriptions of chief executives in the management press in five countries. French CEOs were described as taking autocratic initiatives (high PDI); Germans as stressing the training and responsibilities of their managers and workers (low PDI, high UAI); Japanese as practicing patience and letting the organization run itself, aiming at long-term market share (high LTO); Swedes as taking entrepreneurial risks and at the same time caring for their people's quality of working life (low UAI, low MAS); and the one Taiwanese CEO in the sample as stressing hard work and the family (high LTO, low IDV).[31]

Studies of the satisfaction and productivity of subordinates under different types of leaders show the influence of national cultures. French IBM technicians were most satisfied when they saw their boss as persuasive or paternalistic, unlike their British and German colleagues, who more often liked consultative and democratic bosses. Workers from Peru liked close supervision, unlike similar workers from the United States. Indian assistants showed the highest satisfaction and performance when working under foremen who behaved like elder brothers. What represents appropriate leadership in one setting does not have to be appropriate for a differently programmed group of subordinates.[32]

Leadership behaviors and leadership theories that do not take collective expectations of subordinates into account are basically dysfunctional. What usually happens when foreign theories are taught abroad is that they are preached but not practiced. Wise local managers silently adapt the foreign ideas to fit the values of their subordinates. A country in which this has happened a lot is Japan.[33] Not-so-wise managers may try an unfitting approach once, find out it does not work, and fall back into their old routine.

The existence and functioning of *grievance channels*, through which lower-level organization members can complain about those at the top, is obviously very much culturally influenced. Grievance channels in large-power-distance environments are difficult to establish. On the one hand, subordinates will fear retaliation (for good reason); on the other hand, there will be more unrealistic and exaggerated grievances, and the channels may be used for personal revenge against a superior who is not accessible otherwise. Uncertainty avoidance plays a role too: allowing complaints means allowing the unpredictable.

The term *empowerment* became fashionable in the 1990s. It can refer to any kind of formal and informal means of sharing decision-making power and influence between leaders and subordinates. Earlier terms for such processes *were participative management, joint consultation, Mitbestimmung, industrial democracy, worker representation, worker self-management, shop floor consultation,* and *codetermination*. Their feasibility depends on the value systems of the organization members—of the subordinates at least as much as of the leaders. The first cultural dimension involved is again power distance. Distributing influence comes more naturally to low- than to high-PDI cultures.[34] Ideologies may go the other way around; in the IBM surveys, the statement "Employees in industry should participate more in the decisions taken by management" was more strongly endorsed in high- than in low-PDI countries; an ideology can compensate for reality.

The choice of informal versus formal empowerment is affected by the country's level of uncertainty avoidance. Thus, both PDI and UAI should be taken into account, and the four quadrants of Figure 27.1 represent four different forms of dividing power. In the upper left-hand corner (Anglo countries, Scandinavia, the Netherlands: PDI and UAI both low), the stress is on informal and spontaneous forms of participation on the shop floor. In the lower left-hand corner (German-speaking countries: PDI low, UAI higher), the stress is on formal, legally determined systems (*Mitbestimmung*). On the right-hand side (high PDI), distributing power is basically a contradiction; it will meet with strong resistance from elites and sometimes even from underdogs, or their representatives, such as labor unions. Where it is tried, it has to be pushed by a powerful leader— by a father type such as an enlightened entrepreneur in the high-PDI, low-UAI countries (higher right-hand corner) or by political leadership using legislative tools in the high-PDI, high-UAI countries (lower right-hand corner). Both mean imposed participation, which, of course, is a paradox. One way of making it function is to limit participation to certain spheres of life and to maintain tight control in others; this is the Chinese solution, in which participative structures in work organizations can be combined with a strictly controlled hierarchy in ideological issues.[35]

## CONCLUSION: NATIONALITY DEFINES ORGANIZATIONAL RATIONALITY

In 1980, Geert published an article in the U.S. journal, *Organizational Dynamics*, entitled "Motivation, Leadership, and Organization: Do American Theories Apply Abroad?" It had a stormy history.

The idea that the validity of a theory is constrained by nationality was more obvious in Europe, with all its borders, than in a huge borderless country such as the United States. In Europe, the cultural relativity of the laws that govern human behavior had been recognized as early as the sixteenth century in the skepticism of Michel de Montaigne (1533–92).

Theories, models, and practices are basically culture-specific; they may apply across borders, but this should always be proved. The naive assumption that management ideas are universal is not found only in popular literature: in scholarly journals—even in those explicitly addressing an international readership—the silent assumption of universal validity of culturally restricted findings is frequent.

Lack of awareness of national limits causes management and organization ideas and theories to be exported without regard for the values context in which they were developed. Fad-conscious publishers and gullible readers in those other countries encourage such exports. Unfortunately, to rephrase a famous dictum, there is nothing as impractical as a bad theory.[36]

The economic success of the United States in the decades before and after World War II has led some people in other parts of the world to believe that U.S. ideas about management must be superior and therefore should be copied. They forgot to ask about the kind of society in which these ideas were developed and applied—*if* they were really applied as the books and articles claimed. U.S. management researchers Mark Peterson and Jerry Hunt wrote, "A question for many American normative theories is whether they even apply in the United States,"[37]

The belief in the superiority of American theories is reinforced by the fact that most "international" management journals are published in the United States with U.S.

editors, and it is notoriously difficult for non-North American authors to get their papers accepted.[38]

Just as certain nations excel in certain sports, others are associated with specific disciplines. Psychology, including social psychology, is predominantly a U.S. discipline: individualist and mostly masculine. Sociology is predominantly European,[39] but even European sociologists rarely consider the influence of their nationality on their thinking.

In organization theories, the nationality of the author reflects implicit assumptions as to where organizations came from, what they are, and what they try to achieve. These national "paradigms" all have the same starting point: "In the beginning was ..." After God had created men, men made organizations; but what did they have in mind when making them? Here is Geert's list of the paradigms he observed: *In the beginning was ...*

| | |
|---|---|
| In the United States | the market |
| In France | the power |
| In Germany | order |
| In Poland and Russia | efficiency |
| In the Netherlands | consensus |
| In Scandinavia | equality |
| In Britain | systems |
| In China | the family |
| In Japan | Japan |

The lack of universal solutions to management and organization problems does not mean that countries cannot learn from each other. On the contrary, looking across the border is one of the most effective ways of getting new ideas for management, organization, or politics. But their export calls for prudence and judgment. Nationality constrains rationality.

## NOTES

1. Pugh & Hickson, 1976.
2. Negandhi & Prasad, 1971, p. 128.
3. van Oudenhoven, 2001. The countries were Belgium, Canada, Denmark, France, Germany, Greece, the Netherlands, Spain, the United Kingdom, and the United States.
4. In 2005, the Dutch parliament voted in favor of a system change that involved replacing the appointed mayor by an elected mayor, but the proposal was stranded in the senate.
5. Mouritzen & Svara, 2002, pp. 55–56 and 75.
6. Fayol, 1970 [1916], p. 21. Translation by GH.
7. Weber, 1976 [1930], p. 224.
8. Weber, 1970 [1948], p. 196. Translated from *Wirtschaft and Gesellschaft*, 1921, Part III, Chapter 6, p. 650.
9. Fayol, 1970 [1916], p. 85.
10. Laurent, 1981, pp. 101–14.
11. From a paper presented in 1925, in Metcalf & Urwick, 1940, pp. 58–59.
12. Confucian values were also evident in Sun Yat-sen's extension of the *trias politica*: the examination and control branches had to guarantee the virtue of the civil servants.
13. Williamson, 1975.
14. Ouchi, 1980, pp. 129–41.
15. Kieser & Kubicek, 1983.
16. Crozier & Friedberg, 1977; Pagès, Bonetti, de Gaulejac, & Descendre, 1979.
17. Mintzberg, 1983. Later on (Mintzberg, 1989), the author added a "missionary configuration" with "standardization of norms." To us, this is an aspect of the other types rather than a type by itself. It deals with the "strength" of an organization's culture.
18. Mintzberg, 1983, pp. 34–35.
19. As described in a French classic: organization sociologist Michel Crozier's *The Bureaucratic Phenomenon* (Crozier, 1964).
20. Pedersen & Thomsen, 1997. The countries were Austria, Belgium, Denmark, Finland, France, Germany, Italy, the Netherlands,

Norway, Spain, Sweden, and the United Kingdom.

21. The correlation was $r = 0.65*$.
22. The correlation was $r = 0.52*$. See *Culture's Consequences*, 2001, p. 384.
23. In spite of the Austrian score, the correlation was $r = -0.77**$.
24. Semenov, 2000. The countries were the same as in the study by Pedersen & Thomsen plus Australia, Canada, Ireland, New Zealand, and the United States.
25. Weimer, 1995, p. 336; *Culture's Consequences*, 2001, p. 385.
26. Hofstede, van Deusen, Mueller, Charles, & the Business Goals Network, 2002. Data about China were supplied by Chinese students with work experience in their country but who were studying in Australia and the United States; data from Denmark (Århus, $n = 62$) were added in 2002 (see Hofstede, 2007b).
27. Through a factor analysis of the fifteen goals × seventeen countries matrix: five almost equally strong factors explained 78 percent of the variance.
28. LTO-CVS, $r = -0.59* n = 13$.
29. The countries' factor scores on cluster 5 correlated with their order of similarity to the average ranking with $r = 0.73***$.
30. *Culture's Consequences*, 2001, p. 388.
31. Jackofsky & Slocum, 1988; *Culture's Consequences*, 2001, p. 388.
32. *Culture's Consequences*, 2001, p. 388–89.
33. *Culture's Consequences*, 2001, p. 389.
34. Klidas, 2001.
35. Laaksonen, 1977.
36. "There is nothing as practical as a good theory," attributed to Kurt Lewin.
37. Peterson & Hunt, 1997, p. 214.
38. Generally felt in Europe but proved by Baruch, 2001, based on an analysis of the location of almost two thousand authors in more than one thousand articles in seven top management journals.
39. In the Social Science Citation Index, the most cited psychologists are all Americans; the most cited sociologists are nearly all Europeans, in spite of the fact that the SSCI is mainly based on U.S. journals.

## BIBLIOGRAPHY

Baruch, J. (2001). "Global or North American? A geographical based comparative analysis of publications in top management journals." *International Journal of Cross-Cultural Management* 1: 109–26.

Crozier, M. (1964). *The Bureaucratie Phenomenon.* Chicago: University of Chicago Press.

Crozier, M., and E. Friedberg (1977). *L'acteur et le système: Les contraintes de l'action collective.* Paris: Seuil.

Fayol, H. (1970). *Administration industrielle et générale.* Paris: Dunod. [Original work published 1916.]

Hofstede, G. (1980a). *Culture's Consequences: International Differences in Work-Related Values.* Beverly Hills, CA: Sage.

Hofstede, G. (1980b). "Motivation, leadership, and organization: Do American theories apply abroad?" *Organizational Dynamics* 9(1): 42–63. Hofstede, G. (2001a), *Cultures Consequences: Comparing Values, Behaviors, Institutions, and Organizations Across Nations,* Thousand Oaks, CA: Sage.

Hofstede, G. (2007b). "Asian management in the 21st century." *Asia Pacific Journal of Management* 24: 411–20.

Hofstede, G., C. A. van Deusen, C. B. Mueller, T. A. Charles, and the Business Goals Network (2002). "What goals do business leaders pursue? A study in fifteen countries." *Journal of International Business Studies* 33(4): 785–803.

Jackofsky, E. F., and J. W. Slocum (1988). "CEO roles across cultures." In *The Executive Effect: Concepts and Methods for Studying Top Managers,* ed. D. C. Hambrick, 76–99. Greenwich, CT: JAI.

Kieser, A., and H. Kubicek (1983). *Organisation.* Berlin: Walter de Gruyter.

Klidas, A. K. (2001). "Employee Empowerment in the European Hotel Industry: Meaning, Process and Cultural Relativity." Ph.D. dissertation, University of Tilburg. Amsterdam: Thela Thesis.

Laaksonen, O. J. (1977). "The power of Chinese enterprises." *International Studies of Management and Organization* 7(1): 71–90.

Laurent, A. (1981). "Matrix organiztions and Latin culture." *International Studies of Management and Organization* 10(4): 101–14.

Metcalf, H. C., and L. Urwick (1940). *Dynamic Administration: The Collected Papers of Mary Parker Follett*. New York: Harper & Row.

Mintzberg, H. (1983). *Structure in Fives: Designing Effective Organizations*. Englewood Cliffs, NJ: Prentice-Hall.

Mintzberg, H. (1989). *Mintzberg on Management: Inside Our Strange World of Organizations*. New York: The Free Press.

Mouritzen, P. E., and J. H. Svara (2002). *Leadership at the Apex: Politicians and Administrators in Western Local Governments*. Pittsburgh, PA: University of Pittsburgh Press.

Negandhi, A. R., and S. B. Prasad (1971). *Comparative Management*. New York: Appleton-Century-Crofts.

Ouchi, W. G. (1980). "Markets, bureaucracies and clans." *Administrative Science Quarterly* 25: 129–41.

Pedersen, T., and S. Thomsen (1997). "European patterns of corporate ownership: A twelve-country study." *Journal of International Business Studies* 28: 759–78.

Peterson, M. F., and J. G. Hunt (1997). "International perspectives on international leadership." *Leadership Quarterly* 8(3): 203–31

Pugh, D. S., and D. J. Hickson (1976). *Organizational Structure in Its Context: The Aston Programme I*. Westmead, Farnborough, Hants., UK: Saxon House.

Semenov, R. (2000). *Cross-Country Differences in Economic Governance: As a Major Explanatory Factor*. Ph.D. dissertation, Tilburg, Neth.: Tilburg University.

Stevens, E. P. (1973). "Marianismo: The other face of machismo in Latin America." In *Female and Male in Latin America*, ed. A. Pescatello, 90–101. Pittsburgh, PA: University of Pittsburgh Press.

van Oudenhoven, J. P. (2001). "Do organizations reflect national cultures? A 10-nation study." *International Journal of Intercultural Relations* 25: 89–107.

Weber, M. (1970). *Essays in Sociology*. Edited by H. H. Gerth and C. W. Mills. London: Routledge & Kegan Paul. [Original work published 1948.]

Weiner, J. (1995). *Corporate Financial Goals: A Multiple Constituency Approach to a Comparative Study of Dutch, U.S., and German Firms*. Ph.D. dissertation. Enschede, Neth.: Twente University.

Williamson, O. E. (1975). *Markets and Hierarchies: Analysis and Antitrust Implications*. New York: Free Press.

# 28

# Appreciative Inquiry

*David L. Cooperrider & Diana Whitney*

## AN INVITATION TO THE POSITIVE REVOLUTION IN CHANGE

Appreciative Inquiry (AI) is, as Professor Robert Quinn at University of Michigan has recently written, "creating a positive revolution in the field of organization development and change management."[1] Why? One clue lies in how AI turns the practice of change management inside out. It proposes, quite bluntly, that organizations are not, at their core, problems to be solved. Just the opposite. Every organization was created as a solution designed in its own time to meet a challenge or satisfy a need of society.

Even more fundamentally, organizations are centers of vital connections and life-giving potentials: relationships, partnerships, alliances, and ever-expanding webs of knowledge and action that are capable of harnessing the power of combinations of strengths. Founded upon this lifecentric view of organizations, AI offers a positive, strengths-based approach to organization development and change management.

### AI and the New Model of Change Leadership

Management guru Peter Drucker commented in a recent interview, "The task of organizational leadership is to create an alignment of strengths in ways that make a system's weaknesses irrelevant." Could it be, as Drucker implies, that leading change is *all* about strengths? Why would strength connected to strength create positive change? What would it mean to create an entire change methodology around an economy and ecology of strengths? Where would we—as managers, facilitators, and change leaders—start? What might be the steps and stages of positive change? What about unique skills? How could the discovery and fusion of strengths elevate and extend a system's capacity to adapt, learn, and create *upward spirals* of performance, development, and energizing growth?

Indeed, the field of management has always acknowledged that strengths perform and that their very presence, that is, the visible display of strengths, signals some kind of optimal functioning. The principles and practices of Appreciative Inquiry (AI) suggest the idea that collective strengths do more than perform—*they transform*.

At the surface, this sounds obvious and good. But when we pause and take stock of the way contemporary change management is practiced, we see clearly that positive approaches to change are not yet the norm.

Many, for example, were shocked at the results of the largest, most comprehensive survey ever conducted on approaches to managing change. The study concluded that most schools, companies, families, and organizations function on an unwritten rule. That rule is to fix what's wrong and let the strengths take care of themselves.

Although the results of this study do not sound like the Peter Drucker quote put into practice, where change is all about strengths, the research conclusion unfortunately rings familiar and true. Companies all too often call for low-morale surveys instead of designing rigorous inquiries into extraordinary moments of high engagement, commitment, and passionate achievement.

Managers charter and analyze turnover rates—one report after another—instead of calling for analyses of retention or of *magnetic work environments*, that is, times when people felt so connected to their work, their colleagues, and their organization that the bonds could not be broken.

> *How pervasive is this deficit-based approach to change, which says change begins with the identification of the most pressing problems, the gaps, and their root causes? Do you recognize it? Okay, try this: Think about the last three projects you've worked on and the last half dozen meetings you've attended. How many of the projects were designed to fix something? How many of the meetings were called to address a problem?*

...Could it be that we as a field have reached the end of problem solving as a mode of inquiry capable of inspiring, mobilizing, and sustaining significant human system change? What would happen to our change practices if we began all our work with the positive presumption that organizations, as centers of human relatedness, are alive with infinite constructive capacity? ...

### Approaching Problems From the Other Side

Appreciative Inquiry (AI) begins an adventure. Even in the first steps, one senses an exciting new direction in our language and theories of change—an invitation, as some have declared, to a "positive revolution." The words just quoted *are* strong, but the more we replay the high-wire moments of our five years of work at GTE/Verizon,[2] the more we find ourselves asking the very same kinds of questions that the people of GTE asked their senior executives: "Are you really ready for the momentum that is being generated? This is igniting a grassroots movement ... it is creating an organization in full voice, a center stage for positive revolutionaries!"

Tom White, president of what was then called GTE, Telops (making up 80 percent of GTE's sixty-seven thousand employees), replied with no hesitation: "Yes, and what I see in this meeting are zealots, people with a mission and passion for creating the new GTE. Count me in, I'm your number one recruit, number-one zealot." People cheered.

Fourteen months later, GTE's whole-system change initiative won the ASTD (American Society for Training and Development) award for the best organization change program in the country. This award was based on significant and measurable changes in stock prices, morale survey measures, quality and customer relations, union-management relations, and more. Appreciative inquiry was cited as the "backbone."[3]

To achieve this stunning shift in organizational culture, the team of internal and external change agents asked, "How can we engage the positive potential of all employees toward transforming the company?" The team wanted whatever we did to recognize and invite the positive expression of frontline employee strengths, initiatives, and capabilities. We set a goal of creating a narrative-rich culture with a ratio of five stories of positive performance and success to every negative one as a way of building a vibrant, high-performing, customer-focused culture.

This goal was approached in a number of ways:

- In year one, more than fifty internal change agents (OD consultants, ER managers, Public Affairs and Corporate Communications staff) received extensive training in Appreciative Inquiry. In addition, Appreciative Inquiry was taught to eight hundred frontline employees.
- Opportunities for sharing good news stories were created. One executive volunteered to be the story center. The stories came into his office, and he sent them out to other groups and departments to share and replicate. Many were published in the company newsletter.
- Storytelling was embedded into many existing processes. For example, the annual President's Leadership award focused on relaying stories about winning employees, their teams, and customer service.

- Open-ended questions were added to the company employee survey, and the ratio of positive to negative comments was tracked.
- An Appreciative Inquiry storybook was created as a teaching tool for all employees.
- Appreciative Inquiry was used to introduce a new partnership model for the unions and for company management.[4]

Based on his experience, Tom White described AI in executive language: "Appreciative Inquiry can get you much better results than seeking out and solving problems. That's an interesting concept for me—and I imagine most of you—because telephone companies are among the best problem solvers in the world. We trouble-shoot everything. We concentrate enormous resources on correcting problems that have relatively minor impact on our overall service and performance … when used continually and over a long period of time, this approach can lead to a negative culture. If you combine a negative culture with all the challenges we face today, it could be easy to convince ourselves that we have too many problems to overcome—to slip into a paralyzing sense of hopelessness…. Don't get me wrong. I'm not advocating mindless happy talk. Appreciative Inquiry is a complex science designed to make things better. We can't ignore problems—we just need to approach them from the other side."[5] …

## WHAT IS APPRECIATIVE INQUIRY?

**Ap-pre'ci-ate, v., 1.** Valuing; the act of recognizing the best in people or the world around us; affirming past and present strengths, successes, and potentials; to perceive those things that give life (health, vitality, excellence) to living systems. **2.** To increase in value, e.g., the economy has appreciated in value. Synonyms: value, prize, esteem, and honor.

**In-quire', v., 1.** The act of exploration and discovery. **2.** To ask questions; to be open to seeing new potentials and possibilities. Synonyms: discover, search, systematically explore, and study.

The term AI has been described in a myriad of ways: as a radically affirmative approach to change that completely lets go of problem-based management and in so doing vitally transforms strategic planning, survey methods, culture change, merger integration methods … measurement systems;[6] as a paradigm of conscious evolution geared for the realities of the new century;[7] as the most important advance in action research in the past decade;[8] as offspring and heir to Maslow's vision of a positive social science;[9] and as a methodology that takes the idea of the social construction of reality to its positive extreme, especially with its emphasis on metaphor and narrative, relational ways of knowing, on language, and on its potential as a source of generative theory.[10]

Although AI can be described in many ways—as a philosophy and methodology for change leadership—here is a practice-oriented definition:

> Appreciative Inquiry is the cooperative, coevolutionary search for the best in people, their organizations, and the world around them. It involves systematic discovery of what gives life to an organization or a community when it is most effective and most capable in economic, ecological, and human terms.

In AI, intervention gives way to inquiry, imagination, and innovation. Instead of negation, criticism, and spiraling diagnosis, there is discovery, dream, and design. AI involves the art and practice of asking unconditionally positive questions that strengthen a system's capacity to apprehend, anticipate, and heighten positive potential. Through mass mobilized inquiry, hundreds and even thousands of people can be involved in cocreating their collective future.

AI assumes that every organization and community has many untapped and rich accounts of the positive—what people talk about as past, present, and future capacities, or the positive core. AI links the knowledge and energy of this core directly to an organization or a community's change agenda, and changes never thought possible are suddenly and democratically mobilized.

### The Positive Core

The *positive core* of organizational life is one of the greatest and largely unrecognized resources in the field of change management today. We are clearly in our infancy when it comes to tools for working with the positive core, talking about it, and designing our systems in synergistic alignment with it. But one thing is evident and clear as we reflect on the most important things we have learned with AI:

> Human systems grow in the direction of what they persistently ask questions about, and this propensity is strongest and most sustainable when the means and ends of inquiry are positively correlated. The single most important action a group can take to liberate the human spirit and consciously construct a better future is to make the positive core the common and explicit property of all.

Table 28.1 shows the diverse set of assets, strengths, and resources that, when discussed, broadly constitute an organization or a community's positive core. Conversations about the positive core bring it to life, give it meaning and enable an organization's members and stakeholders to share best practices.

In the process of inquiry into its positive core, an organization enhances its collective wisdom, builds energy and resiliency to change, and extends its capacity to achieve extraordinary results. We call this process mapping the *positive core*....

### A Working Definition of Positive Change

In everything it does, AI deliberately seeks to work from accounts of the positive core. This shift from problem analysis to positive core analysis is at the heart of positive change.

In the old paradigm, change begins with a clear definition of the problem. Problem-solving approaches to change

- Are painfully slow, always asking people to look backward to yesterday's causes
- Rarely result in new vision
- Are notorious for generating defensiveness

With AI, change begins with a rigorous, organization-wide discovery and analysis of the positive core, what we sometimes call a root cause of success analysis. Figure 28.1 illustrates the shift from a problem-solving approach to change management to an AI approach to positive change management.

### TABLE 28.1 • THE POSITIVE CORE OF ORGANIZATIONAL LIFE

| | |
|---|---|
| Achievements | Vital traditions |
| Strategic opportunities | Lived values |
| Product strengths | Positive macrotrends |
| Technical assets | Social capital |
| Breakthrough innovations | Collective spirit |
| Elevated thoughts | Embedded knowledge |
| Best business practices | Financial assets |
| Positive emotions | Visions of positive futures |
| Organization wisdom | Alliances and partnerships |
| Core competencies | Value chain strengths |
| Visions of possibility | Strategic advantages |
| Leadership capabilities | Relational resources |
| Product pipeline | Customer loyalty |

## FIGURE 28.1 • FROM PROBLEM SOLVING TO APPRECIATIVE INQUIRY

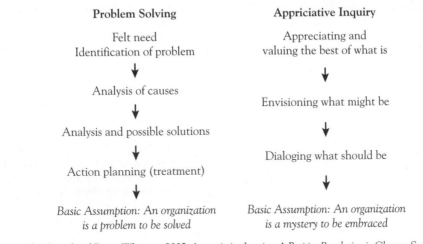

| **Problem Solving** | **Appriciative Inquiry** |
|---|---|
| Felt need<br>Identification of problem | Appreciating and<br>valuing the best of what is |
| ↓ | ↓ |
| Analysis of causes | |
| ↓ | Envisioning what might be |
| Analysis and possible solutions | |
| ↓ | ↓ |
| | Dialoging what should be |
| Action planning (treatment) | |
| ↓ | ↓ |
| *Basic Assumption: An organization*<br>*is a problem to be solved* | *Basic Assumption: An organization*<br>*is a mystery to be embraced* |

Positive change can be defined as follows:

> Any form of organization change, redesign, or planning that begins with a comprehensive inquiry, analysis, and dialogue of an organization's positive core, that involves multiple stakeholders, and then links this knowledge to the organization's strategic change agenda and priorities.

Organizations around the world have made the shift from problem solving to AI to create positive change for a range of strategic agendas including the following: building partnerships and alliances; transforming corporate culture; strategic planning; reducing product development time; enhancing employee retention and morale; and productivity, quality, and financial improvement.

In the spring of 2003, the Denver Office of Finance initiated a citywide inquiry to discover and disseminate financial best practices and to identify revenue-generating opportunities across the city. This initiative was explicitly targeted to save $70 million. To build a grassroots commitment to cost savings, a team of two hundred people were trained and conducted six hundred face-to-face interviews with city employees, local businesses, and community members. They then came together for a one-day AI summit to articulate best practices, envision a stable financial future, and design and initiate individual department-level and cross-agency cost-saving and revenue-generating projects. Margaret Brown, Manager of Budget and Finance, City and County of Denver, and project consultants Lynn Pollard and Amanda Tiosten-Bloom reported the following financial results:

- Extensive consolidation of services reduced duplicated services and led to cost savings. For example, a downsizing of fleet services resulted in a $370,000 savings.
- Relocation and consolidation of agency offices from leased space to city-owned space. Among the many savings this afforded was a reduced cost for building security, saving $358,000 per year.
- Development of a new incentive retirement program. This program-saved $1.5 million per year.

In addition, employee morale, commitment to cost savings, and the ongoing discovery of innovative revenue-generating ideas were elevated through the use of AI. Voluntary suggestions for improved fiscal management continue at a rate of up to fifty e-mails per day. Many of the suggestions reflect the new approach: collaborative and consolidated services, which reduce costs and provide a better quality of service to the citizens of Denver.

Positive change, like what was experienced in Denver, begins with an inquiry into the positive core—what works well when the organization or community is at its best. AI is a process for engaging an entire organization and its stakeholders in creating a future that works for everyone.

At the heart of AI is the *appreciative interview*, a one-on-one dialogue among organization members and stakeholders using questions related to: highpoint experiences, valuing, and what gives life to the organization at its best. Questions such as the following are asked:

- Describe a time in your organization that you consider a highpoint experience, a time when you were most engaged and felt alive and vibrant.
- Without being modest, tell me what it is that you most value about yourself, your work, and your organization.
- What are the core factors that give life to your organization when it is at its best?
- Imagine your organization ten years from now, when everything is just as you always wished it could be. What is different? How have you contributed to this dream organization?

Answers to questions like these and the stories they generate are shared throughout the organization, resulting in new, more compelling images of the organization and its future....

## NOTES

1. Camerson, K.S., Dutton, J.E., and Quinn, R.E. (Editors), *Positive Organizational Scholarship*. San Francisco, CA: Berrett-Koehler, 2003.

2. In 1999, GTE and Bell Atlantic merged, resulting in the formation of Verizon. We worked initially and extensively with GTE and continued with Verizon after the merger.

3. GTE received the ASTD award in 1997 and went on to apply and gain benefit from Appreciative Inquiry in a wide range of settings, such as enhancing call center effectiveness, launching an innovative union-management partnership, and building an appreciative front-line leadership program. After the merger with Bell Atlantic and the creation of Verizon, Appreciative Inquiry was introduced to the companywide diversity network in support of a strength-based approach to diversity.

4. Fry, R., Barrett, F., Seiling, J., and Whitney, D. (Editors). Appreciative Inquiry and Organizational Transformation: Reports from the Field. Westport, CT: Quorum Books, 2002.

5. White, T.W. "Working in Interesting Times." In Vital Speeches of the Day, vol. LXII, no. 15 (1996), pp. 472–474.

6. White, 1996.

7. Hubbard, B.M. Conscious Evolution: Awaking the Power or our Social Potential. Novato, CA: New Word Library, 1998.

8. Bushe, G.R. Clear Leadership. Palo Alto, CA: Davies-Black Publishing, 2001.

9. Chin, A. (1998). Future Visions. Journal of Organization and Change Management. (Spring); Curran, M. (1991). Appreciative Inquiry: A Third Wave Approach to O.D. Vision/Action, December, 12–14.

10. Gergen, K.J. (1994). Realities and Relationships. Cambridge, MA: Harvard University Press.

# CHAPTER 8

# *Theories of Organizations and Environments*

Theoretical models of organizations underwent major changes starting in the 1960s when the "open systems perspective" gained support and essentially displaced "closed system models" (Scott, 2003). The primary focus of research and theory building shifted from the internal characteristics of organizations to the external dynamics of organizational competition, interaction, and interdependency. The *organizations as open systems* perspective views them as systems of interdependent activities embedded in and dependent on wider environments. Organizations not only acquire material, financial, and human resources from their environment, they also gain social support and legitimacy. Thus, the focus of theory and research from the open systems perspective inevitably moved to the interactions and interdependencies among organizations and their environments.

This perspective began to dominate organization theory when, in 1966–1967, two influential modern works on the subject were published: Daniel Katz and Robert Kahn's *The Social Psychology of Organizations* (1966), which articulated the concept of organizations as open systems; and James D. Thompson's *Organizations in Action*, on the rational systems/contingency perspective of organizations(1967).

Systems theories of organization have two major conceptual themes or components: (1) applications of Ludwig von Bertalanffy's (1951, 1968) general systems theory to organizations and (2) the use of quantitative tools and techniques to understand complex relationships among organizational and environmental variables and thereby optimize decisions.

A *system* is an organized collection of parts united by prescribed interactions and designed to accomplish specific goals or general purposes (Boulding, 1956). Thus, it is easy to see why general systems theory provides an important perspective for understanding modern organizations. Systems theory views an organization as a complex set of dynamically intertwined and interconnected elements, including its inputs, processes, outputs, and feedback loops, and the environment in which it operates and with which it continuously interacts. A change in any element of the system causes changes in other elements. The interconnections tend to be complex, dynamic, and often unknown; thus, when management makes decisions involving one organizational element, unanticipated impacts usually occur throughout the organizational system. Systems theorists study these interconnections, frequently using organizational decision processes and information and control systems as their focal points of analysis.

Whereas classical organization theory tends to be single-dimensional and somewhat simplistic, open systems theories tend to be multidimensional and complex in their assumptions about organizational cause-and-effect relationships. The classicalists viewed organizations as static structures; systems theorists see organizations as always-changing processes of interactions among organizational and environmental elements. Organizations are not static, but are rather in constantly shifting states of dynamic equilibrium. They are adaptive systems that are integral parts of their environments. Organizations must adjust to changes in their environments if they are to survive; in turn, virtually all of their decisions and actions affect their environments.

Norbert Wiener's classic model of an organization as an adaptive system, from his 1948 book, *Cybernetics*, epitomizes these basic theoretical perspectives of systems. *Cybernetics*, from a Greek word meaning "steersman," was used by Wiener to mean the multidisciplinary study of the structures and functions of control and information-processing systems in animals and machines. The basic concept behind cybernetics is self-regulation—through biological, social, or technological systems that can identify problems, do something about them, and receive feedback to adjust themselves automatically. Wiener, a mathematician, developed the concept of cybernetics while working on antiaircraft systems during World War II. Variations on this simple model of a system have been used extensively by systems theorists for many years, particularly related to the development and use of management information systems, but we have not been able to locate anyone who used it before Wiener did in 1948.

The *organizational ecology* approach provides an excellent example of organizations adapting to their environments. Organizational ecology focuses on populations of organizations rather than individual organizational units and attempts to explain why certain types or species of organizations survive and multiply whereas others languish and die. Environmental selection is the primary process by which change occurs in organizations; for example, variation in structural forms is more likely to be caused by environmental selection than by adaptation (Carroll & Hannan, 2000; Hannna & Freeman, 1989). Populations of organizations change over time through the processes of founding, growth, decline, transformation, and mortality. Environments differentially select organizations for survival on the basis of the fit between organization forms and environmental characteristics. The stronger the pressures are from within or outside an organization, the less flexibly adaptive it can be and the higher the likelihood that environmental selection will prevail (Baum, 1996; Hannan & Freeman, 1989). Factors leading to higher mortality rates among organizations are the liability of newness, the liability of smallness, and density dependence.

The search for order among these complex variables has led to an extensive reliance on quantitative analytical methods and models. The systems approach is strongly cause-and-effect oriented ("positivist") in its philosophy and methods. In these respects, systems theories have close ties to the scientific management approach of Frederick Winslow Taylor. However, while Taylor used quantitative scientific methods to find "the one best way," the systems theorist uses quantitative scientific methods to identify cause-and-effect relationships and to find *optimal solutions*. In this sense, the conceptual approaches and purposes of the two perspectives are strikingly similar. Systems theories are often called *management sciences* or *administrative sciences*.

Computers, models, and interdisciplinary teams of analysts are the *tools* of the systems perspective. Studies of organizations done by its proponents typically use the scientific method and quasi-experimental research techniques or computer models. This quantitative orientation reflects the systems school's origins in the years immediately following World War II, when the first serious attempts were made to apply mathematical and statistical probability models to organizational processes and decision making. Many of the early efforts were labeled operations analysis or operations research in defense industry-related "think tanks," such as the RAND Corporation of Santa Monica, California. *Operations research* or *operations analysis* refers to the use of mathematical and scientific techniques to develop a quantitative basis for organizational decision-making (Raiffa, 1968). During subsequent decades, defense and aerospace programs provided the development and testing settings for many of the tools and techniques of operations research, including PERT (Program Evaluation and Review Technique), CPM (Critical Path Method), statistical inference, linear programming, gaming, Monte Carlo methods, and simulation.

Daniel Katz and Robert Kahn provided the intellectual basis for merging classical, neoclassical, human relations/behavioral, "modern" structural, and systems perspectives of organizations. They balanced these perspectives through their concept of organizations as open systems—systems that include organizations and their environments. Because organizations are open systems, they must continuously adapt to changing environmental factors, and managers must recognize that all organizational decisions and actions in turn influence their environments. Reprinted here is "Organizations and the System Concept," a chapter from *The Social Psychology of Organizations*, in which Katz and Kahn conclude that the traditional closed-system view of organizations has led to a failure to fully appreciate the interdependencies and interactions between organizations and their environments. Katz and Kahn's concept of open systems has influenced the thinking of many organization theorists since.

Classical organization theorists saw organizations as rational but closed systems that pursued the goal of economic efficiency. Because the systems were "closed" and thus not subject to influence from the external environment, major attention could be focused on such functions as planning and/or controlling. James D. Thompson classifies most organizations as open systems in his influential 1967 book, *Organizations in Action*. Reprinted here are the book's first two chapters, in which he suggests that the closed-system approach may be realistic only at the technical level of organizational operations. Thompson seeks to bridge the gap between open and closed systems by postulating that organizations "abhor uncertainty" and deal with it in the environment by creating specific elements designed to cope with the outside world, while other elements are able to focus on the rational nature of technical operations. The dominant technology used by an organization strongly influences its structure, activities, and evaluation/control processes.

John W. Meyer and Brian Rowan (1977) emphasize cultural and institutional environmental influences while arguing that the modern world contains socially constructed practices and norms that provide the framework for the creation and elaboration of formal organizations. As open systems, organizations gain legitimacy and support to the extent that they accept these norms as appropriate ways to organize. This line of argument, called *institutional theory*, asserts that the world is a product of our ideas and conceptions; our socially created and validated meanings *define* reality. The rise of the modern world as we know it was not caused solely by new production technologies and administrative structures for coordinating complex activities. The growth of certain beliefs and cognitions about the nature of the world and the way things happen—and *should* happen—also shaped the modern world. Beliefs about organizations and institutions are created and reinforced by a wide range of actors and forces, including universities, professional groups, public opinion, the mass media, the state, and laws (Scott, 2003). According to institutional theory, an organization's life chances are significantly improved by its demonstrated conformity to the norms and social expectations of the institutional environments. Thus, environments are sources of legitimacy and support. Many of the environmental forces that affect organizations are not based on the values of efficiency or effectiveness but instead on social and cultural pressures to conform to a prescribed structural form.

Another open systems theory, *resource dependency theory*, stresses that all organizations exchange resources with their environment as a condition for survival. Jeffrey Pfeffer and Gerald Salancik (1978) explain that one cannot understand the structure and behavior of an organization without understanding the context in which it operates. No organizations are self-sufficient, and thus, they must engage in exchanges with their environments in order to survive. Organizations need to acquire resources from their environments, and the importance and scarcity of these resources determine the extent of organizational dependency on the environment. For example, *information* is a resource organizations need to reduce uncertainty and dependency, so organizations seek information to survive.

During the 1980s, a new approach helped theorists cope with the changing dynamics of technical and institutional environments: *theories of organizational networks*. From a network perspective, organizational environments consist of complex relationships and interactions among various actors, including "key suppliers, resource and product consumers, regulatory agencies, and other organizations that produce similar services and products" (DiMaggio and Powell, 1983: 148). While other lines of open system perspective often see the environment as a *place* of transaction, a *source* of resources and legitimacy, and/or a *space* of competition, the network approaches view the organizational environment as a complex *web* of actual interactions and relationships among organizational actors. The networks constrain actors and in turn are shaped by them (Nohria & Eccles, 1992, p. 7).

Today, many formal organizations, including corporations and large nongovernmental organizations (NGOs), are restructuring themselves in network forms and also establishing larger external networks with their partners. This movement is in response to rapidly changing environments and to increasing demands for internal efficiency. The network form of organization is widely viewed as highly effective for adapting to turbulent environments. They permit more flexible interactions among units, people, problems, solutions, and resources. Wayne Baker's article reprinted in this chapter explores the theoretical and methodological features of network organizations. Baker defines a network organization as "an organization integrated across formal groups created by vertical, horizontal, and spatial differentiation for any type of relations." He argues that this network form of organization has comparative advantages, including: "as a flexible and self-adapting organization, it is well-suited to unique customized projects, close customer and supplier involvement in the production process, and complex, turbulent environments (Nohria & Eccles, 1992, p. xiv).

Baker goes beyond theoretical elaboration of network organizations and quantifies their structural properties using the principles of *integration* and *differentiation*. Using a real estate service firm as an example, he concludes that a network organization is *integrated* across formal boundaries while interpersonal ties of different types are formed without respect to vertical, horizontal or spatial *differentiation* (Baker, 1992, p. 422).

Organizational researchers now pay greater attention to the interactions and interdependencies between organizations and their environments as these relations become more complex and dynamic. Theories of organizations and environments view organizations as systems of interdependent activities embedded in wider environments. The early intraorganizational-level theories focused primarily on internal structures, processes, and dynamics of organizations, plus depicted organizations as separate from their environments—as closed entities with clear boundaries. This separation is not apparent in more recent approaches that emphasize the interfaces between organizations and their environments. Organizations govern their task environments in order to acquire material, financial, and human resources. They also manage the institutional and social environments in order to gain social support and legitimacy from outside stakeholders. These environmental factors will become explicit in the readings that are reprinted in this chapter.

We invite you to read the Introduction and readings reproduced in Chapter 9, "Theories of Organizations and Society," which extend the open systems perspective introduced in this chapter.

## BIBLIOGRAPHY

Agranoff, R. (2012). *Collaborating to manage: A primer for the public sector*. Washington, DC: Georgetown University Press.

Amburgey, T. L., & H. Rao (1996). Organizational ecology: Past, present, and future directions. *Academy of Management Journal, 39*, 1265–1286.

Baker, W. (1992). The network organization in theory and practice. In N. Nohria & R. Eccles, eds., *Networks and organizations: Structure, form, and action* (pp. 57–91). Boston: Harvard Business School Press.

Barnett, W. P. (2008). *The red queen among organizations: How competitiveness evolves*. Princeton, NJ: Princeton University Press.

Baum, J. A. C. (1996). Organizational ecology. In S. R. Clegg, C. Hardy, & W. R. Nord, eds., *Handbook of organization studies* (pp. 77–114). Thousand Oaks, CA: Sage.

Baum, J. A. C., & C. Oliver (1996). Toward an institutional ecology of organizational founding. *Academy of Management Journal, 39*, 1378–1427.

Bertalanffy, L. (1951, December). General systems theory: A new approach to unity of science. *Human Biology, 23*, 303–361.

Bertalanffy, L. (1968). *General systems theory: Foundations, development, applications*. New York: George Braziller.

Bolman, L. G., & T. E. Deal. (2013). *Reframing organizations: Artistry, choice and leadership* (5th ed.). San Francisco: Jossey-Bass/Wiley.

Boulding, K. E. (1956, April). General systems theory: The skeleton of science. *Management Science, 2*(3), 197–208.

Brass, D. J., J. Galaskiewicz, H. R. Greve, & W. Tsai (2004). Taking stock of networks and organizations: A multilevel perspective. *Academy of Management Journal, 47*, 795–817.

Brass, D. J., G. Labianca, A. Mehra, D. S. Halgin, & S. P. Borgatti, eds. (2014). *Contemporary perspectives on organizational social networks*. Bingley, UK: Emerald Group.

Burt, R. S. (1992). The social structure of competition. In N. Nohria & R. Eccles, eds., *Networks and organizations: Structure, form, and action* (pp. 57–91). Boston: Harvard Business School Press.

Burt, R. S. (1997). The contingent value of social capital. *Administrative Science Quarterly, 42*, 339–365.

Carroll, G. R., & M. T. Hannan (2000). *Demography of corporations and industries*. Princeton, NJ: Princeton University Press.

Diefenbach, T., & R. Todnem, eds. (2012). *Reinventing hierarchy and bureaucracy: From the bureau to network organizations*. Bingley, UK: Emerald Group.

DiMaggio, P. J., & W. W. Powell (1983). The iron cage revisited: Institutional isomorphism and collective rationality in organizational fields. *American Sociological Review, 48*, 147–160.

Drori, G. S., J. W. Meyer, & H. Hwang (2006). *Globalization and organization: World society and organizational change*. Oxford, UK: Oxford University Press.

Greenwood, R., C. Oliver, R. Suddaby, & K. Sahlin-Andersson (2008). *The Sage handbook of organizational institutionalism*. London, UK: Sage.

Greve, H., T. Rowley, & A. Shipilov. (2014). *Network advantage: How to unlock value from your alliances and partnerships*. San Francisco: Jossey-Bass/Wiley.

Hannan, M. T. (2005). Ecologies of organizations: Diversity and identity. *Journal of Economic Perspectives, 19*, 51–70.

Hannan, M. T., & J. Freeman (1989). *Organizational ecology*. Cambridge, MA: Harvard University Press.

Hannan, M. T., G. R. Carroll, & L. Pòlos (2003). The organizational niche. *Sociological Theory, 21*, 309–340.

Hannan, M. T., L. Pòlos, & G. R. Carroll (2003a). The fog of change: Opacity and asperity in organizations. *Administrative Science Quarterly, 48*, 399–343.

Hannan, M. T., L. Pòlos, & G. R. Carroll (2003b). Cascading organizational change. *Organization Science, 14*, 463–482.

Hannan, M. T., L. Pòlos, & G. R. Carroll (2004). The evolution of inertia. *Industrial and Corporate Change, 13*, 213–242.

Hannan, M. T., L. Pòlos, & G. R. Carroll (2007). *Logics of organization theory: Audiences, codes, and ecologies*. Princeton, NJ: Princeton University Press.

Jackson, M. O. (2008). *Social and economic networks*. Princeton, NJ: Princeton University Press.

Katz, D., & R. L. Kahn (1966). *The social psychology of organizations*. New York: Wiley.

Kilduff, M., & W. Tsai (2003). *Social networks and organizations*. London, UK: Sage.

Lee, M. R. (2014). *Leading virtual project teams: Adapting leadership theories and communications techniques to 21st century organizations*. Boca Raton, FL: CRC Press.

Lepore, D. (2010): *Sechel: Logic, language and tools to manage any organization as a network*. Toronto: Intelligent Management.

Meyer, J. W., & B. Rowan (1977). Institutionalized organizations: Formal structures as myth and ceremony. *American Journal of Sociology, 83*, 340–363.

Nohria, N., & R. Eccles, eds. (1992). *Networks and organizations: Structure, form, and action*. Boston: Harvard Business School Press.

Ott, J. S. (1989). *The organizational culture perspective*. Pacific Grove, CA: Brooks/Cole.

Pfeffer, J., & G. R. Salancik (1978). *The external control of organizations: A resource dependence perspective*. New York: Harper & Row.

Powell, W. W., & P. J. DiMaggio, eds. (1991). *The new institutionalism in organizational analysis*. Chicago, IL: University of Chicago Press.

Powell, W. W., K. W. Koput, & L. Smith-Doerr (1996). Interorganizational collaboration and the locus of innovation: Networks of learning in biotechnology. *Administrative Science Quarterly, 41*, 116–145.

Raiffa, H. (1968). *Decision analysis*. Reading, MA: Addison-Wesley.

Ramos, P. P. (2012). *Network models for organizations: The flexible design of 21st century companies*. New York: Palgrave Macmillan.

Rao, H., & E. H. Neilsen (1992). An ecology of agency arrangements: Mortality of savings and loan associations, 1960–1987. *Administrative Science Quarterly, 37*, 448–470.

Sahlin-Andersson, K., & L. Engwall (2002). *The expansion of management knowledge: Carriers, flows, and sources*. Stanford, CA: Stanford University Press.

Saz-Carranza, A. (2012). *Uniting diverse organizations: Managing goal-oriented advocacy networks*. New York: Routledge.

Scott, W. R. (2003). *Organizations: Rational, natural, and open systems*, 5th ed. Upper Saddle River, NJ: Prentice Hall.

Scott, W. R. (2008). *Institutions and organizations: Ideas and interests*, 3rd ed. Thousand Oaks, CA: Sage.

Scott, W. R., M. Ruef, P. Mendel, & C. Caronna (2000). *Institutional change and healthcare organizations: From professional dominance to managed care*. Chicago, IL: University of Chicago Press.

Thompson, G. F. (2003). *Between hierarchies and markets: The logic and limits of network forms of organization*. Oxford, UK: Oxford University Press.

Thompson, J. D. (1967). *Organizations in action*. New York: McGraw-Hill.

Thornton, P. H. (2002). The rise of the corporation in a craft industry: Conflict and conformity in institutional logics. *Academy of Management Journal, 45*, 81–101.

Thornton, P. H. (2004). *Markets from culture: Institutional logics and organizational decisions in higher education publishing*. Stanford, CA: Stanford University Press.

Uzzi, B. (1997). Social structure and competition in interfirm networks: The paradox of embeddedness. *Administrative Science Quarterly, 42*, 35–67.

Wiener, N. (1948). *Cybernetics*. Cambridge, MA: MIT Press.

## 29

# Organizations and the System Concept

*Daniel Katz & Robert L. Kahn*

The aims of social science with respect to human organizations are like those of any other science with respect to the events and phenomena of its domain. The social scientist wishes to understand human organizations, to describe what is essential in their form, aspects, and functions. He wishes to explain their cycles of growth and decline, to predict their effects and effectiveness. Perhaps he wishes as well to test and apply such knowledge by introducing purposeful changes into organizations—by making them, for example, more benign, more responsive to human needs.

Such efforts are not solely the prerogative of social science, however; common sense approaches to understanding and altering organizations are ancient and perpetual. They tend, on the whole, to rely heavily on two assumptions: that the location and nature of an organization are given by its name; and that an organization is possessed of built-in goals—because such goals were implanted by founders, decreed by its present leaders, or because they emerged mysteriously as the purposes of the organizational system itself. These assumptions scarcely provide an adequate basis for the study of organizations and at times can be misleading and even fallacious. We propose, however, to make use of the information to which they point.

The first problem in understanding an organization or a social system is its location and identification. How do we know that we are dealing with an organization? What are its boundaries? What behavior belongs to the organization and what behavior lies outside it? Who are the individuals whose actions are to be studied and what segments of their behavior are to be included?

The fact that popular names exist to label social organizations is both a help and a hindrance. These popular labels represent the socially accepted stereotypes about organizations and do not specify their role structure, their psychological nature, or their boundaries. On the other hand, these names help in locating the area of behavior in which we are interested. Moreover, the fact that people both within and without an organization accept stereotypes about its nature and functioning is one determinant of its character.

The second key characteristic of the common sense approach to understanding an organization is to regard it simply as the epitome of the purposes of its designer, its leaders, or its key members. The teleology of this approach is again both a help and a hindrance. Since human purpose is deliberately built into organizations and is specifically recorded in the social compact, the bylaws, or other formal protocol of the undertaking, it would be inefficient not to utilize these sources of information. In the early development of a group, many processes are generated which have little to do with its rational purpose, but over time there is a cumulative recognition of the devices for ordering group life and a deliberate use of these devices.

Apart from formal protocol, the primary mission of an organization as perceived by its leaders furnishes a highly informative set of clues for the researcher seeking to study organizational functioning. Nevertheless, the stated purposes of an organization as

*The Social Psychology of Organizations*, Daniel Katz and Robert L. Kahn (New York: Wiley 1966), pp. 14–29. © 1966 John Wiley & Sons, Inc. Reprinted by permission of John Wiley & Sons, Inc.

given by its by-laws or in the reports of its leaders can be misleading. Such statements of objectives may idealize, rationalize, distort, omit, or even conceal some essential aspects of the functioning of the organization. Nor is there always agreement about the mission of the organization among its leaders and members. The university president may describe the purpose of his institution as one of turning out national leaders; the academic dean sees it as imparting the cultural heritage of the past, the academic vice-president as enabling students to move toward self-actualization and development, the graduate dean as creating new knowledge, the dean of men as training youngsters in technical and professional skills which will enable them to earn their living, and the editor of the student newspaper as inculcating the conservative values which will preserve the status quo of an outmoded capitalistic society.

The fallacy here is one of equating the purposes or goals of organizations with the purposes and goals of individual members. The organization as a system has an output, a product or an outcome, but this is not necessarily identical with the individual purposes of group members. Though the founders of the organization and its key members do think in teleological terms about organization objectives, we should not accept such practical thinking, useful as it may be, in place of a theoretical set of constructs for purposes of scientific analysis. Social science, too frequently in the past, has been misled by such short-cuts and has equated popular phenomenology with scientific explanation.

In fact, the classic body of theory and thinking about organizations has assumed a teleology of this sort as the easiest way of identifying organizational structures and their functions. From this point of view an organization is a social device for efficiently accomplishing through group means some stated purpose; it is the equivalent of the blueprint for the design of the machine which is to be created for some practical objective. The essential difficulty with this purposive or design approach is that an organization characteristically includes more and less than is indicated by the design of its founder or the purpose of its leader. Some of the factors assumed in the design may be lacking or so distorted in operational practice as to be meaningless, while unforeseen embellishments dominate the organizational structure. Moreover, it is not always possible to ferret out the designer of the organization or to discover the intricacies of the design which he carried in his head. The attempt by Merton to deal with the latent function of the organization in contrast with its manifest function is one way of dealing with this problem.[1] The study of unanticipated consequences as well as anticipated consequences of organizational functioning is a similar way of handling the matter. Again, however, we are back to the purposes of the creator or leader, dealing with unanticipated consequences on the assumption that we can discover the consequences anticipated by him and can lump all other outcomes together as a kind of error variance.

*It would be much better theoretically*, however, to start with concepts which do not call for identifying the purposes of the designers and then correcting for them when they do not seem to be fulfilled. The theoretical concepts should begin with the input, output, and functioning of the organization as a system and not with the rational purposes of its leaders. We may want to utilize such purposive notions to lead us to sources of data or as subjects of special study, but not as our basic theoretical constructs for understanding organizations.

Our theoretical model for the understanding of organizations is that of an energic input-output system in which the energic return from the output reactivates the system. Social organizations are flagrantly open systems in that the input of energies and the conversion of output into further energic input consist of transactions between the organization and its environment.

All social systems, including organizations, consist of the patterned activities of a number of individuals. Moreover, these patterned activities are complementary or interdependent with respect to some common output or outcome; they are repeated, relatively enduring, and bounded in space and time. If the activity pattern occurs only once or at unpredictable intervals, we could not speak of an organization. The stability or recurrence of activities can be examined in relation to the *energic input* into the system, the *transformation of energies within the system*, and the *resulting product or energic output*. In a factory the raw materials and the human labor are the energic input, the patterned activities of production the transformation of energy, and the finished product the output. To maintain this patterned activity requires a continued renewal of the inflow of energy. This is guaranteed in social systems by the energic return from the product or outcome. Thus the outcome of the cycle of activities furnishes new energy for the initiation of a renewed cycle. The company which produces automobiles sells them and by doing so obtains the means of securing new raw materials, compensating its labor force, and continuing the activity pattern.

In many organizations outcomes are converted into money, and new energy is furnished through this mechanism. Money is a convenient way of handling energy units both on the output and input sides, and buying and selling represent one set of social rules for regulating the exchange of money. Indeed, these rules are so effective and so widespread that there is some danger of mistaking the business of buying and selling for the defining cycles of organization. It is a commonplace executive observation that businesses exist to make money, and the observation is usually allowed to go unchallenged. It is, however, a very limited statement about the purposes of business.

Some human organizations do not depend on the cycle of selling and buying to maintain themselves. Universities and public agencies depend rather on bequests

and legislative appropriations, and in so-called voluntary organizations the output reenergizes the activity of organization members in a more direct fashion. Member activities and accomplishments are rewarding in themselves and tend therefore to be continued, without the mediation of the outside environment. A society of bird watchers can wander into the hills and engage in the rewarding activities of identifying birds for their mutual edification and enjoyment. Organizations thus differ on this important dimension of the source of energy renewal, with the great majority utilizing both intrinsic and extrinsic sources in varying degrees. Most large-scale organizations are not as self-contained as small voluntary groups and are very dependent upon the social effects of their output for energy renewal.

Our two basic criteria for identifying social systems and determining their functions are (1) tracing the pattern of energy exchange or activity of people as it results in some output and (2) ascertaining how the output is translated into energy which reactivates the pattern. We shall refer to organizational functions or objectives not as the conscious purposes of group leaders or group members but as the outcomes which are the energic source for a maintenance of the same type of output.

This model of an energic input-output system is taken from the open system theory as promulgated by von Bertalanffy.[2] Theorists have pointed out the applicability of the system concepts of the natural sciences to the problems of social science. It is important, therefore, to examine in more detail the constructs of system theory and the characteristics of open systems.

System theory is basically concerned with problems of relationships, of structure, and of interdependence rather than with the constant attributes of objects. In general approach it resembles field theory except that its dynamics deal with temporal as well as spatial patterns. Older formulations of system constructs dealt with the closed systems of the physical sciences, in which relatively self-contained structures could be treated successfully as if they were independent of external forces. But living systems, whether biological organisms or social organizations, are acutely dependent upon their external environment and so must be conceived of as open systems.

Before the advent of open-system thinking, social scientists tended to take one of two approaches in dealing with social structures; they tended either (1) to regard them as closed systems to which the laws of physics applied or (2) to endow them with some vitalistic concept like entelechy. In the former case they ignored the environmental forces affecting the organization and in the latter case they fell back upon some magical purposiveness to account for organizational functioning. Biological theorists, however, have rescued us from this trap by pointing out that the concept of the open system means that we neither have to follow the laws of traditional physics, nor in deserting them do we have to abandon science. The laws of Newtonian physics are correct generalizations but they are limited to closed systems. They do not apply in the same fashion to open systems which maintain themselves through constant commerce with their environment, i.e., a continuous inflow and outflow of energy through permeable boundaries.

One example of the operation of closed versus open systems can be seen in the concept of entropy and the second law of thermodynamics. According to the second law of thermodynamics a system moves toward equilibrium; it tends to run down, that is, its differentiated structures tend to move toward dissolution as the elements composing them become arranged in random disorder. For example, suppose that a bar of iron has been heated by the application of a blowtorch on one side. The arrangement of all the fast (heated) molecules on one side and all the slow molecules on the other is an unstable state, and over time the distribution of molecules becomes in effect random, with the resultant cooling of one side and heating of the other, so that all surfaces of the iron approach the same temperature. A similar process of heat exchange will also be going on between the iron bar and its environment, so that the bar will gradually approach the temperature of the room in which it is located, and in so doing will elevate somewhat the previous temperature of the room. More technically, entropy increases toward a maximum and equilibrium occurs as the physical system attains the state of the most probable distribution of its elements. In social systems, however, structures tend to become more elaborated rather than less differentiated. The rich may grow richer and the poor may grow poorer. The open system does not run down, because it can import energy from the world around it. Thus the operation of entropy is counteracted by the importation of energy and the living system is characterized by negative rather than positive entropy.

## COMMON CHARACTERISTICS OF OPEN SYSTEMS

Though the various types of open systems have common characteristics by virtue of being open systems, they differ in other characteristics. If this were not the case, we would be able to obtain all our basic knowledge about social organizations through the study of a single cell.

The following nine characteristics seem to define all open systems.

### 1. Importation of Energy
Open systems import some form of energy from the external environment. The cell receives oxygen from the blood stream; the body similarly takes in oxygen from the air and food from the external world. The personality is dependent upon the external world for stimulation. Studies of sensory deprivation show that when a person is placed in a darkened soundproof room, where he has a minimal amount of visual and auditory stimulation, he develops hallucinations and other signs of mental stress.[3]

Deprivation of social stimulation also can lead to mental disorganization.[4] Kohler's studies of the figural after-effects of continued stimulation show the dependence of perception upon its energic support from the external world.[5] Animals deprived of visual experience from birth for a prolonged period never fully recover their visual capacities.[6] In other words, the functioning personality is heavily dependent upon the continuous inflow of stimulation from the external environment. Similarly, social organizations must also draw renewed supplies of energy from other institutions, or people, or the material environment. No social structure is self-sufficient or self-contained.

## 2. The Through-Put

Open systems transform the energy available to them. The body converts starch and sugar into heat and action. The personality converts chemical and electrical forms of stimulation into sensory qualities, and information into thought patterns. The organization creates a new product, or processes materials, or trains people, or provides a service. These activities entail some reorganization of input. Some work gets done in the system.

## 3. The Output

Open systems export some products into the environment, whether it be the invention of an inquiring mind or a bridge constructed by an engineering firm. Even the biological organism exports physiological products such as carbon dioxide from the lungs, which helps to maintain plants in the immediate environment.

## 4. Systems as Cycles of Events

The pattern of activities of the energy exchange has a cyclic character. The product exported into the environment furnishes the sources of energy for the repetition of the cycle of activities. The energy reinforcing the cycle of activities can derive from some exchange of the product in the external world or from the activity itself. In the former instance, the industrial concern utilizes raw materials and human labor to turn out a product which is marketed, and the monetary return is used to obtain more raw materials and labor to perpetuate the cycle of activities. In the latter instance, the voluntary organization can provide expressive satisfactions to its members so that the energy renewal comes directly from the organizational activity itself.

The problem of structure, or the relatedness of parts, can be observed directly in some physical arrangement of things where the larger unit is physically bounded and its subparts are also bounded within the larger structure. But how do we deal with social structures, where physical boundaries in this sense do not exist? It was the genius of F. H. Allport which contributed the answer, namely that the structure is to be found in an interrelated set of events which return upon themselves to complete and renew a cycle of activities.[7] It is events rather than things which are structured, so that social structure is a dynamic rather than a static concept. Activities are structured so that they comprise a unity in their completion or closure. A simple linear stimulus-response exchange between two people would not constitute social structure. To create structure, the responses of A would have to elicit B's reactions in such a manner that the responses of the latter would stimulate A to further responses. Of course the chain of events may involve many people, but their behavior can be characterized as showing structure only when there is some closure to the chain by a return to its point of origin with the probability that the chain of events will then be repeated. The repetition of the cycle does not have to involve the same set of phenotypical happenings. It may expand to include more subevents of exactly the same kind or it may involve similar activities directed toward the same outcomes. In the individual organism the eye may move in such a way as to have the point of light fall upon the center of the retina. As the point of light moves, the movements of the eye may also change but to complete the same cycle of activity, i.e., to focus upon the point of light.

A single cycle of events of a self-closing character gives us a simple form of structure. But such single cycles can also combine to give a larger structure of events or an event system. An event system may consist of a circle of smaller cycles or hoops, each one of which makes contact with several others. Cycles may also be tangential to one another from other types of subsystems. The basic method for the identification of social structures is to follow the energic chain of events from the input of energy through its transformation to the point of closure of the cycle.

### 5. Negative Entropy

To survive, open systems must move to arrest the entropic process; they must acquire negative entropy. The entropic process is a universal law of nature in which all forms of organization move toward disorganization or death. Complex physical systems move toward simple random distribution of their elements and biological organisms also run down and perish. The open system, however, by importing more energy from its environment than it expends, can store energy and can acquire negative entropy. There is then a general trend in an open system to maximize its ratio of imported to expended energy, to survive and even during periods of crisis to live on borrowed time. Prisoners in concentration camps on a starvation diet will carefully conserve any form of energy expenditure to make the limited food intake go as far as possible.[8] Social organizations will seek to improve their survival position and to acquire in their reserves a comfortable margin of operation.

The entropic process asserts itself in all biological systems as well as in closed physical systems. The energy replenishment of the biological organism is not of a qualitative character which can maintain indefinitely the complex organizational structure of living tissue. Social systems, however, are not anchored in the same physical constancies as biological organisms and so are capable of almost indefinite arresting of the entropic process. Nevertheless the number of organizations which go out of existence every year is large.

### 6. Information Input, Negative Feedback, and the Coding Process

The inputs into living systems consist not only of energic materials which become transformed or altered in the work that gets done. Inputs are also informative in character and furnish signals to the structure about the environment and about its own functioning in relation to the environment. Just as we recognize the distinction between cues and drives in individual psychology, so must we take account of information and energic inputs for all living systems.

The simplest type of information input found in all systems is negative feedback. Information feedback of a negative kind enables the system to correct its deviations from course. The working parts of the machine feed back information about the effects of their operation to some central mechanism or subsystem which acts on such information to keep the system on target. The thermostat which controls the temperature of the room is a simple example of a regulatory device which operates on the basis of negative feedback. The automated power plant would furnish more complex examples. Miller emphasizes the critical nature of negative feedback in his proposition: "*When a system's negative feedback discontinues, its steady state vanishes, and at the same time its boundary disappears and the system terminates.*"[9] If there is no corrective device to get the system back on its course, it will expend too much energy or it will ingest too much energic input and no longer continue as a system.

The reception of inputs into a system is selective. Not all energic inputs are capable of being absorbed into every system. The digestive system of living creatures assimilates only those inputs to which it is adapted. Similarly, systems can react only to those information signals to which they are attuned. The general term for the selective mechanisms of a system by which incoming materials are rejected or accepted and translated for the structure is coding. Through the coding process, the "blooming, buzzing confusion" of the world is simplified into a few meaningful and simplified categories for a given system. The nature of the functions performed by the system determines its coding mechanisms, which in turn perpetuate this type of functioning.

### 7. The Steady State and Dynamic Homeostasis

The importation of energy to arrest entropy operates to maintain some constancy in energy exchange, so that open systems which survive are characterized by a steady state. A steady state is not motionless or a true equilibrium. There is a continuous inflow of energy from the external environment and a continuous export of the products of the system, but the character of the system, the ratio of the energy exchanges and the relations between parts, remains the same. The catabolic and anabolic processes of tissue breakdown and restoration within the body preserve a steady state so that the organism from time to time is not the identical organism it was but a highly similar organism. The steady state is seen in clear form in the homeostatic processes for the regulation of body temperature; external conditions of humidity and temperature may vary, but the temperature of the body remains the same. The endocrine glands are a regulatory mechanism for preserving an evenness of physiological functioning. The general principle here is that of Le Châtelier who maintains that any internal or external factor making for disruption of the system is countered by forces which restore the system as closely as possible to its previous state.[10] Krech and Crutchfield similarly hold, with respect to

psychological organization, that cognitive structures will react to influences in such a way as to absorb them with minimal change to existing cognitive integration.[11]

The homeostatic principle does not apply literally to the functioning of all complex living systems, in that in counteracting entropy they move toward growth and expansion. This apparent contradiction can be resolved, however, if we recognize the complexity of the subsystems and their interaction in anticipating changes necessary for the maintenance of an overall steady state. Stagner has pointed out that the initial disturbance of a given tissue constancy within the biological organism will result in mobilization of energy to restore the balance, but that recurrent upsets will lead to actions to anticipate the disturbance:

> We eat before we experience intense hunger pangs ... energy mobilization for forestalling tactics must be explained in terms of a *cortical tension* which reflects the visceral proprioceptive pattern of the original biological disequilibration. ... *Dynamic homeostasis* involves the maintenance of tissue constancies by establishing a constant physical environment—by reducing the variability and disturbing effects of external stimulation. Thus the organism does not simply restore the prior equilibrium. A new, more complex and more comprehensive equilibrium is established.[12]

Though the tendency toward a steady state in its simplest form is homeostatic, as in the preservation of a constant body temperature, the basic principle is *the preservation of the character of the system*. The equilibrium which complex systems approach is often that of a quasi-stationary equilibrium, to use Lewin's concept.[13] An adjustment in one direction is countered by a movement in the opposite direction and both movements are approximate rather than precise in their compensatory nature. Thus a temporal chart of activity will show a series of ups and downs rather than a smooth curve.

In preserving the character of the system, moreover, the structure will tend to import more energy than is required for its output, as we have already noted in discussing negative entropy. To insure survival, systems will operate to acquire some margin of safety beyond the immediate level of existence. The body will store fat, the social organization will build up reserves, the society will increase its technological and cultural base. Miller has formulated the proposition that the rate of growth of a system—within certain ranges—is exponential if it exists in a medium which makes available unrestricted amounts of energy for input.[14]

In adapting to their environment, systems will attempt to cope with external forces by ingesting them or acquiring control over them. The physical boundedness of the single organism means that such attempts at control over the environment affect the behavioral system rather than the biological system of the individual. Social systems will move, however, toward incorporating within their boundaries the external resources essential to survival. Again the result is an expansion of the original system.

Thus, the steady state, which at the simple level is one of homeostasis over time, at more complex levels becomes one of preserving the character of the system through growth and expansion. The basic type of system does not change directly as a consequence of expansion. The most common type of growth is a multiplication of the same type of cycles or subsystems—a change in quantity rather than in quality. Animal and plant species grow by multiplication. A social system adds more units of the same essential type as it already has. Haire has studied the ratio between the sizes of different subsystems in growing business organizations.[15] He found that though the number of people increased in both the production subsystem and the subsystem concerned with the external world, the ratio of the two groups remained constant. Qualitative change does occur, however, in two ways. In the first place, quantitative growth calls for supportive subsystems of a specialized character not necessary when

the system was smaller. In the second place, there is a point where quantitative changes produce a qualitative difference in the functioning of a system. A small college which triples its size is no longer the same institution in terms of the relation between its administration and faculty, relations among the various academic departments, or the nature of its instruction.

In time, living systems exhibit a growth or expansion dynamic in which they maximize their basic character. They react to change or they anticipate change through growth which assimilates the new energic inputs to the nature of their structure. In terms of Lewin's quasi-stationary equilibrium the ups and downs of the adjustive process do not always result in a return to the old level. Under certain circumstances a solidification or freezing occurs during one of the adjustive cycles. A new baseline level is thus established and successive movements fluctuate around this plateau, which may be either above or below the previous plateau of operation.

## 8. Differentiation

Open systems move in the direction of differentiation and elaboration. Diffuse global patterns are replaced by more specialized functions. The sense organs and the nervous system evolved as highly differentiated structures from the primitive nervous tissues. The growth of the personality proceeds from primitive, crude organizations of mental functions to hierarchically structured and well-differentiated systems of beliefs and feelings. Social organizations move toward the multiplication and elaboration of roles with greater specialization of function. In the United States today medical specialists now outnumber the general practitioners.

One type of differentiated growth in systems is what von Bertalanffy terms progressive mechanization. It finds expression in the way in which a system achieves a steady state. The early method is a process which involves an interaction of various dynamic forces, whereas the later development entails the use of a regulatory feedback mechanism. He writes:

> It can be shown that the primary regulations in organic systems, that is, those which are most fundamental and primitive in embryonic development as well as in evolution, are of such nature of dynamic interaction.... Superimposed are those regulations which we may call secondary, and which are controlled by fixed arrangements, especially of the feedback type. This state of affairs is a consequence of a general principle of organization which may be called progressive mechanization. At first, systems—biological, neurological, psychological or social—are governed by dynamic interaction of their components; later on, fixed arrangements and conditions of constraint are established which render the system and its parts more efficient, but also gradually diminish and eventually abolish its equipotentiality.[16]

### 9. Equifinality

Open systems are further characterized by the principle of equifinality, a principle suggested by von Bertalanffy in 1940.[17] According to this principle, a system can reach the same final state from differing initial conditions and by a variety of paths. The well-known biological experiments on the sea urchin show that a normal creature of that species can develop from a complete ovum, from each half of a divided ovum, or from the fusion product of two whole ova. As open systems move toward regulatory mechanisms to control their operations, the amount of equifinality may be reduced.

## SOME CONSEQUENCES OF VIEWING ORGANIZATIONS AS OPEN SYSTEMS

[In a later chapter] we shall inquire into the specific implications of considering organizations as open systems and into the ways in which social organizations differ from other types of living systems. At this point, however, we should call attention to some of the misconceptions which arise both in theory and practice when social organizations are regarded as closed rather than open systems.

The major misconception is the failure to recognize fully that the organization is continually dependent upon inputs from the environment and that the inflow of materials and human energy is not a constant. The fact that organizations have built-in protective devices to maintain stability and that they are notoriously difficult to change in the direction of some reformer's desires should not obscure the realities of the dynamic interrelationships of any social structure with its social and natural environment. The very efforts of the organization to maintain a constant external environment produce changes in organizational structure. The reaction to changed inputs to mute their possible revolutionary implications also results in changes.

The typical models in organizational theorizing concentrate upon principles of internal functioning as if these problems were independent of changes in the environment and as if they did not affect the maintenance inputs of motivation and morale. Moves toward tighter integration and coordination are made to insure stability, when flexibility may be the more important requirement. Moreover, coordination and control become ends in themselves rather than means to an end. They are not seen in full perspective as adjusting the system to its environment but as desirable goals within a closed system. In fact, however, every attempt at coordination which is not functionally required may produce a host of new organizational problems.

One error which stems from this kind of misconception is the failure to recognize the equifinality of the open system, namely that there are more ways than one of producing a given outcome. In a closed physical system the same initial conditions must lead to the same final result. In open systems this is not true even at the biological level. It is much less true at the social level. Yet in practice we insist that there is one best way of assembling a gun for all recruits, one best way for the baseball player to hurl the ball in from the outfield and that we standardize and teach these best methods. Now it is true under certain conditions that there is one best way, but these conditions must first be established. The general principle, which characterizes all open systems, is that there does not have to be a single method for achieving an objective.

A second error lies in the notion that irregularities in the functioning of a system due to environmental influences are error variances and should be treated accordingly. According to this conception, they should be controlled out of studies of organizations. From the organization's own operations they should be excluded as irrelevant and should be guarded against. The decisions of officers to omit a consideration of external factors or to guard against such influences in a defensive fashion, as if they would go away if ignored, is an instance of this type of thinking. So is the now outmoded "public be damned" attitude of businessmen toward the clientele upon whose support they depend. Open system theory, on the other hand, would maintain that environmental influences are not sources of error variance but are integrally related to the functioning of a social system, and that we cannot understand a system without a constant study of the forces that impinge upon it.

Thinking of the organization as a closed system, moreover, results in a failure to develop the intelligence or feedback function of obtaining adequate information about the changes in environmental forces. It is remarkable how weak many industrial companies are in their market research departments when they are so dependent upon the market. The prediction can be hazarded that organizations in our society will increasingly move toward the improvements of the facilities for research in assessing environmental forces. The reason is that we are in the process of correcting our misconception of the organization as a closed system.

Emery and Trist have pointed out how current theorizing on organizations still reflects the older closed system conceptions. They write:

> In the realm of social theory, however, there has been something of a tendency to continue thinking in terms of a "closed" system, that is, to regard the enterprise as sufficiently independent to allow most of its problems to be analyzed with reference to its internal structure and without reference to its external environment.... In practice the system theorists in social science ... did "tend to focus on the statics of social structure and to neglect the study of structural change." In an attempt to overcome this bias, Merton suggested that "the concept of strain, stress and tension on the structural level, provides an analytical approach to the study of dynamics and change." This concept has been widely accepted by system theorists but while it draws attention to sources of imbalance within an organization it does not conceptually reflect the mutual permeation of an organization and its environment that is the cause of such imbalance. It still retains the limiting perspectives of "closed system" theorizing. In the administrative field the same limitations may be seen in the otherwise invaluable contributions of Barnard and related writers.[18]

## SUMMARY

The open-system approach to organizations is contrasted with common-sense approaches, which tend to accept popular names and stereotypes as basic organizational properties and to identify the purpose of an organization in terms of the goals of its founders and leaders.

The open-system approach, on the other hand, begins by identifying and mapping the repeated cycles of input, transformation, output, and renewed input which comprise the organizational pattern. This approach to organizations represents the adaptation of work in biology and in the physical sciences by von Bertalanffy and others.

Organizations as a special class of open systems have properties of their own, but they share other properties in common with all open systems. These include the importation of energy from the environment, the through-put or transformation of the imported energy into some product form which is characteristic of the system, the exporting of that product into the environment, and the reenergizing of the system from sources in the environment.

Open systems also share the characteristics of negative entropy, feedback, homeostasis, differentiation, and equifinality. The law of negative entropy states that systems survive and maintain their characteristic internal order only so long as they import from the environment more energy than they expend in the process of transformation and exportation. The feedback principle has to do with information input, which is a special kind of energic importation, a kind of signal to the system about environmental conditions and about the functioning of the system in relation to its environment. The feedback of such information enables the system to correct for its own malfunctioning or for changes in the environment, and thus to maintain a steady state or homeostasis. This is a dynamic rather than a static balance, however. Open systems are not at rest but tend toward differentiation and elaboration, both because of subsystem dynamics and because of the relationship between growth and survival. Finally, open systems are characterized by the principle of equifinality, which asserts that systems can reach the same final state from different initial conditions and by different paths of development.

Traditional organizational theories have tended to view the human organization as a closed system. This tendency has led to a disregard of differing organizational environments and the nature of organizational dependency on environment. It has led also to an overconcentration on principles of internal organizational functioning, with consequent failure to develop and understand the processes of feedback which are essential to survival.

## NOTES

1. Merton, R. K. 1957. *Social theory and social structure*, rev. ed. New York: Free Press.

2. von Bertalanffy, L. 1956. General system theory. *General Systems*. Yearbook of the Society for the Advancement of General System Theory, 1, 1–10.

3. Solomon, P., *et al.* (Eds.) 1961. *Sensory deprivation*. Cambridge, Mass.: Harvard University Press.

4. Spitz, R. A. 1945. Hospitalism: An inquiry into the genesis of psychiatric conditions in early childhood. *Psychoanalytic Study of the Child, 1,* 53–74.

5. Kohler, W., & H. Wallach. 1944. Figural after-effects: An investigation of visual processes. *Proceedings of the American Philosophical Society, 88, 269–357.* Also, Kohler, W., & D. Emery. 1947. Figural after-effects in the third dimension of visual space. *American Journal of Psychology, 60, 159–201.*

6. Melzack, R., & W. Thompson. 1956. Effects of early experience on social behavior. *Canadian Journal of Psychology, 10, 82–90.*

7. Allport, F. H. 1962. A structuronomic conception of behavior: Individual and collective. I. Structural theory and the master problem of social psychology. *Journal of Abnormal and Social Psychology, 64, 3–30.*

8. Cohen, E. 1954. *Human behavior in the concentration camp*. London: Jonathan Cape.

9. Miller, J. G. 1955. Toward a general theory for the behavioral sciences. *American Psychologist, 10, 513–531*; quote from p. 529.

10. See Bradley, D. F., & M. Calvin. 1956. Behavior: Imbalance in a network of chemical transformations. *General Systems.* Yearbook of the Society for the Advancement of General System Theory, 1, 56–65.

11. Krech, D., & R. Crutchfield. 1948. *Theory and problems of social psychology*. New York: McGraw-Hill.

12. Stagner, R. 1951. Homeostasis as a unifying concept in personality theory. *Psychological Review, 58, 5–17*; quote from p. 5.

13. Lewin, K. 1947. Frontiers in group dynamics. *Human Relations, 1,* 5–41.

14. Miller, *op. cit.*

15. Haire, M. 1959. Biological models and empirical histories of the growth of organizations. In M. Haire (Ed.), *Modern organization theory*, New York: Wiley, 272–306.

16. von Bertalanffy, L. 1956, *op. cit.*, p. 6.

17. von Bertalanffy, L. 1940. Der organismus als physikalisches system betrachtet. *Naturwissenschaften, 28,* 521 ff.

18. Emery, F. E., & E. L. Trist. 1960. Sociotechnical systems. In *Management sciences models and techniques.* Vol. 2, London: Pergamon Press; quote from p. 84.

# 30

# Organizations in Action

*James D. Thompson*

## STRATEGIES FOR STUDYING ORGANIZATIONS

Complex organizations—manufacturing firms, hospitals, schools, armies, community agencies—are ubiquitous in modern societies, but our understanding of them is limited and segmented.

The fact that impressive and sometimes frightening consequences flow from organizations suggests that some individuals have had considerable insight into these social instruments. But insight and private experiences may generate private understandings without producing a public body of knowledge adequate for the preparation of a next generation of administrators, for designing new styles of organizations for new purposes, for controlling organizations, or for appreciation of distinctive aspects of modern societies.

What we know or think we know about complex organizations is housed in a variety of fields or disciplines, and communication among them more nearly resembles a trickle than a torrent.[1] Although each of the several schools has its unique terminology and special heroes, Gouldner was able to discern two fundamental models underlying most of the literature.[2] He labeled these the "rational" and "natural-system" models of organizations, and these labels are indeed descriptive of the results.

To Gouldner's important distinction we wish to add the notion that the rational model results from a *closed-system strategy* for studying organizations, and that the natural-system model flows from an *open-system strategy*.

### Closed-System Strategy

**The Search for Certainty.** If we wish to predict accurately the state a system will be in presently, it helps immensely to be dealing with a *determinate system*. As Ashby observes, fixing the present circumstances of a determinate system will determine the state it moves to next, and since such a system cannot go to two states at once, the transformation will be unique.[3]

Fixing the present circumstances requires, of course, that the variables and relationships involved be few enough for us to comprehend and that we have control over or can reliably predict all of the variables and relations. In other words, it requires that the system be closed or, if closure is not complete, that the outside forces acting on it be predictable.

Now if we have responsibility for the future states or performances of some system, we are likely to opt for a closed system. Bartlett's research on mental processes, comparing "adventurous thinking" with "thinking in closed systems," suggests that there are strong human tendencies to reduce various forms of knowledge to the closed-system variety, to rid them of all ultimate uncertainty.[4] If such tendencies appear in puzzle-solving as well as in everyday situations, we would especially expect them to be emphasized when responsibility and high stakes are added. Since much of the literature about organizations has been generated as a by-product of the search for improved efficiency or performance, it is not surprising that it employs closed-system assumptions—employs a rational model—about organizations. Whether we

James D. Thompson, *Organizations in Action* (Piscataway, NJ: Transaction Publishers, 2003). Used by permission of Transaction Publishers.

consider *scientific management,*[5] *administrative management,*[6] or *bureaucracy,*[7] the ingredients of the organization are deliberately chosen for their necessary contribution to a goal, and the structures established are those deliberately intended to attain highest efficiency.

**Three Schools in Caricature.** Scientific management, focused primarily on manufacturing or similar production activities, clearly employs economic efficiency as its ultimate criterion, and seeks to maximize efficiency by planning procedures according to a technical logic, setting standards, and exercising controls to ensure conformity with standards and thereby with the technical logic. Scientific management achieves conceptual closure of the organization by assuming that goals are known, tasks are repetitive, output of the production process somehow disappears, and resources in uniform qualities are available.

Administrative-management literature focuses on structural relationships among production, personnel, supply, and other service units of the organization, and again employs as the ultimate criterion economic efficiency. Here efficiency is maximized by specializing tasks and grouping them into departments, fixing responsibility according to such principles as span of control or delegation, and controlling action to plans. Administrative management achieves closure by assuming that ultimately a master plan is known, against which specialization, departmentalization, and controls are determined. (That this master plan is elusive is shown by Simon.[8]) Administrative management also assumes that production tasks are known, that output disappears, and that resources are automatically available to the organization.

Bureaucracy also follows the pattern noted above, focusing on staffing and structure as means of handling clients and disposing of cases. Again the ultimate criterion is efficiency, and this time it is maximized by defining offices according to jurisdiction and place in a hierarchy, appointing experts to offices, establishing rules for categories of activity, categorizing cases or clients, and then motivating proper performance of expert officials by providing salaries and patterns for career advancement. [The extended implications of the assumptions made by bureaucratic theory are brought out by Merton's discussion of "bureaucratic personality."[9]] Bureaucratic theory also employs the closed system of logic. Weber saw three holes through which empirical reality might penetrate the logic, but in outlining his "pure type" he quickly plugged these holes. Policymakers, somewhere above the bureaucracy, could alter the goals, but the implications of this are set aside. Human components—the expert office-holders—might be more complicated than the model describes, but bureaucratic theory handles this by divorcing the individual's private life from his life as an office-holder through the use of rules, salary, and career. Finally, bureaucratic theory takes note of outsiders—clientele—but nullifies their effects by depersonalizing and categorizing clients.

It seems clear that the rational-model approach uses a closed-system strategy. It also seems clear that the developers of the several schools using the rational model have been primarily students of performance or efficiency, and only incidentally students of organizations. Having focused on control of the organization as a target, each employs a closed system of logic and conceptually closes the organization to coincide with that type of logic, for this elimination of uncertainty is the way to achieve determinateness. The rational model of an organization results in everything being functional—making a positive, indeed an optimum, contribution to the overall result. All resources are appropriate resources, and their allocation fits a master plan. All action is appropriate action, and its outcomes are predictable.

It is no accident that much of the literature on the management or administration of complex organization centers on the concepts of *planning* or *controlling*. Nor is it any accident that such views are dismissed by those using the open-system strategy.

### Open-System Strategy

**The Expectation of Uncertainty.** If, instead of assuming closure, we assume that a system contains more variables than we can comprehend at one time, or that some of the variables are subject to influences we cannot control or predict, we must resort to a different sort of logic. We can, if we wish, assume that the system is determinate by nature, but that it is our incomplete understanding which forces us to expect surprise or the intrusion of certainty. In this case we can employ a natural-system model.

Approached as a natural system, the complex organization is a set of interdependent parts which together make up a whole because each contributes something and receives something from the whole, which in turn is interdependent with some larger environment. Survival of the system is taken to be the goal, and the parts and their relationships presumably are determined through evolutionary processes. Dysfunctions are conceivable, but it is assumed that an offending part will adjust to produce a net positive contribution or be disengaged, or else the system will degenerate.

Central to the natural-system approach is the concept of homeostasis, or self-stabilization, which spontaneously, or naturally, governs the necessary relationships among parts and activities and thereby keeps the system viable in the face of disturbances stemming from the environment.

**Two Examples in Caricature.** Study of the *informal organization* constitutes one example of research in complex organizations using the natural-system approach. Here attention is focused on variables which are not included in any of the rational models—sentiments, cliques, social controls via informal norms, status and status striving, and so on. It is clear that students

of informal organization regard these variables not as random deviations or error, but as patterned, adaptive responses of human beings in problematic situations.[10] In this view the formal organization is a spontaneous and functional development, indeed a necessity, in complex organizations, permitting the system to adapt and survive.

A second version of the natural-system approach is more global but less crystallized under a label. This school views the organization as a unit in interaction with its environment, and its view was perhaps most forcefully expressed by Chester Barnard[11] and by the empirical studies of Selznick[12] and Clark.[13] This stream of work leads to the conclusion that organizations are not autonomous entities; instead, the best laid plans of managers have unintended consequences and are conditioned or upset by other social units—other complex organizations or publics—on whom the organization is dependent.

Again it is clear that in contrast to the rational-model approach, this research area focuses on variables not subject to complete control by the organization and hence not contained within a closed system of logic. It is also clear that students regard interdependence of organization and environment as inevitable or natural, and as adaptive or functional.

### Choice or Compromise?

The literature about organizations, or at least much of it, seems to fall into one of the two categories, each of which at best tends to ignore the other and at worse denies the relevance of the other. The logics associated with each appear to be incompatible, for one avoids uncertainty to achieve determinateness, while the other assumes uncertainty and indeterminateness. Yet the phenomena treated by each approach, as distinct from the explanations of each, cannot be denied.

Viewed in the large, complex organizations are often effective instruments for achievement, and that achievement flows from planned, controlled action. In every sphere—educational, medical, industrial, commercial, or governmental—the quality or costs of goods or services may be challenged and questions may be raised about the equity of distribution within the society of the fruits of complex organizations. Still millions live each day on the assumption that a reasonable degree of purposeful, effective action will be forthcoming from the many complex organizations on which they depend. Planned action, not random behavior, supports our daily lives. Specialized, controlled, patterned action surrounds us.

There can be no question but that the rational model of organizations directs our attention to important phenomena—to important "truth" in the sense that complex organizations viewed in the large exhibit some of the patterns and results to which the rational model attends, but which the natural-system model tends to ignore. But it is equally evident that phenomena associated with the natural-system approach also exist in complex organizations. There is little room to doubt the universal emergence of the informal organization. The daily news about labor-management negotiations, interagency jurisdictional squabbles, collusive agreements, favoritism, breeches of contract, and so on, are impressive evidence that complex organizations are influenced in significant ways by elements of their environments, a phenomenon addressed by the natural-system approach but avoided by the rational. Yet most versions of the natural-system approach treat organizational purposes and achievements as peripheral matters.

It appears that each approach leads to some truth, but neither alone affords an adequate understanding of complex organizations. Gouldner calls for a synthesis of the two models, but does not provide the synthetic model.

Meanwhile, a serious and sustained elaboration of Barnard's work[14] has produced a newer tradition which evades the closed-versus open-system dilemma.

## A Newer Tradition

What emerges from the Simon-March-Cyert stream of study is the organization as a problem-facing and problem-solving phenomenon. The focus is on organizational processes related to choice of courses of action in an environment which does not fully disclose the alternatives available or the consequences of those alternatives. In this view, the organization has limited capacity to gather and process information or to predict consequences of alternatives. To deal with situations of such great complexity, the organization must develop processes for *searching* and *learning*, as well as for *deciding*. The complexity, if fully faced, would overwhelm the organization, hence it must set limits to its definitions of situations; it must make decisions in *bounded rationality*.[15] This requirement involved replacing the maximum-efficiency criterion with one of satisfactory accomplishment, decision-making now involving *satisficing* rather than *maximizing*.[16]

These are highly significant notions, and it will become apparent that this book seeks to extend this "newer tradition." The assumptions it makes are consistent with the open-system strategy, for it holds that the processes going on within the organization are significantly affected by the complexity of the organization's environment. But this tradition also touches on matters important in the closed-system strategy; performance and deliberate decisions.

But despite what seem to be obvious advantages, the Simon-March-Cyert stream of work has not entirely replaced the more extreme strategies, and we need to ask why so many intelligent men and women in a position to make the same observations we have been making should continue to espouse patently incomplete views of complex organizations.

**The Cutting Edge of Uncertainty.** Part of the answer to that question undoubtedly lies in the fact that supporters of each strategy have had different purposes in mind, with open-system strategists attempting to understand organizations per se, and closed-system strategists interested in organizations mainly as vehicles for rational achievements. Yet this answer does not seem completely satisfactory, for these students could not have been entirely unaware of the challenges to their assumptions and beliefs.

We can suggest now that rather than reflecting weakness in those who use them, the two strategies reflect something fundamental about the cultures surrounding complex organizations—the fact that our culture does not contain concepts for simultaneously thinking about rationality and indeterminateness. These appear to be incompatible concepts, and we have no ready way of thinking about something as half-closed, half-rational. One alternative, then, is the closed-system approach of ignoring uncertainty to see rationality; another is to ignore rational action in order to see spontaneous processes. The newer tradition with its focus on organizational coping with uncertainty is indeed a major advance. It is notable that a recent treatment by Crozier starts from the bureaucratic position but focuses on coping with uncertainty as its major topic.[17]

Yet in directing our attention to processes for meeting uncertainty, Simon, March, and Cyert may lead us to overlook the useful knowledge amassed by the older approaches. If the phenomena of rational models are indeed observable, we may want to incorporate some elements of those models; and if natural-system phenomena occur, we should also benefit from the relevant theories. For purposes of this volume, then, *we will conceive of complex organizations as open systems, hence indeterminate and faced with uncertainty, but at the same time as subject to criteria of rationality and hence needing determinateness and certainty.*

### The Location of Problems

As a starting point, we will suggest that the phenomena associated with open- and closed-system strategies are not randomly distributed through complex organizations, but instead tend to be specialized by location. To introduce this notion we will start with Parsons' suggestion that organizations exhibit three distinct levels of responsibility and control—*technical, managerial,* and *institutional.*[18]

In this view, every formal organization contains a suborganization whose "problems" are focused around effective performance of the technical function—the conduct of classes by teachers, the processing of income tax returns and the handling of recalcitrants by the bureau, the processing of material and supervision of these operations in the case of physical production. The primary exigencies to which the technical suborganization is oriented are those imposed by the nature of the technical task, such as the materials, which must be processed and the kinds of cooperation of different people required to get the job done effectively.

The second level, the managerial, *services* the technical suborganization by (1) mediating between the technical suborganization and those who use its products—the customers, pupils, and so on—and (2) procuring the resources necessary for carrying out the technical functions. The managerial level *controls*, or administers, the technical suborganization (although Parsons notes that its control is not unilateral) by deciding such matters as the broad technical task which is to be performed, the scale of operations, employment and purchasing policy, and so on.

Finally, in the Parsons formulation, the organization which consists of both technical and managerial suborganizations is also part of a wider social system which is the source of the "meaning," or higher-level support which makes the implementation of the organization's goals possible. In terms of "formal" controls, an organization may be relatively independent; but in terms of the meaning of the functions performed by the organization and hence of its "rights" to command resources and to subject its customers to discipline, it is never wholly independent. This overall articulation of the organization and the institutional structure and agencies of the community is the function of the third, or institutional, level of the organization.

Parsons' distinction of the three levels becomes more significant when he points out that at each of the two points of articulation between them there is a *qualitative* break in the simple continuity of "line" authority because the functions at each level are qualitatively different. Those at the second level are not simply lower-order spellings-out of the top level functions. Moreover, the articulation of levels and functions rests on a two-way interaction, with each side, by withholding its important contribution, in a position to interfere with the functioning of the other and of the larger organization.

If we now reintroduce the conception of the complex organization as an open system subject to criteria of rationality, we are in a position to speculate about some dynamic properties of organizations. As we suggested, the logical model for achieving complete technical rationality uses a closed system of logic—closed by the elimination of uncertainty. In practice, it would seem, the more variables involved, the greater the likelihood of uncertainty, and it would therefore be advantageous for an organization subject to criteria of rationality to remove as much uncertainty as possible from its *technical core* by reducing the number of variables operating on it. Hence, if both resource-acquisition and output-disposal problems—which are in part controlled by environmental elements and hence to a degree uncertain or problematic—can be removed from the technical core, the logic can be brought closer to closure, and the rationality, increased.

Uncertainty would appear to be greatest, at least potentially, at the other extreme, the institutional level. Here the organization deals largely with elements of the environment over which it has no formal authority or control. Instead, it is subjected to generalized norms, ranging from formally codified law to informal standards of good practice, to public authority, or to elements expressing the public interest.

At this extreme the closed system of logic is clearly inappropriate. The organization is open to influence by the environment (and vice versa) which can change independently of the actions of the organization. Here an open system of logic, permitting the intrusion of variables penetrating the organization from outside, and facing up to uncertainty, seems indispensable.

If the closed-system aspects of organizations are seen most clearly at the technical level, and the open-system qualities appear most vividly at the institutional level, it would suggest that a significant function of the managerial level is to mediate between the two extremes and the emphases they exhibit. If the organization must approach certainty at the technical level to satisfy its rationality criteria, but must remain flexible and adaptive to satisfy environmental requirements, we might expect the managerial level to mediate between them, ironing out some irregularities stemming from external sources, but also pressing the technical core for modifications as conditions alter. One exploration of this notion was offered in Thompson.[19]

**Possible Sources of Variation.** Following Parsons' reasoning leads to the expectation that differences in technical functions, or *technologies*, cause significant differences among organization, and since the three levels are interdependent, differences in technical functions should also make for differences at managerial and institutional levels of the organization. Similarly, differences of the institutional structures in which organizations are imbedded should make for significant variations among organizations at all three levels.

Relating this back to the Simon-March-Cyert focus on organizational processes of searching, learning, and deciding, we can also suggest that while these adaptive processes may be generic, the ways in which they proceed may well vary with differences in technologies or in environments.

### Recapitulation

Most of our beliefs about complex organizations follow from one or the other of two distinct strategies. The closed-system strategy seeks certainty by incorporating only those variables positively associated with goal achievement and subjecting them to a monolithic control network. The open-system strategy shifts attention from goal achievement to survival, and incorporates uncertainty by recognizing organizational interdependence with environment. A newer tradition enables us to conceive of the organization as an open system, indeterminate and faced with uncertainty, but subject to criteria of rationality and hence needing certainty.

With this conception the central problem for complex organizations is one of coping with uncertainty. As a point of departure, we suggest that organizations cope with uncertainty by creating certain parts specifically to deal with it, specializing other parts in operating under conditions of certainty or near certainty. In this case, articulation of these specialized parts becomes significant.

We also suggest that technologies and environments are major sources of uncertainty for organizations, and that differences in those dimensions will result in differences in organizations. To proceed, we now turn to a closer examination of the meaning of "rationality," in the context of complex organizations.

## RATIONALITY IN ORGANIZATIONS

Instrumental action is rooted on the one hand in *desired outcomes* and on the other hand in *beliefs about cause/effect relationships.* Given a desire, the state of man's knowledge at any point in time dictates the kinds of variables required and the manner of their manipulation to bring that desire to fruition. To the extent that the activities thus dictated by man's beliefs are judged to produce the desired outcomes, we can speak of technology, or *technical rationality.*

Technical rationality can be evaluated by two criteria: instrumental and economic.

The essence of the instrumental question is whether the specified actions do in fact produce the desired outcome, and the instrumentally perfect technology is one which inevitably achieves such results. The economic question in essence is whether the results are obtained with the least necessary expenditure of resources, and for this there is no absolute standard. Two different routes to the same desired outcome may be compared in terms of cost, or both may be compared with some abstract ideal, but in practical terms the evaluation of economy is relative to the state of man's knowledge at the time of evaluation.

We will give further consideration to the assessment of organizational action in a later chapter, but it is necessary to distinguish at this point between the instrumental and economic questions because present literature and organization gives considerable attention to the economic dimension of technology but hides the importance of the instrumental question, which in fact takes priority. The cost of doing something can be considered only after we know that something can be done.

Complex organizations are built to operate technologies which are found to be impossible or impractical for individuals to operate. This does not mean, however, that technologies operated by complex organizations are instrumentally perfect. The instrumentally perfect technology would produce the desired outcome inevitably, and this perfection is approached in the case of continuous processing of chemicals or in mass manufacturing—for example, of automobiles. A less perfect technology will produce the desired outcome only part of the time; nevertheless, it may be incorporated into complex organizations, such as the mental hospital, because the desire for the possible outcome is intense enough to settle for possible rather than highly probable success. Sometimes the intensity of desire for certain kinds of outcomes, such as world peace, leads to the creation of complex organizations, such as the United Nations to operate patently imperfect technologies.

## Variations in Technologies

Clearly, technology is an important variable in understanding the actions of complex organizations. In modern societies the variety of desired outcomes for which specific technologies are available seems infinite. A complete but simple typology of technologies which has found order in this variety would be quite helpful. Typologies are available for industrial production[20] and for mental therapy[21] but are not general enough to deal with the range of technologies found in complex organizations. Lacking such a typology, we will simply identify three varieties which are (1) widespread in modern society and (2) sufficiently different to illustrate the propositions we wish to develop.

**The Long-linked Technology.**[22] A long-linked technology involves serial interdependence in the sense that act Z can be performed only after successful completion of act Y, which in turn rests on act X, and so on. The original symbol of technical rationality, the mass production assembly line, is of this long-linked nature. It approaches instrumental perfection when it produces a single kind of standard product, repetitively and at a constant rate. Production of only one kind of product means that a single technology is required, and this in turn permits the use of clear-cut criteria for the selection of machines and tools, construction of work-flow arrangements, acquisition of raw materials, and selection of human operators. Repetition of the productive process provides experience as a means of eliminating imperfections in the technology; experience can lead to the modification of machines and provide the basis for scheduled preventive maintenance. Repetition means that human motions can also be examined, and through training and practice, energy losses and errors minimized. It is in this setting that the scientific-management movement has perhaps made its greatest contribution.

The constant rate of production means that, once adjusted, the proportion of resources involved can be standardized to the point where each contributes to its capacity; none need to be underemployed. This of course makes important contributions to the economic aspect of the technology.

**The Mediating Technology.** Various organizations have, as a primary function, the linking of clients or customers who are or wish to be interdependent. The commercial bank links depositors and borrowers. The insurance firm links those who would pool common risks. The telephone utility links those who would call and those who would be called. The post office provides a possible linkage of virtually every member of the modern society. The employment agency mediates the supply of labor and the demand for it.

Complexity in the mediating technology comes not from the necessity of having each activity geared to the requirements of the next but rather from the fact that the mediating technology requires operating in *standardized ways*, and *extensively*; e.g., with multiple clients or customers distributed in time and space.

The commercial bank must find and aggregate deposits from diverse depositors; but however diverse the depositors, the transaction must conform to standard terms and to uniform bookkeeping and accounting procedures. It must also find borrowers; but no matter how varied their needs or desires, loans must be made according to standardized criteria and on terms uniformly applied to the category appropriate to the particular borrower. Poor risks who receive favored treatment jeopardize bank solvency. Standardization permits the insurance organization to define categories of risk and hence to sort its customers or potential customers into appropriate aggregate categories; the insured who is not a qualified risk but is so defined upsets the probabilities on which insurance rests. The telephone company became viable only when the telephone became regarded as a necessity, and this did not occur until equipment was standardized to the point where it could be incorporated into one network. Standardization enables the employment agency to aggregate job applicants into categories which can be matched against standardized requests for employees.

Standardization makes possible the operation of the mediating technology over time and through space by assuring each segment of the organization that other segments are operating in compatible ways. It is in such situations that the bureaucratic techniques of categorization and impersonal application of rules have been most beneficial.[23]

**The Intensive Technology.** This third variety we label *intensive* to signify that a variety of techniques is drawn upon in order to achieve a change in some specific object; but the selection, combination, and order of application are determined by feedback from the object itself. When the object is human, this intensive technology is regarded as "therapeutic," but the same technical logic is found also in the construction industry[24] and in research where the objects of concern are nonhuman. ...

The intensive technology is a custom technology. Its successful employment rests in part on the availability of all the capacities potentially needed, but equally on the appropriate custom combination of selected capacities as required by the individual case or project.

**Boundaries of Technical Rationality.** Technical rationality, as a system of cause/effect relationships which lead to a desired result, is an abstraction. It is instrumentally perfect when it becomes a closed system of logic. The closed system of logic contains all relevant variables, and only relevant variables. All other influences, or *exogenous variables*, are excluded; and the variables contained in the system vary only to the extent that the experimenter, the manager, or the computer determines they should.

When a technology is put to use, however, there must be not only desired outcomes and knowledge of relevant cause/effect relationships, but also power to control the empirical resources which correspond to the variables in the logical system. A closed system of action corresponding to a closed system of logic would result in instrumental perfection in reality.

The mass production assembly operation and the continuous processing of chemicals are more nearly perfect, in application, than the other two varieties discussed above because they achieve a high degree of control over relevant variables and are relatively free from disturbing influences. Once started, most of the action involved in the long-linked technology is dictated by the internal logic of the technology itself. With the mediating technology, customers or clients intrude to make difficult the standardized activities required by the technology. And with the intensive technology, the specific case defines the component activities and their combination from the larger array of components contained in the abstract technology.

Since technical perfection seems more nearly approachable when the organization has control over all the elements involved,

> Proposition 2.1: Under norms of rationality, organizations seek to seal off their core technologies from environmental influences.

### Organizational Rationality

When organizations seek to translate the abstractions called technologies into action, they immediately face problems for which the core technologies do not provide solutions.

Mass production manufacturing technologies are quite specific, *assuming* that certain inputs are provided and finished products are somehow removed from the premises before the productive process is clogged; but mass production technologies do not include variables which provide solutions to either the input-or output-disposal problems. The present technology of medicine may be rather specific if certain tests indicate an appendectomy is in order, if the condition of the patient meets certain criteria, and if certain medical staff, equipment, and medications are present. But medical technology contains no cause/effect statements about bringing sufferers to the attention of medical practitioners, or about the provision of the specified equipment, skills, and medications. The technology of education rests on abstract systems of belief about relationships among teachers, teaching materials, and pupils; but learning theories assume the presence of these variables and proceed from that point.

One or more technologies constitute the core of all purposive organizations. But this technical core is always an incomplete representation of what the organization must do to accomplish desired results. Technical rationality is a necessary component but never alone sufficient to provide *organizational rationality*, which involves acquiring the inputs which are taken for granted by the technology, and dispensing outputs which again are outside the scope of the core technology.

At a minimum, then, organizational rationality involves three major component activities, (1) input activities, (2) technological activities, and (3) output activities. Since these are interdependent, organizational rationality requires that they be appropriately geared to one another. The inputs acquired must be within the scope of the technology, and it must be within the capacity of the organization to dispose of the technological production.

Not only are these component activities interdependent, but both input and output activities are interdependent with environmental elements. Organizational rationality, therefore, never conforms to closed-system logic but demands the logic of an open system. Moreover, since the technological activities are embedded in and interdependent with activities which are open to the environment, the closed system can never be completely attained for the technological component. Yet we have offered the proposition that organizations subject to rationality norms seek to seal off their core technologies from environmental influences. How do we reconcile these two contentions?

> Proposition 2.2: Under norms of rationality, organizations seek to buffer environmental influences by surrounding their technical cores with input and output components.

To maximize productivity of a manufacturing technology, the technical core must be able to operate as if the market will absorb the single kind of product at a continuous rate, and as if inputs flowed continuously, at a steady rate and with specified quality. Conceivably both sets of conditions could occur; realistically they do not. But organizations reveal a variety of devices for approximating these "as if" assumptions, with input and output components meeting fluctuating environments and converting them into steady conditions for the technological core.

Buffering on the input side is illustrated by the stockpiling of materials and supplies acquired in an irregular market, and their steady insertion into the production process. Preventive maintenance, whereby machines or equipment are repaired on a scheduled basis, thus minimizing surprise, is another example of buffering by the input component. The recruitment of dissimilar personnel and their conversion into reliable performers through training or indoctrination is another; it is most dramatically illustrated by basic training or boot camp in military organizations.[25]

Buffering on the output side of long-linked technologies usually takes the form of maintaining warehouse inventories and items in transit or in distributor inventories, which permits the technical core to produce at a constant rate, but distribution to fluctuate with market conditions.

Buffering on the input side is an appropriate and important device available to all types of organizations. Buffering on the output side is especially important for mass-manufacturing organizations, but is less feasible when the product is perishable or when the object is inextricably involved in the technological process, as in the therapeutic case.

Buffering of an unsteady environment obviously brings considerable advantages to the technical core, but it does so with costs to the organization. A classic problem in connection with buffering is how to maintain inventories, input or output, sufficient to meet all needs without recurring obsolescence as needs change. Operations research recently has made important contributions toward this problem of "run out versus obsolescence," both of which are costly.

Thus, while a fully buffered technological core would enjoy the conditions for maximum technical rationality, organizational rationality may call for compromises between conditions for maximum technical efficiency and the energy required for buffering operations. In an unsteady environment, then, the organization under rationality norms must seek other devices for protecting its technical core.

Proposition 2.3: Under norms of rationality, organizations seek to smooth out input and output transactions.

Whereas buffering absorbs environmental fluctuations, smoothing or leveling involves attempts to reduce fluctuations in the environment. Utility firms—electric, gas, water, or telephone—may offer inducements to those who use their services during "trough" periods, or charge premiums to those who contribute to "peaking." Retailing organizations faced with seasonal or other fluctuations in demand, may offer inducements in the form of special promotions or sales during slow periods. Transportation organizations such as airlines may offer special reduced fare rates on light days or during slow seasons.

Organizations pointed toward emergencies, such as fire departments, attempt to level the need for their services by activities designed to prevent emergencies, and by emphasis on the early detection so that demand is not allowed to grow to the point that would overtax the capacity of the organization. Hospitals accomplish some smoothing through the scheduling of nonemergency admissions.

Although action by the organization may thus reduce fluctuations in demand, complete smoothing of demand is seldom possible. But a core technology interrupted by constant fluctuation and change must settle for a low degree of technical rationality. What other services do organizations employ to protect core technologies?

Proposition 2.4: Under norms of rationality, organizations seek to anticipate and adapt to environmental changes which cannot be buffered or leveled.

If environmental fluctuations penetrate the organization and require the technical core to alter its activities, then environmental fluctuations are exogenous variables within the logic of technical rationality. To the extent that environmental fluctuations can be anticipated, however, they can be treated as *constraints* on the technical core within which a closed system of logic can be employed.

The manufacturing firm which can correctly forecast demand for a particular time period can thereby plan or schedule operations of its technical core at a steady rate during that period. Any changes in technical operations due to changes in the environment can be made at the end of the period on the basis of forecasts for the next period.

Organizations often learn that some environmental fluctuations are patterned, and in these cases forecasting and adjustment appear almost automatic. The post office knows, for example, that in large commercial centers large volumes of business mail are posted at the end of the business day, when secretaries leave offices. Recently the post office has attempted to buffer that load by promising rapid treatment of mail posted in special locations during morning hours. Its success in buffering is not known at this writing, but meanwhile the post office schedules its technical activities to meet known daily fluctuations. It can also anticipate heavy demand during November and December, thus allowing its input components lead time in acquiring additional resources.

Banks likewise learn that local conditions and customs result in peak loads at predictable times during the day and week, and can schedule their operations to meet these shifts.[26]

In cases such as these, organizations have amassed sufficient experience to know that fluctuations are patterned with a high degree of regularity or probability; but when environmental fluctuations are the result of combinations of more dynamic factors, anticipation may require something more than the simple projection of previous experience. It is in these situations that forecasting emerges as a specialized and elaborate activity, for which some of the emerging management-science or statistical-decision theories seem especially appropriate.

To the extent that environmental fluctuations are unanticipated they interfere with the orderly operation of the core technology and thereby reduce its performance. When such influences are anticipated and considered as constraints for a particular period of time, the technical core can operate as if it enjoyed a closed system.

Buffering, leveling, and adaptation to anticipated fluctuations are widely used devices for reducing the influence of the environment on the technological cores of organizations. Often they are effective, but there are occasions when these devices are not sufficient to ward off environmental penetration.

Proposition 2.5: When buffering, leveling, and forecasting do not protect their technical cores from environmental fluctuations, organizations under norms of rationality resort to rationing.

Rationing is most easily seen in organizations pointed toward emergencies, such as hospitals. Even in nonemergency situations, hospitals may ration beds to physicians by establishing priority systems for nonemergency admissions. In emergencies, such as community disasters, hospitals may ration pharmaceutical dosages or nursing services by dilution—by assigning a fixed number of nurses to a larger patient population.

Mental hospitals, especially state mental hospitals, may ration technical services by employing primarily organic-treatment procedures—electroshock, drugs, insulin—which can be employed more economically than psychoanalytic or *milieu* therapies.[27] Teachers and caseworkers in social welfare organizations may ration effort by accepting only a portion of those seeking service, or if not empowered to exercise such discretion, may concentrate their energies on the more challenging cases or on those which appear most likely to yield satisfactory outcomes.[28]

But rationing is not a device reserved for therapeutic organizations. The post office may assign priority to first-class mail, attending to lesser classes only when the priority task is completed. Manufacturers of suddenly popular items may ration allotments to wholesalers or dealers, and if inputs are scarce, may assign priorities to alternative uses of those resources. Libraries may ration book loans, acquisitions, and search efforts.[29]

Rationing is an unhappy solution, for its use signifies that the technology is not operating at its maximum. Yet some system of priorities for the allocation of capacity under adverse conditions is essential if a technology is to be instrumentally effective—if action is to be other than random.

**The Logic of Organizational Rationality.** Core technologies rest on closed systems of logic, but are invariably embedded in a larger organizational rationality which pins the technology to a time and place, and links it with the larger environment through input and output activities. Organizational rationality thus calls for an open-system logic, for when the organization is opened to environmental influences, some of the factors involved in organizational action become *constraints*; for some meaningful period of time they are not variables but fixed conditions to which the organization must adapt. Some of the factors become *contingencies*, which may or may not vary, but are not subject to arbitrary control by the organization.

Organizational rationality therefore is some result of (1) constraints which the organization must face, (2) contingencies which the organization must meet, and (3) variables which the organization can control.

### Recapitulation

Perfection in technical rationality requires complete knowledge of cause/effect relations plus control over all of the relevant variables, or closure. Therefore, under norms of rationality (Prop. 2.1), organizations seek to seal off their core technologies from environmental influences. Since complete closure is impossible (Prop. 2.2), they seek to buffer environmental influences by surrounding their technical cores with input and output components.

Because buffering does not handle all variations in an unsteady environment, organizations seek to smooth input and output transactions (Prop. 2.3), and to anticipate and adapt to environmental changes which cannot be buffered or smoothed (Prop. 2.4), and finally, when buffering, leveling, and forecasting do not protect their technical cores from environmental fluctuations (Prop. 2.5), organizations resort to rationing.

These are maneuvering devices which provide the organization with some self-control despite interdependence with the environment. But if we are to gain understanding of such maneuvering, we must consider both the direction toward which maneuvering is designed and the nature of the environment in which maneuvering takes place.

## NOTES

1. William R. Dill, "Desegregation or Integration? Comments about Contemporary Research in Organizations," in *New Perspectives in Organization Research*, eds. W. W. Cooper, Harold J. Leavitt, & Maynard W. Shelly II (New York: John Wiley & Sons, Inc., 1964). James G. March, "Introduction," in *Handbook of Organizations*, ed. James G. March (Chicago: Rand McNally, 1965).

2. Alvin W. Gouldner, "Organizational Analysis," in *Sociology Today*, eds. Robert K. Merton, Leonard Broom, and Leonard S. Cottrell, Jr. (New York: Basic Books, 1959).

3. W. Ross Ashby, *An Introduction to Cybernetics* (London: Chapman and Hall, Ltd., 1956).

4. Sir Frederic Bartlett, *Thinking: An Experimental and Social Study* (New York: Basic Books, 1958).

5. Frederick W. Taylor, *Scientific Management* (New York: Harper & Row, 1911).

6. Luther Gulick, & L. Urwick, eds., *Papers on the Science of Administration* (New York: Institute of Public Administration, 1937).

7. Max Weber, *The Theory of Social and Economic Organization*, ed. Talcott Parsons, trans. A. M. Henderson and Talcott Parsons (New York: Free Press, 1947).

8. Herbert A. Simon, *Administrative Behavior*, 2nd ed. (New York: Macmillan, 1957).

9. Robert K. Merton, "Bureaucratic Structure and Personality," in *Social Theory and Social Structure*, rev. ed., ed. Robert K. Merton (New York: Free Press, 1957).

10. Fritz J. Roethlisberger, & W. J. Dickson, *Management and the Worker* (Cambridge, Mass.: Harvard University Press, 1939).

11. Chester I. Barnard, *The Functions of the Executive* (Cambridge, Mass.: Harvard University Press, 1938).

12. Philip Selznick, *TVA and the Grass Roots* (Berkeley, Calif.: University of California Press, 1949).

13. Burton R. Clark, *Adult Education in Transition* (Berkeley, Calif.: University of California Press, 1956).

14. Herbert A. Simon, *Administrative Behavior*. James G. March, & Herbert A. Simon, Organizations (New York: Wiley, 1958). Richard M. Cyert, & James G. March, A *Behavioral Theory of the Firm* (Englewood Cliffs, N.J.: Prentice-Hall, 1963).

15. Herbert A. Simon, *Models of Man, Social and Rational* (New York: Wiley, 1957).

16. Ibid.

17. Michel Crozier, *The Bureaucratic Phenomenon* (Chicago: The University of Chicago Press, 1964).

18. Talcott Parsons, *Structure and Process in Modern Societies* (New York: Free Press, 1960).

19. James D. Thompson, "Decision-making, the Firm, and the Market," in New *Perspectives in Organization Research,* eds., W. W. Cooper et al. (New York: Wiley, 1964).

20. Joan Woodward, *Industrial Organization: Theory and Practice* (London: Oxford University Press, 1965).

21. Robert W. Hawkes, "Physical Psychiatric Rehabilitation Models Compared" (Paper presented at the Ohio Valley Sociological Society, 1962).

22. The notions in this section rest especially on conversations some years ago with Frederick L. Bates. For a different but somewhat parallel analysis of work flows, see Robert Dubin, "Stability of Human Organizations," in *Modern Organization Theory,* ed. Mason Haire (New York: Wiley, 1959).

23. Weber, *Theory of Organization.* Merton, *Social Theory and Structure.*

24. Arthur L. Stinchcombe, "Bureaucratic and Craft Administration of Production: A Comparative Study," *Administrative Science Quarterly 4* (September 1959): 168–187.

25. Sanford M. Dornbusch, "The Military Academy as an Assimilating Institution," *Social Forces 33* (May 1955): 316–321.

26. Chris Argyris, *Organization of a Bank* (New Haven, Conn.: Labor and Management Center, Yale University, 1954).

27. Ivan Belknap, *The Human Problems of a State Mental Hospital* (New York: McGraw-Hill, 1956).

28. Peter M. Blau, *The Dynamics of Bureaucracy* (Chicago: The University of Chicago Press, 1955).

29. Richard L. Meier, "Communications Overload," *Administrative Science Quarterly 7* (March 1963): 521–544.

# 31

# Institutionalized Organizations: Formal Structure as Myth and Ceremony

*John W. Meyer & Brian Rowan*

...Formal organizations are generally understood to be systems of coordinated and controlled activities that arise when work is embedded in complex networks of technical relations and boundary-spanning exchanges. But in modern societies formal organizational structures arise in highly institutionalized contexts. Professions, policies, and programs are created along with the products and services that they are understood to produce rationally. This permits many new organizations to spring up and forces existing ones to incorporate new practices and procedures. That is, organizations are driven to incorporate the practices and procedures defined by prevailing rationalized concepts of organizational work and institutionalized in society. Organizations that do so increase their legitimacy and their survival prospects, independent of the immediate efficacy of the acquired practices and procedures.

Institutionalized products, services, techniques, policies, and programs function as powerful myths, and many organizations adopt them ceremonially. But conformity to institutionalized rules often conflicts sharply with efficiency criteria and, conversely, to coordinate and control activity in order to promote efficiency undermines an organization's ceremonial conformity and sacrifices its support and legitimacy. To maintain ceremonial conformity, organizations that reflect institutional rules tend to buffer their formal structures from the uncertainties of technical activities by becoming loosely coupled, building gaps between their formal structures and actual work activities.

This paper argues that the formal structures of many organizations in postindustrial society (Bell 1973) dramatically reflect the myths of their institutional environments instead of the demands of their work activities. The first part describes prevailing theories of the origins of formal structures and the main problem the theories confront. The second part discusses an alternative source of formal structures: myths embedded in the institutional environment. The third part develops the argument that organizations reflecting institutionalized environments maintain gaps between their formal structures and their ongoing work activities. The final part summarizes by discussing some research implications.

Throughout the paper, institutionalized rules are distinguished sharply from prevailing social behaviors. Institutionalized rules are classifications built into society as reciprocated typifications or interpretations (Berger and Luckmann 1967, p. 54). Such rules may be simply taken for granted or may be supported by public opinion or the force of law (Starbuck 1976). Institutions inevitably involve normative obligations but often enter into social life primarily as facts which must be taken into account by actors. Institutionalization involves the processes by which social processes, obligations, or actualities come to take on a rule-like status in social thought and action. So, for example, the social status of doctor is a highly institutionalized rule

John W. Meyer and Brian Rowan, "Institutionalized Organizations: Formal Structure as Myth and Ceremony," *American Journal of Sociology* 83, no. 2 (1977): 340–363. © 1977 by The University of Chicago. Reprinted by permission of The University of Chicago Press.

(both normative and cognitive) for managing illness as well as a social role made up of particular behaviors, relations, and expectations....

In a smaller way, a No Smoking sign is an institution with legal status and implications, as well as an attempt to regulate smoking behavior. It is fundamental to the argument of this paper that institutional rules may have effects on organizational structures and their implementation in actual technical work which are very different from the effects generated by the networks of social behavior and relationships which compose and surround a given organization.

## PREVAILING THEORIES OF FORMAL STRUCTURE

A sharp distinction should be made between the formal structure of an organization and its actual day-to-day work activities. Formal structure is a blueprint for activities which includes, first of all, the table of organization: a listing of offices, departments, positions, and programs. These elements are linked by explicit goals and policies that make up a rational theory of how, and to what end, activities are to be fitted together. The essence of a modern bureaucratic organization lies in the rationalized and impersonal character of these structural elements and of the goals that link them.

One of the central problems in organization theory is to describe the conditions that give rise to rationalized formal structure. In conventional theories, rational formal structure is assumed to be the most effective way to coordinate and control the complex relational networks involved in modern technical or work activities (see Scott 1975 for a review). This assumption derives from Weber's (1930, 1946, 1947) discussions of the historical emergence of bureaucracies as consequences of economic markets and centralized states. Economic markets place a premium on rationality and coordination. As markets expand, the relational networks in a given domain become more complex and differentiated, and organizations in that domain must manage more internal and boundary-spanning interdependencies. Such factors as size (Blau 1970) and technology (Woodward 1965) increase the complexity of internal relations, and the division of labor among organizations increases boundary-spanning problems (Aiken and Hage 1968; Freeman 1973; Thompson 1967). Because the need for coordination increases under these conditions, and because formally coordinated work has competitive advantages, organizations with rationalized formal structures tend to develop.

The formation of centralized states and the penetration of societies by political centers also contribute to the rise and spread of formal organization. When the relational networks involved in economic exchange and political management become extremely complex, bureaucratic structures are thought to be the most effective and rational means to standardize and control subunits. Bureaucratic control is especially useful for expanding political centers, and standardization is often demanded by both centers and peripheral units (Bendix 1964, 1968). Political centers organize layers of offices that manage to extend conformity and to displace traditional activities throughout societies.

*The problem. Prevailing theories assume that the coordination and control of activity are the critical dimensions on which formal organizations have succeeded in the modern world.* This assumption is based on the view that organizations function according to their formal blueprints: coordination is routine, rules and procedures are followed, and actual activities conform to the prescriptions of formal structure. But much of the empirical research on organizations casts doubt on this assumption. An earlier generation of researchers concluded that there was a great gap between the formal and the informal organization (e.g., Dalton 1959; Downs 1967; Homans 1950). A related observation is that formal organizations are often loosely coupled (March and Olsen

1976; Weick 1976): structural elements are only loosely linked to each other and to activities, rules are often violated, decisions are often unimplemented, or if implemented have uncertain consequences, technologies are of problematic efficiency, and evaluation and inspection systems are subverted or rendered so vague as to provide little coordination.

Formal organizations are endemic in modern societies. There is need for an explanation of their rise that is partially free from the assumption that, in practice, formal structures actually coordinate and control work. Such an explanation should account for the elaboration of purposes, positions, policies, and procedural rules that characterizes formal organizations, but must do so without supposing that these structural features are implemented in routine work activity.

## INSTITUTIONAL SOURCES OF FORMAL STRUCTURE

By focusing on the management of complex relational networks and the exercise of coordination and control, prevailing theories have neglected an alternative Weberian source of formal structure: the legitimacy of rationalized formal structures. In prevailing theories, legitimacy is a given: assertions about bureaucratization rest on the assumption of norms of rationality (Thompson 1967). When norms do play causal roles in theories of bureaucratization, it is because they are thought to be built into modern societies and personalities as very general values, which are thought to facilitate formal organization. But norms of rationality are not simply general values. They exist in much more specific and powerful ways in the rules, understandings, and meanings attached to institutionalized social structures. The causal importance of such institutions in the process of bureaucratization has been neglected.

Formal structures are not only creatures of their relational networks in the social organization. In modern societies, the elements of rationalized formal structure are deeply ingrained in, and reflect, widespread understandings of social reality. Many of the positions, policies, programs, and procedures of modern organizations are enforced by public opinion, by the views of important constituents, by knowledge legitimated through the educational system, by social prestige, by the laws, and by the definitions of negligence and prudence used by the courts. Such elements of formal structure are manifestations of powerful institutional rules which function as highly rationalized myths that are binding on particular organizations.

In modern societies, the myths generating formal organizational structure have two key properties. First, they are rationalized and impersonal prescriptions that identify various social purposes as technical ones and specify in a rulelike way the appropriate means to pursue these technical purposes rationally (Ellul 1964). Second, they are highly institutionalized and thus in some measure beyond the discretion of any individual participant or organization. They must, therefore, be taken for granted as legitimate, apart from evaluations of their impact on work outcomes.

Many elements of formal structure are highly institutionalized and function as myths. Examples include professions, programs, and technologies:

> Large numbers of rationalized professions emerge (Wilensky 1965; Bell 1973). These are occupations controlled, not only by direct inspection of work outcomes but also by social rules of licensing, certifying, and schooling. The occupations are rationalized, being understood to control impersonal techniques rather than moral mysteries. Further, they are highly institutionalized: the delegation of activities to the appropriate occupations is socially expected and often legally obligatory over and above any calculations of its efficiency.

> Many formalized organizational programs are also institutionalized in society. Ideologies define the functions appropriate to a business—such as sales, production, advertising, or accounting; to a university—such as

instruction and research in history, engineering, and literature; and to a hospital—such as surgery, internal medicine, and obstetrics. Such classifications of organizational functions, and the specifications for conducting each function, are prefabricated formulae available for use by any given organization. Similarly, technologies are institutionalized and become myths binding on organizations. Technical procedures of production, accounting, personnel selection, or data processing become taken-for-granted means to accomplish organizational ends. Quite apart from their possible efficiency, such institutionalized techniques establish an organization as appropriate, rational, and modern. Their use displays responsibility and avoids claims of negligence.

The impact of such rationalized institutional elements on organizations and organizing situations is enormous. These rules define new organizing situations, redefine existing ones, and specify the means for coping rationally with each. They enable, and often require, participants to organize along prescribed lines. And they spread very rapidly in modern society as part of the rise of postindustrial society (Bell 1973). New and extant domains of activity are codified in institutionalized programs, professions, or techniques, and organizations incorporate the packaged codes. For example:

The discipline of psychology creates a rationalized theory of personnel selection and certifies personnel professionals. Personnel departments and functionaries appear in all sorts of extant organizations, and new specialized personnel agencies also appear.

As programs of research and development are created and professionals with expertise in these fields are trained and defined, organizations come under increasing pressure to incorporate R & D units.

As the prerational profession of prostitution is rationalized along medical lines, bureaucratized organizations—sex-therapy clinics, massage parlors, and the like—spring up more easily.

As the issues of safety and environmental pollution arise, and as relevant professions and programs become institutionalized in laws, union ideologies, and public opinion, organizations incorporate these programs and professions.

The growth of rationalized institutional structures in society makes formal organizations more common and more elaborate. Such institutions are myths which make formal organizations both easier to create and more necessary. After all, the building blocks for organizations come to be littered around the societal landscape; it takes only a little entrepreneurial energy to assemble them into a structure. And because these building blocks are considered proper, adequate, rational, and necessary, organizations must incorporate them to avoid illegitimacy. Thus, the myths built into rationalized institutional elements create the necessity, the opportunity, and the impulse to organize rationally, over and above pressures in this direction created by the need to manage proximate relational networks:

**Proposition 1.** As *rationalized institutional rules arise in given domains of work activity, formal organizations form and expand by incorporating these rules as structural elements.*

Two distinct ideas are implied here: (1A) As institutionalized myths define new domains of rationalized activity, formal organizations emerge in these domains. (1B) As rationalizing institutional myths arise in existing domains of activity, extant organizations expand their formal structures so as to become isomorphic with these new myths.

To understand the larger historical process it is useful to note that:

**Proposition 2.** *The more modernized the society, the more extended the rationalized institutional structure in given domains and the greater the number of domains containing rationalized institutions.*

Modern institutions, then, are thoroughly rationalized, and these rationalized elements act as myths giving rise to more formal organization. When propositions 1 and 2 are combined, two more specific ideas follow: (2A) Formal organizations are more likely to emerge in more modernized societies, even with the complexity of immediate relational networks held constant. (2B) Formal organizations in a given domain of activity are likely to have more elaborated structures in more modernized societies, even with the complexity of immediate relational networks held constant.

Combining the ideas above with prevailing organization theory, it becomes clear that modern societies are filled with rationalized bureaucracies for two reasons. First, as the prevailing theories have asserted, relational networks become increasingly complex as societies modernize. Second, modern societies are filled with institutional rules which function as myths depicting various formal structures as rational means to the attainment of desirable ends. Figure 31.1 summarizes these two lines of theory. Both lines suggest that the postindustrial society—the society dominated by rational organization even more than by the forces of production—arises both out of the complexity of the modern social organizational network and, more directly, as an ideological matter. Once institutionalized, rationality becomes a myth with explosive organizing potential, as both Ellul (1964) and Bell (1973)—though with rather different reactions—observe.

### The Relation of Organizations to Their Institutional Environments

The observation is not new that organizations are structured by phenomena in their environments and tend to become isomorphic with them. One explanation of such isomorphism is that formal organizations become matched with their environments by technical and exchange interdependencies. This line of reasoning can be seen in the works of Aiken and Hage (1968), Hawley (1968), and Thompson (1967). This explanation asserts that structural elements diffuse because environments create boundary-spanning exigencies for organizations, and that organizations which incorporate structural elements isomorphic with the environment are able to manage such interdependencies.

A second explanation for the parallelism between organizations and their environments—and the one emphasized here—is that organizations structurally reflect socially constructed reality (Berger and Luckmann 1967). This view is suggested in the work of Parsons (1956) and Udy (1970), who see organizations as greatly conditioned by their general institutional environments and therefore as institutions themselves in part. Emery and Trist (1965) also see organizations as responding directly to environmental structures and distinguish such effects sharply from those that occur through boundary-spanning exchanges. According to the institutional conception as developed here, organizations tend to disappear as distinct and bounded units. Quite beyond the environmental interrelations suggested in open-systems theories, institutional theories in their extreme forms define organizations as dramatic enactments of the rationalized myths pervading modern

FIGURE 31.1 • THE ORIGINS AND ELABORATION OF FORMAL ORGANIZATIONAL STRUCTURES

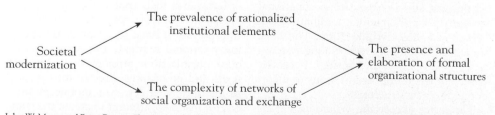

John W. Meyer and Brian Rowan, "Institutionalized Organizations: Formal Structure as Myth and Ceremony," *American Journal of Sociology* 83, no. 2 (1977): 340–363. © 1977 by The University of Chicago. Reprinted by permission of The University of Chicago Press. Organizational Survival

societies, rather than as units involved in exchange—no matter how complex—with their environments.

The two explanations of environmental isomorphism are not entirely inconsistent. Organizations both deal with their environments at their boundaries and imitate environmental elements in their structures. However, the two lines of explanation have very different implications for internal organizational process, as will be argued below.

### The Origins of Rational Institutional Myths
Bureaucratization is caused in part by the proliferation of rationalized myths in society, and this in turn involves the evolution of the whole modern institutional system. Although the latter topic is beyond the scope of this paper, three specific processes that generate rationalized myths of organizational structure can be noted.

*The elaboration of complex relational networks.* As the relational networks in societies become dense and interconnected, increasing numbers of rationalized myths arise. Some of them are highly generalized: for example, the principles of universalism (Parsons 1971), contracts (Spencer 1897), restitution (Durkheim 1933), and expertise (Weber 1947) are generalized to diverse occupations, organizational programs, and organizational practices. Other myths describe specific structural elements. These myths may originate from narrow contexts and be applied in different ones. For example, in modern societies the relational contexts of business organizations in a single industry are roughly similar from place to place. Under these conditions a particularly effective practice, occupational specialty, or principle of coordination can be codified into mythlike form. The laws, the educational and credentialing systems, and public opinion then make it necessary or advantageous for organizations to incorporate the new structures.

*The degree of collective organization of the environment.* The myths generated by particular organizational practices and diffused through relational networks have legitimacy based on the supposition that they are rationally effective. But many myths also have official legitimacy based on legal mandates. ... Legislative and judicial authorities create and interpret legal mandates; administrative agencies—such as state and federal governments, port authorities, and school districts—establish rules of practice; and licenses and credentials become necessary in order to practice occupations. The stronger the rational-legal order, the greater the extent to which rationalized rules and procedures and personnel become institutional requirements. New formal organizations emerge and extant organizations acquire new structural elements.

*Leadership efforts of local organizations.* The rise of the state and the expansion of collective jurisdiction are often thought to result in domesticated organizations (Carlson 1962) subject to high levels of goal displacement (Clark 1956; Selznick 1949; Zald and Denton 1963). This view is misleading: organizations do often adapt to their institutional contexts, but they often play active roles in shaping those contexts (Dowling and Pfeffer 1975; Parsons 1956; Perrow 1970; Thompson 1967). Many organizations actively seek charters from collective authorities and manage to institutionalize their goals and structures in the rules of such authorities.

Efforts to mold institutional environments proceed along two dimensions. First, powerful organizations force their immediate relational networks to adapt to their structures and relations. For instance, automobile producers help create demands for particular kinds of roads, transportation systems, and fuels that make automobiles virtual necessities; competitive forms of transportation have to adapt to the existing relational context. But second, powerful organizations attempt to build their goals and procedures directly into society as institutional rules. Automobile producers, for instance, attempt to create the standards in public opinion defining desirable cars, to influence legal standards defining satisfactory cars, to affect judicial rules defining cars adequate enough to avoid manufacturer liability, and to force agents of the collectivity to purchase only their cars. Rivals must then compete both in social networks or markets and in contexts of institutional rules which are defined by extant organizations. In this fashion, given organizational forms perpetuate themselves by becoming institutionalized rules....

### The Impact of Institutional Environments on Organizations

Isomorphism with environmental institutions has some crucial consequences for organizations: (*a*) they incorporate elements which are legitimated externally, rather than in terms of efficiency; (*b*) they employ external or ceremonial assessment criteria to define the value of structural elements; and (*c*) dependence on externally fixed institutions reduces turbulence and maintains stability. As a result, it is argued here, institutional isomorphism promotes the success and survival of organizations. Incorporating externally legitimated formal structures increases the commitment of internal participants and external constituents. And the use of external assessment criteria—that is, moving toward the status in society of a subunit rather than an independent system—can enable an organization to remain successful by social definition, buffering it from failure.

*Changing formal structures.* By designing a formal structure that adheres to the prescriptions of myths in the institutional environment, an organization demonstrates that it is acting on collectively valued purposes in a proper and adequate manner (Dowling and Pfeffer 1975; Meyer and Rowan 1975). The incorporation of institutionalized elements provides an account (Scott and Lyman 1968) of its activities that protects the organization from having its conduct questioned. The organization becomes, in a word, legitimate, and it uses its legitimacy to strengthen its support and secure its survival.

From an institutional perspective, then, a most important aspect of isomorphism with environmental institutions is the evolution of organizational language. The labels of the organization chart as well as the vocabulary used to delineate organizational goals, procedures, and policies are analogous to the vocabularies of motive used to account for the activities of individuals (Blum and McHugh 1971; Mills 1940). Just as jealousy, anger, altruism, and love are myths that interpret and explain the actions of individuals, the myths of doctors, of accountants, or of the assembly line explain organizational activities. Thus, some can say that the engineers will solve a specific problem or that the secretaries will perform certain tasks, without knowing who these engineers or secretaries will be or exactly what they will do. Both the speaker and the listeners understand such statements to describe how certain responsibilities will be carried out.

Vocabularies of structure which are isomorphic with institutional rules provide prudent, rational, and legitimate accounts. Organizations described in legitimated vocabularies are assumed to be oriented to collectively defined, and often collectively mandated, ends. The myths of personnel services, for example, not only account for the rationality of employment practices but also indicate that personnel services are valuable to an organization. Employees, applicants, managers, trustees, and governmental agencies are predisposed to trust the hiring practices of organizations that follow legitimated procedures—such as equal opportunity programs, or personality testing—and they are more willing to participate in or to fund such organizations. On the other hand, organizations that omit environmentally legitimated elements of structure or create unique structures lack acceptable legitimated accounts of their activities. Such organizations are more vulnerable to claims that they are negligent, irrational, or unnecessary. Claims of this kind, whether made by internal participants, external constituents, or the government, can cause organizations to incur real costs. For example:

> With the rise of modern medical institutions, large organizations that do not arrange medical-care facilities for their workers come to be seen as negligent—by the workers, by management factions, by insurers, by courts which legally define negligence, and often by laws. The costs of illegitimacy in insurance premiums and legal liabilities are very real.

> Similarly, environmental safety institutions make it important for organizations to create formal safety rules, safety departments, and safety programs. No Smoking rules and signs, regardless of their enforcement, are necessary to avoid charges of negligence and to avoid the extreme of illegitimation: the closing of buildings by the state.

> The rise of professionalized economics makes it useful for organizations to incorporate groups of economists and econometric analyses. Though no one may read, understand, or believe them, econometric analyses help legitimate the organization's plans in the eyes of investors, customers (as with Defense Department contractors), and internal participants. Such analyses can also provide rational accountings after failures occur: managers whose plans have failed can demonstrate to investors, stockholders, and superiors that procedures were prudent and that decisions were made by rational means.

Thus, rationalized institutions create myths of formal structure which shape organizations. Failure to incorporate the proper elements of structure is negligent and irrational; the continued flow of support is threatened and internal dissidents are strengthened. At the same time, these myths present organizations with great opportunities for expansion. Affixing the right labels to activities can change them into valuable services and mobilize the commitments of internal participants and external constituents.

*Adopting external assessment criteria.* In institutionally elaborated environments organizations also become sensitive to, and employ, external criteria of worth. Such criteria include, for instance, such ceremonial awards as the Nobel Prize, endorsements by important people, the standard prices of

professionals and consultants, or the prestige of programs or personnel in external social circles. For example, the conventions of modern accounting attempt to assign value to particular components of organizations on the basis of their contribution—through the organization's production function—to the goods and services the organization produces. But for many units—service departments, administrative sectors, and others—it is utterly unclear what is being produced that has clear or definable value in terms of its contribution to the organizational product. In these situations, accountants employ shadow prices: they assume that given organizational units are necessary and calculate their value from their prices in the world outside the organization. Thus modern accounting creates ceremonial production functions and maps them onto economic production functions: organizations assign externally defined worth to advertising departments, safety departments, managers, econometricians, and occasionally even sociologists, whether or not these units contribute measurably to the production of outputs. Monetary prices, in postindustrial society, reflect hosts of ceremonial influences, as do economic measures of efficiency, profitability, or net worth (Hirsch 1975).

Ceremonial criteria of worth and ceremonially derived production functions are useful to organizations: they legitimate organizations with internal participants, stockholders, the public, and the state, as with the IRS or the SEC. They demonstrate socially the fitness of an organization. The incorporation of structures with high ceremonial value, such as those reflecting the latest expert thinking or those with the most prestige, makes the credit position of an organization more favorable. Loans, donations, or investments are more easily obtained. Finally, units within the organization use ceremonial assessments as accounts of their productive service to the organization. Their internal power rises with their performance on ceremonial measures (Salancik and Pfeffer 1974).

*Stabilization.* The rise of an elaborate institutional environment stabilizes both external and internal organizational relationships. Centralized states, trade associations, unions, professional associations, and coalitions among organizations standardize and stabilize (see the review by Starbuck 1976).

Market conditions, the characteristics of inputs and outputs, and technological procedures are brought under the jurisdiction of institutional meanings and controls. Stabilization also results as a given organization becomes part of the wider collective system. Support is guaranteed by agreements instead of depending entirely on performance. For example, apart from whether schools educate students, or hospitals cure patients, people and governmental agencies remain committed to these organizations, funding and using them almost automatically year after year.

Institutionally controlled environments buffer organizations from turbulence (Emery and Trist 1965; Terreberry 1968). Adaptations occur less rapidly as increased numbers of agreements are enacted. Collectively granted monopolies guarantee clienteles for organizations like schools, hospitals, or professional associations. The taken-for-granted (and legally regulated) quality of institutional rules makes dramatic instabilities in products, techniques, or policies unlikely. And legitimacy as accepted subunits of society protects organizations from immediate sanctions for variations in technical performance:

> Thus, American school districts (like other governmental units) have near monopolies and are very stable. They must conform to wider rules about proper classifications and credentials of teachers and students, and of topics of study. But they are protected by rules which make education as defined by these classifications compulsory. Alternative or private schools are possible, but must conform so closely to the required structures and classifications as to be able to generate little advantage.
>
> Some business organizations obtain very high levels of institutional stabilization. A large defense contractor may be paid for

following agreed-on procedures, even if the product is ineffective. In the extreme, such organizations may be so successful as to survive bankruptcy intact—as Lockheed and Penn Central have done—by becoming partially components of the state. More commonly, such firms are guaranteed survival by state-regulated rates which secure profits regardless of costs, as with American public utility firms.

Large automobile firms are a little less stabilized. They exist in an environment that contains enough structures to make automobiles, as conventionally defined, virtual necessities. But still, customers and governments can inspect each automobile and can evaluate and even legally discredit it. Legal action cannot as easily discredit a high school graduate.

*Organizational success and survival.—* Thus, organizational success depends on factors other than efficient coordination and control of productive activities. Independent of their productive efficiency, organizations which exist in highly elaborated institutional environments and succeed in becoming isomorphic with these environments gain the legitimacy and resources needed to survive. In part, this depends on environmental processes and on the capacity of given organizational leadership to mold these processes (Hirsch 1975). In part, it depends on the ability of given organizations to conform to, and become legitimated by, environmental institutions. In institutionally elaborated environments, sagacious conformity is required: leadership (in a university, a hospital, or a business) requires an understanding of changing fashions and governmental programs. But this kind of conformity—and the almost guaranteed survival which may accompany it—is possible only in an environment with a highly institutionalized structure. In such a context an organization can be locked into isomorphism, ceremonially reflecting the institutional environment in its structure, functionaries, and procedures. Thus, in addition to the conventionally defined sources of organizational success and survival, the following general assertion can be proposed:

FIGURE 31.2  •  ORGANIZATIONAL SURVIVAL

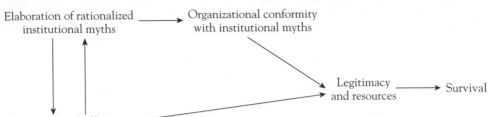

**Proposition 3.** *Organizations that incorporate societally legitimated rationalized elements in their formal structures maximize their legitimacy and increase their resources and survival capabilities.*

This proposition asserts that the long-run survival prospects of organizations increase as state structures elaborate and as organizations respond to institutionalized rules. In the United States, for instance, schools, hospitals, and welfare organizations show considerable ability to survive, precisely because they are matched with—and almost absorbed by—their institutional environments. In the same way, organizations fail when they deviate from the prescriptions of institutionalizing myths: quite apart from technical efficiency, organizations which innovate in important structural ways bear considerable costs in legitimacy.

Figure 31.2 summarizes the general argument of this section, alongside the established view that organizations succeed through efficiency.

## INSTITUTIONALIZED STRUCTURES AND ORGANIZATIONAL ACTIVITIES

Rationalized formal structures arise in two contexts. First, the demands of local relational networks encourage the development of structures that coordinate and control activities. Such structures contribute to the efficiency of organizations and give them competitive advantages over less efficient competitors. Second, the interconnectedness of societal relations, the collective organization of society, and the leadership of organizational elites create a highly institutionalized context. In this context rationalized structures present an acceptable account of organizational activities, and organizations gain legitimacy, stability, and resources.

All organizations, to one degree or another, are embedded in both relational and institutionalized contexts and are therefore concerned both with coordinating and controlling their activities and with prudently accounting for them. Organizations in highly institutionalized environments face internal and boundary-spanning contingencies. Schools, for example, must transport students to and from school under some circumstances and must assign teachers, students, and topics to classrooms. On the other hand, organizations producing in markets that place great emphasis on efficiency build in units whose relation to production is obscure and whose efficiency is determined, not by a true production function, but by ceremonial definition.

Nevertheless, the survival of some organizations depends more on managing the demands of internal and boundary-spanning relations, while the survival of others depends more on the ceremonial demands of highly institutionalized environments. The discussion to follow shows that whether an organization's survival depends primarily on relational or on institutional demands determines the tightness of alignments between structures and activities.

## Types of Organizations

Institutionalized myths differ in the completeness with which they describe cause and effect relationships, and in the clarity with which they describe standards that should be used to evaluate outputs (Thompson 1967). Some organizations use routine, clearly defined technologies to produce outputs. When output can be easily evaluated a market often develops, and consumers gain considerable rights of inspection and control. In this context, efficiency often determines success. Organizations must face exigencies of close coordination with their relational networks, and they cope with these exigencies by organizing around immediate technical problems.

But the rise of collectively organized society and the increasing interconnectedness of social relations have eroded many market contexts. Increasingly, such organizations as schools, R & D units, and governmental bureaucracies use variable, ambiguous technologies to produce outputs that are difficult to appraise, and other organizations with clearly defined technologies find themselves unable to adapt to environmental turbulence. The uncertainties of unpredictable technical contingencies or of adapting to environmental change cannot be resolved on the basis of efficiency. Internal participants and external constituents alike call for institutionalized rules that promote trust and confidence in outputs and buffer organizations from failure (Emery and Trist 1965).

Thus, one can conceive of a continuum along which organizations can be ordered. At one end are production organizations under strong output controls (Ouchi and McGuire 1975) whose success depends on the management of relational networks. At the other end are institutionalized organizations whose success depends on the confidence and stability achieved by isomorphism with institutional rules. For two reasons it is important not to assume that an organization's location on this continuum is based on the inherent technical properties of its output and therefore permanent. First, the technical properties of outputs are socially defined and do not exist in some concrete sense that allows them to be empirically discovered. Second, environments and organizations often redefine the nature of products, services, and technologies. Redefinition sometimes clarifies techniques or evaluative standards. But often organizations and environments redefine the nature of techniques and output so that ambiguity is introduced and rights of inspection and control are lowered. For example, American schools have evolved from producing rather specific training that was evaluated according to strict criteria of efficiency to producing ambiguously defined services that are evaluated according to criteria of certification (Callahan 1962; Tyack 1974; Meyer and Rowan 1975).

## Structural Inconsistencies in Institutionalized Organizations

Two very general problems face an organization if its success depends primarily on isomorphism with institutionalized rules. First, technical activities and demands for efficiency create conflicts and inconsistencies in an institutionalized organization's efforts to conform to the ceremonial rules of production. Second, because these ceremonial rules are transmitted by myths that may arise from different parts of the environment, the rules may conflict with one another. These inconsistencies make a concern for efficiency and tight coordination and control problematic.

Formal structures that celebrate institutionalized myths differ from structures that act efficiently. Ceremonial activity is significant in relation to categorical rules, not in its concrete effects (Merton 1940; March and Simon 1958). A sick worker must be treated by a doctor using accepted medical procedures; whether the worker is treated effectively is less important. A bus company must service required routes whether or not there are many passengers. A university must maintain appropriate departments independently of the departments' enrollments. Activity, that is, has ritual significance: it maintains appearances and validates an organization.

Categorical rules conflict with the logic of efficiency. Organizations often face the dilemma that activities celebrating institutionalized rules, although they count as virtuous ceremonial expenditures, are pure costs from the point of view of efficiency. For example, hiring a Nobel Prize winner brings great ceremonial benefits to a university. The celebrated name can lead to research grants, brighter students, or reputational gains. But from the point of view of immediate outcomes, the expenditure lowers the instructional return per dollar expended and lowers the university's ability to solve immediate logistical problems....

Yet another source of conflict between categorical rules and efficiency is the inconsistency among institutionalized elements. Institutional environments are often pluralistic (Udy 1970), and societies promulgate sharply inconsistent myths. As a result, organizations in search of external support and stability incorporate all sorts of incompatible structural elements. Professions are incorporated although they make overlapping jurisdictional claims. Programs are adopted which contend with each other for authority over a given domain. For instance, if one inquires who decides what curricula will be taught in schools, any number of parties from the various governments down to individual teachers may say that they decide.

In institutionalized organizations, then, concern with the efficiency of day-to-day activities creates enormous uncertainties. Specific contexts highlight the inadequacies of the prescriptions of generalized myths, and inconsistent structural elements conflict over jurisdictional rights. Thus the organization must struggle to link the requirements of ceremonial elements to technical activities and to link inconsistent ceremonial elements to each other.

### Resolving Inconsistencies

...An organization can resolve conflicts between ceremonial rules and efficiency by employing two interrelated devices: decoupling and the logic of confidence.

*Decoupling.*—Ideally, organizations built around efficiency attempt to maintain close alignments between structures and activities. Conformity is enforced through inspection, output quality is continually monitored, the efficiency of various units is evaluated, and the various goals are unified and coordinated. But a policy of close alignment in institutionalized organizations merely makes public a record of inefficiency and inconsistency.

Institutionalized organizations protect their formal structures from evaluation on the basis of technical performance: inspection, evaluation, and control of activities are minimized, and coordination, interdependence, and mutual adjustments among structural units are handled informally.

**Proposition 4.** *Because attempts to control and coordinate activities in institutionalized organizations lead to conflicts and loss of legitimacy, elements of structure are decoupled from activities and from each other.*

Some well-known properties of organizations illustrate the decoupling process:

Activities are performed beyond the purview of managers. In particular, organizations actively encourage professionalism, and activities are delegated to professionals.

Goals are made ambiguous or vacuous, and categorical ends are substituted for technical ends. Hospitals treat, not cure, patients. Schools produce students, not learning. In fact, data on technical performance are eliminated or rendered invisible. Hospitals try to ignore information on cure rates, public services avoid data about effectiveness, and schools deemphasize measures of achievement.

Integration is avoided, program implementation is neglected, and inspection and evaluation are ceremonialized.

Human relations are made very important. The organization cannot formally coordinate activities because its formal rules, if applied, would generate inconsistencies. Therefore individuals are left to work out technical interdependencies informally. The ability to coordinate things in violation of the rules—that is, to get along with other people—is highly valued.

The advantages of decoupling are clear. The assumption that formal structures are really working is buffered from the inconsistencies and anomalies involved in technical activities. Also, because integration is avoided disputes and conflicts are minimized, and an organization can mobilize support from a broader range of external constituents.

Thus, decoupling enables organizations to maintain standardized, legitimating, formal structures while their activities vary in response to practical considerations. The organizations in an industry tend to be similar in formal structure—reflecting their common institutional origins—but may show much diversity in actual practice.

*The logic of confidence and good faith.* Despite the lack of coordination and control, decoupled organizations are not anarchies. Day-to-day activities proceed in an orderly fashion. What legitimates institutionalized organizations, enabling them to appear useful in spite of the lack of technical validation, is the confidence and good faith of their internal participants and their external constituents.

Considerations of face characterize ceremonial management (Goffman 1967). Confidence in structural elements is maintained through three practices—avoidance, discretion, and overlooking (Goffman 1967, pp. 12–18). Avoidance and discretion are encouraged by decoupling autonomous subunits; overlooking anomalies is also quite common. Both internal participants and external constituents cooperate in these practices. Assuring that individual participants maintain face sustains confidence in the organization, and ultimately reinforces confidence in the myths that rationalize the organization's existence.

Delegation, professionalization, goal ambiguity, the elimination of output data, and maintenance of face are all mechanisms for absorbing uncertainty while preserving the formal structure of the organization (March and Simon 1958). They contribute to a general aura of confidence within and outside the organization....

Decoupling and maintenance of face, in other words, are mechanisms that maintain the assumption that people are acting in good faith. Professionalization is not merely a way of avoiding inspection—it binds both supervisors and subordinates to act in good faith. So in a smaller way does strategic leniency (Blau 1956). And so do the public displays of morale and satisfaction which are characteristic of many organizations. Organizations employ a host of mechanisms to dramatize the ritual commitments which their participants make to basic structural elements. These mechanisms are especially common in organizations which strongly reflect their institutionalized environments.

**Proposition 5.** *The more an organization's structure is derived from institutionalized myths, the more it maintains elaborate displays of confidence, satisfaction, and good faith, internally and externally.*

The commitments built up by displays of morale and satisfaction are not simply vacuous affirmations of institutionalized myths. Participants not only commit themselves to supporting an organization's ceremonial facade but also commit themselves to making things work out backstage. The committed participants engage in informal coordination that, although often formally inappropriate, keeps technical activities running smoothly and avoids public embarrassments. In this sense the confidence and good faith generated by ceremonial action is in no way fraudulent. It may even be the most reasonable way to get participants to make their best efforts in situations that are made problematic by institutionalized myths that are at odds with immediate technical demands.

*Ceremonial inspection and evaluation.* All organizations, even those maintaining high levels of confidence and good faith, are in environments that have institutionalized the rationalized rituals of inspection and evaluation. And inspection and evaluation can uncover events and deviations that undermine legitimacy. So institutionalized

## FIGURE 31.3 • THE EFFECTS OF INSTITUTIONAL ISOMORPHISM ON ORGANIZATIONS

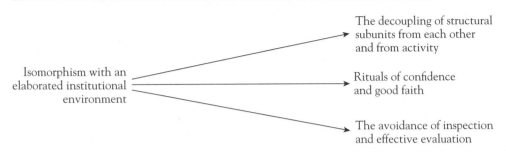

organizations minimize and ceremonialize inspection and evaluation.

In institutionalized organizations, in fact, evaluation accompanies and produces illegitimacy. The interest in evaluation research by the American federal government, for instance, is partly intended to undercut the state, local, and private authorities which have managed social services in the United States. The federal authorities, of course, have usually not evaluated those programs which are completely under federal jurisdiction; they have only evaluated those over which federal controls are incomplete. Similarly, state governments have often insisted on evaluating the special fundings they create in welfare and education but ordinarily do not evaluate the programs which they fund in a routine way.

Evaluation and inspection are public assertions of societal control which violate the assumption that everyone is acting with competence and in good faith. Violating this assumption lowers morale and confidence. Thus, evaluation and inspection undermine the ceremonial aspects of organizations.

**Proposition 6.** *Institutionalized organizations seek to minimize inspection and evaluation by both internal managers and external constituents.*

Decoupling and the avoidance of inspection and evaluation are not merely devices used by the organization. External constituents, too, avoid inspecting and controlling institutionalized organizations (Meyer and Rowan 1975). Accrediting agencies, boards of trustees, government agencies, and individuals accept ceremonially at face value the credentials, ambiguous goals, and categorical evaluations that are characteristic of ceremonial organizations. In elaborate institutional environments, these external constituents are themselves likely to be corporately organized agents of society. Maintaining categorical relationships with their organizational subunits is more stable and more certain than is relying on inspection and control.

Figure 31.3 summarizes the main arguments of this section of our discussion.

## SUMMARY AND RESEARCH IMPLICATIONS

Organizational structures are created and made more elaborate with the rise of institutionalized myths, and, in highly institutionalized contexts, organizational action must support these myths. But an organization must also attend to practical activity. The two requirements are at odds. A stable solution is to maintain the organization in a loosely coupled state.

No position is taken here on the overall social effectiveness of isomorphic and loosely coupled organizations. To some extent such structures buffer activity from efficiency criteria and produce ineffectiveness. On the other hand, by binding participants to act in good faith, and to adhere to the larger rationalities of the wider structure, they may maximize long-run effectiveness. It should not be assumed that the creation of microscopic rationalities in the daily activity of workers effects social ends more efficiently than commitment to larger institutional claims and purposes....

## NOTE

Work on this paper was conducted at the Stanford Center for Research and Development in Teaching (SCRDT) and was supported by the National Institute of Education (contract no. NE-C-00-3-0062). The views expressed here do not, of course, reflect NIE positions. Many colleagues in the SCRDT, the Stanford Organizations Training Program, the American Sociological Association's work group on Organizations and Environments, and the NIE gave help and encouragement. In particular, H. Acland, A. Bergesen, J. Boli-Bennett, T. Deal, J. Freeman, P. Hirsch, J. G. March, W. R. Scott, and W. Starbuck made helpful suggestions.

## REFERENCES

Aiken, Michael, and Jerald Hage. 1968. "Organizational Interdependence and Intraorganizational Structure." *American Sociological Review* 33 (December): 912–30.

Bell, Daniel. 1973. *The Coming of Post-industrial Society.* New York: Basic Books.

Bendix, Reinhard. 1964. *Nation-Building and Citizenship.* New York: Wiley.

___. 1968. "Bureaucracy." pp. 206–19 in *International Encyclopedia of the Social Sciences,* edited by David L. Sills. New York: Macmillan.

Berger, Peter L., and Thomas Luckmann. 1967. *The Social Construction of Reality.* New York: Doubleday.

Blau, Peter M. 1956. *Bureaucracy in Modern Society.* New York: Random House.

___. 1970. "A Formal Theory of Differentiation in Organizations." *American Sociological Review* 35 (April): 201–18.

Blum, Alan F., and Peter McHugh. 1971. "The Social Ascription of Motives." *American Sociological Review* 36 (December): 98–109.

Callahan, Raymond E. 1962. *Education and the Cult of Efficiency.* Chicago: University of Chicago Press.

Carlson, Richard O. 1962. *Executive Succession and Organizational Change.* Chicago: Midwest Administration Center, University of Chicago.

Clark, Burton R. 1956. *Adult Education in Transition.* Berkeley: University of California Press.

Dalton, Melville. 1959. *Men Who Manage.* New York: Wiley.

Dowling, John, and Jeffrey Pfeffer. 1975. "Organizational Legitimacy." *Pacific Sociological Review* 18 (January): 122–36.

Downs, Anthony. 1967. *Inside Bureaucracy.* Boston: Little, Brown.

Durkheim, Émile. 1933. *The Division of Labor in Society.* New York: Macmillan.

Ellul, Jacques. 1964. *The Technological Society.* New York: Knopf.

Emery, Fred L., and Eric L. Trist. 1965. "The Causal Texture of Organizational Environments." *Human Relations* 18 (February): 21–32.

Freeman, John Henry. 1973. "Environment, Technology and Administrative Intensity of Manufacturing Organizations." *American Sociological Review* 38 (December): 750–63.

Goffman, Erving. 1967. *Interaction Ritual.* Garden City, N.Y.: Anchor.

Hawley, Amos H. 1968. "Human Ecology." pp. 328–37 in *International Encyclopedia of the Social Sciences,* edited by David L. Sills. New York: Macmillan.

Hirsch, Paul M. 1975. "Organizational Effectiveness and the Institutional Environment." *Administrative Science Quarterly* 20 (September): 327–44.

Homans, George C. 1950. *The Human Group.* New York: Harcourt, Brace.

March, James G., and Johan P. Olsen. 1976. *Ambiguity and Choice in Organizations.* Bergen: Universitetsforlaget.

March, James G., and Herbert A. Simon. 1958. *Organizations*. New York: Wiley.

Merton, Robert K. 1940. "Bureaucratic Structure and Personality." *Social Forces* 18 (May): 560–68.

Meyer, John W., and Brian Rowan. 1975. "Notes on the Structure of Educational Organizations." Paper presented at annual meeting of the American Sociological Association, San Francisco.

Mills, C. Wright. 1940. "Situated Actions and Vocabularies of Motive." *American Sociological Review* 5 (February): 904–13.

Ouchi, William, and Mary Ann Maguire. 1975. "Organizational Control: Two Functions." *Administrative Science Quarterly* 20 (December): 559–69.

Parsons, Talcott. 1956. "Suggestions for a Sociological Approach to the Theory of Organizations I." *Administrative Science Quarterly* 1 (June): 63–85.

___. 1971. *The System of Modern Societies*. Englewood Cliffs, N.J.: Prentice-Hall.

Perrow, Charles. 1970. *Organizational Analysis: A Sociological View*. Belmont, Calif.: Wadsworth.

Salancik, Gerald R., and Jeffrey Pfeffer. 1974. "The Bases and Use of Power in Organizational Decision Making." *Administrative Science Quarterly* 19 (December): 453–73.

Scott, Marvin B., and Stanford M. Lyman. 1968. "Accounts." *American Sociological Review* 33 (February): 46–62.

Scott, W. Richard. 1975. "Organizational Structure." pp. 1–20 in *Annual Review of Sociology*. Vol. 1, edited by Alex Inkeles. Palo Alto, Calif.: Annual Reviews.

Selznick, Philip. 1949. *TVA and the Grass Roots*. Berkeley: University of California Press.

Spencer, Herbert. 1897. *Principles of Sociology*. New York: Appleton.

Starbuck, William H. 1976. "Organizations and their Environments." pp. 1069–1123 in *Handbook of Industrial and Organizational Psychology*, edited by Marvin D. Dunnette. New York: Rand McNally.

Terreberry, Shirley. 1968. "The Evolution of Organizational Environments." *Administrative Science Quarterly* 12 (March): 590–613.

Thompson, James D. 1967. *Organizations in Action*. New York: McGraw-Hill.

Tyack, David B. 1974. *The One Best System*. Cambridge, Mass.: Harvard University Press.

Udy, Stanley H., Jr. 1970. *Work in Traditional and Modern Society*. Englewood Cliffs, N.J.: Prentice-Hall.

Weber, Max. 1930. *The Protestant's Ethic and the Spirit of Capitalism*. New York: Scribner's.

___. 1946. Essays in Sociology. New York: Oxford University Press.

___. 1947. *The Theory of Social and Economic Organization*. New York: Oxford University Press.

Weick, Karl E. 1976. "Educational Organizations as Loosely Coupled Systems." *Administrative Science Quarterly* 21 (March): 1–19.

Wilensky, Harold L. 1965. "The Professionalization of Everyone?" *American Journal of Sociology* 70 (September): 137–58.

Woodward, Joan. 1965. *Industrial Organization, Theory and Practice*. London: Oxford University Press.

Zald, Mayer N., and Patricia Denton. 1963. "From Evangelism to General Service: The Transformation of the YMCA." *Administrative Science Quarterly* 8 (September): 214–34.

## 32

# External Control of Organizations:
# A Resource Dependence Perspective

*Jeffrey Pfeffer & Gerald R. Salancik*

... To understand the behavior of an organization you must understand the context of that behavior—that is, the ecology of the organization. This point of view is important for those who seek to understand organizations as well as for those who seek to manage and control them. Organizations are inescapably bound up with the conditions of their environment. Indeed, it has been said that all organizations engage in activities which have as their logical conclusion adjustment to the environment (Hawley, 1950:3).

At first glance, this position seems obvious. An open-systems perspective on organizations is not new (Katz and Kahn, 1966), and it is generally accepted that contexts, organizational environments, are important for understanding actions and structures. One of the purposes of [this chapter] is to note that, in spite of the apparent obviousness of this position, much of the literature on organizations still does not recognize the importance of context; indeed, there are some reasons why such a neglect of contextual factors is likely to be maintained.

## OVERVIEW

Most books about organizations describe how they operate, and the existence of the organizations is taken for granted. This book discusses how organizations manage to survive. Their existence is constantly in question, and their survival is viewed as problematic. How managers go about ensuring their organization's survival is what this book is about.

Our position is that organizations survive to the extent that they are effective. Their effectiveness derives from the management of demands, particularly the demands of interest groups upon which the organizations depend for resources and support. As we shall consider, there are a variety of ways of managing demands, including the obvious one of giving in to them.

The key to organizational survival is the ability to acquire and maintain resources. This problem would be simplified if organizations were in complete control of all the components necessary for their operation. However, no organization is completely self-contained. Organizations are embedded in an environment comprised of other organizations. They depend on those other organizations for the many resources they themselves require. Organizations are linked to environments by federations, associations, customer-supplier relationships, competitive relationships, and a social-legal apparatus defining and controlling the nature and limits of these relationships. Organizations must transact with other elements in their environment to acquire needed resources, and this is true whether we are talking about public organizations, private organizations, small or large organizations, or organizations which are bureaucratic or organic (Burns and Stalker, 1961). ...

The fact that organizations are dependent for survival and success on their environments does not, in itself, make their existence problematic. If stable supplies were assured from the sources of needed resources, there would be no problem. If the resources needed by the organization were continually available, even if outside their control, there would be no problem. Problems arise not merely because organizations are dependent on their environment, but because this environment is not dependable. Environments can change, new organizations enter and exit, and the supply of resources becomes more or less scarce. When environments change, organizations face the prospect either of not surviving or of changing their activities in response to these environmental factors. ...

Both problems of using resources and problems of acquiring them face organizations, but the use of resources always presupposes their existence. A good deal of organizational behavior, the actions taken by organizations, can be understood only by knowing something about the organization's environment and the problems it creates for obtaining resources. What happens in an organization is not only a function of the organization, its structure, its leadership, its procedures, or its goals. What happens is also a consequence of the environment and the particular contingencies and constraints deriving from that environment.

Consider the following case, described by a student at the University of Illinois. The student had worked in a fast-food restaurant near the campus and was concerned about how the workers (himself) were treated. Involved in what he was studying, the student read a great deal about self-actualizing, theories of motivation, and the management of human resources. He observed at the restaurant that workers would steal food, make obscene statements about the boss behind his back, and complain about the low pay. The student's analysis of the situation was a concise report summarizing the typical human relations palliatives: make the boring, greasy work more challenging and the

indifferent management more democratic. The student was asked why he thought management was unresponsive to such suggestions. He considered the possibility that management was cruel and interested only in making a profit (and the operation was quite profitable). He was then asked why the employees permitted management to treat them in such a fashion—after all, they could always quit. The student responded that the workers needed the money and that jobs were hard to obtain.

This fact, that the workers were drawn from an almost limitless labor pool of students looking for any kind of part-time employment was nowhere to be found in the student's discussion of the operation of the restaurant. Yet, it was precisely this characteristic of the labor market which permitted the operation to disregard the feelings of the workers. Since there were many who wanted to work, the power of an individual worker was severely limited. More critical to the organization's success was its location and its ability both to keep competition to a minimum and to maintain a steady flow of supplies to serve a virtually captive market. If the workers were unsatisfied, it was not only because they did not like the organization's policies; in the absence of any base of power and with few alternative jobs, the workers had neither the option of voice nor exit (Hirschman, 1970).

More important to this organization's success than the motivation of its workers was its location on a block between the campus and dormitories, the path of thousands of students. Changes in policies and facilities for housing and transportation of students would have a far greater effect than some disgruntled employees. Our example illustrates, first, the importance of attending to contextual variables in understanding organizations, but also that organizational survival and success are not always achieved by making internal adjustments. Dealing with and managing the environment is just as important a component of organizational effectiveness.

A comparison of the phonograph record and the pharmaceutical industries (Hirsch, 1975) illustrates this point more directly. These two industries, Hirsch noted, are strikingly different in profitability. This difference in profits is more striking because the industries in many ways are otherwise similar: both sell their products through intermediaries, doctors in the case of pharmaceuticals, disc jockeys in the case of records; both introduce many new products; both protect their market positions through patent or copyright laws. What could account for the difference in profit? Hirsch argued that the pharmaceutical industry's greater profits came from its greater control of its environment; a more concentrated industry, firms could more effectively restrict entry and manage distribution channels. Profits resulted from a favorable institutional environment. Aware of the importance of the institutional environment for success, firms spent a lot of strategic effort maintaining that environment. They would engage in activities designed to modify patent laws to their advantage and in other efforts to protect their market positions.

### The Environment as Treated in the Social Sciences

The social sciences, even if not frequently examining the context of behavior, have long recognized its importance. The demography of a city has been found to affect the particular form of city government used, and particularly the use of a city manager (Kessel, 1962; Schnore and Alford, 1963). Some political economists have argued that party positions are developed with reference to the distribution of preferences for policies in the population (e.g., Davis and Hinich, 1966), which means that political platforms are affected by context. The importance of external influences on individual voting behaviors has been recognized, while participation in political activities, as well as other forms of voluntary associations, is also partially determined by the context,

particularly the demographic and socioeconomic dimensions of the community.

As in the case of political science, some theorists writing about organizational behavior have recognized that the organization's context shapes the activities and structures of formal organizations. Katz and Kahn (1966) argued for the necessity of viewing organizations as open systems, and Perrow (1970) forcefully illustrated the analytical benefits to be gained by considering the environment of the organization in addition to its internal operating characteristics. Bendix (1956) showed how ideologies shaped the use of authority in organizations, and Weber (1930) proposed a theory of economic development that held the religion of a country to be critical. He suggested that the development of mercantile capitalism depended on a legitimating ideology which stressed hard work and delayed gratification, such as that provided by Protestantism, as contrasted with Catholicism.

Economists were even more explicit in giving critical importance to the context of organizations, but they tended to take the environment as a given. Competition is a critical variable distinguishing between the applicability of models of monopoly, oligopoly, imperfect competition, or perfectly competitive behavior. The study of oligopoly is explicitly the study of interorganizational behavior (e.g., Fellner, 1949; Phillips, 1960; Williamson, 1965). And, the study of antitrust policy implicitly recognizes the fact that organizations do make efforts to limit or otherwise manage the competitiveness of their environments.

In recent years, it has become fashionable for those writing about management and organizations to acknowledge the importance of the open-systems view and the importance of the environment, particularly in the first chapter or in a special section of the book. Except for some special terminology, however, the implications of the organization's context for analyzing and managing organizations remains undeveloped....` Prescriptions for, and discussions of, the operation of organizations remain predominantly concerned with the internal activities, organizational adjustments, and the behavior of individuals.

## INTERNAL VERSUS EXTERNAL PERSPECTIVES ON ORGANIZATIONS

The interest in intraorganizational phenomena is not difficult to understand. First, internal processes are the most visible. Walking into any organization, one finds people who are involved in a variety of activities important to the performance of the organization. As Perrow (1970) aptly noted, at first glance, the statement that organizations are, after all, composed of people is patently obvious.... People inside the organization are visible, accessible, and willing to express their opinions. They are a convenient, if not always adequate, research focus.

In addition to convenience, attention to intraorganizational phenomena is fostered by a cognitive bias to attribute causality to the actions of individuals. Research on the behavior of individuals asked to select causative factors suggests that while actors and participants in an event tend to attribute the outcome to situational factors, observers tend to interpret outcomes as the result of the personal motivation and capabilities of the actors (Jones and Nisbett, 1971). The observers of organizations and organizational behavior share this bias. In one recent illustration of this phenomenon (Wolfson and Salancik, 1977), individuals were given the task of controlling an electric car as it traveled over a model track. Unknown to the individuals, their performance was controlled by alterations in the amount of electrical power reaching various sections of the track. All the actual subjects were motivated to do well, but observers tended to see a performer's success as reflecting the amount of effort expended. In fact, it was the result of the experimenter's manipulation of electricity....

Kelley (1971) perceptively noted that attributions are guided not only by the desire to be correct, but also to provide a feeling of control over situations. Clearly, by attributing outcomes to individual action, the observer has a theory of behavior that implies how to control outcomes. When one does not like what is going on, the simple solution is to replace the individual or change the activities. When, on the other hand, a model is used which attributes causality to contextual factors, one faces a much more difficult task in altering activities or outcomes. Therefore, the feelings of control that derive from attributing organizational actions to individuals reinforce the perceptual and cognitive biases, tending to produce a consistent, self-reinforcing system of perception and attribution that emphasizes the importance of individual action. ...

### The Importance of Individuals in Organizations

The basic, important question of how much of the variance in organizational activities or outcomes is associated with context and how much with individuals has been infrequently addressed. Pfeffer (1977) noted various theoretical reasons for expecting that individuals would have less effect on organizational outcomes than would an organization's context. First, he argued that both personal and organizational selection processes would lead to similarity among organizational leaders. This means that there is a restriction on the range of skills, characteristics, and behaviors of those likely to achieve positions of importance in organizations. Second, even when a relatively prominent position in the organization has been achieved, the discretion permitted to a given individual is limited. Decisions may require the approval of others in the organization; information used in formulating the decisions comes from others; and persons may be the targets of influence attempts by others in their role set—these social influences further constrain the individual's discretion. Finally, it is simply the case that many of the things that affected organizational results are not controlled by organizational participants. In the case of business firms, the economic cycle, tariff and other regulations, and tax policies are either not subject to control by the organization or are controlled only indirectly through persuasion. In school districts, budgets and educational demands, which are largely a function of state legislative action, local economic growth, and demographic factors are largely outside the control of the district administration. Considering all these factors, it is not likely administrators would have a large effect on the outcomes of most organizations.

In a study of 167 companies, Lieberson and O'Connor (1972) attempted to partition variance in sales, profit, and profit margin to the effects of year (economic cycle), industry, company, and finally, administrators. While the estimate of administrative impact varied by industry and was largest in the case of profit margin, the magnitude of the administrative effect was dwarfed by the impact of the organization's industry and the stable characteristics of a given organization. Extending this perspective, Salancik and Pfeffer (1977) examined the effects of mayors on city budget categories for a sample of 30 United States cities. These authors found that the mayoral impact was greatest for budget items such as parks and libraries not directly the subject of powerful interest-group demands, but that, in general, the mayor accounted for less than 10 percent of the variation in most city budget expenditures.

The conditions under which there would be more or less administrative effect is an important issue, and the theoretical perspective developed in this book will suggest some answers. But, it is fair to state that, based on the presently available research evidence, there is much less evidence for profound administrative effects than is reflected in the predominance of an internal orientation in the literature on organizations.

## BASIC CONCEPTS FOR A CONTEXTUAL PERSPECTIVE

...In the remainder of this chapter, we will briefly describe a number of key concepts that develop this perspective. These concepts will assist in bringing coherence to the large body of work on organization and environment and will provide us with the tools for systematically understanding the effect of environments on organizations and the effect of organizations on environments.

### Organizational Effectiveness

The first concept is organizational effectiveness.... The effectiveness of an organization is its ability to create acceptable outcomes and actions. It is important to avoid confusing organizational effectiveness with organizational efficiency, a confusion that is both widespread and more a real than a semantic problem. The difference between the two concepts is at the heart of the external versus internal perspective on organizations. Organizational effectiveness is an *external* standard of how well an organization is meeting the demands of the various groups and organizations that are concerned with its activities. When the automobile as a mode of transportation is questioned by consumers and governments, this is an issue of the organizational effectiveness of automobile manufacturers. The most important aspect of this concept of organizational effectiveness is that the acceptability of the organization and its activities is ultimately judged by those outside the organization. As we shall see, this does not imply that the organization is at the mercy of outsiders. The organization can and does manipulate, influence, and create acceptability for itself and its activities.

The effectiveness of an organization is a sociopolitical question. It may have a basis in economic considerations, as when an individual declines purchase of a product because it is priced too high. The concept is not restricted, however, to decisions that are economically motivated. Rather, it reflects both an assessment of the usefulness of what is being done and of the resources that are being consumed by the organization.

Organizational efficiency is an *internal* standard of performance. The question whether what is being done should be done is not posed, but only how well is it being done. Efficiency is measured by the ratio of resources utilized to output produced. Efficiency is relatively value free and independent of the particular criteria used to evaluate input and output. Because efficiency involves doing better what the organization is currently doing, external pressures on the organization are often defined internally as requests for greater efficiency.... .

The difference between efficiency and effectiveness can be illustrated easily. In the late 1960s, Governor Ronald Reagan of California curtailed the amount of money going to the state university system. He was concerned that state university campuses, particularly Berkeley, were indoctrinating students in radical, left-wing ideas. In response to these political pressures and to forestall further budget cuts, the administrators attempted to demonstrate that they were educating students at an ever lower cost per student. Not surprisingly, this argument had little impact on the governor; indeed, it missed the point of his criticism. Producing revolutionaries at lower cost was not what the governor wanted; rather, he questioned whether the universities produced anything that justified giving them state funds.

### Organizational Environment

The external basis for judging organizational effectiveness makes the concept of environment important. The concept of environment, however, is elusive. In one sense, the environment includes every event in the world which has any effect on the activities or outcomes of the organization. Primary schools are a part of other organizations' environment. Thus, when primary schools fail to teach reading and grammar properly, some organizations may be affected more than others. An organization which does not require people to read as part of their task may be minimally affected.

Other organizations may feel profound effects, as in the case of universities which found themselves spending more and more resources teaching basic reading, grammar, and mathematics skills. Even more affected were publishers, who found it necessary to rewrite many of their textbooks at a seventh- or eighth-grade reading level. The Association of American Publishers had to revise the pamphlet "How to Get the Most Out of Your Textbook" because the college students for whom it was written could not understand it.

Although one can conceive of an organization's environment as encompassing every event that affects it, doing so would not be useful for understanding how the organization responds. Every event confronting an organization does not necessarily affect it. A baking company which has a large inventory of sugar will be less affected by changes in the price of sugar than one which must purchase supplies on the open market continually. Thus, one reason why elements of an environment may have little impact is that the organization is isolated or buffered from them. A second reason why organizations do not respond to every event in the environment is that they do not notice every event, nor are all occurrences important enough to require a response. The term "loosely coupled" has been used to denote the relationship between elements in a social system, such as those between organizations. The effects of organizations on one another are frequently filtered and imperfect (March and Olsen, 1975; Weick, 1976). Loose-coupling is an important safety device for organizational survival. If organizational actions were completely determined by every changing event, organizations would constantly confront potential disaster and need to monitor every change while continually modifying themselves. The fact that environmental impacts are felt only imperfectly provides the organization with some discretion, as well as the capability to act across time horizons longer than the time it takes for an environment to change.

Perhaps one of the most important influences on an organization's response to its environment is the organization itself. Organizational environments are not given realities; they are created through a process of attention and interpretation. Organizations have information systems for gathering, screening, selecting, and retaining information. By the existence of a department or a position, the organization will attend to some aspects of its environment rather than others. Organizations establish subunits to screen out information and protect the internal operations from external influences. Organizational perception and knowledge of the environment is also affected because individuals who attend to the information occupy certain positions in the organization and tend to define the information as a function of their position. If the complaint department is located in the sales division, the flow of information may be interpreted as problems with the marketing and promotion of the product. If it is located in the public relations department, the complaints may be seen as a problem in corporate image. If the function were located in the production department, the complaints might be interpreted as problems of quality control or product design. Since there is no way of knowing about the environment except by interpreting ambiguous events, it is important to understand how organizations come to construct perceptions of reality.

Organizational information systems offer insight to those seeking to analyze and diagnose organizations. Information which is not collected or available is not likely to be used in decision making, and information which is heavily represented in the organization's record keeping is likely to emphatically shape decisions. Some organizations, such as Sears, collect information on a regular basis about worker opinions and morale, while others do not. It is inevitable that those organizations not collecting such information will make decisions that do not take those factors into account. Information systems both determine what will be considered in organizational choice and also provide information about what the organization considers important.... Information, regardless of its actual validity, comes to take on an importance and meaning just because of its collection and availability.

The kind of information an organization has about its environment will also vary with its connections to the environment. Organizational members serve on boards of directors, commissions, and are members of clubs and various other organizations. By sending representatives to governmental hearings or investigatory panels, organizations learn about policies that may affect their operations. Research personnel in industry maintain regular contacts with university research projects that may result in knowledge vital to their interests. In one instance, the director of research for the Petroleum Chemicals Research Division of the Ethyl Corporation, a major producer of lead additives for gasoline, made a personal visit to a university research group one month after it had received a large grant to study the impact of lead in the environment (Salancik and Lamont, 1975). Ethyl had learned of the project from contacts in the government. As the project's major objective was to determine the impact of lead on the environment so that policies regarding the manufacture, sale, and distribution of lead might be assessed, the project was of obvious concern to Ethyl.

How an organization learns about its environment, how it attends to the environment, and how it selects and processes information to give meaning to its environment are all important aspects of how the context of an organization affects its actions.

### Constraints

A third concept important for understanding organization-environment relationships is constraint. Actions can be said to be constrained whenever one response to a given situation is more probable than any other response to the situation, regardless of the actor responding. That is, constraint is present whenever responses to a situation are not random. A person driving down a city street will tend to drive between 25 and 35 miles per hour. The same person on a state or federal highway will tend to drive between 50 and 65 miles per hour. Whatever the reason, the fact that behavior—of drivers, for example—is not random or, in other words, is somewhat predictable suggests that something is constraining behavior in these situations.

Constraints on behavior are often considered to be undesirable, restricting creativity and adaptation. However, in most cases action is not possible without constraints, which can facilitate the choice and decision process. Consider an undergraduate student attempting to decide on a course of study for a given semester. At a large university, there may be hundreds of courses, and if there were no constraint, literally millions of possible program combinations could be constructed. Deciding among these millions of programs would, of course, be difficult and time consuming, if not impossible. Fortunately, program choices are constrained. First, there may be a limit on the number of courses a student is allowed to take, and then, there is the constraint of not being able to be in two places at the same time. A third constraint is that some courses are defined as being appropriate for certain categories of student, such as graduate courses or freshman courses, while others have necessary prerequisites that limit their being chosen. Further constraints are added by general university requirements, and then, requirements particular to the student's own department and chosen degree program. Thus, out of millions of possible programs of study, only a few options will be feasible, permitted by all the various constraints. Instead of facing a difficult information-processing task, the student need choose only among a very limited set of alternatives.

Behavior is almost inevitably constrained—by physical realities, by social influence, by information and cognitive capacity, as well as by personal preferences.

And, in many cases, constraints can be manipulated to promote certain behaviors. In the study of human behavior, when an experimenter designs an experimental situation, he presupposes that he has imposed enough constraints on the situation so that most individuals will behave as he predicts. In a similar fashion, the behavior of larger social units, such as groups and formal organizations, is generally constrained by the interests of others—governments, consumers, unions, competitors, etc.

The concept of constraint explains why individuals account for relatively little variance in the performance and activities of organizational systems. Every individual operates under constraint. Even leaders are not free from it. In a recent study of leadership behavior in an insurance company, it was found that the extent to which supervisors were able to do as their workers wanted was inversely related to the extent to which the supervisors were constrained by other departments (Salancik et al., 1975). Supervisors forced to coordinate and meet the demands of other departments had to behave in ways necessary to meet those demands; they did not have the opportunity to satisfy the desires of their subordinates. The point is that behaviors are frequently constrained by situational contingencies and the individual's effect is relatively small.

## THE ROLE OF MANAGEMENT

We have emphasized the importance of contexts, or situational contingencies, as determinants of organizational behavior. We have attempted to question the internal perspective of organizational functioning and the concomitant belief in the omnipotence of individual administrative action. We have not, however, defined the role of the manager out of existence. It is important to conclude this introductory chapter by making explicit our view of the role of the manager within the theoretical perspective we are developing.

### The Symbolic Role of Management

As has been noted by others (e.g., Kelley, 1971; Lieberson and O'Connor, 1972), individuals apparently desire a feeling of control over their social environments. The tendency to attribute great effect to individual action, particularly action taken by persons in designated leadership positions, may be partially accounted for by this desire for a feeling of personal effectiveness and control. Thus, one function of the leader or manager is to serve as a symbol, as a focal point for the organization's successes and failures—in other words, to personify the organization, its activities, and its outcomes. Such personification of social causation enhances the feeling of predictability and control, giving observers an identifiable, concrete target for emotion and action....

The symbolic role of administrators is, occasionally, constructed with elaborate ritual and ceremony. The inauguration of the president is an uncommon event invested with pomp and expectation. This even though three months earlier both voters and commentators were saying that there was no difference between the candidates. The ritual, however, is necessary.

Why organizations vary in the ritual they associate with their offices of power is little understood. One possibility is that more care and trouble is taken in selecting and installing organizational leaders when they do have influence. Another possibility is just the reverse. The very impotence of leadership positions requires that a ritual indicating great power be performed. People desire to believe in the effectiveness of leadership and personal action. When, in fact, administrators have only minor effects, it might be plausibly argued that ritual, mythology, and symbolism will be most necessary to keep the image of personal control alive. When the administrator really does make a difference and really does affect organizational performance, his effect will be obvious to all and there will be little need to make a show of power and control. It is only when the administrator makes little or no

difference that some symbol of control and effectiveness is needed.

It is interesting to note that the ritual of the inauguration of American presidents has grown over time as the executive bureaucracy has grown. The president personally probably has come to have less and less effect on the basic operations of government, while the rituals associated with the office have increased in scope and grandeur.

That managers serve as symbols is not to deny their importance. Important social functions are served by the manipulation of symbols. The catharsis achieved by firing the unsuccessful football coach or the company executive, or by not reelecting some political figure, is too real to dismiss as unimportant. Those who remain in the organization are left with the hope that things will be improved. And, belief in the importance of individual action itself is reinforced—a belief which, even if not completely true, is necessary to motivate individuals to act at all.

The manager who serves as a symbol exposes himself to personal risks. He is accountable for things over which he has no control, and his personal career and fortunes may suffer as a consequence. The sportscasters' cliche that managers are hired to be fired reflects a great amount of truth about all managers. One of the reasons for having a manager is to have someone who is responsible, accountable for the organization's activities and outcomes. If the manager has little influence over these activities or outcomes, it is still useful to hold him responsible. His firing itself may permit loosening some of the constraints facing the organization.

Since most organizational researchers have assumed that managers were the critical element in actual organizational outcomes, the symbolic role of management has been virtually neglected, except for the brief mention by Mintzberg (1973). We would argue that this is one of the more important functions of management, deserving of more explicit empirical attention.

## The Possibilities of Managerial Action

Saying that managers are symbols to be held accountable does not suggest many purposeful actions for them; yet, there are many possibilities for managerial action, even given the external constraints on most organizations. Constraints are not predestined and irreversible. Most constraints on organizational actions are the result of prior decision making or the resolution of various conflicts among competing interest groups. For instance, the requirement for companies doing business with the government to develop (and, possibly, implement) affirmative action hiring plans for recruiting minorities and women did not suddenly materialize. This constraint has a lengthy history and resulted from the interaction of a variety of groups and individuals. The fact that a constraint exists indicates that sufficient social support has been mustered to bring it into existence. In the social context of organizations, behind every constraint there is an interest group that has managed to have that constraint imposed. Since this is the case, the constraint is potentially removable if it is possible to organize the social support and resources sufficient to remove it.

The social context of an organization is, itself, the outcome of the actions of social actors. Since many constraints derive from the actions of others, one important function of management is influencing these others as a means of determining one's own environment. Organizations frequently operate on their environments to make them more stable or more munificent. One function of management, then, is to guide and control this process of manipulating the environment. Much of this book will describe just how organizations attempt to influence and control their social context.

Another component of managerial action involves both the recognition of the social context and constraints within which the organization must operate and the choice of organizational adjustments to these social realities. Even when there is no possibility for managerial alteration of the social environment, management can still be difficult, for recognizing the realities of the social context is not easy or assured. Many organizations have gotten into difficulty by failing to understand those groups or organizations on which they depended for support or by failing to adjust their activities to ensure continued support.

One image of the manager we have developed is that of an advocator, an active manipulator of constraints and of the social setting in which the organization is embedded. Another image is that of a processor of the various demands on the organization. In the first, the manager seeks to enact or create an environment more favorable to the organization. In the second, organizational actions are adjusted to conform to the constraints imposed by the social context. In reality, both sets of managerial activities are performed. We would like to emphasize that both are problematic and difficult. It requires skill to perceive and register accurately one's social context and to adjust organizational activities accordingly. And, it requires skill to alter the social context that the organization confronts. Both images of the role of management imply a sensitivity to the social context in which the organization is embedded and an understanding of the relationship between the organization and its environment. Both, in other words, require the adoption of an external orientation to guide the understanding of organizational functioning.

## SUMMARY

… We have noted that we are dealing with the problems of the acquisition of resources by social organizations, of the organization's survival, as well as of the use of such resources within organizations to accomplish something. To acquire resources, organizations must inevitably interact with their social environments. No organization is completely self-contained or in complete control of the conditions of its own existence. Because organizations import resources from their environments, they depend on their environments. Survival comes when the organization adjusts to, and copes with, its environment, not only when it makes efficient internal adjustments.

The context of an organization is critical for understanding its activities. Despite considerable pro forma acknowledgment of the environment, managers and researchers continue to attribute organizational actions and outcomes to internal factors. Such attributional processes flow from cognitive and perceptual biases that accompany the observation of organizations, as well as from the desire to view social behavior with a feeling of control. These attributions have led to the neglect and serious underestimation of the importance of social context for understanding organizational behavior. Studies estimating the effects of administrators (e.g., Lieberson and O'Connor, 1972; Salancik and Pfeffer, 1977) have found them to account for about 10 percent of the variance in organizational performance, a striking contrast to the 90 percent of the intellectual effort that has been devoted to developing theories of individual action.

While organizational actions are constrained, and contextual factors do predict organizational outcomes and activities, there are several perspectives on the role of management in organizations consistent with such a theoretical position. In the first place, management serves as a symbol of the organization and its actions. Managers are people to fire when things go poorly, an act that reinforces the feeling of control over organizational actions and results. The symbolic role of management, though as yet unexplored, can be systematically empirically examined. In addition to its symbolic role, management can adjust and alter the social context surrounding the organization or can facilitate the organization's adjustment to its context. Both activities require understanding the social context and the interrelationship between context and the organization. Even as a processor of external demands, management has a problematic task. Many organizational troubles stem from inaccurate perceptions of external demands or from patterns of dependence on the environment. Indeed, we would argue that the image of management as a processor of demands is one that implies a high degree of skill and intelligence. After all, anyone can make decisions or take actions—it requires much more skills to be correct.

# REFERENCES

Bendix, R. 1956. *Work and Authority in Industry*. New York: Wiley.

Burns, T., and G. M. Stalker. 1961. *The Management of Innovation*. London: Tavistock.

Davis, O. A., and M. Hinich. 1966. "A mathematical model of policy formulation in a democratic society." In J. L. Bernd (ed.), *Mathematical Applications in Political Science II*, 175–208. Dallas, Tex.: Southern Methodist University Press.

Fellner, W. 1949. *Competition Among the Few*. New York: Knopf.

Hawley, A. H. 1950. *Human Ecology*. New York: Ronald Press.

Hirsch, P. M. 1975. "Organizational effectiveness and the institutional environment." *Administrative Science Quarterly*, 20: 327–344.

Hirschman, A. O. 1970. *Exit, Voice, and Loyalty*. Cambridge: Harvard University Press.

Jones, E. E., and R. E. Nisbett. 1971. *The Actor and the Observer: Divergent Perceptions of the Causes of Behavior*. Morristown, N.J.: General Learning Press.

Katz, D., and R. L. Kahn. 1966. *The Social Psychology of Organizations*. New York: Wiley.

Kelley, H. H. 1971. *Attribution in Social Interaction*. Morristown, N.J.: General Learning Press.

Kessel, J. H. 1962. "Government structure and political environment: a statistical note about American cities." *American Political Science Review*, 56: 615–620.

Lieberson, S., and J. F. O'Connor. 1972. "Leadership and organizational performance: a study of large corporations." *American Sociological Review*, 37: 117–130.

March, J. G., and J. P. Olsen. 1975. "Choice situations in loosely coupled worlds." Unpublished manuscript, Stanford University.

Mintzberg, H. 1973. *The Nature of Managerial Work*. New York: Harper & Row.

Perrow, C. 1970. *Organizational Analysis: A Sociological View*. Belmont, Calif.: Wadsworth.

Pfeffer, J. 1977. "The ambiguity of leadership." *Academy of Management Review*, 2: 104–112.

Phillips, A. 1960. "A theory of interfirm organization." *Quarterly Journal of Economics*, 74: 602–613.

Salancik, G. R., B. J. Calder, K. M. Rowland, H. Leblebici, and M. Conway. 1975. "Leadership as an outcome of social structure and process: a multidimensional approach." In J. G. Hunt and L. Larson (eds.), *Leadership Frontiers*, 81–102. Ohio: Kent State University Press.

Salancik, G. R., and V. Lamont. 1975. "Conflicts in societal research: a study of one RANN project suggests that benefitting society may cost universities." *Journal of Higher Education*, 46: 161–176.

Salancik, G. R., and J. Pfeffer. 1977. "Constraints on administrator discretion: the limited influence of mayors on city budgets." *Urban Affairs Quarterly*, June.

Schnore, L. F., and R. R. Alford. 1963. "Forms of government and socio-economic characteristics of suburbs." *Administrative Science Quarterly*, 8: 1–17.

Weber, M. 1930. *The Protestant Ethic and the Spirit of Capitalism*. New York: Scribner.

Weick, K. E. 1976. "Educational organizations as loosely coupled systems." *Administrative Science Quarterly*, 21: 1–19.

Williamson, O. E. 1965. "A dynamic theory of interfirm behavior." *Quarterly Journal of Economics*, 79: 579–607.

Wolfson, M. R., and G. R. Salancik. 1977. "Actor-observer and observer-observer attributional differences about an achievement task." *Journal of Experimental Social Psychology*, June.

# 33

# The Network Organization in Theory and Practice

*Wayne E. Baker*

The *network organization* has become a concept in theory and practice. The use of this organizational form has been documented in manufacturing and service firms (see, e.g., Burns and Stalker 1961; Mintzberg 1979; Miles and Snow 1986; Eccles and Crane 1987), and the concept has been promoted by the popular business press (e.g., Guterl 1989) and management consultants (e.g., Nolan, Pollock, and Ware 1988). Prior studies have compiled a useful qualitative base of knowledge about the network organization. In this chapter, I develop the network organization concept with grater theoretical and methodological precision in order to advance the concept in theory and inform the adoption of the network organizational form in practice.

The concept of the network organization may be placed in the context of current debates in organizational theory. Organizational change has "provoked some of the most spirited debates in contemporary organization studies" (Aldrich and Marsden 1988:380). Strategic-choice theorists emphasize the ability of managers to redesign organizations to fit changing tasks and environments. In contrast, population ecologists stress organizational inertia—the inability to change structures and processes once established. In essence, population ecologists view organizational design as a wager on fitness that, once placed, consigns an organization to its fate.

The network organization evades organizational inertia by its very nature. The network form is designed to handle tasks and environments that demand flexibility and adaptability. A network organization can flexibly construct a unique set of internal and external linkages for each unique project. Unlike a bureaucracy, which is a fixed set of relationships for processing all problems, the network organization molds itself to each problem. Moreover, it adapts itself not by top-management fiat but by the interactions of problems, people, and resources; within the broad confines of corporate strategy, organizational members autonomously work out relationships. This self-adaptability feature led Eccles and Crane (1988) to call the network form a "self-designing" organization. At least in metaphor, the network organization is a market mechanism that allocates people and resources to problems and projects in a decentralized manner. Like a market, efficiency is assumed. For example, in a network organization a novel problem is routed by the shortest path to the right people, while in a hierarchy a novel problem takes long paths by wending its way through channels established for familiar (routine) problems. The intrinsic ability of the network organization to repeatedly redesign itself to accommodate new tasks, unique problems, and changing environments enables such organizations to escape the plight of forms such as bureaucracy, which ossify and become incapable of change.

All known network organizations evolved unplanned or resulted from the redesign of a non-network organization. In this chapter, I study a professional

Baker, Wayne E. (1992). "The Network Organization in Theory and Practice," in N. Nohria and R. G. Eccles (Eds.), *Networks and Organizations* (pp. 397–429). Boston, Mass.: Harvard Business School Press.

service firm in which the network design was a strategic choice of the founders. The organization, a commercial real estate development firm; began with the network concept as a *conscious* design *prior* to its creation.[2] This provides a rare opportunity to explore the limits and possibilities of the network model where it was implemented in a setting (relatively) uncontaminated by the residues of previous structures, processes, and history. Further, it permits the evaluation of organizational theory put into practice: the network organization as an ideal-type versus real organizational structure.

The presentation is organized in three sections. In section 1, I develop the concept of the network organization in theory. After discussing various conceptions and misconceptions about the network organization, I provide a concrete theoretical definition. In short, it is a social network that is *integrated* across formal boundaries. Interpersonal ties of any type are formed without respect to formal groups or categories. This conceptual definition, as I discuss, is akin to Blau's macrostructual theory of formal differentiation and intergroup relations (e.g., Blau 1977; Blau and Schwartz 1984; Calhoun, Meyer, and Scott 1990) but applied at the organizational level.

In section 2, I describe the data collected on the various networks of relationships among members of the commercial real estate development firm and present a simulation-based method for hypothesis testing. This approach adopts the general logic of blockmodeling (e.g., White, Boorman, and Breiger 1976) but replaces structural equivalence as a basis of subgroup formation with Blau' focus on formal differentiation (cf. Marsden 1981). A priori blockmodels are created, using formal group membership to partition actors into blocks and simulation techniques to compare real a priori blockmodels against the baseline of a theoretical ideal-typical network organization.

Concluding remarks are presented in section 3.

# 1. THE NETWORK ORGANIZATION IN THEORY

## *Some Clarifications*

The concept of a "network organization" suffers from semantic ambiguity, multiple interpretations, and imprecise definitions. Therefore the term must be clarified before we use it further.

**1.** The network organization is a specific organizational type, but the mere presence of a network of ties is not its distinguishing feature. *All* organizations are networks—patterns of roles and relationships—whether or not they fit the network organization image. Organizational type depends on the particular pattern and characteristics of the network. For example, a network characterized by a rigid hierarchical subdivision of tasks and roles, vertical relationships, and an administrative apparatus separated from production is commonly called a bureaucracy. In contrast, a network characterized by flexibility, decentralized planning and control, and lateral (as opposed to vertical) ties is closer to the network organization type. The chief structural characteristic of a network organization is the high degree of integration across formal boundaries.

**2.** A network organization is characterized by integration across; formal boundaries of *multiple types* of *socially important* relations. Such "thick" network organizations are integrated over many relations—strong and Weak task-related communication, informal socializing, advice-giving and advice-getting, promotion decisions, and so on. The thick network concept is consistent with descriptions of known network organizations (see, e.g., Burns and Stalker 1961; Mintzberg 1979; Eccles and Crane 1987). In contrast, management consultants and other practitioners often think of what can be called "thin" network organizations: firms with extensive electronic communication networks (see, e.g., Nolan and Pollock 1986; Nolan, Pollock, and Ware 1988). Though communication technology may help integrate an organization, there is scant consideration of the extent to which the organization is integrated over multiple types of socially important relations.

**3.** For a network organization, integration covers *vertical* and *spatial* differentiation as well as *horizontal* differentiation. Considerations of organizational integration are often confined to coordination and interaction between horizontal units such as production, marketing, and research and development. Lawrence and Lorsch's (1967) classic study of differentiation and integration is a case in point. To define and study a network organization, however, the concept of integration must be extended to include interaction across vertical boundaries (hierarchical levels) and across spatial boundaries (multiple geographic locations) as well.

**4.** The network organization form is not limited to professional service firms. The task and environmental characteristics that induce integration in professional service firms (see, e.g., Eccles and Crane 1987) also appear in force in other industries—manufacturing (Burns and Stalker 1961), Hollywood feature film making (Baker and Faulkner 1991), book publishing (Powell 1985; Miles and Snow 1986), and aerospace and petrochemicals (Mintzberg 1979)—and induce the emergence of network organizations in these settings as well.

### Differentiation and Integration

To advance both theory and practice, it is necessary to move beyond the typical qualitative definitions of a network organization (Eccles and Crane 1987; Mintzberg 1979) and quantify its structural properties. To do so, I examine two key principles of organizational design—*differentiation* and *integration*. Differentiation refers to the formal

division of an organization into ranks, functions, departments, work teams, and so on. It includes vertical differentiation such as hierarchical levels, horizontal differentiation such as functional areas, and spatial differentiation such as multiple locations.[3] Integration refers to the degree of coordination (or, in a broader sense, interaction) among organizational units, however differentiated.[4] The critical distinguishing feature of a network organization, is a high degree of *integration*. In the ideal-typical network organization, all members are well integrated: formal categories or groups such as formal position, geographic location, and market focus are not significant barriers to interaction. Interpersonal ties of all types—task-related communication, advice, socializing, and so on—are as easily established *between* as *within* formal groups or categories.

Concepts from Blau's macrostructural theory of intergroup relations (e.g., Blau 1977; Blau and Schwartz 1984; Calhoun, Meyer, and Scott 1990) may be used to relate differentiation and integration in an ideal-typical network organization. According to Blau, rates of social interaction between groups (e.g., intermarriage) are a function of "ingroup bias" and "opportunities for contact." Ingroup bias is a preference to associate with similar alters, such as a preference to marry within the same ethnic group. Opportunities for contact refers to differentiation of a population, including *heterogeneity* (division into nominal categories or groups such as race and religion) and *inequality*: differences in income or education, for example, along an interval scale, usually measured as the Gini index. Only heterogeneity is of concern here.

The relationship of formal differentiation and integration in an ideal-typical network organization can now be stated precisely: intergroup relations in a network organization are associated with heterogeneity—opportunities for contact—not with ingroup biases. Interaction in an ideal-typical network organization does not exhibit preferences for ingroup instead of outgroup ties; in other words, formal boundaries do not inhibit relationships. The probability of a tie between members of two different formal groups is a function of the number and relative sizes of formal groups in the organization.

Note that the *reason* for a high degree of integration does not enter into the structural definition of a network organization. A network organization can result naturally from integration-producing forces such as the task and environmental characteristics we will discuss, or from the intentional use of integrating mechanisms—formal liaison positions, multifunctional task forces, role-set composition,[5] formal job rotation, multigroup conferences, facility design, and so on—that act to offset disintegrating forces.

### Ingroup and Intergroup Relationships

What induces ingroup ties and intergroup affiliations? For managers, this is more than an academic question. Because many forces act against integration, a network organization may not arise spontaneously and must be intentionally created by the use of integrating mechanisms. (Of course, many forces are outside management control and cannot be altered directly.) The forces that induce or inhibit integration may be classified into three types: task characteristics, organizational characteristics, and environmental factors. I will summarize the three types briefly, focusing particularly on their effects on the integration of organizational networks across formal boundaries.

*Task Characteristics* The nature of tasks may require interaction across formal boundaries. In investment banks, for example, three task characteristics—the need to process large amounts of information quickly, the production of unique products ("deals"), and the close involvement of customers and suppliers (e.g., law firms) in the production process— create the need for flexible and frequent intergroup ties (Eccles

and Crane 1987). The production of unique products, for example, creates regular and frequent cross-group interaction because the mix of experts (e.g., product specialists) and client managers changes from deal to deal. Task characteristics may also necessitate specialization, especially when tasks are nonroutine and require particular knowledge and expertise. Specialization is evident in professional services (such as the proliferation of product specialists in investment banks) and would be expected to reduce integration (but see the potential countervailing effect of heterogeneity discussed in the following section).

Commercial real estate development shares some task characteristics with investment banking, especially the production of unique products and close interaction with clients and suppliers (e.g., law firms, builders, architects, municipal authorities), which should induce integrated organizational networks. However, real estate projects are typically fewer and of longer duration than investment banking deals; such differences should yield less natural integration in real estate firms, compared with the integration of investment banks. These effects, however, could be offset by the use of generalists as integrative devices. Even though real estate development has experienced task specialization and the proliferation of specialists, the firm studied here requires partners and leasing agents to be generalists. Generalists help to integrate an organization because they have wider and more diverse egocentric networks than do specialists.

It is important to emphasize that integration-inducing task characteristics are found in both service and manufacturing firms. Whenever products or projects are unique, require input from various experts, and must be solved creatively, an integrated organization is more effective (see, e.g., Mintzberg 1979)—whether a service is provided or a tangible product is made.

*Organizational Characteristics* Many organizational characteristics influence and shape social interaction. As system size increases, for example, the expected number of contacts per person increases at a multiplicative rate, but time and energy constraints eventually dampen the effect (Mayhew and Levinger 1976). But as *group* size increases, the probability of *outgroup* ties decreases (Blau and Schwartz 1984), suggesting that it is increasingly difficult to sustain integration as an organization grows and differentiates. Indeed, the partners of the real estate firm intuitively recognized the potential deleterious effect of size.

Size also influences integration via its relationship to differentiation. Organizational size is positively associated with the extent of vertical differentiation (more layers), horizontal differentiation (greater division of labor and more functional specialization), and, though the evidence is mixed, with spatial differentiation (more locations) (e.g., Meyer 1972; Mayhew et al. 1972; Blau and Schoenherr 1971). The units formed by differentiation can become loci of ingroup biases, impeding the integration of the organization. For example, as Lawrence and Lorsch (1967) documented in their classic study, members of different departments develop divergent emotional and cognitive orientations that can obstruct the formation of interdepartmental ties. Similarly, geographic separation can permit the emergence of divergent subcultures and decrease the probability of intergroup affiliations. Spatial distance decreases the likelihood of contact (e.g., Blau and Schwartz 1984; Mayhew and Levinger 1976) so that geographic dispersion, which raises the costs of (intergroup) interaction, can decrease outgroup ties and increase ingroup ties. In short, differentiation can create favorable circumstances for the emergence of ingroup biases. These biases can occur for social psychological reasons (the tendency to associate with like others, such as those from the same subculture) and for economizing reasons (the efficient allocation of finite time and energy).[6]

But differentiation can have paradoxical effects. Differentiation means more differences among individuals, which reduce the rate of intergroup ties, but differentiation itself increases the likelihood of intergroup ties because it constrains available choices (Blau and Schwartz 1984:40–42). The opportunity structure created by heterogeneity can increase the chance of intergroup contacts and even overwhelm strong tendencies for ingroup choice. Despite common intuition, a well-integrated organization can be created naturally by the formal division of an organization, even in the face of ingroup tendencies.

Other organizational factors that facilitate a well-integrated organization include personnel selection, control systems, facility design, and cultural norms and values. For example, the senior partners of the real estate firm select personnel that "fit" the culture of a network organization (e.g., gregarious generalists, not reclusive specialists). Recruitment is highly selective, involving a lengthy and intensive process of repeated interviews and mandatory participation at social events and recreational activities, and powerful socialization takes place on the job.

An intensified need for frequent communication and interaction across formal boundaries can be created by vague roles and responsibilities (Eccles and Crane 1987), which at the real estate firm is exacerbated by the absence of written policies or objectives, lack of formal strategic planning, and lack of formal performance appraisals. Senior partners play down status distinctions that might discourage intergroup ties.

Finally, organizational form reflects the personal preferences and choices of key decision makers (Andrews 1980). At the real estate firm, the network model reflects the preferences of the CEO and senior partners. The CEO, for example, expressed a clear dislike for formal administration. The network form, which emphasizes decentralized planning, decision making, and control, does not require a traditional (hierarchical) administrator. But the senior partners' preference for a network organization is more than a mere taste for informality; they believe that this form is more efficient and effective internally, as well as a better fit to environmental demands (discussed in next section). For example, it is considered to be cost efficient because it can produce the same as a hierarchically organized firm but with fewer people. The use of generalists reduces costs because project teams can be smaller, outside consultants are required less often, and the firm is not burdened with excessive overhead costs in the form of expensive internal consultants (specialists).[7] Such cost efficiencies helped the firm survive a predicted downturn in the real estate market. Planned integration of deal makers and support staff may offer similar benefits. For example, locating the accounting staff at headquarters and working to create connections between accountants and deal makers ensures quick and accurate transmission of vital information.

*Environmental Characteristics* A principal tenet of organizational theory is that structure is related to environment (e.g., Aldrich and Marsden 1988). Organizations that fit their environments will perform better and are more likely to survive than those that do not (Emery and Trist 1965; Wholey and Brittain 1986). Network (or organic) structures are better suited to complex, rapidly changing, and turbulent environments than hierarchical (or mechanistic) structures, which do better in stable, simple, routine environments (Burns and Stalker 1961; Mintzberg 1979; Miles and Snow 1986). While many organizations buffer their "technological core" from the environment (Thompson 1967), the organization and its environment are closely intermeshed in the production of professional services.

At the real estate firm, many partners believe the network design is a good fit to the dynamic real estate environment, permitting quick and flexible responses to project and market demands. Internal ties among partners, leasing agents, project engineers, accountants, and others easily intermix with externalties to brokers, lawyers, architects, contractors, and municipalities—all of which shift and remix as projects progress through stages of development, new projects come on-line, and other projects are completed. In addition,

partners believe that an integrated organization enables the firm to present "one front" to brokers and customers, and to "cross-sell" customers (e.g., marketing the development of industrial warehouse space to a client who had already employed the firm to develop office space).

While a turbulent and complex environment might induce integration, it can also exacerbate ingroup biases. For example, the complexity of a market is simplified by classifying it into types and establishing internal divisions that mirror them. The real estate firm in my study has three market foci with internal divisions to match: retail, industrial, and office real estate. Each market group revolves around a unique "focus" of interest (Feld 1981) with specialized task requirements and personnel. Each interacts with a specialized organizational subenvironment, including distinct economic and political conditions and specialized external relationships with customers and suppliers (e.g., architects, contractors). Such differences can engender divergent cognitive and emotional orientations (Lawrence and Lorsch 1967) and impede integration. Thus the match of internal organizational structure with external market structure can seriously obstruct overall integration.

## 2. DATA AND METHODS

### Data
A multimethod/multistage approach was used to collect qualitative and quantitative data. Informal interviews were conducted with all senior partners, most partners and leasing agents, and a small sample of support staff personnel. In sum, 77 usable surveys were obtained, yielding a 95 percent response rate.

### A Method for Hypothesis Testing
To evaluate real organizational networks I have developed simulation procedures that

permit hypothesis testing. The approach uses the general logic of blockmodeling (e.g., White, Boorman, and Breiger 1976).

The approach used in the present study was developed for two main reasons: (1) It permits a simple, straightforward, and valid operationalization of the network organization and tests of hypotheses. (2) The simplicity and intuitive nature of the approach improves communication with and between the diverse audiences represented.

*The Method* In the basic blockmodeling approach, one attempts to derive a model of social structure from social network data that is a simpler, reduced representation of the underlying data. This model (called an image) is generated by aggregating nodes into distinct sets (or blocks), using the rule of structural equivalence,[8] and treating each set as internally homogeneous and homogeneous in its relations to every other set.

## 3. CONCLUSION

Organizational design is a solution to problems. As a purposive social system that directs concerted collective action toward a common goal (Aldrich and Marsden 1988), an organization must be designed to process raw materials, people, and information; to do so, it must delineate a division of labor, roles and relationships, coordination mechanisms, and so on. As an incomplete social system, an organization must be designed to relate to its environment—suppliers, customers, regulators, competitors, and the like. Firms with organizational designs that solve such problems more efficiently or effectively tend to outperform rivals with ill-suited organizational designs. The multidivisional form, for example, is considered to be a more efficient solution than the traditional unitary form to problems created by large size and complexity (Armour and Teece 1978; Chandler 1977; Williamson 1975).

So too with the network organization. As a flexible and self-adapting organization, it is well suited to unique customized projects, close customer and supplier involvement in the production process, and complex turbulent environments. These task and environmental characteristics are often found together in professional services, contributing to the widespread appearance of the network organizational form in financial services, engineering and architectural services, commercial real estate development, advertising, and management consulting. In the present case, the real estate firm adopted the network model because it was considered to be cost efficient, suited to tasks and environment, and compatible with the antibureaucratic values of key decision makers. Several competitors in the same market were organized more hierarchically and suffered known difficulties in fostering ties across formal boundaries. Though comparative performance data are not available,[9] senior partners claimed that the firm was doing well, which was consistent with all outward appearances and reputation in the business community. Most important, the firm has never laid off an employee, unlike all its competitors, even in the recent downturn in the real estate market. But the ultimate test of the network design will be the extent to which its self-designing capabilities will enable it to escape organizational inertia.

Is the real estate firm integrated? I used a strong test to evaluate the integration of the organization: comparison of real networks against the network organization as an ideal type. In theory, a network organization is *integrated* across formal boundaries; interpersonal ties of all types are formed without respect to vertical, horizontal, or spatial differentiation. Against this high standard, real organizational networks fared well:

1. For the firm as a whole, spatial differentiation impedes integration by both strong and weak ties, but weak ties integrate the firm across formal groups created by horizontal differentiation, and the firm

is integrated by strong and weak ties across formal group boundaries created by vertical differentiation.

**2.** The networks of deal makers are integrated across formal boundaries created by vertical and spatial differentiation. Formal, position is not a barrier to strong ties, weak ties, or informal socializing ties. Further, weak ties, social ties, and promote ties integrate deal makers across the dimension of geography (though strong and advice ties tend to occur within geographic units). Despite integration across vertical and spatial boundaries, horizontal boundaries strongly impede integration, especially for strong, advice, promote, and social ties.

**3.** The CEO is not a critical node in the deal-maker networks. Even though the CEO occupies a very central position, especially in strong-tie networks, removal of the CEO does not cause existing strong-tie and weak-tie networks in the "operating core" (Mintzberg 1979) of deal makers to become substantially more or less integrated than they already are.

Of the three formal dimensions, horizontal differentiation proved to be the greatest impediment to integration: market groups created the highest hurdle for intergroup interaction. This may be because the formal dimension of horizontal differentiation is more directly linked to and influenced by the firm's environment than either vertical or spatial differentiation. The internal division of the firm into retail, office, and industrial groups mirrors the external structure of the real estate market. Each market group revolves around a "focus" of interest (Feld 1981) that induces ingroup bias; each market group conducts unique projects and specialized tasks, and engages in specialized external relationships, with customers, suppliers (e.g., architects, contractors), and regulatory agencies. Neither natural integrative forces nor intentional integration, mechanisms were able to fully overcome barriers created by market groups.

Although the real estate firm is not fully integrated, I conclude that it is moderately well integrated because none of the three dimensions of formal differentiation is a significant barrier to interaction at *two* levels: the firm as a whole and the operating core of deal makers. Lack of integration at one level is compensated by integration at the other. Spatial dispersion is a barrier for the firm as a whole, but deal makers are able to overcome the "friction'" of space. Horizontal divisions impede the integration of deal makers, but the firm as a whole is integrated by weak ties across these groups. *Both* levels are well integrated across vertical boundaries. Finally, the relative integration of the real estate firm is evident in an analysis of reachability. As shown in Figure 33.1, more than 95 percent of all pairs in the firm are "reachable" with more than 65 percent reachable in paths of two links or less. Figure 33.2 shows comparable percentages for the bank wiring room.[10]

In general, this study makes contributions to theory, methods, and practice. For theory, a contribution is a precise structural definition of a network organization. A network organization is *integrated* across formal groups created by vertical, horizontal, and spatial differentiation for any type of relation. This structural definition of a network organization can be easily operationalized as an amorphous a priori blockmodel (i.e., when partitions are formed on the basis of formal group membership). For network methods, a contribution is the development of simulation techniques for statistical hypothesis that compare the goodness-of-fit (*b*) of real blockmodels against the baseline of the amorphous image. These techniques are generally applicable. They can be used to assess the statistical significance of social networks by formal groups, as in this case, or on bases such as structural equivalence or other attributes. Finally, for practice, the

## FIGURE 33.1 • MINIMUM DISTANCES FOR STRONG AND WEAK TIES, REAL ESTATE FIRM

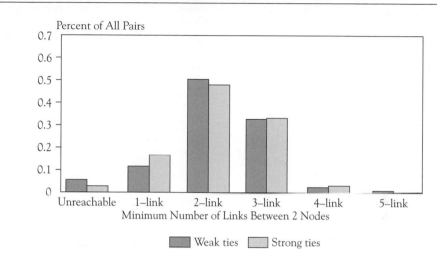

application of the theory and methods to evaluate a real network organization provides insights into specific; management questions about the actual integration of the firm. The approach can be used, to evaluate any management question that can be posed and operationalized as a particular network pattern.

## FIGURE 33.2 • MINIMUM DISTANCES FOR HELPING AND LIKING TIES, BANK WIRING ROOM

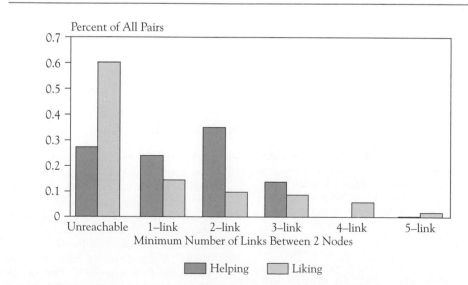

## NOTES

1. The chapter is the revision of a paper prepared for the symposium on Networks and Organizations: Theory and Practice, Harvard Business School, August 20–23, 1990. The original symposium paper was presented under the title "Ideal versus Real Structure in an Intentional Network Organization."

2. The real estate firm used Gore's (n.d.) *lattice organization* as its organizational blueprint. Gore defines the characteristics of the lattice organization as (1) no fixed or assigned authority; (2) direct person-to-person communication; (3) natural leadership defined by skills and experiences; (4) journeyman apprentice environment; (5) group-imposed discipline; and (6) constant interaction with other members of the organization. (The sixth characteristic is my primary focus in this analysis.)

3. I limit the use of differentiation to the division of a social system into *formal* categories or groups, like Blau and associates (e.g., Blau and Schwartz 1984; Calhoun, Meyer, and Soott 1990), but I fully acknowledge the existence and importance of *informal* differentiation, such as groups formed on the basis of structural equivalence (e.g., White, Boorman, and Brieger 1976), consistent with network theory.

4. In their classic study, Lawrence and Lorsch define integration as "the quality of the state of collaboration that exists among departments [i.e., horizontal differentiation] that are required to achieve unity of effort by the demands of the environment" (1967:11).

5. Role set composition includes the use of generalists instead of specialists. Generalists, by virtue of multiple roles, have wider and more diverse egocentric networks than specialists, who occupy single roles. Dual-role occupancy, such as "artistic hyphenate" (screenwriter-director) in Hollywood film making, is another example (Baker and Faulkner 1991).

6. Ingroup biases can also develop when structural differentiation intersects gender stratification. Consider the differentiation of the firm into deal makers and accounting staff. A partner told me that integra-tion of the two groups was inhibited by the fact that most deal makers are male and most account ants female, but participation in sports (an informal integrating mechanism) was almost exclusively male.

7. Real estate generalists were easily switched from development activities in weal markets or products to strong markets products, or from an inactive stage (e.g., initiation of new developments) to an active stage (e.g., leasing or managing existing properties).

8. Two actors are structurally equivalent if they have the same relationships to all other actors. That is, $a$ and $b$ are structurally equivalent if and only if $aRc <=> bRc$ and $cRa <=> cRb$ for any $c$ and any relation (e.g., Breiger, Boorman, and Arabie 1975:330).

9. Comparative performance data are almost impossible to obtain or determine because most commercial real estate firms are privately held and secretive, and properties are held as freestanding units, making it difficult to determine aggregate values.

10. Though the comparison may be tenuous due to important differences in tasks and contexts, reachability in the 77 person real estate firm can be contrasted with the distribution of minimum distances for "helping" and "linking" ties in the 14-person bank wiring room depicted in Figure 33.2. For example, 60 percent of all pairs are unreachable for liking ties, and almost 30 percent are unreachable for helping ties. Even though the bank wiring room was one-fifth the size of the real estate firm, it was clearly much more fragmented.

## REFERENCES

Aldrich Howard E., and Peter Marsden. 1988. "Environments and Organizations." In Neil. J. Smelser, ed., *Handbook of Sociology*. Beverly Hills: Sage, pp. 361–392.

Andrews, Kenneth R. 1980. *The Concept of Corporate Strategy*. Homewood, IL: Irwin.

Armour, Henry Ogden, and David J. Teece. 1978. "Organizational Structure and Economic Performance: A Test of the Multidivisional Hypothesis." *Bell Journal of Economics* 9:106–122.

Baker, Wayne E., and Robert R. Faulkner. 1991. "Role as Resource in the Hollywood Film Industry." *American Journal of Sociology* 97:279–309.

Blau, Peter M. 1977. *Inequality and Heterogeneity.* New York: Free Press.

Blau, Peter M., and Richard A. Schoenherr 1971. *The Structure of Organizations*, New York: Basic Books.

Blau, Peter M., and Joseph E. Schwartz. 1984. *Crosscutting Social Circles.* New York: Academic Press.

Burns, Tom, and George M. Stalker. 1962. *The Management of Innovation.* London: Tavistock.

Calhoum, Craig, Marshall W. Meyer, and W. Richard Scott. 1990. *Structures of Power and Constraint* Cambridge: Cambridge University Press.

Chandler Alfred D. 1977. *The Visible Hand: The Managerial Revolution in American Business.* Cambridge, MA: Harvard University Press.

Eccles, Robert G., and Dwight B. Crane. 1987. "Managing Through Networks In Investment Banking." *California Management Review* 30:176–195.

—. 1988. *Doing Deals: Investment Banks at Work.* Boston: Harvard Business School Press.

Emery, F. E., and E. L. Trist. 1965. "The Causal Texture of Organizational Environments." *Human Relations* 18:21–32.

Feld, Scott. 1981. "The Focused Organization of Social Ties." *American Journal of Sociology* 86:1015–1035.

Guterl, Fred V. 1989. "Goodbye, Old Matrix." *Business Month* (February): 32, 34, 35, 38.

Lawrence, Paul R., and Jay W. Lorsch. *Organization and Environment: Managing Differentiation and Integration.* Boston: Harvard Business School Division of Research.

Marsden, Peter V. 1981. "Models and Methods for Characterizing the Structural Parameters of Groups." *Social Networks* 3:1–27.

Mayhew, Bruce H., Roger L. Levinger, J. Miller McPherson, and Thomas R. James. 1972. "System Size and Structural Differentiation in Formal Organizations: A Baseline Generator for Two Major Theoretical Propositions." *American Sociological Review* 37:629–633.

Mayhew, Bruce H., and Roger L. Levinger. 1976. "Size Density of Interaction in Human Aggregates." *American Journal of Sociology* 82:86–110.

Miles, Raymond E., and Charles C. Snow. 1986. "Organizations: New Concepts for New Forms." *California Management Review* 28:62–73.

Mintzberg, Henry. 1979. *The Structuring of Organizations.* Englewood Cliffs, NJ: Prentice-Hall.

Nolan, Richard L., and Alex J. Pollock. 1986. "Organization and Architecture, or Architecture and Organization." *Stage by Stage* 6:1–10.

Nolan, Richard L., Alex J. Pollock, and James P. Ware. 1988. "Toward the Design of Network Organizations." *Stage by Stage* 8:1–12.

Powell, Walter W. 1985. *Getting into Print.* Chicago: University of Chicago Press.

Rohatgi, V. K. 1976. *An Introduction to Probability Theory and Mathematical Statistics.* New York: Wiley.

Thompson, James D. 1967. *Organizations in Action.* New York: McGraw-Hill.

White, Harrison C., Scot A. Boorman, and Ronald L. Brieger. 1976. "Social Structure form Multiple Networks, I: Blockmodels of Roles and Positions." *American Journal of Sociology* 81:730–780.

Wholey, Douglas R., and Jack W. Brittain. 1986. "Organizational Ecology: Findings and Implications." *Academy of Management Review* (July): 513–533.

Williamson, Oliver E. 1975. *Markets and Hierarchies.* New York: Free Press.

# CHAPTER 9

# *Theories of Organizations and Society*

Chapter 8, "Theories of Organizations and Environments," describes how open systems organization theories have evolved and developed over the past four to five decades from viewing organizations as systems that *are in the environment and interact with it* into systems that *are integral components of their environment.* Changes in society and in society's views of organizations separate this chapter from Chapter 8, "Theories of Organizations and Environments." Perhaps this chapter should be titled "Theories of Organizations in Changing Societies."

The concept of open systems has thus evolved beyond its original meaning—interactive flows of influences and effects across organization boundaries and into the rest of the environment—to include the understanding that organizations are inseparable from the "rest of the environment." In reality as well as in theory, organizations truly are integral parts of the environment—including their society.

Long-standing open systems theory explains: A company builds automobiles, for example, that when driven affect the social, political, economic, and physical environment which, in turn, affects the public's goodwill toward the firm and therefore people's inclination to buy its automobiles or to work for the firm. The firm thus needs to take into account that its effects on its environments come back to affect its well-being.

More recent open *societal* systems theories go farther in arguing that because the automobile-producing firm is part of the environment—a member of its local, national, and international community—it has obligations that go well beyond its own well-being. Because a company reaps many benefits from its existence in a "healthy community" or "healthy society," it is responsible for and benefits from making decisions and acting in ways that *are in society's best interests*—as a responsible citizen.

Classical economists counter that a firm should remain focused on its economic interests. If a firm pursues ends other than profit maximization, it will make decisions that are not in its financial best interests. As other firms do the same, the economy will suffer. The government agencies and nonprofit organizations that are responsible for improving social conditions depend on revenue generated by profitable businesses to provide the tax revenues and philanthropic support. Therefore, asking businesses to pursue ends other than profit maximization is not in the best interest of a society.

Newer open systems organization theorists disagree, counter-arguing that a healthy society and a healthy economic environment are inexorably interrelated. It is short-sighted for firms to limit their interests to profits, not only because corporations are part of and affected by their societal environments but also because they are products of them. They are created under the laws of the society, protected by society's courts, and obtain capital from society's financial institutions. Furthermore, their employees are citizens of the society, and they sell their products to employees of government agencies that regulate them, deliver their products and services on society's transportation networks, and employ citizens educated in society's schools and universities.

In this chapter, we focus on four societal consciousness themes that have received considerable attention from organization theorists and researchers especially since the turn of this century: *diversity/cultural competency*, *social responsibility*, *social entrepreneurship*, and the *blending and blurring* of *the government, nonprofit, and for-profit sectors*. We include the diversity theme in this chapter although it has existed for several decades because its contributions to organization theory have sharpened in recent years—including the notion of *cultural competence*—and have markedly influenced the intellectual development of theories in the other themes.

## DIVERSITY AND CULTURAL COMPETENCY

Two readings are included here that reflect the diversity and cultural competency perspective of organization theory: Joan Acker's "Gendering Organizational Theory," and Mitchell Rice and Audrey Mathews', "A New Kind of Public Service Professional." We have included these two readings in this chapter because of the overarching reasons that diversity and cultural competency are in an organization's long-term best interest—as well as society's best interest. Whereas most of the earlier arguments for diversity were centered on workforce representation and expanding the supply of skilled potential employees, newer theories also emphasize that diverse organizations with culturally competent employees and managers increase organizational effectiveness and thereby improve communities and societies overall—and positively affect the organization's environment.

Joan Acker's "Gendering Organizational Theory" reflects a theme originally popularized by Gareth Morgan (1986): "The way we 'read' organizations influences how we produce them." Feminist organization theorists argue that long-standing male control of organizations has been accompanied and maintained by male perspectives of organization theory. Thus, it is through male lenses that we *see* and analyze organizations. At least four sets of gendered processes perpetuate this male reality of organizations: (1) gender divisions that produce gender patterning of jobs, (2) creation of symbols and images, (3) interactions characterized by dominance and subordination, and (4) "the internal mental work of individuals as they consciously construct their understandings of the organization's gendered structure of work and opportunity and the demands for gender-appropriate behaviors and attitudes." Ordinary activities in organizations are not gender neutral. They perpetuate the "gendered substructure within the organization itself and within the wider society," as well as in organization theory.

"A New Kind of Public Service Professional," by Mitchell Rice and Audrey Mathews asserts, "The resulting effects and affects for organizations and public agencies that manage diversity well are creative problem solving, innovation, and improvements in the organizations' abilities to adapt to other inevitable forces of change." These organizations are able to deliver services and products effectively "to clients and customers with different cultural backgrounds, beliefs, practices, and languages." Theories and knowledge about managing diversity well in today's world require an expanded vision of diversity that uses "a new framework and lenses" that include multiculturalism and cultural competency. Rice and

Mathews base their assertions about organizational diversity and cultural competency in theories of organizational culture (Chapter 7) and organizational behavior (Chapter 3). Cultural competency requires cultural awareness, cultural knowledge, and cultural skills and therefore is dynamic—not static—and "requires frequent learning, relearning, and unlearning about different cultural groups."

## SOCIAL RESPONSIBILITY

The central theme in the literature on social responsibility parallels that of diversity and cultural competency but takes different directions. Organizations and their agents are responsible for the effects of their decisions and actions on the totality of the environment. Obviously, organizations have economic and legal obligations, but from a corporate social responsibility perspective, they also have obligations to make decisions and to act in ways that benefit the full spectrum of corporate stakeholders—not shareholders only (Epstein, 1987). For example, an organization would be acting in a socially responsible manner if it produces products with social or environmental attributes or characteristics, or if it offers its employees a paid day off per month if they use the day to volunteer with selected nonprofit organizations.

It is important to appreciate that social responsibility is about much more than organizations being "nice." As more organizations adopt responsible policies and strategies, the overall social, economic, and physical environments in their communities will improve, and these organizations will benefit in many ways including, for example, having access to better and healthier labor markets and workforces, lower transaction costs, better quality of life, better ecosystems, and stronger markets for products and services.

In "Corporate Citizenship: Social Responsibility, Responsiveness, and Performance," a reading reprinted in this chapter, Archie Carroll and Ann Buchholtz explain it is "partially business's fault that many of today's social problems arose in the first place and, consequently, that business should assume a role in remedying these problems.... Deterioration of the social condition must be halted if business is to survive and prosper in the future." Carroll and Buchholtz view corporate social responsibility as encompassing economic, legal, ethical, and philanthropic components. They use Carroll's "Corporate Social Performance Model" (1979) to integrate economic concerns into a social performance framework and to insert ethical and philanthropic expectations into an economic and legal framework.

## SOCIAL ENTREPRENEURSHIP

Social entrepreneurship has emerged as a global phenomenon in recent years, "driven by a new breed of pragmatic, innovative, and visionary social activities and their networks, social entrepreneurship [and] borrows from an eclectic mix of business, charity, and social movement models to reconfigure solutions to community problems and deliver sustainable new social value" (Nicholls, 2006, p. 2). The movement consists of creative, problem-solving individuals and organizations in the private, nonprofit, and government sectors that are attacking an array of local and global social problems (Bornstein, 2004). "Social entrepreneurs are those people—the practical dreamers who have the talent and the skill and the vision to solve the problems, to change the world for the better... operating in a free market where success is measured not just in financial profit but also in the improvement of the quality of people's lives" (Skoll, 2006, v).

Social entrepreneurship is also partly a reaction to economic, socio-economic, and political pressures (Light, 2008). Over the past several decades, the once clearly visible differences between nonprofit organizations and business firms have been blurring. Most of the longtime revenue sources for nonprofits have been holding steady or declining, and competition among 501(c)(3) nonprofit organizations for these shrinking dollars has increased. Concurrently, pressure on nonprofits to be more business-like and entrepreneurial has intensified. "They [nonprofit organizations] have been challenged to find and develop new sources of income, increase their efficiency,... create venture partnerships with business—to be more like businesses in all respects" (Ott, 2001, p. 358). Thus, many nonprofit organizations have become highly successful at selling products and services in the marketplace and at investing in financial markets (Mosher-Williams, 2006). Meanwhile, many for-profit businesses have been attempting to provide benefits to a wide array of stakeholders across different geographic communities and among communities of interest—as well as shareholders.

These two trends have responded to economic changes for many years, and they also reflect pervasive changes in socioeconomic perspectives. Since the 1980s, business values have been dominant in our society. Governments and nonprofit organizations have been widely viewed as less competent organizational forms that need to learn how to operate more like businesses. Business men and women have been recruited aggressively onto the boards of trustees of 501(c)(3) organizations. Over the past several decades, many nonprofits learned their lessons well and became highly adept at using the funds from entrepreneurial ventures to support their largely tax-exempt social missions.

Social entrepreneurship is an "umbrella term" that includes many types of activities including, for example, cause-related marketing, enterprising individuals committing themselves and their resources, social purpose business ventures dedicated to adding for-profit motivations to the nonprofit sector, new types of philanthropists supporting venture capital-like investment portfolios, and nonprofit organizations "reinventing" themselves.

The context has been more complex since the Great Recession, however. And, a seemingly endless series of well-publicized scandals and failures has shaken confidence in corporations and financial institutions over the past decade: AIG, Enron, Fannie Mae, Freddie Mac, Goldman-Sachs, Global Crossing, Halliburton, Martha Stewart Omnimedia, and Tyco—as well as incredibly high corporate executive compensation packages—to name only a few. Many businesses began engaging in socially beneficial activities to offset widespread public perceptions of uncontrolled corporate greed.

Paul Light's chapter reprinted here, "The Search of Social Entrepreneurship: Drawing Conclusions," presents findings from a wide-ranging study on the differences between highly, moderately, and not very socially entrepreneurially-oriented organizations, using interviews of senior executives in 131 high-performing social benefit organizations. The findings are in four areas: the role of entrepreneurs in stimulating socially entrepreneurial activities; the entrepreneurial ideas; environments that provide opportunities for social entrepreneurship; and characteristics of organizations that tend to be more socially entrepreneurial. Light concludes, "Social entrepreneurship is evolving rapidly both as a concept and as a cause... The field is coalescing around the notion that intractable social problems may not be as intractable as once believed."

The emergence of and interest in social entrepreneurship has resulted from rising social consciousness and social responsibility, and the intersecting trends of creative cross-sector solutions to social problems and the responses of businesses and nonprofits to profound changes in economic and socio-political pressures. Few would have predicted the rapid rise of social entrepreneurship or the nature of its path over the recent decades. It will be interesting to observe its course into the future.

## THE BLENDING AND BLURRING OF THE GOVERNMENT, NONPROFIT AND FOR-PROFIT SECTORS

Although the long-term trend toward the "blurring and blending" of the private, nonprofit, and government sectors has been widely acknowledged for many years, the nature, substance, and magnitude of the blending and blurring continue to change and therefore, also the implications (USGAO, 2007). Indeed, the implications are unclear for the future of many of our core societal institutions and for civil society in general.

In the 1980s and 1990s, this phrase primarily referred to first, contract arrangements for the delivery of government services by nonprofits and the resulting heavy dependence of these nonprofits on the government for revenue; and second, to rapidly expanding entrepreneurial ventures by nonprofits that competed directly with for-profit firms. Overall, government funding has been on a long-term decline. Republicans and Democrats alike in Washington, DC, and in statehouses across the country are clamoring for governments to be *downsized*, for the *devolution* of government services and fiscal responsibility to the lowest levels of government, and for the *diffusion* of government services and responsibility into the nonprofit and for-profit sectors (Ott & Dicke, 2012). Meanwhile, nonprofits are told they must they must be more entrepreneurial in pursuing alternative sources of revenue, and they need to manage their resources and programs efficiently.

While these long-standing meanings of "blending and blurring among the sectors" continue to expand, some relationships among organizations in the three sectors have become deeper and more subtle in recent years, adding complexities to the long-standing meanings. *Network organizations* are a leading example: "horizontal network organizations" span organizational and sectoral boundaries usually with no one person or organization totally in charge (Chapter 8).

*Hybrid organizations*, are partly government agencies, partly for-profit businesses, and/ or partly nonprofit organizations. Hybrid organizations have emerged as it has become increasingly evident to legislative bodies, policy makers, and service providers that no single organization or sector can have effective impact on our most intractable social problems. As the title of David Billis' chapter, which is reprinted here, suggests, "Towards a Theory of Hybrid Organizations" develops a foundation for theory building about organizations that are partly in one sector and partly in another. Billis identifies underlying principles, "ideal type sectors and accountabilities," "hybrid zones," and the most difficult challenges facing hybrid organization theory builders: ownership, appropriate models-in use, and primary accountability.

# BIBLIOGRAPHY

Acker, J. (1992). Gendering organizational theory. In A. J. Mills & P. Tancred (eds.), *Gendering organizational analysis* (pp. 248–260). Thousand Oaks, CA: Sage.

Acker, J. (2006). *Class questions: Feminist answers*. Lanham, MD: AltaMira Press/Rowman & Littlefield.

Alkadry, M. G., & L. E. Tower (2014). *Women and public service: Barriers, challenges, and opportunities*. Armonk, NY: M. E. Sharpe.

Andriof, J., & M. McIntosh, eds. (2001). *Perspectives on corporate citizenship*. London: Greenleaf.

Austin, J. E., & M. M. Seitanidi (2014). *Creating value in nonprofit-business collaborations*. San Francisco: Jossey-Bass/Wiley.

Billis, D. ed. (2010). *Hybrid organizations and the third sector: Challenges for practice, theory and policy*. Houndmills, Basingstoke, Hampshire, UK: Palgrave Macmillan.

Bornstein, D., & S. Davis (2010). *Social entrepreneurship: What everyone needs to know*. New York: Oxford University Press.

Brooks, A. C. (2008). *Social entrepreneurship: A modern approach to social value creation*. Upper Saddle River, NJ: Cengage Learning Prentice Hall.

Carroll, A. B., & A. K. Buchholtz (1989). *Business and society: Ethics and stakeholder management*. Cincinnati, OH: Publishing Co.

Child, C. (2010). Wither the turn? The ambiguous nature of nonprofits' commercial revenue. *Social Forces*, 89, 1–17.

Cox, T., Jr. (2001). *Creating the multicultural organization: The challenge of managing diversity*. New York: John Wiley.

Davis, G. F., D. McAdam, W. R. Scott, & M. N. Zald, eds. (2005). *Social movements and organization theory*. New York: Cambridge University Press.

Dees, J. G., & B. B. Anderson (2006). Framing a theory of social entrepreneurship: Building on two schools of practice and thought. In R. Mosher-Williams, ed., *Research on social entrepreneurship: Understanding and contributing to an emerging field* (pp. 39–66). ARNOVA Occasional Paper Series, 1(3). Indianapolis, IN: Association for Research on Nonprofit Organizations and Voluntary Action.

Dees, J.G., J. Emerson, & P. Economy (2002). *Strategic tools for social entrepreneurs: Enhancing the performance of your enterprising nonprofit*. Hoboken, NJ: Wiley.

Elkington, J. (2008). *The power of unreasonable people: How social entrepreneurs create markets that change the world*. Boston: Harvard Business School Press.

Epstein, E. M. (1987). The corporate social policy process: Beyond business ethics, corporate social responsibility and corporate social responsiveness. *California Management Review*, 29, 99–114.

Ferguson, K. E. (1984). *The feminist case against bureaucracy*. Philadelphia: Temple University Press.

Gardenswartz, L., & A. Rowe (2003). *Diverse teams at work: Capitalizing on the power of diversity*. Alexandria, VA: Society for Human Resource Management.

Guo, C., & W. Bielefeld (2014). *Social entrepreneurship: An evidence-based approach to creating social value*. San Francisco: Jossey-Bass/Wiley.

Guy, M. E., M. A. Newman, & S. H. Mastracci (2010). Are we there yet? From Taylor's triangle to Follett's web; from knowledge work to emotion work. In R. O'Leary, D. M. Van Slyke, & S. Kim, eds., *The future of public administration around the world: The Minnowbrook perspective* (pp. 33– 44). Washington, DC: Georgetown University Press.

Haugh, H. (2006). Social enterprise: Beyond economic outcomes and individual returns. In J. Mair, J. Robinson, &. K. Hockerts, eds., *Social entrepreneurship* (pp. 180–205). New York: Palgrave Macmillan.

Hesselbein, F., M. Goldsmith, R. Beckhard, & R. F. Schubert, eds. (1998). *The community of the future*. San Francisco: Jossey-Bass.

Husted, B. (2000). A contingency theory of corporate social performance. *Business and Society,* *39*(1), 24–48.

Johnston, W. B., & A. H. Packer (1987). *Workforce 2000: Work and workers for the twenty-first century.* Indianapolis, IN: Hudson Institute; Washington, DC: U. S. Department of Labor.

Light, P. C. (2006). Searching for social entrepreneurs: Who they might be, where they might be found, what they do. In R. Mosher-Williams, ed., *Research on social entrepreneurship: Understanding and contributing to an emerging field* (pp. 13–37). ARNOVA Occasional Paper Series, *1*(3). Indianapolis, IN: Association for Research on Nonprofit Organizations and Voluntary Action.

Light, P. C. (2008). *The search for social entrepreneurship.* Washington, DC: Brookings Institution Press.

Mair, J., J. Robinson, & K. Hockerts, eds. (2006). *Social entrepreneurship.* New York: Palgrave Macmillan.

McWilliams, A., & D. Siegel (2001). Corporate social responsibility: A theory of the firm perspective. *Academy of Management Review, 26*(1), 117–127.

Mendel, S. C. (2010). Are private government, the nonprofit sector, and civil society the same thing? *Nonprofit and Voluntary Sector Quarterly, 29,* 717–733.

Morgan, G. (1986, 1997, 2006). *Images of organization.* Thousand Oaks, CA: Sage.

Mosher-Williams, R., ed. (2006). *Research on social entrepreneurship: Understanding and contributing to an emerging field.* Indianapolis, IN: Association for Research on Nonprofit Organizations and Voluntary Action.

Nicholls, A., ed. (2006). *Social entrepreneurship: New models of sustainable social change.* 2nd ed. New York: Oxford University Press.

Nicholls, A., & A. Murdock, eds. (2012). *Social innovation: Blurring boundaries to reconfigure markets.* New York: Palgrave Macmillan.

Ott, J. S. and L. A. Dicke (forthcoming, 2015). The blending and blurring of the sectors. In J. S. Ott and L. A. Dicke, eds., *The nature of the nonprofit sector.* 3rd ed. Boulder, CO: Westview Press/Perseus Books.

Ott, J. S. and L. A. Dicke (2012). Managing under government contracts, through networks, and in collaborations. In J. S. Ott and L. A. Dicke, eds., *Understanding nonprofit organizations.* 2nd ed. (pp. 327–335) Boulder, CO: Westview Press/Perseus Books.

Rice, Mitchell F. & Audrey L. Mathews (2012). A New Kind of Public Service Professional: Processing Cultural Competency Awareness, Knowledge, and Skills, In Kristen A. Norman-Major and Susan T. Gooden, eds., *Cultural Competency for Public Administrators.* (pp. 19-31). Armonk, NY: M. E. Sharpe.

Schwartz, R. (2006). Profit taboo in social enterprise country. *Alliance, 11*(3), 21–32.

Skoll, J., (2006). Preface. In A. Nicholls, ed., *Social entrepreneurship: New models of sustainable social change.* 2nd ed. (pp. v–vi). New York: Oxford University Press.

Smith, S. R., & K. Grønbjerg (2006). Scope and theory of government-nonprofit relations. In W. W. Powell and R. Steinberg, eds., *The nonprofit sector: A research handbook.* 2nd. ed. (pp. 221–242). New Haven, CT: Yale University Press.

Sonenshein, S. (2006). Crafting social issues at work. *Academy of Management Journal, 49*(6), 1158–1172.

Stivers, C. (1993). *Gender images in public administration: Legitimacy and the administrative state.* Newbury Park, CA: Sage.

Thiederman, S. (1991). *Bridging cultural barriers for corporate success: How to manage the multicultural work force.* New York: Lexington.

US GAO (United States Government Accountability Office. (July 24, 2007). *Nonprofit sector: Increasing numbers and key role in delivering federal services*. Testimony before the Subcommittee on Oversight, Committee on Ways and Means, House of Representatives. Washington, DC: U.S. GAO-07-1084T.

Wei-Skillern, J. C., J. E., Austin, H. B. Leonard, & H. H. Stevenson (2008). *Entrepreneurship in the social sector*. Thousand Oaks, CA: Sage.

## 34

# Gendering Organizational Theory

*Joan Acker*

Although early critical analyses of organizational theory (e.g., Acker and Van Houten 1974; Kanter 1977) led to few immediate further efforts, feminist examination of organizational theory has developed rapidly in the last few years (Ferguson 1984; Calás and Smircich 1989a, 1989b; Hearn and Parkin 1983, 1987; Burrell 1984, 1987; Mills 1988; Hearn et al., 1989; Acker 1990; Martin 1990a, 1990b). The authors of these critiques are responding to and helping to create the conditions for a fundamental reworking of organizational theories to account for the persistence of male advantage in male organizations and to lay a base for new critical and gendered theories of organizations that can better answer questions about how we humans come to organize our activities as we do in contemporary societies.

The conditions for a new critique began with the rapid proliferation of studies about women and work, conceptualized in theoretical terms of prefeminist social science. For example, studies of women's economic and occupational inequality, sex segregation, and the wage gap document the extent of the problems but give us no convincing explanations for their persistence or for the apparently endless reorganization of gender and permutations of male power. Similarly, the extensive literature on women and management documents difficulties and differences but provides no adequate theory of gendered power imbalance. The need for new theory was implicit in the inadequacies of old theory.

Developments within feminist theory also provide foundations for a new criticism of organizational theory....

## THINKING ABOUT GENDER

*Gender* refers to patterned, socially produced, distinctions between female and male, feminine and masculine. Gender is not something that people are, in some inherent sense, although we may consciously think of ourselves in this way. Rather, for the individual and the collective, it is a daily accomplishment (West and Zimmerman 1987) that occurs in the course of participation in work organizations as well as in many other locations and relations.

... Gender, as patterned differences, usually involves the subordination of women, either concretely or symbolically, and, as Joan Scott (1986) points out, gender is a pervasive symbol of power.

The term *gendered processes* "means that advantage and disadvantage, exploitation and control, action and emotion, meaning and identity, are patterned through and in terms of a distinction between male and female, masculine and feminine" (Acker 1990: 146; see also Scott 1986; Harding 1986; Connell 1987; Flax 1990). Gendered processes are concrete activities, what people do and say, and how they think about these activities, for thinking is also an activity. The daily construction, and sometimes deconstruction, of gender occurs within material and ideological constraints that set the limits of possibility. For example, the boundaries of sex segregation, themselves continually constructed and reconstructed, limit the actions of particular women and men at particular times. Gendered processes do not occur outside other social processes but are integral parts of these processes—for example, class and race relations—which cannot be fully understood without a comprehension of gender (Connell 1987). At the same time, class and race processes are integral to gender relations. The links between class and race domination and gender are ubiquitous. For example, at the top of the typical Southern California high-tech firm stands the rational, aggressive, controlling white man (occasionally a woman but one who has learned how to operate in the class/gender structure), while at the very bottom there are often women of color working on a production line where they have little control over any aspect of their working lives (Fernandez Kelly and Garcia 1988). Examining how the organization was started and is controlled by these particular men and how these particular women came to be the production workers leads us back into the class/gender/race relations of that time and place. Similarly, if we look at the work processes and organizational controls that keep the firm going, we will see the intertwining of gender, race, and class.

Gendered processes and practices may be open and overt, as when managers choose only men or only women for certain positions or when sexual jokes denigrating women are part of the work culture. On the other hand, gender may be deeply hidden in organizational processes and decisions that appear to have nothing to do with gender. For example, deregulation and internationalization of banking has altered the gender structure of banks in both Sweden (Acker 1991) and Britain (Morgan and Knights 1991). In Sweden, these changes contributed to a growing wage gap between women and men, as women remained in low-wage branch banking and men, chosen more

often for the growing international banking departments, were rewarded with disproportionate salary increases. In Britain, deregulation, and the resulting increase in competitiveness in the industry, was an important cause of reorganization in one bank that gave women new tasks at the expense of some men but still protected the privileges of men in traditional managerial positions. To understand the persistence of gender patterns, even as external changes cause internal organizational restructuring, I think we should consider the gender substructure of organizations and the ways that gender is used as an organizational resource, topics discussed below.

## ELEMENTS IN A THEORY OF GENDERED ORGANIZATIONS

### Gendered Processes

Gendered organizations can be described in terms of four sets of processes that are components of the same reality, although, for purposes of description, they can be seen as analytically distinct. As outlined above, gendering may occur in gender-explicit or gender-neutral practices; it occurs through concrete organizational activities; and its processes usually have class and racial implications as well. Sexuality, in its diverse forms and meanings, is implicated in each of these processes of gendering organizations.

The first set of processes is the production of gender divisions. Ordinary organizational practices produce the gender patterning of jobs, wages, and hierarchies, power, and subordination (e.g., Kanter 1977). Managers make conscious decisions that re-create and sometimes alter these patterns (Cohn 1985); unions, where they exist, often collude, whether intentionally or not. For example, while employers can no longer, by law, advertise for female workers for some jobs and male workers for others, many still perceive women as suited for certain work and men as suited for other work. These perceptions help to shape decisions. The introduction of new technology may offer the possibility for the reduction of gender divisions but most often results in a reorganization, not an elimination, of male predominance (e.g., Cockburn 1983, 1985). The depth and character of gender divisions vary dramatically from one society to another and from one time to another. In Britain, for example, when women first began to enter clerical work, separate offices were often set up so that women and men would not have to meet on the job, thus avoiding the possibility of sexual encounters and resulting in extreme gender segregation (Cohn 1985). Whatever the variation, there is overwhelming evidence that hierarchies are gendered and that gender and sexuality have a central role in the reproduction of hierarchy.

Gendering also involves the creation of symbols, images, and forms of consciousness that explicate, justify, and, more rarely, oppose gender divisions. Complex organizations are one of the main locations of the production of such images and forms of consciousness in our societies. Television, films, and advertising are obvious examples, but all organizations are sites of symbolic production. Gender images, always containing implications of sexuality, infuse organizational structure. The top manager or business leader is always strong, decisive, rational, and forceful—and often seductive (Calás and Smircich 1989b). The organization itself is often defined through metaphors of masculinity of a certain sort. Today, organizations are lean, mean, aggressive, goal oriented, efficient, and competitive but rarely empathetic, supportive, kind, and caring. Organizational participants actively create these images in their efforts to construct organizational cultures that contribute to competitive success.

The third set of processes that reproduce gendered organizations are interactions between individuals, women and men, women and women, men and men, in the multiplicity of forms that enact dominance and subordination and create alliances and exclusions. In these interactions, at various levels of hierarchy, policies that create divisions are developed and images of gender are created and affirmed. Sexuality is involved here, too, in overt or hidden ways; links between dominance and sexuality shape interaction and help to maintain hierarchies favoring men (Pringle 1989). Interactions may be between supervisors and subordinates, between coworkers, or between workers and customers, clients, or other outsiders. Interactions are part of the concrete work of organization, and the production of gender is often "inside" the activities that constitute the organization itself.

The fourth dimension of gendering of organizations is the internal mental work of individuals as they consciously construct their understandings of the organization's gendered structure of work and opportunity and the demands for gender-appropriate behaviors and attitudes (e.g., Pringle 1989; Cockburn 1991). This includes creating the correct gendered persona and hiding unacceptable aspects of one's life, such as homosexuality. As Pringle (1989: 176) says, "Sexual games are integral to the play of power at work, and success for women depends on how they negotiate their sexuality." Such internal work helps to reproduce divisions and images even as it ensures individual survival.

### Gender and Sexuality as Organizational Resources

Gender, sexuality, and bodies can be thought of as organizational resources, primarily available to management but also used by individuals and groups of workers. Simultaneously, however, gender, sexuality, and bodies are problems for management. Solutions to these problems become resources for control. Both female and male bodies have physical needs on the job. Management often controls lunch and toilet breaks as well as physical movement around the workplace as integral elements in furthering productivity. Numbers of researchers, from Crozier on (Acker and Van Houten 1974), have observed that women workers are more tightly controlled in these ways than men workers. Higher-level employees are often rewarded with fewer bodily constraints and special privileges in regard to physical needs—for example, the executive washroom and dining room.

Reproduction and sexuality are often objects of and resources for control. As Burrell (1984: 98) argues, "Individual organizations inaugurate mechanisms for the control of sexuality at a very early stage in their development." Reproduction and sexuality may disrupt ongoing work and seriously undermine the orderly and rational pursuit of organizational goals. Women's bodies, sexuality, and procreative abilities are used as grounds for exclusion or objectification. On the other hand, men's sexuality dominates most workplaces and reinforces their organizational power (Collinson and Collinson 1989). In addition, talk about sex and male sexual superiority helps construct solidarity and cooperation from the bottom to the top of many organizations, thus promoting organizational stability and control.

Gender is also a resource in organizational change. Hacker (1979) showed how technological transformation at AT&T in the 1970s was facilitated by moving women into formerly male jobs slated to be eliminated. Today, in the drive for organizational "flexibility," managements often consciously create part-time jobs, low paid and dead end, to be filled by women (see, e.g., Cockburn 1991). It is gender, and often race, that makes women ideal employees. These are only examples from a multiplicity of processes that suggest the possibilities for research about gender and sexuality in organizational control and change.

### The Gendered Substructure of Organization

The more or less obvious manifestations of gender in organizational processes outlined above are built upon, and in turn help to reproduce, a gendered substructure of organization. The gendered substructure lies in the spatial and temporal arrangements of work, in the rules prescribing workplace behavior, and in the relations linking workplaces to living places. These practices and relations, encoded in arrangements and rules, are supported by assumptions that work is separate from the rest of life and that it has first claim on the worker. Many people, particularly women, have difficulty making their daily lives fit these expectations and assumptions. As a consequence, today, there are two types of workers, those, mostly men, who, it is assumed, can adhere to organizational rules, arrangements, and assumptions, and those, mostly women, who, it is assumed, cannot, because of other obligations to family and reproduction.

Organizations depend upon this division, for, in a free market economy, in contrast to a slave economy, they could not exist without some outside organization of reproduction to take care of supplying workers. In this sense, the gender substructure of organization is linked to the family and reproduction. This relationship is not simply a functional link. It is embedded in and re-created daily in ordinary organizational activities, most of which do not appear on the surface to be gendered. In the exploration of some of these processes, it is possible to see how integral to modern organization this gendered substructure is, and how relatively inaccessible to change it remains.

I began this discussion by considering some of the problems posed by the gendered nature of existing, ostensibly gender-neutral, organizational theory and processes. Feminist critics of traditional theory now widely recognize that this body of theory is gendered, that it implicitly assumes that managers and workers are male, with male-stereotypic powers, attitudes, and obligations (e.g., Acker 1990; Calás and Smircich 1992; Mills 1989).

What is problematic is the discontinuity, even contradiction, between organizational realities obviously structured around gender and ways of thinking and talking about these same realities as though they were gender neutral. What activities or practices produce the facade of gender neutrality and maintain this disjuncture between organizational life and theory? These questions can provide a point of entry into the underlying processes that maintain gender divisions, images, interactions, and identities.

This analytic strategy is based on Dorothy Smith's _The Conceptual Practices of Power_ (1990) in which she argues that concepts that feminists may see as misrepresenting reality—here the concept of gender-neutral structure—indicate something about the social relations they represent. That is, such concepts are not "wrong." On the contrary, they are constructed out of the working knowledge of those who manage and control, thus they say something about processes of power, including the suppression of knowledge about gender. While it is important to "deconstruct" these concepts, revealing hidden meanings, we can, in addition, investigate the concrete activities that produce them.

The break between a gendered reality and gender-neutral thought is maintained, I believe, through the impersonal, objectifying practices of organizing, managing, and controlling large organizations. As Smith (1987) argues, these processes are increasingly textually mediated. Bureaucratic rules and written guides for organizational processes have been around for a long time, but their proliferation continues as rationalization of production and management expands on a global scale. The fact that much of this is now built into computer programs may mystify the process but only increases objectification and the appearance of gender neutrality. The continuing replication of the assumption of gender neutrality is part of the production of texts that can apply to workers, work processes, production, and management as general phenomena. Thus gender neutrality, the suppression of knowledge about gender, is embedded in organizational control processes.

This work of re-creating gender neutrality as part of the construction of general phenomena that can be organized and controlled through the application of documentary processes is evident in job evaluation,[1] a textual tool used by management to rationalize wage setting and the construction of organizational hierarchies. Other managerial processes produce assumptions of gender neutrality, but job evaluation provides a particularly good example because it is widely used in every industrial country (International Labour Office 1986).

Job evaluators use documents, or instruments, that describe general aspects of jobs, such as knowledge, skill, complexity, and responsibility, to assess the "value" of particular, concrete jobs in comparison with other particular, concrete jobs. The content of the documents and the way evaluators discuss and interpret them in the course of the job evaluation process provide an illustration of how concrete organizational activities reproduce the assumption of gender neutrality (Acker 1989, 1990).

Job evaluation, as most experts will tell you, evaluates jobs, not the people who do the jobs. Job evaluation consultants and trainers admonish evaluators to consider only the requirements of the job, not the gender or other characteristics of the incumbent. The tasks, skill requirements, and responsibilities of a job can be reliably described and assessed, while people who fill the jobs vary in their knowledge and commitment. Jobs can be rationalized and standardized; people cannot. A job exists separate from those who fill it, as a position in the hierarchy of an organizational chart. It is a reified, objectified category. But the abstract job must contain the assumption of an abstract worker if it is to be more than a set of tasks written on a piece of paper. Such a worker has no obligations outside the demands of the job, which is a bounded, abstract entity. To fit such demands, the abstract worker does not eat, urinate, or procreate, for these activities are not part of the job. Indeed, the abstract worker has no body and thus no gender. Jobs and hierarchies are represented as gender neutral, and every time such a job evaluation system is used, the notion of gender-neutral structure and the behavior based on that notion are re-created within the organization. Gender-neutral organizational theories reflect this gender-neutral rendering of organizational reality.

Real jobs and real workers are, of course, deeply gendered and embodied. The abstract worker transformed into a concrete worker turns out to be a man whose work is his life and whose wife takes care of everything else. Thus the concept of a job is gendered, in spite of its presentation as gender neutral, because only a male worker can begin to meet its implicit demands. Hidden within the concept of a job are assumptions about separations between the public and private spheres and the gendered organization of reproduction and production. Reproduction itself, procreation, sexuality, and caring for children, the ill, and the aged, unless transferred to the public sphere, are outside job and organizational boundaries. Too much involvement in such activities makes a person unsuitable for the organization. Women do not fit the assumptions about the abstract worker. Thus they are less than ideal organization participants, best placed in particular jobs that separate them from "real" workers.

The exclusion of reproduction is, as I argue above, linked to the ideology of the gender-neutral, abstract worker who has no body and no feelings, along with no gender. This abstraction facilitates the idea that the organization and its goals come first before the reproductive needs of individuals and society, such as, for example, the need to preserve and restore the natural environment. The concept of the abstract worker, completely devoted to the job, also supports the idea that strong commitment to the organization over and above commitment to family and community are necessary and normal.... As a consequence, management can more easily make the tough decisions, such as those to close factories while opposing all efforts to protect actual, concrete bodies and minds through plant closure legislation.

The theory and practice of gender neutrality covers up, obscures, the underlying gender structure, allowing practices that perpetuate it to continue even as efforts to reduce gender inequality are also under way (e.g., Cockburn 1991). The textual tools of management, as they are employed in everyday organizational life, not only help to create and then obscure gender structures that disadvantage women but are also part of complex processes that daily re-create the subordination of reproduction to production and justify the privileging of production over all other human necessities.

The gender-neutral character of the job and the worker, central to organizational processes and theories discussed above, depends upon the assumption that the worker has no body. This disembodied worker is a manifestation of the universal "citizen" or "individual" fundamental to ideas of democracy and contract. As Carole Pateman (1986: 8) points out, the most fundamental abstraction in the concept of liberal individualism is "the abstraction of the 'individual' from the body. In order for the individual to appear in liberal theory as a universal figure, who represents anyone and everyone, the individual must be disembodied." If the individual had bodily form, it would be clear that he represents one gender and one sex rather than a universal being. The universal individual is "constructed from a male body so that his identity is always masculine" (Pateman 1988: 223). Even with the full rights of citizens, women stand in an ambiguous relation to this universal individual. In a similar way, the concept of the universal worker, so common in talk about work organizations, "excludes and marginalizes women who cannot, almost by definition, achieve the qualities of a real worker because to do so is to become like a man" (Acker 1990: 150).

## SUMMARY AND CONCLUSIONS

A gendered organization theory should produce better answers to questions about both the organization of production and the reproduction of organization

(Burrell and Hearn 1989). I have suggested one strategy for developing such a theory, starting with an inventory of gendered processes that necessarily include manifestations of sexuality. In any concrete organization, these processes occur in complex interrelations. Gendered processes are often resources in organizational control and transformation. Underlying these processes, and intimately connected to them, is a gendered substructure of organization that links the more surface gender arrangements with the gender relations in other parts of the society. Ostensibly gender neutral, everyday activities of organizing and managing large organizations reproduce the gendered substructure within the organization itself and within the wider society. I think that this is the most important part of the process to comprehend, because it is hidden within abstract, objectifying, textually mediated relations and is difficult to make visible. The fiction of the universal worker obscures the gendered effects of these ostensibly gender-neutral processes and helps to banish gender from theorizing about the fundamental character of complex organizations. Gender, sexuality, reproduction, and emotionality of women are outside organizational boundaries, continually and actively consigned to that social space by ongoing organizational practices. Complex organizations play an important role, therefore, in defining gender and women's disadvantage for the whole society.

What are the practical implications of analyses, such as mine, in which ordinary organizational practices and thinking about those practices are grounded in the prior exclusion of women? The implications are not a return to an imaginary, utopian past where production is small scale and reproduction and production are fully integrated in daily life. Nor are the implications an Orwellian future where sexuality, procreation, and child raising would be integrated

in superorganizations where all of life is paternalistically regulated.

Instead, we might think about alternative possibilities, some short term and others long term. Short-term, new strategies to transform parts of large organizations from the inside are possible.[2] One way to do this is to take control of, or at least to influence and use, the textual tools of management. This is what comparable worth activists aim to do, as they attempt to affect the construction and use of job evaluation instruments to increase the value placed on women's jobs. Comparable worth experience shows that this is difficult and time consuming but not impossible (Acker 1989; Blum 1991). Many other practices could be similarly altered, but union organization controlled by women is the essential condition for doing such things. In the meantime, individual women can become experts in using and manipulating organizational texts; superior knowledge of rules and procedures can often facilitate change....

Long-term strategies will have to challenge the privileging of the "economy" over life and raise questions about the rationality of such things as organizational and work commitment ... as well as the legitimacy of organizations' claims for the priority of their goals over other broader goals. The gendered structure of organizations will only be completely changed with a fundamental reorganization of both production and reproduction. The long term is very long term and impossible to specify, but this should not lead us to abandon the search for other ways of organizing complex collective human activities.

## NOTES

1. The following discussion of job evaluation is based on Acker (1989).
2. This has been suggested by Beatrice Halsaa, Hildur Ve, and Cynthia Cockburn, who are proposing an international feminist activist/researcher conference on the topic.

# REFERENCES

Acker, J. 1989. *Doing Comparable Worth: Gender, Class and Pay Equity.* Philadelphia: Temple University Press.

___. 1990. "Hierarchies, Jobs, Bodies: A Theory of Gendered Organizations." *Gender & Society* 4: 139–58.

___. 1991. "Thinking About Wages: The Gendered Wage Gap in Swedish Banks." *Gender & Society* 5: 390–407.

Acker, J., and D. R. Van Houten. 1974. "Differential Recruitment and Control: The Sex Structuring of Organizations." *Administrative Science Quarterly* 19(2): 152–63.

Blum, L. M. 1991. *Between Feminism and Labor: The Significance of the Comparable Worth Movement.* Berkeley: University of California Press.

Burrell, G. 1984. "Sex and Organizational Analysis." *Organization Studies* 5(2): 97–118.

___. 1987. "No Accounting for Sexuality." *Accounting, Organizations, and Society* 12: 89–101.

Burrell, G., and J. Hearn. 1989. "The Sexuality of Organization." In *The Sexuality of Organization,* edited by J. Hearn, D. L. Sheppard, P. Tancred-Sheriff, and G. Burrell. London: Sage.

Calás, M. B., and L. Smircich. 1989a. "Voicing Seduction to Silence Leadership." Paper presented at the Fourth International Conference on Organizational Symbolism and Corporate Culture, Fountainbleau, France.

___. 1989b. "Using the 'F' Word: Feminist Theories and the Social Consequences of Organizational Research." pp. 355–59. In *Academy of Management Best Papers Proceedings.* Washington, DC: Academy of Management.

___. 1992. "Re-writing Gender into Organization Theorizing: Directions from Feminist Perspectives." In *Re-thinking Organization: New Directions in Organizational Research and Analysis,* edited by M. I. Reed and M. D. Hughes. London: Sage.

Cockburn, C. 1981. "The Material of Male Power." *Feminist Review* 9: 51.

___. 1983. Brothers: Male Dominance and Technological Change. London: Pluto.

___. 1985. *Machinery of Dominance.* London: Pluto.

___. 1991. *In the Way of Women: Men's Resistance to Sex Equality in Organizations.* Ithaca: ILR Press.

Cohn, S. 1985. *The Process of Occupational Sex-Typing.* Philadelphia: Temple University Press.

Collinson, D. L., and M. Collinson. 1989. "Sexuality in the Workplace: The Domination of Men's Sexuality." In *The Sexuality of Organization,* edited by J. Hearn, D. L. Sheppard, P. Tancred-Sheriff, and G. Burrell. London: Sage.

Connell, R. W. 1987. *Gender and Power.* Stanford, CA: Stanford University Press.

Ferguson, K. E. 1984. *The Feminist Case Against Bureaucracy.* Philadelphia: Temple University Press.

Fernandez Kelly, M. P., and A. M. Garcia. 1988. "Invisible Amidst the Glitter: Hispanic Women in the Southern California Electronics Industry." In *The Worth of Women's work,* edited by A. Statham, E. M. Miller, and H. O. Mauksch. Albany: SUNY Press.

Flax, J. 1990. *Thinking Fragments: Psychoanalysis, Feminism, and Postmodernism in the Contemporary West.* Berkeley: University of California Press. Foucault, M. 1972. *The Archeology of Knowledge.* New York: Pantheon.

Hacker, S. L. 1979. "Sex Stratification, Technology and Organizational Change: A Longitudinal Case Study of AT&T." *Social Problems* 26: 539–57.

Harding, S. 1986. *The Science Question in Feminism.* Ithaca, NY: Cornell University Press.

Hearn, J., and P. W. Parkin. 1983. "Gender and Organizations: A Selective Review and a Critique of a Neglected Area." *Organization Studies* 4(3): 219–42.

___. 1987. *"Sex" at "Work": The Power and Paradox of Organizational Sexuality.* Brighton: Wheatsheaf.

Hearn, J., D. Sheppard, P. Tancred-Sheriff, and G. Burrell, eds. 1989. *The Sexuality of Organization.* London: Sage.

Hill-Collins, P. 1990. *Black Feminist Thought: Knowledge, Consciousness, the Politics of Empowerment.* Boston: Unwin Hyman.

International Labour Office. 1986. *Job Evaluation.* Geneva: Author.

Kanter, R. M. 1977. *Men and Women of the Corporation.* New York: Basic Books.

MacKinnon, C. 1979. *Sexual Harassment of Working Women.* New Haven, CT: Yale University Press.

Martin, J. 1990a. "Deconstructing Organizational Taboos: The Suppression of Gender Conflict in Organizations." *Organizational Science* 1: 1–21.

___. 1990b. "Re-reading Weber: Searching for Feminist Alternatives to Bureaucracy." Paper presented at the annual meeting of the Academy of Management, San Francisco.

Mills, A. J. 1988. "Organization, Gender and Culture." *Organization Studies* 9(3): 351–69.

___. 1989. "Gender, Sexuality and Organization Theory." In *The Sexuality of Organization,* edited by J. Hearn, D. L. Sheppard, P. Tancred-Sheriff, and G. Burrell. London: Sage.

Morgan, G. and D. Knights. 1991. "Gendering Jobs: Corporate Strategy, Managerial Control and the Dynamics of Job Segre-gation." *Work, Employment & Society* 5: 181–200.

Pateman, C. 1986. "Introduction: The Theoretical Subversiveness of Feminism." In *Feminist Challenges,* edited by C. Pateman and E. Gross. Winchester, MA: Allen & Unwin.

___. 1988. *The Sexual Contract.* Cambridge, MA: Polity.

Pringle, R. 1989. "Bureaucracy, Rationality and Sexuality: The Case of Secretaries." In *The Sexuality of Organization,* edited by J. Hearn, D. L. Sheppard, P. Tancred-Sheriff, and G. Burrell. London: Sage.

Scott, J. 1986. "Gender: A Useful Category of Historical Analysis." *American Historical Review* 91: 1053–75.

Smith, D. 1987. *The Everyday World as Problematic: A Feminist Sociology.* Toronto: University of Toronto Press.

___. 1990. *The Conceptual Practices of Power: A Feminist Sociology of Knowledge.* Toronto: University of Toronto Press.

West, C., and D. H. Zimmerman. 1987. "Doing Gender." *Gender & Society* 1: 125–51.

## 35

# A New Kind of Public Service Professional Possessing Cultural Competency Awareness, Knowledge, and Skills

*Mitchell F. Rice & Audrey L. Mathews*

Demographic changes in the United States can be largely attributed to growth in the Hispanic/Latino, Asian, and other minority populations (see U.S. Census Bureau 2000, 2005a, 2005b). These demographic changes are impacting American society in many ways. Ongoing research, initiated in the late 1980s and 1990s, documented the effects of demographic changes in workplaces (see, e.g., Johnston and Parker 1987; Morrison and Glinow 1990). More recent research is raising questions about demographic changes and the delivery of public programs and public services (Rice 2008, 2010). Presently, due to demographic changes, there is a much different mix of individuals—consumers, customers, clients, and workers—in communities all across the United States than there was two decades ago. Now an encounter between individuals, clients, constituents, or service recipients and the professionals of public service agencies are often exchanges involving different cultural backgrounds, beliefs, practices, and languages (Rice 2010). This is to say that public agency service delivery professionals are typically from one culture and the service recipients or clients are from or closely connected to or strongly influenced by another culture. These demographic changes provided a vision and agenda for the workplace diversity movement initiated by scholars such as Taylor Cox and Stacey Blake (1991) and Roosevelt Thomas (1991).

Research indicates that organizations that manage diversity well show a reduction in workforce turnover, an increase in productivity, an edge in attracting talented women and minorities, and public agencies providing more effective programs and service delivery (Mathews 2010). In spite of recessions, collapses, and reductions in the size and operations of major organizations and public agencies and their workforces, the impact of the demographic changes are continuing. The resulting effects and affects for the organizations and public agencies that manage diversity well are creative problem solving, innovation, and improvements in the organizations' abilities to adapt to other inevitable forces of change. The bottom line for these organizations and public agencies is the successful and effective implementation and delivery of programs and services to communities of underserved clients and/or clients with different cultural backgrounds, beliefs, practices, and languages.

It appears that organizations that have effectively used the framework and lenses of cultural competency to manage the demographic changes of clients with their organizations have improved the quality and delivery of programs and services to constituents and clients. There are numerous successful examples in both the business and public sectors, such as Hewlett Packard, Ford Motor Company, Harvard Pilgrim Healthcare, and IBM from the business sector and the City of Laredo, Texas; Salinas, California Police Department; the U.S. Department of Defense and the Center for the Advanced Study of Language; the City of Phoenix, Arizona and the Seattle, Washington, Police Department from the public sector (see Rice 2008). These organizations thus fortify by example the answer to the question whether public organizations can become culturally competent (Cox and Blake 1991; Mathews 2010; Rice 2010; Thomas 1991). The common thread certifying that these multicultural/cultural organizations are culturally competent is a diversity management orientation built on the strengths and perspectives of beliefs that individuals from different cultures can make positive contributions to the organization or public agency. The objective is to establish culturally appropriate internal and external program and service delivery strategies and approaches. The cultural competency theoretical framework's underpinnings include elements from many theories or permutations-amalgamations, definitive properties, relationship differentials, knowledge derivatives, and applied practice outcomes and effects.

## A NEW CULTURAL COMPETENCY BEHAVIOR IN THE PRACTICE OF PUBLIC ADMINISTRATION

As prescribed by Strauss and Corbin (1990), theoretical sampling and testing of existing literature and models are used to buttress and expand on the theoretical modeling of cultural competency for public administration and public agency service delivery. The theory building initiated by Bailey (2005), continued by Rice (2010), and reexamined by Mathews (2010) sets the foundation for this chapter. To reiterate, according to Mathews in "Diversity Management and Cultural Competency" (2010), as the workplace diversity movement's framework and lenses moved into the last decade of the twentieth century, the focus of the movement was expanded by the notions

of multiculturalism and core cultural competencies. The theoretical framework for this emerging model's foundation has its origin in organization culture and behavior research conducted by social and behavioral scientists and applied practices in both the private sector and in the social sciences (Mathews 1999, 2002). Cultural competency in public programs and public agency service delivery has arrived at *cultural proficiency* when the agency, its professionals, and staffs understand and effectively respond to the challenge and opportunity posed by the presence of sociocultural diversity in a defined social system. Rice (2008, 24–26) proffers that organizations have an obligation to modify their administration service delivery strategies and approaches to encompass a development process that leads to cultural proficiency. Modifications such as recruitment and communication represent "surface structure" or "first cut changes" (see Kumpfer et al. 2002, 242).

One of the first steps to take in moving toward cultural competency in a public agency or public program is to make public services programming and public services delivery visible and accessible by translating program materials and providing the program in the primary client's language—sometimes known as a *translated* program (see Cheng Gorman 1996; Cheng Gorman and Balter 1997). This would include translating a public agency's program and service delivery literature into the language of the target population to increase awareness that services are available. Also, awareness and visibility are increased by modifying recruitment strategies, such as placing radio ads on the Spanish radio stations or in Spanish or other specific language newspapers.

Cultural competency also involves a public agency's operation ridding itself of cultural discomforts or cultural discontinuities (Uttal 2006). For example, attendance and participation in a health education workshop are more effective if culturally relevant activities, terms, and lessons that are meaningful to the participants are used.

Without these adaptations, the workshop may fail to convey the knowledge it is trying to impart. Cultural discomforts created by strange examples will also undermine the retention of participants and even possibly culturally offend participants. Some programs that serve racial ethnic populations are beginning to acknowledge that their effectiveness may also depend on taking a more familistic approach, such as bringing the whole family into a workshop or to a counseling session (Malley-Morrison and Hines 2004). Other programs have found it effective to recruit and retain Latino couples in a parent education program, instead of inviting only one individual parent (usually the mother) to participate (see Powell 1995). These types of adaptations are reflective of the changes necessary to provide culturally adapted programs that are going to work for a culturally different population.

Yet cultural adaptations in public agency services delivery and programming may still not go far enough. Cheng Gorman (1996) distinguishes between culturally adapted programs and those that are culturally specific. In culturally adapted programs, the examples that are used in a workshop are transformed or modified to respect the target culture's behaviors and practices. For example, activities that require a lot of writing would be replaced with oral exercises in a workshop for people from an orally expressive culture. Activities that require handholding would be removed from a workshop for individuals who are members of a low-touch culture. The key aspect of a culturally adapted program is that these changes leave the original points of a workshop or program intact but take into account the participants' cultural style of learning. In culturally specific programs, the transformations go beyond adding culturally adapted components to public service programming. Unlike the culturally adapted program, a public program or public agency that is culturally specific will integrate the target group's values, attitudes, and beliefs (Cheng Gorman 1996). This change requires that the assumptions of the overall workshop, program, and/or agency are critically examined and its philosophy is altered to reflect the value systems and worldview of the target population. For example, in a culture that does not verbally express self-emotions, the expectation for people to talk about themselves is dropped. A parenting program might use a familistic approach rather than the more commonly accepted child-centered approach used in the United States (see Kumpfer et al. 2002). Mock (2001) and Boyd-Franklin (2001) are in agreement that among ethnic families a family focused strategy is preferred rather than a youth-only focused prevention strategy because of the cultural emphasis on the "we" family identity as opposed to "I" self-identity. Culturally specific programs are designed with the purpose of facilitating success within a specific group's culture and are formatted to be culturally relevant.

## ADDING CULTURAL COMPETENCY IN PUBLIC ADMINISTRATION HIGHER EDUCATION PROGRAMS

Operationally, within an organization, cultural competency is achieved by integrating and transforming knowledge about individuals and groups into specific practices, standards, policies, and attitudes applied in appropriate cultural settings to increase the quality of services, thereby producing better outcomes (Davis 1997). The idea of cultural competency is an explicit acknowledgement that a one-size-fits-all public agency service delivery process cannot meet the needs of an increasingly diverse U.S. population. This means learning new patterns of behavior and applying them in appropriate situations (National Association of Social Workers 2001).

Before the new public agency service delivery professionals can appropriately step into their roles in the organization, public administration communities—both in practice and in education—need to reinvent themselves in order to produce a new public agency service delivery professional who is well grounded in cultural competency. This reinvention is necessary because evidence points to poorly working or failed community-oriented programs in housing, education, and health care. One area that stands out in these poorly working or failed programs and services is public administration's inability to embrace cultural competency and recognize the significance of understanding the cultural context in which any direct public service encounter occurs (Applewhite 1998). Other areas that support the need for a new kind of public agency service delivery professional are the following:

- the deficient and often inaccurate and inadequate public services and programs provided to minority populations (Geron 2002);
- public agencies' administration, services, and programs' lack of relevancy to the minority populations who really need them (Boyle and Springer 2001); and
- public program and public agency service delivery professionals who are not prepared to deliver relevant programs and services due to a lack of awareness and skills in cultural competency (Suzuki, McRae, and Short 2001).

It is also important that this new kind of public agency service delivery professional reinvention takes place through public administration education. According to Rice (2006, 91–92), "the teaching of cultural competency in university based public administration education programs and core curricula must be required. Second, steps must be taken to get public agencies to implement cultural competency programs, strategies, and practices in service delivery."

However, as Susan White's survey findings of twenty top MPA programs reveal, "Fewer than half of the top ranked MPA programs exposed students to core courses that relate to any aspect of diversity" (2004, 120). In a much larger study conducted by Wyatt-Nichol and Antwi-Boasiako (2008), online survey invitations were distributed to 246 MPA/MPP (Master of Public Policy) program directors, 92 of whom responded,

resulting in a 38 percent response rate. Interestingly, every respondent indicated that it was important (78 percent very important, 22 percent somewhat important) for graduate programs to promote awareness of cultural diversity issues. Yet course offerings on diversity have been somewhat limited. Rice (2004, 153–154) notes that "the teaching of social equity and diversity must be included in curricular and coursework in public administration education … to be more relevant to contemporary students and a concentrated effort must be made to provide students with a racially and ethnically diverse faculty." Yet a racially and ethnically diverse public administration faculty may be very difficult to achieve.

Further exacerbating the problem of little or no focus on diversity and cultural competency, the major textbooks in the field of public administration provide little or no coverage on cultural competency—except for the Rice text (2010) and another text by Espiridion Borrego and Richard Greggory Johnson III (2011)—or equity measures (Svara and Brunet 2004). Overall, public administration's higher education community is failing public sector and nonprofit organizations, because it does not impart the nuances of cultural competency to students in both teaching and training, leading to poorly working, failed, or inappropriate programs and the lack of organizational support systems to implement culturally appropriate and culturally responsive programs and services.

## DEVELOPING CULTURALLY COMPETENT PUBLIC AGENCY SERVICE DELIVERY PROFESSIONALS

Cultural competency is the ability of public agency service delivery professionals to integrate into their theoretical and technical approach to assessment and intervention relevant human diversity factors that are important to the process and successful outcome of the service or program (Fuertes and Ponterotto 2003). Figure 35.1 illustrates the important elements of the cultural competency cycle. The elements shown must occur in order to develop a culturally competent professional and/or a culturally competent public agency. The key elements of the cultural competency cycle are (1) learning about other cultures; (2) becoming aware and knowledgeable of cultural differences and their effect and impact on program agency and public service delivery outcomes; (3) engaging and integrating cultural awareness, cultural knowledge, and cultural sensitivity into public agency service delivery practices; and (4) thereby leading to culturally competent public agency service delivery professionals and providers. Cultural competency operates at the individual, professional level in the application of specific awareness,

knowledge, and skills in the context of public agency service delivery encounters and at the institutional level in the promotion of organizational practices to meet the needs of diverse populations.

Table 35.1 shows the attributes of a culturally competent public agency service delivery professional. Cultural competency consists of three distinctive areas focusing on cultural awareness, cultural knowledge, and cultural skills (Sue et al. 1998) that enable a system, agency, or professional to work effectively in cross-cultural settings and to deliver public services and public programs to diverse constituents and communities. These three distinctive areas must take place in this order. In other words, cultural awareness leads to cultural knowledge, and cultural knowledge contributes to the acquisition of cultural skills.

## FIGURE 35.1 • THE CULTURAL COMPETENCY CYCLE

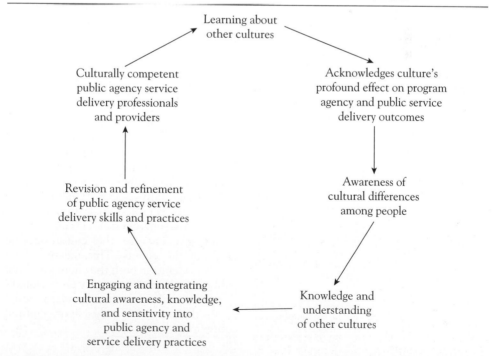

Learning about other cultures

Culturally competent public agency service delivery professionals and providers

Acknowledges culture's profound effect on program agency and public service delivery outcomes

Revision and refinement of public agency service delivery skills and practices

Awareness of cultural differences among people

Engaging and integrating cultural awareness, knowledge, and sensitivity into public agency and service delivery practices

Knowledge and understanding of other cultures

*Mitchell F. Rice & Audrey L. Mathews, M.E. Sharpe, Inc. Cultural Competency for Public Adminstrators, p. 25*

Cultural awareness takes into account those values, attitudes, and assumptions essential to working with clients and service recipients who are culturally different from a public agency service delivery professional (Pope and Reynolds 1997; see also Campinha-Bacote 1999). Table 35.1 shows eleven aspects of cultural awareness. A highly important aspect of cultural awareness is self-awareness. Self-awareness is especially important because it involves self-evaluation and reflection about one 's views of a particular culture in the form of stereotypes, biases, or culturally based assumptions (Pope and Reynolds 1997). Stated another way, self-awareness stresses understanding our own individual personal beliefs and attitudes as well as how we are the products of our own cultural conditioning. Further, understanding cultural awareness also takes into account a willingness to consider various worldviews, perspectives, and cultural differences.

Cultural knowledge consists of understanding the worldviews of various cultural groups and possessing knowledgeable professional expertise relevant to persons in other cultures. Public agency service delivery professionals must gather information about cultural groups that they are working with and learn in what ways cultural constructs influence how these groups respond to the helping process. Specifically, knowledge about cultures presumes the following specific competencies:

1. knowledge about the histories of cultures other than one's own;
2. knowledge about the role of education, money, values, attitudes, and behaviors in other cultures;
3. knowledge about the language and slang of another culture;
4. knowledge about the resources available for teaching and learning in other cultures;
5. knowledge about how each individual's own culture is perceived by members of other cultures;

6. knowledge about identity development models and the acculturation process for members of oppressed or underserved groups and their impact on individuals, groups, intergroup relations, and society;
7. knowledge about how helping services are delivered in other cultures;
8. knowledge about the ways cultural differences affect verbal and nonverbal communications;
9. knowledge about how change occurs for values and behaviors in individuals who are members of other cultures; and
10. knowledge about other cultures' views about gender, class, race and ethnicity, language, nationality, sexual orientation, age, religion or spirituality, and disability (see Table 35.1).

Cultural skills consist of those attributes that allow public service agency delivery professionals to effectively apply cultural awareness and cultural knowledge they have learned (see Table 35.1). Not having a foundation of cultural awareness and cultural knowledge makes it difficult to possess cultural skills that allow one to decide on culturally sensitive and culturally appropriate interventions and strategies. Deciding on culturally sensitive and culturally appropriate interventions and strategies requires the ability to identify and openly discuss cultural differences and issues, to assess the impact of cultural differences on communication, to genuinely connect to individuals who are different and gain their trust and respect, and to initiate individual, group, and institutional multicultural interventions, along with other attributes and skills. Overall, culturally competent public agency service delivery professionals should be able to adjust assessments and recommendations regarding clients to the culture-specific needs of the clients. This means taking into consideration both the client's and the public agency service delivery professional's culture as well as a cultural understanding of how the service fits in the client's cultural context (see Table 35.1).

**TABLE 35.1 • ATTRIBUTES OF CULTURALLY COMPETENT PUBLIC AGENCY SERVICE DELIVERY PROFESSIONALS**

| Cultural awareness | Cultural knowledge | Cultural skills |
| --- | --- | --- |
| Awareness of their own behavior and its impact on others. | | Ability to identify and openly discuss cultural differences and issues. |
| Awareness of the interpersonal process that occurs within a multicultural dyad. | | |
| A belief that differences are valuable and that learning about others who are culturally different is necessary and rewarding. | | |
| A willingness to take risks and see them as necessary and important for personal and professional growth. | Knowledge of diverse cultures and groups. | Ability to assess the impact of cultural differences on communication and to effectively communicate across those differences. |
| A strong commitment to justice, social change, and social equity. | Knowledge about how change occurs in values and behaviors of individuals from other cultures. | Ability to empathize and genuinely connect with individuals who are different from themselves. |
| A belief in the value and significance of their own cultural heritage and worldview as a starting place for understanding others who are culturally different from them. | Knowledge about the ways that cultural differences affect verbal and nonverbal communication. Knowledge about other cultures' views about gender, class, race, ethnicity, language, nationality, sexual orientation, age, religion or spirituality, and disability. | Ability to incorporate new learning and prior learning in new situations. |
| A willingness to examine, challenge, and change their own values, worldview, assumptions, and biases. | Knowledge about culturally appropriate resources and how to make culturally appropriate referrals. | Ability to gain the trust and respect of individuals who are culturally different from themselves. |
| An openness to change and a belief that change is necessary and positive. | Knowledge about the nature of institutional power in other cultures. | Ability to accurately assess their own multicultural skills, comfort level, growth, and development. |
| An acceptance of other worldviews and perspectives and a willingness to acknowledge that they, as individuals, do not have all the answers. | Knowledge about identity development models and the acculturation process for members of oppressed or underserved groups and their impact on individuals, groups, Intergroup relations, and society. | Ability to differentiate individual differences, cultural differences, and universal similarities. |
| A belief that cultural differences do not have to interfere with effective communication or meaningful relationships. | Knowledge and understanding of discrimination and its impact on identity and self-esteem. | Ability to support individuals and systems that identify oppression issues in a manner that optimizes multicultural interventions. Ability to undertake individual, group, and institutional multicultural interventions. |
| Awareness that one's own cultural heritage and background affects one's worldview, values, and assumptions. | Knowledge about other cultures' views about education and other areas. | Ability to use culture to undertake culturally sensitive and appropriate interventions. |

## CONCLUSION

Incorporating cultural competency into the study of public administration and moving public agency service delivery professionals and public agencies toward cultural competence is an ongoing effort that requires the recognition of several activities. First, the study of public administration must acknowledge that cultural differences are important in the delivery of public agency services and programs. Second, continuous internal leadership and support are required by all members of the public agency. Third, culturally competent public administration and public agency service delivery requires the following attributes: (1) cultural appropriateness; (2) cultural accessibility; and (3) cultural acceptability. Culturally appropriate public service delivery recognizes the needs of the target population or populations and the types of services provided. Culturally accessible public agency service delivery opens the door to services for different cultural groups. This includes addressing the structural barriers that can impede cultural competency. Once these barriers are addressed, culturally acceptable services are more likely to occur in all areas of the public agency.

Fourth, public administration and public agency service delivery professionals' use of cultural competency builds on the strengths and perspectives of minority cultures beliefs, habits, behaviors, and value systems to establish public agency service delivery intervention strategies and approaches. In other words, public agency professionals work from inside the public agency and utilize the beliefs, behaviors, perspectives, and values of minority cultures to help frame and provide culturally appropriate and responsive services (U.S. DHHS 2001,5). In this way, public agency service professionals are acknowledging the significance of culture in minority groups' problems as well as in their solutions. Fifth, acquiring cultural competency awareness, knowledge, and skills is a developmental process whereby public agencies and public service delivery professionals

attain cultural awareness, cultural knowledge, and cultural skills through both training and cultural encounters with individuals from different cultural groups. This process acknowledges that cultural competence is not static and requires frequent learning, relearning, and unlearning about different cultural groups. Finally, cultural competency in public administration and among public agency service delivery professionals will require new thinking outside of traditional public administration and incorporating different, nontraditional, and nonmainstream sources and approaches as articulated in the five observations above. This new thinking recognizes that the practice of public administration has a major impact on society and, as a result, must focus on cultural competency in a contemporary, multicultural era by providing cultural competency skills to future public agency service delivery professionals. Traditional public administration operations and programs have been "generic" and heavily influenced by white, middle-class values, resulting in professional training that has stressed "the melting pot" model of American culture, resulting in few culturally specific models and programs (see Kumpfer et al. 2002, 242).

Therefore, there is a strong need for effective cultural competency modeling. This modeling must take place in both teaching and practice in accordance with and as promoted within existing federal and state legislation (Bailey 2005). The cultural competency model should integrate and transform knowledge about individuals and groups into culturally specific practices, standards, and policies to increase the quality and effectiveness of services. Further, the model should contain the basis for developing criteria, assessing needs both internal and external to the organization, and adjusting the developmental processes to reflect the sociocultural diversity in a defined social system. The model also needs to acknowledge that cultural competency does not mean acquiring an encyclopedic knowledge of the world's cultures and their specific behaviors and views about values, customs, practices, or beliefs. It does, however, require that public agency service providers and service delivery professionals understand and acknowledge the role that culture plays in the success or failure of programs and services. In the end, cultural competency has its start with the dominant culture becoming self-aware of its own customs and then showing responsiveness to and understanding of the cultural differences of others—clients, employees, or services recipients within a defined program or system.

## REFERENCES

Applewhite, Steven L. 1998. Culturally competent practice with elderly Latinos. *Journal of Gerontological Social Work* 30(1/2): 1 15.

Bailey, Margo L. 2005. Cultural competency and the practice of public administration. In *Diversity and Public Administration: Theory, Issues, and Perspectives*, ed. Mitchell F. Rice, 177–196. Armonk, NY: ME. Sharpe.

Borrego, Espiridion, and Richard Greggory Johnson. 2011. *Cultural Competence for Public Managers: Managing Diversity in Today's World*. New York: CRC Press-Taylor Francis Group.

Boyd-Franklin, Nancy. 2001. Reaching out to larger systems. *Family Psychologist* 17(3): 1–4.

Boyle, David P., and Alyson Springer. 2001. Toward cultural competency measures for social work with specific populations. *Journal of Ethnic and Cultural Diversity in Social Work* 9(3/4): 53–77.

Campinha-Bacote, Josepha. 1999. A model and instrument for addressing cultural competence in health care. *Journal of Nursing Education* 38(5): 203–206.

Cheng Gorman, Jean. 1996. Culturally-Sensitive Parent Education Programs for Ethnic Minorities (PC Reports 7–96–26). New York: New York University, Psychoeducational Center.

Cheng Gorman, Jean, and Lawrence Baiter. 1997. Culturally sensitive parent education: A critical review of quantitative research.

*Review of Educational Research* 67(3): 339–369.

Cox, Taylor, and Stacey Blake. 1991. Managing Cultural Diversity: Implications for Organizational Competitiveness. *The Academy of Management Executive* 5 (3): 45–56.

Davis, King. 1997. *Exploring the Intersection between Cultural Competency and Managed Behavioral Health Care Policy: Implications for State and County Mental Health Agencies*. Alexandria, VA: National Technical Assistance Center for State Mental Health Planning.

Fuertes, Jairo N., and Joseph G. Ponterotto. 2003. Culturally appropriate intervention strategies. In *Multicultural Counseling Competencies 2003: Association of Multicultural Counseling Competencies*, eds. Gargi Roysircar, Patricia Arredondo, Jairo N. Fuertes, Joseph G. Ponterotto, and Rebecca L. Toporek, 51–58. Alexandria, VA: Association for Multicultural Counseling and Development.

Geron, Scott M. 2002. Cultural competency: How is it measured? Does it make a difference? *Generations* 26(3): 39–45.

Johnston, William B., and Arnold H. Parker. 1987. *Workforce 2000*. Indianapolis, IN: Hudson Institute.

Kumpfer, Karol L., Rose Alvarado, Paula Smith, and Nikki Bellamy. 2002. Cultural sensitivity and adaptation in family-based prevention interventions. *Prevention Science* 3(3): 241–246.

Malley-Morrison, Kathleen, and Denise A. Hines. 2004. *Family Violence in a Cultural Perspective*. Thousand Oaks, CA: Sage.

Mathews, Audrey L. 1999. The Sum of the Differences: Diversity and Public Organizations. New York: McGraw-Hill.

____. 2002. The mosaic of formal and informal mentoring relationships. DPA diss., University of Southern California.

____. 2010. Diversity Management and Cultural Competency. In *Diversity and Public Administrate Theory, Issues and Perspectives*, 2nd ed. Mitchell F. Rice 210–263. Armonk, NY: M.E. Sharpe.

Mock, Matthew. 2001. Working with Asian American Families. *The Family Psychologist* 17(3): 5–7.

Morrison, Ann M., and Mary-Ann Von Glinow. 1990. Women and minorities in management. *American Psychologist* 45(2): 200–208.

National Association of Social Workers. 2001. Standards for Cultural Competence in Social Work Practice. www .socialworkers.org/practice/standards/ NASWCulturalStandards.pdf.

Pope, Raechele L., and Amy L. Reynolds. 1997. Student affairs core competencies: Integrating multicultural awareness, knowledge, and skills. *Journal of College Student Development* 38(3): 271–281.

Powell, Douglas. 1995. Including Latino fathers in parent education and support programs. In *Understanding Latino Families: Scholarship, Policy and Practice*, ed. Ruth Zambrana, 85–106. Thousand Oaks, CA: Sage.

Rice, Mitchell F. 2004. Organizational culture, social equity, and diversity: Teaching public administration in the postmodern era. *Journal of Public Affairs Education* 10(2): 143–154.

———. 2006. Cultural competency: A missing framework in contemporary public administration and public service delivery. In *Proceedings: Taking Social Equity to the Streets*, ed. Mary Hamilton, Appendix J, 89–100. Fifth Social Equity Leadership Conference, University of Nebraska at Omaha, February 2–3.

———. 2008. A primer for developing a public agency service ethos of cultural competency in public services programming and public services delivery. *Journal of Public Affairs Education* 14(1): 21–38.

———. 2010. Cultural competency, public administration, and public service delivery in an era of diversity. In *Diversity and Public Administration: Theory, Issues, and Perspectives* (2nd ed.), ed. Mitchell F. Rice, 189–209. Armonk, NY: M.E. Sharpe.

Strauss, Anselm and Juliet Corbin. 1990. *Basics of Qualitative Research: Grounded Theory Procedures and Techniques*. Newbury Park, CA: Sage.

Sue, Derald Wing., Robert T. Carter, J. Manual Casas, Nadya A. Fouad, Allen E. Ivey, Margaret Jensen, Teresa LaFromboise, Jeanne E. Manese, Joseph G. Ponterotto, and Ena Vasquez-Nutall. 1998. *Multicultural Counseling Competencies*. Thousand Oaks, CA: Sage.

Suzuki, Lisa A., Mary B. McRae, and Ellen L. Short. 2001. The facets of cultural competence: Searching outside the box. *Counseling Psychologist* 29(6): 842–849.

Svara, James, and James Brunet. 2004. Filling in the skeleton pillar: Addressing social equity in introductory courses in public administration. *Journal of Public Affairs Education* 10(2): 99–109.

Thomas, Roosevelt. 1991. *Beyond Race and Gender: Unleashing the Power of Your Total Workforce by Managing Diversity*. New York: AMACOM.

U.S. Census Bureau. 2000. *Statistical Abstract of the United States*. Washington, DC: Government Printing Office.

U.S. Census Bureau News. 2005a. Texas becomes nation's newest majority-minority state, Census Bureau announces. News release, August 11.

———. 2005b. Hispanic population passes 40 million, Census Bureau reports. News release, June 9.

U.S. Department of Health and Human Services (U.S. DHHS), Administration on Aging. 2001. *Achieving Cultural Competence: A Guidebook for Providers of Services to Older Americans and Their Families*. www.AOA .gov/prof/addive/culturally/addiv_cult.asp.

Uttal, Lynet. 2006. Organizational cultural competency: Shifting programs for Latino immigrants from a client-centered to a community-based orientation. *American Journal of Community Psychology* 38:251–262.

White, Susan. 2004. Multicultural MPA curriculum: Are we preparing culturally competent public administrators? *Journal of Public Affairs Education* 10(2): 111–123.

Wyatt-Nichol, Heather, and Kwame Badu Antwi-Boasiako. 2008. Diversity across curriculum: Perceptions and practices. *Journal of Public Affairs Education* 14(1): 79–90.

## 36

# Corporate Citizenship: Social Responsibility, Responsiveness, and Performance

*Archie B. Carroll & Ann K. Buchholtz*

... For the past three decades, business has been undergoing the most intense scrutiny it has ever received from the public. As a result of the many allegations being leveled at it—charges that it has little concern for the consumer, cares nothing about the deteriorating social order, has no concept of acceptable ethical behavior, and is indifferent to the problems of minorities and the environment—concern is continuing to be expressed as to what responsibilities business has to society. These concerns have generated an unprecedented number of pleas for corporate social responsibility (CSR). More recently, CSR has been embraced in the broader term—*corporate citizenship*. Concepts that have evolved from CSR include corporate social *responsiveness* and corporate social *performance*. Today, many business executives prefer the term *corporate citizenship* as an inclusive reference to social responsibility issues.

CSR continues to be a "front-burner" issue within the business community, and this is highlighted by the formation and growth since 1992 of an organization called **Business for Social Responsibility (BSR)**. According to BSR, it was formed to fill an urgent need for a national business alliance that fosters socially responsible corporate policies. In 2004, BSR reported over 1,400 business member firms, including among its membership such recognizable names as Levi Strauss & Co., Stride Rite, Ford, GM, Reebok, Honeywell, Coca-Cola, Liz Claiborne, Inc., The Timberland Co.,

and hundreds of others. Further, BSR publishes reports such as *Corporate Social Responsibility: A Guide to Better Business Practice* to help its member firms and the business world.[1]...

### THE CORPORATE SOCIAL RESPONSIBILITY CONCEPT

...An early view of CSR was stated as follows: "**Corporate social responsibility** is seriously considering the impact of the company's actions on society."[2] Another definition was that "the idea of social responsibility ... requires the individual to consider his [or her] acts in terms of a whole social system, and holds him [or her] responsible for the effects of his [or her] acts anywhere in that system."[3]

Both of these definitions provide preliminary insights into the idea of social responsibility that will help us appreciate some brief history.

...[T]he commitment to social responsibility by businesses has led to increased corporate *responsiveness* to stakeholders and improved social (stakeholder) *performance*—ideas that are developed more fully in this chapter.

...[S]ome today prefer the language of "corporate citizenship" to collectively embrace the host of concepts related to CSR. However, for now, a useful summary of the themes or emphases of each of the chapter title concepts helps us see the flow of ideas accentuated as these concepts have developed:

## CORPORATE CITIZENSHIP CONCEPTS

Corporate social *responsibility*—emphasizes obligation, accountability

⬇

Corporate social *responsiveness*—emphasizes action, activity

⬇

Corporate social *performance*—emphasizes outcomes, results

From Carroll/Buchholtz. Business and Society, 6E. © 2006 South-Western, a part of Cengage Learning, Inc. Reproduced by permission. www.cengage.com/permissions.

The growth of these ideas has brought about a society more satisfied with business. However, this satisfaction, although it has reduced the number of factors leading to business criticism, has at the same time led to increased expectations that have resulted in more criticism.... The net result is that the overall levels of business social performance and societal satisfaction should increase with time in spite of this interplay of positive and negative factors. Should business not be responsive to societal expectations, it could conceivably enter a downward spiral, resulting in significant deterioration in the business/society relationship. The corporate fraud scandals beginning in 2001 have seriously called businesses' concern for society into question.

### Historical Perspective on CSR

The concept of business responsibility that prevailed in the United States during most of our history was fashioned after the traditional, or classical, *economic model*. Adam Smith's concept of the "invisible hand" was its major point of departure. The classical view held that a society could best determine its needs and wants through the marketplace. If business is rewarded on the basis of its ability to respond to the demands of the market, the self-interested pursuit of that reward will result in society getting what it wants. Thus, the "invisible hand"

of the market transforms self-interest into societal interest. Unfortunately, although the marketplace did a reasonably good job in deciding what goods and services should be produced, it did not fare as well in ensuring that business always acted fairly and ethically.

Years later, when laws constraining business behavior began to proliferate, it might be said that a *legal model* emerged. Society's expectations of business changed from being strictly economic in nature to encompassing issues that had been previously at business's discretion. Over time, a *social model* or *stakeholder model* has evolved.

...As McKie observed, "The business community never has adhered with perfect fidelity to an ideologically pure version of its responsibilities, drawn from the classical conception of the enterprise in economic society, though many businessmen (people) have firmly believed in the main tenets of the creed."[4]

### Modification of the Economic Model

A modification of the classical economic model was seen in practice in at least three areas: philanthropy, community obligations, and paternalism.[5] History shows that businesspeople did engage in **philanthropy**—contributions to charity and other worthy causes—even during periods characterized by the traditional economic view. Voluntary **community obligations** to improve, beautify, and uplift were evident. One early example of this was the cooperative effort between the railroads and the YMCA immediately after the Civil War to provide community services in areas served by the railroads. Although these services economically benefited the railroads, they were at the same time philanthropic.[6]

During the latter part of the nineteenth century and even into the twentieth century, **paternalism** appeared in many forms. One of the most visible examples was the company town. Although business's motives for creating company towns (e.g. the Pullman/Illinois experiment) were mixed, business had to do a considerable amount of the work in governing them. Thus, the company accepted a form of paternalistic social responsibility.[7]

The emergence of large corporations during the late 1800s played a major role in hastening movement away from the classical economic view. As society grew from the economic structure of small, powerless firms governed primarily by the marketplace to large corporations in which power was more concentrated, questions of the responsibility of business to society surfaced.[8]

Although the idea of corporate social responsibility had not yet fully developed in the 1920s, managers even then had a more positive view of their role. Community service was in the forefront. The most visible example was the Community Chest movement, which received its impetus from business. Morrell Heald suggests that this was the first large-scale endeavor in which business leaders became involved with other nongovernmental community groups for a common, nonbusiness purpose that necessitated their contribution of time and money to community welfare projects.[9] The social responsibility of business, then, had received a further broadening of its meaning.

The 1930s signaled a transition from a predominantly laissez-faire economy to a mixed economy in which business found itself one of the constituencies monitored by a more activist government. From this time well into the 1950s, business's social responsibilities grew to include employee welfare (pension and insurance plans), safety, medical care, retirement programs, and so on. McKie has suggested that these new developments were spurred both by governmental compulsion and by an enlarged concept of business responsibility.[10]

Neil J. Mitchell, in his book *The Generous Corporation*, presents an interesting thesis regarding how CSR evolved.[11] Mitchell's view is that the ideology of corporate social responsibility, particularly philanthropy, was developed by American business leaders as a strategic response to the antibusiness fervor that was beginning in the late 1800s and early 1900s. The antibusiness reaction was the result of specific business actions, such as railroad price gouging, and public resentment of the emerging gigantic fortunes being made by late nineteenth-century moguls, such as Andrew Carnegie and John D. Rockefeller.[12]

As business leaders came to realize that the government had the power to intervene in the economy and, in fact, was being encouraged to do so by public opinion, there was a need for a philosophy that promoted large corporations as a force for social good. Thus, Mitchell argued, business leaders attempted to persuade those affected by business power that such power was being used appropriately. An example of this early progressive business ideology was reflected in Carnegie's 1889 essay, "The Gospel of Wealth," which asserted that business must pursue profits but that business wealth should be used for the benefit of the community. Philanthropy, therefore, became the most efficient means of using corporate wealth for public benefit. A prime example of this was Carnegie's funding and building of more than 2,500 libraries.

...

**Acceptance and Broadening of Meaning.** The period from the 1950s to the present may be considered the modern era in which the concept of corporate social responsibility gained considerable acceptance and broadening of meaning. During this time, the emphasis has moved from little more than a general awareness of social and moral concerns to a period in which specific issues, such as product safety, honesty in advertising, employee rights, affirmative action, environmental sustainability, ethical behavior, and global CSR have been emphasized. The issue orientation eventually gave way to the more recent focus on social performance and corporate citizenship. First, however, we can expand upon the modern view of CSR by examining a few definitions or understandings of this term that have developed in recent years.

## A Four-Part Definition of CSR

We would like to present Carroll's four-part definition of CSR that focuses on the *types* of social responsibilities it might be argued that business has. Carroll's definition helps us to understand the component parts that make up CSR, and it is the definition that we will build upon in this book:

> The social responsibility of business encompasses the economic, legal, ethical, and discretionary (philanthropic) expectations that society has of organizations at a given point in time.[13]

Carroll's four-part definition attempts to place economic and legal expectations of business in context by relating them to more socially-oriented concerns. These social concerns include ethical responsibilities and philanthropic (voluntary/discretionary) responsibilities.

**Economic Responsibilities.** First, there are business's **economic responsibilities**. It may seem odd to call an economic responsibility a social responsibility, but, in effect, this is what it is. First and foremost, the American social system calls for business to be an economic institution. That is, it should be an institution whose orientation is to produce goods and services that society wants and to sell them at fair prices—prices that society thinks represent the true value of the goods and services delivered and that provide business with profits adequate to ensure its perpetuation and growth and to reward its investors. While thinking about its economic responsibilities, business employs many management concepts that are directed toward financial effectiveness—attention to revenues, costs, strategic decision making, and the host of business concepts focused on maximizing the long-term financial performance of the organization. In the mid-2000s, the worldwide hyper-competition in business has highlighted business's economic responsibilities. But, economic responsibilities are not enough.

**Legal Responsibilities.** Second, there are business's **legal responsibilities**. Just as society has sanctioned our economic system by permitting business to assume the productive role mentioned earlier, as a partial fulfillment of the social contract, it has also laid down the ground rules—the laws—under which business is expected to operate. Legal responsibilities reflect society's view of "codified ethics" in the sense that they embody basic notions of fair practices as established by our lawmakers. It is business's responsibility to society to comply with these laws. If business does not agree with laws that have been passed or are about to be passed, our society has provided a mechanism by which dissenters can be heard through the political process. In the past 35 years, our society has witnessed a proliferation of laws and regulations striving to control business behavior. A recent *Newsweek* cover story titled "Lawsuit Hell: How Fear of Litigation Is Paralyzing Our Professions" emphasizes the burgeoning role that the legal responsibility of organizations is assuming.[14]

As important as legal responsibilities are, legal responsibilities do not embrace the full range of behaviors expected of business by society. On its own, law is inadequate for at least three reasons. First, the law cannot possibly address all the topics, areas, or issues that business may face. New topics continually emerge such as Internet-based business (e-commerce) and genetically modified foods. Second, the law often lags behind more recent concepts of what is considered appropriate behavior. For example, as technology permits more exact measurements of environmental contamination, laws based on measures made by obsolete equipment become outdated but not frequently changed. Third, laws are made by lawmakers and may reflect the personal interests and political motivations of legislators rather than appropriate ethical justifications. A wise sage once said: "Never go to see how sausages or laws are made." It may not be a pretty picture. Although we would like to believe that our lawmakers are focusing on "what is right," political maneuvering often suggests otherwise.

**Ethical Responsibilities.** Because laws are important but not adequate, **ethical responsibilities** embrace those activities and practices that are expected or prohibited by societal members even though they are not codified into law. Ethical responsibilities embody the full scope of norms, standards, and expectations that reflect what consumers, employees, shareholders, and the community regard as fair, just, and in keeping with the respect for or protection of stakeholders' moral rights.[15]

In one sense, changes in ethics or values precede the establishment of laws because they become the driving forces behind the initial creation of laws and regulations. For example, the civil rights, environmental, and consumer movements reflected basic alterations in societal values and thus may be seen as ethical bellwethers foreshadowing and leading to later legislation. In another sense, ethical responsibilities may be seen as embracing and reflecting newly emerging values and norms that society expects business to meet, even though they may reflect a higher standard of performance than that currently required by law. Ethical responsibilities in this sense are often ill defined or continually under public scrutiny and debate as to their legitimacy and thus are frequently difficult for business to agree upon. Regardless, business is expected to be responsive to newly emerging concepts of what constitutes ethical practices. In recent years, ethics in the global arena have complicated things.

Superimposed on these ethical expectations emanating from societal and stakeholder groups are the implied levels of ethical performance suggested by a consideration of the great ethical principles of moral philosophy, such as justice, rights, and utilitarianism.[16]

...[L]et us think of ethical responsibilities as encompassing those areas in which society expects certain levels of moral or principled performance but for which it has not yet articulated or codified into law.

**Philanthropic Responsibilities.** Fourth, there are business's voluntary/discretionary or **philanthropic responsibilities**. These are viewed as responsibilities because they reflect current expectations of business by the public. These activities are voluntary, guided only by business's desire to engage in social activities that are not mandated, not required by law, and not generally expected of business in an ethical sense. Nevertheless, the public has an expectation that business will engage in philanthropy and thus this category has become a part of the social contract between business and society. Such activities might include corporate giving, product and service donations, volunteerism, partnerships with local government and other organizations, and any other kind of voluntary involvement of the organization and its employees with the community or other stakeholders. Examples of companies fulfilling their philanthropic responsibilities, and "doing well by doing good" are many:

- Chick-fil-A, the fast-food restaurant, through the WinShape Centre Foundation, operates foster homes for more than 120 children, sponsors a summer camp that has hosted more than 21,000 children since 1985, and has provided college scholarships for more than 16,500 students.
- Merck & Co., the drug giant, supports science education in and around Rahway, New Jersey.
- IBM gives away computers and computer training to schools around the country.
- UPS has committed $2 million to a two-year program, the Volunteer Impact Initiative, designed to help nonprofit organizations develop innovative ways to recruit, train, and manage volunteers.

The distinction between ethical responsibilities and philanthropic responsibilities is that the latter typically are not expected in a moral or an ethical sense. Communities desire and expect business to contribute its money, facilities, and employee time to humanitarian programs or purposes, but they do not regard firms as unethical if they do not provide these services at the desired levels. Therefore, these responsibilities are more discretionary, or voluntary, on business's part, although the societal expectation that they be provided is always present. This category of responsibilities is often referred to as good "corporate citizenship."

In essence, our definition forms a four-part conceptualization of corporate social responsibility that includes the economic, legal, ethical, and philanthropic expectations placed on organizations by society at a given point in time. Figure 36.1 summarizes the four components, society's expectation regarding each component, and examples. The implication is that business has accountability for these areas of responsibility and performance. This four-part definition provides us with categories within which to place the various expectations that society has of business. With each of these categories considered to be an indispensable facet of the total social responsibility of business, we have a conceptual model that more completely describes the kinds of expectations that society expects of business. One advantage of this model is that it can accommodate those who have argued against CSR by characterizing an economic emphasis as separate from a social emphasis. This model offers these two facets along with others that collectively make up corporate social responsibility.

... In summary, the total social responsibility of business entails the concurrent fulfillment of the firm's economic, legal, ethical, and philanthropic responsibilities. In equation form, this might be expressed as follows:

### FIGURE 36.1 • UNDERSTANDING THE FOUR COMPONENTS OF CORPORATE SOCIAL RESPONSIBILITY

| *Type of Responsibility* | *Societal Expectation* | *Explanations* |
| --- | --- | --- |
| **Economic** | REQUIRED of business by society | Be profitable. Maximize sales, minimize costs. Make sound strategic decisions. Be attentive to dividend policy. Provide investors with adequate and attractive returns on their investments. |
| **Legal** | REQUIRED of business by society | Obey all laws, adhere to all regulations. Environmental and consumer laws. Laws protecting employees. Obey Sarbanes–Oxley Act. Fulfill all contractual obligations. Honor warranties and guarantees. |
| **Ethical** | EXPECTED of business by society | Avoid questionable practices. Respond to spirit as well as letter of law. Assume law is a floor on behavior, operate above minimum required. Do what is right, fair, and just. Assert ethical leadership. |
| **Philanthropic** | DESIRED/EXPECTED of business by society | Be a good corporate citizen. Give back. Make corporate contributions. Provide programs supporting community—education, health/human services, culture and arts, civic. Provide for community betterment. Engage in volunteerism. |

*Economic Responsibilities*
*+ Legal Responsibilities*
*+ Ethical Responsibilities*
*+ Philanthropic Responsibilities*
*= Total Corporate*<br>*Social Responsibility*

Stated in more practical and managerial terms, the socially responsible firm should strive to:

- Make a profit.
- Obey the law.
- Be ethical.
- Be a good corporate citizen.

It is especially important to note that the four-part CSR definition ... represents a stakeholder model. That is, each of the four components of responsibility addresses different stakeholders in terms of the varying priorities in which the stakeholders are affected. Economic responsibilities most dramatically impact owners/shareholders and employees (because if the business is not financially successful, owners and employees will be directly affected). When the Arthur Andersen accounting firm went out of business in 2002, employees were displaced and significantly affected. Legal responsibilities are certainly crucial with respect to owners, but in today's society the threat of litigation against businesses emanates frequently from employees and consumer stakeholders. Ethical responsibilities affect all stakeholder groups, but an examination of the ethical issues business faces

today suggests that they involve consumers and employees most frequently. Because of the fraud of the early 2000s, investor groups have also been greatly affected. Finally, philanthropic responsibilities mostly affect the community, but it could be reasoned that employees are next affected because some research has suggested that a company's philanthropic performance significantly affects its employees' morale. Figure 36.2 presents this stakeholder view of CSR, along with a hypothetical priority scheme in which the stakeholder groups are addressed/affected by the companies' actions in that realm. The numbers in the cells are not based on empirical evidence but are only suggestive to illustrate how stakeholders are affected. Other priority schemes could easily be argued.

...[O]ur model's four facets (economic, legal, ethical, and philanthropic) provide us with a useful framework for conceptualizing the issue of corporate social responsibility. The social contract between business and society is to a large extent formulated from mutual understandings that exist in each area of our basic model. But, it should be noted that the ethical and philanthropic categories, taken together, more nearly capture the essence of what people generally mean today when they speak of the social responsibility of business. Situating these two categories relative to the legal and economic obligations, however, keeps them in proper perspective.

### FIGURE 36.2 • A STAKEHOLDER VIEW OF CORPORATE SOCIAL RESPONSIBILITY

| CSR Component | *Stakeholder Group Addressed and Primarily Affected* | | | | |
| --- | --- | --- | --- | --- | --- |
| | Owners | Consumers | Employees | Community | Others |
| **Economic** | 1 | 4 | 2 | 3 | 5 |
| **Legal** | 3 | 2 | 1 | 4 | 5 |
| **Ethical** | 3 | 1 | 2 | 4 | 5 |
| **Philanthropic** | 3 | 4 | 2 | 1 | 5 |

NOTE: Numbers in cells suggest one prioritization of stakeholders addressed and affected within each CSR component. Numbers are illustrative only. Do you agree with these priorities? Why? Why not? Discuss.

From Carroll/Buchholtz. *Business and Society*, 6E. © 2006 South-Western, a part of Cengage Learning, Inc. Reproduced by permission. www.cengage.com/permissions.

## ARGUMENTS AGAINST AND FOR CORPORATE SOCIAL RESPONSIBILITY

In an effort to provide a balanced view of CSR, we will consider the arguments that traditionally have been raised against and for it. We should state clearly at the outset, however, that those who argue against corporate social responsibility are not using in their considerations the comprehensive four-part CSR definition and model presented here. Rather, it appears that the critics are viewing CSR more narrowly—as only the efforts of the organization to pursue social goals (primarily our philanthropic category)....

### Arguments Against CSR

Let us first look at the arguments that have surfaced over the years from the anti-CSR school of thought. Most notable has been the classical economic argument. This traditional view holds that management has one responsibility: to maximize the profits of its owners or shareholders. This classical economic school, led by economist Milton Friedman, argues that social issues are not the concern of businesspeople and that these problems should be resolved by the unfettered workings of the free-market system.[17] Further, this view holds that if the free market cannot solve the social problem, then it falls upon government and legislation to do the job.... [I]t is clear that the economic argument views corporate social responsibility more narrowly than we have in our conceptual model.

A second major objection to CSR has been that business is not equipped to handle social activities. This position holds that managers are oriented toward finance and operations and do not have the necessary expertise (social skills) to make social decisions.[18] Although this may have been true at one point in time, it is less true today. Closely related to this argument is a third: If managers were to pursue corporate social responsibility vigorously, it would tend to dilute the business's primary purpose.[19] The objection here is that CSR would put business into fields not related, as F. A. Hayek has stated, to their "proper aim."[20]

A fourth argument against CSR is that business already has enough power—economic, environmental, and technological—and so why should we place in its hands the opportunity to wield additional power?[21] In reality, today, business has this social power regardless of the argument. Further, this view tends to ignore the potential use of business's social power for the public good.

One other argument that merits mention is that by encouraging business to assume social responsibilities we might be placing it in a risky position in terms of global competition. One consequence of being socially responsible is that business must internalize costs that it formerly passed on to society in the form of dirty air, unsafe products, consequences of discrimination, and so on. The increase in the costs of products caused by including social considerations in the price structure might necessitate raising the prices of products, making them less competitive in international markets. The net effect might be to dissipate the country's advantages gained previously through technological advances. This argument weakens somewhat when we consider the reality that social responsibility is quickly becoming a global concern, not one restricted to U.S. firms and operations.

The arguments presented here constitute the principal claims made by those who oppose the CSR concept, as it once was narrowly conceived. Many of the reasons given appear logical. Value choices as to the type of society the citizenry would like to have, at some point, become part of the total social responsibility question. Whereas some of these objections might have had validity at one point in time, it is doubtful that they carry much weight today.

### Arguments for CSR

Authorities have agreed upon two fundamental points: "(1) Industrial society faces serious human and social problems brought on largely by the rise of the large corporations, and (2) managers must conduct the affairs of the corporation in ways to solve or at least ameliorate these problems."[22] This generalized justification of corporate social responsibility is appealing. It actually comes close to what we might suggest as a first argument for CSR—namely, that it is in business's long-range self-interest to be socially responsible. These two points provide an additional dimension by suggesting that it was partially business's fault that many of today's social problems arose in the first place and, consequently, that business should assume a role in remedying these problems. It may be inferred from this that deterioration of the social condition must be halted if business is to survive and prosper in the future.

The long-range self-interest view holds that if business is to have a healthy climate in which to exist in the future, it must take actions now that will ensure its long-term viability. Perhaps the reasoning behind this view is that society's expectations are such that if business does not respond on its own, its role in society may be altered by the public—for example, through government regulation or, more dramatically, through alternative economic systems for the production and distribution of goods and services.

It is sometimes difficult for managers who have a short-term orientation to appreciate that their rights and roles in the economic system are determined by society. Business must be responsive to society's expectations over the long term if it is to survive in its current form or in a less restrained form.

One of the most practical reasons for business to be socially responsible is to ward off future government intervention and regulation. Today there are numerous areas in which government intrudes with an expensive, elaborate regulatory apparatus to fill a void left by business's inaction. To the extent that business polices itself with self-disciplined standards and guidelines, future government intervention can be somewhat forestalled. Later, we will discuss some areas in which business could

have prevented intervention and simultaneously ensured greater freedom in decision making had it imposed higher standards of behavior on itself.

Two additional arguments supporting CSR deserve mention together: "Business has the resources" and "Let business try."[23] These two views maintain that because business has a reservoir of management talent, functional expertise, and capital, and because so many others have tried and failed to solve general social problems, business should be given a chance. These arguments have some merit, because there are some social problems that can be handled, in the final analysis, only by business. Examples include a fair workplace, providing safe products, and engaging in fair advertising. Admittedly, government can and does assume a role in these areas, but business must make the final decisions.

Another argument supporting CSR is that "proacting is better than reacting." This position holds that proacting (anticipating and initiating) is more practical and less costly than simply reacting to problems once they have developed. Environmental pollution is a good example, particularly business's experience with attempting to clean up rivers, lakes, and other waterways that were neglected for years. In the long run, it would have been wiser to have prevented the environmental deterioration from occurring in the first place. A final argument in favor of CSR is that the public strongly supports it. A 2000 *Business Week/Harris* poll revealed that, with a stunning 95 percent majority, the public believes that companies should not only focus on profits for shareholders but that companies should be responsible to their workers and communities, even if making things better for workers and communities requires companies to sacrifice some profits.[24]

### The Business Case for CSR

...The business case reflects why businesspeople believe that CSR brings distinct benefits or advantages to business organizations and the business community. Often, these benefits directly affect the "bottom line."... According to Porter: "Today's companies ought to invest in corporate social responsibility as part of their business strategy to become more competitive." In a competitive context, "the company's social initiatives—or its philanthropy—can have great impact. Not only for the company but also for the local society."[25]

In his book, *The Civil Corporation*, Simon Zadek has identified four ways in which firms respond to CSR pressures, and he holds that these form a composite business case for CSR. His four approaches are as follows:[26]

- *Defensive approach.* This is an approach designed to alleviate pain. Companies will do what they have to do to avoid pressure that makes them incur costs.
- *Cost-benefit approach.* This traditional approach holds that firms will undertake those activities if they can identify a direct benefit that exceeds costs.
- *Strategic approach.* In this approach, firms will recognize the changing environment and engage with CSR as part of a deliberate emergent strategy.
- *Innovation and learning approach.* In this approach, an active engagement with CSR provides new opportunities to understand the marketplace and enhances organizational learning, which leads to competitive advantage....

### Millennium Poll on Corporate Social Responsibility

As we think about the first decade of the new millennium, it is useful to consider the results of the millennium poll on CSR that was sponsored by Environics International, the Prince of Wales Business Leaders Forum, and The Conference Board. This representative survey of 1,000 persons in each of 23 countries on 6 continents revealed how important citizens of the world felt corporate social responsibility really was. The survey revealed the following expectations that major companies would be expected to do in the twenty-first century.[27]

---

## CORPORATE RESPONSIBILITY IN THE TWENTY-FIRST CENTURY

In the twenty-first century, major companies will be expected to do all of the following:

- Demonstrate their commitment to society's values and their contribution to society's social, environmental, and economic goals through actions.
- Fully insulate society from the negative impacts of company operations and its products and services.
- Share the benefits of company activities with key stakeholders as well as with shareholders.
- Demonstrate that the company can make more money by doing the right thing, in some cases reinventing its business strategy. This "doing well by doing good" will reassure stakeholders that the new behavior will outlast good intentions.

---

From Carroll/Buchholtz. Business and Society, 6E. © 2006 South-Western, a part of Cengage Learning, Inc. Reproduced by permission. www.cengage.com/permissions.

The survey findings suggest that CSR is fast becoming a global expectation that requires a comprehensive strategic response. Ethics and CSR need to be made a core business value integrated into all aspects of the firm.

## CORPORATE SOCIAL RESPONSIVENESS

...A general argument that has generated much discussion over the past several decades holds that the term *responsibility* is too suggestive of efforts to pinpoint accountability or obligation. Therefore, it is not dynamic enough to fully describe business's willingness and activity—apart from obligation—to respond to social demands. For example, Ackerman and Bauer criticized the CSR term by stating, "The connotation of 'responsibility' is that of the process of assuming an obligation. It places an emphasis on motivation rather than on performance." They go on to say, "Responding to social demands is much more than deciding what to do. There remains the management task of doing what one has decided to do, and this task is far from trivial."[28] They argue that "social responsiveness" is a more apt description of what is essential in the social arena.

Their point was well made, especially when it was first set forth. *Responsibility*, taken quite literally, does imply more of a state or condition of having assumed an obligation, whereas *responsiveness* connotes a dynamic, action-oriented condition. We should not overlook, however, that much of what business has done and is doing has resulted from a particular motivation—an assumption of obligation—whether assigned by government, forced by special-interest groups, or voluntarily assumed. Perhaps business, in some instances, has failed to accept and internalize the obligation, and thus it may seem odd to refer to it as a responsibility. Nevertheless, some motivation that led to social responsiveness had to be there, even though in some cases it was not articulated to be a responsibility or an obligation....

Thus, the corporate social responsiveness dimension that has been discussed by some as an alternative focus to that of social responsibility is, in actuality, an *action phase* of management's response in the social sphere. In a sense, the responsiveness orientation enables organizations to rationalize and operationalize their social responsibilities without getting bogged down in the quagmire of accountability, which can so easily occur if organizations try to get an exact determination of what their true responsibilities are before they take any action.

In an interesting study of social responsiveness among Canadian and Finnish forestry firms, researchers concluded that the social responsiveness of a corporation will proceed through a predictable series of phases and that managers will tend to respond to the most powerful stakeholders.[29] This study demonstrates that social responsiveness is a *process* and that stakeholder power, in addition to a sense of responsibility, may sometimes drive the process.

## CORPORATE SOCIAL PERFORMANCE

For the past few decades, there has been a trend toward making the concern for social and ethical issues more and more pragmatic. The responsiveness thrust that we just discussed was a part of this trend. It is possible to integrate some of the concerns into a model of **corporate social performance (CSP)**. The performance focus is intended to suggest that what really matters is what companies are able to accomplish—the results or outcomes of their acceptance of social responsibility and adoption of a responsiveness philosophy. In developing a conceptual framework for CSP, we not only have to specify the nature (economic, legal, ethical, philanthropic) of the responsibility, but we also need to identify a particular philosophy, pattern, mode, or strategy of responsiveness. Finally, we need to identify the stakeholder issues or topical areas to which these responsibilities are manifested. One need not ponder the stakeholder issues that have evolved under the rubric of social responsibility to recognize how they have changed over time. The issues, and especially the degree of organizational interest in the issues, are always in a state of flux. As the times change, so does the emphasis on the range of social issues that business must address....

Also of interest is the fact that particular issues are of varying concern to businesses, depending on the industry in which they exist as well as other factors. A bank, for example, is not as pressed on environmental issues as a manufacturer. Likewise, a manufacturer is considerably more absorbed with the issue of environmental protection than is an insurance company.

### Carroll's CSP Model
... Carroll's **corporate social performance model**... brings together the three major dimensions we have discussed:

1. Social responsibility categories—economic, legal, ethical, and discretionary (philanthropic)
2. Philosophy (or mode) of social responsiveness—e.g., reaction, defense, accommodation, and proaction
3. Social (or stakeholder) issues involved—consumers, environment, employees, etc.)[30]

One dimension of this model pertains to all that is included in our definition of social responsibility—the economic, legal, ethical, and discretionary (philanthropic) components. Second, there is a social responsiveness continuum. Although some writers have suggested that this is the preferable focus when one considers social responsibility, the model suggests that responsiveness is but one additional aspect to be addressed if CSP is to be achieved. The third dimension concerns the scope of social or stakeholder issues (e.g. consumerism, environment, produce safety, and discrimination) that management must address.

The corporate social performance model is intended to be useful to both academics and managers. For academics, the model is primarily a conceptual aid to perceiving the distinction among the concepts of corporate social responsibility that have appeared in the literature....

The conceptual model can assist managers in understanding that social responsibility is not separate and distinct from economic performance. The model integrates economic concerns into a social performance framework. In addition, it places ethical and philanthropic expectations into a rational economic and legal framework. The model can help the manager systematically think through major stakeholder issues....

## CORPORATE CITIZENSHIP

Business practitioners and academics alike have grown fond of the term *corporate citizenship* in reference to businesses' corporate social performance. But, what does

**corporate citizenship** really mean? Does it have a distinct meaning apart from the concepts of corporate social responsibility, responsiveness, and performance discussed earlier? A careful look at the concept and its literature shows that although it is a useful and attractive term, it is not distinct from the terminology we have described earlier, except in the eyes of some writers who have attempted to give it a specific, narrow meaning. If one thinks about companies as "citizens" of the countries in which they reside, corporate citizenship just means that these companies have certain responsibilities that they must perform in order to be perceived as good corporate citizens. ...

*Corporate citizenship* has been described by some as a broad, encompassing term that basically embraces all that is implied in the concepts of social responsibility, responsiveness, and performance. Graves, Waddock, and Kelly, for example, define good corporate citizenship as "serving a variety of stakeholders well."[31] ...

Carroll has recast his four categories of corporate social responsibility as embracing the "four faces of corporate citizenship,"—economic, legal, ethical, and philanthropic. Each face, aspect, or responsibility reveals an important facet that contributes to the whole. He poses that "just as private citizens are expected to fulfill these responsibilities, companies are as well."[32]

At the narrow end of the spectrum, Altman speaks of corporate citizenship in terms of corporate community relations. In this view, it embraces the functions through which business intentionally interacts with nonprofit organizations, citizen groups, and other stakeholders at the community level.[33] ...

What are the benefits of good corporate citizenship to business itself? A literature review of studies attempting to discern the benefits to companies of corporate citizenship, defined broadly, revealed empirical and anecdotal evidence supporting the following:[34]

- Improved employee relations (e.g., improves employee recruitment, retention, morale, loyalty, motivation, and productivity)
- Improved customer relationships (e.g., increased customer loyalty, acts as a tie-breaker for consumer purchasing, enhances brand image)
- Improved business performance (e.g., positively impacts bottom-line returns, increases competitive advantage, encourages cross-functional integration)
- Enhanced company's marketing efforts (e.g., helps create a positive company image, helps a company manage its reputation, supports higher prestige pricing, and enhances government affairs activities)

The terminology of corporate citizenship is especially attractive because it resonates so well with the business community's attempts to describe their own socially responsive activities and practices. Therefore, we can expect that this concept will be around for some years to come. Generally speaking, as we refer to CSR, social responsiveness, and social performance, we are also embracing activities that would typically fall under the purview of a firm's corporate citizenship.[35]

## SOCIAL PERFORMANCE AND FINANCIAL PERFORMANCE

One issue that comes up frequently in considerations of corporate social performance is whether or not there is a demonstrable relationship between a firm's social responsibility or performance and its financial performance. Unfortunately, attempts to measure this relationship are typically hampered by measurement problems....

Over the years, studies on the social responsibility–financial performance relationship have produced varying results.[36] In one important study of this relationship, Preston and O'Bannon, examined data from 67 large U.S. corporations covering the years 1982–1992. They concluded that "there is a positive association between social and financial performance in large U.S. corporations."[37] Research by Waddock

and Graves has concluded that corporate social performance (CSP) was positively associated with prior financial performance (CFP) and future financial performance.[38] In a study of the chemical industry, Griffin and Mahon found that perceptual CSP measures are "somewhat related" to the financial information. Overall, however, they found contradictory results in studies they examined.[39] Finally, a study by Roman, Hayibor, and Agle, reanalyzing the Griffin and Mahon data, concluded that the "vast majority of studies support the idea that, at the very least, good social performance does not lead to poor financial performance." They go on to say that most of the studies they reviewed indicated a positive correlation between CSP and CFP.[40]

In qualifying the research, it is important to note that there have been at least three different views, hypotheses, or perspectives that have dominated these discussions and research.

**Perspective 1.** Perhaps the most popular view is built on the belief that socially responsible firms are more financially profitable. To those who advocate the concept of social performance, it is apparent why they would like to think that social performance is a driver of financial performance and, ultimately, a corporation's reputation. If it could be demonstrated that socially responsible firms, in general, are more financially successful and have better reputations, this would significantly bolster the CSP view, even in the eyes of its critics.

Perspective 1 has been studied extensively. Unfortunately, the findings of most of the studies that have sought to demonstrate this relationship have been either flawed in their methodology or inconclusive. Numerous studies have been done well, but even these have failed to produce conclusive results. In spite of this, some studies have claimed to have successfully established this linkage....

Part of the problem with Perspective 1 is that positive correlations may be found, but causality is not clearly established.

**Perspective 2.** This view, which has not been studied as extensively, argues that a firm's financial performance is a driver of its social performance. This perspective is built somewhat on the notion that social responsibility is a "fair weather" concept; that is, when times are good and companies are enjoying financial success, we witness higher levels of social performance. In their study, Preston and O'Bannon found the strongest evidence that financial performance either precedes, or is contemporaneous with, social performance. This evidence supports the view that social–financial performance correlations are best explained by positive synergies or by "available funding."[41]...

**Perspective 3.** This position argues that there is an interactive relationship among social performance, financial performance, and corporate reputation. In this symbiotic view, the three major factors influence each other, and, because they are so interrelated, it is not easy to identify which factor is driving the process. Regardless of the perspective taken, each view advocates a significant role for CSP, and it is expected that researchers will continue to explore these perspectives for years to come....

Finally, it should be mentioned that the "contingency" view of Husted suggests that CSP should be seen as a function of the fit between specific strategies and structures and the nature of the social issue. He argues that the social issue is determined by the expectational gaps of the firm and its stakeholders that occur within or between views of what is and/or what ought to be, and that high corporate social performance is achieved by closing these expectational gaps with the appropriate strategy and structure.[42]

### A Stakeholder Bottom-Line Perspective

A basic premise of all these perspectives is that there is only one "bottom line"—a corporate bottom line that addresses primarily the stockholders', or owners', investments in the firm. An alternative view is that the firm has "multiple bottom lines" that

benefit from corporate social performance. This stakeholder-bottom-line perspective argues that the impacts or benefits of CSP cannot be fully measured or appreciated by considering only the impact of the firm's financial bottom line.

To truly operate with a stakeholder perspective, companies need to accept the multiple-bottom-line view. Thus, CSP cannot be fully comprehended unless we also consider that its impacts on stakeholders, such as consumers, employees, the community, and other stakeholder groups, are noted, measured, and considered. Research may never conclusively demonstrate a relationship between CSP and financial performance. If a stakeholder perspective is taken, however, it may be more straightforward to assess the impact of CSP on multiple stakeholders' bottom lines. This model of CSP and stakeholders' bottom lines might be depicted as shown in Figure 36.3.

**The Triple Bottom Line.** A variant of the "multiple bottom line" perspective is popularly known as the **Triple Bottom Line** concept. The phrase *triple bottom line* has been attributed to John Elkington. The concept seeks to encapsulate for business the three key spheres of **sustainability**— *economic, social,* and *environmental.* The "economic bottom line" refers to the firm's creation of material wealth, including financial income and assets. The "social" bottom line is about the quality of people's lives and about equity between people, communities, and nations. The "environmental" bottom line is about protection and conservation of the natural environment.[43] It may quickly be seen that these three areas ... represent a version of the stakeholder-bottom line concept. At its narrowest, the term is used as a framework for measuring and reporting corporate performance in terms of economic, social, and environmental indicators. At its broadest, the concept is used to capture the whole set of values, issues, and processes that companies must address to minimize harm resulting from their activities and to create economic, social, and environmental value.[44] As a concept, it is

## FIGURE 36.3 • RELATIONSHIP BETWEEN CORPORATE SOCIAL PERFORMANCE (CSP) AND STAKEHOLDERS' "MULTIPLE BOTTOM LINES"

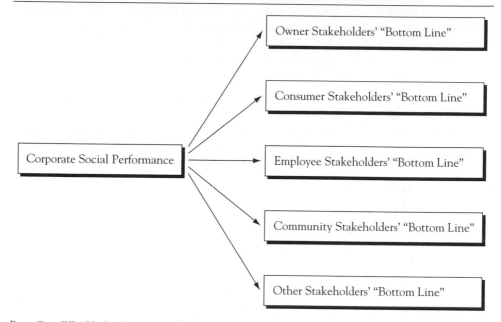

From Carroll/Buchholtz. Business and Society, 6E. © 2006 South-Western, a part of Cengage Learning, Inc. Reproduced by permission. www.cengage.com/permissions.

a more detailed spelling out of the idea of corporate social performance.

As mentioned earlier, **corporate sustainability** is the goal of the triple-bottom-line approach. The goal of sustainability is to create long-term shareholder value by taking advantage of opportunities and managing risks related to economic, environmental, and social developments. Leaders in this area try to take advantage of the market's demand for sustainability products and services while successfully reducing and avoiding sustainability costs and risks. To help achieve these goals, the Dow Jones Sustainability Indexes were created to monitor and assess the sustainability of corporations.[45]...

## SUMMARY

Important and related concepts include those of corporate citizenship, corporate social responsibility, responsiveness, and performance. The corporate social responsibility concept has a rich history. It has grown out of many diverse views and even today does not enjoy a consensus of definition. A four-part conceptualization was presented that broadly conceives CSR as encompassing economic, legal, ethical, and philanthropic components....

The concern for corporate social responsibility has been expanded to include a concern for social responsiveness. The responsiveness focus suggests more of an action-oriented theme by which firms not only must address their basic obligations but also must decide on basic modes of responding to these obligations. A CSP model was presented that brought the responsibility and responsiveness dimensions together into a framework that also identified realms of social or stakeholder issues that must be considered. The identification of social issues has blossomed into a field now called "issues management" or "stakeholder management."

The interest in corporate social responsibility extends beyond the academic community. On an annual basis, *Fortune* magazine polls executives on various dimensions of corporate performance; one major dimension is called "Social Responsibility." A vibrant organization, Business for Social Responsibility, promises to be on the cutting edge of CSR practice. Walker Information has investigated how the general consuming public regards social responsibility issues. The term *corporate citizenship* has arrived on the scene to embrace a whole host of socially conscious activities and practices on the part of businesses. This term has become quite popular in the business community.

...Studies of the relationship between social responsibility and economic performance do not yield consistent results, but social efforts are nevertheless expected and are of value to both the firm and the business community. In the final analysis, sound corporate social (stakeholder) performance is associated with a "multiple-bottom-line effect" in which a number of different stakeholder groups experience enhanced bottom lines.

## NOTES

1. Business for Social Responsibility, *Corporate Social Responsibility: A Guide to Better Business Practice* (San Francisco: BSR Education Fund, 2000). BSR's website is http://www.bsr.org.

2. *Quoted in John L. Paluszek, Business and Society: 1976–2000* (New York: AMACOM, 1976), 1.

3. Keith Davis, "Understanding the Social Responsibility Puzzle," *Business Horizon* (Winter 1967), 45–50.

4. James W. McKie, "Changing Views," in *Social Responsibility and the Business Predicament* (Washington, DC: The Brookings Institute, 1974), 22.

5. *Ibid.*

6. See Morrell Heald, *The Social Responsibilities of Business: Company and Community,*

1900–1960 (Cleveland: Case Western Reserve University Press, 1970), 12–14.

7. McKie, 23.

8. *Ibid.*, 25.

9. Heald, 119.

10. McKie, 27–28.

11. Neil J. Mitchell, *The Generous Corporation: A Political Analysis of Economic Power* (New Haven, CT: Yale University Press, 1989).

12. Ronald E. Berenbeim, "When the Corporate Conscience Was Born" (A review of Mitchell's book). *Across the Board* (October 1989), 60–62.

13. Archie B. Carroll, "A Three-Dimensional Conceptual Model of Corporate Social Performance," *Academy of Management Review* (Vol. 4, No. 4, 1979), 497–505.

14. Stuart Taylor, Jr., and Evan Thomas, "Civil Wars," *Newsweek* (December 15, 2003), 43–53.

15. Archie B. Carroll, "The Pyramid of Corporate Social Responsibility: Toward the Moral Management of Organizational Stakeholders," *Business Horizons* (July–August 1991), 39–48. Also see Archie B. Carroll, "The Four Faces of Corporate Citizenship," *Business and Society Review* (Vol. 100–101, 1998), 1–7.

16. *Ibid.*

17. Milton Friedman, "The Social Responsibility of Business Is to Increase Its Profits," *The New York Times* (September 1962), 126.

18. Christopher D. Stone, *Where the Law Ends* (New York: Harper Colophon Books, 1975), 77.

19. Keith Davis, "The Case For and Against Business Assumption of Social Responsibilities," *Academy of Management Journal* (June 1973), 312–322.

20. F. A. Hayek, "The Corporation in a Democratic Society: In Whose Interest Ought It and Will It Be Run?" in H. Ansoff (ed.), *Business Strategy* (Middlesex: Penguin, 1969), 225.

21. Davis, 320.

22. Thomas A. Petit, *The Moral Crisis in Management* (New York: McGraw-Hill, 1967), 58.

23. Davis, 316.

24. Cited in Aaron Bernstein, "Too Much Corporate Power," *Business Week* (September 11, 2000), 149.

25. "CSR—A Religion with Too Many Priests," *European Business Forum* (Issue 15, Autumn 2003).

26. Simon Zadek, *The Civil Corporation*. See also Lance Moir, "Social Responsibility: The Changing Role of Business," Cranfield School of Management, U.K.

27. The Millennium Poll on Corporate Social Responsibility (Environics, Intl., Ltd., Prince of Wales Business Leaders Forum, The Conference Board, 1999), http://www .Environics.net.

28. Robert Ackerman and Raymond Bauer, *Corporate Social Responsiveness: The Modern Dilemma* (Reston, VA: Reston Publishing Company, 1976), 6.

29. Juha Näsi, Salme Näsi, Nelson Phillips, and Stelios Zyglidopoulos, "The Evolution of Corporate Responsiveness," *Business and Society* (Vol. 36, No. 3, September 1997), 296–321.

30. Carroll, 1979, 502–504.

31. Samuel P. Graves, Sandra Waddock, and Marjorie Kelly, "How Do You Measure Corporate Citizenship?" *Business Ethics* (March/April 2001), 17.

32. Archie B. Carroll, "The Four Faces of Corporate Citizenship," *Business and Society Review* (100/101, 1998), 1–7.

33. Barbara W. Altman, *Corporate Community Relations in the 1990s: A Study in Transformation*, unpublished doctoral dissertation, Boston University.

34. Archie B. Carroll, Kim Davenport, and Doug Grisaffe, "Appraising the Business Value of Corporate Citizenship: What Does the Literature Say?" Proceedings of the International Association for Business and Society, Essex Junction, VT, 2000.

35. For more on corporate citizenship, see the special issue "Corporate Citizenship," *Business and Society Review* (105:1, Spring 2000), edited by Barbara W. Altman and Deborah Vidaver-Cohen. Also see Jorg Andriof and Malcolm McIntosh (eds.), *Perspectives on Corporate Citizenship* (London: Greenleaf Publishing, 2001). Also see,

Isabelle Maignan, O. C. Ferrell, and G. Tomas M. Hult, "Corporate Citizenship: Cultural Antecedents and Business Benefits," *Journal of the Academy of Marketing Science* (Vol. 27, No. 4, Fall 1999), 455–469. Also see Malcolm McIntosh, Deborah Leipziger, Keith Jones, and Gill Coleman, *Corporate Citizenship: Successful Strategies for Responsible Companies* (London: Financial Times/Pitman Publishing), 1998.

36. See, for example, Mark Starik and Archie B. Carroll, "In Search of Beneficence: Reflections on the Connections Between Firm Social and Financial Performance," in Karen Paul (ed.), *Contemporary Issues in Business and Society in the United States and Abroad* (Lewiston, NY: The Edwin Mellen Press, 1991), 79–108; and I. M. Herremans, P. Akathaporn, and M. McInnes, "An Investigation of Corporate Social Responsibility, Reputation, and Economic Performance," *Accounting, Organizations, and Society* (Vol. 18, No. 7/8, 1993), 587–604.

37. Lee E. Preston and Douglas P. O'Bannon, "The Corporate Social–Financial Performance Relationship: A Typology and Analysis," *Business and Society* (Vol. 36, No. 4, December 1997), 419–429.

38. Sandra Waddock and Samuel Graves, "The Corporate Social Performance–Financial Performance Link," *Strategic Management Journal* (Vol. 18, No. 4, 1997), 303–319.

39. Jennifer Griffin and John Mahon, "The Corporate Social Performance and Corporate Financial Performance Debate," *Business and Society* (Vol. 36, No. 1, March 1997), 5–31.

40. Ronald Roman, Sefa Hayibor, and Bradley Agle, "The Relationship Between Social and Financial Performance," *Business and Society* (Vol. 38, No. 1, March 1999), 121. For a reply to this study, see John Mahon and Jennifer Griffin, "Painting a Portrait: A Reply," *Business and Society* (Vol. 38, No. 1, March 1999), 126–133.

41. Preston and O'Bannon, 428.

42. Bryan Husted, "A Contingency Theory of Corporate Social Performance," *Business and Society* (Vol. 39, No. 1, March 2000), 24–48, 41.

43. Simon Zadek, *The Civil Corporation: The New Economy of Corporate Citizenship* (London: Earthscan, 2001), 105–114.

44. "What Is the Triple Bottom Line?" (January 8, 2004), http://www.sustain ability.com/philosophy/triple-bottom /tbl-intro.asp.

45. Dow Jones Sustainability Indexes, http://www.sustainability-index.com /html/sustainability/corpsustainability .html.

## 37

# The Search for Social Entrepreneurship: Drawing Conclusions

*Paul C. Light*

This study challenges and confirms much of the conventional wisdom about socially entrepreneurial activity and social entrepreneurship. The study may be exploratory in nature, but it does yield strong insights about the nature of socially entrepreneurial activity, especially as it occurs among high-performing social benefit organizations.

The most I can claim is that the study reflects an effort to explore potential differences among the highly, moderately, and not-too entrepreneurial organizations that emerged from my sample of reputed high-performing social benefit organizations in 2001.

Nevertheless, there is grist for further research embedded in this study, not the least of which is the relatively large amount of socially entrepreneurial activity that appears to exist among high-performing social benefit organizations. This study cannot prove that a quarter of all high-performing social benefit organizations are highly socially entrepreneurial, nor can it prove that another third are moderately so. But the study does suggest that there may be significant opportunities to expand socially entrepreneurial activity in the social benefit sector and that such activity can change the social equilibrium, given adequate resources. It can also ask whether this socially entrepreneurial activity might be enhanced through the spin-off of programs and units from their moderately entrepreneurial hosts or through scale-up to much greater organizational engagement.

However, the key question is not how much socially entrepreneurial activity

exists, but how it can be expanded to maximum impact. Given the promise involved in the general movement toward altering a persistent and resistant social equilibrium, the field needs to be much more supportive in helping social entrepreneurs achieve their goals, whether it should be through organizational development, capacity-building infrastructure, more aggressive research and development, stronger networks of other social entrepreneurs and socially entrepreneurial organizations, or further encouragement and funding of management improvements. This help must involve careful research, however, not hunch.

## FINDINGS

The key findings of this study rest on the interviews of senior executives at 131 high-performing social benefit organizations as well as a detailed literature review across the fields of business and social entrepreneurship. The surveys provide conditional insights on how highly socially entrepreneurial organizations differ from their less entrepreneurial peers, provided, of course, that the initial coding of the organizations was accurate.

### Entrepreneurs

This study confirms the important role of entrepreneurs in stimulating socially entrepreneurial activity. Indeed, the most important difference in the 2006 survey may well involve the significant engagement of the

Paul C. Light, "Drawing Conclusions," Ch. 7 in Light (2008), *The Search for Social Entrepreneurship*. Brookings Institution Press.

original founders in their organizations. Fully one in five of the highly socially entrepreneurial organizations were still headed by their original founder, while another three out of five still engaged their founder in some meaningful way. One can only assume that they are holding fast to their mission, helping their organizations maintain a clear focus on social change.

This continued engagement may help explain the role of *commitment to vision* as the most important factor in both organization performance and socially entrepreneurial activity. Highly socially entrepreneurial organizations clearly put a greater emphasis on this commitment than on being well managed. They do not neglect management per se, at least according to respondents' ratings of their own organization's performance. But it is performance based on vision that appears to drive the ratings.

Given the fact that the highly socially entrepreneurial organizations were just as likely to be large and old as the moderately and not-too socially entrepreneurial comparison groups, this focus on vision emerges as a potentially critical characteristic of entrepreneurs. Logically it would exist somewhere in the middle layers of the pyramid of characteristics presented earlier in this book. Vision would certainly affect agility, for example, including tolerance for ambiguity and risk, and surely vision affects alertness. Although there is ample room for further research on the link between vision and other core characteristics, such research should focus clearly on core characteristics that link to vision. Bluntly put, if a core characteristic does not contribute to commitment to vision, it is not a core characteristic at all.

### Ideas

The study clearly suggests that ideas matter to a variety of organizational indicators, most notably the remarkably high levels of growth in the demand for programs and the perceived level of budgetary growth. The highly socially entrepreneurial organizations either choose ideas with great potential for growth or the growth itself created the resources for socially entrepreneurial activity.

There is also good evidence that the highly socially entrepreneurial organizations prefer certain kinds of socially entrepreneurial activity. There appeared to be a clear preference by highly socially entrepreneurial organizations for ideas that might alter the basic structure of the social equilibrium. Again, this is not to argue that the organizations that were coded as highly socially entrepreneurial organizations did not care about management—indeed, almost half of the respondents at these highly socially entrepreneurial organizations said that their organizations were involved in program design and administrative systems.

This commitment to vision creates consequences for management nonetheless, indicated by the somewhat lower levels of enthusiasm among respondents at the highly socially entrepreneurial organizations toward providing resources such as time and funding for the development of new ideas. At the same time, these organizations were also more committed to asking employees to participate in key decisions that affect their missions. These organizations clearly believe in their vision and, by implication, their ideas for achieving it. They seem less interested in developing new ideas per se but quite committed to a strategy for driving that vision throughout the organization.

### Opportunities

The study shows that highly socially entrepreneurial organizations have a preference for working in certain kinds of environments that may provide more opportunities to establish their presence and scale up toward challenging the prevailing social equilibrium. According to the 2006 survey, respondents at the organizations that were coded as highly socially entrepreneurial reported that their organizations worked in less competitive and regulated corners of their environments, a finding that was confirmed in the 2001 survey as well. As already noted, they seem to "go where they ain't," meaning that they focus on opportunities with the greatest room to challenge the prevailing wisdom.

Their external environment is hardly forgiving to such efforts, however. Despite their remarkable growth, the highly socially entrepreneurial organizations either do not operate in areas of the environment with the potential for revenue diversification or choose to avoid diversification as a potential deadweight on their vision. Although this lack of diversification does create vulnerabilities that might occur because of the eventual evaporation of support as seed grants expire, the organizations that were coded as highly socially entrepreneurial may simply view diversification as an obstacle to their vision. Hence, they may justifiably focus on single streams of revenue.

These organizations may have plenty of practical reasons for rejecting diversification, however. They may focus on single streams of revenue because of concerns regarding the administrative burdens of managing multiple streams. As past research suggests, each additional stream carries its own costs, whether in duplicative accounting streams, different deadlines for reporting, or new evaluation systems. It is one thing for these organizations to measure results about their programs, for example, and quite another to measure results using the many different languages of results management that currently burden social benefit organizations in general. Not only is focused funding a way to maintain the commitment to vision, it also may be a way to keep the highly socially entrepreneurial organizations as agile as possible in reacting to new opportunities.

Strategic planning is one way to manage the different kinds of uncertainties facing organizations created by external threats, few though they might be at highly socially entrepreneurial organizations. However, as the surveys show, these organizations assign

less importance to strategic planning than their less entrepreneurial peers do. Once again, they may be worried about the administrative burdens involved in strategic planning—done well, it is a time-consuming task. But the lack of implied interest in strategic planning may also reflect the intense commitment to vision. These organizations may eschew planning because they already know where they want to go, which can be a strength or a vulnerability.

### Organizations
Finally, the study shows that the highly socially entrepreneurial organizations share many of the attributes of their less socially entrepreneurial peers in most areas of organizational life:

— Except for assigning lower importance to strategic planning, they manage their external relations just as effectively, assigning the same level of importance to setting clear missions and measuring results.
— Except for lower confidence in their accounting systems (a finding from the 2001 survey), they also have similar internal management structures, operating with relatively flat hierarchies (another finding from the 2001 survey), while assigning the same level of importance to encouraging units within the organization to work together.
— Except for assigning lower importance to encouraging employees to take risks in developing new ideas, they have similar commitments to participatory leadership, assigning roughly the same levels of importance to having a shared vision for the organization's future and to encouraging employees to participate in key decisions as did their less entrepreneurial peers.
— Except for assigning lower importance to providing training and information technology and having less active boards (still another finding from the 2001 survey), they have similar commitments to providing enough resources to succeed, assigning the same importance to having enough staff.

The exceptions listed above raise questions about *sustaining* high performance as the highly socially entrepreneurial organizations continue to challenge the prevailing wisdom. Organizations cannot survive long without the firm direction that strategic planning provides, for example, or the accountability that strong board governance provides. Nor can they expect high performance from their employees if they neglect information technology and training.

This is not to argue that highly socially entrepreneurial organizations are poorly governed. Indeed, some research suggests that they use very different forms of governance than those used by their less entrepreneurial peers and that they have much more agile systems. Nevertheless, they must also pay attention to the vulnerabilities embedded in the exceptions cited above. If they are growing so fast that they do not have the resources for training and information technology, their investors should provide it. And if their governance does not meet contemporary demands for active engagement by the board and better understanding of the board's role in providing policy guidance, their investors should demand it.

It is impossible to know, of course, whether assigning lower importance to training and information technology means that the highly socially entrepreneurial organizations are actually providing less of these key resources. But the 2006 survey suggests potential vulnerabilities in basic operating capacity. There is simply no reason why socially entrepreneurial organizations should not be competitive on these kinds of resources, unless they are either so committed to vision that they neglect the basics or because their investors are so committed to vision that they are only willing to invest in the idea.

If the idea matters, so does management. To the extent management systems produce bureaucratic inertia, socially entrepreneurial organizations need to be deliberate about protecting their flexibility, through strategic planning, capacity building, training, or other interventions. But to the extent that management is essential for

scale-up and impact, socially entrepreneurial organizations need to embrace it.

## TRUE OR FALSE

This study hardly resolves the debate over definitions and assumptions, which is still central to the development of the field. To the contrary, the field is still some distance from even discussing the underlying assumptions that guide contemporary research, let alone determining which assumptions matter most in separating different forms of social entrepreneurship; shaping strategies for the launch, acceleration, and scale-up of actual interventions; or building an inventory of advice on how to increase the odds that the prevailing equilibrium will change.

### Revisiting Assumptions

This study does provide a set of admittedly conditional findings that may help advance the search for social entrepreneurship. Building on the literature review and surveys discussed in this book, there is enough soft evidence to make speculative decisions on my forty assumptions.

*False* is the default position in the absence of at least some evidence to the contrary. This study led me to change twenty of my past assumptions, from false to true and just two from true to false, suggesting that social entrepreneurship is an uncommon but not impossible act.

Regarding entrepreneurs, the study suggests that social entrepreneurs (1) never rest as they move forward toward change; (2) think differently from other high achievers; (3) persevere against the odds; (4) share common histories, with occasional exceptions; and (5) continue to imagine, in part because they are high achievers. It is important to note that these assumptions need not always be true, nor do they necessarily limit the number of entrepreneurs. Socially entrepreneurial activity can become "natural" through organizational design, while the number of entrepreneurs can be increased by helping motivated individuals, teams, and networks learn how to think like an entrepreneur.

Regarding ideas, the study also suggests that socially entrepreneurial ideas are (6) designed to change the world and (7) must grow at least minimally to achieve success. Even as they surprise the social equilibrium, socially entrepreneurial ideas do not necessarily have to be absolutely new. Indeed, in the study of government innovation, there is a long history of using old stuff in new ways—that is, cobbling together a set of familiar ideas in an entirely new combination. Similarly, scaling to success does not necessarily require global scale. It can involve moving from one city block to an entire neighborhood, for example, or one neighborhood to a larger community. The key is to pay attention to the dissemination of the breakthrough, not to its visibility to the world. In a sense, modesty becomes social entrepreneurship, if only to lull the prevailing wisdom into complacency.

Regarding opportunities, the study suggests that socially entrepreneurial opportunities (8) are rare, though not so much so that they only arise once in a great while; (9) cannot be predicted; (10) tend to occur in great punctuations when the demand for change rises to a tipping point; (11) emerge where entry costs are low; (12) open and close quickly as entrepreneurs surge toward action; (13) favor competition over collaboration; and (14) appear to the special few. These last two assumptions are linked to the notion that entrepreneurs think differently from other high achievers—competition has tended to improve ideas across the equilibrium, while alertness to opportunity is one of the key characteristics of success. Once again, not all these assumptions are fixed into the future—investors can easily help entrepreneurs identify opportunities, while training and education can improve the quality of competition.

Regarding organizations, the study suggests that socially entrepreneurial organizations (15) tend to nurture a stream of new ideas as they move forward into conflict with the prevailing equilibrium, (16) rarely pause as they pursue change, (17) are constructed differently from other high-performing organizations, (18) need unrestricted revenue to invest in organizational capacity and research and development, (19) can use diversified revenue to protect against fluctuations in a single stream of revenue, and (20) do insulate themselves from aging. This last assumption takes us all the way back to the concept of corporate entrepreneurship, which argues that organizational rejuvenation is a central challenge for maintaining market position. Just as corporations must change or die, socially entrepreneurial organizations must blend their pursuit of managerial excellence with a constant vigilance against bureaucracy, which is exactly what Apple and so many other firms do.

Two assumptions regarding ideas and organizations changed from true to false. The study suggests that (1) socially entrepreneurial ideas involve both radical new combinations *and* dramatic expansions of existing ideas and that (2) socially entrepreneurial organizations maintain constant forward motion, even as they create their organizational infrastructure—put another way, they build the plane while flying it. Levels of socially entrepreneurial activity clearly varied greatly among my sample of high-performing social benefit organizations and appear to vary among businesses.

As Ebenezer Scrooge might put it, the question about these changes is whether they reflect the future that will be or one that might be. Lacking a strong infrastructure and solid research base, it may be that future social entrepreneurs will always have to work 24/7, persevere against the odds, and sacrifice themselves to succeed. But the field could make life so much easier with relatively small investments in capacity building. There is no need for social entrepreneurship to be so difficult and no proof whatsoever that hardship improves the quality of ideas and level of impact.

Quite the contrary, socially entrepreneurial activity can be a natural product of life in agile, alert, adaptive, and aligned organizations, which can be built through deliberate action.

More exclusive assumptions does not mean that social entrepreneurs must be mythical heroes, even though their efforts may have heroic effects. But this change toward exclusivity does suggest that entrepreneurs play *the* central role in the change process. The field may not agree on just which characteristics are actually tied to success, but there is no question that some characteristics matter greatly. As such, this study suggests that Dees was on target in his 1998 description of social entrepreneurship as an exceptional act by exceptional people:

Social entrepreneurship describes a set of behaviors that are exceptional. These behaviors should be encouraged and rewarded in those who have the capabilities and temperament for this kind of work. We could use many more of them. Should everyone aspire to be a social entrepreneur? No. Not every social sector leader is well suited to being entrepreneurial.... Social entrepreneurs are a special breed of leader, and they should be recognized as such. This definition preserves their distinctive status and assures that social entrepreneurship is not treated lightly.[1]

Social entrepreneurship is much more difficult than I originally believed. Although I still maintain that there is more socially entrepreneurial behavior across the sectors than previously imagined, success still involves a struggle against an entrenched equilibrium that often denies simple common sense. Indeed, if I had to pick one core characteristic of successful social entrepreneurs beyond commitment to vision, it would be perseverance against an array of obstacles, a point well made by Dees in arguing that social entrepreneurs act boldly without regard to resources in hand.

This is not to argue that business entrepreneurship is easy by comparison—witness the high failure rates of new businesses. But private markets provide significant incentives for new ideas, ample legal protection for inventions, and access to capital that simply does not exist for socially entrepreneurial activity. Thus many of the moderately entrepreneurial organizations in this study may be using subsidies from contracts, grants, and fees for service to subsidize their change efforts.

Although the literature of social entrepreneurship focuses almost exclusively on success, that success is not a foregone conclusion. At the very least, advocacy must remain part of the skill set that entrepreneurs bring to their task, whether as a primary component of the change effort or as a holstered weapon, so to speak, that must be brought to bear to achieve durable policy change. Advocacy is surely part of the policy impact that Ashoka uses to measure the success of its fellows, just as it is part of the defense against existing organizations that refuse to yield ground as a new idea emerges.

New ventures face enormous pressure to become more bureaucratic over time and start their lives highly centralized around a specific idea. At the same time, existing organizations must shed their bureaucracies if they are to stimulate innovation within. Staying agile is not a foregone characteristic of social entrepreneurship, and it may require aggressive actions such as strategic planning, reorganization, and the use of business tools to maintain the acceleration that socially entrepreneurial organizations achieved early in the development process.

Entrepreneurs can actually be seen as organizational products—sometimes, they bolt their organizations in search of autonomy; other times, they find the encouragement to build from within. Viewed as such, social entrepreneurship has a dual meaning. It focuses on the social equilibrium, while being the product of social interactions. As Pino Audia and Christopher Rider (2005) argued from their own literature review, successful entrepreneurship involves a host of social networks inside and outside the endeavor. These networks are hard to build if the entrepreneur toils without contact with the outside world.

Bill Drayton may be quite right that the number of actual entrepreneurs is quite low today but may underestimate efforts to spur potential entrepreneurs into action through education and training. The federal government has a host of programs for increasing the number of business entrepreneurs, for example, not to mention whole departments and agencies, while the Ewing Marion Kauffman Foundation has embarked on an ambitious effort to strengthen entrepreneurship education at the nation's business schools. Perhaps a similar focus on potential social entrepreneurs might work just as well.

Building on the evidence in this study, I am convinced that lonely entrepreneurs are not the only source of social entrepreneurship. There is more than enough evidence that socially entrepreneurial activity can come from more than one individual. The assumption that entrepreneurship belongs to the few may help narrow our vision in the search for promising investments and fellowships, but this clearly limits potential support for ideas that emerge from large dissemination networks such as CARE.

I am also convinced that socially entrepreneurial ideas do not have to grow to the maximum to succeed, though grow they must to some larger level of impact. Some entrepreneurs want to change the social equilibrium one small step at time, while others might seek replication by other organizations. Either path might produce global change, but entrepreneurs do not necessarily start with that ambition.

I saw many examples of small ideas that stayed small and still had great impact. Moreover, in an age of high-speed knowledge transfer, it seems reasonable to argue that dissemination of system-changing ideas has never been easier, provided that someone is keeping watch. Although the ultimate impact of a given idea rests in its launch, scale-up, sustained momentum, and diffusion, the invention of a new idea can involve existing organizations. After all, the incandescent light was invented

seventy-five years before Edison imagined a system for disrupting the status quo.

I also remain convinced that the social equilibrium can be nibbled away through multiple attacks. Moreover, a "thousand flowers" approach can create a healthy competition among ideas that produces stronger initiatives. This may mean that some ideas simply disappear over time, for example, while others may be elevated in prominence only to be acquired by organizations with greater access to capital. Private firms may even come to see the value of a profitable idea and establish their own presence in a market. The point is that ideas often evolve over time, switching sectors and winning new entrepreneurs along the way.

Finally, I am unalterably convinced that social entrepreneurship can emerge from existing organizations, especially if entrepreneurs have access to investment capital and protection as their ideas advance. The advantages of new ventures are clear: They focus their mission on a specific idea that has the novelty and familiarity to undermine the existing social equilibrium, and they tend to remain agile as they age. But just because existing organizations face extraordinary challenges in creating an entrepreneurial culture does not mean they are doomed to failure. To the contrary, entrepreneurial organizations have the resources to help new ideas scale up, provided that these organizations want to be part of a new equilibrium.

## RECOMMENDATIONS

### Entrepreneurs

For those who care about assisting social entrepreneurs, the study suggests the need for further learning and recruitment opportunities through fellowship programs. There is simply too much isolation in the effort to create pattern-breaking change. If social entrepreneurs cannot find what they need from the usual sources of support, then this support needs to be built from the ground up. Social entrepreneurs may be intuitive thinkers, but they easily could avoid mistakes by talking with others. As much as such interaction may take time and energy from the vision, it is well worth the effort.

The study also suggests that entrepreneurs must create an appropriate balance between the single-minded pursuit of their vision and the need for high-performance management. Despite worries that management will somehow overwhelm vision, I believe the evidence suggests that entrepreneurs need management skills to succeed. Some might bring it with them as individual entrepreneurs, while pairs, teams, and networks may already contain it. But wherever it resides, entrepreneurs must accept the reality that management is essential to successful implementation. If they want evidence, they need only talk to their own employees—there is nothing more demoralizing than pursuing a strong vision without the resources to succeed. Working 24/7 without enough "stuff" to succeed is a recipe for turnover and pause. Either entrepreneurs must start talking about management, including governance, at the very beginning, or they will be addressing it in the midst of a crisis.

Working 24/7 can also be dangerous to one's health. Generally, social entrepreneurs are expected to persevere without pause, sometimes without a living wage to support them. It would be no surprise if they exhibited high rates of physical and emotional duress that go with pursuing their vision. If investors want to sustain high rates of engagement, they must be willing to invest in the entrepreneurs who provide it, which means the administrative support (including pension and health insurance) to continue the entrepreneurial chase.

### Ideas

For those who care about designing socially entrepreneurial ideas that drive change, the study suggests the potential value of moderately entrepreneurial organizations as a source of pattern-breaking change.

Investors and entrepreneurs should not ignore the potential contributions of these organizations as incubators of ideas and sources of potential spin-offs, and they should not underestimate the power of research and development for producing effective socially entrepreneurial ideas.

Nor should investors and entrepreneurs ignore the value of traditional research and development in producing the new combinations needed to disturb the social equilibrium. Currently, most social entrepreneurs must present a business plan to receive fellowships and venture capital. But there is virtually no source of funding for the core work needed to develop the "social value proposition" that drives these plans. Providing this support may be the single best investment for increasing the odds that entrepreneurs can move their ideas into the social marketplace faster.

It could well be, for example, that incubators and eventual spin-offs could become an important marketplace for matching entrepreneurial ideas to specific opportunities. Instead of excluding these organizations from the field, some investors might create intermediary organizations to harvest particularly promising ideas, while others might invest more heavily in ensuring that such ideas exist in welcoming environments with the resources necessary to achieve high impact.

The search for ideas could easily expand to small-scale efforts at the neighborhood and community level, too. Much of the contemporary conversation about socially entrepreneurial activity emphasizes broad geographic change; however, there are thousands of organizations that pursue pattern-breaking change through much more focused efforts. Such efforts might involve an effort to break a particularly vicious equilibrium in a specific setting, such as a crime-ridden city or beleaguered neighborhood. Replication of these ideas might be a much more efficient method of breaking similarly localized equilibriums in other regions, and replication should be considered frequently as part of the socially entrepreneurial skill set.

### Opportunities

For those who care about identifying socially entrepreneurial opportunities, this study suggests ample room for building a search infrastructure to help entrepreneurs identify potential targets of change. Although alertness to opportunity appears to be a core characteristic of the social entrepreneur, some opportunities may appear for such a short time or in such a disguise that it goes unnoticed. Such an environmental scanning effort could also include support for the kind of hybrid organizations featured in Martin and Osberg's work, especially to the extent that these organizations use advocacy and activism to exploit or create wedges in the social equilibrium.

The search for opportunities could also involve innovative funding mechanisms that might allow social entrepreneurs to attack and navigate barriers to success. Without urging greater diversification for diversification's sake, investors could help entrepreneurs secure the needed capital and flexibility to survive the early threats to success. Such mechanisms already exist for investors, including the revolving loan fund operated by the Acumen Fund. But such funding may not be enough to provide the security to protect socially entrepreneurial organizations against the backlash created by a resilient social equilibrium. Without recommending government engagement on the level of the Bush administration's faith-based initiative per se, there may be ways to provide new streams of support that could provide needed diversification.

### Organizations

For those concerned about building stronger socially entrepreneurial organizations, this study has been quite clear on the need for further investment in high-performance capacity. Alongside investments in the core idea, investors could easily support the research and capacity-building infrastructure needed to help these organizations build sustainable structures. Also, they could develop templates and other assessment tools for helping socially entrepreneurial organizations remain agile *and* accountable. The last thing the field needs today is a scandal that might give the social equilibrium the fodder to resist change.

High performance demands more than just occasional attention, however. It also involves the recruitment of committed managers. To those who argue that managers and leaders are fundamentally different and often incompatible, I suggest that leaders who cannot manage are high risks indeed. One reason so many business ventures involve teams is precisely to compensate for weaknesses in the single entrepreneur, particularly the weaknesses that undermine effective performance.

Social entrepreneurs and their investors must confront their own views of managers as little more than bureaucratic ciphers that do things right, not the right things. Nothing could be further from their role in high-performing organizations. If one accepts Joseph Schumpeter's (1934;1939) distinction between inventors and innovators, managers could easily lay claim to the latter term.

This study also suggests social entrepreneurs and their investors must confront their long-standing belief that socially entrepreneurial activity simply cannot take place in existing organizations. Call it intrapreneurship or entrepreneurship, but whatever it is called, socially entrepreneurial activity appears to flourish in settings that provide the high performance needed for sustainable impact. This high performance can exist in many locations, including social benefit organizations, businesses, governments, and organizations in between. It can also exist in new organizations and old, small and large. The coding that underpins this study suggests that socially entrepreneurial activity is possible in existing organizations, including some with remarkably large dissemination systems that might provide the opportunity for much faster scale-up of promising ideas. The field simply cannot ignore such capacity by fiat.

## CONCLUSION

Social entrepreneurship is evolving rapidly both as a concept and as a cause.

As a concept, social entrepreneurship has captured interest across a wide range of academic disciplines. But the field is coalescing around the notion that intractable social problems may not be as intractable as once believed. The number of case studies is increasing rapidly, even as researchers design new work that will distinguish social entrepreneurship as a distinctive field of endeavor.

As a cause, social entrepreneurship is attracting a new generation of change agents who have the core characteristics needed for sustainable change. Driven by commitment to their vision of sustainable success in addressing problems such as poverty, hunger, and disease and supported by an increasingly energetic community of investors, these change agents are moving rapidly to design and implement a broad mix of ideas for changing the social equilibrium. Although it is difficult to estimate just how many change efforts are currently under way, this study suggests that the number is certainly growing and includes new and old organizations alike.

The question facing the field is not whether a new generation of social entrepreneurs will accept the call to action—that much is clear from the remarkable increase in student interest in coursework on the topic Rather, the question is how researchers can work together to increase the odds of success. Although failure is always an option for a business entrepreneur, it could not be more costly for a social entrepreneur. After all, every decision to support one idea involves an untold number of decisions to delay or deny others. The field of social entrepreneurship simply cannot tolerate the high failure rates found in business entrepreneurship. There is too much at stake, whether in sunk costs, missed opportunities, or needless sacrifice. Social entrepreneurs deserve more than respect; they also deserve the best odds possible.

## NOTES

1. Dees (1998, p. 5)

## REFERENCES

Audia, Pino G., and Christopher I. Rider. 2005. "A Garage and an Idea: What More Does an Entrepreneur Need?" *California Management Review* 48, no. 1 (Fall): 6–28.

Martin, Roger L., and Sally Osberg. 2007. "Social Entrepreneurship: The Case for Definition." *Stanford Social Innovation Review* 5 (Spring): 29–39.

Dees, J. Gregory. 1998. "Enterprising Nonprofits." *Harvard Business Review* 76 (January–February): 55–67.

_____. 2003. "Social Entrepreneurship Is about Innovation and Impact, Not Income" (www.fuqua.duke.edu/centers/case/articles/1004/corner.htm).

Schumpeter, Joseph A. 1934. *The Theory of Development*. Cambridge, MA: Harvard University Press.

_____. 1939. *Business Cycles: A Theoretical, Historical and Statistical Analysis of the Capitalist Process*. New York: McGraw-Hill.

## 38

# Towards a Theory of Hybrid Organizations

*David Billis*

## INTRODUCTION

Hybrid organizations are ubiquitous. They are international, multi-sector phenomena and their unclear sector accountability often engenders unease and distrust. And in our area of concern we appear to have stumbled into a period of intense organizational hybridity in which we appear to be drifting up the (welfare hybrid) creek not only without a paddle, but also without a reliable map. Expressed in a somewhat more scholarly fashion, the first priority is the need to develop 'tentative theories' (Popper, 1972) of hybrid organizations.

The objective of this chapter is therefore to begin to get to grips with the agenda of questions. It is laid out as a 'building blocks' exercise and contains five parts.

1. Any study of hybridity must inevitably begin by establishing the nature of the "non-hybrid" state of the phenomenon. At the heart of the model is an approach to "ownership" in terms of decision-making accountability that is intended to be applicable to all three main sectors.
2. This part develops a model for the third sector. Reflecting on previous research, it is suggested that the archetypal characteristics of the Third Sector Organization (TSO) are most closely found in the associational form of organization. A new approach to membership and ownership leads to a re-evaluation of the role of some paid staff in the association.
3. The third, pivotal level proposes a "principal sector" hypothesis which is intended to resolve the paradox of strong sectors in the midst of the growth of hybrid types. The centerpiece of this part is a model of sectors and their hybrid zones.

4. The final level of analysis considers the nature of hybridity in the third sector. In order to do this, the concepts of "shallow," "entrenched," "organic," and "enacted" hybrids are introduced.
5. The chapter concludes with a summary and a few thoughts as to how this approach to hybridity might prove helpful.

## PART ONE: BUILDING AN IDEAL MODEL: THE PUBLIC AND PRIVATE SECTORS

This part constructs *an ideal* type *model* of the public *and private* sectors.

### Sectors and ideal types

Sectors are treated as collections of (non-hybrid) organizations. It is suggested that (a) all organizations have broad generic structural features or *elements* (such as the need for resources) but that (b) their nature and logic or *principles* are distinctly different in *each sector*. These principles have a logical interdependence and provide a coherent explanation for meeting objectives and solving problems. Together they represent the "rules of the game" of the ideal model for each sector.

For my purposes the model or "type" must draw sufficiently from empirical reality so that it can be used in both practice and in policy-making. Following this broad (Weberian) approach, the "pure" ideal type very rarely exists (Weber and Parsons, 1964). But, notwithstanding the wide variations in structures, organizations within each sector appear to derive their strength

Edited by David Billis, *Hybrid Organizations and the Third Sector*, published 2010 Palgrave Macmillan. Reproduced with permission of Palgrave Macmillan.

and legitimacy (Suchman, 1995) from the characteristics and rules of the game of their own distinctive ideal type. In reality, organizations within any sector, whilst adhering to the core principles, will vary in the degree to which they fully match the ideal model. And individuals, particularly those in powerful roles or organizational positions, who can contribute to shaping hybridity, will encounter the tensions between the ideal type and organizational reality.

### Core structural elements in the public and private sector

My choice is selective and based on the search for the predominant structural features of organizations.

It can be seen that the following five core *elements* persistently appear:

(1) ownership
(2) governance
(3) operational priorities
(4) human resources
(5) other resources

Clarifying the nature of ownership is essential if any model building that includes the third sector is not to be scuppered at the onset. The reason for this is, as Grønbjerg points out in her summary of the literature, that the third sector is usually regarded as not possessing "owners" as usually defined (Grønbjerg, 2001). This is discussed in the following section.

### Revisiting the definition of ownership

Economists have been energetic in defining ownership.

In this chapter, ownership is defined according to different levels of decision-making accountability (formal, active and principal) *within* the broad category of ownership. For the moment, the discussion is confined to the private and the public sectors. Here can be identified groups of people who have the "formal rights" to elect the board of directors and political representatives respectively known as shareholders

and the electorate. Nevertheless a sizeable percentage of this *formal/legal ownership* can be inactive. In reality they may have little interest or motivation to participate in any of the decision-making activities of business or government.

In both sectors people can be found within the formal ownership who (at least) *do* exercise their votes at the annual board meeting and who *do* vote in government elections. These can be regarded as *active owners* even if their influence on Hansmann's small set of fundamental issues is slight.

The third group are the *principal owners*: those who *in effect* can close the organization down and transfer it to another sector – what Weisbrod (1998) refers to as "conversion" – or change the fundamental boundary and mission of the organization through mergers or other actions (Gray, 1997). In the private sector, it may be large pension funds or other major investors. In the public sector, it likely to be the elected representatives or a caucus of those representatives.

### Building the foundations: A model of the public and private sectors

So far, five *elements* which might serve as a basis for building a model of the public and private sectors have been identified. *Each element comes with a distinctive set of principles for each sector.*

What emerge are tentative models of

- A *private sector* which is (a) owned by shareholders and (b) governed according to the principle of size of share ownership, working according to (c) operational priorities driven by principles of market forces in individual choice, with typical (d) human resources consisting of paid employees in a managerially controlled *firm* and (e) other resources primarily from sales and fees.
- A *public sector* which is (a) owned by the citizens and (b) governed according to principles of public elections with work driven (c) by principles of public services

and collective choice and as its typical (d) human resources consisting of paid public servants in legally backed bureaus and (f) resourced by taxation.

## PART TWO: DEVELOPING A MODEL FOR THE THIRD SECTOR

### The search for distinctive principles

There is an impressive list of authors who have sought to uncover the sector's general distinctive features.

Much of this literature has been summarized and analyzed by Grønbjerg who identified five major attributes: (1) private auspices, (2) absence of formal ownership rights, (3) volunteerism, (4) particular missions and substantive goals and (5) the challenge of changing people (Grønbjerg, 2001). The extensive international mapping exercise undertaken by Johns Hopkins University (Salamon and Anheier, 1992) identified the key "common features" as self-governing, nonprofit distribution, private and nongovernmental in basic structure and voluntary to 'some meaningful extent' (Salamon et al., 2000).

In sum, the literature highlights a number of principles which are seen to be distinctive. These include independence, use of voluntary labor, sensitivity and closeness to users and being mission driven.

However, much of the research, as Smith (2000) points out, ignores the vast number of small grass roots organizations, a similar point made in a comprehensive review of community movements and local organizations (Cnaan and Milofsky, 2008). Also, rather neglected in current third sector research are social movements (Davis, 2005) and, at the other end of the scale, many huge membership organizations such as the National Trust (which has 3.5 million members and 52,000 volunteers), let alone political parties. It is likely therefore that a more balanced overview of the third sector would give increased emphasis to the role of volunteers and the distinctive type of resources of these organizations.

All this, in addition to the actual history of many organizations, indicates that an ideal type of the third sector is best typified by the association. In this model people establish a formal organization in order to resolve their own or other people's problems. These members, through a process of private elections, elect committees and officers to guide the work of the organization. The organization may need additional volunteer labor to forward its policies. Other resources may also be sought and these are typically membership dues, donations and legacies. Work is driven neither by the need to make a profit nor by public policies but primarily by the association's own agenda. This approach differs from most prevailing theoretical approaches to the sector. The association, rather than being a rather peripheral component is now seen as the "ideal model" and source of the distinctive sector attributes (Rothschild-Whitt, 1979).

Nevertheless, in the development of a model comparable to the private and public sectors, one stumbling block still remains: the place of members and "owners" in the third sector model.

### Ownership in membership associations

This section of the chapter explores whether the preceding analysis of different layers of owners helps in the model building of the sector.

In the association, the gap between *formal*, *active* and *principal* owners may be small. However, even in small, tightly knit groups, it is possible to differentiate between those (formal members) who stay in the shadows (see Putnam [2000] for a seminal study); those who play an active part in committee and other activities; and a core group of those (principal owners) "who everybody knows" will really be the key players in the defining moments of the group's history.

The distinctive characteristics of associations are the linkage and logical flow between its ownership by members, principles of governance, reliance on volunteer resources for its operational work and principles of membership accountability which together enable it to function as a robust and effective organization. Critically, although there may be clear differentiation in the roles of governing body, committees and volunteer workers, all will usually be part of the active and membership/ownership groups as defined. In addition, those receiving services may be past or present members, or have close links through family, neighborhood, friendship and other groups. Active members will be dedicated to the cause which may be expressed tangibly both through financial contributions and through a preparedness to take on unpopular and sometimes unpleasant work, readiness to recruit others into the organization and, if necessary, advocacy – the determination to persuade those outside the group of the rightness of the mission.

According to this approach, *formal, active* and *principal* member/owners can also be identified according to their different levels of accountability for decision-making.

### The model of the three sectors

Employing a decision-making approach to the issue of membership/ownership enables their core elements and principles to be laid out together with those of the private and public sectors in the form of a table (Table 38.1)

According to this model, the ideal type "work doing" operational units of the sectors are the firm, bureau and association.

Underpinning the model of sectors is the notion of accountability and the role of principal owners. By organizational accountability, I am referring to those individuals and groups (governing bodies of all sorts, and individuals) who have the *authority* to carry out their designated duties and can be held to account to higher level individuals and institutions if they fail to carry out those duties.

### PART THREE: BUILDING A MODEL OF HYBRID ORGANIZATIONS

#### *Approaches to the study of hybridity*

Despite recent increased interest in hybrid organizations, the literature remains sparsely spread across many academic disciplines over several decades. For case of analysis, much of the disparate literature might be loosely grouped into three approaches.

1. A popular approach regards hybrid organizations as occupying points on a *continuum* between sectors (e.g., Dahl and Lindblom, 1953; Demone and Gibelman, 1989).
2. Other writers have adopted what might be called a *single sector emphasis*. Here, their main concern is either with the public or

### TABLE 38.1 • IDEAL TYPE SECTORS AND ACCOUNTABILITY

| Core elements ↓ | Private sector principles | Public sector principles | Third sector principles |
|---|---|---|---|
| 1. Ownership | Shareholders | Citizens | Members |
| 2. Governance | Share ownership size | Public elections | Private elections |
| 3. Operational Priorities | Market forces and individual choice | Public service and collective choice | Commitment about distinctive mission |
| 4. Distinctive human resources | Paid employees in managerially controlled *Firm* | Paid public servants in legally backed *Bureau* | Members and volunteers in *Association* |
| 5. Distinctive other resources | Sales, fees | Taxes | Dues, donations and legacies |

private sector, and organizations on their boundary are usually studied from the perspective of the implications for one particular sector (Gray, 1990; Courpasson and Dany, 2003; Koppell, 2003; Skelcher et al., 2005).

3. A few writers, mainly from continental Europe, appear to have gone one step further in a *separate sector* approach. For them, hybridization and hybrid organizations have replaced the sector metaphor and are now *the* permanent features in the welfare system (Brandsen et al., 2005; Evers, 2005). In an earlier paper, James (1983), although focusing on US nonprofits, seems to be arguing an almost similar case.

Any theory will need to (a) handle the paradox of a strong sector concept in a period of increased hybridity (b) cover all three sectors and (c) address the issue of accountability.

The following section attempts to address these issues.

### The model of hybridity: The prime sector approach

My working hypothesis is that organizations will have "roots" and have primary adherence to the principles of one sector (Biilis, 1991; 1993; 2003). This is based on the inherent contradictory distinctive and conflicting *principles* (rules of the game) for each sector outlined in Table 38.1.

According to a prime sector approach, stakeholders and public policy makers need to be clear whether the organizations they are working with, and in, fundamentally adhere to the principles of accountability inherent in either the public, private or third sector. Thus, hybrids are not on a continuum but have a clear cut off point evident when principal owners take the boundary-shaping decisions (closures, conversions mergers etc.) according to the principles of the different sectors.

But neither are hybrids a separate sector since there is no evidence that they have distinctive and explicit *principles* of management and operation which set them apart from other sectors.

Figure 38.1 depicts the three sectors and their hybrid zones. The model of the three sectors requires a few words of explanation.

The figure is unable to capture an important aspect of my argument: that is – whereas the move across sectors is a fundamental organizational decision – it is possible to slide into one or more of the nine hybrid zones. (See the later discussion on shallow and entrenched, and organic and enacted hybridity.)

A few tentative examples (without explanation) from the public and private sectors may help a very modest fleshing out of the model and perhaps stimulate debate.

| | |
|---|---|
| *Public/Third* | *NHS Foundation Trusts* |
| *Public/Private/ Third* | *The BBC* |
| *Public/Private* | *Nationalised industries, Fannie Mae* |
| *Private/Public* | *Partnership UK (51 per cent private equity)* |
| *Private/Public / Third* | *The National Lottery* |
| *Private/Third* | *The John Lewis Partnership* |

## PART FOUR: THE CASE OF HYBRID TSOs

The following discussion is restricted to some key theoretical and practical issues for the third sector raised by the prime sector approach to hybridity. It opens by distinguishing firstly between 'shallow' and 'entrenched' hybridity and secondly between 'organic' and 'enacted' hybrids. These sections are followed by a consideration of one of the chronic dilemmas of third sector theory: the role of paid staff.

### Shallow hybridity

Hybridity in the third sector is not a new phenomenon. For many years, some organizations have moved into hybridity in a rather gentle fashion, causing minor disturbances,

## FIGURE 38.1 • THE THREE SECTORS AND THEIR HYBRID ZONES

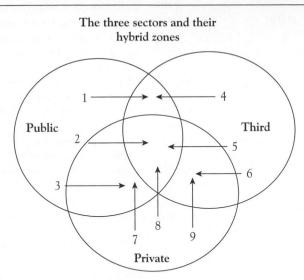

The three sectors and their
hybrid zones

Key: The hybrid zones

| | | |
|---|---|---|
| 1. Public/Third | 4. Third/Public | 7. Private/Public |
| 2. Public/Private/Third | 5. Third/Public/Private | 8. Private/Public/Third |
| 3. Public/Private | 6. Third/Private | 9. Private/Third |

David Billis, Palgrave-Macmillan. Hybrid Organizations and the Third Sector. P.57

but not necessarily calling into question their basic third sector identity.

The introduction of a modest form of hybridity often arises from the desire to maintain or perhaps extend the range of activities. Board members with a business background might be keen for more commercial approaches. For example, in one case study, the appointment of an NHS consultant led to pressure to work more closely with the health service. Resources and grants from government or business might be received to support the general purposes of the organization.

Field work over several decades indicates that taking on the first paid staff (the typical human resources of the public and private sectors) can be felt as an important step into shallow hybridity for TSOs (Billis, 1984). This can be uncomfortable but most TSOs appear to have survived this early discomfort and have preserved the

integrity of their core missions. Initially, they may employ staff to handle their supporting non-operational activities.

At some point, the organization may decide that it needs one, or even a few, paid staff to undertake operational work to meet the needs of its users. A special grant might be sought, or an appeal launched, and workers are recruited. Often, the first paid staff may themselves have been committed members, perhaps founders of the organization. Even where tensions arise between volunteer workers and those who get paid for the same work, this may still be regarded as belonging to the shallow form of hybridity.

### Entrenched hybridity in the third sector

Whether planned at all or not, entrenched hybridity can arrive both at the (a) governance and (b) operational levels of organizations in all sectors.

At the governance level, the board or other form of governing body may find itself compelled to, or under pressure to, accept permanent government or private sector representatives in return for resources and influence.

More usually, entrenched hybridity in the third sector begins as a result of receiving private and public sector resources through grants, contracts and sales. These resources will increase and decrease according to political preferences and market forces but they may become sufficiently reliable that, together with third sector sources, they represent a flow of income adequate to maintain a structure of management. (But entrenched hybridity need not take this 'organic' route; it can arrive immediately through 'enactment' – see the following section.)

At the operational level, entrenchment arises when paid staff become dominant in the delivery of the operational work of the organization and a management structure with several hierarchical levels is established. Then the organization can be considered to have embedded into its structure core features of the firm and bureau. The rules of the game begin to change and associational principles have to coexist with alien principles drawn from the private and public sectors (see Table 38.1). This is because maintaining a structure of staff leads to increased pressure towards considerations of individual and organizational survival. Significant resources have increasingly to be secured often through the political process (that they meet public policy needs), and/or through the market principles of cost and price.

Entrenched paid staff structures bring with them a different language and way of operation. People are then dependent on the organization for their livelihood and – quite naturally – hours and conditions of service, promotion and career development have to be accommodated. Formal job descriptions, managerial accountability, sanctions and reward systems all become daily features and replace the 'group' and 'committee' as the prime ways of organizing and solving problems. It becomes increasingly likely that such structures are influenced by political and commercial priorities and activities. There are other possible consequences. Volunteers might wonder why others should receive payment, whilst they give their labor freely on the basis of belief and commitments.

Although entrenched hybridity may increase the propensity for mission drift, I am far from arguing that this is inevitable. If third sector resources are themselves adequate, then entrenched hybrids can be established from within the sector itself. It seems reasonable to assume that despite the tensions that arrive with the introduction of employment hierarchies, this type of hybrid TSO will be less susceptible to mission drift. More importantly, paid staff may also be active or principal members/owners: an essential part of this analysis which is discussed shortly.

### Organic and enacted hybrids

Much of the third sector literature has been occupied with organizations where hybridity has resulted from the steady accumulation of external resources. Over many years, organizations may have moved from shallow to entrenched hybridity. However, in this new era of frenzied organizational experimentation, there are a growing number of hybrid organizations that are enacted, that are established from day one as hybrids, usually by other organizations.

Enacted hybrids arise for different reasons, in different sectors and under different broad headings. Although they may be seen as part of the broader category of numerous collaborative mechanisms across sectors (including partnerships, networks, project groups, joint ventures and joint operating groups), they are distinguished by the fact that they have an *apparently* independent, often legal, structure. Thus governments can create or sponsor new organizational forms oil companies can collaborate with national governments in separate legal forms and TSOs can establish trading companies.

Enacted hybrids may present complex problems of accountability. The only point that might be made in this chapter is to question the extent to which these arrangements are time-limited and the extent to which they affect the basic sector identity of individual organizations involved in the collaborations.

### Paid staff as members/owners?

Another problem remains unresolved. The theoretical quandary is as follows. Hybrid TSOs are usually and increasingly dependent on paid staff and may have few if any 'formal members,' so how can these agencies be part of the third sector whose core principles, I have argued, are based on the association?

My argument is that in hybrid TSOs paid staff may also be part of the *active* membership by similarly (to other active members) demonstrating their genuine commitment to organizational purposes through their freely given and un-coerced contributions to the operations and governance of the organization. Thus, additional to their normal work role, they may undertake voluntary work or provide other resources. They may participate in committees and other governance activities. They may have a more flexible approach to precise hours of work flowing from a belief in the purposes of the organization. 'Voluntary' must mean what it says. As Bacchiega and Borzaga put it in their analysis of social enterprises, "incentives for workers are not based exclusively on monetary rewards; rather, they derive mainly from workers' involvement in shaping and sharing the organization's goals and mission'" (Bacchiega and Borzaga, 2001, p. 274).

Being part of the governance process is more than a consultation exercise in which staff opinions are solicited in order to help managers do *their* work. In contrast, in these meetings, the active TSO members combine their work role with a personal commitment to the cause to discuss broader

organizational issues informally or perhaps in a more structured fashion. There is a degree of overlap and hybridity in their paid work and membership roles.

From this pool of paid staff of active members, there may be those who are sufficiently committed and influential to be considered a natural part of the ownership of the organization which makes the critical decisions discussed earlier.

## PART FIVE: DISCUSSION AND CONCLUSIONS

In view of the contested boundaries of the third sector, the chapter began the process of model building by drawing on research and literature from the private and particularly from the public sectors. It rapidly became clear that if a similar model were to be developed for the third sector, several intellectual challenges would need to be confronted. The first of these was the problem of *ownership*, a core component of these models. Applying the traditional economic definitions of ownership inevitably leads to the familiar conclusion that TSOs have no owners. Rather than abandon the concept in the model building, ownership was revisited and redefined in terms of its accountability for different levels of decision-making. Principal, active and formal owners were defined. Principal owners were seen to be those that take the major boundary shaping or strategic decisions. Approaching ownership in this way enabled the concept to be more realistically employed in the third sector model.

The second challenge was to uncover an 'ideal type' of the third sector which possessed an equally robust set of core distinctive principles. After reflecting on the policy and research literature, the conclusion was reached that the positive attributes most frequently claimed for the sector were found in their most pristine form in the archetypal association. This does not mean that such groups are unproblematic utopian communities, or that they are the most significant players in public policy. Placing the association and its claimed virtues at the heart of the third sector is comparable to the powerful ideal models of the public and private sectors under whose own general *principles* can be found equally diverse groups of institutions.

These two threads of argument (ownership and distinctive principles) and the proposition that organizations had *primary accountability* to the principles of one sector, led to the model presented in Table *38.1* and eventually to the depiction of hybrid organizations in Figure 38.1.

In an attempt to get to grips more closely with the nature of hybridity, *shallow* was differentiated from *entrenched states* of hybrid TSOs. It was hypothesized that entrenchment is likely to be associated with the development of hierarchical levels of paid staff and the associated resource demands, usually from public and private sector sources. In the belief that these may prove to have different problems, it was suggested that it might be worthwhile differentiating *organic* from *enacted types* of hybrid – those established by other organizations.

Finally, the chapter returned to what currently appears to be a central theme of the 'optimistic-pessimistic' debate, the position of large paid staff TSOs. I raised the possibility that based on the discussion about principal owners/members, paid staff may under certain circumstances be part of this group.

This chapter has primarily concentrated on the organic hybrids with a single accountable ownership body. I think that a strong case can be made that if we can ask more penetrating questions and get closer to an answer about ownership in these forms of hybrid TSOs, this would represent a major step forward. Nevertheless, as noted earlier, there is a growing body of more complex TSOs with interlocking layers of ownership and accountability that remains to be explored. To complicate matters even further, the tendency to enact hybrid organizations appears also to be increasing, with the possibility of another distinctive set of issues and challenges.

## REFERENCES

Bacchicga, A. and C. Borzaga (2001) Social enterprises as incentive structures: an economic analysis *in* C. Borzaga and J. Defourny (eds.) *The Emergence of Social Enterprise*, London: Roudedge.

Billis, D. (1984a) *Voluntary Sector Management: Research and Practice*. Uxbridge: Brunel University, Programme of Research and Training in Voluntary Action (PORTVAC).

Billis, D. (1991) The Roots of Voluntary Agencies: A Question of Choice. *Nonprofit and Voluntary Sector Quarterly*, 20(1), pp. 57–70.

Billis, D. (1993) Sector Blurring and Nonprofit Centres: The Case of the United Kingdom. *Nonprofit and Voluntary Sector Quarterly*, 22(3), pp. 241–257.

Billis, D. (2003) *Sectors, Hybrids, and Public Policy: The Voluntary Sector in Context*, paper presented to the annual meeting of ARNOVA, November, Denver.

Brandsen, T., W. van de Donk and K. Putters (2005) Griffins or Chameleons? Hybridity as a Permanent and Inevitable Characteristic of the Third Sector. *International Journal of Public Administration*, 28, pp. 749–765.

Cnaan, R. A. and C. Milofsky (eds.) (2008) *Handbook of Community Movements and Local Organizations*, Handbooks of Sociology and Social Research, New York: Springer.

Courpasson, D. and F. Dany (2003) Indifference or Obedience? Business Firms as Democratic Hybrids. *Organization Studies*, 24(8), pp. 1231–1260.

Dahl, R. A. and C. E. Lindblom (1953) *Politics, Economics and Welfare: Planning and Politico-Economic Systems Resolved into Basic Social Processes*. New York: Harper.

Davis, G. F. (2005) *Social Movements and Organization Theory*. Cambridge and New York: Cambridge University Press.

Demone, H. W. and M. Gibelman (1989) *Services for Sale: Purchasing Health and Human Services*. New Brunswick, NJ: Rutgers University Press.

Evers, A. (2005) Mixed Welfare Systems and Hybrid Organizations: Changes in the Governance and Provision of Social

Services. *International Journal of Public Administration*, 28, pp. 737–748.

Gray, B. (1997) Conversion of HMOs and Hospitals: What's At Stake? *Health Affairs*, 16(2), pp. 29–47.

Gray, B. H. (1990) Nonprofit Hospitals and the For-Profit Challenge. *The Bulletin of the New York Academy of Medicine*, 66(4), pp. 366–375.

Grønbjerg, K. A. (2001) Foreword in S. J. Ott (ed.) *The Nature of the Nonprofit Sector*, Boulder, CO: Westview Press.

James, E. (1983) How Nonprofits Grow: A Model. *Journal of Policy Analysis and Management*, 2(3), pp. 350–366.

Koppell, J. G. S. (2003) *The Politics of Quasi-Government. Hybrid organizations and the Dynamics of Bureaucratic Control*. Cambridge: Cambridge University Press.

Popper, K. R. (1972) *Objective Knowledge: An Evolutionary Approach*. Oxford: Clarendon Press.

Putnam, R. D. (2000) *Bowling Alone: The Collapse and Revival of American Community*, New York and London: Simon & Schuster.

Rothschild-Whitt, J. (1979) The Collectivist Organization: An Alternative to Rational-Bureaucratic Models. *American Sociological Review*, 44, pp. 509–527.

Salamon, L. M. and H. K. Anheier (1992) *In Search of the Nonprofit Sector 1: The Question of Definitions*, Baltimore: Johns Hopkins University Institute for Policy Studies.

Salamon, L. M., L. C. Hems, and K. Chinnock (2000) The Nonprofit Sector: For What and For Whom? *Working Papers*, J.H.C.N.S. Project, Baltimore: The John Hopkins Center for Civil Society Studies.

Skelcher, C, N. Mathur and M. Smith (2005) The Public Governance of Collaborative Spaces: Discourse, Design and Democracy. *Public Administration*, 83(3), pp. 573–596.

Smith, D. H. (2000) *Grassroots Associations*, Thousand Oaks, CA: Sage Publications.

Suchman, M. C. (1995) Managing Legitimacy: Strategic and Institutional Approaches. *Academy of Management Review*, 20(3), pp. 571–610.

Weber, M. and T. Parsons (1964) *The Theory of Social and Economic Organization*, New York: Free Press.

Weisbrod, B. A. (1998) *To Profit or Not to Profit: The Commercial Transformation of the Nonprofit Sector*, Cambridge: Cambridge University Press.